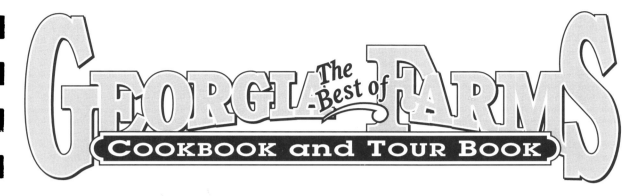

The Best of Georgia Farms

Cookbook and Tour Book

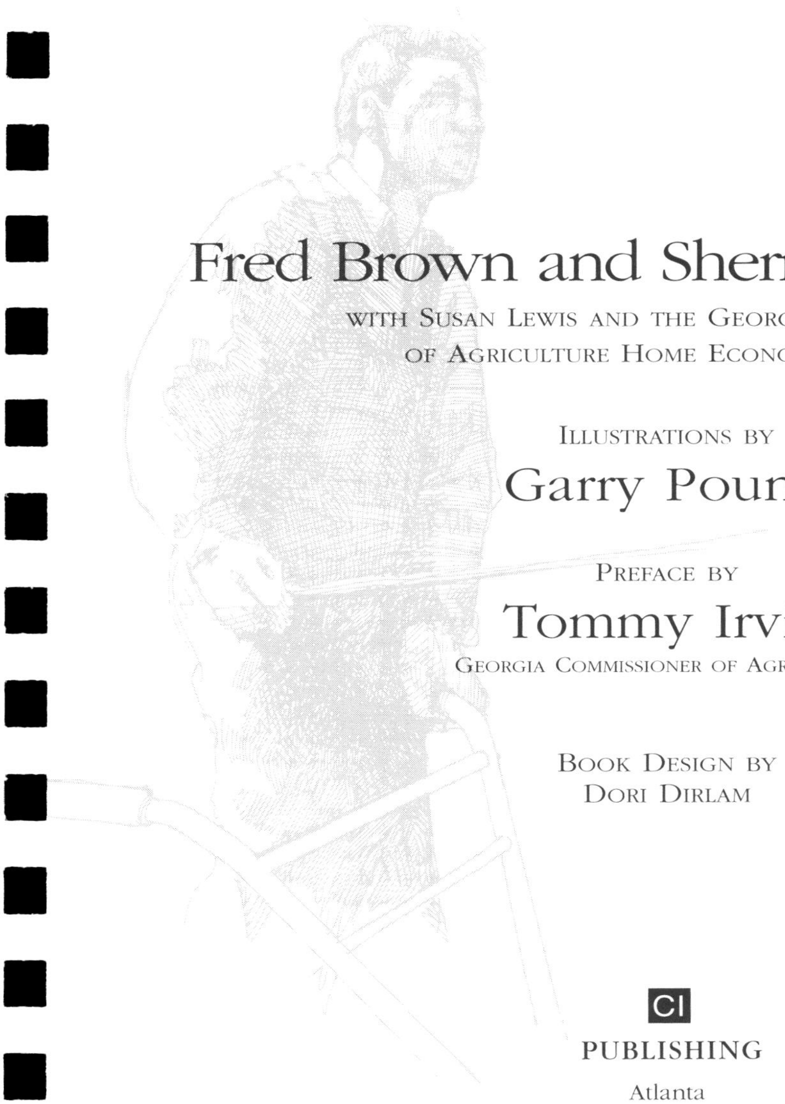

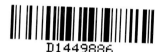

Fred Brown and Sherri M. L. Smith

WITH SUSAN LEWIS AND THE GEORGIA DEPARTMENT
OF AGRICULTURE HOME ECONOMIST STAFF

ILLUSTRATIONS BY

Garry Pound

PREFACE BY

Tommy Irvin

GEORGIA COMMISSIONER OF AGRICULTURE

BOOK DESIGN BY
DORI DIRLAM

CI
PUBLISHING
Atlanta

CI Publishing, 1401 Peachtree Street, Suite 100, Atlanta, Georgia 30309

Grateful acknowledgement is made to the following for permission to reprint previously published material:

Alfred A. Knopf, Inc.: Excerpts from *New Southern Cooking* by Nathalie Dupree. Copyright © 1986 by Nathalie Dupree. Excerpt from *The Story of Corn* by Betty Fussell. Copyright © 1992 by Betty Fussell. Excerpt from *The Taste of Country Cooking* by Edna Lewis. Copyright © 1976 by Edna Lewis. Ballantine Books, A Division of Random House, Inc.: Excerpts from *Crackers* by Roy Blount, Jr. Copyright © 1980 by Roy Blount, Jr. Excerpt from *Food and Healing* by Annemarie Colbin. Copyright © 1996 by Annemarie Colbin. Excerpt from *Rainey* by Clyde Edgerton. Copyright © 1986 by Clyde Edgerton. Crown Publishing Group: Excerpt from *White Columns in Georgia* by Medora Field Perkerson. Copyright © 1982 by Medora Field Perkerson. Dell Publishing Co.: Excerpt from *Cold Sassy Tree* by Olive Ann Burns. Copyright © 1984 by Olive Ann Burns. Doubleday, a division of Bantam Doubleday Dell Publishing Group, Inc.: Excerpts from Savannah Seasons: Food and Stories from Elizabeth on 37th by Elizabeth Terry with Alexis Terry. Copyright © 1996 by Elizabeth Terry and Alexis Terry. Doubleday & Co., Inc.: Excerpt from *The Hog Book* by William Hedgepeth. Copyright © 1978 by William B. Hedgepeth. Galahad Books: Excerpt from *Grace Hartley's Southern Cooking* by Grace Hartley. Copyright © 1980 by Grace Hartley. Published by permission of Doubleday & Company, Inc. Grosset and Dunlap: Excerpt from *Southern Cooking* by Mrs. S. R. Dull. Copyright © 1968 by Grosset and Dunlap. Harcourt Brace Jovanovich: Excerpt from *The Color Purple* by Alice Walker. Copyright © 1982 by Alice Walker. Historic Sims-Mitchell House: Excerpt from *Soul on Rice: African Influences on American Cooking* by Patricia B. Mitchell. Copyright © 1993 by Patricia B. Mitchell. Longstreet Press, Inc.: Excerpt from *The Dillard House Cookbook and Mountain Guide* compiled and written by Fred Brown. Copyright © 1996 by The Dillard House, Inc. Excerpt from *In My Father's Garden* by Lee May. Copyright © 1995 by Lee May. McIntosh County Board of Commissioners: Excerpt from *Early Days on the Georgia Tidewater: The Story of McIntosh County and Sapelo* by Buddy Sullivan. Copyright © 1990 by Buddy Sullivan. Peachtree Publishers Limited: Excerpt from *Guess Who's Coming to Dinner: Entertaining at the Governor's Mansion: Menus, Recipes and Anecdotes* by Mary Beth Busbee and Jan Busbee Curtis. Copyright © 1986 by Mary Beth Busbee and Jan Busbee Curtis. Excerpt from *Run with the Horsemen* by Ferrol Sams. Copyright © 1982 by Ferrol Sams. Poseidon Press: Excerpts from *A Harry Crews Reader* by Harry Crews. Copyright © 1993 by Harry Crews. St. Simon Press, Inc.: Excerpt from *The Blue Willow Inn Cookbook* by Louis and Billie Van Dyke. Copyright © 1996 by Louis and Billie Van Dyke. Starr Toof: *Famous Recipes from Mrs. Wilkes' Boarding House* in Historic Savannah by Mrs. L. H. Wilkes. Copyright © 1976 by Mrs. L. H. Wilkes. Taylor Publishing Company: *Gardening in the South with Don Hastings, Volume 2, Vegetables and Fruits* by Don Hastings. Copyright © 1988 by Don Hastings. The Columbus Museum Guild: Excerpt from *Seasoned Skillets and Silver Spoons: A Culinary History of Columbus*, Georgia by Mary Hart Brumby. Copyright © 1993 by The Columbus Museum Guild. The Junior League of Savannah: Excerpt from *Savannah Style, A Cookbook* by the Junior League of Savannah. Copyright © 1980 by the Junior League of Savannah. The University of Michigan: Excerpt from *Principles and Privilege: Two Women's Lives on a Georgia Plantation* by Frances A. Kemble and Frances A. Butler Leigh. Copyright © 1995 by the University of Michigan. The University of North Carolina Press: Excerpt from *The Foxfire Book of Appalachian Cookery* edited by Linda Garland Page and Eliot Wigginton. Copyright © 1984 by The Foxfire Fund, Inc. Ticknor & Fields, Houghton Mifflin Company: Excerpt from *Leaving Cold Sassy* by Olive Ann Burns. Copyright ©1992 by Olive Ann Burns. University of Georgia Press: Excerpts from *Storytellers: Folktales and Legends from the South* edited by John A. Burrison. Copyright © 1991 by University of Georgia. Wayne Erbsen Music Company: Excerpt from *Backpocket Old Time Song Book: Words and Music to 40 Timeless Mountain Tunes* by Wayne Erbsen. Copyright © 1992 by Wayne Erbsen Music Company International.

ISBN 58072-001-3

Manufactured in Canada

First edition, first printing

Contents

The Foods and Their Recipes

CONTENTS

SPECIAL FEATURES

FAMOUS GEORGIANS' RECIPES

FOLD-OUTS

INTERVIEWS

TOURS

CONTENTS

SPECIAL FEATURES

SIDEBARS

Contents

Special Features

Sidebars

ACKNOWLEDGEMENTS

This book could not have begun, much less have finished, without the complete support of the Georgia Department of Agriculture. The idea of compiling a cookbook of the best recipes from Georgia's popular *Farmers and Consumers Market Bulletin* had been discussed for many years. In April of 1996 Don Rogers, the department's assistant commissioner for marketing, pushed the idea forward and made it a reality. Don also suggested adding travel destinations so readers could see the beautiful locations where Georgia crops are grown and visit historic sites that reflect the state's rich agricultural heritage. From day one, Mary Ellen Lawson, the department's director of international marketing, was an enthusiastic supporter and was invaluable in developing a strategy for producing the book. Rita Bagwell McDuffie, assistant to Georgia agricultural commissioner Tommy Irvin for more than thirty years, coordinated meetings and interviews, expedited memos, rewrote copy and produced original text for the book. She kept the entire project going when momentum lagged or logjams developed. Marsha Crowley has been overseeing the collecting and testing of *Market Bulletin* recipes for years and her behind-the-scenes work provided the book's foundation. Susan Lewis compiled, tested and formatted all the recipes, wrote original sidebar text and gathered numerous resources. There would not be *The Best of Georgia Farms Cookbook and Tour Book* without her professionalism and expertise.

From the beginning, Georgia Commissioner of Agriculture Tommy Irvin was an enthusiastic supporter of the cookbook and tour book idea. He gave writers and editors free reign with regard to the editorial material, insisting only that we turn out a book that was worthy in editorial quality to the products cultivated by Georgia farmers.

Others in the department of agriculture who provided valuable assistance are:

Martha Mead and Benita Johnston for recipe proofreading; Sylvia Willis and Carlton Moore for *Market Bulletin* research; Nancy Werling and Roselyn Davenport who processed paperwork, handled phone calls and countless other details; Brenda James Griffin, director of press and consumer services and Gabe Jordan, press officer. Thanks also to the statisticians and staff of the Georgia Agriculture Statistics Service in Athens who are experts in tracking agricultural data.

Harvey Robertson provided valuable ideas on distribution and marketing; Mike Bonner, director of the Atlanta Farmer's Market, allotted generous amounts of his time to locate resource material and explain how the largest farmer's market in the world works; Danette Amstein with the Georgia Beef Board and Judy Harrison with The University of Georgia Cooperative Extension Service assisted in recipe research; and Anne Byrn provided recipe consultation. The Georgia Apple Commission, the

Georgia Egg Commission, the Georgia Milk Commission, the Georgia Peach Commission, the Georgia Pecan Commission, the Georgia Sweet Potato Commission, the Vidalia Onion Committee, the Southeast United Dairy Industry Association, Inc., the National Watermelon Board, the Georgia Beekeeper Association and the Georgia Peanut Commission all provided recipes.

Also included in *The Best of Georgia Farms* are recipes from well-known Georgians. Many thanks to those who graciously responded to our requests: Mary Beth Busbee, Kent Butler (for Mrs. Brumby's cookbook), Virginia Carnes (Lester Maddox's daughter), Elizabeth Harris, Grace Hartley, Bernice Irvin, Shirley Miller, Lynda Talmadge, Louis and Billie Van Dyke, Lazell Vinson, Ruth A. Wells (Senator Sam Nunn's secretary), and L. H. and Sema Wilkes.

Former President and Georgia Governor Jimmy Carter; Gold Kist founder D. W. Brooks; farmers Tim Mercier, Willie Adams and James Lee Adams; and chefs and cookbook authors Nathalie Dupree and Elizabeth Terry provided hours of interviews which were edited for these pages.

Although their publishers are credited elsewhere, we say thanks again to the authors whose books and articles are excerpted throughout the book. The pleasures of eating Georgia and Southern food is in itself a rich experience, but somehow reading what these authors have written about it makes it even better: Roy Blount Jr., Olive Ann Burns, Harry Crews, Clyde Egerton, Fannie Flagg, Bill Hedgepeth, Edna Lewis, Margaret Mitchell, Medora Perkinson, Ferroll Sams, Buddy Sullivan and Alice Walker.

Also, many thanks to *Fried Green Tomatoes* director/producer Jon Avnet for writing a wonderful sidebar for us about his first visit to Juliette.

This is the second book on which we have been privileged to work with illustrator Garry Pound of Columbus. Hopefully, it will not be the last. Garry's wonderfully detailed line drawings convey moods, feelings and a sense of humor that often surpasses the limited ability of words. He produces beautiful work under the most difficult time constraints and always exceeds our expectations of quality and quantity.

Many thanks to our expert and industrious proofreader Kim Blass who more than does her part in keeping us on deadline, to writer Hal Jacobs who came through for us with humorous and insightful sidebars when we were down to the wire and to Lillian Sands who carefully transcribed our many hours of taped interviews.

Others who aided us in our endless quest for information are: Carl Black, the Cagle family, Carolyn Cary, Mike Dollar, Tal DuVall, Don Hastings, Cynthia Hizer, Eda Kenny, Janet Mack, Lee May, Walter Reeves, John Singleton, Lloyd Swartzentruber, Betty Talmadge and Gene Talmadge.

DEDICATION

Since 1917 the *Farmers and Consumers Market Bulletin* has been published continuously in Georgia under various names, the *Market Bulletin*, the *Farmers' Market Bulletin* and now the *Farmers and Consumers Market Bulletin*. In 1992, to celebrate its seventy-fifth anniversary, the editors asked for letters from its 250,000 weekly readers, telling what the bulletin had meant to them over the years.

Among the hundreds of letters was this one from Mrs. Raymond R. Hughes of Carrollton, Georgia: "When farm chores and field work were completed and during the long after-supper hours, Mama read aloud to all the family. The only reading material in our home then was the Bible, the *Market Bulletin*, our bi-monthly county newspaper and a few school text books... Mama read and reread every page of each issue of the *Market Bulletin*...."

Letters came from octogenarians: "... I have been taking the *Market Bulletin* since July 1918. It has been wonderful in pleasure and business. I have sold lots of things through the years including seed, animals, rabbit and bird boxes, bird feeders, quilting frames, butter molds, dasher lids for churns and other things. I am 89 years old and still advertise and look forward for it to come every Wednesday."—*P. D. Webb of Elberton.*

And teenagers: "... I'm an 18 year-old college freshman, and I've been reading the *Market Bulletin* for about four years. My family and I own show horses so I've found your equine editions very beneficial. I especially like your listings of equine events in the Bulletin Calendar and we've attended many shows we've read about in this section."—*Dana Nichols of Lawrenceville.*

The *Market Bulletin* is a valuable and beloved institution of Georgia. For most of the twentieth century, the pages of this modest tabloid have faithfully recorded the state's agricultural history. Through its colorful ads the personal history of Georgia farmers through wars, the scourge of the boll weevil, the Great Depression, the New Deal and presidents since Woodrow Wilson have been poignantly revealed. A small selection of these personal ads are reproduced as "page turners" on the bottom right hand pages of this book.

The Best of Georgia Farms, whose recipes are collected from the pages of the *Farmers and Consumers Market Bulletin,* is dedicated to present and past bulletin readers and to the editors and commissioners of agriculture who, over the years, have faithfully sustained this one-of-a-kind Georgia institution. Commissioners of Agriculture: J. J. Brown, 1917-1927; Eugene Talmadge, 1927-1933; George C. Adams, 1933-1934; Tom Linder, 1935-1936; Columbus Roberts, 1937-1941; Tom Linder, 1941-1955; Phil Campbell, 1955-1969 and Tommy Irvin, 1969 to the present. *Market Bulletin* Editors: Carlton B. Moore, Toby D. Moore, Lisa Ray, Valera Jessee, Deborah Pullin, D. Anglin and Jack Gilchrist.

FARMERS AND CONSUMERS
MARKET BULLETIN
GEORGIA DEPARTMENT OF AGRICULTURE · TOMMY IRVIN, COMMISSIONER

PREFACE BY TOMMY IRVIN

The happiest memories of my life as a young lad growing up on our modest farm in North Georgia are those pertaining to the many delicious foods my mother prepared from the products that grew right there on our land.

Not only did we have the good fortune of eating fresh corn, beans and other crops we grew; but we also enjoyed wonderful cobblers and other delights Mama made from the blackberries and strawberries picked off wild vines and the apples I gathered for her which dropped off our big apple tree in the fall. I remember well the innovative ways my mother converted one of those scrawny yard chickens into a tasty Sunday dinner. The great aromas that came from Mama's kitchen will always dwell in my mind and heart.

I guess I haven't changed much as far as my food preferences are concerned. My wife Bernice says, "I wish I had a nickel for every time you've called and said, 'Honey, put the cornbread on, I'm on the way home.' "

She says I'm easy to fix for. I love home-cooked vegetables and cornbread. She can make me happy with a bowl of beans, sliced onion, cornbread and sweetmilk.

Like most traditional country cooks, Bernice seldom follows a recipe for cooking vegetables, corn bread and biscuits. Like most southern ladies, she has a little secret or two that makes her cooking special to me. She tells me she adds a little margarine to fresh peas or lima beans—a little bacon grease to green beans and turnip greens. She says she always puts a little sugar in her vegetable soup.

I smiled, but was not surprised, when, looking over the proofs of this book, I read where former President and Georgia Governor Jimmy Carter said his favorite meal was one like his mama used to cook and one which Rosalynn had qualified as an expert: black-eyed peas, string beans, collard greens, cornbread, butter milk or ice tea with some potato, pumpkin or apple pie as dessert. He said it makes his mouth water just to talk about it. Mine too.

I would guess that for most of us some of our most important memories are memories that have to do with food.

Because the native products of Georgia have given such nourishment, pleasure and memories to so many different people from every possible walk of life, it is a special pleasure for me to bring to you this cookbook and tour book that we have called *The Best of Georgia Farms*.

Most of the recipes here come from the pages of the Georgia *Farmers and Consumers Market Bulletin* that has been published continuously by the Georgia Department of Agriculture since 1917. All of the *Market Bulletin* recipes and have been tested and tasted by the professionals on our home economist staff.

Other recipes come from a cross-section of well-known Georgians—some professionals and some traditional family cooks. All of the recipes rely mostly on Georgia-produced ingredients.

Our state is truly blessed with a mild climate, long growing season, a variety of beautifully rich soils and plentiful rainfall. These God-given resources, combined with the ingenuity and resourcefulness of our farmers, provide a variety of Georgia-grown products that take second place to no other state.

Other parts of the book take you on self-guided tours to locations around the state where specific products are grown or where the rich agricultural history of our state is illustrated in parks, historic sites, museums and demonstration gardens.

Also, in these pages, you will meet some of the fascinating personalities who have enriched our agricultural history and continue to do so today.

I hope you will enjoy *The Best of Georgia Farms* and that you will keep one copy in the kitchen for cooking and one in your car for touring. I hope it will be a genuine source of cooking, traveling and reading pleasure to you and a continual reminder of the outstanding products that are gown and produced in our great State of Georgia.

INTRODUCTION BY FRED BROWN

Cagle Dairy in Holly Springs, the oldest and only dairy producer-distributor in Georgia, puts together dairy tours for school-age children. "We love for them to come," says matriarch Bernice Cagle. "Especially the children from the city. This is the first time some of them have ever seen a cow. They think milk comes from the grocery store."

Not long ago, while I was having my hair cut in a Buckhead barber shop, I overheard the men and women stylists talking about a bizarre—for Buckhead—event that had occurred the day before. A nearby resident's small pet pig had escaped and terrorized the merchants of the Peachtree Battle Shopping Center. The humane society was called and a large crowd of upscale shopping center patrons witnessed the pig capture. "It was *wonderful*," my barber, a woman, said. "*So exciting*! I hadn't seen a pig in forty years."

Many of us who live in Georgia's cities have a misconception about the state. We see it as a state of freeways, traffic jams and shopping centers. In reality, Georgia's cities are urban islands in a great rural sea where peaches grow on peach trees, cotton grows in cotton fields and pecans grow in pecan groves; where milk comes from cows and pig wrangling is a common everyday occurrence.

Georgia is the largest state east of the Mississippi. With 58,910 square miles, it is about the same size as the states of Maine, Vermont, New Hampshire, Massachusetts and Rhode Island combined. Georgia has more land area than the nations of Ireland, Greece, Portugal or England. Georgia is not just a state, it is a *region* with two different mountain ranges, a Piedmont, a Coastal Plain and a seacoast—and much of it is rural farm land.

As recently as 1950, nearly one-third of Georgia's population lived on farms. That has changed over the years as people have left farms and migrated to cities. But, even though the actual number of people living on farms has decreased, agriculture has maintained its importance, and in some ways, has become more important to the state's economy. It takes fewer people to grow corn; but it takes numerous people to shuck it, wash it and wrap it in a plastic-covered cardboard tray and get it to the supermarket where it is attractively displayed for consumers. It takes fewer people to grow lettuce but more people to chop it and package it into the individual servings sold by fast food franchises. Farming and agribusiness, including the processing and packaging of food, is the largest employer in the state of Georgia.

Perhaps more than any other state, the history of Georgia is intimately connected to the development of agriculture.

Georgia's earliest settlers, the colonists who came with James Oglethorpe to set up the thirteenth American colony in 1733, came specifically to farm. A stipulation of the original charter for the colony was that the settlers were to establish small fifty-acre farms. The most important thing they brought with them on the passage from England was seeds.

In the 127 years between the settlement of the state and the Civil War, Georgia became the most important cotton producing state in the Union. When the Civil War began, Georgia had more plantations than any other state. Because of the devastation from the Civil War, followed by the boll weevil plague in the 1920s and the Great Depression in the '30s, Georgia's agriculture, and therefore, Georgia's economy, languished for almost one hundred years.

In 1933 when D. W. Brooks, the founder of Gold Kist and one of the individuals interviewed in this book, gathered the farmers of Carroll County on the courthouse lawn to preach to them about how to improve their farming techniques, the average farmer in the crowd was making seventy-two dollars a year.

Franklin Roosevelt, whose New Deal policies began to lift America out of the depression, maintained a residence, The Little White House, at Warm Springs, Georgia. There in Georgia's Piedmont, he saw firsthand the poverty and poor agricultural practices that were plaguing Georgia and the South. His Georgia observations and experiences translated directly into some of the New Deal's most innovative agricultural practices.

Like its history, Georgia's culture is inextricably bound to agriculture. Scarlett O'Hara, the prototype Southern heroine, speaks for Georgia and the entire South when she returns to Tara after the Yankees have devastated it and vows that she will never be hungry again. There must be ten thousand roadside stands in Georgia selling boiled peanuts. We have a Watermelon Queen, crowned every year in Cordele. We have a Pig Jig in Vienna. We have the Vidalia Onion. In 1962 the city of Gainesville passed an ordinance making it illegal to eat fried chicken with a fork. In 1992 popular Atlanta newspaper and nationally syndicated columnist Lewis Grizzard wrote about the fine fried green tomatoes served at the Blue Willow Inn in Social Circle and turned that restaurant into an overnight success. Each week since 1917, Georgians have eagerly awaited the arrival of the *Georgia Farmers and Consumers Market Bulletin*. In 1992 a deluge of letters celebrating its seventy-fifth anniversary poured into the Georgia Department of Agriculture—more than a few ranking the bulletin next to the Bible in importance in their homes.

From the Apple Festival in Ellijay to the Blessing of the Fleet in Darien, most of the dozens of fairs and festivals held each year around the state are agriculture based. Cane grinding, pottery turning and corn shuck dolls are just a few festival events, activities and crafts for sale that celebrate our agricultural heritage. In 1997 antique tractor collector Rick Minter and a partner organized an antique tractor show in

Fayette County—once farm land but now a rapidly growing suburban Atlanta county. They expected about five hundred people to show up—more than five thousand people came to relive a part of their agricultural past.

Many of Georgia's most interesting and popular tourist attractions reflect our agricultural heritage: The Agrirama in Tifton, Hofwyl-Broadfield Plantation on the coast near Darien, Jarrell Plantation in Middle Georgia and the Foxfire Museum in Rabun County are just a few of the many examples. This book takes that into account by designing tours, along with directions and maps, to the major agriculture related attractions and historic sites in Georgia. Here are twenty-eight tours from Rabun County in Georgia's northeast corner to Decatur County in the southwest corner.

Often times driving to a tour location is as interesting and inspiring as the tour itself. The route through southwest Georgia along Georgia Highway 39 passes through some of the most beautiful and productive farm land anywhere in the world. The mountain roads of Rabun County, lined on both sides with cabbage farms, are as pretty as any Caribbean beach. The miles and miles of pecan groves that line both sides of US Highway 19 north of Albany are worth a special trip.

During an interview with President Carter that I recorded for this book, it was gratifying to hear him describe in detail the different routes he and Mrs. Carter take driving back and forth from their home in Plains to The Carter Center in Atlanta. I have taken those same routes, and the views he described of peanut farms, cotton fields and pine tree farms are views I have enjoyed many times.

The interviews in this book are still more examples of Georgia's rich agricultural heritage. D. W. Brooks, the founder of Gold Kist; Willie Adams, a small poultry and beef farmer in Greene County; Tommy Irvin, Georgia's Commissioner of Agriculture; Tim Mercier, the largest apple grower in the state; and James Adams, who runs a large, multifaceted agricultural operation in Camilla, all reflect Georgia's agricultural past and it's future. Nathalie Dupree and Elizabeth Terry, chefs and cookbook authors whose interviews are recorded in this book, demonstrate a genuine love for and understanding of Georgia food and have done as much as any one to bring the glories of Georgia and Southern cooking to national attention.

The book's sidebars are designed to provide brief insights into Georgia agriculture and food. Some of my personal favorites are the book excerpts by authors such as Ferroll Sams, Olive Ann Burns and William Hedgepeth, who have written—sometimes elegantly, sometimes humorously—about Georgia food and farming. Even native Georgians who think they know the food personalities of the state will be surprised to learn of the connections between food legends Margaret Lupo, Sara Spano, Steve Nygren and Margaret Mitchell.

Among the many pleasures of compiling this book, one of the most interesting and satisfying was slowly leafing through the yellowed, bound volumes of the

Georgia Market Bulletin, now called the *Georgia Farmers and Consumers Market Bulletin,* which has been published since 1917. Today, 250,000 people receive this free weekly publication. Both sets of my grandparents subscribed to it, my mother and father subscribed and now I get it. The bulletin's ads for seeds, used farm equipment, farm animals, help wanted, positions wanted and land for sale, along with periodic editorials by legendary characters, such as former Georgia Governor Gene Talmadge, weave a personal and touching story of Georgia agriculture through boll weevil plague, depression and a world war, as well as good times. Excerpts from the bulletin are presented somewhat chronologically as page turners, and they provide some of the book's most interesting reading.

First and foremost, of course, this is a cookbook specializing in Georgia-grown products. Most of the recipes come from the pages of the *Farmers and Consumers Market Bulletin* and have been formatted and tested by the professional home economists in the Georgia Department of Agriculture. Favorite recipes, using Georgia-grown food, from well-known Georgians supplement these and can be found in sidebars throughout the book.

This is a book about Georgia food, the land where it is grown and the people who grow it. Putting it together was a special privilege because Georgia agriculture touches everyone. *Agriculture* touches everyone. After all, we all eat. We wanted this book also to touch everyone—to have the same broad appeal and be nourishing in its own way.

We hope you will cook a recipe, take a tour and enjoy meeting some of the colorful and interesting personalities that make up Georgia agriculture.

An Introduction to the Recipes

Commissioner Tommy Irvin created the Georgia Cooking recipe column in the *Farmers and Consumers Market Bulletin* in 1969 after polling readers and discovering their desire for recipes using Georgia-grown foods. Through the years recipes have been submitted by readers and tested by department of agriculture home economists to insure quality and good taste. This give-and-take process has ensured that the recipes reflect the culture and tastes of farmers and consumers across the state.

Responding to an interest in healthy eating, department home economists began providing nutritional analysis and hints on modifying recipes to meet specific nutritional needs, with the strong belief that all foods can be part of a healthy diet and lifestyle. Diabetic exchanges have been included on some recipes and have become increasingly popular. Consequently, the *Market Bulletin's* Georgia Cooking column has evolved from its original mission of sharing the bounty of good Georgia foods to educating its readers on food trends and nutrition information. Our choices for this book reflect the variety of recipes and good foods that have been the most popular and sought after through the years.

Meats/Poultry

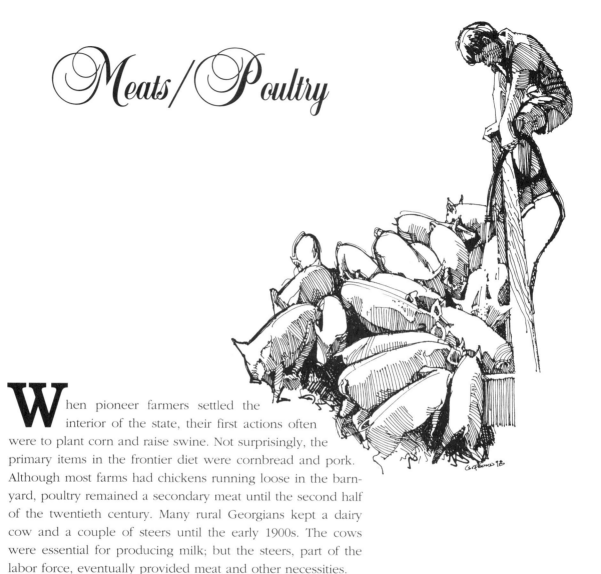

When pioneer farmers settled the interior of the state, their first actions often were to plant corn and raise swine. Not surprisingly, the primary items in the frontier diet were cornbread and pork. Although most farms had chickens running loose in the barnyard, poultry remained a secondary meat until the second half of the twentieth century. Many rural Georgians kept a dairy cow and a couple of steers until the early 1900s. The cows were essential for producing milk; but the steers, part of the labor force, eventually provided meat and other necessities.

Beef and pork production have become comparatively small agricultural industries in modern Georgia. The state ranked fifteenth in number of hogs and twenty-fourth in number of cattle and calves in 1996. Poultry production, however, has become by far the state's leading commodity. Ranking second in number of broilers produced and first in value of broiler production, the state produced 1.1 billion birds, 15 percent of the nation's total, with a farm value exceeding $2.2 billion in 1996.

BEEF

Cattle have been domesticated in the Near East since at least 6500 B.C. Contemporary domestic breeds evolved from a single early ancestral breed, the aurochs. In addition to prehistoric cave paintings that help identify the breed, some aurochs actually survived until comparatively modern times. The last documented auroch was killed by a poacher in 1627 on a hunting reserve near Warsaw, Poland. Although there's no direct evidence, some believe living aurochs could still remain in remote parts of Europe.

Early cattle served three purposes, providing meat, milk and labor. Eventually, horses and machinery took over the labor function, and cattle were bred specifically for the meat and milk purposes. Some common breeds of beef cattle include Agnus Charloise, Beefmaster, Brahma, Polled and Horned Hereford and Limousin.

In eighteenth-century Georgia, settlers from the Carolinas brought their cattle with them. In the extreme southern part of the state, settlers mixed their stock with that of the Spanish explorers who brought along cattle and other livestock on their expeditions. Large herds of free range cattle foraged clearings among the vast pine forests of South Georgia, causing the South in some ways to resemble the Wild West. Roundups, branding and long drives were common. Settlers, skillfully snapping long, rawhide whips to make a cracking noise, most likely gave rise to the name "cracker" – as in Georgia cracker.

Many rural Georgians kept a dairy cow and a couple of steers for the family's food supply until the early 1900s. In addition to the fresh and preserved meat, the animals provided hides, horns

Country Pot Roast

Onion soup mix adds flavor to an old standard

3 to 3½	pounds boneless chuck roast
1	tablespoon shortening
1	1-ounce package onion soup mix
2	cups water
4	medium-sized potatoes, cut into 1-inch cubes
4	carrots, thinly sliced
2	tablespoons all-purpose flour
½	cup water

In a Dutch oven, brown roast in shortening. Combine onion soup mix with 2 cups water and pour over roast; simmer, turning occasionally for 1½ to 2 hours or until tender. Add vegetables and cook 30 minutes or until potatoes are tender. Remove roast onto serving platter. Blend flour and remaining water and stir into gravy. Bring to a boil; reduce heat and simmer until thickened. Yields 6 servings.

Wanda McDaniel
Sparta, Georgia

Beef and Noodle Casserole

Just add a salad to this easy skillet dish and dinner's ready

1	pound ground beef
1	large onion, chopped
2	cloves garlic, minced
½	bell pepper, chopped
1	4-ounce can green peas, drained
1	16-ounce can whole tomatoes, drained
1	6-ounce can sliced mushrooms, drained
1	10.75-ounce can Cheddar cheese soup
1	8-ounce package noodles, cooked and drained
1	tablespoon Worcestershire sauce
	Dash hot sauce
	Salt and pepper to taste
½ to 1	cup grated Cheddar cheese

Preheat oven to 350°. In a large skillet, brown beef, onion, garlic and pepper. Drain. Combine with remaining ingredients, except cheese, and place in a 9x13-inch casserole. Top with cheese. Bake for 40 minutes. Yields 6 servings.

Sandy West
Milledgeville, Georgia

Deep Dish Taco Squares

Biscuit mix is the key to this unusual taco

- ½ pound ground beef
- ½ cup sour cream
- ⅓ cup mayonnaise
- ½ cup (2 ounces) shredded, sharp Cheddar cheese
- 1 tablespoon chopped onion
- 1 cup biscuit mix
- ¼ cup water
- 1 medium tomato, thinly sliced
- ½ cup chopped green pepper
- Paprika (optional)

Preheat oven to 375°. Grease 8-inch square baking dish. In medium skillet, brown ground beef; drain. In a small bowl, mix sour cream, mayonnaise, cheese and onion; reserve. In a separate bowl, combine biscuit mix and water until soft dough forms. Pat dough in pan, pressing ½ inch up sides. Layer beef, tomato and green pepper in pan; spoon sour cream mixture over top. Sprinkle with paprika if desired. Bake until edges of dough are light brown, 25 to 30 minutes. Yields 6 servings.

Sandy Bailey
Mableton, Georgia

Vegetable Meatloaf

Rice and vegetable soup make this a hearty meatloaf

- 2 pounds lean ground beef
- 2 cups cooked rice
- 1 egg, beaten
- 1½ cups chopped onion
- 1½ cups chopped bell pepper
- ¼ teaspoon pepper
- ¼ teaspoon garlic salt
- 2 tablespoons Worcestershire sauce
- 1 19-ounce can chunky-style vegetable soup
- 1 cup grated Cheddar cheese

Preheat oven to 350°. Combine all ingredients except cheese; place in large loaf pan or two small ones. Bake for 90 minutes or until done. Top with grated cheese while hot. Yields 6 servings.

Pat Newman
Augusta, Georgia

and tallow, the fat used in soap and candles. Since World War II cattle production has become predominantly a specialized industry. Most Georgia cattle farmers raise calves and send them to giant feedlots in the Midwest for fattening and slaughter. Today, cattle are found in all of Georgia's 159 counties. Cattle production is the state's sixth largest cash commodity, contributing about $250 million a year to the economy. Of the 1.4 million head in Georgia in 1996, Morgan County led the way with 31,000.

An all-American favorite, beef can be an important part of a healthy diet. A nutrient-rich food with high-quality protein, iron, zinc and five B-complex vitamins, beef today is 27 percent leaner than beef raised twenty-five years ago.

Resolved, that realizing that a wornout soil means a wornout man, I will not rob my farm of its fertility.
Resolved, that even if I have discouraging experiences, I will keep my good spirits and my faith that the Creator of the Land and of all things animate and inanimate with which I work, will not forsake a faithful tiller of the soil.

New Year Resolutions, Market Bulletin,
January 7, 1926

Apple Glazed Beef Brisket

Baked or grilled, apple jelly adds a taste of fall to this brisket

4 to 5	pounds boneless beef brisket
1	medium onion, quartered
2	large garlic cloves, halved
10	whole cloves
1	10-ounce jar apple jelly
⅓	cup dry white wine
3	tablespoons Dijon-style or spicy brown mustard
3	tablespoons minced green onions, including tops
1½	teaspoons salt
¾	teaspoon curry powder
¾	teaspoon coarse ground black pepper
	Parsley
	Tomato roses

Place brisket, onion, garlic and cloves in large Dutch oven. Add water to cover. Bring to a boil; reduce heat, cover and simmer 2½ to 3 hours until tender. Drain brisket, cover and refrigerate up to 24 hours. To prepare glaze, combine apple jelly, wine, mustard, green onions, salt, curry powder and pepper in small saucepan and heat until jelly melts, stirring occasionally. Preheat oven to 325°. Place brisket in shallow roasting pan. Brush with glaze and roast 45 minutes, basting frequently with glaze. Place brisket on heated serving platter and garnish with parsley and tomato roses. Carve brisket into thin slices and serve with remaining glaze. Yields 8 servings.

Vicki Wadlington
Tennessee
1984 National Beef Cook-Off Winner

Hint: Brisket may also be cooked on charcoal grill for 30 minutes, basting often with glaze.

Buyer's Guide to Beef

When purchasing beef, refer to the package label that identifies the type of meat and the wholesale and retail cuts. Look for USDA choice or select grades; these are the lowest in fat and calories.

The leanest cuts of beef are loin and round cuts. The "skinniest" six cuts of beef are round tip, top round, eye of round, top loin, tenderloin and sirloin. The words "round" or "loin" mean lean steaks or roasts.

When selecting beef, look at the appearance and color. The lean part should be a cherry-red color, unless it has been cured or smoked.

Beef, including vacuum-packaged beef, is a dark, purplish-red color when first cut. Marbling, the small flecks of fat throughout the lean, improves the meat's flavor and juiciness.

Look for a fat covering of one-eighth inch or less on steaks or roasts, or trim the extra fat to one-eighth inch. The fat cover keeps beef from drying out and helps retain juices during cooking.

Fresh beef should be refrigerated as packaged and can be stored for one to four days.

Beef can be frozen in the packaging for up to two weeks.

The best way to defrost beef is in the refrigerator, but a microwave oven can also be used.

Tenderize lean cuts by cooking slowly with moist heat, cooking in liquid or marinating.

To prepare beef without adding fat, try roasting, broiling, pan broiling, grilling and microwaving.

Mushroom Stuffed Sirloin

Mushroom stuffing makes this an elegant dish

- 1 tablespoon olive oil
- ⅓ cup finely chopped mushrooms (about 1 ounce)
- ⅛ cup minced shallots or green onions
- ½ teaspoon red wine
- Dash each of salt, dried thyme leaves and black pepper
- 1 pound boneless beef top sirloin steak, cut 2 inches thick

Heat oil in large, heavy nonstick skillet over medium-high heat. Add mushrooms and shallots; cook 4 to 5 minutes or until vegetables are tender, stirring occasionally. Add wine and cook until evaporated. Stir in salt, thyme and pepper. Remove from heat; cool thoroughly.

Meanwhile, trim excess fat from boneless beef top sirloin steak. To cut pocket in steak, make a horizontal cut through the center, parallel to the surface of the meat, about 1 inch from each side. Cut to, but not through, opposite side. Spoon cooled stuffing into pocket, spreading evenly. Secure opening with wooden picks.

Place steak on rack in broiler pan so surface of meat is 4 to 5 inches from heat. Broil 25 minutes for rare (140°), 30 minutes for medium (160°) or to desired doneness, turning once. Place on warm serving platter. Let stand 10 to 15 minutes. Remove picks; carve into ½-inch slices. Yields 4 servings.

Georgia Beef Board

Ginger Beef

Use a wok to cook this easy Oriental dish

- ¾ pound round steak
- ½ teaspoon ground ginger
- 1 tablespoon vegetable oil
- 3 scallions, thinly sliced
- 1 10-ounce package frozen Japanese-style crispy vegetables with seasoning
- 2 tablespoons water
- 2 cups hot cooked rice

Thinly slice steak, then cut slices into slivers. Sprinkle with ginger. Heat oil in a large skillet or wok over medium heat. Add scallions and sauté for 1 minute. Add steak and brown until all pink disappears. Remove from pan. Remove seasoning pouch from vegetables. Spread vegetables in hot skillet, cover and cook 2 to 3 minutes, stirring once. Sprinkle contents of seasoning pouch over vegetables; stir in water and steak. Serve with rice. Yields 3 servings.

Carol Sarmir
Roswell, Georgia

The Department of Agriculture

Founded in 1874, the Georgia Department of Agriculture, the nation's oldest such department, operates primarily as a regulatory and enforcement agency to protect consumers and promote farmers. Elected every four years, the Commissioner of Agriculture directs nearly nine hundred employees in half a dozen divisions. The Administrative Division takes care of internal support services, such as accounting, budget and personnel, and directs public outreach programs through the office of public affairs, which serves as the department's liaison with the news media and oversees the weekly tabloid *The Farmers and Consumers Market Bulletin.*

Animal Industry inspects poultry, beef and milk; licenses and enforces laws dealing with livestock, bird and pet operations; tests fertilizer, feed and seed; and inspects kennels, pet shops and animal shelters.

Consumer Protection Field Forces administers regulations regarding food processing, packaging, sales and storage; and licenses all food handling establishments except for restaurants.

Plant Industry deals with pesticides, nurseries, the bee industry, entomology and chemical labs, seed labs, crop industry inspections and boll weevil eradication.

Fuel and Measures regulates the state's motor fuel industry; enforces laws governing grain, cotton and tobacco storage; and verifies the accuracy of commercial weighing and measuring devices.

The Marketing Division, through farmer's markets, commodities promotion and international trade units, actively promotes Georgia agricultural products to retail and wholesale markets at home and abroad.

THE GEOGRAPHY OF AGRICULTURE

From the mountains to the coast, where crops or livestock thrive depends in large part on regional growing conditions. The elevation, soil, topography and climate of a particular area will determine how well a particular plant or animal does. For example, in Northeast Georgia the conditions favor apples and wine grapes. These crops grow well in the cool evenings and warm days of a mountain summer. Further south, the fruit would lose their flavor and color because of the hotter temperatures. While most vegetable production takes place in South Georgia because of the long growing season, Rabun County at the northeast tip of the state stands out as an exceptionally strong produce growing area in North Georgia. The reason: an unusually large, flat valley combined with fertile mountain soils. In the Piedmont, the rolling hills have prevented the widespread use of modern farming machines such as large harvesters, which has meant the almost complete disappearance of row crops such as cotton, tobacco, peanuts and soybeans. In this section of the state, chicken and cattle farms continue to operate, unaffected by the terrain, and the mild climate prevents the heat stresses that the animals can experience further south.

In South Georgia, where the topography flattens out into the Coastal Plain, modern mechanized equipment can navigate the level, sandy soils with relative ease. The region, therefore, can host large farms with row crops, as well as orchards which require huge machines for harvesting. The region also offers much less risk of frost, which can seriously damage many crops, like peaches.

Some crops depend on more specific conditions. For instance,

SWEET AND SAUCY MEATBALLS

Peach preserves and chili sauce bring zip to this appetizer

1	green onion, chopped
1	tablespoon butter or margarine
1	pound ground chuck
½	cup fine, dry breadcrumbs
1	egg, beaten
¼	teaspoon dry mustard
⅛	teaspoon pepper
1	16-ounce jar peach preserves
1	12-ounce bottle chili sauce
1	tablespoon minced green onions
½	teaspoon ground ginger

Combine chopped green onion and butter in a large bowl; microwave, uncovered, at HIGH for 2 minutes or until onion is tender. Stir in ground chuck, breadcrumbs, egg, mustard and pepper; shape into ¾-inch meatballs. Arrange meatballs in a 12x8x2-inch baking dish; cover with wax paper and microwave at HIGH for 6-8 minutes or until no longer pink, stirring after 3 minutes. Set aside.

Combine preserves, chili sauce, minced green onions and ginger in a 1½-quart casserole, stirring until blended. Cover with heavy-duty plastic wrap and microwave at HIGH for 5½ to 6 minutes or until preserves melt, stirring after 3 minutes. Spoon sauce over meatballs; serve immediately in your prettiest chafing dish. Yields 2 dozen appetizer servings.

Georgia Department of Agriculture Test Kitchen

Sesame Steak and Mushrooms

Sesame oil adds a terrific touch of the Orient!

2 to 2½	pounds boneless sirloin steak
1	8-ounce package mushrooms, sliced thin
3 to 4	green onions, sliced thin, with some green
	Leaf lettuce
	Green onions
	Carrot curls for garnish

Dressing

¼	cup low-sodium soy sauce
¼	cup wine vinegar
2	tablespoons Dijon mustard
3	tablespoons dry sherry
2	tablespoons honey
1	teaspoon finely-minced fresh ginger root
1	large garlic clove, finely minced
¼	cup corn oil
3	tablespoons Oriental sesame oil

Broil steak to desired doneness. (Rare to medium-rare is best.) Let cool and slice into bite-size pieces. Combine all ingredients for dressing except oils and mix well. Add oils and shake in a tightly capped jar. (Dressing can be made several days ahead and refrigerated.) Pour dressing over steak and mushrooms. Toss gently, cover and let marinate in refrigerator 1 to 2 hours, stirring several times. To serve: drain excess dressing and spoon onto lettuce-lined platter. Sprinkle with chopped onions and carrot curls if desired. Can be served hot or cold. Yields approximately 6 servings.

Gail Greenblatt
Columbus, Georgia
1988 Georgia Beef Cook-Off Winner

Hint: The dressing has an oriental spicy flavor without being overly salty.

vidalia onions grow well in Southeast Georgia largely because of the low sulphur content of the soil. The Georgia package bee industry, which ships starter and queen honey bees to other parts of the country, centers around Southeast Georgia mostly because of its proximity to the Okefenokee Swamp. Like cattle, bees require large spaces to graze, and the vast public wetlands offer a massive supply of swamp flowers. Watermelons grow in largest concentration around the Cordele region. Besides the long growing season, the soil type lends itself to a superior tasting melon.

Peaches grow best along a belt just south of the Fall Line in Middle Georgia. South of there, the trees aren't exposed to enough low temperatures before they blossom to ensure that the tree will fruit. Yet north of the Fall Line, the fruit trees suffer the risk of frosts after the blossom, which can diminish a harvest. Other crops do well in most any circumstances. Corn, for example, while concentrated in South Georgia, grows in every Georgia county.

Reaves Farm & Orchard Co., Cleveland, Ga. Farmers to run 3 two horse crops on shares; will furnish stock but not supplies; will give some work so party will have means to run until crops are made and gathered; near church and school.

Farm Help Wanted, Market Bulletin, *January 7, 1926*

Ernie's Beef Stew

Baking is the secret to this hearty, winter main dish

1½ to 2	pounds stew beef, cut into 2-inch pieces
3	tablespoons all-purpose flour
2	cups water
1½	cups coarsely chopped onion
2	16-ounce cans tomatoes, chopped
1	clove garlic, minced
1	tablespoon parsley flakes (optional)
2½	teaspoons salt
¼	teaspoon pepper
1	bay leaf
6	medium carrots, cut into 2-inch pieces
3	medium potatoes, cut into 1½-inch cubes
½	cup chopped celery

In a large pot over medium heat, brown beef in its own fat. In a small bowl, mix flour and water for thickening. Preheat oven to 350°. Add flour mixture, onion, tomatoes, garlic, parsley, salt, pepper and bay leaf to beef. Bring mixture to a boil. Pour into 3-quart casserole and cover. Bake for 1½ hours, stirring once or twice. Add carrots, potatoes and celery. Continue baking covered for 1 hour or until vegetables are tender, adding more water if needed. Remove bay leaf before serving. Yields 6 to 8 main dish servings.

Ernestine Lewis
Rincon, Georgia

Good Taste in Music

Over the years a lot of country song writers have put to music their thoughts on food. Some of the song titles describing southern delicacies are:

A Corn Licker Still in Georgia
Bacon and Collards
Chicken in the Bread Tray
Hog in the Cane Break
Home Brew Rag
How Many Biscuits Can You Eat?
I Love Molasses
Little Brown Jug
Milk Cow Blues
Mister Chicken
Pass Around the Bottle and We'll All Take a Drink
Peach Pickin' Time in Georgia
Peel Me a Nanner
Polly Put the Kettle on
Rabbit Soup
Short'nin' Bread
Southern Fried
Streak-o-Lean, Streak-o-Fat
The Old Hen Cackled and the Rooster's Going to Crow
The Taffy-Pulling Party
Turkey in the Straw
Watermelon on the Vine

A few southern bands have also felt that food names make for memorable band names:

Corn Dodgers
Corn Huskers
Dilly and His Dill Pickles
Goober and the Peas
Lick Skillet Orchestra
Light Crust Doughboys
Moo Cow Band
Skillet Lickers
Sorghum Band

Brunswick Stew

Ground beef adds flavor and texture to this Georgia tradition!

2	3-pound fryer chickens
	Salt to taste
	Chopped onion to taste
	Chopped celery to taste
3	pounds ground beef
4	cups chopped onion
3	15-ounce cans chopped tomatoes
1	10.75-ounce can cream of mushroom soup
1	cup barbecue sauce
½	cup chili sauce (hot)
1	teaspoon pepper
1	teaspoon Worcestershire sauce
1	10.75-ounce can cream of chicken soup
4	cups chicken broth (as needed)
1	cup ketchup
1	teaspoon salt or to taste
1	teaspoon ground ginger
1	teaspoon hot sauce
2	15-ounce cans cream-style corn

Combine chicken, salt, onion and celery in large stock pot; cover with water. Bring to a boil, then reduce heat and simmer for 45 minutes or until done. Reserve broth for stew. When chicken is cool, remove skin, debone and cut into bite-sized pieces. In large skillet, brown ground beef. Drain off excess fat and add onions. Simmer mixture until onions are transparent. In large stock pot, combine cooked chicken, hamburger mixture and the next 12 ingredients. Cook over low heat for several hours. Best if simmered all day. During the last hour of cooking, add corn. Yields 8 quarts.

Mary White
Doraville, Georgia

Hint: To reduce fat and calories in this recipe, remove skin from chicken before boiling and skim fat from broth before adding to stew. Substitute lean ground turkey for the ground beef and use 99% fat-free cream of mushroom soup. To reduce sodium content, omit salt and use low-sodium canned tomatoes and low-sodium soup. Result: One serving contains 216 calories, 5.8g of fat (24% of calories).

Brunswick Stew

The origins of this thick, spicy stew are disputed—whether it was derived from Brunswick County, Virginia or North Carolina, or the city of Brunswick, Georgia—but cooks agree on most of the ingredients: chicken, onions, potatoes, tomatoes, butter beans, corn and plenty of pepper.

As for its origins, John Egerton, author of *Southern Food*, passes along a story about a black cook named Jimmy Matthews who concocted a squirrel stew for his master Creed Haskins in Brunswick County, Virginia, in 1828. However, one should note, as Egerton does in his book, "It seems safe to say that Indians were making stews with wild game long before any Europeans arrived, and in that sense there was Brunswick stew before there was a Brunswick."

HOG-KILLING TIME

From *A Childhood: The Biography of a Place* by Harry Crews …

Before it was over, everything on the hog would have been used. The lights (lungs) and liver—together called haslet—would be made into a fresh stew by first pouring and pouring again fresh water through the slit throat—the exposed throat called a goozle—to clean the lights out good. Then the fat would be trimmed off and put with the fat trimmed from the guts to cook crisp into cracklins to mix with cornbread or else put in a wash pot to make soap…. After the guts had been covered with salt overnight, they were used as casings for sausage made from shoulder meat, tenderloin, and—if times were hard—any kind of scrap that was not entirely fat…. Whatever meat was left, cheeks, ears, and so on, would be picked off, crushed with herbs and spices and packed tightly into muslin cloth for hog's head-cheese. The fat from the liver, lungs, guts, or wherever was cooked until it was as crisp as it would get and then packed into tin syrup buckets to be ground up later for cracklin cornbread. Even the feet were removed, and after the outer layer of split hooves was taken off, the whole thing was boiled and pickled in vinegar and peppers. If later in the year the cracklins started to get rank, they would be thrown into a cast-iron wash pot with fried meat's grease, any meat for that matter that might have gone bad in the smokehouse, and some potash and lye and cooked into soap, always made on the full of the moon so it wouldn't shrink.

BEEF STEAK WITH VEGETABLES

4	beef boneless chuck eye steaks, cut ½ inch thick (about 4 to 5 ounces each)
1	teaspoon pepper
½	teaspoon salt
3	tablespoons peanut oil (divided)
1	cup radishes, cut julienne
1	cup yellow squash, cut julienne
1	teaspoon garlic, pressed
1	medium sweet red bell pepper, chopped
2	teaspoons freshly squeezed lime juice
2	teaspoons chopped fresh basil leaves
½	teaspoon pepper
¼	teaspoon salt

Rub steaks with ½ teaspoon salt and 1 teaspoon pepper; set aside. In a large skillet, heat 1½ tablespoons of peanut oil over moderate heat until hot. Add radishes and squash; sauté until soft, stirring occasionally. Add garlic, chopped pepper and lime juice. Continue to sauté until pepper is soft. Add basil and season with remaining salt and pepper; stir and remove to serving dish. In the same skillet, heat 1½ tablespoons of peanut oil over medium heat; add steaks and cook for 6 to 8 minutes for medium-rare or until desired doneness is reached, turning once. Serve steaks with vegetables. Yields 4 servings.

Carolyn Toole
Hoschton, Georgia
1994 Georgia Beef Cook-Off Winner

HAM AND BROCCOLI CASSEROLE

1	10-ounce package frozen broccoli spears
1½	cups cubed cooked ham
1	10.75-ounce can cream of mushroom soup
½	cup mayonnaise
¼	teaspoon tumeric
½	cup grated Cheddar cheese
½	cup bread crumbs
2	tablespoons butter, melted

Partially cook broccoli spears approximately 3 to 4 minutes, until thawed but not done. Preheat oven to 325°. Place broccoli in an 8-inch square baking dish. Sprinkle ham over broccoli. In a small bowl, combine soup, mayonnaise and tumeric; pour on top of ham. Sprinkle grated cheese over soup mixture. Mix bread crumbs with butter and place on top of casserole. Bake for 30 minutes. Yields 4 servings.

Sandra Bracewell
Alpharetta, Georgia

Downtown Pork Tenderloin

Peaches and a rosemary cream sauce make this a beautiful dish

1½	pounds pork tenderloin, cut crosswise into 1-inch slices
4	tablespoons unsalted butter, divided
	Salt and pepper to taste
4	peaches, peeled and each cut into 8 wedges
4	shallots, minced
1	teaspoon rosemary leaves
½	cup peach nectar
4	tablespoons lemon juice
1	cup chicken broth
½	cup cream (half and half)

Flatten pork slices to about ¼-inch thickness between sheets of plastic wrap. In a large, heavy skillet, heat 2 tablespoons butter over medium-high heat. Pat the pork slices dry; season with salt and pepper. Sauté in butter for 4 minutes, turning once. Transfer the cooked pork to a platter; keep warm and covered.

Add the remaining butter to the skillet. Cook the peach wedges in butter, covered, over medium-high heat for 2 minutes, or until peaches are just tender. Transfer the peaches to the platter of pork; keep warm and covered. Add the shallots to the skillet; cook over medium heat, stirring for 2 minutes. Add the rosemary, peach nectar and lemon juice. Deglaze the skillet, scraping up brown bits and boil the liquid, stirring occasionally, until it is reduced to about ¼ cup. Add the broth and boil the mixture, stirring until the liquid is reduced by half. Add the cream and the pork with any juices that have accumulated on the platter; leave the peaches on the platter. Boil the mixture, stirring and turning the pork occasionally for 1 minute or until the sauce is thickened slightly. Transfer the pork to the platter and pour the sauce over it. Yields 6 servings.

Georgia Peach Commission

History of Hogs
From *The Hog Book* by William Hedgepeth …

So far as scientists, anthropologists and historians are able to determine, pigs have been rooting about the globe's surface for at least 45 million years now, whereas men emerged and commenced to root around only about a million years ago, a mere gnat of time as such things are reckoned on the hogspan scale. And in all the ensuing aeons, hogs have remained structurally intact: the same skull and skeletal pattern, the same fourteen ribs and basic bone-fittings, the same forty-four teeth and seventy-five feet of intestine, the same cloven hoofs, the same sweet snout, the same apparent passions and ardent desires.

M. C. Blackwell, Farrar, Ga. 1 open buggy good except body slightly busted $17.50 with harness; 1 two horse wagon $15.

Second Hand Machinery For Sale, Market Bulletin, *January 14, 1926*

PORK

One of the oldest livestock on earth, pigs were domesticated in China around 7000 B.C. Egyptian drawings from 3000 B.C. show pigs as prized animals eaten only once each year. Hernando de Soto introduced hogs to North America in Florida in 1539. Upon his death three years later, his original fifteen had bred to almost a thousand. Before becoming president, George Washington imported special hogs to establish breeding herds. Some common breeds today include Berkshire, Chester White, Hampshire, Poland China, Yorkshire, Landrace, Duroc and Spot.

In the early days of Georgia's settlement, hog production was both limited and haphazard. During Colonial times, hogs often were raised on the coastal islands where they could not stray too far. They ranged freely and foraged for themselves, but were not allowed in towns. Oglethorpe once ordered some hogs shot for trespassing into Fort Frederica where they damaged the foundations by rooting into them. When left to forage in the open pasture, the hogs tended to revert to a state of semi-wildness. The descendants of theses "razorbacks" or "land pikers" live in remote parts of the state today.

The hogs brought with the interior settlers were little tamer than the wild razorbacks in the woods. High in the shoulder, low in the rear, thin, with a long head and snout and swift of foot, they were often killed in the woods or rounded up in the fall, some marked in the ear and released, others taken home to be fattened on corn and killed.

Hogs were killed usually after the first long spell of cold weather in the fall. Edible parts that can't be preserved, such as

PORK ROAST WITH GEORGIA PEACH SAUCE

Marinate the pork ahead of time for deep rich flavor

- ¼ cup soy sauce
- 3 tablespoons sherry
- 1 large clove of garlic, minced
- 1 teaspoon dry mustard
- ½ teaspoon ground cinnamon
- ½ teaspoon rubbed thyme
- 1 3 to 4-pound center cut pork loin roast
- ⅔ cup puréed peaches or peach preserves
- ¼ cup chili sauce or ketchup
- 1 cup water, divided

In small bowl combine first 6 ingredients. Marinate pork 2 to 3 hours or overnight in refrigerator. Reserve marinade for later use. Preheat oven to 325°. Roast pork for about 30 minutes per pound or until meat thermometer reaches at least 160°. Meanwhile, in small saucepan combine reserved marinade, peach purée, chili sauce and ½ cup water; boil then reduce to simmer. Baste pork during last 20 minutes of cooking. After pork is cooked, add remaining ½ cup water to oven pan and scrape up pan juices. Add pan juices to sauce. Yields 9 servings or about 3 servings per pound.

Georgia Peach Commission

SAUSAGE SQUASH CASSEROLE

Yellow squash and sausage combine for a great look and taste!

- ¾ pound ground sausage
- 4 cups sliced, cooked yellow squash
- ¾ cup bread crumbs
- ½ cup grated Parmesan cheese
- ¾ cup milk
- 1 teaspoon garlic powder
- 2 tablespoons parsley flakes
- ½ teaspoon oregano leaves
- ½ teaspoon salt
- 2 eggs, well beaten

Preheat oven to 325°. In a large skillet, brown sausage; drain and set aside. In a medium bowl, combine squash, bread crumbs, cheese, milk and spices. Add sausage and fold in eggs. Turn into an 8-inch square baking dish. Bake for 25 to 30 minutes. Yields 6 servings.

Wendy Love
Riverdale, Georgia

Baked Pork Apple Dinner

This contest winner combines two Georgia products

- 2 pounds boneless pork chops, trimmed of fat
- ⅓ cup all-purpose flour, divided
- 2 tablespoons canola oil
- 1½ cups apple juice
- 1 teaspoon salt
- 1 teaspoon pepper
- 2 pounds medium new potatoes, halved
- 1 pound carrots, cut into 2-inch pieces
- 2 medium onions, chopped
- 2 cooking apples, peeled, cored and quartered

Preheat oven to 350°. Coat pork chops in 2 tablespoons of flour. In large skillet, heat oil over medium heat and add pork chops. Brown chops on both sides. Remove chops from pan and drain well on paper towels. Reduce heat and immediately add remaining flour, stirring well to combine. Stir in apple juice, salt and pepper. Heat to boil, then reduce heat to simmer. Using a 9x13-inch pan and an 8x8-inch pan, add new potatoes, carrots and onions, distributing evenly. Top with browned chops. Pour apple juice mixture over top. Cover with aluminum foil and bake for 30 minutes. Add apples, distributing evenly to each pan; re-cover and bake 10 minutes. Remove foil and bake 10 minutes. Serve hot. Yields 8 to 10 main dish portions.

Janice Tatum-Barbour
Albany, Georgia
Second Place Main Dish,
1994 Macon Great Tastes of Georgia Recipe Contest

Potato Stuffed Pork Chops

- 4 medium-sized potatoes
- 6 pork chops, cut 1-inch thick
- ½ cup blue cheese dressing
- 1 tablespoon butter or margarine
- ¼ teaspoon salt
- ⅛ teaspoon pepper
- 6 orange slices

Preheat oven to 350°. Peel and cut up potatoes. Place in a medium-sized saucepan with small amount of water and boil until tender. Cut a pocket in the side of each chop. Drain and mash potatoes; measure 1½ to 1¾ cups of potatoes. Blend with dressing, butter, salt and pepper. Fill chops with potato mixture. (Chops can be closed with toothpicks or left open to allow potatoes to brown.) Place chops in two 9x12-inch baking dishes. Sprinkle with salt. Top each chop with an orange slice. Bake for 90 minutes. Yields 6 servings.

Georgia Department of Agriculture Test Kitchen

chitterlings, livers, knuckles and brains, spurred great feasts after the slaughter. Hams, shoulders, jowls and bacon sides, cured indefinitely, were trimmed, buried in salt for a month, then smoked in the smokehouse, preferably with hickory wood. Farmers differed on what spices to use, but most rubbed red pepper into the meat to prevent infestations of insects.

As long as the supply lasted, Southerners ate at almost every meal either ham, shoulder, bacon, sausage, pork or vegetables flavored with pork fat. Nonetheless, few farmers in Georgia in the 1800s and early 1900s raised hogs for much more than their families, devoting most of their energy and acres to lucrative cash crops.

The industry changed in the early 1900s. During World War I, pork demand skyrocketed and in 1919 hog production reached its all-time peak in the state at 2,350,000. Large packing plants opened in Moultrie, Statesboro, Macon and Tifton. Improved breeds were introduced to produce meatier, healthier pigs. New crops like peanuts and other legumes offered cheap forage. In the 1920s, more than 80 percent of farms had hogs and pigs, although most were still raised for farm consumption.

In 1996 there were about eight hundred thousand hogs and pigs on Georgia farms, totaling about $69 million in value. The industry is concentrated in South Georgia, where Colquitt County led the state with thirty-nine thousand head in 1996.

Compared to a decade ago, today's pork after cooking and trimming has 31 percent lower total fat, 20 percent less saturated fat, 14 percent less calories and 10 percent less cholesterol. Pork also provides a host of important nutrients, including protein, B-vitamins, iron and zinc.

The Georgia National Fair

Each October fireworks and midway neon light up the nighttime sky as the Georgia National Fair takes over the National Fairgrounds and Agricenter in Perry. Farm people from across the state come to show their prize horse, cow or pig; try out their secret casserole or canned preserves recipe; or display their latest quilt. And everyone comes for the fun—pig races and livestock shows; country music stars; antique tractors; agricultural exhibits on poultry, beef, dairy, cotton and peanuts; booths with quilters, weavers, honey producers, jam and jelly makers and farm product sellers; roasted corn, barbecue, funnel cakes, alligator meat and fried catfish; and twisting, turning and looping ferris wheels, spider barrels and roller coasters.

1. The bell tower is a welcome landmark for fairgoers.
2. Cotton candy and caramel apples are two of the many popular fair-time foods.
3. Competing for a blue ribbon is an agricultural fair tradition.
4. Uncle Sam greets visitors in front of the Sheep, Swine and Goat Barn.
5. The Georgia National Fairgrounds and Agricenter sits on 628 landscaped acres.
6. Fireworks light up the sky each night at the fair.
7. The midway skyline promises and delivers family fun.

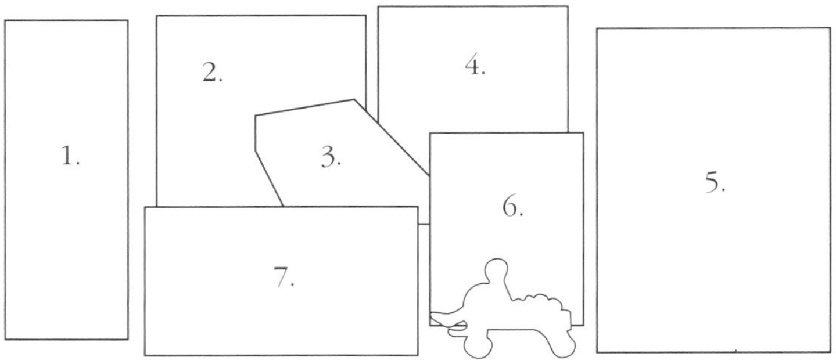

Willie Adams

Willie Adams's sixty-acre poultry and livestock farm is in Greene County between Greensboro and the Oconee River, about one mile north of I-20. It is bordered by Richland Creek on the east, the Seaboard System rail line on the south, an unnamed creek on the west and US 278, designated in this part of the state as Jefferson Davis Memorial Highway, to the north. Jim Adams Road, named for Willie Adams's grandfather, leads to the farm. The white frame farm house, weathered barn and several outbuildings sit on a north-to-south trending ridge, which forms the highest elevation on the farm. For the interview we made our way through a clutter of old farm machinery to a one-story, white-washed cinder block structure. Inside, we stood at a plywood table piled waist high with papers and talked.

My great, great-grandfather, he was farming back at the turn of the century. They owned some land in the east part of Greene County, which is now under Lake Oconee. His son, James Adams, my grandfather, farmed, sharecropped up until 1938. Then President Roosevelt had a plan they called the New Deal, and he applied for funds to purchase a house and ninety-two acres and some mules. He began farming, raising cotton, corn, oats, watermelons, sweet potatoes, peanuts. He did that for about ten years or so. Then he went just basically cotton and corn; until the boll weevil hit and he had to sell. He sold about thirty acres of land to pay off the rest of it, so that cut it down in the neighborhood of about sixty acres, what we have now. He farmed that on up until around 1941 up until the time World War II began. His two sons had to leave to go to service so my grandfather and his wife and his three daughters continued to farm on up until 1950, '55. Then he cut back. He had got kinda up into age. He was growing small acres of cotton and a little bit of corn.

I'm Willie Adams, the grandson. What I did, I came in and started raising livestock for Future Farmers of America and 4-H while I was in school, and we continued that on until 1968. At that time I finished high school and took a few courses at Fort Valley State College and some night courses at the University of Georgia. I went to work with Wayne Egg Company. I worked there for about ten years. I was in charge of egg processing and basic inventory. I was working there full time on the night shift and during the daytime I was running the farm, raising cows and whatever. In 1977 I began growing broilers for Central Sawyer. I worked at Wayne Egg at night and ran those two broiler houses for about six or eight months. After that I discontinued my job at Wayne Egg and went full-time farming. I was raising beef cows and broilers.

A small poultry farmer, Adams works with large poultry companies who supply the baby chicks that he then grows to maturity, a system common throughout North Georgia.

In North Georgia you have somewhere in the neighborhood of ten or twelve poultry companies, but down in this area you only have four. You got Harrison, you have Gold Kist and you got Cagle and Seaboard. But basically in Greene County there's only two, Cagle and Seaboard. Seaboard is the main one. I'm the only grower in this area for Cagle.

You build the houses; you furnish the labor. The poultry company, they furnish the chickens and the supervision and the feed. The University of Georgia says for a person to make a pretty fair living growing poultry you need four houses which are about forty feet wide and five hundred feet long. And you need to produce one hundred thousand chickens every seven weeks. That's your average-size poultry farm.

Basically, you're talking somewhere in the neighborhood of about eighty thousand dollars, yearly gross revenue, on the lower side. It depends. The cost coming out of that for you to operate, you got gas, you got the electricity, upkeep and maintenance of your houses.

One forty foot-by five hundred-foot poultry house costs you around $125,000. And like I said, the University of Georgia says you need to have four houses to make a decent living. You talking about... Whew! A half a million dollars. That's right. That's a lot of money! You need to have chickens in those houses.

Five years ago I had to spend thirty-five thousand dollars on three houses to put in fans and some drinkers. Five years later they said those drinkers was obsolete and I had to change to another type and I didn't have the money to do it with. So at the present time I'm operating two of my houses. I have five houses. Three of the houses been vacant for about two years. So the poultry business has its ups and downs I would say.

Adams receives baby chicks from the poultry company and grows them to maturity in seven weeks.

You have your houses prepared and ready. You have it set at about eighty-five degrees inside the house. The chickens be roughly two or three hours old. They hatched at the hatchery. You bring 'em in. You have your house divided in half, long ways, with a plastic curtain. That's called a "half brood." With Cagle you're talking somewhere in the neighborhood of about twenty-five thousand chickens per house. You hand feed 'em. You have your feeders running down your house. You put your pans under your feeders and then you put your feed in there by hand scoop for about two or three days. When they get older they learn how to jump over into the self-feeder. You have your water there and you have your little mini cups on your water where they can get to drink the water out of the cups. After they get five days old, you take the cups off where they can get it off the nipple and they be on the self drinkers. Each day as they age you raise your drinkers and feeders up. Then after three weeks you take your bowls up and raise your curtain and go to the whole house. Then you turn your feeders on and they start to feeding and then they automatically grow.

After they get up to seven weeks they come in and they catch 'em. It takes about two buses to bring in eighty-five or ninety thousand baby chickens. When they get ready to take 'em away it takes somewhere in the neighborhood of from ten to twelve eighteen-wheeler road tractors to haul 'em away. You have roughly about two weeks to clean the houses out and get ready to go again.

Willie Adams's formula for a successful small farmer:

Basically growing chickens and livestock and, if possible, growing hay for a cash crop. My suggestion is if a person has a good bit of open land, two poultry houses and raising cows is about one of the best things you can do, even with livestock prices being flexible. Because you don't have any cost for fertilizer. You have your fertilizer right there. You can grow silage and hay without using any commercial fertilizer because you got that poultry litter to spread on there. Poultry litter is one of the best things that ever happened. I haven't used any commercial fertilizer in twenty years. I grow silage and hay with poultry litter. I grow beef cattle, but I know farmers around who run poultry and dairy. Poultry and dairy run real good together.

Will there be a fifth generation on the Adams Farm?

To obtain any capital to get into the business is so hard. Then after you get into it your children can see how hard it is for you to struggle. I have two children, a girl and a boy. She's seventeen and finishing high school this year. Thinking about going to school taking nursing. Got a son that's twelve. He likes sports and computers. And not really interested in agriculture and I can't too much blame him.

AFRICAN AMERICAN FARMERS

- In 1920, 1 in every 7 farmers was African American.
- In 1982, 1 in every 67 farmers was African American.
- In 1910, African American farmers owned 15.6 million acres of farm land nationally.
- In 1982, African American farmers owned 3.1 million acres of farm land nationally.
- Between 1920 and 1992 the number of African American farmers in the U.S. declined from 925,710 to 18,816, or by 98 percent.
- In 1984 and 1985 the U.S. Department of Agriculture lent $1.3 billion to farmers nationwide to buy land. Of the almost 16,000 farmers who received those funds only 209 were African American.
- Almost half of all African American-operated farms are smaller than 50 acres.
- In the late 1980s, there were less than 200 African American farmers in the United States under the age of 25.

SOURCE: *Black Farmers and Agriculturist Association, 1025 Thomas Jefferson St., Suite 407 West, Washington, DC 20007.* Voice: 202/342-1300; Fax: 202/342-5880.

- In 1930 in Greene County, Georgia, there were 615 white farmers and 942 African American farmers. In 1992 there were 204 white farmers and 8 African American farmers.

SOURCE: *Willie Adams*

BUYER'S GUIDE TO PORK

A key to selecting pork is to read the label. The label explains the kind of meat, the cut and where on the animal it's from. The leanest pork cuts are those with "leg" or "loin" in the names.

Fresh pork comes mainly from the loin and shoulder area and sometimes the leg and side. Cuts include chops, roasts, ribs, leg cutlets, ground pork and blade steaks. Cured or prepared pork, like sausage, cold cuts, ham and bacon, offer extended shelf life.

Trim external fats from pork before cooking to reduce calories, fat and cholesterol.

Fresh pork will have a light-pink color.

The lean part of the cut should be firm, fine-grained and free from excess moisture. The thin outside rim of fat should be white.

Pork should be cooked to an internal temperature of 160° to 170°, medium to well-done, according to the USDA. Pork cooked to 160° will be slightly pink in the center. Bone-in cuts will be slightly pinker, but are safe to eat. Well-done pork will have little to no pink color.

To keep pork lean, use a low-fat cooking method that lets fat drip away or requires a minimum of added fat. Try roasting, broiling, grilling, microwaving, stir frying and pan broiling.

Marinades tenderize lean cuts and add flavor.

Keep pork in the meat tray or coldest part of the refrigerator. Wrap pork in plastic film or aluminum foil before refrigerating.

Freeze pork if you plan to keep it longer than three days.

To freeze, divide pork into convenient portions and wrap tightly in wax paper, heavy duty aluminum foil or freezer bags.

NACHO DIP

Great for parties and entertaining!

1 pound mild pork sausage
1 pound hot pork sausage
1 10.75-ounce can cream of chicken soup
1 10.75-ounce can cream of mushroom soup
1 5-ounce can evaporated whole milk
2 pounds processed American cheese
2 4-ounce cans chopped green chilies
1 4-ounce jar pimentos
1 8-ounce jar taco sauce, mild or hot

In large skillet, cook sausage; crumble into ½-inch pieces. Drain. Combine sausage and remaining ingredients in crock pot. Cook on high until cheese is melted and all ingredients are combined, stirring often. Adjust to low heat. Serve with tortilla chips. Yields 80 servings.

Molly Horton
Griffin, Georgia

Hint: To reduce fat and calories, substitute 1 pound of turkey sausage for the 2 pounds of pork sausage, evaporated skim milk for the evaporated milk and use 99% fat-free soups. Result: Each serving contains 63 calories and 4.5g of fat.

SAVANNAH RED RICE

2 cups raw long grain rice
2 teaspoons salt
4 cups water
6 slices bacon
2 medium onions, chopped fine
1 8-ounce can tomato sauce
1 6-ounce can tomato paste
2 teaspoons sugar
2 teaspoons Worcestershire sauce
Dash red hot pepper sauce

Cook rice in salted water according to package directions. Fry bacon and set aside; reserve bacon fat. In a large skillet, sauté onion in 4 tablespoons bacon fat until clear. Add tomato sauce, paste, sugar, Worcestershire sauce and hot sauce; simmer 10 minutes. Place cooked rice in a large casserole and stir in tomato mixture. Cover and bake at 325° for 45 minutes. Crumble bacon on top. Yields 8 to 10 servings.

Bettie G. Wright
Atlanta, Georgia

Hint: One pound cooked shrimp or fried smoked sausage may be added.

Apple Fall Squash

Sage and thyme enhance the flavor of this colorful side dish

3	1-pound acorn squash
12	ounces bulk light pork-turkey sausage
¼	cup chopped onion
1½	cups Golden Delicious apples, cored and chopped
¼	teaspoon ground sage
¼	teaspoon rubbed thyme
⅛	teaspoon pepper
⅛	teaspoon salt
½	cup chopped pecans

Preheat oven to 350°. Halve squash and remove seeds. Place cut-side down in 13x9-inch baking dish. Add small amount of water to cover bottom of dish and bake for 45 minutes. Sauté sausage and onion until brown and crumbly. Drain excess fat. Add apples and seasonings. Sauté 5 minutes longer. Turn squash cut-side up and discard water. Fill squash cavities with apple and sausage mixture. Sprinkle with pecans. Cover with foil and bake for 30 minutes or until squash is tender. Yields 6 servings.

Georgia Apple Commission

Apple Barbecued Ribs

5 to 6	pounds pork spareribs
4	quarts water
½	cup chopped onion
¼	cup vegetable oil
½	cup ketchup
⅓	cup fresh chopped parsley
2	tablespoons honey
2	tablespoons lemon juice
1	tablespoon Worcestershire sauce
1	teaspoon salt
1	teaspoon prepared mustard
½	teaspoon ground ginger
¼	teaspoon black pepper
1	clove garlic, minced
2	cups applesauce

Cut ribs into serving pieces; place in a large Dutch oven. Add water, cover and simmer 20 to 30 minutes. In a large saucepan, heat oil and sauté onion until tender. Add next 11 ingredients; simmer 15 minutes. Place ribs on grill over low coals. Baste with sauce. Grill about 40 minutes, turning frequently. Serve with remaining sauce. Yields 6 servings.

Georgia Apple Commission

A Pig for Fun

A hog breeder from Decatur County in South Georgia brought a special breed of hog to Atlanta for Zoo Atlanta. He flew the hog into Hartsfield Airport but the flight was late and he had another appointment in town. So he took the pig out in front of the airport and hailed a cab and told the cabbie, "Look, I'm running late. How about taking the pig to the zoo."

He put the pig in the cab, gave the driver some money and off they went.

He had his meeting, went to dinner and spent the night at the Buckhead Ritz. Next morning he got up and walked out of the hotel. There's the cab driver and the pig's in the back seat. He had on sunglasses, a baseball cap and a fielder's glove on the seat next to him.

The farmer was stunned. He ran up to the cab driver.

"Hey, I thought I told you to take that pig to the zoo."

"He had a wonderful time at the zoo. Today he wants to go to a Braves game."

E. H. George, Madison Ga. Man with cultured wife, good and neat housekeeper, to take 1, 2, or 3 horse farm on shares on large plantation; also take young man to board; will finance; come and bring references; must be sober, honest, intelligent and industrious; fine proposition to right parties.

Farm Help Wanted, Market Bulletin, *January 28, 1926*

CHICKEN

The domestication of the chicken is believed to have taken place about 3000 B.C. in India. In America, the chicken has been bred into a number of general classes: Rhode Island Reds, Wyandottes, Plymouth Rocks, Jersey Giants and New Hampshires. Other common breeds originating across the world include Cornish, Leghorns and Andalusians. Many breeds are becoming endangered as small farms become less common and the commercial poultry industry focuses on only a few breeds.

A part of Southern cuisine for years, fried chicken in the 1800s was the meal of honor served at the farmer's table, often to important guests such as the local preacher, whose fondness of fried chicken inspired many a tale. Practically every farm had chickens, which ran loose in the barnyard, survived off a minimum of feed and could be conveniently slaughtered compared to pigs or cattle. Nevertheless, the yard bird was served far less frequently than pork, the meat that dominated the Southern diet in the 1800s and early 1900s.

For most of the twentieth century, however, the demand for chicken has risen and today far exceeds pork and beef. During this time chicken production has changed dramatically. A few generations ago rural Southerners were largely self-sufficient. They supplied their own chickens and sold excess poultry and eggs to retail town merchants.

From the 1930s to 1950s, poultry pioneers like Jesse Dixon Jewell of Gainesville transformed poultry into a specialized industry using mass production techniques. Jewell, a small feed store owner, and others began providing feed and chicks on credit to

Broccoli Chicken Rolls

Microwave this family favorite

- 4 boneless chicken breast halves, flattened to ¼ inch
- 2 slices (¼ ounce each) low-fat cheese
- 1 10-ounce package frozen chopped broccoli, defrosted and drained
- ½ cup skim milk
- 1 tablespoon all-purpose flour
- 1 tablespoon white wine
- 1 teaspoon parsley flakes
- ¼ teaspoon pepper

Cut one cheese slice into fourths. Place one ¼ piece on each chicken breast. Spoon approximately 2 tablespoons broccoli onto chicken. Roll up and secure with wooden toothpicks. Place rolls seam side down in a lightly greased glass casserole. Cover with wax paper. Microwave on high for 8 to 10 minutes; drain.

Blend remaining ingredients in a 2-cup measure. Microwave on high for 1½ to 3 minutes, stirring halfway through. Add remaining cheese. Pour sauce over chicken and cook on high for 1 minute. Yields 4 servings.

Catherine Courchaine
Covington, Georgia

Hot Chicken Salad

A ladies' luncheon favorite

- 1 fryer chicken, cooked and boned
- 1½ cups diced celery
- ⅔ cup crushed saltine crackers
- 1 medium onion, grated
- 1 cup mayonnaise
- 4 hard cooked eggs, chopped
- 1 10.75-ounce can cream of chicken soup
- 2 tablespoons chopped pimento, optional
- 2 cups crushed potato chips

Preheat oven to 400°. Cut chicken into chunks and combine with remaining ingredients, except potato chips. Pour mixture into a greased 2-quart casserole; top with potato chips. Cover and bake for 15 minutes. Uncover and bake 15 minutes longer. Yields 6 to 8 servings.

Betty Jo Smith
LaGrange, Georgia

Capital Chicken Casserole

Tarragon, white wine and artichoke hearts add sophistication

- 4 tablespoons butter
- 1 tablespoon vegetable oil
- 1 broiler-fryer chicken, cut in parts
- 1 8-ounce package fresh mushrooms, sliced
- 1 tablespoon flour
- 1 10.75-ounce can cream of chicken soup
- 1 cup dry white wine
- 1 cup water
- ½ cup cream
- 1 teaspoon salt
- ¼ teaspoon tarragon leaves
- ¼ teaspoon pepper
- 1 15-ounce can artichoke hearts, drained
- 6 green onions, green and white parts included, chopped
- 2 tablespoons chopped parsley

Preheat oven to 350°. In large frying pan, place butter and oil and heat over medium temperature until butter melts. Add chicken and cook, turning after about 10 minutes or until brown on all sides. Remove chicken and place in baking pan or casserole. In same frying pan, sauté mushrooms about 5 minutes or until tender. Stir in flour. Add soup, wine and water; simmer, stirring, about 10 minutes or until sauce thickens. Stir in cream, salt, tarragon and pepper; pour over chicken. Bake uncovered for 60 minutes. Mix in artichoke hearts, green onions and parsley. Bake about 5 minutes more or until fork can be inserted in chicken with ease. Yields 4 servings.

Sheila Hoban
$10,000 Winner,
1980 National Chicken Cooking Contest

farmers to raise broilers, the chickens commonly sold for meat. When the chickens were ready for market, Jewell provided the transportation to haul them to markets. The farmers were happy to raise something besides cotton, which the boll weevil had nearly wiped out in the Piedmont region of the state. One of the first modern agribusiness arrangements, Jewell's efforts helped change Northeast Georgia poultry production from a sideline activity to a major commercial venture.

The typical poultry farmer has one or more chicken houses, growing ten to twenty thousand birds per house. Usually, each batch is grown about seven weeks under a contract with an agribusiness company. The chickens are delivered to processing plants for slaughtering, dressing and packing, and then transported by refrigerated truck to a variety of markets, including supermarkets and fast food chains.

Today, the chicken population worldwide exceeds 7 billion, higher than the human population. In Georgia more than 1 billion broilers, also called fryers, are grown each year in large commercial flocks. The largest commodity in the state, chickens contribute more than $2 billion each year to the Georgia economy. To compare, the value of poultry production in Hall County alone is worth more than that of peaches, pecans, apples, blueberries, grapes and onions combined in the entire state. More than eighty counties, mostly in the northeastern part of the state, earn $1 million or more from poultry income.

Chickens continue to grow in popularity. Since 1960 consumption has increased 154 percent in America. Lower in calories and fat than most other meats, chicken provides important nutrients like protein, iron and zinc.

Classic Country Captain

In 1993 the Columbus Museum published a book containing recipes collected by Mary Hart Brumby, a Columbus native. Many years ago Mrs. Brumby had set out to record family recipes given to her by her beloved grandmother, Miss Mamie. She had intended to share the recipes, along with the family stories that she had written, with her own children, nieces and nephews. But as she wrote, she realized that there were numerous recipes and anecdotes from other Columbus families and friends that would be wonderful to include. As people learned about her project, they began asking for copies of the forgotten recipes and the book, *Seasoned Skillets and Silver Spoons*, came to be.

One very famous recipe included in the book, Country Captain Mira Hart, is Mira Hart's (Mrs. Brumby's mother) version of a chicken curry recipe by Alexander Filippini, a chef at Delmonico's in the early 1900s.

Kent Butler, the publication's co-chairman, says that this recipe has been famous among Columbus citizens for years. Legend has it that when General George Patton was stationed at Fort Benning he would order buckets of Country Captain brought to the base.

To make the dish, which serves a small dinner party, Mira Hart would place 12 pieces of chicken in a little flour, mixed with salt and black pepper, and fry it in hot lard until lightly browned. She would then remove the chicken to a large casserole and keep it hot in the oven. Next, she poured out most of the lard until she had about 2 tablespoons left. Then over a low heat, Mrs. Hart would wilt 2 medium onions, finely sliced, and 2 green peppers, seeded and

Chicken Pie with Sweet Potato Crust

A low-fat, family favorite!

	Vegetable cooking spray
1	cup diced carrots
½	cup diced celery
1	cup diced onion
1	cup diced cooked potato
1	cup cooked peas
2	cups diced cooked chicken
1	tablespoon dried parsley
3	tablespoons all-purpose flour
1	cup skim milk
1	cup low-sodium chicken broth
¼	teaspoon pepper
½	teaspoon rubbed sage
	Sweet Potato Pie Crust

Preheat oven to 350°. Coat a large skillet with cooking spray and place over medium heat. Add carrots, celery and onions and stir-fry for 2 minutes, until vegetables are slightly tender. Remove from heat. In a 2½-quart casserole dish, combine vegetable mixture with potatoes, peas and chicken. Sprinkle with parsley and toss thoroughly. Set aside. Combine flour and a small amount of milk in a saucepan over medium-high heat, blending until smooth. Gradually stir in remaining milk and chicken broth. Cook on low heat, stirring constantly. Cook until thickened. Stir in pepper and sage. Pour sauce over chicken and vegetables in casserole dish. Cover mixture with Sweet Potato Pie Crust. Bake 45 minutes. Yields 6 to 8 servings.

Sweet Potato Pie Crust

1	cup all-purpose flour
½	teaspoon baking powder
¼	teaspoon salt
3	tablespoons diet margarine
½	cup cold mashed sweet potatoes
1	egg white

Combine flour, baking powder and salt; cut in margarine until mixture resembles coarse crumbs. Add sweet potatoes and egg whites, blending well. Roll dough out on a lightly floured surface to ¼-inch thickness. Yields crust for 1 pie.

Agriculture Test Kitchen

Southwestern Oven-Fried Chicken

This main dish has a winning combination of spices!

- 3 slices white bread, torn in small pieces
- 3 tablespoons fresh cilantro leaves
- 2 tablespoons yellow cornmeal
- 2 tablespoons pine nuts
- 2 large garlic cloves, peeled
- 1½ teaspoons ground cumin
- ½ teaspoon oregano leaves
- ½ teaspoon salt, divided
- ¼ teaspoon cayenne pepper
- ⅛ teaspoon ground cloves
- 2 teaspoons egg white
- 2 tablespoons Dijon mustard
- 1 tablespoon water
- 2 teaspoons honey
- 4 broiler-fryer chicken drumsticks, skinned
- 4 broiler-fryer chicken thighs, skinned
- ¼ teaspoon pepper

In food processor container, place bread, cilantro, cornmeal, pine nuts, garlic, cumin, oregano, ¼ teaspoon of the salt, cayenne pepper and ground cloves. Process to form fine crumbs. Add egg white and mix until moist. Place mixture on a large, shallow plate and set aside. In small bowl, mix together mustard, water and honey; brush evenly over chicken.

Preheat oven to 400°. Sprinkle chicken with pepper and remaining ¼ teaspoon salt. Dip chicken, one piece at a time, in breadcrumb mixture and press gently to adhere thin coating. Place chicken on rack in greased jellyroll pan. Bake for 40 minutes until chicken is crisp and brown and fork can be inserted with ease. Yields 4 servings.

Judith Markiewicz
1989 National Chicken Cooking Contest Winner

sliced, with a clove of garlic that she had crushed. She then seasoned this with 1 heaping teaspoon of salt, ½ teaspoon of white pepper, 2 teaspoons of curry powder, ½ teaspoon of chopped parsley and 2 saltspoons of thyme. Mrs. Hart would add 2 20-ounce cans of Italian tomatoes, cooking the sauce until it was bubbling hot. She then poured the mixture over the chicken in the casserole. If the sauce did not cover the chicken, she would heat some chicken stock in the same skillet and add it to the casserole. Covering it tightly, she would return the pan to the oven and cook the chicken very slowly until it was "perfectly done." This meant that the meat should still be "attached to the bone, but just clinging."

Mrs. Brumby wrote, "If there is too much sauce now to comfortably take up the rice, remove the chicken and reduce the sauce to a thicker consistency and then check for salt, acidity, pepper and strength of curry." To reduce the acidity, Mrs. Hart would add a little sugar.

Just before serving, Mrs. Hart would stir in 3 heaping tablespoons of currants that had been soaked in a little sherry. She would arrange 2 cups of dry, fluffy cooked rice in a ring on a platter, remove the chicken to the center and pour the sauce over the rice and chicken. For a final touch, Mira sprinkled ½ pound of toasted almonds over the dish.

Mrs. Brumby believed that "a good curry must be prepared hours or, preferably, the day before it is to be served. Curry takes time to infuse into the meat. I think it is really best of all on the day after the party when you re-heat the leftover for the third time."

What's Dinner? What's Supper?

There has always been confusion in what the South calls dinner. In the rest of the country, dinner is the evening meal. But in the South, dinner is "lunch" and the evening meal is called supper.

Nathalie Dupree, author of *New Southern Cooking,* tells a story about a former husband's grandmother which attempts to explain the situation.

"David's grandmother used to cook up a big lunch and then afterwards she would just cover it with a snowy white tablecloth to keep the flies away. She would just take the table cloth off at night and that's what we would eat for the evening meal. We would just sup on it... Supper. Dinner wasn't the main meal of the day. The main meal of the day was lunch. Dinner is lunch and supper is when you eat leftovers."

Chicken Tetrazzini

Use leftover chicken to make this an easy mid-week meal

- 1 8-ounce package fresh mushrooms, sliced
- 3 tablespoons butter or margarine
- 3 cups chopped, cooked chicken
- 1 12-ounce can evaporated whole milk
- 4 ounces dry spaghetti (cooked according to package directions)
- ½ cup grated Parmesan cheese
- Salt and pepper to taste

Preheat oven to 325°. Sauté mushrooms in butter. Add chicken and cover with evaporated milk. Simmer on low heat for 10 minutes. Place spaghetti in bottom of 9x12-inch baking dish; sprinkle with cheese and dot with butter. Pour chicken mixture over spaghetti. Add more milk if desired. Bake for 20 minutes. Yields 6 servings.

Kathryn Raiche
Atlanta, Georgia

Yes! Another Chicken Casserole

And another great way to combine chicken and noodles

- 3 to 4 chicken breasts, cooked and cut up
- 2 10.75-ounce cans cream of chicken soup
- 1 8-ounce can sliced water chestnuts, drained
- 1 small onion, chopped
- ¾ cup sliced almonds
- 1 cup chopped celery
- ¾ cup mayonnaise
- 2 cups cooked egg noodles
- Potato chips, crushed

Preheat oven to 350°. Combine above ingredients, except potato chips, and place in a buttered 9x12-inch casserole dish. Top with crushed potato chips. Bake for 30 minutes. Yields 8 servings.

Mollie Shrader
Trenton, Georgia

Roasted Chicken

Cook 2 chickens! Serve one for dinner, save the other for salads and casseroles

¼	cup olive oil
¼	cup soy sauce
1	teaspoon garlic powder
1	teaspoon salt
1	teaspoon coarse grind black pepper
2	teaspoons celery seed
2	teaspoons rosemary leaves
2	teaspoons oregano leaves
1	lemon, quartered
2	3 to 4-pound broiler-fryer chickens

Preheat oven to 400°. Combine olive oil, soy sauce and all spices in measuring cup. Rinse chickens and pat dry. Carefully separate skin from body of chickens at neck area, working down to breast and thigh area. Evenly pour half of olive oil mixture between skin and meat of both chickens; brush remaining mixture on outer skin. Squeeze lemon juice into cavity of birds and place ½ lemon in each. Place chickens on two vertical roasting racks or on lightly greased broiler rack in roasting pan. Bake until meat thermometer placed in thigh of chicken registers 180°, or for approximately 60 minutes. One chicken yields 6 main dish servings.

Georgia Department of Agriculture Test Kitchen

Hint: Experiment with your own unique combination of herbs and spices, sauces, mustards and salad dressings. To reduce fat and sodium in this recipe, eliminate olive oil, soy sauce and salt. Remove skin from chicken. Lightly coat chicken with 2 teaspoons olive oil and sprinkle herb spice combination on skin. Cook as directed. Results: Each serving contains 327 calories, 9g fat and 204mg sodium.

Pickrick Skillet Fried Chicken

From the time it opened on Hemphill Avenue in Atlanta in 1947 until it closed in 1965, the Pickrick Restaurant, owned by former Governor Lester Maddox and his wife Virginia, was famous for its pan-fried chicken, biscuits and gravy. At one time the Pickrick's special of two pieces of chicken, two vegetables and biscuit for 45 cents attracted Atlantans and tourists for miles around.

Two rules for cooks at the Pickrick: use only the heavy metal skillets especially designed and manufactured for the Pickrick to fry chicken and never completely submerge the chicken in shortening when frying. Deep fry kettles and pressure cookers were banned from the kitchen—and so were cooks who used them.

To make the Pickrick's famous skillet fried chicken, restaurant cooks would cut broilers, weighing from 2½ to 2¾ pounds into 8 pieces, 10 if liver and gizzard were included.

Pieces of chicken were dipped into a milk and egg mixture, drained and dredged in flour seasoned with salt, pepper and Accent. Shortening was then heated to about 350º in a skillet. Cooks placed each piece of battered chicken in the hot shortening with skin side down and open flesh side up. The shortening never covered any more than ⅔ the height, or thickness, of the chicken being fried. The chicken was cooked for 12 minutes with the skin side down, then it was turned over and cooked an additional 10 minutes. The cooks then removed the chicken from the skillet and drained it on paper towels or on a wire shelf in a metal pan.

Buyer's Guide to Chicken

One whole broiler-fryer serves four and yields more than three cups of cooked, diced chicken meat without skin.

Leg quarters are the most economical way to buy chicken.

Select specialty chicken parts to suit specific needs.

When buying, check the label's "Sell By" date, which indicates the last day the product should be sold. Chicken will maintain its quality for up to two days after the date if properly refrigerated. If frozen, it can be kept longer.

Look for the safe food handling messages on fresh chicken packages as a reminder for proper cooking, serving and storing.

Chicken's skin color doesn't indicate a difference in nutritional value, flavor, tenderness or fat content. Skin color ranges from white to deep yellow, depending on the chicken's diet.

Refrigerate raw chicken immediately. Never leave it sitting out at room temperature.

Packaged fresh chicken can be refrigerated in its original wrappings in the coldest part of the refrigerator.

Cooked, cut-up chicken can be stored in the refrigerator for up to two days; a whole, cooked chicken can be refrigerated for three days.

If chicken is stuffed, place stuffing in a separate container before refrigerating.

Freeze uncooked chicken that won't be used within two days of purchase.

To freeze fresh chicken, wrap parts separately in foil or plastic bags. Gather individual parts together in a freezer bag and label. Press all the air out of the bag before freezing.

Cooked chicken should be prepared for freezing the same way, unless topped with sauce or gravy. If sauce or gravy is

Italian Chicken Casserole

Low-fat and delicious!

4	ounces (1½ cups) uncooked mostaccioli (tube-shaped pasta)
1	tablespoon olive oil
½	cup chopped onion
½	cup chopped green bell pepper
1	14.5 or 16-ounce can chopped tomatoes, undrained
1	6-ounce can tomato paste
2	teaspoons sugar
¼	teaspoon salt
½	teaspoon Italian seasoning
⅛	teaspoon ground red pepper (cayenne)
2	cups cubed cooked chicken
½	cup sliced mushrooms
¼	cup water (as needed)
4	ounces (1 cup) shredded mozzarella cheese

Cook mostaccioli pasta as directed on package. Drain and keep warm.

Preheat oven to 350°. In large skillet, heat oil over medium-high heat until hot. Add onion and bell pepper; cook and stir 2 to 5 minutes or until crisp-tender. Stir in tomatoes and their liquid, tomato paste, sugar, salt, Italian seasoning and ground red pepper. Bring to a boil. Reduce heat to low and simmer uncovered 5 minutes. Stir in chicken, mushrooms and cooked mostaccioli pasta. Add up to ¼ cup water if mixture is too dry. Adjust seasoning to taste. Spoon into ungreased 2-quart casserole; cover.

Bake for 45 to 50 minutes or until bubbly. Uncover; sprinkle with cheese. Bake uncovered an additional 5 minutes or until cheese is melted. Yields 5 servings.

Georgia Department of Agriculture Test Kitchen

Hint: This delicious casserole is sure to become a family favorite. And, it's low-fat...Enjoy!

Chicken Black Bean Salad

Dressing

½	cup peach preserves
¼	cup lime juice
1	tablespoon vegetable oil
1	teaspoon chili powder
¼	teaspoon ground red pepper (cayenne)

Salad

2	cups cubed cooked chicken
1	medium red bell pepper, chopped
2	cups cooked kernel corn
1	15-ounce can black beans, drained, rinsed
5 to 6	Boston or Bibb lettuce leaves

In small bowl, combine all dressing ingredients and mix well. Finely chop large chunks of peaches, if needed. In large bowl, combine all salad ingredients, except lettuce. Add dressing; blend well. Refrigerate at least one hour before serving. Adjust seasonings to taste. Serve salad on lettuce-lined plates. Yields 5 servings.

Georgia Department of Agriculture Test Kitchen

Stuffed Turkey Breast

1	6-ounce package seasoned stuffing mix
¼	cup butter or margarine, divided
½	cup chopped celery
¼	cup chopped onion
1	3-pound boneless turkey breast, skinned
2	tablespoons honey

Prepare stuffing mix according to package directions. In a saucepan, sauté celery and onion in 2 tablespoons butter or margarine until celery is tender and onion is transparent. Mix celery and onion with stuffing mix.

Preheat oven to 325°. Lay turkey breast flat on wax paper, skin side down. Remove any tendons, skin or fat. Pound the breast to flatten and form a more even thickness. Spoon stuffing mixture into center of turkey leaving a 2-inch border at sides. Starting at bottom, fold in sides of turkey breast over filling. Tie turkey breast roll securely in several places with string. Place, seam side down, on rack in roasting pan. Mix honey and remaining butter or margarine together. Pour half of honey mixture over roll. Insert meat thermometer making sure bulb rests in meat of turkey. Bake, covered, for 30 minutes. Uncover, baste with remaining honey mixture and continue baking for 1½ hours or until meat thermometer registers 170°. Transfer turkey to cutting board; remove string; let stand 10 minutes before slicing. Yields 8 servings.

Georgia Department of Agriculture Test Kitchen

included, pack chicken in a rigid container with a tight-fitting lid. Keep frozen until ready to use.

Thaw chicken in the refrigerator, in cold water, or in the microwave —never on a counter top.

It takes about twenty-four hours to thaw a four-pound chicken in the refrigerator. Cut-up chicken parts will thaw in three to nine hours.

To thaw chicken in cold water, place it in the water in its original wrap or a watertight plastic bag. Change water often. A whole chicken will thaw in two hours.

Don't refreeze cooked or uncooked chicken once it has been thawed.

Always cook chicken well-done, not medium or rare. The internal temperature should reach 180° for chicken with bones, 170° for boneless parts.

To see if done, pierce chicken with a fork. It should insert easily and juices should run clear. Never leave chicken at room temperature for more than two hours. If not eaten immediately, cooked chicken should be kept either hot (above 140°) or refrigerated.

Cover leftovers to retain moisture and ensure that chicken is heated all the way through. Bring gravies to a rolling boil before serving.

Almost half the chicken's fat is found in the skin. Remove it before or after cooking to reduce calories and fat.

W. H. Mitchell, Barnesville, Ga. 3 to 5 good farm mules for sale now or in August, or will trade 1 or 2 mules for a real good tractor.

Horses and Mules For Sale, Market Bulletin, *July 21, 1927*

TURKEY

Native to northern Mexico and the eastern United States, the turkey is the most recognizable symbol of Thanksgiving, the annual American feast held in honor of the first harvest celebration by Native Americans and Pilgrims in the 1600s.

The wild turkey is brown with buff-colored feathers on the tail and tips of the wings. The male turkey, known as a Tom, is larger and has brighter plumage. He has a long wattle—a wrinkled, brightly colored fold of skin, hanging from the neck at the base—and a conspicuous tuft of bristles that look like a beard extending downward from his chest. The female, called a Hen, usually is smaller and more muted in color. First domesticated in Mexico, the turkey was brought into Europe in the early 1700s. Since then turkeys have been raised for the superb quality of their meat and eggs.

Commercial production of turkeys in Georgia is small compared to the state's broiler and egg industry. The turkey industry is centered in Northeast Georgia, but with no processing plants in state, all birds are shipped, mostly to North Carolina, South Carolina and Virginia. (North Carolina leads the nation in turkey production.) Turkeys produced in Georgia during 1996 totaled six hundred thousand birds, 38 percent below 1995. This reduction translated into a production drop from 44 million pounds to 17 million pounds between the two years.

TURKEY AND GOUDA IN A LOAF

This combination creates a beautiful appetizer or main dish

1	tablespoon butter
½	cup chopped onion
½	cup chopped celery
2	cups diced, cooked turkey or chicken
1	teaspoon Italian seasoning
½	teaspoon salt
¼	teaspoon pepper
⅓	cup sliced, pitted ripe olives
1	2-ounce jar chopped pimiento, drained
2	cups (8 ounces) shredded Gouda cheese
1	16-ounce package hot roll mix or 1 10-ounce can refrigerated pizza crust
*1	cup hot water
*1	egg
1	egg white, slightly beaten
1	tablespoon sesame seeds
	Vegetable cooking spray

* For use with hot roll mix only!

Melt butter in a skillet. Sauté onion and celery about 2 minutes. In large bowl, combine turkey, onion mixture, Italian seasoning, salt, pepper, olives, pimiento and cheese; set aside.

Preheat oven to 375°. If using hot roll mix, combine flour and yeast packet from inside box in a bowl. Add water and egg. Stir until dough leaves sides of bowl. Knead 5 minutes. Cover bowl and let stand 5 minutes. (Note: If using refrigerated pizza crust, unroll dough and proceed as follows.) Roll dough on floured surface into 14x10-inch rectangle. Spray baking sheet with vegetable cooking spray. Place dough on baking sheet and spoon turkey mixture lengthwise down center third of dough, leaving a little room at top and bottom. Make cuts ½-inch apart on each side of rectangle just to edge of filling. To give a braided appearance, fold strips of dough at an angle halfway across filling, slightly overlapping ends and alternating from side to side. Fold ends under to seal. Brush with egg white. Sprinkle with sesame seeds. Bake for 30 to 35 minutes or until golden brown. Cool slightly; cut into slices and serve. Yields 8 servings for entree, 16 for appetizer.

Variation: Add ½ cup prosciutto to turkey mixture and substitute Provolone for Gouda cheese.

Kevin Davis
Decatur, Georgia

Turkey Corn Chowder

An easy main dish for the day after Thanksgiving!

1	medium onion, chopped
¼	cup butter or margarine, melted
2	cups water
2	chicken bouillon cubes
3	cups diced cooked turkey
1	cup chopped celery
6	carrots, peeled and sliced
1	15-ounce can golden whole kernel corn, drained
1	15-ounce can golden cream-style corn
1	quart milk
	Salt and pepper to taste

Sauté onion in butter in a Dutch oven until tender. Add water, bouillon cubes, turkey, celery and carrots; cook 20 to 30 minutes or until carrots are tender. Add corn, milk and salt and pepper to taste; simmer until hot. Yields 8 to 10 servings.

Trisha Taylor
Hampton, Georgia

Turkey Salad Bake

1	5-ounce package potato chips
1	cup shredded sharp Cheddar cheese, divided
1	tablespoon butter
½	cup chopped pecans
2	cups diced, cooked turkey
1	cup chopped celery
2	teaspoons grated onion
¼	teaspoon salt
¼	teaspoon pepper
½	cup mayonnaise
2	tablespoons lemon juice

Preheat oven to 450°. Crush potato chips to make 2 cups; combine potato chips and 1/2 cup cheese. Place half of potato chip mixture in bottom of a lightly greased 8-inch square baking dish. Set remaining potato chip mixture aside.

Melt butter in a small skillet over low heat; add pecans and sauté until brown. Drain on paper towel. In a large bowl, combine pecans with remaining ingredients and spoon over potato chip mixture. Sprinkle remaining potato chips over turkey and top with remaining cheese. Bake for 12 to 15 minutes. Yields 5 to 6 servings.

Priscilla Steele
Smyrna, Georgia

Buyer's Guide to Turkey

When buying a whole turkey, calculate one pound of uncooked turkey for each person served.

Most whole turkeys are frozen when purchased. The best way to thaw a turkey is to leave it in the original wrapping and place it the refrigerator. Allow five hours per pound defrosting time. A sixteen pound-turkey, for example, will require about three or four days to defrost completely. If the turkey has not completely thawed when ready to cook, place it under cold tap water to hasten the thawing process.

Check the "Buyer's Guide to Chicken" on pages 30 and 31 for general poultry handling tips.

Georgia Should Lead in Agriculture Diversified Farming, Its Benefits and Possibilities. Buy Georgia Products First.

Headline on article by Mrs. Norman Sharp, Assistant Director, State Bureau of Markets, Market Bulletin, *July 28, 1927*

Poultry Production

Georgia's poultry industry, consisting of chickens, eggs and turkeys, represents the state's largest agricultural sector, contributing nearly 40 percent of the state's farm income each year. The industry pumps more than $10 billion annually through the Georgia economy. According to the University of Georgia Extension Service, on an average day, Georgia processes about 18 million pounds of chicken meat, 8 million pounds of table eggs, 5 million pounds of hatching eggs and 75 tons of turkey.

Mediterranean Turkey Pizza

Turkey and squash make this a very untraditional pizza

- 1 tablespoon olive oil
- 1 pound turkey cutlets, cut into ½ -inch strips
- 2 cloves garlic, minced
- ½ medium Vidalia® onion, thinly sliced
- 1 medium zucchini, cut in half lengthwise and sliced
- 1 medium yellow squash, cut in half lengthwise and sliced
- 4 medium plum tomatoes, diced
- ¼ cup chopped sun-dried tomatoes
- 1 tablespoon chopped fresh basil
- 1 tablespoon chopped fresh oregano
- 1 large (12-inch) ready-made pizza crust
- 1½ cups shredded mozzarella cheese, divided
- 1 2.25-ounce can sliced black olives, drained

In large skillet over medium-high heat, heat olive oil and sauté turkey cutlets, garlic and onion for 3 to 4 minutes or until onion is soft. Add zucchini and yellow squash and cook until crisp-tender. Stir in plum and sun-dried tomatoes, basil and oregano. Remove from heat and set aside.

Preheat oven to 375°. Sprinkle pizza crust with half of cheese and top with turkey mixture. Sprinkle remaining cheese and olives over top of pizza. Bake for approximately 10 minutes or until cheese melts. Yields 4 main dish servings.

Recipe adapted from National Turkey Federation

Hint: Sun-dried tomatoes have an intense flavor and are added to this recipe because of their Mediterranean influence. You may omit them if they are unavailable in your area. Substitute about 1½ teaspoons of dried basil and oregano if fresh is unavailable. To reduce the calories and fat in this recipe, substitute part skim mozzarella cheese.

Ostrich Stir Fry

Serve over rice for an unusual but delicious meal

1	teaspoon cornstarch
¼	cup light soy sauce
¼	cup dry sherry
½	teaspoon sugar
1	teaspoon peeled and grated ginger
1	pound emu, ostrich or rhea, sliced very thin
3	tablespoons olive oil
¼	teaspoon salt
1	clove garlic, minced (more to taste)
1	8-ounce package fresh mushrooms, sliced

In small bowl, blend cornstarch with soy sauce until smooth. Add sherry, sugar and ginger. Combine the sauce and meat and marinate for one hour. Strain marinade from meat and reserve marinade. In wok or large heavy skillet, heat olive oil and salt until very hot. Add meat and brown on both sides. Add garlic and mushrooms; stir fry for 2 minutes. Add marinade and heat through. (If necessary, thicken with a small amount of cornstarch diluted in water.) Yields 4 servings.

Kate Boyd
Augusta, Georgia

Hint: To reduce fat and calories in this recipe, reduce olive oil to 1½ tablespoons. Result: Each serving contains 195 calories and 6.4g fat.

Emu

A bird that roamed the Australian outback for millions of years, the emu has provided sustenance to the Aborigines since prehistoric times. In recent decades, limited commercial production of emus has taken place in America. Thousands of emu ranchers raise flocks of the bird, a cousin of the African ostrich. They believe the emu will play a larger role in the American diet as consumers seek healthier, leaner meats.

Emu ranching has many attractive qualities for those seeking a relatively low-maintenance agricultural business. The emu operations require little land; the average ranch has fewer than fifteen acres. And a breeder hen can produce about twenty chicks a year for twenty years or more.

Currently available in only a handful of restaurants or specialty markets across the United States, emu is a very lean meat, 97 percent fat free. Similar to beef in both appearance and taste, it is higher in protein, vitamin C and iron than beef and lower in cholesterol than chicken.

Emu, ostrich and rhea, all members of the ratite family, are being raised in Georgia and marketed as an alternative to red meat. Various cuts are available, including steaks, roasts, strips and ground meat. It is important not to overcook the meat since it is low in fat. The meat is easier to slice if partially frozen.

Sober young man wants job for 1928. Experienced in operating turpentine still and grist mill. Write Leroy Calhoun, Soperton, Ga.

Positions Wanted, Market Bulletin, *January 5, 1928*

Woodmanston Plantation

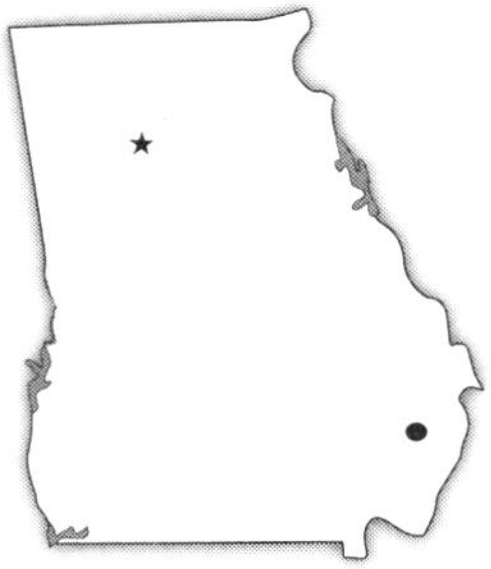

Woodmanston Plantation

This former rice plantation located in coastal swamplands is in ongoing development as an educational center for those interested in ecology, botany, natural history and the plantation heritage of coastal Georgia.

Days/Hrs.: Weekdays, 8am-4:30pm.

Fees: $1 contribution.

Directions: From Midway, go south on US 17 for 2.5 miles to Barrington Ferry Road. Continue south on Barrington Ferry Road for 4.8 miles. Entrance is about 0.5 mile on the left after the Sandy Run Road intersection.

More Information: LeConte-Woodmanston, P.O. Box 179, Midway, GA 31320; 912/884-6500.

In 1760, about thirty years after James Oglethorpe landed on the Georgia coast, John Eatton LeConte established Woodmanston Plantation, one of the first rice plantations in Georgia. Indians raided the property and British troops set fire to the house during the Revolution, but despite the setbacks, by the late 1700s, Woodmanston had become one of the largest rice plantations in Liberty County. An inland plantation on high ground between Bulltown and Briary Bay swamps, Woodmanston's rice production relied on a method of irrigation known as the gravity-flow system (see page 59).

Begin a tour of Woodmanston at the two-mile trail that follows the perimeter of one of the rice fields, a three-acre rectangle bordered by dikes. The rice fields have remained abandoned since the Civil War; but with help from the state, the LeConte-Woodmanston Foundation and the Garden Club of Georgia, some of the slave constructed channels, dikes and fields have recently been cleared of a hundred years of overgrowth from swamp gums, cypress and Ogeechee lime trees. At the trailhead, a bridge crosses an eight-foot canal. Underneath once stood a wooden trunk gate, which controlled the level of the water, used not only to irrigate the rice but also to kill undesired weeds and support the forming rice grain. The fields usually received four separate floodings before the rice was ready for harvest. Built on swamps, inland rice plantations like Woodmanston used the gravity-flow system to irrigate the fields. Canals diverted slow moving swamp creeks into a reservoir created by earthen dams. The reservoir occupied the depression to the right of the main dike dam trail. Released through gates in a series of canals, the water from the reservoir inundated fields at lower elevations to nourish the rice. After irrigation, the water moved through other trunk gates into canals at lower elevations to return to the swamp, where it continued its flow to the ocean.

Follow the trail around the rice fields and continue to the clearing with a garden, the location of the plantation house.

Shortly after John Eatton LeConte's son Louis inherited the plantation in 1810, he married a local girl, Anne Quarterman, and cultivated an experimental horticultural garden renowned on both sides of the Atlantic. (The Foundation is currently restoring the garden.) While devoting much of his work to ornamentals, LeConte, like all planters, necessarily cultivated fruits and vegetables for consumption on the estate. Moreover, the LeContes developed what would become the state's first successful commercial pear variety the LeConte Pear, thus, beginning the South's pear industry (see page 200).

The LeContes did not reach their scientific peak until Louis's sons John and Joseph came of age. Watching their father tinker in his experimental garden, the boys picked up a natural curiosity for nature. Brilliant students, both excelled at Ivy League schools and returned to teach at the University of Georgia, the elder John physics and the younger Joseph natural history. Eventually, the brothers headed west to the newly formed University of California at Berkeley, where John served as the first president and Joseph a professor of geology. Gaining an international reputation, the younger LeConte became president of the American Association for the Advancement of Science and a founder of the Sierra Club. Today, a pear, sparrow, thrasher, glacier, lake, two mountains, fossils, plants, buildings and avenues in Athens, Atlanta and Berkeley all bear the name LeConte, acknowledgements of two remarkably distinguished careers in natural science.

TRUSTEES' GARDEN

When James Oglethorpe left England to found what would become the state of Georgia, he brought with him the idea of planting a garden with specific crops that England wanted to grow in the Colonies to relieve its dependence on other countries—grapes for wine, silkworms to develop its own silk industry and cotton, peaches, herbs and spices. This experimental garden would serve as a laboratory to determine which crops would thrive in the new land.

Authorized by the Original Trustees of the Colony of Georgia, Oglethorpe set sail carrying diagrams and instructions for what would become known as the Trustees' Garden. Within a month of his landing on Yamacraw Bluff, on the banks of the Savannah River in 1733, Oglethorpe laid out a plot for the garden. Ships brought bundles of roots and baskets of seeds from all over the world. Many of the crops, including the silkworm project, failed. Others, like hemp, cotton and indigo, did well. In fact, a handful of seeds from the Chelsea Physic Garden in London became the first upland cotton successfully planted in the United States.

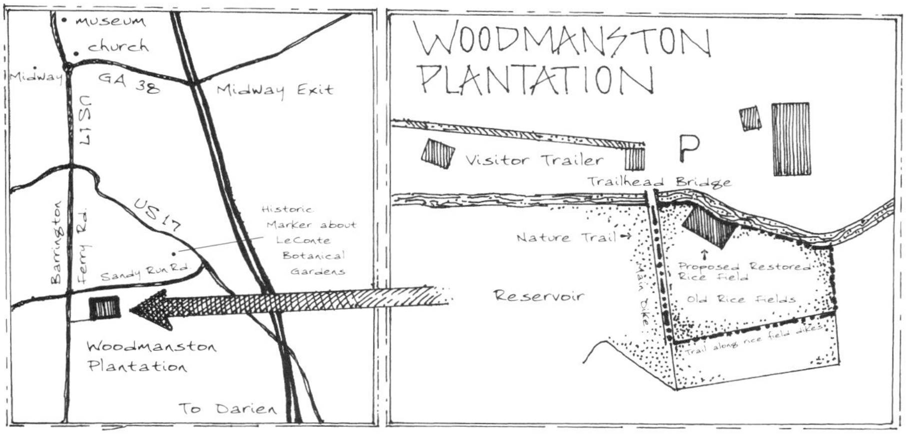

SAPELO ISLAND

THE STORY OF GEORGIA AGRICULTURE BEGINS ALONG ITS COAST. These marshlands and coastal, or barrier, islands were the site of the earliest Colonial and later American settlements. One barrier island, Sapelo, became the primary residence of Thomas Spalding, one of the most successful and innovative plantation owners on the Georgia tidewater. In 1802, Spalding, who would eventually own most of the island, purchased four thousand acres on Sapelo's south end. With considerable slave labor, he cleared and drained the interior and planted cotton, sugar cane and corn to develop Sapelo into one of the Deep South's most productive antebellum plantations.

Spalding's great love of farming led him to experiment with crop diversification and agricultural engineering, the results of which he was generous in sharing with others. He developed sea island cotton, a long-staple variety favored by English textile mills for fine fiber, that he grew on Sapelo and at another plantation on St. Simons Island. He is considered the father of the sugar industry (see page 40). Spalding also revived and improved the use of tabby, an extremely practical and versatile building material first used on the coast by the Colonists. Made of equal parts crushed shell, water, sand and lime, the last of which came from burning oyster shells, the raw supply of tabby on the coast was nearly limitless. Yet tabby remained little used until Spalding wrote extensively about it in agricultural journals in the early 1800s, explaining that tabby would allow the inexpensive building of grain mills, warehouses and dwellings. Shortly thereafter a tabby construction boom took place until the 1850s. Spalding built his own home of the material in 1812 and oversaw the construction of tabby warehouses in nearby Darien (see page 49). Rice and sugar mills, slave quarters and manor homes, all tabby, soon appeared all over the coast on island river delta plantations (see page 60).

A trip to Sapelo, which can only be reached by ferry, is a good lesson in history. Here is where some of the earliest agricultural experiments in Georgia took place. From the main

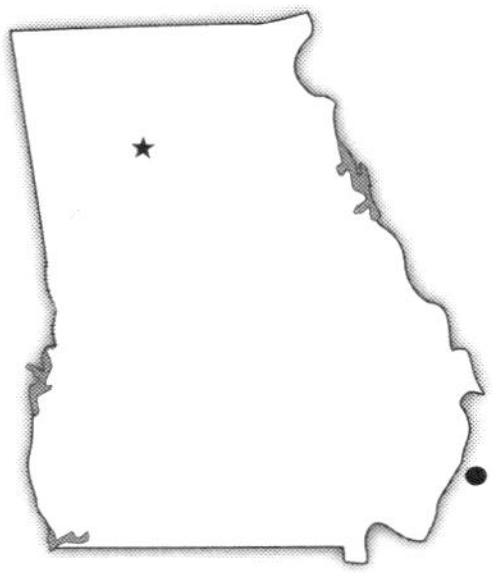

SAPELO ISLAND

All but four hundred acres of this barrier island located to the north of Darien is owned by the State of Georgia. It is home to the 8,240-acre R. J. Reynolds State Wildlife Refuge, the University of Georgia's Marine Institute and the Sapelo Island National Estuarine Research Reserve. Residents of a 434-acre privately owned community, Hog Hammock, trace their Sapelo ancestry back to the early nineteenth century.

Facilities/Rentals: Professional, educational and other groups of 14-29 adults can stay at the South End House. The $100 daily cost per person, two-day minimum, includes meeting facilities, transportation, lodging and meals. Contact the Reynolds Mansion, P.O. Box 15, Sapelo Island, GA 31327; 912/485-2299. Groups, minimum of 25 people for 2 nights, may camp near the beach in a Sapelo Island pioneer camp, which has hot showers and comfort station. Contact the Reynolds Mansion for details. Without a DNR tour or mansion reservation, visitors cannot take the DNR ferry unless a guest of island residents. Some residents rent weekend trailers, cottages and camp sites and island cars and bikes, the only transportation allowed on Sapelo Island. With any type of dock (1), in a rented car or bicycle, take the main dirt road heading east. Take the first left on the main north-south artery and head north. On the left is a two-mile long grass airstrip (2). Spalding first cleared the pines from this section of dry land and planted his sea island cotton and sugar. Continuing north, just before the intersection with a dirt road to the right, an overgrown cemetery (3) of ex-slaves remains hidden in the woods to the right.

Continue north about three miles to the tabby ruins of Spalding's circa 1809 mule-powered sugar mill (4). Spalding wrote in a popular South Carolina agricultural magazine: "The mill house I have erected is 41 feet in diameter, of tabby, and octagonal in its form ... the danger of fire, the superiority durability, and the better appearance of the buildings, should make us prefer either tabby or brick." A twelve-foot high arch marks the entrance where mules entered the mill. Inside, attached by a tether to a pole, they moved the gears that powered the cane crusher. Many historians in the early 1900s misidentified this tabby ruin on Sapelo and others on the coast as Spanish in origin. Spain sent priests and soldiers on ventures to the coast in the 1700s, but there remain no signs of their brief occupations. Nonetheless, in the 1920s and 1930s the *Atlanta Constitution*, *New York Times* and *National Geographic* all published articles, quoting respected scholars, that referred to these ruins as the San Jose Missions.

Circulation in 1932 of a letter from Kate McKinley Treanor resolved the matter of their true origin. A relative of Spalding who lived on the island in her youth, she recalled her uncle showing her the remains of the sugar works, which he explained were built by the slaves of his grandfather, Thomas Spalding. A long tabby house, where Mrs. Treanor actually lived for awhile, used for curing and boiling the sugar, stood next to the mill. The sugar house, as it was called, was remodeled into guest accommodations by a later owner and now houses a state Department of Natural Resources unit and a small post office.

To see the best preserved tabby ruins on the island, return to the main north-south road and continue north about six miles to Le Chatelet (5). Sometimes called Chocolate, it is the

reservation, the island entrepreneurs reserve your spot on the ferry and pick you up at the dock. The Weekender at 912/485-2277 rents a cottage duplex. The Baileys at 912/485-2206 rent a trailer. Family camping can be arranged at 912/838-2257. For car or bike rental try the above numbers, George and Lulu at 912/485-2270 or Yvonne Grovner at 912/485-2262.

Days/Hrs./Tours: DNR-guided bus tours that highlight the historical and ecological resources on the island begin from the Meridian dock at 9am and return from the island at 1pm on Sat. and 8:30am and 12:30pm on Wed. Friday tours from June 1 to Labor Day run the same times as Wed. An extended tour takes place from 8:30am-2:30pm the last Tues. of each month from March to Oct. For all tours, space is limited and reservations are required. Contact the Sapelo Island Visitors Center, located at the Meridian Ferry Dock, P.O. Box 15, Sapelo Island, GA 31327; 912/437-3224. To book a special group tour or school field trip, available on a reserved basis on Tues. and Thurs. (and Fridays from Sept. through May), call 912/485-2251. Maurice Bailey drives a mule-driven cart for guests to tour the island. Call 912/485-2170.

Fees: DNR-sponsored island tours, $10 per person, includes $2 round trip ferry ride.

Directions: A public ferry to Sapelo departs several times daily from the state dock in Meridian off GA 99. From Darien go north on GA 99 for 8 miles. Turn right at the sign for the Sapelo Island Research Reserve.

More Information: Sapelo Island National Estuarine Research Reserve, P.O. Box 15, Sapelo Island, GA 31327; 912/485-2251.

SPALDING AND SUGAR

From *Early Days on the Georgia Tidewater: The Story of McIntosh County and Sapelo* by Buddy Sullivan ...

Thomas Spalding's greatest hopes for crop diversification, besides cotton, lay in the cultivation and processing of sugar cane.

The first report of sugar cane being introduced to coastal Georgia...was in 1784 when John McQueen introduced plants acquired in Jamaica. Spalding notes that he began cultivation of cane on Sapelo Island in 1805 with one hundred plants.

Spalding, quite correctly, emphasized that he was the first to plant sugar cane for sugar "as a crop." He was certainly the first to do so on a successful basis. He began experimenting with sugar cane on Sapelo in 1805, then became fully engaged in sugar milling operations after the construction of his tabby works on the southwest side of the island ca. 1809. By 1814...Spalding had realized earnings of $12,500 from his sugar crop. It certainly is no exaggeration to refer to Spalding as the father of the Georgia sugar industry.

In the War of 1812, the British had designs on Spalding's ample sugar supply on Sapelo but were unable to get it.

former property of a wealthy French planter and contemporary of Spalding who also obviously recognized the importance of tabby as a building material. The lime for tabby came from burning oyster shells. Ready-made supplies cover much of the coastal islands as middens, or long, extensive mounds of discarded shells left by Indians. A particularly impressive one remains close to the northwest tip of the island and is accessible by the main road, near Chocolate.

Sapelo Island has one of the few surviving nineteenth century former slave settlements on the coast. To reach Hog Hammock (6), return south on the main road about eight miles and turn left at the cemetery. Soon one reaches a cluster of mobile homes, weathered shacks, a church and several small stores. About seventy residents, most descendants of slaves who worked on the Spalding plantation, live in Hog Hammock. Founded shortly after the Civil War and named for a former slave, Hog Hammock reflects the man's former trade on the plantation—working with pigs. His family later changed their surname to Hall, but the name of the community remains.

From here, go south, bearing left at the fork, and continue south on a second north-south road to the South End House (7). In an oak grove on the south end of the island, Spalding built his impressive tabby mansion. Lawn grass now grows where cotton and cane fields once stood. The house, designed to withstand terrific storms, survived a hurricane in 1824 when waves broke in powerful surges at the foundation. It did not survive vandals after the Civil War, however. On the original tabby foundation, Hudson Motor chief Howard Coffin of Detroit in 1925 completed a palatial home based partly on Spalding's original architectural designs. The carmaker also constructed a shrimp and oyster cannery on Sapelo. During the Depression, tobacco heir R. J. Reynolds of North Carolina purchased the estate and most of Sapelo. The mansion has priceless furnishings, murals and European works of art; eighteen bathrooms and thirteen bedrooms; and a bowling alley in the basement, still used by guests. In front of the main south entrance are two large Cuban urns, once used to store sugar in a cane mill. Facing the front of the house, to the right a road leads to the ocean beach. Reynolds added some farm buildings on the north side of the South End House, including a dairy barn, complete with movie theater on the top floor. Wild cows from his farm roam the island. By the 1960s, the Reynolds heirs had donated the mansion, farm buildings and island property to the University of Georgia for use as a marine research laboratory. Most of the island has since become the R. J. Reynolds State Wildlife Refuge or the Sapelo Island National Estuarine Research Reserve.

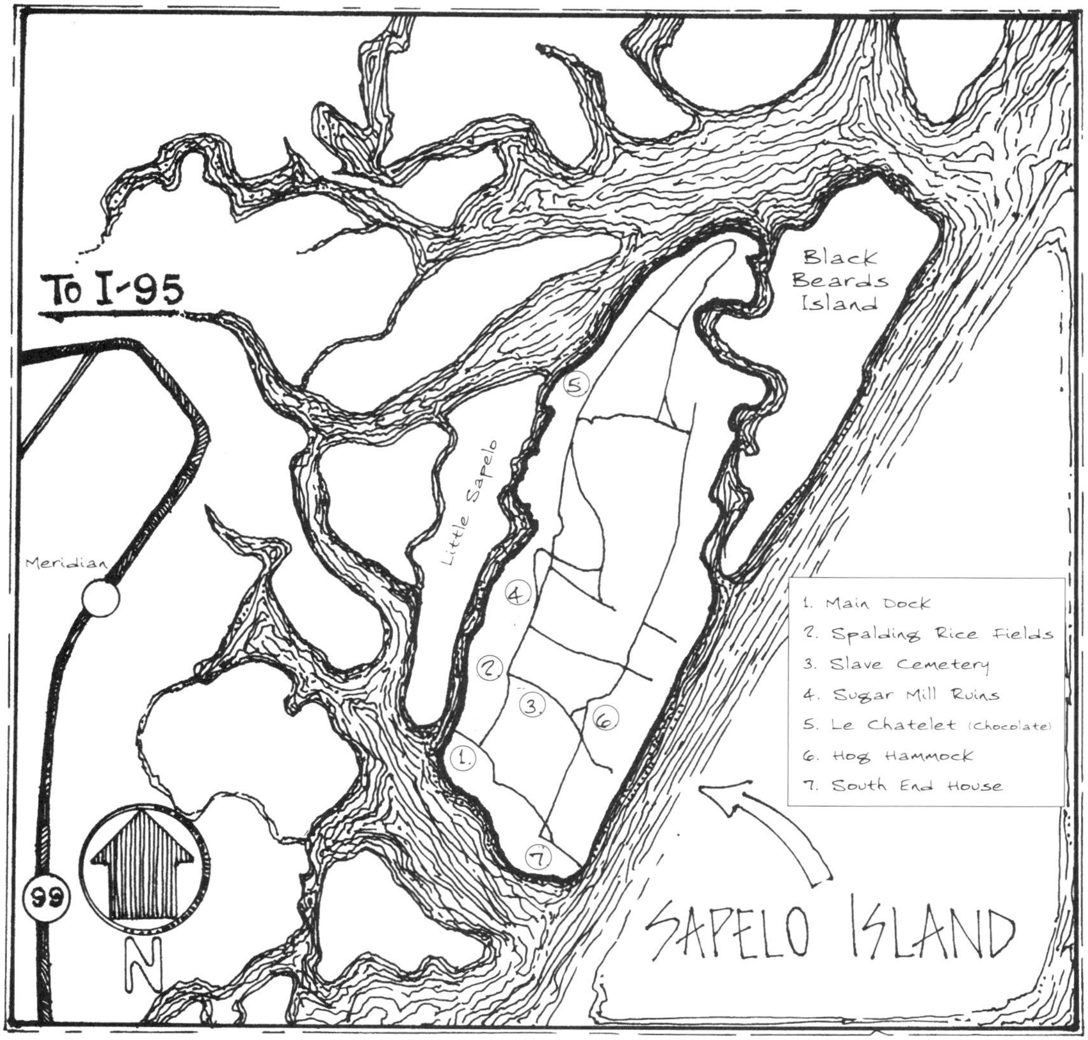

McIntosh Sugar Works

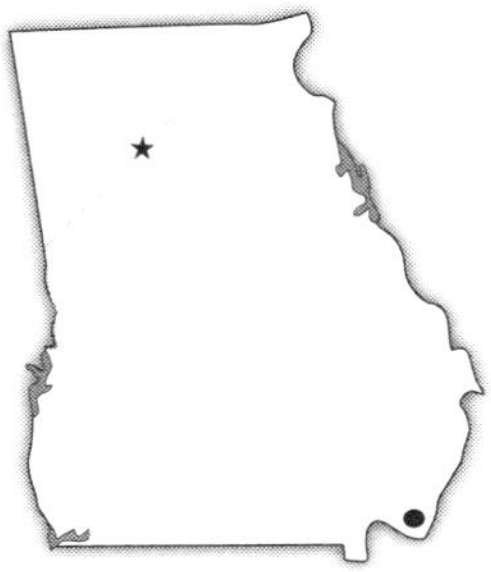

McIntosh Sugar Works

This historic sugar works is one of the most visually stunning displays of tabby ruins on the Georgia coast.

Days/Hrs.: Daily, from sunrise to sunset.

Directions: From St. Marys, go west 3 miles on GA 40, then north about 4 miles on Spur 40. The sugar works is on the left, just past the intersection of Spur 40 and Kings Bay Road.

More Information: St. Marys Tourism Council, P.O Box 1019, St. Marys, GA 31558; 912/882-6200 or 912/882-4000.

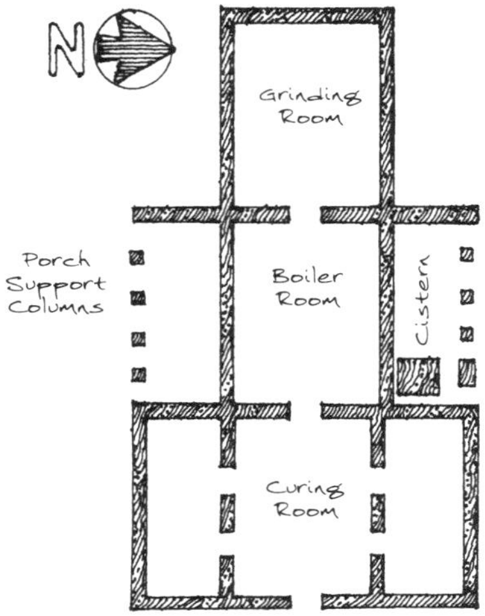

This nineteenth-century sugar refinery is one of the largest and most visually stunning displays of tabby ruins on the entire Georgia coast. Although slightly eroded, the ruins reveal much of the sugar work's original functions. It was believed that the thick walls of the building helped insure the warmth needed for superior production of sugar. The 75-foot wide and 120-foot long building is divided into three main rooms. In the two-story grinding room draft animals such as horses, mules or cattle went up ramps from the outside through the low, wide openings onto the reinforced first floor where they powered the mill. The boiler room held four large vats. Cane juice flowed through a gutter from the mill into the first vat, a clarifier, where the sediment settled from the juice. The juice then went to the largest boiler, where it distilled into a granulating syrup. From there it went into a cooling vat. After it cooled workers poured it into hogsheads, large casks or barrels that each held from sixty to one hundred gallons. The room has huge columns, which once supported the roof of the porches on the south and north sides where the wood supply was kept. The long chamber was the curing room. The low tabby walls built near the middle supported the heavy timbers required to hold the barrels of raw sugar during the process of curing. The molasses drained from the sugar crystal into flat troughs in the floor and ran into a cistern. Workers next packaged the product and hauled it to St. Marys for shipping.

Planters began growing cane in the early 1800s, but the War of 1812 and the Embargo and Non-Intercourse Acts prevented its export, and the Hurricane of 1824 obliterated sugar works and cane fields around Savannah. By the late 1820s, sugar had moved south to regions near the Altamaha and St. Marys rivers, where cane grew on about one hundred plantations. John Houstoun McIntosh built these sugar works. His friend Thomas Spalding (see page 38), who had seen steam-propelled horizontal cane mills in Louisiana, convinced him to build the first similar type structure, powered by animals, in Georgia.

Seafood

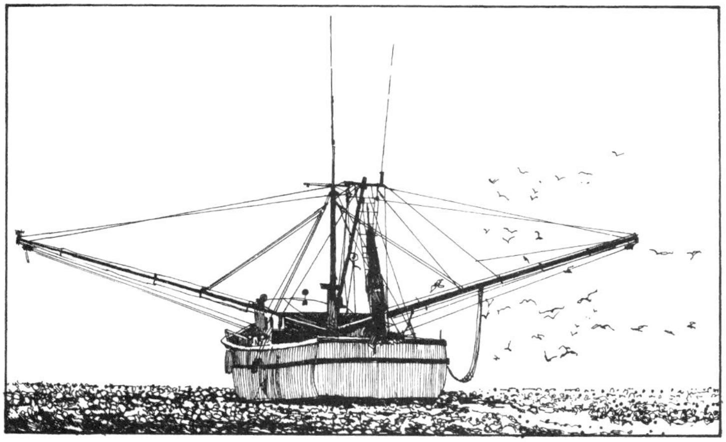

The bounty of the sea has been harvested along the world's coastal areas since prehistoric times. From large and small communities dotting the Georgia coast, such as Brunswick, Darien, Thunderbolt and Meridian, fishermen and women take boats out year-round, collecting shrimp, oysters, clams, blue-crabs and saltwater fish for regional restaurants and markets. From early to late summer, sweet white shrimp is the biggest haul from these rich, coastal marshes.

Compared to other agricultural industries in the state, seafood represents a relatively small industry. Yet, the great taste and health benefits ensure a steady demand for seafood, which is high in protein, contains unsaturated rather than saturated fat and has plenty of B vitamins. Nutritionists suggest incorporating fish and seafood into a healthy diet. Among deep-water species, white-meat fish have less fat and oil than red-meat and blue-skinned varieties. Moreover, slow-moving shellfish, like clams and oysters, have less fat and cholesterol than faster-moving ones, such as crabs, lobsters and shrimp.

Buyer's Guide to Seafood

For fresh seafood, look for good color, smooth skin, clear rather than cloudy eyes, good odor without the smell of decay, clean and intact gills and resiliency when pressed.

For frozen seafood, look for seafood that is rock hard, free of ice crystals, has no signs of thawed juices and no white spots, which can indicate freezer burn.

At home, when defrosting frozen seafood, do so gradually to preserve the quality of the fish. The best way is to thaw it overnight in the refrigerator. Avoid thawing at room temperature. If you must thaw fish quickly, seal fish in a plastic bag and immerse in cold water for about and hour, or microwave on the "defrost" setting, stopping when fish is still icy but pliable.

Marinades or rubs enhance flavor. Refrigerate seafood when marinating. Dispose of used marinade as it contains raw fish juices. Serve the cooked seafood on a clean platter.

Fish is best cooked quickly at high heat. For every inch of thickness, cook eight to ten minutes.

When microwaving boneless fish, cook on "high" for three minutes per pound. Let stand three minutes to finish cooking.

Determine if fish are done by the color and flakiness of the flesh. Slip the point of a sharp knife into the flesh and pull aside; the edges should be opaque and the center slightly translucent with the flakes just beginning to separate.

Shrimp cook quickly in two to three minutes, just until the meat loses its glossy appearance, curls up and turns pink. To stop the cooking process, immediately rinse shrimp in cool water.

Vidalia® Shrimp Dip

Two great Georgia favorites in a low-fat dip!

8	ounces fat-free cream cheese, softened
½	cup reduced-fat mayonnaise
1½	cups finely chopped Vidalia® onion
1	10.75-ounce can reduced-sodium-and-fat condensed tomato soup
1	cup cooked, chopped shrimp
8 to 10	drops hot sauce
	Parsley for garnish (optional)

In medium bowl, beat softened cream cheese with mayonnaise until smooth. Fold in remaining ingredients. Chill in covered bowl for several hours or overnight. Garnish with parsley sprig if desired. Serve with reduced-fat or fat-free crackers or toasted, quartered pita bread. Yields 40 servings.

Aurelia Wood
Athens, Georgia

Marinated Shrimp

Marinating overnight adds extra flavor to this colorful dish

1	cup extra virgin olive oil
¾	cup white wine vinegar
¼	cup capers with brine
¼	cup sugar
2	teaspoons salt
1	teaspoon chopped fresh parsley
1	teaspoon dry mustard
3	bay leaves
1	garlic clove, mashed
2	pounds cooked shrimp, peeled with tails attached
1	large, thinly sliced Vidalia® onion
	Olives (garnish)
	Lemon slices (garnish)

In medium bowl, mix oil, wine vinegar, capers, sugar, salt, parsley, mustard, bay leaves and garlic. Add shrimp and onion. Cover and refrigerate at least 3 hours or overnight. Transfer shrimp with marinade to decorative 2-quart serving bowl. Garnish with olives and lemon slices. Yields approximately 12 servings.

Georgia Department of Agriculture Test Kitchen

Hint: A variety of marinated or pickled vegetables may be added, including artichoke hearts, baby corn and sliced red pepper.

Savannah Gumbo

This winner contains the best from Georgia and the coast

½	cup peanut oil
½	cup all-purpose flour
1	large Vidalia® onion, chopped
1	large bell pepper, chopped
4	banana peppers, diced
2	cloves garlic, finely minced
1	8-ounce can tomato sauce
1	10-ounce can diced tomatoes with green chili peppers
1	cup chopped okra
2	pounds shrimp, peeled
	Salt
	Pepper
	Cajun seasoning salt
3	cups cooked rice
	Red pepper slices (garnish)
	Chives (garnish)

To make a roux: heat oil in heavy pot or saucepan. Sprinkle flour into oil, stirring constantly. Cook over low heat for 40 to 45 minutes, stirring often. Cook until the mixture is the color of caramel and has a gravy-like consistency.

Add onion, bell pepper, banana peppers and garlic to the roux; cook 15 minutes. Add tomato sauce, diced tomatoes and okra; cook additional 15 minutes. Add shrimp and cook for 10 minutes. Season to taste. Serve over hot rice. Garnish with red pepper slices and chives. Yields 6 servings.

Karen Nelson
Savannah, Georgia
First Place Main Dish,
Savannah 1994 Great Taste of Georgia Recipe Contest

Clams, mussels and oysters are done when they pop their shells open, usually after about five minutes. Discard those that stay closed.

To store fresh seafood in the refrigerator, place in the coldest part, usually the lowest shelf at the back or in the meat keeper.

Keep raw and cooked seafood separate to prevent bacterial cross contamination. After handling raw seafood, thoroughly wash knives, cutting surfaces, sponges and hands with hot, soapy water.

It is well for all farmers to realize that this is a year for electing a President of the United States. Past history has proven that these years are generally accompanied by financial depressions and uncertain business conditions until after the election. I would hate to see a large cotton crop made in the South this year. A ten million bale crop will bring more money than a fifteen million bale crop....Don't try to plant more than you can cultivate well, fertilize well and gather when it needs it. Don't go too much in debt.

Editorial by Eugene Talmadge, Georgia Commissioner of Agriculture, Market Bulletin, *January 12, 1928*

MIDDAY DINNER

In her book about antebellum homes, *White Columns in Georgia*, Medora Field Perkerson described a midday dinner where she was the only non-relative among twelve family members of the Johnson family in Washington, Georgia:

It was a meal to remember, but routine for the long-time family cook. The damask-laid table was set with old family silver and white and gold bone china—the decoration painted on by Mrs. Johnson's mother years before. Flanking the silver bowl of early pink camellias were small cut-glass dishes containing watermelon-rind pickles and fig preserves.

First came a fresh fruit cocktail which included the sweet almondy bitter of late Georgia peaches. Was there rum in it too? Then, baked hen and dressing passed on a garnished silver platter, followed immediately by another great platter of baked Wilkes County ham. The invariable Southern combination of chicken (fried, baked, broiled or otherwise) with baked country ham is a marriage most surely made in heaven. Rice and gravy are always served with them of course, and every grain of rice must stand apart. (Every grain did.)

Vegetables were all fresh from the host's early fall garden. Tender young butter beans. Small pods of okra cooked in butter. Corn soufflé. Candied sweet potatoes. A salad of curly green garden lettuce and tomatoes. Two kinds of hot bread, of course—feather-light rolls and corn-meal egg bread.

Finally, tall glasses of syllabub, that airy mixture of milk, cream, sugar and sherry, always made in a special churn at the very last moment before serving. Coffee.

CRAB PECAN DELIGHT

Serve as a main dish or with crackers as a hot hors d'oeuvre

- ½ stick (¼ cup) butter
- ½ cup chopped celery
- 2 tablespoons chopped green onions
- 1½ cups chopped pecans, divided
- Dash minced garlic
- ½ teaspoon salt
- ⅛ teaspoon pepper
- 1 pound crab meat
- 1 10.75-ounce can cream of celery soup
- ¾ cup evaporated whole milk
- ¼ cup dry bread crumbs
- 1 teaspoon butter

Preheat oven to 350°. In large sauté pan, heat butter. Add celery, onion, 1 cup pecans and garlic. Sauté until vegetables are tender. Add salt and pepper. Stir in crab and soup; slowly stir in milk and simmer 10 minutes. Spoon into lightly greased 8-inch square casserole dish. Top with crumbs, remaining pecans and dot with butter. Bake for 25 minutes. Yields 6 servings.

Carroll Hart
Surrency, Georgia

OYSTER STEW

Serve with crackers and a salad for a quick and easy meal

- ½ cup chopped onion
- 2 tablespoons butter or margarine, melted
- 1 12-ounce container fresh Standard oysters, undrained
- 1 quart 2% milk
- ¼ teaspoon salt
- ¼ teaspoon white pepper
- ⅛ teaspoon red pepper

Sauté onions in butter in Dutch oven until onions are tender. Add remaining ingredients to onion mixture. Cook over low heat until edges of oysters begin to curl and mixture is hot but not boiling. Serve stew with crackers. Yields 6 servings.

Kaye Thigpen
Waycross, Georgia

Tomato Feta Shrimp

This pasta dish goes great with a salad and French bread

4	tablespoons olive oil, divided
4	garlic cloves, minced and divided
4	large tomatoes peeled, seeded, quartered
1	teaspoon basil leaves
1	teaspoon oregano leaves
½	cup dry white wine
1¼	pounds medium shrimp, peeled
1	teaspoon crushed red pepper
8	ounces feta cheese
½	cup Parmesan cheese (more to taste)
4	cups cooked ziti pasta (more to taste)

Heat 3 tablespoons olive oil on medium-high heat in saucepan or skillet. Add 3 minced cloves of garlic and sauté for 2 to 3 minutes. Add tomatoes, basil and oregano and cook for 15 minutes on low heat. Add wine and continue to simmer on low. In separate saucepan, heat remaining 1 tablespoon olive oil on medium-high heat. Add remaining garlic, shrimp and red pepper. Cook until shrimp are just pink (5 to 7 minutes). Preheat oven to 400°. Fold feta cheese and shrimp mixture into tomato sauce. Pour into 8x12-inch baking dish and sprinkle with Parmesan cheese. Bake for 20 minutes. Serve over cooked ziti pasta. Yields 4 main dish servings.

Mary Swanson
Atlanta, Georgia

Hint: To lower the calories, fat and sodium in this recipe, reduce olive oil to 2 tablespoons and feta cheese to 6 ounces. Omit Parmesan cheese. Result: One serving contains 569 calories, 19.7g fat and 699mg sodium.

Potlikker

From *Every Man a King* by Huey P. Long ...

Potlikker is the juice that remains in a pot after greens or other vegetables are boiled with proper seasoning. The best seasoning is a piece of salt fat pork, commonly referred to as "dry salt meat" or "side meat." If a pot be partly filled with well-cleaned turnip greens and turnips (the turnips should be cut up), with a half-pound piece of the salt pork, and then with water, and boiled until the greens and turnips are cooked reasonably tender, then the juice remaining in the pot is the delicious, invigorating, soul-and-body sustaining potlikker. The turnips and greens, or whatever other vegetable is used, should be separated from the juice; that is, the potlikker should be taken as any other soup and the greens eaten as any other food.

Attention Georgia Farmers. Make a New Year's resolution to read some good books each month during 1929. You do not have to Buy these books. You may Borrow them from the Georgia Library Commission entirely free for the slight cost of return postage. We have books on all subjects pertaining to agriculture, poultry, live stock as well as many other interesting lines of study, information and recreation. A postal to us will bring you a book by return mail for a month's loan. Address: Georgia Library Commission, State Capitol, Atlanta.

Announcement, Market Bulletin, *January 10, 1929*

THE COHUTTA FISHERIES CENTER

A division of the University of Georgia Cooperative Extension Service, the Cohutta Fisheries Center in Northwest Georgia provides valuable research into aquaculture for the farmers who operate the nearly eight thousand acres of commercial fish ponds in the state. To research and teach about fisheries and aquaculture, the sixty-five-acre center has thirty-six ponds stocked with rainbow trout, striped bass, largemouth bass, channel catfish and blue gill. Feeding all the fish ponds is a cold spring, which produces 350 million gallons of water a year. Gravity moves the water from pond to pond, getting warmer as it travels. The water has a good pH and high levels of calcium and magnesium.

Center researchers study the nutritional needs of fish; ways for farmers to increase the production of their fisheries; stocking methods; and pond water quality. They provide farmers with information on the economics of growing fish and the markets available. The center also conducts workshops for fish farmers and summer programs for high school and graduate students.

The center has a long tradition of public use. At the turn of the century, a large hotel and one of the most popular spas in the eastern United States stood on the grounds. Guests swam in the mineral rich waters formed from a large natural spring. Later, a federal fish hatchery occupied the site. Today, about one thousand people a year fish the two ponds open to the public. Anglers don't need a fishing license and pay for the fish by the pound. An aquarium, with fish native to Georgia, is also open to the public.

The Fisheries Center is north of Dalton near the town of Cohutta, just off GA 71. For more information, call 706/694-8830.

FISH KEBOBS

Use this deliciously different recipe as an entrée or appetizer

- 2 pounds whitefish, steamed and flaked
- 1 egg
- 1/8 teaspoon salt
- 1/8 teaspoon pepper
- 2 tablespoons chopped fresh cilantro
- Hot pepper sauce to taste
- 2 teaspoons minced garlic
- 3 teaspoons minced onion
- 1 teaspoon minced ginger root
- 3 teaspoons chives
- 2 teaspoons lime juice
- All-purpose flour
- 3 tablespoons vegetable oil

Mix fish with next 10 ingredients; adjust seasoning to desired taste. Shape mixture into balls; dust with flour and flatten. Heat oil in large skillet over medium heat. Fry fish kebobs until golden brown, turning once. Serve hot with ketchup or chutney. Yields 8 servings. If using kebobs as a cocktail snack, make the balls smaller.

Merle Barefoot
Grantville, Georgia

Hint: To reduce the fat in this recipe, coat skillet with vegetable cooking spray first, then add 1 tablespoon vegetable oil for frying the kebobs. Result: One serving contains 148 calories and 4.2g fat (27% of calories).

Darien

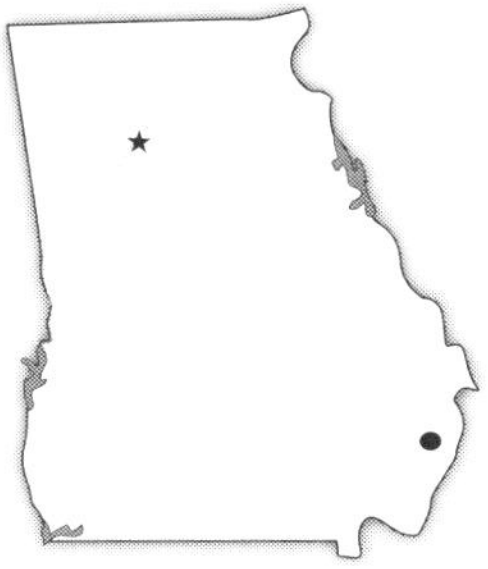

With the largest watershed in the state and the largest swamp ecosystem on the East Coast, the Altamaha River has made possible a considerable bounty of natural and cultivated crops for Darien, the town that has sat at its mouth for more than two hundred years. Rice, indigo and cotton. Pines, cypress and oak. Shrimp, oysters and fish.

Begin a tour of Darien at the intersection of US 17 and GA 99, where a monument (1) honors the Highland Scots who settled the outpost in 1736, three years after James Oglethorpe founded Savannah. Darien evolved into a thriving commercial port, sending rice, cotton and indigo from coastal and river plantations across the world.

Darien's fortunes quickly changed during the Civil War. The burn marks on the trunks and limbs of three oaks (2) beside

Darien

One of the prettiest views on all the Sea Islands Coast is at sunset from the bridge over the Darien River, looking east down onto the shrimp docks where boats are hung with drying shrimp nets.

Days/Hrs.: Visitor Center, 9am-5pm daily except Sunday.

Directions: From US 95, take exit 10 and head east briefly on CR 251, which ends in Darien at the intersection of US 17. Downtown is a few blocks south.

More Information: McIntosh County Chamber of Commerce Visitor Center, 105 Fort King George Drive, Darien, GA 31305; 912/437-4192.

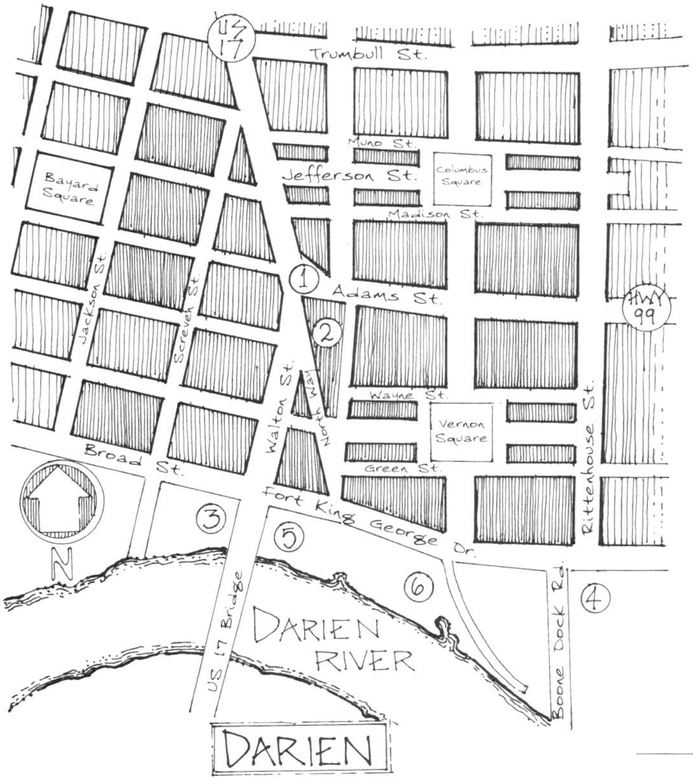

Chatham Artillery Punch

According to Savannah's Junior League cookbook *Savannah Style*, Chatham Artillery Punch is the city's most famous drink—and has been for a number of years:

"It is said that the concoction possesses a kick greater than the two brass cannons presented the Chatham Artillery by George Washington. It was first devised in the 1850s to honor a rival military organization, the Republican Blues, and since then has laid to rest, at least temporarily, many an unknown soldier and countless known ones.

"The original recipe was brewed in ice-filled horse buckets into which were placed sugar, lemon and a quart each of brandy, whiskey and rum. Then the bucket was filled with champagne. Revised recipes call for the addition of green tea, but the popular punch still, though it tastes as mild as syllabub, conquers like a cyclone."

To make the punch, mix 2 gallons of tea (Green tea— 1 pound of tea to 2 gallons of water. Soak overnight in tin bucket and strain) with the juice of 3 dozen lemons, preferably in a cedar tub. Then add 5 pounds of brown sugar, 2 gallons of Catawba wine, 2 gallons of rum, 1 gallon of brandy, 1 gallon of dry gin and 1 gallon of whiskey. Let the mixture set for at least 1 or 2 weeks in a covered container. After setting period is over and when ready to serve, pour the liquid over a cake of ice. Never chill it in the refrigerator or use crushed ice. Add 2 quarts of cherries, 2 quarts of pineapple cubes and 10 quarts of champagne, pouring in slowly and mixing with a circular motion.

The punch, which serves 200, is ready to do its damage.

the Community Center, one block south on US 17, reportedly came from the torch of Federal troops, mostly black, who paid a visit from a garrison on St. Simons Island in 1863, an event chronicled in the movie *Glory*. Further south one block are the old ruins of the city's riverfront (3) on West Broad Street. Made of tabby, a common coastal building material (see page 60), the warehouses—built from 1810 to 1845 to store cotton before export—are practically all that remain of the town from the antebellum era.

East of US 17, Broad Street becomes Fort King George Drive. Continue down this road for three blocks to the intersection of Boon Dock Road to the tabby structure, St. Cyprian's Episcopal Church (4). Built in the early 1870s by former slaves of the nearby Butler Plantation (see page 56), the church received assistance, curiously, from Pierce Butler's daughter and son-in-law, Francis Butler and James Leigh, both of whom held pro-slavery sentiments.

Turn back west on Fort King George Drive and stop along the waterfront. The tabby foundations of other buildings (5) along the waterfront road mark the site of a construction boom from from 1870 to 1910 to support a bustling timber economy. At the turn of the century, the city had became one of the largest lumber exporting ports in America. The Altamaha was choked with pines, cypress and oaks harvested from up river which were floated down to Darien sawmills. By the early 1900s overcutting of the forests ended the timber boom. The land that formed the largest watershed in the state, the heart of Georgia, had been timbered out. The mills shut down.

To make a living Darien looked again to the water. Few estuaries match the productive commercial fisheries of the fertile Altamaha delta, where the main channel breaks up near the coast into the Altamaha, Champney, Butler and Darien Rivers, separated by islands where cotton, rice and indigo once grew. Every day shrimp and fishing boats trudge up and down the Darien River, the northernmost delta tributary, from the waterfront docks (6) on either side of US 17. From the setting sun and the boats docking and hanging their nets to dry to the sweeping tidal flats in the distance, the US 17 bridge offers one the most memorable views on the Georgia coast.

Head back north on US 17 to its intersection with GA 99 at the Highlander Monument and turn right on GA 99. As it leaves Darien, GA 99 makes a gentle east to north to west curve, winding through the coastal marshes and sand ridges, before rejoining US 17 about 15 miles later.

Mile 1: Ashantilly, which adjoins St. Andrews Cemetery along the dirt road to the right, once served as a second home for the Spaldings of Sapelo Island (see page 38). Like many planter families, the Spaldings retreated to houses in inland towns during the summer when the coastal plantations were rife with heat and malaria. Thomas Spalding, credited with reviving and improving the use of tabby, directed the building of warehouses along the Darien waterfront, some of whose remains still exist. In the early twentieth century, the Haynes family restored the home, where today William Haynes operates the nationally known Ashantilly Press, which hand sets and prints fine editions of books.

Mile 3: The Ridge, a quiet residential community, has picturesque Victorian homes built during the early 1900s by timber barons and bar pilots, local captains who navigated ships into the Darien harbor, dodging the sand bars that threatened to beach them.

Mile 5: A historic marker points the way down a road to the tabby ruins of a sugar mill and rum distillery on Carnochan Creek in an area known as the Thicket. Built by Thomas Spalding and William Carnochan, the tabby works functioned until destroyed by the hurricane of 1824. The ruins, difficult to locate, are on private property.

Mile 8: The Sapelo Island Dock road goes by shrimp docks on Hudson Creek before ending at the DNR visitor center, where people catch the ferry to the island where Thomas Spalding had one of the coast's most innovative plantations.

Mile 10: Valona, a particularly scenic commercial shrimping community on Shellbluff Creek, began in the 1890s. Most of the families here are descended from the Atwoods, the original settlers.

Mile 12: George Troup, governor of Georgia in the 1820s, grew up near the Sapelo River on the Belleville plantation, which was a mile northeast of GA 99.

Ansley-Hodges Project

The Ansley-Hodges Memorial Project observation platform just south of Darien between the Champney and South Altamaha rivers in the Altamaha Wildlife Management area overlooks about 145 acres of former rice fields that flourished on Champney Island 150 years ago.

Barely discernible lines of grass, trees and shrubs reveal the location of the canals that divided these acres into fields of twenty to thirty acres each. Flat-bottomed boats were towed along the canals and slaves loaded them with bundles of cut rice. About 250 feet north of the platform, a line of trees parallel to the Champney River grow on an original plantation dike. Slaves used wooden shovels to scoop up the thick Champney River mud that forms that dike—backbreaking labor under a blazing Sea Island sun. (See map on page 59.)

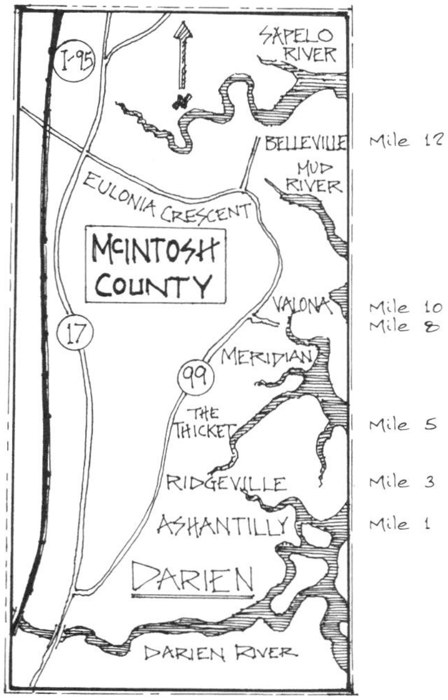

The Bountiful Marshes

Georgia's coastal marshlands encompass approximately 475,000 acres in a four-to-six mile band between the barrier islands and the mainland. Thriving in the nutrient-rich waters of the estuaries, these marshes have been identified as one of the most extensive and productive marshlands systems in the United States.

These marshes, sounds and nearshore ocean waters produce more food and energy than any other estuarine zone on the eastern seaboard. The coastal marshlands are also an essential life support system for the state's multimillion dollar seafood industry. The marshes serve as a nursery ground for juvenile fish and shellfish that have sport as well as commercial value. They also export food into nearshore water of the ocean to nourish marine species that spend the earlier portions of their lives in the marshes.

1. Prehistoric Indians were the first to harvest oysters from Georgia coastal waters.
2. Born on Daufuskie Island, South Carolina, shrimper Thomas Stefford, fifty-two, has trolled the coast of South Carolina and Georgia since he was fifteen years old.

3 and 4. Dozens of species of fish come from Georgia's coastal waters.

5. The setting sun over the Georgia marshlands silhouettes a live oak draped with Spanish moss.
6. Shrimp produces more revenue than any other Georgia seafood.
7. Crab is the second largest seafood revenue producer.
8. Shrimp boats docked on Lazaretto Creek make a picturesque site from the Tybee Island bridge. Thomas Stefford's boat is the one farthest on the left.
9. A shrimp boat heads out to sea for a day's work.

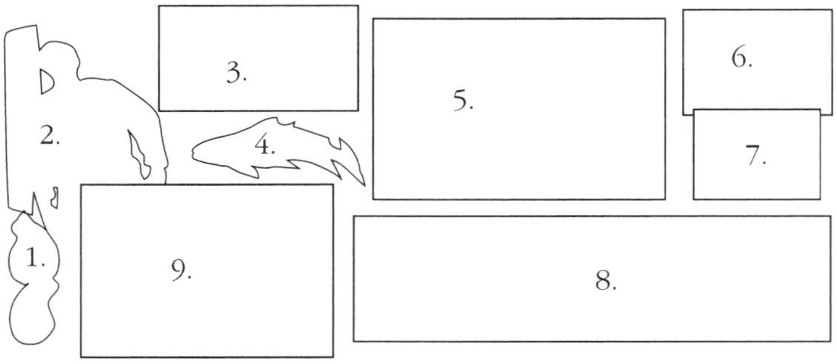

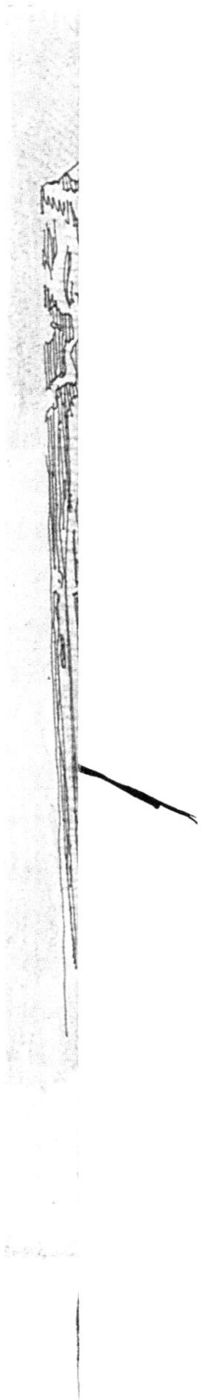

ELIZABETH TERRY

Elizabeth Terry, 56, began her cooking career as a home cook entertaining friends; first in Cambridge, Massachusetts, where her husband, Michael, was studying law at Harvard, and later in Atlanta where Michael practiced law and she ran a small soup-and-sandwich shop, Thyme For You, on the lower level of Lenox Square. Twenty years from the time she concocted her first béarnaise sauce, her restaurant, Elizabeth on 37th, in Savannah was named one of the top twenty-five restaurants in the country and she was named one of the top ten women chefs in America. Her cookbook, Savannah Seasons, *published in 1996, may be, when all is said and done, "The Southern cookbook" for this generation. In his lengthy, personal introduction to* Savannah Seasons, *Pat Conroy (whose* Beach Music *main character Jack McCall ate at Elizabeth on 37th), says, "(Elizabeth)... treated Southern food with the same reverence that Andre Soltner brought to the preparation of French produce or Marcella Hazan invoked when speaking of the regional cooking of her native Italy." In Conroy's view, Elizabeth has, "altered the history of food in the American Southeast."*

We talked at a table in her restaurant, which is located in a renovated, Edwardian-style, twelve-room mansion on 37th Street in Savannah. She and Michael and their two children, Alexis and Celeste, live above the restaurant. A bright Savannah sun was streaming in the front window.

There have really been two styles of Southern cooking. This wonderful back-of-the-stove, long-simmering, feeding great numbers of people with what was available. In other words, black-eyed peas with onion and a little fatback. That kind of cooking. Greens. Then there is also this tradition that is particularly evident in coastal Savannah, of rice plantations and Madeira Society entertaining. Remember that Savannah is a port and also the railroad came down here. So cotton went north, but then on the same trains coming down to pick up the cotton they brought lobsters and things from the north. There's always been fine dining in this area. There were rice birds when there were rice plantations. People have always hunted venison and deer, quail. The Ogeechee River, the whole river system that flows into middle Georgia. It's almost shad season and Ogeechee River shad was a celebrated delicacy in Savannah and Darien and throughout coastal Georgia all the way up into the Piedmont. Then of course, we have all the bounty of the sea right here: oysters, shrimp, flounder, snapper, mussels, clams. I went to the Georgia Historical Society and looked through old manuscripts. There were lists of seeds that people ordered. They grew pomegranates and oranges under glass in green houses. Wonderful food has been prepared here for a long time. This is not something that I've made up—serving oysters in pastry with country ham. I'm not the first person to have rosemary bushes.

Fortunately because I'm right here on the coast, I'm really very tied to the sea. There are dozens and dozens of dozens of different fish. You learn when a fish is just out of water. I learned this from fishing. We would fish and come home and I would cook the fish. I would see how it tasted. And how it cooks differently when it was broiled and when it was pan sautéed and when it was steamed. It was so interesting just to look at that. Then when I bought fish commercially, I would see when it didn't look the way it looked when I caught it. And I would return it and say, "Its not that I have to have red snapper every day. It's that I have to have fresh fish every day." That became the important thing to me. I mean our whole staff has caught king mackerel and tasted it the next day, so they know. And I still, to this day, talk to the fish people and say, "What do you have for me today?" and they know that that means I will take whatever they say is the freshest and will come up with a wonderful recipe for whatever fish that is. I always start with the fish but I carry that through into pork or venison.

A Miro or a Matisse apparently sees colors in a way that normal humans do not. Mozart must have heard sounds that no one else heard. Do the five senses of a chef like Elizabeth produce combinations of tastes that the rest of us are not aware of until they are stimulating our taste buds?

I just eat and pay attention to what it tastes like. And then depending on the season, put it with seasonal things. People are hunting venison in the fall. In the fall the marsh is brown like the fur of a deer. In the fall red cabbages and apples and sweet potatoes are fall colors and also fall tastes. It's all related. Now in the spring the marsh is turning bright green and the food we have is also bright green. Asparagus that's coming into season. There are new shoots of green onions. So it's the brighter flavors. That's really what it is. It's all the weather and the day and the season and the colors. Its the whole...thing. I know what two things are going to taste like together. Or maybe four things. I probably have an inordinate passion for food. I spend a shocking amount of time with food. Reading about food, touching food, listening to food cook. There are sounds that food makes when it's almost finished. There's a touch. There's a feel. So its really just alerting all of my senses to this particular thing. It all ...happens. It excites me. And its easy for me to consider all of those things at one time.

Cooking genius is one thing but Elizabeth, along with her husband Michael, runs a million-dollar a year manufacturing business. In the introduction to her book she says that she and Michael are not ambitious, but they are perfectionists.

When I was sixteen, I took sewing classes and the whole class was encouraged to enter a sewing contest. I just felt... if I was going to enter the sewing contest I was going to win it. So I suppose that I have a little bit... a lot... of the sense of doing it well. If we were ambitious, we would have several restaurants. But we are perfectionists so we have one highly regarded and one well-run and well-organized restaurant. That's what interests us. I have always been fascinated with learning how to do something and learning how to do it extremely well. I love watching myself getting better and better and better at something. I truly have learned that practice makes perfect. I know that anybody can learn to play the tuba or learn to cook. But anybody doesn't learn to play the tuba or learn to cook because they don't have a passion for it. I'm compulsive about everything. That's just how I am. I'm never late. I just sit down and do it, even though that means I have to stay up late. I just get it off my table that day. I love having half a case of oranges and planning how I'm going to use them. I won that contest, Make It Yourself With Wool. I won a trip to Europe... Sewing.

So if Elizabeth has written what may be "The" Southern cookbook of her generation and if she is perhaps "The" Southern cook cooking today, what is her definition of Southern cooking?

People in the South have always entertained. So people are not just cooking because it's this meal and then there's another meal. There's a sharing and a giving. People in the South when they present a meal to someone they are giving more than nourishment. They are giving part of themselves.

Touring the Georgia Coast with Elizabeth and Michael Terry ...

Michael keeps a sixteen-foot Cobia in a boat shed in McIntosh County, an hour south of Savannah. We'll pack cheese sandwiches with lettuce and mustard; a cooler full of sparkling water; strips of pepper, celery, and carrots and a bag of gumdrops, and then fish the incoming tide. From the anchored boat we see shorebirds, sea gulls, sandpipers, terns, brown pelicans, and often oyster catchers, avocets, ibis, herons, and wood storks. After lunch, Michael starts the motor, and as we move out, we see crab fishermen hauling in, emptying, and resetting their traps. We always see dolphin and occasionally alligators. We hear clapper rails calling across the marsh as Michael guides the boat along the rivers and creeks of coastal Georgia between his favorite fishing drops. I love the changing colors of the marsh grass, bright green in summer, brown in winter; and turning from one to another in between times. I see the sky best when I'm on the water in a boat with Michael. The big white clouds, or the clear, still day with no clouds, or the swirling clouds with gray edges, and the clouds with silver linings. Here we talk or not as we cast our lines and watch the bobbers.

Elizabeth's Favorite Fish Recipes

Broiled Fish with Lemon Parsley-Dill Marinade

Serves 6

6 (6-ounce) fillets of Flounder; ½-inch thick
⅓ cup extra virgin olive oil
2 tablespoons dry vermouth
1 tablespoon minced garlic
2 tablespoons lemon pulp, all membrane and skin discarded
2 tablespoons sliced fresh chives or green onion
2 tablespoons minced fresh Italian parsley
2 tablespoons minced fresh dill
1 teaspoon kosher salt
½ teaspoon fresh cracked black pepper

Combine all ingredients (except flounder) in the bowl of a food processor and process briefly until thoroughly combined and well minced. Alternatively, all the ingredients may be minced very fine by hand and whisked together.

Spoon the marinade on both sides of the fillet in a shallow non reactive dish, using all the marinade. Cover and refrigerate to develop the flavors 30 minutes before broiling. Do not marinate longer.

Preheat the broiler and then the broiler pan.

Place the fish and marinade on the hot pan under the broiler and broil 5 - 8 minutes until lightly browned and cooked through. Pour any accumulated pan juices over the cooked fish to serve.

Roasted Grouper with Sesame Almond Crust

Serves 6

6 (6-ounce) boneless and skinless Black Grouper fillets, each ½-inch thick
2 tablespoons sesame oil *(available in the Oriental food section of the grocery store)*
2 tablespoons vegetable oil
2 tablespoons lemon juice
1 egg, beaten
2 tablespoons water
¼ teaspoon salt
¼ teaspoon pepper
1 teaspoon hot chili sauce
1 cup crushed Weston Stoned Wheat Thins or other crisp wheat crackers
½ cup Asiago cheese, grated
¼ cup almonds, toasted
2 tablespoons sesame seeds, toasted
¼ cup minced fresh Italian parsley
2 tablespoons minced fresh tarragon
½ teaspoon fresh cracked black pepper
2 tablespoons butter, melted
2 tablespoons extra virgin olive oil

Preheat the oven to 425°. Butter a shallow baking pan.

In a medium bowl, combine the sesame oil, vegetable oil, lemon juice, water, beaten egg, salt, pepper, and chili sauce. Set aside.

Combine the wheat thins, cheese, almonds, sesame seeds, parsley, tarragon, and pepper in the bowl of the food processor and process to a crumb. Set aside.

Dip the fish fillets in the marinade, then in the crumbs. Place on a buttered shallow baking pan. Do not allow the fillets to touch each other. Combine the butter and olive oil and drizzle over the fish, then roast in the oven for 20 minutes, until the fillets are browned and cooked through.

Light Lemon Parsley-Dill Marinade

Yields ½ cup

⅓ cup virgin olive oil
2 tablespoons dry vermouth
1 tablespoon minced garlic
2 tablespoons sliced fresh chives or green onion
2 tablespoons lemon pulp, all membrane and skin discarded
2 tablespoons minced fresh Italian parsley
2 tablespoons minced fresh dill
½ teaspoon fresh cracked black pepper.
1 teaspoon kosher salt

Combine all the ingredients in the bowl of a food processor and process briefly until thoroughly combined and well minced. Alternately, all the ingredients may be minced very fine by hand and whisked together. Refrigerate until needed.

Butler Plantation

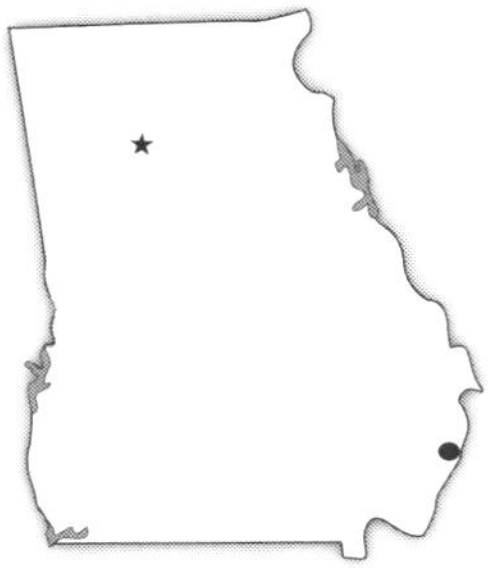

Butler Plantation

The importance of rice growing on the coast is signified by the seventy-five-foot high rice mill chimney which is still a prominent part of the landscape marking the site of this former prestigious rice plantation in the Altamaha delta.

Facilities: None for the public. The Huston House serves as a residence for a DNR ranger.

Days/Hrs.: Daily, sunrise to sunset.

Directions: From Darien take US 17 south. Less than a mile after crossing the bridge over the Butler River, turn right just past the rice mill chimney down the second dirt road, which leads to parking next to the DNR office in the Huston House.

More Information: Georgia Department of Natural Resources, Game Management Section, 1 Conservation Way, Brunswick, GA 31520; 912/262-3173.

About a mile south of Darien, between the Butler and Champney rivers, lies Butler Island, site of Butler Plantation, a large and profitable antebellum rice plantation. Owned by the Major Pierce Butler family and built and maintained by slave labor, the estate employed the latest methods of rice production. Dutch engineers designed the extensive slave-built systems of canals and dikes between the two rivers. Butler used the tidal flow system to irrigate the rice fields, a much more efficient method than the inland swamp reservoir method employed by LeConte and other eighteenth century planters. But as important as this plantation is to the story of rice production, it is perhaps even more important as the subject of a journal kept by British actress and abolitionist Frances "Fanny" Kemble Butler, wife of Major Butler's heir, Pierce. Several decades after divorcing Butler and returning to England, Kemble published the journal which is said to have helped sway public opinion in England against the Confederacy during the Civil War; thus helping to end the institution of slavery and changing the agricultural economy of the South forever.

Begin a tour of Butler Island at the seventy-five-foot high brick smoke stack, the nineteenth century remnant of the Butler rice mill. In the 1920s, the tower reportedly saved the life of a Darien resident who clung to the top during a ferocious storm which covered all but the tip in water. Closer to the highway, a short distance away, a short, squat brick cylinder, identified by different accounts as an old brick kiln or a tidal-powered mill, remains partly concealed in a canal.

The large home, in the middle of the well-manicured lawn behind the mill ruins, built in 1926 by Col. T. L. Huston, stands on the site of the original plantation house. Huston, a part-time owner of the New York Yankees, established a dairy on the property. The long white building a little further south on the same side of US 17, now a maintenance shed for the Georgia Department of Natural Resources, originally had a glass front for motorists to watch the milking. Today the main house houses offices of the DNR, which acquired the property in 1954 and manages the former rice plantation as part of the twenty-one thousand-acre Altamaha Waterfowl Management Area.

Walk from the house, west along the Butler River where many of the plantation's original levees and canals remain. Cattails, honeysuckle and yellow and purple wildflowers run along the border of the old fields. One of the original trunks, or gates which let in the tidal flow of the river to the fields, is on the main dike along the river's edge, marked by a fading interpretive sign.

Return to the main house, walking on its southern side to the site of former slave cabins and the infirmary, marked by an interpretive sign. On her visit in 1838, Kemble cleaned up the infirmary and protested the lashing of a worker, attempting to improve the lot of the hundreds of Butler slaves whom she observed living and working in extremely inhumane conditions. Her appeals fell on the deaf ears of her husband.

More old rice fields extend further south on both sides of US 17. A jumble of different colors, shades and heights, the marsh grasses don't immediately reveal their past. Yet concentrate for a moment and the outlines of the fields begin to appear, marked by darker and higher grass growth.

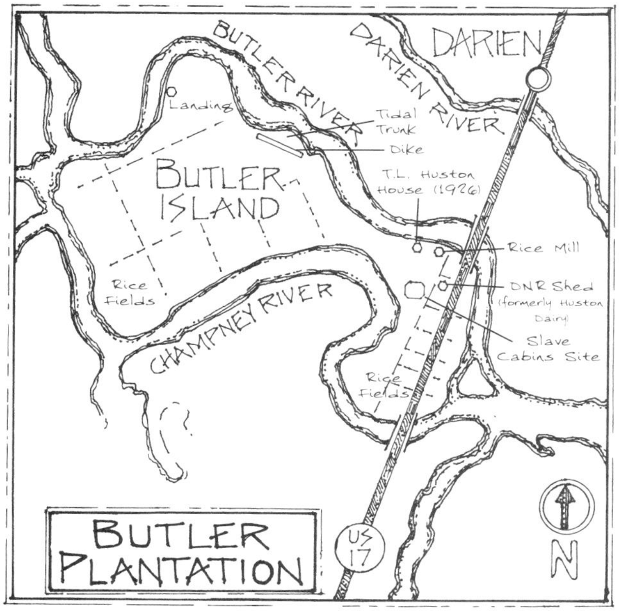

FANNY'S JOURNAL

From *Journal of a Residence on a Georgian Plantation in 1838-1839* by Frances Kemble …

In taking my first walk on the island, I directed my steps toward the rice mill, a large building on the banks of the river, within a few yards of the house we occupy.... Immediately opposite to this building is a small shed, which they call the cook's shop, and where the daily allowance of rice and corn grits of the people is boiled and distributed to them by an old woman, whose special business this is. There are four settlements or villages on the island, consisting of from ten to twenty houses, and to each settlement is annexed a cook's shop with capacious cauldrons, and the oldest wife of the settlement for officiating priestess....

My walks are rather circumscribed, inasmuch as the dikes are the only promenades. On all sides of these lie either the marshy rice-fields, the brimming river, or the swampy paths of yet unreclaimed forest.... As I skirted one of these thickets today, I stood still to admire the beauty of the shrubbery. Every shade of green, every variety of form, every degree of varnish, and all in full leaf and beauty in the very depth of winter. The stunted dark colored oak, the magnolia bay, the wold myrtle, most beautiful of all, that pride of the South, the magnolia graniflora, whose lustrous dark green perfect foliage would alone render it an object of admiration, without the queenly blossom whose color, size, and perfume are unrivaled in the whole vegetable kingdom....

I should like the wild savage loneliness, if it were not for slavery.

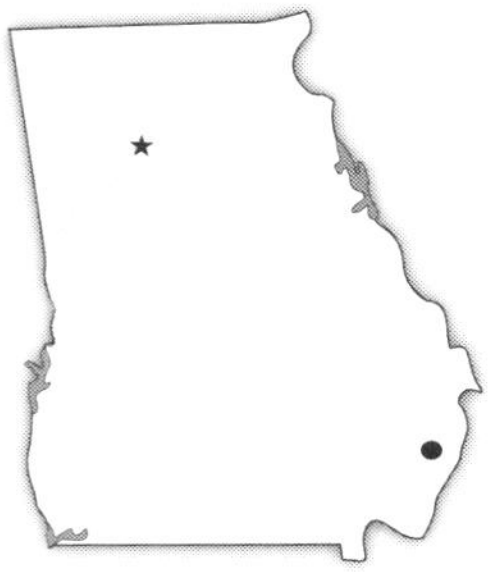

HOFWYL-BROADFIELD PLANTATION

Once a thriving rice plantation on the Altamaha River between Darien and Brunswick, Hofwyl-Broadfield, a state historic site, provides visitors with a look into the lives and culture of the Georgia rice coast from 1800 to 1915.

Facilities: Visitor's center with interpretive displays, films, books and gifts; nature trail, marsh overlook, self-guided tour of the dairy farm and guided tours of the main house. Opened in late 1997, a 2.5-mile nature trail loop starts across US 17 from the main entrance and goes through 400 acres of grass, sand and pines. Mostly dry, the trail does pass by a wetland area often visited by egrets and ducks to catch fish.

Days/Hrs.: Open year-round, Tues.-Sat., 9am-5pm; Sun., 2pm-5:30pm. Main house closes 30 minutes earlier.

Fees: Adults, $2.50; ages 6 to 18, $1.50.

Directions: From Darien, go south on US 17 for 1-2 miles. A small sign marks the Hofwyl-Broadfield entrance on the left.

More Information: Hofwyl-Broadfield Plantation, State Historic Site, 5556 US 17N, Brunswick, GA 31525; 912/264-7333.

HOFWYL-BROADFIELD PLANTATION

NO ONE LIVED IN MORE REFINEMENT THAN THE RICE PLANTERS. Nowhere is their life better documented than Hofwyl-Broadfield. No one worked under worse conditions than the rice slaves. And nowhere is their life better remembered than this plantation. Boasting the finest rice culture museum in the state and a panoramic view of the old rice fields, the plantation estate also offers a personal look into the antebellum home of a rice planting family that owned the property for almost two hundred years.

In 1806 the slaves of William Brailsford and his son-in-law James Troup carved a rice plantation out of a cypress swamp along the Altamaha. When Troup died in 1849, the plantation had seventy-three hundred acres, 375 slaves, and an eighty thousand dollar debt, a crushing financial obligation that ill-affected the family for generations. Troup's daughter Ophelia and her husband, George Dent, inherited the estate and built the house which stands today.

With the best interpretive history of coastal rice culture in the state, the visitor center has a diorama illustrating the layout of the fields and excellent displays of the tools and technology used in rice cultivation. A seventeen-minute documentary offers a revealing look into the lives of whites and blacks on the plantation while another documents rice cultivation. Graphic models and displays chronicle the contributions slaves made to rice culture. Many came directly from West Africa, bringing with them valuable knowledge about rice cultivation and tools, such as rice fans, flat baskets and a mortar and pestle to remove rice hulls. Some worked as engineers, boatmakers and carpenters to create the impressive rice field infrastructure.

Outside the visitor center, a short nature trail to the left goes to the edge of a river marsh that once grew the Hofwyl-Broadfield rice. Shortly before it reaches the marsh, the tabby ruins of a rice mill appear on the right. Continue straight ahead through a gate and onto a historic dike, made in large part with shells, which leads to a platform that overlooks the old rice fields. Looking at the inhospitable marsh, one can easily imagine the perils faced by the slaves: malaria, mosquitoes and burning heat. Cultivating rice proved a most unhealthy occupation, much worse than picking cotton. Rampant sickness meant an extremely high turnover rate.

Slaves made the technological feat possible through tedious work. They cleared fifty yard swaths, between fifty to eighty feet from the river water line, dug ditches eight feet wide and five feet deep, scooping up the thick Champney River mud to form the dikes. They sowed the seeds in early spring, covering them with mud by hoe, followed by constant weeding and four managed floods over the summer. During harvest, the workers cut the grain by hand with a rice hook, left the grain on the stubble for a day to dry and tied it in sheaves. They then loaded the sheaves aboard flat boats, transported it to the mill house or yard for curing and put them away in large stacks about fourteen feet in diameter. Each contained about three hundred bushels of rice when threshed. Either a threshing mill removed the seed from the harvested rice plant, or slaves threshed it manually, using hand flails like those used since Biblical times. Then the rice was winnowed, mostly by hand, which separated the grain from the hull and other chaff.

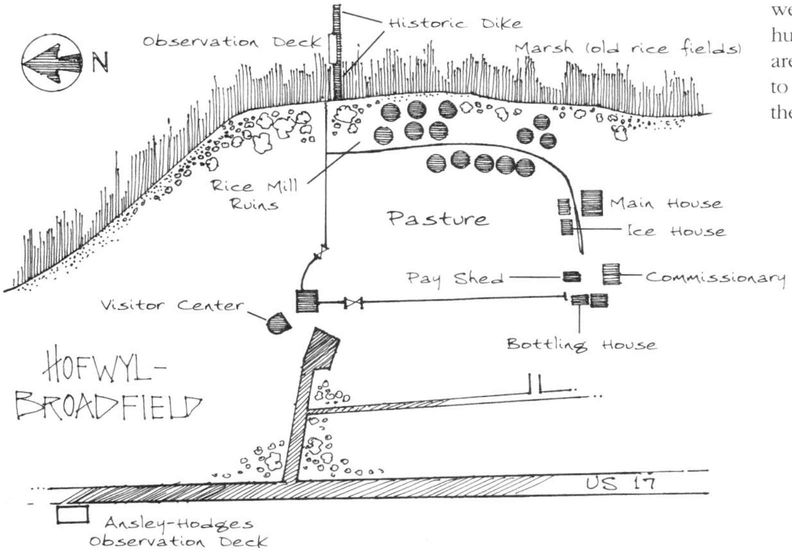

Rice Growing in Early America

Inland swamp rice production, which depended on a method of irrigation called gravity-flow, originated in the American Southeast in 1724. Plantations like Woodmanston relied on the diversion of slow moving swamp creeks into a reservoir created by earthen dams. Water from this reservoir was then released through trunk gates into fields at lower elevations of the swamp where rice was grown. After irrigation, this water was released into even lower elevations of the swamp where it continued its flow toward the ocean.

At the turn of the nineteenth century, inland swamp rice production was being replaced by a more efficient method of production known as the tidal flow system, which used the natural ebb and flow of the marsh tides to irrigate the rice fields. Plantations of this type, like Howfyl-Broadfield, were built along major coastal rivers and were not as susceptible to flood and drought as were inland swamp plantations. However, they were susceptible to the storms and hurricanes that swept through the areas, sometimes causing damage to the rice fields by inundating them with salt water.

Tabby: An Early American Building Material

Scattered along Georgia's coast and barrier islands are eighteenth - and nineteenth - century labyrinthine ruins, weathered and worn as if from antiquity. In these intricate mazes of windows, doorways, columns, rooms and walls, the sharp edges of oyster shells are felt; afternoon sunlight, flickers and spreads in a changing kaleidoscope on the walls opposite the cracks and crevices. These are tabby ruins, and they reflect a time before highways, motels and beaches—a time in Georgia's history when sugar cane and rice were cash crops and only a few wealthy planters traveled this coast.

Tabby construction was an inexpensive process. The materials needed were easily available in the tidal estuaries and shell middens left by Indians who had once inhabited the coastal areas. The procedure involved burning oysters shells to produce lime and then combining equal amounts by measure of the lime, shells and sand. When water was added, a cement-like mixture resulted. Poured into great wooden molds and tapped into form, the mixture became known as "tappy" or tabby.

Noted historians once believed that many of the tabby ruins along Georgia's coast were those of seventeenth-century Spanish missions, but this has since been proven false. Tabby construction in the region only goes back to the 1730s when General James Oglethorpe used it extensively in constructing Fort Frederica on St. Simons Island. Most of the ruins are the result of Thomas Spalding's (see page 38) influence and his expertise in tabby construction. Spalding revived tabby use in the early 1800s. On Sapelo Island he built his own home, sugar mill and other buildings from the material. He wrote detailed instructions on making tabby and extensively on its application in agricultural journals of the period.

Many of today's tabby ruins were once sugar mills. Especially significant are the ruins of Spalding's sugar mill on Sapelo, William Carnochan's sugar mill at the Thicket near Carneghan (see page 51) and the McIntosh Sugar Works near St. Marys (see page 42).

Other ruins include the powder magazine and foundations at Fort Frederica, the ruins at Retreat Plantation on St. Simons, the Horton House and Horton's Brewery site on Jekyll Island, the ruins of the mansion Dungeness on Cumberland Island and the waterfront at Darien (see page 50).

TABBY RUINS - RICE MILLS, SAPELO ISLAND, GEORGIA

Fresh Fish

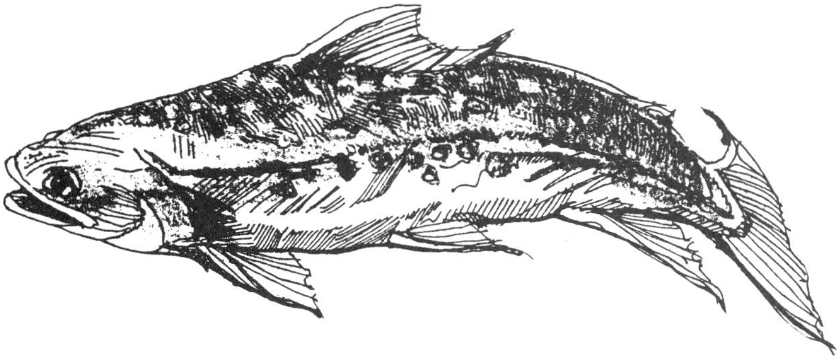

Man has long fished Georgia's rivers and streams, and today, as people consume more and more fish, aquaculture, the intensive cultivation of aquatic animals or plants, has become the fastest growing agriculture business in the nation.

Catfish cultivation, the most dominant type of aquaculture, is concentrated in the Southeastern part of the United States, primarily because of the length of the growing season. Georgia farmers produce well over 12 million pounds of catfish each year, representing a market value of more than $14 million. Most Georgia fish farmers raise channel catfish, a native, wild species that populates local streams and lakes.

Of course, Georgians will never give up their passion for catching their own fish dinner. Trout — which have a hard time living in Georgia streams since the soil tends to have little calcium, a necessary nutrient for their growth — is just one type of fish raised on fish farms in Georgia for stocking rivers, streams and lakes. Trout farms generally are located in the northern part of the state since the fish need clean, cold water to survive and reproduce.

Sheepshead Fillets, Wild Rice

Mary Beth Busbee, wife of former Georgia Governor George Busbee, is a well-known southern cook who has put together her own cookbook, *Guess Who's Coming to Dinner: Entertaining at the Governor's Mansion*. Her recipe for sheepshead fillets with wild rice and mushroom-pecan sauce combines two of the couple's favorite pastimes, cooking and fishing.

"Since moving out of the governor's mansion in 1983, we have had more time to spend enjoying fishing in the marshes and rivers along Georgia's beautiful Atlantic Coast. This recipe uses one of our favorite fish to catch (they pull like crazy!) and to eat. I also like to use pecans from Albany in the sauce."

To make 6 servings of her recipe, Mrs. Busbee takes 2 pounds of sheepshead fillets or other fish fillets, thaws them if they are frozen, cuts them into serving-size portions and seasons them with 1 teaspoon of salt and ¼ teaspoon of pepper. Next, she chops up 3 slices of bacon and cooks it in a 10-inch skillet until it is lightly browned. She adds 1 cup of chopped fresh mushrooms, ¼ cup of minced onion and ¼ cup of minced celery to the bacon, cooking the mixture until it is tender. She then stirs in 2 cups of cooked wild rice, or white and wild rice, and ½ teaspoon of salt. Mrs. Busbee places the fish in a well-greased baking pan, approximately 12 x 8 x 2 inches, and spoons the rice mixture on top of the fish. She melts 2 tablespoons of margarine or butter and drizzles it over the rice. Covering the dish, she places it in a 350° preheated oven and bakes it for 20 minutes, or until the fish flakes easily when tested with a fork.

Pecan Crusted Trout

A crunchy coating gives this fresh trout special appeal.

- 4 large trout fillets (about 6 to 8 ounces each)
- Salt and pepper to taste
- 1 tablespoon fresh lemon juice
- ½ cup seasoned bread crumbs, divided
- 1 cup toasted pecan halves
- 2 teaspoons dried rosemary leaves
- ⅓ cup all-purpose flour
- 1 egg, beaten with 2 to 3 teaspoons water
- 2 tablespoons vegetable oil, divided in half
- 2 tablespoons butter, divided in half

Season trout fillets with salt, pepper and lemon juice. Let stand at room temperature for 10 to 15 minutes. Combine 2 tablespoons of bread crumbs with pecans in blender or food processor. Grind pecans finely, combine with remaining bread crumbs and rosemary and transfer to plate. Dredge fillets in flour; shake off excess. Dip in egg wash. Place fillets skin-side up on crumb mixture, pressing into flesh. In large skillet, heat 1 tablespoon each of oil and butter over medium-high heat. Place 2 fillets skin-side up in skillet and cook until golden brown, about 3 minutes. Using spatula, turn fillets and cook until opaque in center, about 3 more minutes. Transfer to plate. Repeat with remaining butter, oil and fillets. Yields 4 main dish servings.

Georgia Pecan Commission

Crisp Fried Catfish

A cornmeal coating adds crispiness to this Southern favorite

- 6 small catfish, filleted
- 1 teaspoon salt
- ¼ teaspoon pepper
- 2 cups self-rising cornmeal
- Vegetable oil

Sprinkle catfish with salt and pepper. When ready to cook, coat pieces of catfish with cornmeal. Fry fish in hot oil about 4 minutes on each side or until golden brown. Drain on absorbent paper. Serve hot. Yields 6 servings.

Agriculture Test Kitchen

Fish Parmigiano

Basil, oregano and mozzarella cheese add an Italian touch

2	eggs, beaten
1	teaspoon salt
¼	teaspoon pepper
1	cup dry bread crumbs
½	cup grated Parmesan cheese
2	pounds fresh or frozen (thawed) fish fillets
1	15-ounce can tomato sauce
¼	cup lemon juice
½	teaspoon basil leaves
½	teaspoon oregano leaves
8	slices (1 ounce each) mozzarella cheese

Preheat oven to 350°. Combine eggs, salt and pepper. Combine crumbs and Parmesan cheese. Dip fish in egg mixture, then in crumb mixture. Place in buttered jelly roll pan, skin side down. Combine tomato sauce, lemon juice, basil and oregano; pour over fish. Top with mozzarella cheese. Bake 15 to 20 minutes or until fish flakes when tested with a fork. Yields 6 to 8 servings.

Agriculture Test Kitchen

Trout in Wine Sauce

This elegant dish is a good dinner party entrée

2	tablespoons butter
¾	cup sliced mushrooms
⅓	cup chopped green onion
2	tablespoons chopped parsley
¼	cup white wine
4	large trout fillets
	Salt and pepper
1	tablespoon butter
1	tablespoon flour
½	cup light cream

Preheat oven to 350°. In a skillet, melt 2 tablespoons butter and sauté mushrooms, green onion and parsley until tender. Remove from heat; stir in wine. Place fish in an ungreased shallow baking dish; sprinkle with salt and pepper. Spoon mushroom mixture over fillets and dot with butter. Bake uncovered for 10 minutes; drain, reserving liquid. In a saucepan, mix flour and cream; stir in reserved liquid and heat until thickened, stirring constantly. Pour over fillets. Bake uncovered for 10 more minutes or until fish flakes easily with fork. Yields 4 servings.

Chris Ward
Douglas, Georgia

While the fish are baking, Mrs. Busbee makes her mushroom-pecan sauce. She melts 3 tablespoons of margarine or butter in a 1-quart saucepan and adds 1 cup of sliced, fresh mushrooms and 1 tablespoon of minced onion, cooking them until tender. Next, she stirs in 3 tablespoons of all-purpose flour, ½ teaspoon of dry mustard, ½ teaspoon of salt and ¼ teaspoon of thyme leaves. Stirring constantly, she gradually adds 2 cups of half-and-half and cooks the mixture until it is thick and smooth. Her last step is to add ¼ cup of pecans, which she has toasted, to the sauce. Mrs. Busbee's recipe makes about 2½ cups of sauce to pour over her fish.

Buyer's Guide to Fish

For fresh fish, look for good color, smooth skin, clear rather than cloudy eyes, good odor, clean and intact gills and resiliency when pressed.

For frozen fish, look for fish that is rock hard, free of ice crystals, has no signs of thawed juices and no white spots, which can indicate freezer burn.

At home, when defrosting frozen fish, do so gradually to preserve its quality. The best way is to thaw it overnight in the refrigerator.

Fish is best cooked quickly at high heat. For every inch of thickness, cook eight to ten minutes.

When microwaving boneless fish, cook on "high" for three minutes per pound. Let stand three minutes to finish cooking.

Determine if fish are done by the color and flakiness of the flesh. Slip the point of a sharp knife into the flesh and pull aside; the edges should be opaque and the center slightly translucent with the flakes just beginning to separate.

Callaway Plantation

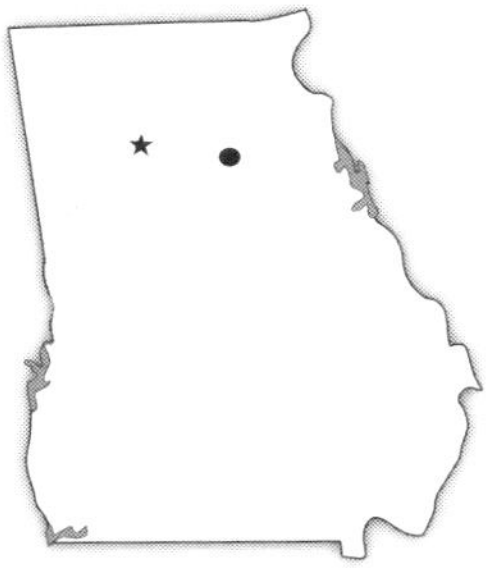

Callaway Plantation

This Piedmont plantation is a fifty-six-acre historic restoration project deeded to the City of Washington by the Callaway family.

Facilities: Historic farm with log cabin, Federal-style house, plantation manor and other period structures and crops. The site recently acquired a circa 1891 school house and 1900 country store, the second being restored into offices and a gift shop.

Days/Hrs.: Tues.-Sat., 10am-5pm, Sun., 2pm-5pm.

Fees: Adults $4, children 6-12 $2, 5 and under free.

Directions: From Washington, go west 5 miles on US 78. The plantation is across from the Washington-Wilkes airport.

More Information: Callaway Plantation, P.O. Box 9, Washington, GA 30673; 706/678-7060. Web site:www.washingtonga.org.

As late as the early 1770s, Georgia's boundaries were mostly within the coastal region. In only a confined area beyond Augusta were the Piedmont's heavier soils and hardwood forests included within Georgia's boundary. Frontiersmen were trickling down into this area from their homes in Virginia, Maryland and the Carolinas. Self-reliant, with few slaves and little love for coastal aristocrats, they brought a new way of life centered around the cultivation of tobacco and corn.

As the population grew, Georgia needed more of this Piedmont land—land inhabited by the Creek and Cherokee Indians. In 1773 Georgia's Royal Governor, James Wright, purchased two tracts of land from the Cherokees and Creeks: one strip of coastal plain, stretching between the Ogeechee and Altamaha rivers, which made way for the cultivation of rice; the other on the Piedmont, stretching north to Hart County on the Savannah River and almost to Athens on the west. Out of these Piedmont "ceded lands," Wilkes County was formed along with the first Constitution of Georgia in 1777.

Settlers flooded into the new area via the Piedmont route from the north. Most of these families were non-slaveholders who took farm-size tracts of two hundred acres or less, thus blending well with the tobacco and corn growing frontiersmen who had preceded them into the Piedmont a few years earlier.

One such pioneer family was that of Job Callaway, who came down from Bedford County, Virginia, by way of South Carolina, with his three brothers, John, Joseph and Joshua, in 1782. Callaway received a huge 1783 Revolutionary War grant of about three thousand acres near the town of Washington, property that remains in the family to this day. Descendants of John's created Callaway Gardens in Pine Mountain (see page 208); but the Callaways of Washington left a notable legacy as well: a public park with restored homes and farm buildings that chronicle the history of a pioneer family which rose to prominence from the richness of the Georgia soil.

Begin a visit to Callaway Plantation at the oldest building

on the property, a late eighteenth-century log cabin, that represents the original home of Job Callaway. While the original cabin no longer exists, this circa 1785 example would have been very similar. During the 1790s, Job's son Jacob built the gray, two-story, four-bedroom Federal-style home, which stands directly in front of the cabin. For three generations, the family cooked and ate in the cabin and lived and slept in the house. During this period, the Callaways and other farmers in the region were growing tobacco, hemp and wheat. But with the invention of the cotton gin in 1793, cotton became Georgia's cash crop, growing particularly well in the Piedmont region where it began to dramatically change the character of agriculture and life. By the Civil War, Job's grandson Parker was growing cotton with the help of under one hundred slaves.

The next rise in the Callaway fortune saw Job's great-grandson Aristedes build the property's impressive Greek revival manor. Constructed of heart or Virginia Pine and hand-made brick, produced in kilns on the farm, the classic, circa 1869, two-story home was the focal point of a postbellum cotton estate that stretched in all directions as far as the eye could see. The plantation was not in the path of Sherman's March to the Sea, allowing the Callaways to continue growing cotton with the use of tenant farmers. Virtually unaltered, the dwelling retains the original doors, plaster and mantels, all in remarkably good condition. Other period structures, such as a barn, smokehouse and blacksmith shop, are located on the property as well as a vegetable garden and a cotton patch.

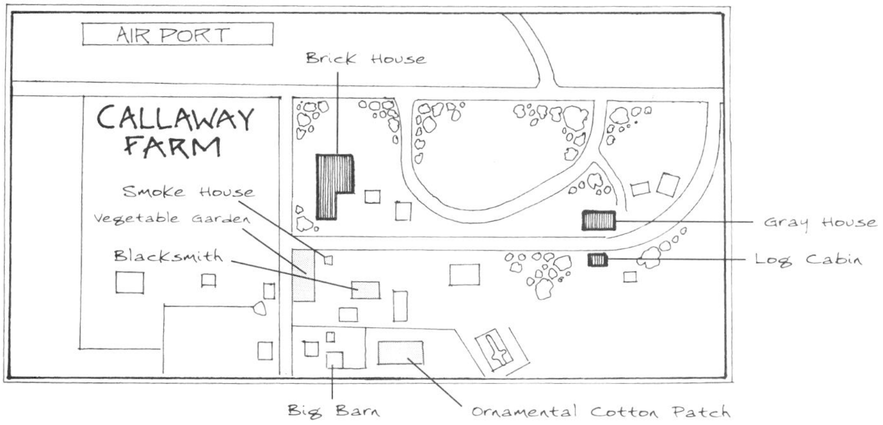

King Cotton

By the end of the 1700s, Georgia was epitomized by two types of farmers: the slaveholding plantation owners of the coastal plain and the pioneer tobacco and corn farmers of the Piedmont. These two groups formed two societies living in distinctly different environments, following diverging economic paths and inheriting different social traditions. But one Georgia crop would be the glue to bond these two increasingly disparate ways of life. That crop would be cotton. In the late 1800s, South Carolina was growing cotton; but it was the long staple fiber suitable for cultivation in Georgia only along the coastal margins and islands. The upland cotton variety that grew best in the Piedmont had a short staple fiber, making hand removal of seeds a prohibitively laborious process.

In 1793, Massachusetts-born Eli Whitney solved Georgia's cotton problem with his invention of the cotton gin. The gin cleaned cotton as fast as fifty persons. Cotton became profitable to produce on small farms, using only family labor, as well as large plantations with hundreds of slaves. Soon Georgia became the world's largest producer of cotton, unifying the state as no other crop ever would. Cotton was King.

Atlanta History Center

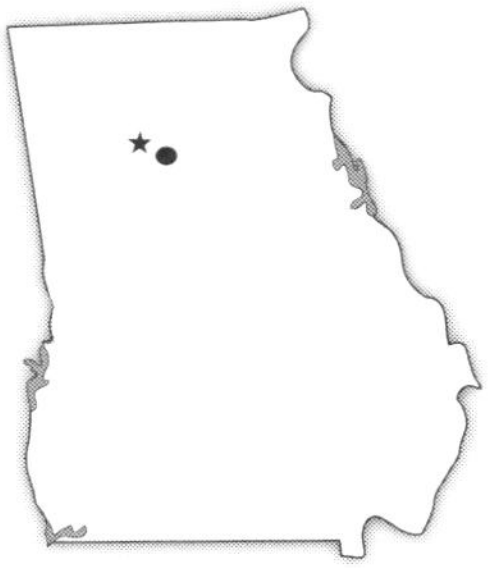

Atlanta History Center

The thirty-three-acre Atlanta History Center preserves the cultural record of the city from the 1840s to the present.

Facilities: Museum with historical exhibits, cafe, Tullie Smith Farm, Swan House, gardens, and library/archives.

Days/Hrs.: Mon.-Sat., 10am-5:30pm; Sun., noon-5:30pm. The library is closed Sun.-Mon.

Fees: For adults, museum exhibits and garden $7, Tullie Smith Farm additional $1, Swan House additional $2.

Directions: From Peachtree Street in Buckhead, turn west on West Paces Ferry Road and continue several blocks. The well-marked history center has an entrance on the left.

More Information: Atlanta History Center, 130 West Paces Ferry Road, NW, Atlanta, Georgia 30305; 404/814-4000. Web site: www.atlhist.org.

NO WHERE IS THE HISTORY OF GEORGIA FARM LIFE AS WELL DEFINED as it is at the Atlanta History Center. Here, the Tullie Smith Farm, an authentic nineteenth-century Georgia Piedmont farm reconstruction, and a permanent museum exhibition, *Shaping Traditions: Folk Arts in a Changing South*, offer some of the best visual, written and audio interpretations of traditional farm culture in the state.

The folk arts exhibition in the museum (1) is a good place to start a tour of the center. More than five hundred examples of pottery, woodwork, basketry, weaving, quilting and metal work from the John A. Burrison collection is the basis for the exhibit. Burrison, a Georgia State University professor and exhibit curator, salvaged many of the artifacts from junk shops, old farms and mountain hamlets all over the Southeast.

The most extensive collection relates to folk pottery, once vital to farm life. Before plastic and cans, rural families relied on potters—often congregated in small "jug towns" across the Georgia Piedmont where natural clay was readily available—to provide butter churns, syrup holders, food containers, water and milk pitchers and medicine holders.

There are cotton baskets made of white oak splits, illustrations of an old cotton gin with baling press, a detailed model of a sorghum maker and hand held-rice mills (wooden mortars with deep holes and specialized grinding tools, used by African-Americans in the nineteenth century on the coast). Mountain fiddle songs and African American gospels play throughout the exhibit. Traditional folk remedies are explored. A quilt exhibit displays—on command—one of a half dozen works representing different styles. There are illustrations and examples of corn shucking contests and corn husk dolls. A recreated primitive Baptist church resounds with old sermons and gospel songs.

From the exit in the back of the history museum, go left on a short trail to the Tullie Smith Farm (2), surrounded by acres of hilly, densely wooded terrain. The farm consists of six historic buildings, including a farmhouse, built in 1845 about five miles east of this location. The Robert Smith family and their descendants lived in the home until 1967. The furnishings reflect the modest life of the inhabitants. Out the back door a few steps stands the kitchen, completely separate from the house; the prevalence of grease inside and lack of running water nearby made fires a frequent experience. Next to the kitchen stands the circa 1850 smokehouse. It contains real cured hams, which resemble stones covered in a thin crust, partly green. Other mid-nineteenth century structures include a corn crib, and a barn with sheep, chickens and goats.

In sharp contrast to the simple lifestyle of the Smiths, but also connected with agriculture, is the palatial circa 1928 Swan House (3). A short walk along a marked trail through the woods, it once served as the home of the Inmans, a prominent Atlanta family that made a fortune in the cotton brokerage business. Regular tours go through the home, which, besides magnificent furnishings on the inside, has luxurious, European-style gardens and fountains on the outside.

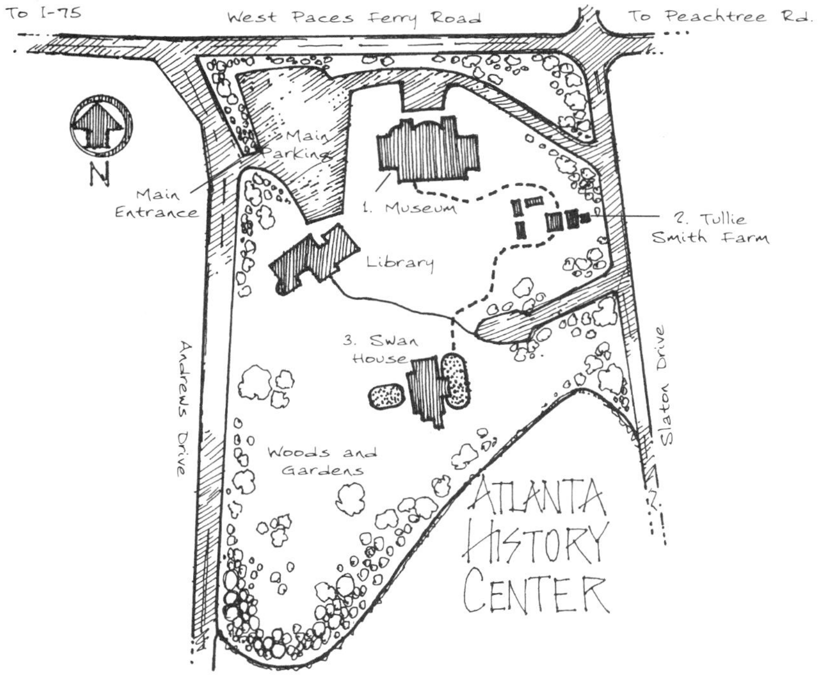

WESTVILLE

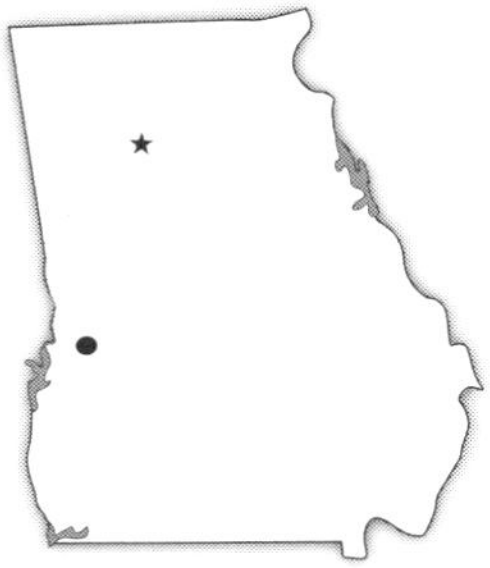

WESTVILLE

Westville is a sixty-seven-acre functioning living history village that realistically depicts Georgia's pre-industrial life and culture of 1850—when agriculture was the way of life.

Facilities: Historic village and gift shop with limited snacks.

Days/Hrs.: Tues.-Sat., 10am-5pm; Sun., 1-5 pm. Open Mon. when federal holidays observed. Closed New Year's Day, Thanksgiving and Christmas.

Fees: Adults $8, seniors $7, K-12 students $4, under 5 and youth groups with reservations are free.

Directions: From downtown Lumpkin, go southeast about 1 mile on MLK Drive. Westville is on the left.

More Information: Westville, MLK Drive, Lumpkin, GA 31815; 912/838-6310 or 888/733-1850. Web site: www.westville.org.

In 1850, towns in Georgia's coastal plain, such as Savannah and Darien, had been settled for more than one hundred years, but Atlanta was not yet even fifteen years old. And even though towns were springing up along the rivers and railroad lines throughout its interior, Georgia was still mostly frontier. Lumpkin's village of Westville is an authentic recreation of how people lived in west Georgia's pre-industrial period a decade before the Civil War, portraying farm people who came to town to buy supplies, went to church and socialized and brought their cotton and grain to sell. Most of Westville's thirty-three structures, all dating from before 1855, are concentrated on the town's main streets where craftspersons answer questions as they work their trades, tilling, spinning, quilting, weaving, woodworking, blacksmithing and basket and pottery making. Although everything in Westville reflects a time when agriculture dominated the way of life for Georgians, listed are just a few notable stops.

The circa 1850 General Store (1), originally from Webster County, serves as a gift shop selling jams, jellies, old-fashioned biscuit cutters and crafts made on site, such as replica butter churns. The Singer House (2) was built in 1838 in Lumpkin by German immigrants Johann George and Louisa Singer, who started the Singer Company, the oldest hardware store in Georgia, which is located on Lumpkin's town square. Built in Stewart County in 1831, the Federal-style Bryan-Worthington House (3) represents the dwelling of the operator of the screw press (4) and 1840 cotton gin (5) across the road.

The Patterson-Marrett Farmhouse (6) is a log, dog-trot style dwelling, typical of the mid-eighteenth century. Inside to the right is a bedroom, always unlocked, reserved for travelers who commonly relied on the hospitality of strangers while on the remote, dirt roads of the South; in exchange, the travelers brought rare scraps of news from afar. Inside is a spinning jenny, iron coffee grinder, corn-husk broom and other authentic period furnishings. Good aromas float from the kitchen, separated from the main house by a walkway. The matron of the house, in simple dress and apron, is cooking biscuits, her Dutch oven in the fireplace, underneath a brick mantle covered in large iron skillets. Primitive roads and transportation made rural families remarkably self-reliant. Household labor produced a variety of necessities from the farm, such as preserved meats, canned goods, homemade syrup and vegetables. A vegetable garden outside includes common crops such as beans, corn, greens and sugar cane. Essential on the farm, the mule dragged the plow, turned the cane mill and pulled the wagon. The barn (7) houses the mule along with chickens, geese and turkeys. A genuine copper whiskey distillery is housed in this small building (8). As in the cotton screw press, mules power the mill (9), which in this case grinds cane stalks. During the Harvest Fair, Westville makes a dark red cane syrup that is a popular drink poured over ice. The rest, boiled in the kettle, becomes the syrup sold in the general store. Village potters work in this cluster of small buildings (10). There's one pug mill to make clay, although potters traditionally had a second to make bricks. The old wood-fuel kiln is still used to fire stoneware vessels. The pottery shop is where potters shape native clay into necessities commonly found in nineteenth century homes, like stoneware, jars, churns, pitchers and jugs.

Cotton Gin and Screw Press

Each fall during Westville's Harvest Festival, mules attached to the end of a long horizontal pole bring to life the only antebellum animal-powered cotton gin remaining in the world. The pole is attached to a drive that moves a set of gears and belts, powering the gin machine and removing the seed from the lint, or white fiber which makes fabrics. In the gin house upstairs, a ginner piles cotton into the machine. Like teeth, mechanical gears take the seed, which falls into a tray underneath, out of the cotton lint.

Also powered by draft animal, Westville's cotton screw press is perhaps one of a half dozen remaining in the United States. A huge wooden screw, carved by hand from white oak, tightens loose cotton lint into round bales as it turns. Mules, attached to levers, power the screw as they walk in a circle around the machine's perimeter. When tight, a leather strap went around the bale.

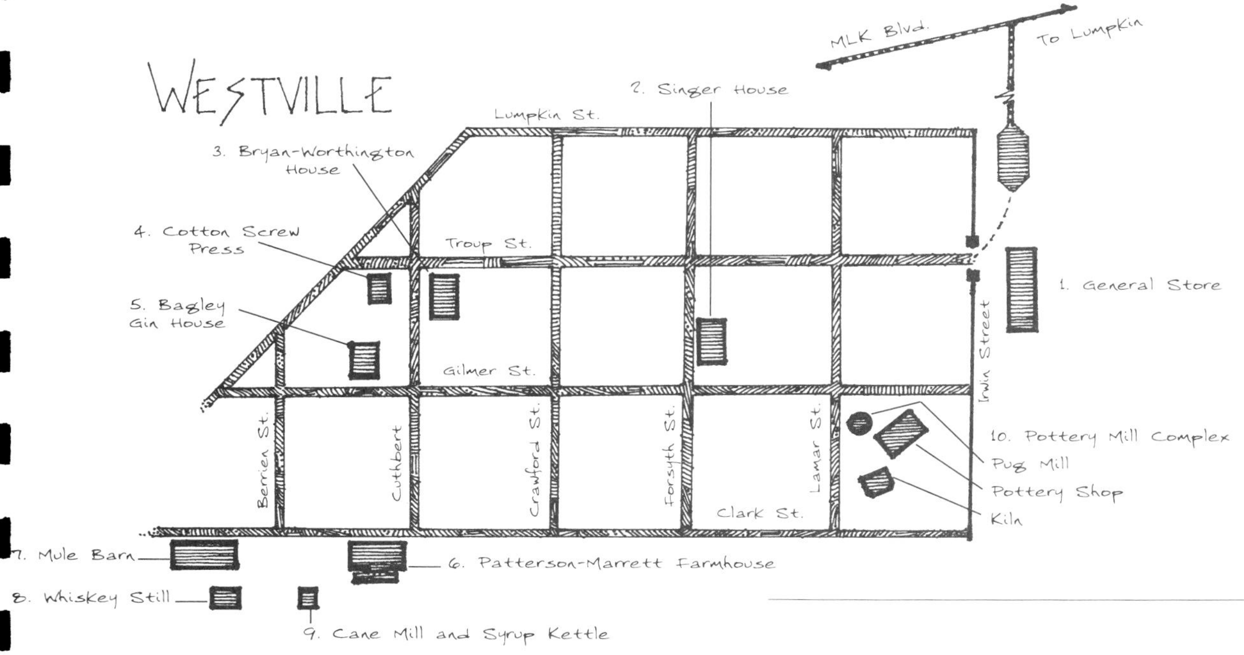

Prehistoric Agriculture

The history of agriculture in the region that would become Georgia goes back thousands of years to the Paleo Indians, nomadic hunters of large mammals who roamed the region looking for food before 9000 BC, when the climate was much colder and ice still covered much of the earth. The daily routine of these Indians was mostly centered around hunting. They traveled in small bands, or families, searching for the large animals of their day—-the mastodon, the giant bison, the mammoth. These animals provided them with meat and fat for food, skins for clothing and bones for tools. The Indians stayed in one place for only a few days, eating the animals and plants in the area and moving on. They built shelters only if they found enough food in an area to last a few weeks or months.

By the Archaic Period, from 9000 to 1000 BC, the ice covering much of the earth had retreated, the climate had gradually warmed and the large animals roaming the region had disappeared. White-tailed deer, boars, black bear and many small animals, which can still be found today, appeared. The Indians of this period were hunters and gatherers who utilized these new food sources as well as shellfish and seasonal plants. Rivers and their rich food sources became available. Acorn and nut-bearing trees, extending from the Fall Line to the upper Coastal Plain, were probably of great importance to these people, providing them with needed protein and fatty acids. The large stands of hickory and oak trees growing in the region were probably as important in bringing these Indians into the area as the large amounts of game.

The first steps to farming were taken when hunters began to understand more and more about the plants and animals they used for food. They possibly noticed that a plant would grow where seeds had fallen on the ground, or learned how to raise animals by taking care of young animals whose mothers they had killed. In this region it is known that during the Woodland period, 1000 BC to AD 900, people planted sunflower, marsh elder and goosefeet—plants considered weeds today. Eventually, squash and gourds and later corn and beans were cultivated. The Indians also learned to make pottery, which was a monumental step, as it was used to cook and store food and transport water. People began to live in villages at least part of the year. After about 2.5 million years as hunters, people no longer had to roam to obtain food. Farmers settled in one area for several years at a time and built villages near their cropland, living there as long as the crops grew well. Once the land became unproductive because of continuous planting, the Indians moved to an new area and built another village.

During the Mississippian Period, 700 to 1600 AD, the Indians built large villages usually on rivers or streams, using the rich bottomlands for farming and the rivers and streams for transportation. Village areas surrounded huge, flat-topped temple mounds where social and religious ceremonies took place. The Mississippian Indians still hunted and gathered, but this culture discovered that the bottomland soils produced better crops and the periodic flooding that occurred restored the nutrients in the soil. They cultivated seed plants, pumpkins, beans, squash, probably tobacco and especially corn. So important was the staple corn that the Mississippians gave it religious significance, connecting it to the king-gods who led them. The great mounds they built, full of burial plots and artifacts, still stand, some protected as public property. Etowah Mounds State Park near Cartersville on the Etowah River was perhaps the most powerful Mississippian center in Georgia. Rood Mounds on the Chattahoochee, part of the Florence Marina State Park in Florence, once felt the examining hands of explorer William Bartram. Other important mound sites from where great corn cultures sprang include the Kolomoki Mounds State Historic Site near Blakely and the Ocmulgee National Monument in Macon.

Native Americans in Georgia:

10,000 BC – Paleo Indians migrate over North America

9000 BC – Archaic Indians adapt to extinction of many large animals like mammoth and mastodon due to warming of climate

2000 BC – People of coastal Georgia independently invent pottery, which allows for cooking year-round storage of food

1000 BC – Southeastern Woodland Indians begin a mixed economy of agriculture and forest use (hunting, fishing, wild plants).

700s AD – Mississippian period of intensive agriculture and town developing; major temple mounds built at Etowah and Ocmulgee

1500s AD – Population declines due to introduction of European diseases

1733 – First European settlers arrive on Georgia soil

1763 – Creek Indians cede first of their Georgia lands in the interior

1790 – Creeks yield Piedmont lands, which are made valuable soon by the invention of the cotton gin

1803 – Former Indian lands distributed to white settlers in a land-lottery system

1820-1840 – Mass expulsion of Indians, known as the Trail of Tears, to the western Indian Territory

Vegetables

Vegetables are versatile. They can be eaten raw, steamed, boiled, baked, microwaved, fried and stir-fried. They are among the oldest known of man's food sources. Most vegetables are cholesterol free, high in fiber and low in calories, fat and sodium.

The dictionary defines a vegetable as any of many nutritious foods that come from the parts of a plant. Horticultural scientists define a vegetable as the edible product of a herbaceous plant, a plant with stems that are softer and less fibrous than the wood stems of trees and shrubs. Vegetables are grouped according to the part of the plant from which they come. Plant parts eaten as vegetables include bulbs, flower clusters, fruits, leaves, roots, seeds, stems and tubers. Most vegetables are annuals, plants that live for only one growing season.

Among Southeastern states, Georgia is a leader in vegetable production, both in acreage and cash receipts. With Georgia's mild climate and long growing season, farmers can harvest some type of vegetable or fruit year-round. Most of the state's vegetable crops are supplied to the fresh market and are readily available at any of the seventeen state farmer's markets.

Lima Beans

Believed to be at least four thousand years old, beans, members of the legume family, are among the oldest foods known to man. Many of the popular beans in Southern cuisine, like snap beans and lima beans, originated in South or Central America. Ancient Peruvians placed large lima beans of various colors in the tombs of their dead. Southwestern Indians in North America stored them in their dwellings. On his first voyage to the New World, Columbus found lima beans cultivated by Indians in Cuba.

The lima is also known as the Sieva bean, Butter bean, Civet bean, Sewee bean, Carolina bean and Sugar bean. When mottled with purple, lima beans are called calico or speckled butter beans. Lima bean pods are 3 1/2 inches long and 3/4 of an inch wide. The main varieties are vining and bush. Small seed baby bush limas and large seed Fordhook bush limas are the main ones sold commercially.

Lima beans are quick and easy to prepare and provide great nutritional value. Loaded with nutrients such as protein, thiamine, riboflavin, folate, iron, potassium and fiber, they are an excellent addition to any meal.

Available in Georgia from June to November, lima beans are grown in the central and southern part of the state.

Lima Bean Casserole

Mustard and lemon juice add tang and flavor!

- 2 cups water
- 4 cups fresh, shelled baby lima beans
- 4 slices bacon
- 2 tablespoons all-purpose flour
- 3 tablespoons brown sugar
- 1½ teaspoons salt
- ¼ teaspoon pepper
- 1½ teaspoons dry mustard
- 1½ tablespoons lemon juice
- ½ cup breadcrumbs
- 2 tablespoons butter, melted
- ½ cup (2 ounces) shredded Cheddar cheese

Bring water to a boil in medium saucepan. Add lima beans; return to a boil. Reduce heat and simmer until tender (about 20 minutes); drain reserving 1 cup liquid. Place lima beans in a lightly greased 8-inch square baking dish; set aside. Cook bacon in large skillet until crisp, remove bacon, reserving 2 tablespoons drippings in skillet. Crumble bacon and set aside.

Preheat oven to 350°. Heat bacon drippings in skillet; add flour, stirring until smooth. Cook 1 minute, stirring constantly. Gradually add reserved bean liquid; cook over medium heat, stirring constantly, until mixture is thickened. Stir in brown sugar and next four ingredients. Pour sauce over beans. Combine breadcrumbs and butter; sprinkle over top. Bake for 25 minutes; sprinkle with cheese. Bake 5 more minutes or until cheese melts. Sprinkle crumbled bacon over top. Yields 6 servings.

Georgia Department of Agriculture Test Kitchen

LEMON PECAN GREEN BEANS

Add a Southern crunch to this fresh favorite

1	pound fresh green beans
¼	teaspoon salt, or to taste
1	tablespoon olive oil
¼	cup sliced green onions
¼	cup chopped pecans, toasted
2	teaspoons finely chopped fresh rosemary or dried rosemary leaves
2	teaspoons fresh lemon juice
2	teaspoons grated lemon rind
	Garnishes: lemon slice, fresh rosemary sprigs (optional)

Wash beans and remove ends. Sprinkle with salt. Arrange beans in a steamer basket and place over boiling water. Cover and steam approximately 10 minutes or until crisp-tender. Plunge green beans into cold water to stop cooking process; drain and set aside.

In a large skillet, heat olive oil over medium heat. Add green onions and cook, stirring constantly, about 3 minutes. Add green beans, pecans, rosemary and lemon juice; cook, stirring constantly until mixture is thoroughly heated. Sprinkle with lemon rind and garnish with lemon slices and fresh rosemary if desired. Serve immediately. Yields 4 servings.

Georgia Pecan Commission

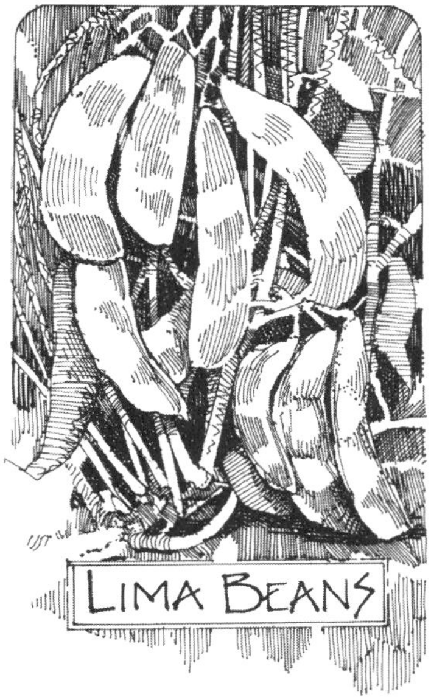

BUYER'S GUIDE TO LIMA BEANS

Lima beans can be purchased fresh in the pods, frozen, canned or dried as seeds.

Lima bean pods should be fresh, well-filled and dark green in color.

When buying shelled lima beans, look for dry, plump limas with tender skin, green or greenish white in color.

Shelled lima beans will stay fresh for about one week.

Lima beans with hard skins have less flavor because they are over-mature.

Snap Beans

Sparked by an interest in beans with stringless pods, Americans began planting snap beans in 1890. Because of their stringless, fiberless pods, snap beans don't split when ripe like most shell and dry beans. Also known as string beans or green beans, they can play an important part in a healthy, well-balanced diet.

Served steamed or boiled, they give flavor, color and texture to meals and are a good source of fiber, with no fat, sodium or cholesterol.

Most snap beans grow east of the Mississippi River. They thrive in warm climates with bright sunshine, like the central and southern parts of Georgia, where snap bean production takes place from May to August.

Marinated Italian Beans

Marinating enhances garlic, basil, oregano and tarragon flavors

- 1½ pounds fresh green beans
- ¾ cup water
- 1 16-ounce bottle Italian salad dressing
- ½ cup lemon juice
- 2 tablespoons tarragon vinegar
- ½ teaspoon basil leaves
- ¼ teaspoon pepper
- ⅛ teaspoon oregano leaves
- 2 cloves garlic, crushed
- 1 2-ounce jar pimiento
- Garnish: lemon slices (optional)

Wash beans. Trim ends and remove strings. Place beans in a 12x8x2-inch baking dish; add water. Cover with heavy-duty plastic wrap and microwave at high for 12 to 14 minutes or until crisp-tender, stirring after 6 minutes. Let stand covered 2 minutes; drain. Combine dressing and next 7 ingredients in a small bowl, stirring well. Pour dressing mixture over beans; cover and refrigerate 6 to 8 hours. Garnish with lemon slices if desired. Yields 6 servings.

Georgia Department of Agriculture Test Kitchen

Hint: Cider vinegar or wine-based vinegar may be substituted for the tarragon vinegar listed in this recipe.

Cucumber Salad

A cool as a cucumber summertime salad

- 1 4-ounce package lime gelatin
- ½ cup boiling water
- 2 medium cucumbers, grated
- 1 small onion, minced
- 1 cup cottage cheese
- 1 cup chopped pecans
- ½ cup mayonnaise
- 1 tablespoon lemon juice
- ½ teaspoon salt
- 1 tablespoon white vinegar
- 1 cucumber, sliced

Dissolve gelatin in boiling water. Add next 8 ingredients; mix and pour into mold and congeal. Garnish with sliced cucumber when ready to serve. Yields 8 servings.

Mrs. Reita Medum
Molena, Georgia

Cabbage Casserole

A family reunion favorite

1	small cabbage or ½ large cabbage
1	medium Vidalia® onion
½	stick (¼ cup) margarine
	Salt and pepper, to taste
¼	cup mayonnaise
1	10.75-ounce can cream of mushroom or cream of chicken soup

Topping

1	stick (½ cup) margarine
1	cup grated sharp Cheddar cheese
1	stack round butter crackers, crushed

Coarsely chop cabbage and place in 2-to-3-quart casserole dish. Chop onion and place on top of cabbage. Melt ½ stick margarine and pour over cabbage. Sprinkle with salt and pepper to taste. In small bowl, mix soup and mayonnaise together. Spread over top of cabbage mixture.

Preheat oven to 350°. To make topping, melt the remaining stick of margarine. In small bowl, mix melted margarine, grated cheese and crushed crackers. Sprinkle cracker-cheese mixture over top of casserole. Bake for about 45 minutes or until top is browned and inside is bubbly. Yields 8 servings.

Janice Webb
Lawrenceville, Georgia

Hint: To reduce calories, fat, cholesterol and sodium in this recipe, use reduced-fat margarine and reduced-fat mayonnaise. Cut the shredded cheese to ½ cup and margarine to ½ stick (¼ cup) in the topping. You can also substitute low-fat or reduced-sodium crackers. Result: Each serving contains 221 calories, 16.7g fat, 10mg cholesterol and 500mg sodium.

Buyer's Guide to Snap Beans

Look for snap beans with a fresh, bright green color, preferably young, tender beans with crisp, firm pods. Avoid buying snap beans with blemishes or wilted, flabby pods.

Snap beans, thin and round, differ slightly from pole beans, thin and flat.

Snap beans should be refrigerated and will stay fresh three to five days.

To help preserve color and retain nutrients, cook snap beans in a covered pot.

CABBAGE

Cabbage has been grown in the eastern Mediterranean and Asia Minor for thousands of years. Jacques Carter introduced cabbage, one of the first crops grown by colonists, to North America on his third voyage to the continent in 1541. The vegetable comes from a large family that includes Brussels sprouts, kale, collards, rutabagas, turnips and cauliflower.

Cabbage are packed with nutrition. Ounce for ounce they provide as much vitamin C as orange juice. A member of the cruciferous family, they contain a substance that might reduce the risk of some forms of cancer. One of the most versatile vegetables, cabbage can be cooked or served raw.

Hundreds of cabbage varieties grow in the United States. The main ones cultivated in Georgia are smooth-leaved green cabbage, crinkled-leaved green Savoy cabbage and red cabbage. Georgia cabbage is available year-round but primarily in the spring and fall. A significant amount of cabbage is grown around Dillard in Rabun County (see page 214), but most of Georgia's cabbage is grown in the Moultrie area.

CHINESE FIRECRACKERS

These homemade eggrolls are a great low-fat appetizer!

- 1 teaspoon vegetable oil
- ½ pound ground turkey
- 1½ cups finely chopped cabbage
- 1 medium carrot, shredded (about ½ cup)
- 2 tablespoons finely chopped green onion
- ¼ teaspoon chili powder
- ¼ teaspoon salt
- ¼ teaspoon pepper
- 2 tablespoons dry white wine or apple juice
- 1 teaspoon cornstarch
- 14 frozen phyllo sheets (13x9-inches each), thawed
- Vegetable cooking spray
- Sweet and sour sauce

Heat vegetable oil in medium non-stick skillet. Cook ground turkey, cabbage, carrot and onion in oil over medium heat about 5 minutes, stirring frequently, until turkey is done and vegetables are crisp-tender. Stir in chili powder, salt and pepper. Mix wine and cornstarch; stir into turkey mixture. Cook uncovered, stirring occasionally, until slightly thickened.

Preheat oven to 375°. Cut phyllo sheets crosswise in half. Cover with damp towel to keep from drying out. Place 1 piece phyllo on flat surface. Cover lightly with vegetable cooking spray. Top with a second piece of phyllo. Place about 2 tablespoons of turkey mixture on short end of phyllo; shape into about 4-inch log. Roll up phyllo and turkey mixture. Twist phyllo 1 inch from each end to form firecracker shape. Repeat with remaining phyllo and turkey mixture. Spray lightly with oil.

Bake on ungreased cookie sheet 18 to 22 minutes or until phyllo is crisp and golden brown. Serve with sweet and sour sauce. Yields 14 eggrolls.

Frank Sams
Burnt Hickory, Georgia

KILLER COLE SLAW

Oriental noodles and sunflower seeds bring an added crunch

- ½ cabbage, chopped
- 5 green onions, chopped
- ¼ cup slivered almonds
- ¼ cup sunflower seeds
- 1 8-ounce package Oriental noodle soup mix, crushed (save seasoning packet for dressing)

DRESSING

- ¼ cup vinegar
- ¼ cup salad oil
- Seasoning packet from noodles

Combine first 4 ingredients. In separate bowl combine dressing ingredients. Toss salad with dressing. Add noodles and toss again. Yields 4 servings.

Megan Hankinson
Atlanta, Georgia

BUYER'S GUIDE TO CABBAGE

Cabbage heads should be hard and heavy for their size.

Look for bright green or red outer leaves, depending on the variety, that are fresh and blemish-free.

A cabbage head should not have too many loose outer leaves because they must be discarded.

Worm-eaten outer leaves often indicate damage to the whole head.

Avoid cabbage with wilted or yellowing leaves.

Cabbage refrigerated in the vegetable crisper should keep fresh at least one month.

Trim cabbage conservatively because the outer leaves are extra-rich in nutrients like vitamins A and C.

MOCK OYSTER STEW

Eggplant is the key ingredient to this soup

- 2 eggplants (about 1 pound each)
- 1 quart milk
- 4 tablespoons butter or margarine
- 1 teaspoon salt
- 12 saltine crackers, crushed

Peel eggplants and cut into 1-inch cubes. Boil in small amount of water for 10 minutes and drain. Add milk, butter, salt and crackers; simmer for 5 minutes. Serve hot.

Hint: I usually sauté ½ cup chopped onions and ½ cup chopped celery in 3 tablespoons butter and add to the milk mixture and sprinkle in some Durkee's Red Hot Sauce. The name beats eggplant soup, which it could be called.

Ruth Horton
Atlanta, Georgia

Want a good boy (farmers') who has no home, to make home with us and help farm a 1 mule farm. From 15 to 17 yrs. of age. Must not be a town bum, not chew, smoke nor have bad habits. Be a good worker (not have to follow and tell what to do). Will also teach him to do other work. If you know of such a boy, let me know before crop time. Mrs. S. M. King, Faceville, Ga.

Farm Help Wanted, Market Bulletin, *January 10, 1929*

Cabbage Casserole

The Dillard House has been cooking and serving Southern food to visitors of Rabun County in the North Georgia mountains ever since Carrie and Arthur Dillard founded the restaurant and boarding house back in 1916. Today, Lazell Vinson is just one of the many Dillard House cooks who carry on that tradition. Her cabbage casserole is one of several found in the *Dillard House Cookbook and Mountain Guide*. It is a restaurant favorite that reflects the area's bounty of Georgia-grown cabbages (see page 214).

To prepare her casserole, Mrs. Vinson begins by shredding 1 large head of cabbage. She then cooks the cabbage in a pot of boiling water with 1 teaspoon of salt for 5 to 8 minutes, draining it well when done. She cautions not to overcook the cabbage; it should remain crisp. To make the casserole sauce, she melts 1 cup of margarine in a sauce pot. Next she adds 3 tablespoons of all-purpose flour and salt and pepper to make a paste. Stirring constantly, she adds 1 quart of milk and cooks the sauce until it is thick. She then takes a buttered 2-quart casserole and layers the cabbage, enough sauce to cover, a second layer of cabbage, the remaining sauce and 2 cups of grated cheddar cheese. Mrs. Vinson tops the casserole with 1½ cups of buttered bread crumbs and bakes it in a 300° preheated oven for 15 to 20 minutes.

Eggplant Dip

Fresh garlic and ginger add spice to this dip

1 to 1¼	pounds large, whole eggplant
1	tablespoon finely minced garlic
1	tablespoon finely minced fresh ginger
¼	cup thinly sliced green onion
¼	teaspoon dried red chili flakes (more to taste)
3	tablespoons soy sauce
3	tablespoons packed brown sugar
1	teaspoon unseasoned rice vinegar
1	tablespoon hot water
2	tablespoons corn or peanut oil
½	teaspoon sesame oil
	Garlic croutons or crackers
	Garnish: thinly sliced green onion

Preheat oven to 475°. Prick eggplant in several places with fork. Place on baking sheet and bake for 20 to 40 minutes, until fork-tender, turning once. Remove eggplant and slit lengthwise to speed cooling. While still warm, remove tough stem end and peel, scraping and saving any pulp. Cube pulp. Process pulp and any thick baking juices in food processor or blend until nearly smooth. In small bowl, combine garlic, ginger, ¼ cup green onion and red chili flakes. In medium bowl, combine soy sauce, brown sugar, rice vinegar and hot water; mix until smooth.

Heat oil in wok or large heavy skillet on high heat. Add garlic-ginger mixture and stir fry about 15 seconds until fragrant, being careful not to burn. Add the soy sauce-brown sugar mixture and stir until simmering, lowering heat if necessary. Add eggplant; stir well to blend and heat through. Remove from heat, add sesame oil and adjust spices if necessary to achieve zesty flavor. Allow to cool, then cover and refrigerate several hours or overnight if possible. Serve at room temperature, spooned over croutons or crackers and garnished with green onion. Yields approximately 25 servings.

Joy Manbeck
Alpharetta, Georgia

Hint: Substitute white vinegar if rice vinegar is unavailable.

Eggplant and Rice Provençale

This casserole makes a great dinner party entrée

- 4 tablespoons olive oil
- 2 pounds eggplant, peeled and cut into 1-inch cubes
- 3 cups finely chopped onion
- 1 cup green pepper, cut into 1-inch cubes
- 2 cloves garlic, minced
- 1 teaspoon thyme
- 1 bay leaf
- 3 tomatoes, peeled, chopped and cored
- 1 cup rice, uncooked
- 3¾ cups chicken broth
- Salt and pepper to taste
- ½ cup grated Parmesan cheese
- 2 tablespoons butter

Preheat oven to 400°. Heat oil in large skillet over high heat. Add eggplant cubes, stirring constantly. Add next five ingredients, continuing to stir. Add tomatoes, lower heat and cook until vegetables are tender, approximately 7 minutes. Stir in rice and chicken broth. Season with salt and pepper to taste. Spoon mixture into 4-quart baking dish or two 2-quart dishes. Sprinkle Parmesan cheese over top. Dot with butter and bake uncovered for 40 minutes. Yields 16 servings.

Robyn Jackson
Duluth, Georgia

Hint: This recipe may be cut in half if you are feeding a smaller group. To reduce fat and calories in this recipe, reduce olive oil to 3 tablespoons and omit butter. Results: Each serving contains 121 calories and 3.9g fat (28% of calories).

Eggplant

A member of the nightshade family that includes the potato, tomato and sweet pepper, the eggplant was cultivated as far back as the fifth century A.D. by the Chinese. Asian ladies once made black dye from eggplant to stain their teeth before polishing. In contrast to the small eggplants of China, large-fruited varieties were cultivated in India, a major center of distribution for eggplant in the sixteenth century; eggplants continue to grow wild there. Europeans had differing opinions about the purple vegetable. The Spanish, who introduced eggplant to America, called it the apple of love. Northern Europeans, however, called it the apple of madness. Before 1900, many ornamental varieties of eggplant grew in the United States.

A favorite fall food, this egg-shaped vegetable can be baked, sauteéd, fried, broiled, grilled, scalloped and stuffed. Mostly the large-fruited variety is grown commercially in Georgia, primarily in the southwest where it thrives in the long growing season and high temperatures. The harvest takes place from June through August.

Buyer's Guide to Eggplant

Select an eggplant that is firm, heavy for its size and well-shaped.

Eggplant should have dark purple to purple-black skin.

Avoid buying eggplant that is poorly colored, soft, shriveled or cut.

Eggplant will stay fresh for up to seven days if stored in the refrigerator.

Cucumbers

Related to pumpkins, squashes, gourds and melons, cucumbers probably originated in India and spread over much of the civilized world thousands of years ago. Cucumbers are one of the few vegetables mentioned in the Bible, and they were introduced into China in the second century B.C. Royalty loves the cucumber. Emperor Tiberius had cucumbers at every meal. Charlemagne ordered that cucumbers be grown on his estate. The English tried to make cucumbers grow straight by placing them in glass cylinders. Perhaps from prehistoric exchanges the cucumber reached the Americas. In 1535 the French found Indians growing cucumbers near what is now Canada; in 1539 the Spanish recorded seeing it cultivated in what became Florida.

Many Americans enjoy cucumbers because they are easy to prepare and complement many side dishes and salads. Made up of 95 percent water, they add no fat, sodium and very few calories. There are two main varieties in America: slicing or table cucumbers, which feature white spines, grow fairly large and retain their color for a long time; and pickling cucumbers, which are smaller and don't keep their color as long.

Georgia has a long growing season for cucumbers, primarily when grown in the southern part of the state. Fresh ones are available from May through November.

Southern Pasta and Vegetables

A colorful vegetable combination creates a pasta winner

- 1 tablespoon oil
- ½ cup chopped onion
- 1 garlic clove, minced
- 1 small eggplant, cut into ½-inch cubes (2 cups)
- 1 zucchini, cut lengthwise in half and into ¼-inch slices
- 1 14.5-ounce can diced, peeled, seasoned tomatoes, undrained
- ½ cup chopped green bell pepper
- ½ teaspoon dried basil leaves
- ¼ teaspoon salt
- ¼ teaspoon pepper
- ⅛ teaspoon fennel seed
- 1 9-ounce package refrigerated reduced-calorie cheese ravioli or 2 cups frozen ravioli

In Dutch oven or large saucepan, heat oil over medium-high heat. Add onion and garlic; cook until tender. Stir in remaining ingredients except ravioli. Bring to a boil. Reduce heat; cover and simmer 20 minutes or until vegetables are tender. Cook uncovered for an additional 5 to 10 minutes or until thickened, stirring occasionally.

Meanwhile, cook ravioli to desired doneness as directed on package. Drain. Add cooked ravioli to vegetable mixture; toss to combine. Yields 4 servings.

Georgia Department of Agriculture Test Kitchen

Turnip Green Dip

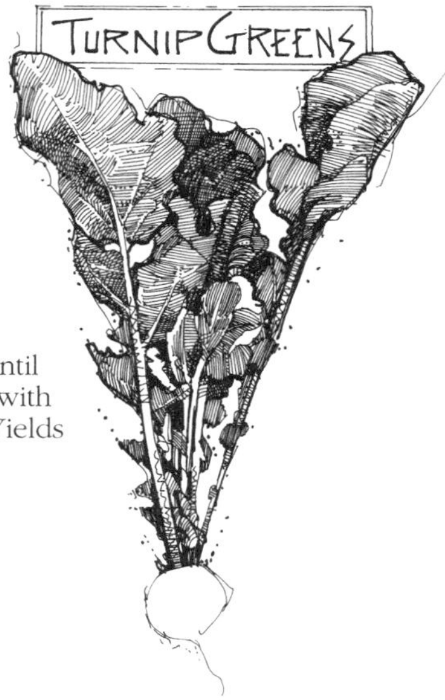

An easy and different party dip!

- 1 .9-ounce envelope dry vegetable soup mix
- 1 cup sour cream
- 1 cup mayonnaise
- 1 10-ounce package frozen turnip greens, thawed and drained

In a medium bowl, combine ingredients until well-blended. Chill several hours. Serve with crackers, raw vegetables or corn chips. Yields 3 cups.

Lloyd Sherrod
Midville, Georgia

MUSHROOM MUSTARD KALE

A good side dish with any type of meat

- 3 tablespoons oil
- 1 medium onion, thinly sliced
- 1 cup sliced fresh mushrooms
- 1 garlic clove, mashed
- 1 large bunch kale (about 16 leaves), heavy stems removed, finely chopped
- 2 tablespoons water
- 2 to 3 teaspoons Dijon mustard
- Salt and pepper to taste

Heat oil in large skillet over medium-high heat. Add onion and sauté until softened. Stir in mushrooms and garlic and sauté 2 to 3 minutes more. Reduce heat to low and mix in kale. Cook covered, stirring frequently, about 15 minutes, or until kale is tender. If needed, add water so vegetables don't burn. Just before serving, add mustard, salt and pepper to taste. Serve immediately. Yields 4 to 5 servings.

Leafy Greens Council

BUYER'S GUIDE TO CUCUMBERS

Cucumbers should be a true green color and firm all over. They may have some white or greenish-white color and still be top quality.

Look for well-shaped, well-developed cucumbers, not too large in diameter.

Even the best cucumbers could have small lumps on their surfaces.

Avoid overgrown cucumbers that are large in diameter and have a dull, yellow color.

Withered or shriveled ends are signs of toughness and bitter flavor.

TURNIP GREEN SOUP

Puréed potatoes and turnips make up this delicious soup

- 2 tablespoons butter
- 1 medium onion, chopped
- 4 cups water
- 4 medium potatoes (about 1½ pounds), peeled and cut in chunks
- 2 cups tightly packed turnip greens, fresh or frozen
- 1 to 1¼ cups milk
- 1 teaspoon vinegar (optional)
- Salt and pepper to taste

Melt butter in large saucepan; add onion and sauté until transparent. Add water; bring to a boil and add potatoes and greens. Simmer for 15 to 20 minutes or until potatoes are soft. Put through a food mill. (A blender or food processor could be used instead of a food mill if desired.) Add milk to achieve desired consistency and vinegar (optional). Salt and pepper to taste. Serve hot. Yields 6 servings.

Mrs. Hardy Edwards
Winterville, Georgia

GREENS

Descendants of wild cabbage, greens, such as kale, mustard and collards, are among the oldest cultivated plants in the world. The Bible mentions the life cycle of mustard greens. Europeans have records from the first century A.D. of growing collards, which later turned up in the gardens of Colonial Americans. Since antebellum times, greens have been a common part of the fare of Southerners, black and white. One popular tradition that has survived to this day is eating boiled greens, black-eyed peas and hog jowls on New Year's Day to bring good luck for the coming year.

A variety of different plants are grown for greens, but all offer excellent nutrition and taste. Most leafy greens are good sources of antioxidant vitamins like A, C and E, which might reduce the risk of heart disease. They also contain calcium, iron, folic acid, fiber and other important nutrients.

Greens grow in all parts of Georgia. They are available year-round with the highest volume harvested from late December through March. Some of the most popular varieties include: collard greens, a durable wide-leaved plant with a cabbage-like flavor that can withstand heat, drought and light freezes; kale, with ruffly, greenish-blue leaves and a mild cabbage flavor as versatile as spinach or cabbage; mustard greens, which feature oval-shaped leaves with frilled edges and a sharp taste; and turnip greens, which have thin dark green leaves with a distinct, pleasant taste.

WONDERFUL WINTER STEW

Chunks of steak, potatoes and turnips make this a hearty meal

- 2 tablespoons vegetable oil
- 1 pound boneless beef sirloin steak, cut into 1-inch cubes
- 2 slices thick cut bacon, cut into thirds
- 2 medium red or white potatoes, peeled and quartered
- 1 medium turnip, peeled and cubed
- 3 carrots, sliced
- 3 celery ribs, sliced
- 2 onions, cubed
- 1 clove garlic, minced
- 1 teaspoon basil leaves
- 1 teaspoon oregano leaves
- 1 15-ounce can tomatoes, okra and corn
- Salt and pepper to taste

In large Dutch oven, heat oil on medium-high heat. Add beef and brown on all sides. Add bacon and cook several minutes. Reduce heat to medium-low and add remaining ingredients. Simmer for 1 hour. Yields 8 servings.

Molly Morehead
Shakerag, Georgia

SPINACH ORIENTAL

This quick and easy side dish goes great with fish

- 1 pound fresh spinach
- 2 tablespoons vegetable oil
- 1 teaspoon grated onion
- 2 tablespoons sesame seeds
- 2 tablespoons soy sauce

Wash spinach well. Drain and remove tough stems. In a skillet, heat the oil. Add onion and sesame seeds. Cook and stir over medium-high heat until the seeds are browned. Add spinach and soy sauce, cover and cook about 5 minutes or until tender. Yields 4 servings.

Mrs. Florrie Johnston
Mableton, Georgia

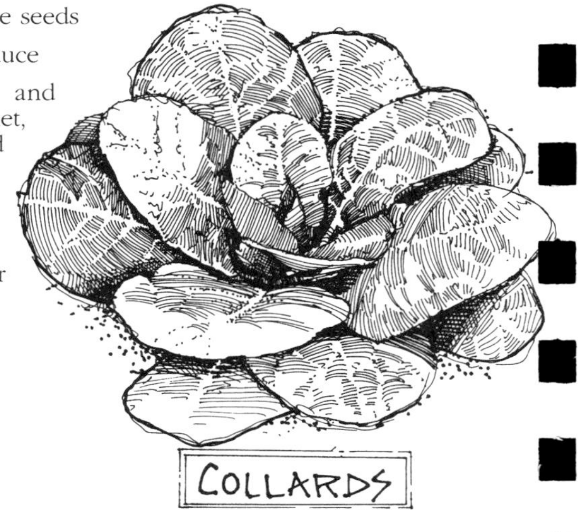

Creamed Spinach

Bacon and onion are key flavors to this dish

4	bacon slices, finely chopped
1	cup chopped onion
¼	cup all-purpose flour
2	teaspoons seasoned salt
½	teaspoon seasoned pepper
½	teaspoon garlic powder
1½ to 2	cups milk
2	10-ounce packages chopped frozen spinach, cooked and drained

In a medium skillet, cook bacon until almost crisp. Add onion and cook until tender; remove from heat. Add flour and seasonings; gradually stir in milk, starting with 1½ cups. Cook, stirring constantly over low heat until thickened. Add spinach and mix thoroughly. If too thick, add remaining milk. Yields 8 servings.

Toni Favors
Lithonia, Georgia

Shrimp and Spinach Pizza

This unique combination makes a colorful pizza

½	teaspoon olive oil
⅓	cup thinly sliced red onion
3	cups chopped fresh spinach
¼	teaspoon dried oregano
1	cup shredded mozzarella cheese, divided
2	7-inch flat pizza bread rounds
2	plum tomatoes, sliced
10	large shrimp, cooked and peeled
	Fresh cracked pepper (optional)

Preheat oven to 400°. In small nonstick skillet, heat oil over medium heat. Cook onion 1 minute. Add spinach and cook 1 minute or until wilted. Stir in oregano. Sprinkle ¼ cup mozzarella cheese on each flat bread. Top with spinach mixture, tomato, shrimp and remaining cheese. Bake directly on oven rack 10 minutes or until cheese is melted. Sprinkle with fresh cracked pepper if desired. Yields 2 individual pizzas.

Agriculture Test Kitchen

Buyers Guide to Greens

When selecting greens, look for leaves that are fresh, young, tender and free from blemishes.

Select greens with healthy, green leaves. Avoid them with course, fibrous or yellow-green leaves.

Most greens can be stored for up to two weeks. To maintain quality, refrigerate greens in a plastic bag.

The young, tender leaves of most greens can be used for salads, while the older, but still tender leaves are good for cooking.

For best results cook turnip greens only until crisp-tender, in as little water as will keep them from sticking, for about twenty to twenty-five minutes. To preserve their green color, cover them as they boil for about one minute, just long enough for them to wilt and compact. Then remove the cover for a minute to let the vapors escape. Repeat several times while cooking.

Cook mustard greens in a covered pan with a little water for fifteen to twenty minutes.

To prepare kale, cut off and discard root ends, tough stems, mid-ribs and discolored leaves.

Want boy 17 or 18 yrs. to help make 1 horse crop for 1929. Will give $50 for 12 mos., not $50 a mo., furnish clothes, shoes and board and washing free. No hard work. Treat you right. If make good hand, will give more next yr. T. Lester Massey, Danielsville, Ga., Rt. 1.

Farm Help Wanted, Market Bulletin, *January 10, 1929*

OKRA

A staple in Southern diets for generations, okra originated in Ethiopia, spread across the eastern Mediterranean and North Africa and came to New Orleans with slaves, who gave okra its common name of gumbo. Gumbo z'herbs (with herbs) was once a traditional dish thought to bring good luck on Good Friday. It included okra and at least seven kinds of greens.

A member of the hibiscus family, okra's relatives include many ornamental flowering plants and cotton. Okra is a podded vegetable that has natural thickening properties when cooked, a quality used to enrich Creole gumbos. Whether mixed in gumbo, served with tomatoes or fried, okra is a great-tasting Southern specialty that provides fiber, vitamin C, calcium and potassium.

Okra is available in Georgia from June through November. Growing is concentrated in the southern part of the state, where the consistently warm and humid conditions offers okra an ideal climate.

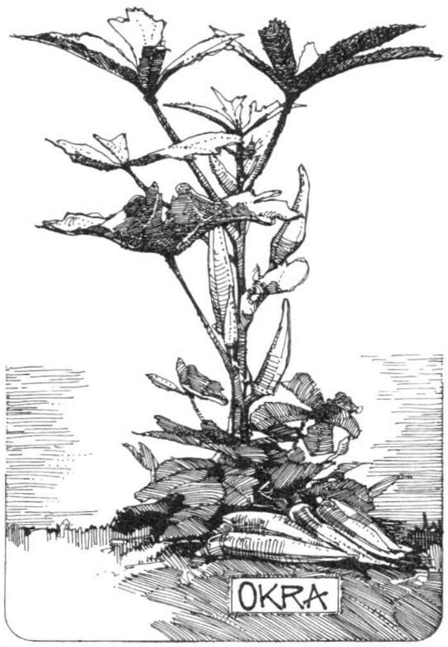

After NAFTA Hobo Soup

Low-fat and full of vegetables

- 3 tablespoons butter
- 1 medium onion, chopped fine
- 1 clove garlic, minced
- 1 16-ounce can diced tomatoes
- 4 cups water
- 1 medium potato, peeled and diced
- 3 tablespoons rice
- ¼ cup elbow macaroni
- 1 cup cut okra, fresh or frozen
- 1 cup small butter beans, fresh or frozen
- 1 tablespoon sugar
- 1 tablespoon Worcestershire sauce
- 1 tablespoon cider vinegar
- Salt and pepper to taste

In Dutch oven, melt butter. Add onions and garlic; sauté for 2 to 3 minutes. Add remaining ingredients and mix thoroughly. Bring soup to boil; reduce heat. Let simmer for 45 minutes to 1 hour, stirring frequently. Yields 8 servings.

W. J. Rawlins
Newnan, Georgia

Okra Patties

- 1 pound fresh okra, chopped, or 1 bag (18-ounce) frozen cut okra
- ½ cup chopped onion
- 1 teaspoon salt
- ¼ teaspoon pepper
- 1 egg
- ½ cup water
- ½ cup all-purpose flour
- 1 teaspoon baking powder
- ½ cup cornmeal
- Pinch garlic powder (optional)
- Oil

Combine cut okra, onion, salt, pepper, egg and water; mix well. Combine flour, baking powder, corn meal and garlic powder. Add to okra mixture, stirring well. Spoon patties into about ½-inch hot oil. Fry over medium heat until well browned on both sides. Drain on paper towels. Yields 8 servings.

Connie Walker
Norcross, Georgia

Okra Pilaf

A new way to serve rice!

4	bacon slices, cut into 1-inch pieces
½	pound okra, cut into 1-inch pieces
1	cup long grain rice
2	cups water
	Salt and pepper to taste

Fry bacon and okra in large skillet until okra is tender and bacon is browned. Add rice, water, salt and pepper. Pour mixture into double-boiler and simmer for about 1 hour until rice is fluffy. Yields 4 servings.

Evalyn H. Hadden
Augusta, Georgia

Elvira's Fried Pea Patties

Black-eyed peas never tasted so good!

1	15-ounce can black-eyed peas
1	large egg
⅛	teaspoon salt
¼	teaspoon seasoned pepper
6	heaping tablespoons self-rising flour
1½	cups chopped onions
¼	cup vegetable oil

Pour peas in medium bowl; mash well with a potato masher. Add egg, spices, flour and onions; mix well. Pour oil into skillet and heat on medium-high. Drop mixture by heaping tablespoons into hot oil. Brown on both sides. Drain on paper towel. Yields 12 large patties.

Elvira Buice
Buford, Georgia

Hint: To reduce the fat and calories in this recipe, reduce oil to 2 tablespoons. Result: Each serving contains 68 calories and 1.8g fat (24% of calories).

Buyer's Guide to Okra

Okra is the immature seed pod of the okra plant.

Look for pods that are tender; tips should bend with very slight pressure.

Pods should be under 4.5 inches long, bright green and free from blemishes.

Fresh okra bruises easily so handle with care.

If refrigerated, okra will keep for ten days.

Cook okra in aluminum, porcelain, earthenware or glass. Metal cookware causes okra to turn black, but doesn't harm the taste.

A short time after I was in office my good old friend Mr. Shannon of Commerce, who was formerly Editor of the Commerce News, came into the office to see me. He looked over and said, "Well Talmadge, how are you getting along?" I jumped up right quick and shook hands with him and said, "Well Mr. Shannon, I'm doing the best that I can." He backed off and said, "No, you are telling a lie now. There was never but one man who did the best that he could and that was 'The man the bull was after.'"

Excerpt from an editorial by Eugene Talmadge, Georgia Commissioner of Agriculture, Market Bulletin, *January 2, 1930*

A Garden is a Personal Thing

The custom of growing vegetables for the table in a garden patch is part of the South's heritage. These functional vegetable gardens, sometimes called garden patches, kitchen gardens or garden plots, have been a part of the culture since Indian women cultivated corn, beans and squash in small plots around their village homes.

Planting a garden of experimental crops for England was one of the reasons white settlers first came to Georgia, but they also had to garden for their own subsistence—something that proved difficult for the colonists in those first few years. Gardens were a necessary and common part of life on rural farms and plantations for both whites and blacks. African Americans continued their West African tradition of growing yams, okra, beans and collards. There was always a garden near the main plantation house and often slaves had their own individual gardens behind their cabins. After the Civil War, whenever land was available to them, tenant farmers and mill workers realized the necessity and luxury of being able to grow their own food.

Today, a garden is still a good way to supply a family with a variety of nutritious vegetables to be enjoyed fresh or preserved for later use. Planting and harvesting favorite Southern vegetables, such as squash, tomatoes, field peas and watermelon, is often considered a relaxing and rewarding experience for the entire family as well as a way to pass on a Southern tradition.

Four of Georgia's top gardeners share their personal thoughts on the pleasures of gardening:

1. Walter Reeves, DeKalb County extension agent, co-wrote the *Georgia Gardener's Guide* and hosts "The Lawn and Garden Show with Walter Reeves," each Saturday from 6am to 10am on WSB 750AM in Atlanta.
2. Lee May, gardening columnist for the *Atlanta-Journal Constitution*, is the author of *In My Father's Garden*, a memoir centering on how he and his father nurtured a long-lost connection through their mutual love of digging in the dirt.
3. Don Hastings comes from a well-known Georgia gardening family. He wrote the three-volume *Gardening in the South with Don Hastings* and co-authored *Month-by-Month Gardening in the South* with his son, Chris.
4. Virginia native Edna Lewis grew up on a farm where gardening was a basic part of life. She has written several cookbooks, including the acclaimed The *Taste of Country Cooking.*

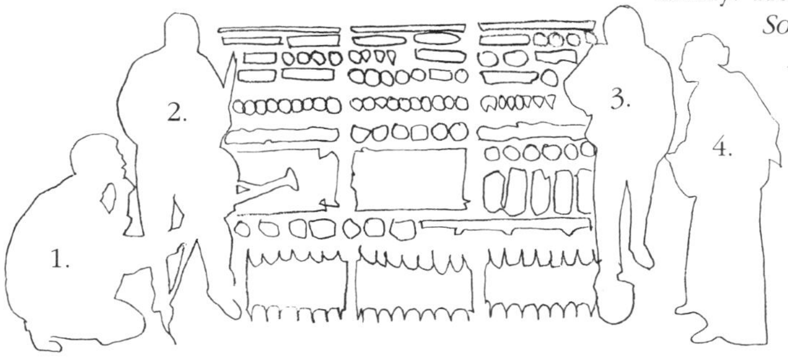

Tommy Irvin

Tommy Irvin, Georgia's Commissioner of Agriculture, has held office almost thirty years, longer than any other elected official in Georgia.

I was born July fourteenth in Hall County in a little community called Lula. My childhood days were spent in several different locations because my father was a sharecropper. Sharecroppers were known to move from one farm to another. So over a period of several years, I lived in four or five different locations. I guess we would like to think we were moving up with each move.

We had these so-called sharecrop homes. You cut the wood off the farm and you cooked with a wood stove. The only heat you had was a fireplace. If it rained, you had to have pots and pans to catch the water from the leaks in the roof. They had cracks in the doors and cracks in the floors. You could count all your yard chickens through the cracks in the floors, and you could see the stars though holes in the roof.

We grew our own livestock. We had our own hogs, milked our own cows. I remember like it was yesterday, my mother and I picking cotton by hand. I saw how hard my mother worked and how we struggled to make ends meet.

There were what you used to call one-horse farms, two-horse farms and multiple horse farms. All of our years we were classified most of the time as a one-horse farm.

You had one, either mule or horse on the farm, and you did all the plowing with that one animal. I started plowing when I was eight years old because I seemed to sprout right up. By the time I was ten years old, I was as good at doing farm labor as most adults. The most difficult job that I had to do was trying to gee whiz cotton in that red soil. I had already gotten to be rather tall and the handle bars on a gee whiz are relatively low. I was having to try to hold that gee whiz and keep it from jumping from side to side and jerking the cotton out of the ground. I had to go somewhat stooped over, and it was very uncomfortable for me. I liked to plow with a one-horse turner because you could stand upright. I was good at that and I was good at using the plows and sweeps to plow our corn and plow our cotton once it got larger.

I was the tallest kid in the community for my age, so everything seemed to be a misfit for me. My overalls would be too short. It was difficult to pick cotton because I was so tall I had to get on my knees.

The traveling stores came through our community to bring us things that we couldn't grow on the farm, like a little sugar, a little coffee and a little salt and pepper. We would trade for them with eggs and chickens and if we had an extra ham we would trade them that. It was a bartering system; we had practically no cash. We were poor and didn't know it.

After living in a succession of sharecrop houses, the Irvins were able to purchase their first home.

My first home, the farm my daddy was able to buy with borrowed money, was called the Skelton Place, in White County. By then Mama and I were farming and Daddy was trying to run a sawmill. He had some fairly wore out equipment. During the war you couldn't buy anything new and the only thing new he had was an engine to pull the mill with. Everything else was old and pretty dilapidated. We raised chickens on that farm. I often slept in the feed room of the chicken house so I wouldn't have to go out in the middle of the night to fire the wood brooders. That was the farm where Daddy gave me my own cotton patch. I don't remember exactly the acreage, just a small plot of land but I had my own cotton patch where I earned my first money.

A family tragedy stunned the Irvin family and pushed young Tommy into a business that would change his life.

My mother and I were doing the farming, basically, and Daddy would help us on the side. Then my daddy got killed at the sawmill, in a sawmill accident.

I just turned seventeen. I was the oldest of five children. I had two younger brothers and two younger sisters. We settled up any obligations my father had. Mama was going to take the old equipment and pile it up in the barn shelter. I said, "Mama, let me see what I can do with it."

I had been around it ever since I was eight or nine years old, and Daddy used to carry me around with him a lot when he was in the lumber business, so I knew a little bit about all of it.

I had that cotton money, two hundred dollars. I found a fellow who had a little patch of timber, and he said he would sell it to me for two hundred dollars. I worked out an arrangement with Mama that I would take the equipment and set it up on that little patch of timber and I would cut it and after I got my two hundred dollars for the timber back, we would split any profit we made. That is the way I started in business.

I remember going up to Clarkesville—this was about 1947, I was eighteen years old—and talking to Mr. Randolph Reeves—by the way Mr. Reeves is still living—and I said, "I want to buy a saw mill." So I bought me a little mill, a brand new engine and started my own business.

The young Irvin found he had a knack for politics. Prohibited from finishing his own education by economic necessity, he vowed to do what he could to keep that from happening to others.

I had been a trustee in a couple of our schools back in the days when that was a position appointed by the county board of education. The first actual public office I held was a member of the Habersham County Board of Education. I went there in January of 1956. I thought I needed to do something else where I could really make things happen. So that following fall I ran for the state legislature and got elected. I served as a member of the state legislature and a member of the county school board at the same time. During that time, I sought a district office on the school board. I later ran for statewide office and also served as president of the Georgia School Boards Association.

I never attended one day of what we call regular college. I don't even have a high school diploma. I had to drop out because of family obligations. That's one of the things that made me want to try so hard to make up for those things that I felt like I missed out on—having the opportunity to get a good education and to enjoy growing up as most young people do today. I wanted the next generation to come along to have it better than I did. I brought my five children up to be good workers, but I didn't think they ought to have it as tough as I did. When I told them how things were when I was a young boy, they couldn't relate to it.

Irvin was recruited to manage Lester Maddox's campaign for governor and then served as Maddox's executive secretary. During this period he sold his lumber operations to devote all of his time to his state government duties. In 1969 Maddox appointed Tommy Irvin Commissioner of Agriculture.

When I came over here one of the reporters from the *Constitution* called me up and said, "Irvin, what do you know about farming?"

I said, "Well I know how to put on a set of Johnson wings."

He said, "What does that mean?"

I said, "That means you don't know anything about farming."

I said, "I know how to tie a set of hame strings. I know how to put a harness on a horse and how to hitch them up and I know how to plow. If you discount that, I'm proud of my success in the lumber business."

It's interesting to see how other people look at you. If they were looking for something to justify the fact that they didn't think I would be a very good commissioner, I had to find some way to prove myself.

Two years later the paper ran an editorial that said, "We think Tommy Irvin performed better than most people's expectations. We think he is deserving of a full term." It was a complete reversal. This was in the state's largest newspaper.

It kind of embarrassed me in a way when Governor Maddox was asked why are you going to appoint Tommy Irvin commissioner of agriculture. He said, "He's been a very successful business man. He is a millionaire and he recognizes the fact that agriculture is the biggest business in Georgia." I was not a millionaire. I had a lot of resources, but resources back in those days weren't worth what they are worth today. I just never did seem to have any difficulty knowing how to make money in the business community. I use that same criteria in managing the budget of this department and promoting Georgia agriculture. You've got to manage. There is an old saying, "You can't spend yourself rich." But you can't be too stingy either. My daddy told me when I was a young boy, he said, "Son watch your nickels and dimes. If you manage those well, the dollars will take care of themselves." I always remember that.

As commissioner of agriculture for nearly thirty years— the senior elected official in Georgia— Tommy Irvin has worked with and advised governors, senators and presidents, including Herman Talmadge, Carl Sanders, Lester Maddox, George Busbee, Joe Frank Harris, Zell Miller, Sam Nunn, Jimmy Carter and Bill Clinton.

I've always been a person that felt you should talk about your assets and let other people criticize your inadequacies. They will do that. I used to tell that to George Busbee—he and I were freshmen legislators together before he was governor. I used to hear him say some things, and he would criticize himself. I would say, "Governor, I don't want to hear you doing that. You leave your criticism up to your enemies. They'll do a good job of that. You talk about the things that you are excellent at."

A major player in Georgia politics and American agriculture for over three decades, Irvin has remained faithful to his rural roots and the simple wisdom that his farm upbringing taught him.

I was speaking at a Kiawanis club meeting recently and I got a lot of excellent questions. This particular one came from someone in the audience who said, "Commissioner, what do you contribute your success in being the longest serving elected official in Georgia?"

I said, "Well I've asked myself that same question many times. I don't know if there is a real good answer to it, but I would like to answer it truthfully. My daddy was a hard worker; my mama was a hard worker. I never expected anything else. Getting up early and staying until the job is done is an integral part of anything that you do. I have a farm background. I was raised on a farm. I've done all the things that farmers do. I have proven to be a good businessman. I think I have a record of doing a good job here. I've always tried to maintain your confidence. I've always been focused on the duties of my office. I put that first. I never, ever tried to use this job for a stepping stone to a higher office. My commitment is to be absolutely the best at what I'm doing and that is still the thing that drives me."

I guess the greatest blessing a man can have is to spend his life in a career that he truly loves and enjoys. I was as excited and eager to come to work this morning as I was my very first day here over twenty-nine years ago. A man knows God has placed him in the right spot when he feels that way about himself and his job.

Black-Eyed Peas

A legume in the Southern pea family, black-eyed peas originated in Asia or Africa. The first slaves brought them to America, where they thrived in the warm climates and long growing seasons of the South. Also known as field peas, this Southern staple makes a tasty, healthy side dish, low in fat and high in fiber.

Other Southern peas include Queen Anne peas, the closest relative of black-eyed peas; purple hull peas, like Coronets; crowder peas, like Mississippi Silver; and cream types, like Texas Cream and Dixiecream.

Southern peas grow well in most Georgia soils but primarily grow in the central and southern parts of the state. They are harvested from June through November, with the heaviest volume from June through mid-August.

Buyer's Guide to Peas

Black-eyed peas are most commonly in the pods when sold retail. Select young, tender peas with crisp, firm pods.

Peas with thick, tough, fibrous pods are over-mature.

Unshelled peas should be refrigerated and will stay fresh for up to one week.

To help preserve color and retain nutrients, cook peas in a covered pot.

Consider having peas shelled for you at the one of the state farmer's markets to save preparation time.

Layered Tex-Mex Dip

Sweet green peas instead of avocado make this dip low-fat

- 1 15-ounce can spicy chili beans, drained
- 1 8-ounce container low-fat sour cream
- 1 tablespoon taco seasoning mix
- ½ cup chopped mild jalapeño peppers or chili peppers
- 3 cups sweet green peas, cooked or 1 16-ounce pack frozen sweet peas, cooked
- 3 tablespoons lime juice
- 1 teaspoon minced garlic
- 1 cup (4 ounces) shredded Cheddar cheese
- ½ cup finely chopped Vidalia® onions
- 1 cup chopped tomatoes

In food processor bowl with metal blade or blender container, process beans until smooth. On large, shallow serving platter, thinly spread bean mixture to approximately 7-inch circle or equivalent size. In small bowl combine sour cream and taco seasoning mix; blend well. Spread over bean mixture; sprinkle with peppers.

In food processor bowl with metal blade or blender container, combine drained peas, lime juice and garlic; process until smooth. Spread over peppers. Sprinkle with cheese, onions and tomatoes. Serve with tortilla chips. Yields 7 cups.

Hoppin' John

This recipe uses sausage to vary a Southern tradition

- 1 16-ounce bag black-eyed peas
- 1 cup chopped onion
- 1 cup rice, uncooked
- 1 pound sausage, browned
- ½ green pepper, chopped
- ½ red pepper, chopped
- Salt and pepper to taste

In a large saucepan, cook peas according to package directions until two-thirds done. Add remaining ingredients to peas and simmer until peas are tender, about 30 minutes. Add warm water so there is enough "pot-likker." Serve with cornbread. Yields 8 servings.

Charlie Ruth Ross
Chatsworth, Georgia

GERI'S PASTA SALAD

Cool and inviting with lots of fresh vegetables!

½	cup rice, uncooked
½	cup macaroni, uncooked
½	cup (approximately) broken spaghetti, uncooked
1	cup broccoli florets in bite-size pieces
½	cup chopped celery
2	carrots, grated
1	8-ounce can sliced water chestnuts
1	2.25-ounce can sliced black olives
½	cup cooked English peas
2	tablespoons chopped green onion
	Dressing

Cook rice, macaroni and spaghetti, each according to package directions. Drain well and allow to cool. In large bowl, toss together rice, macaroni, spaghetti and other salad ingredients.

DRESSING

⅓	cup lemon juice
1	teaspoon sugar
½	cup vegetable oil
¼	cup mayonnaise
½	teaspoon prepared mustard
¾	cup grated Parmesan cheese
2	teaspoons black pepper

In jar or bottle (2-cup size) with lid, combine dressing ingredients and shake well. Pour dressing over salad, mixing well. Refrigerate until ready to serve. Yields 12 servings.

Geri Land
Fayetteville, Georgia

Hint: To reduce calories, fat and cholesterol in this recipe, reduce oil to ¼ cup and Parmesan cheese to ½ cup. Substitute reduced-calorie mayonnaise. Results: Each serving contains 170 calories, 9g fat and 4mg cholesterol.

HOPPIN' JOHN

"The half-million Africans surviving the dreary and formidable passage across the Atlantic to America," writes Patricia B. Mitchell in her cookbook *Soul on Rice, African Influences on American Cooking*, "brought virtually no material possessions with them. However, they did bring something of even greater value: a rich cultural heritage. Native African foodways were an important part of this legacy."

One dish that Africans brought from across the Atlantic, Hoppin' John, consists primarily of rice and black-eyed peas, two staples in the diet of most Africans. Despite its humble origins, the white aristocracy quickly adopted this simple but tasty dish. Today, Hoppin' John can be found on the table of all southerners, especially on New Year's Day, when eating black-eyed peas is considered to bring good luck.

To make Patricia Mitchell's version of Hoppin' John, cover 1 pound of dried black-eyed peas with 3 pints of cold water in a large kettle and soak overnight or bring the peas to a boil, simmer for 2 minutes and let stand for an hour. Add ½ pound of sliced salt pork or bacon, 1 teaspoon of Tabasco sauce and 1 teaspoon of salt. Cover and cook over low heat for about 30 minutes or until peas are tender. Meanwhile, chop 2 medium onions and cook them in 2 tablespoons of bacon fat or lard until they are yellow. Add this to the peas along with 1 cup of uncooked long-grain rice and 1½ cups of boiling water. Cook, stirring occasionally, until the rice is tender and the water is absorbed, about 20 minutes. Cayenne pepper, salt and black pepper can be added if desired. Serves 8.

PEPPERS

Columbus found Indians in the Caribbean growing peppers. His find was described on his return as "pepper more pungent than that of the Caucasus," a reference to the dried, ground seeds and berries of black pepper commonly used in Europe but in no way related to the New World pepper. Nonetheless, Europeans immediately adopted the new vegetable. Within one hundred years, bell and chile peppers grew from England to Austria.

The common bell peppers are perhaps the most familiar peppers to Americans. Most varieties have a mild, sweet flavor, in sharp contrast to the hot and usually more tapered, smaller chili peppers.

All bell peppers are good sources of vitamins C and A.

Whether green, yellow or red, bell peppers add color, flavor and nutrients to many dishes. Green peppers are harvested before they reach maturity and will turn bright red if left on the vine. Bell peppers are available from mid-June through October in Georgia. Commercial production concentrates in the southwest part of the state.

PEPPER STEAK-HIGHTOWER STYLE

Low-fat and delicious

1½ to 2	pounds lean, beef round steak, cut into strips or cubed
2	tablespoons margarine
2	teaspoons garlic powder
½	teaspoon pepper
½	cup water
2	cups vegetable juice
1	cup sliced green onion
2	medium green bell peppers, cut in strips
2	large tomatoes, cut in wedges
3	cups hot cooked rice

Brown steak in margarine. Add garlic powder, pepper, water, vegetable juice and onions. Cover and simmer 30 minutes or until meat is tender. Stir in peppers and gently fold in tomatoes. Cook 10 minutes or until peppers are tender. Serve over hot rice. Yields 6 servings.

Reba Hightower
Doraville, Georgia

Vegetable Tart

Peppers add crunch and flavor

- Prepared refrigerated pie crust
- 2 tablespoons butter or margarine
- 1 cup chopped celery
- ½ cup chopped onion
- ½ cup kernel corn
- 1 cup chopped green pepper
- 2 cups sliced mushrooms
- 1 cup chopped baked ham
- ¼ teaspoon rubbed thyme
- ⅛ teaspoon ground nutmeg
- 3 eggs
- ¼ teaspoon salt
- ¼ teaspoon black pepper
- ¾ cup half-and-half
- Vegetable cooking spray

Preheat oven to 450°. Spray tart pan with vegetable spray. Arrange prepared pie crust in tart pan. (Best to use a pan with removable bottom.) Prick crust with fork at 1-inch intervals. Bake for 10 minutes. Meanwhile, in a large skillet, melt butter or margarine over low heat. Add celery and sauté for 2 minutes. Add onion, corn, green pepper, mushrooms, ham, thyme and nutmeg; cook for about 10 minutes. Set aside. Drain vegetables if mixture contains moisture. Set aside. Beat eggs with salt and pepper and half-and-half. Add vegetable mixture. Pour into tart shell and bake at 400° for 25 to 30 minutes or until pale golden and slightly puffed. Cool for about 15 minutes and remove from tart pan. Yields 8 servings.

Georgia Department of Agriculture Test Kitchen

Hint: Serve for breakfast or brunch as an alternative to quiche.

Buyer's Guide to Bell Peppers

Bell peppers should be well-shaped and firm.

Look for bell peppers with uniform, glossy color and thick walls.

Soft, watery spots found on the sides of bell peppers indicate signs of decay.

Avoid bell peppers with pale skins and soft, pliable flesh, which indicates immaturity.

Store bell peppers in the refrigerator crisper, where they'll stay fresh for up to two weeks.

Want to exch. 1 mare mule, little lame, about 10 yrs. old, wt. 1200 or 1300 lbs. (if fat) for 50 pecan trees, Stuart, Schleys, Money-Makers and Success 8 to 10 ft. high. Party to deliver trees and get mule. J. P. Anderson Sr., Lithonia, Ga. Box 160. Pecan and Other Fruit Trees Wanted,

Market Bulletin, *January 8, 1931*

THE GEORGIA FARM BUREAU

Farmers banding together to help each other is the basic concept behind the American Farm Bureau Federation, the largest general farm organization in the United States. The federation works to protect and advance the business and economic interests of farmers and ranchers by supporting educational programs, promoting favorable legislation and sponsoring helpful services. It is an independent and voluntary organization that operates on local, state, national and international levels.

Georgia farmers along with farmers from twenty-seven other state farm bureaus formed the American Farm Bureau Federation in 1920, but this early Georgia Farm Bureau nearly vanished with the Depression in the early 1930s. Then in 1937, fifty dirt farmers, representing twenty-five counties in Northwest Georgia, formed what was to become today's Georgia Farm Bureau Federation. By 1997, membership approached three hundred thousand families, the largest general agricultural organization in the state.

Farm Bureau offices offer many services for the public, such as general insurance and real estate brokering. But farmers—who make up the boards of county offices—remain the driving force behind the Farm Bureau, which offers them farm insurance, commodities marketing and agricultural programs in print as well as on cable television and Georgia News Network radio. Farm credit is available to construct buildings and homes and buy machinery and vehicles as well as seed and fertilizer. And from tires to fencing and posts, when farmers need more traditional items, they can buy them from the local bureau.

PICKLED PEPPERS

Hungarian, banana and other varieties!

4	quarts long red, green or yellow peppers
1½	cups salt
2	tablespoons prepared horseradish
2	cloves garlic
10	cups vinegar
2	cups water
¼	cup sugar

Wash and drain peppers. Cut 2 small slits in each pepper. Dissolve salt in 1 gallon water. Pour over peppers and let stand 12 to 18 hours in a cool place. Drain peppers; rinse again and drain thoroughly. Combine remaining ingredients; simmer 15 minutes. Remove garlic.

Pack peppers into hot jars, leaving ½-inch head space. Bring liquid to a boil. Fill jar ½-inch from top with boiling liquid. Remove air bubbles. Wipe jar rims. Adjust lids. Process 10 minutes in a boiling water bath. Yields 8 pint jars.

The University of Georgia Cooperative Extension Service

SOUTHERN VEGGIE PIZZA

A healthy snack or lunch idea

⅔	cup light mayonnaise
2	8-ounce packages light cream cheese, softened
1	package ranch dressing mix
2	8-ounce packages refrigerated crescent roll dough
1	medium sweet red pepper, chopped
1	medium green pepper, chopped
½	cup coarsely chopped broccoli florets
½	cup coarsely chopped fresh mushrooms
¼	cup chopped Vidalia® onion
¼	cup grated Cheddar cheese

In medium bowl, blend mayonnaise, cream cheese and dressing mix together. Place crescent roll dough in a 12-inch pizza-shaped pan and bake following the directions on the package. Cool the crescent dough. After dough is cooled, spread on the cream cheese mixture. Sprinkle vegetables on top of cream cheese mixture. Top with grated cheese. Cut and serve. Yields 8 slices.

Debra Cox
Pelam, Georgia
Second Place, Light Cuisine,
1995 Atlanta Great Tastes of Georgia Recipe Contest

Hint: Great treat for children after school—especially when vegetables are at their peak.

Fried Jalapeños

Recreate this popular Southwestern appetizer at home!

15	medium-sized fresh jalapeño peppers
1	8-ounce package cream cheese, softened
1	cup milk
1	egg
	Salt and pepper to taste
½	cup all-purpose flour
2	cups seasoned bread crumbs
	Oil for frying

Blanch jalapeño peppers in boiling water for 3 minutes. Cool in ice water. Slice each jalapeño through the top and lengthwise down one side. Gently scrape out seeds and membranes. Reserve seeds in small bowl. Add softened cream cheese and mix well. Stuff peppers with this mixture and place in freezer 30 to 45 minutes. In shallow bowl, combine milk, egg, salt and pepper. Place flour in shallow bowl or plate and bread crumbs in a separate bowl or plate. After jalapeños are frozen, roll in flour, dip in milk mixture and roll in bread crumbs. Dip again in milk mixture and once again roll in bread crumbs. Press the mixture firmly around the peppers. Return to freezer until ready to fry. At serving time, heat oil to 325°. Carefully lower frozen peppers into hot oil, cook until crispy and brown, 2 to 3 minutes. Serve hot. Yields 15 peppers.

Agriculture Test Kitchen

Hint: A restaurant favorite, this recipe has been requested by many *Market Bulletin* readers. Increasing or decreasing the amount of seeds added to the cheese greatly influences the "heat" of the peppers. For crispy peppers heated throughout, make sure the oil is really hot and use a candy thermometer to check the temperature. Make several batches now and freeze for later use.

Pick-Your-Own

Pick-your-own farms are fast becoming a popular way for city dwellers to make a connection between the food they eat and the place it was grown.

The farms are a win-win situation for farmers and customers alike. For farmers, they offer a substantial source of income on a relatively small area of land. Since customers buy direct from the farmer, the farmer receives 100 percent of the final price of the product. Farmers also don't have to pay workers to harvest the crop, saving labor costs. And some commercial produce farmers report that they began their operations because people who saw their fields kept calling to see if they could pick the vegetables!

For consumers, pick-your-own farms provide a fresh alternative to supermarket produce at a fraction of the price. Vegetables and fruits come right off the land locally, not off a truck or train from far away. Pick-your-own tomatoes, for example, ripen on the vine, giving them more flavor and color. By buying straight from a farmer, customers pay on average 25 to 30 percent of the price they would find for the same produce in a grocery store.

Generally farmers devote from five to fifteen acres for pick-your-own operations. Strawberry pick-your-owns open first in early spring, followed by ones with general produce in summer and autumn. Tomatoes are the primary crop grown on pick-your-own farms. Other popular crops include blueberries, blackberries, melons, apples, peaches, peppers, corn, peas and potatoes. For information on pick-your-farms in Georgia, see page 296.

PUMPKINS

Most pumpkins and squashes were cultivated by Indians in the Americas. The first recorded people to grow crops in North America, cliff dwellers grew pumpkins in what became the Southwestern United States. As American settlers and Europeans became familiar with it in the eighteenth century, the pumpkin became part of legends and fairy tales, from Cinderella's pumpkin coach to Peter the Pumpkin Eater to the jack-o'-lantern in the Legend of Sleepy Hollow. And halloween celebrations wouldn't be complete without a carved pumpkin face!

Many also enjoy the bright orange winter squash for its excellent taste and nutrition. Pumpkins are a great source of vitamin A, calcium, potassium, phosphorus, vitamin C and fiber.

Some of the common varieties grown in Georgia—one of the ten top pumpkin producers in the United States—include the Big Mac, Mammoth Gold, Baby Moon and Connecticut Field, the most common pumpkin used for jack-o-lanterns. Fresh pumpkins are available from late September through October and most production takes place in the northern part of the state.

PUMPKIN BARS

A cream cheese frosting makes these bars even better

2	eggs
½	cup sugar
½	cup packed light brown sugar
½	cup vegetable oil
1	cup cooked, mashed pumpkin
1	cup all-purpose flour
½	teaspoon baking soda
½	teaspoon salt
¾	teaspoon ground cinnamon
¼	teaspoon ground ginger
¼	teaspoon ground nutmeg
	Cream Cheese Frosting

Preheat oven to 350°. In medium bowl, mix eggs, sugar, brown sugar and oil. Add pumpkin and beat well. In separate bowl, combine flour, baking soda, salt, cinnamon, ginger and nutmeg. Add flour mixture to pumpkin mixture; combining well. Grease 9x13x2-inch pan and pour in mixture. Bake for 25 minutes, then cool.

CREAM CHEESE FROSTING

3	ounces cream cheese
⅓	stick margarine, softened
1	cup powdered sugar
1	teaspoon vanilla extract

In medium bowl, beat cream cheese and margarine. Add powdered sugar and vanilla and beat until smooth and spreadable. Spread thinly on top of cooled pumpkin dessert. Cut into bars. Yields 36 bars.

Brenda Toby
Alpharetta, Georgia

Stuffed Pumpkin Stew

This stew looks and tastes like a winner!

- 1 medium whole pumpkin
- ½ teaspoon salt
- ½ teaspoon pepper
- 1 tablespoon butter

Preheat oven to 350°. Wash outside of pumpkin with soap and water. Cut top or lid from pumpkin and reserve. Scoop out seeds and fibers and discard. Season inside pumpkin with salt and pepper. Spread rim with butter. Replace top on pumpkin and bake for 1 hour or until flesh is tender.

Filling for Pumpkin

- 3 tablespoons butter
- 2 cloves garlic, minced
- 1 onion, chopped
- 1½ pounds bottom round beef, cut into 1-inch cubes
- 1 green bell pepper, chopped
- 3 medium white potatoes, cubed
- 3 medium sweet potatoes, cubed
- 1½ teaspoon salt, more to taste
- 1 teaspoon pepper
- 1 tablespoon sugar
- 1½ cups beef broth (as needed)
- 6 ears sweet corn, cut from cob (or 1 medium can whole kernel corn)
- 2 medium tomatoes, chopped
- 4 peaches, peeled and sliced (or 1 can sliced, drained)

In large Dutch oven, melt butter over medium heat; add onion and garlic and cook until transparent. Add beef, bell pepper, white potatoes, sweet potatoes, salt, pepper and sugar. Bring to a boil. Reduce heat and cook 40 minutes, stirring occasionally and adding beef broth ½ cup at a time if mixture is too dry. Stir in corn, tomatoes and peaches; cook at least 10 minutes more or until vegetables are tender. Spoon into cooked whole pumpkin. Serve stew mixture along with a scoop of pumpkin. Yields 8 to 10 main dish portions.

Betty McKnight
Cordele, Georgia
First Place, Main Dish,
1994 Macon Great Tastes of Georgia Recipe Contest

Buyer's Guide to Pumpkins

When buying, select a firm, heavy pumpkin without blemishes or spots.

Look for pumpkins with a rich, orange color and an attached, dry stem.

A well-formed, heavy pumpkin will have more meat, less waste and sweeter flavor than a lighter one.

Avoid pumpkins with scars or cracks.

If stored in a cool, dry, well-ventilated place, pumpkins will last up to three months.

Pumpkin purée can be refrigerated for three to five days or frozen for later use.

Want a 2 or 3 mule farm on halves, or to work for wages part of time. Have 3 boys and self, 4 regular hands and others to do day work. Will work for $15 per mo. or will take 2 horse on halves and have one of the boys for wages. All raised on farm. Do not smoke or drink and am reliable, etc. and can give ref. H. A. McLane, Colbert, Ga. Rt. 2.

Positions Wanted, Market Bulletin, *January 15, 1931*

SOYBEANS

The Chinese first cultivated this bean five thousand years ago; and for thousands of years they, the Koreans and the Japanese relied on it as an important food source. First brought to the United States in 1804 as a forage crop, soybeans and soy seed became an important source for edible oils and fats during World War II. A rich source of protein, soybeans today are a staple throughout the world.

Soybeans have been popular with Georgia farmers. They are more drought tolerant than other crops and do well double-cropped with wheat. The increased use of soybean for human and livestock consumption has increased demand for the crop. Soybeans grow on about one half million acres in Georgia, primarily in the east central portion of the state. The 1996 crop had a value of $66 million.

BUYER'S GUIDE TO SOYBEANS

The versatile beans grow similar to snap beans and in dried form can be sprouted, ground into flour or made into soybean oil, milk or a curd called tofu.

Gardeners use soybeans in the green state when the pods are easily shelled after plunging them into boiled water.

Shelled soybeans take about fifteen minutes to cook and are good with any garnish used for limas.

A shortcut for all dried beans is to cover them with water in a kettle and boil for about two minutes, allow to stand one hour covered with water, then cook until tender.

SOY CASSEROLE

- ¼ cup diced salt pork
- 2 cups chopped celery
- 2 tablespoons chopped onions
- 2 tablespoons chopped green pepper
- 6 tablespoons all-purpose flour
- 2 cups milk (or cooking water and ⅔ cup dry milk)
- 1 teaspoon salt
- 2 cups cooked soybeans
- 1 cup buttered bread crumbs

Preheat oven to 350°. Brown the salt pork in frying pan. Add the celery, onion and green pepper and cook for 5 minutes. Add thickening made from the flour, milk and salt. Stir until it reaches boiling point. Stir in the cooked beans. Pour the mixture into a greased 2-quart baking dish. Cover with the buttered bread crumbs. Bake for 30 minutes or until the crumbs are brown. Yields 8 servings.

Georgia Department of Agriculture Test Kitchen

SOY BURGERS

Soy replaces ground beef in this healthy burger

- 2 cups cooked soybeans
- 1 medium onion
- ½ green bell pepper
- 1 stalk celery
- 1 carrot
- 1 egg, beaten
- 1 cup cracked wheat
- 2 tablespoons soybean oil

Coarsely grind soybeans, onion, green pepper, celery and carrot. If done by hand, mash the soybeans and chop the vegetables. Add egg and cracked wheat. Mix well; shape into patties. Fry in oil, 10 to 15 minutes on each side, until crispy. Drain on paper towel. Yields 8 burgers.

Georgia Department of Agriculture Test Kitchen

Yellow Squash Gingerbread

- 2½ cups all-purpose flour
- ⅓ cup firmly packed brown sugar
- 2 teaspoons baking soda
- 2 teaspoons ground ginger
- 1 teaspoon ground cinnamon
- ½ teaspoon ground cloves
- 2 cups coarsely shredded yellow squash, well drained
- ⅔ cup molasses
- 3 tablespoons vegetable oil
- 1 teaspoon vanilla extract
- 1 egg or 1 egg substitute

Preheat oven to 350°. In large bowl, combine flour and next 5 ingredients. Stir well. Add squash and stir well. Make a well in the center of the mixture. In small bowl, combine molasses, vegetable oil, vanilla and egg; stir well. Add molasses mixture to ingredients, stirring until just moistened. Pour batter into 9x5x3-inch loaf pan coated with cooking spray. Bake for 55 minutes or until a wooden pick inserted in the center comes out clean. Cool in pan for 10 minutes. Remove from pan and cool completely. Sprinkle with powdered sugar. Yields 12 slices.

Mariah Thompson
Smyrna, Georgia

Spaghetti Squash Pie

- 1 medium spaghetti squash
- ½ cup sugar
- ½ cup finely packed brown sugar
- 2 tablespoons all-purpose flour
- 1 cup evaporated whole milk
- 1 cup water
- 3 egg yolks, beaten
- 5 tablespoons butter, melted
- 1 teaspoon coconut extract
- 1 10-inch pie shell, unbaked

Preheat oven to 450°. Wash squash, cut in half and discard seeds. Place squash, cut side down, in a Dutch oven and add 2 inches of water. Bring to a boil and cook covered 25 to 30 minutes or until tender. Drain squash and cool. Using a fork, remove spaghetti-like strands from inside squash. Measure 1½ cups of squash strands to be used in pie. Combine next 8 ingredients, mixing well; stir in reserved squash strands. Pour mixture into pie shell. Bake for 5 minutes; reduce oven to 350° and bake 40 minutes or until pie is set. Serve warm or cold. Yields 8 servings.

Bernice C. Cobb
Atlanta, Georgia

Squash

Squash has been a staple in the Indian diet for thousands of years. The word "squash" comes from an Indian word meaning "raw or uncooked" and probably applied to summer squash, which can be eaten raw.

There are winter and summer squash varieties, but the names are misleading in that they don't relate to when they are harvested or available. Winter squashes, such as acorn, spaghetti and butternut, are characterized by hard shells and are harvested at maturity. Generally, they must be cooked before consumption. Summer squashes, such as yellow crookneck and zucchini, have soft shells, edible skins and seeds and are harvested before maturity. Many types of squash are perfect ingredients for everything from entrées and appetizers to salads and desserts. Both summer and winter varieties are low calorie and a good source of vitamin C, carotene, riboflavin, calcium and iron.

Georgia grows varieties of both summer and winter squash, mostly concentrated in South Georgia. Georgia winter squash is available from late August through March. Summer squash is available almost year-round, with peak harvests in late spring.

Want a good blacksmith. Must be good hand to shoe mules, and build wheels. E. R. Yarbrough, Meershon, Ga.

Farm Help Wanted, Market Bulletin, *July 10, 1931*

WINTER SQUASH BUYER'S GUIDE

Look for winter squash that is fully mature, indicated by a hard, tough rind.

Winter squash should be heavy for its size. The added weight indicates a thick wall and more edible flesh.

Slight color variations within winter squash won't affect flavor.

Avoid winter squash with cuts, punctures, sunken or moldy spots on the rind, all signs of decay.

Avoid winter squash with a tender rind; the eating quality is probably poor.

Acorn squash should have a dark green surface with a little yellow-orange color.

The rind of butternut squash should be completely buff to light tan.

BLENDER SQUASH PUDDING

Squash for dessert!

PUDDING

- 3 cups puréed cooked yellow squash
- 3 tablespoons all-purpose flour
- ¾ cup sugar
- ¼ cup margarine, melted
- 2 egg yolks
- ½ cup milk
- 1 teaspoon vanilla extract
- ¼ teaspoon ground nutmeg (optional)

MERINGUE

- 2 egg whites
- ¼ teaspoon cream of tartar
- ¼ cup sugar
- ¼ teaspoon vanilla extract

Preheat oven to 350°. In large bowl, combine puréed squash, flour, sugar and melted margarine. Blend well. Add egg yolks, milk and flavorings. Blend until well-mixed. Pour pudding into 9-inch baking pan or a 10-inch pie plate. Bake for 50 to 60 minutes or until well done. Remove and top with meringue while still warm. To prepare meringue, beat egg whites and cream of tartar until foamy. Beat in sugar, 1 tablespoon at a time; continue beating until stiff and glossy. Do not overbeat. Beat in vanilla. Seal meringue to edge of crust to prevent shrinking or weeping. Bake until delicate brown, about 10 minutes. Cool away from draft. Yields 8 servings.

Evelyn Rainey
Atlanta, Georgia

Squash Macaroni Casserole

A new variation on traditional macaroni and cheese

- 1 cup sliced, cooked yellow squash
- 1 cup cooked macaroni
- 1 cup grated Cheddar cheese
- 1 egg, beaten
- ½ cup milk
- 2 tablespoons butter, melted
- 4 saltine crackers, crushed

Preheat oven to 350°. In a medium bowl, combine squash, macaroni and cheese. In another bowl, combine egg, milk and butter; stir into squash mixture. Place mixture in a 1-quart casserole or pie plate; top with crushed crackers. Bake for 40 minutes or until light brown. Yields 6 servings.

Marie S. Kinder
Colquitt, Georgia

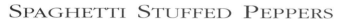

Spaghetti Stuffed Peppers

Two types of squash make up this main dish

- ¼ cup low-sodium chicken broth
- 1 cup chopped zucchini or yellow crookneck squash
- ½ cup shiitake or brown mushrooms, chopped
- ¼ cup sliced green onions
- 1 tablespoon chopped fresh basil or 1 teaspoon dried basil leaves
- 1 tablespoon chopped fresh thyme or 1 teaspoon dried thyme leaves
- 1 clove garlic, minced
- ¼ teaspoon pepper
- 1½ cups spaghetti squash, cooked, seeded and fluffed into strands
- 4 sweet bell peppers, any color
- ¼ cup shredded nonfat or low-fat Swiss or Cheddar cheese

Preheat oven to 375°. In a skillet, heat chicken broth to simmering. Add squash, mushrooms, onions, herbs, garlic and pepper. Simmer uncovered, stirring occasionally, for 4 minutes, or until vegetables are tender. Remove from heat. Stir in spaghetti squash. Slice tops off bell peppers and discard seeds. Spoon filling into peppers; sprinkle on shredded cheese. Add tops. Place in shallow baking dish sprayed with vegetable cooking spray. Cover and bake for 30 to 35 minutes or until heated through. Yields 4 servings.

5-A-Day Recipe, encouraging you to eat 5 servings of fruits and vegetables a day!

Summer Squash Buyer's Guide

Look for squash that are well-formed, with no cuts or bruises in the flesh.

Squash should be tender, with skin that is glossy, not dull, hard or tough.

Avoid stale or over-mature squash which will have a dull appearance and a hard, tough surface. Such squash usually have enlarged seeds and dry, stringy flesh.

If refrigerated, summer squash will keep up to two weeks.

Sweet Potatoes

This member of the morning glory family originated in the Americas. Columbus observed their cultivation in the Caribbean during his fourth voyage; DeSoto found sweet potatoes in what became Louisiana; and the Pilgrims feasted on them during the first Thanksgiving.

Sweet potatoes were grown by early settlers on raised ridges. The crop usually came from vines cut from older plants and were planted following corn in July. After the sweet potatoes were harvested, hogs often grazed over the fields. Farmers cured their sweet potato harvest in oblong pits lined and covered with corn stalks. Soil then covered the pit to protect the vegetables from rain and frost. An opening in the pit allowed some ventilation. The tuber was known as the staff of life during the Civil War, providing the main sustenance, to civilians and soldiers alike, either baked, fried, roasted or served in pudding and pie. The state led the nation in sweet potato production from 1836 to 1936, at one time devoting more than 150,000 acres to the crop. Today Georgia is the seventh-largest sweet potato producer in acreage with 1,700 acres devoted to sweet potato production.

A tasty holiday tradition in pies, puddings and casseroles, sweet potatoes are also one of the most nutritionally complete foods available, packed with fifteen essential vitamins and minerals, including twice the recommended daily allowance of vitamin A. Sweet potatoes are low in sodium and high in thiamine, riboflavin, vitamin C, iron, potassium, calcium and fiber.

Sweet Potato Dessert

A moist bread with a pudding-like texture

- 2 cups cooked, mashed sweet potatoes (about 3 medium)
- ½ cup sugar
- 1 stick (½ cup) butter, melted
- 2 eggs
- ½ cup self-rising flour
- 1 14-ounce can sweetened condensed milk
- 1 teaspoon vanilla extract
- 1 teaspoon ground cinnamon
- ½ teaspoon almond flavoring
- 1 cup chopped pecans
- 1 cup raisins

Preheat oven to 300°. In large bowl, cream sweet potato, sugar and butter. Add eggs, self-rising flour, condensed milk, vanilla, cinnamon and almond flavoring. Mix well. Fold in pecans and raisins. Pour into a greased 14x11-inch pan. Bake for 45 to 60 minutes or until done. Yields 20 servings.

Irene Smith
Cochran, Georgia

Hint: Top bread with whipped cream that has a little sugar added.

Sweet Potato Biscuits

A taste that's worth the time

- 1 cup baked, mashed sweet potatoes
- ⅛ teaspoon salt
- 2 cups self-rising flour
- ⅓ cup shortening
- ⅓ cup milk

Preheat oven to 400°. Grease cookie sheet. Sprinkle salt on potatoes. Sift flour. Cut shortening and potatoes into flour. Add milk gradually (more or less according to potatoes). Mix well and roll out. Cut with biscuit cutter or shape with hands. Bake on greased pan for 12 to 15 minutes. Butter and serve hot. The dough hook on your mixer works very well in mixing this dough. Yields 12 biscuits.

Georgia Department of Agriculture Test Kitchen

Sweet Potato Soufflé Crunch

A rich Southern favorite!

3	cups cooked, mashed sweet potatoes
1	cup sugar
½	teaspoon salt
2	eggs, slightly beaten
2½	tablespoons butter or margarine, melted
½	cup milk
1	teaspoon vanilla extract
	Crunch Topping

Preheat oven to 350°. Mix all ingredients together and pour into a greased 8-inch square baking dish. Cover with crunch topping.

Crunch Topping

2½	tablespoons margarine
1	cup brown sugar
⅓	cup all-purpose flour
1	cup chopped pecans

In small saucepan, melt margarine and stir in remaining ingredients. Sprinkle over souffle before baking. Bake for 35 minutes. Yields 6 to 8 servings.

Debbie Healy
Atlanta, Georgia

Sweet Potato Cheesecake Pie

This will delight any and all cheesecake eaters!

1	8-ounce package cream cheese, softened
6	tablespoons sugar
1	cup cooked, mashed sweet potatoes
½	teaspoon ground nutmeg
½	teaspoon ground cinnamon
	Dash of salt
1	egg
1	9-inch unbaked pie shell

Preheat oven to 350°. In a medium bowl, combine cream cheese and sugar; beat at medium speed until smooth. Blend in sweet potatoes and spices. Add egg and beat well. Pour into unbaked pie shell. Bake for about 1 hour. Refrigerate until ready to serve. Yields 8 servings.

Darlene Coley
Gordon, Georgia

Two types of sweet potato are available in Georgia: the moist-flesh sweet potatoes which are soft and sweet when cooked; and the Jersey-type sweet potatoes, which have a dry, mealy flesh and stay firm when cooked.

The names sweet potatoes and yams are often used interchangeably. Yet, despite the fact that the two have resemblances in appearance and taste, they are from two different families. Yams aren't grown in the United States, but close to the Equator.

Sweet potatoes, available from late October through December, grow in all parts of the state, but primarily in South Georgia in the Tifton area, where they flourish in the hot, humid climate.

Sweet Potatoes Buyer's Guide

When buying sweet potatoes, look for a firm, smooth potato, uniform in shape and color.

Select thick, chunky, medium-sized vegetables which taper at both ends.

Handle sweet potatoes gently to avoid bruising.

Georgia sweet potatoes range from pale yellow to dark orange-red, depending on the variety.

Avoid buying sweet potatoes that show signs of decay or blemishes.

Store sweet potatoes in a cool, dark, well-ventilated place.

Sweet Potato Pecan Cookies

- ½ cup margarine, softened
- 1½ cup firmly packed brown sugar
- 2 eggs
- 1 cup cooked, mashed sweet potatoes
- ½ teaspoon lemon extract
- ½ teaspoon vanilla extract
- 2½ cups all-purpose flour
- 1 tablespoon baking powder
- ½ teaspoon salt
- 2 teaspoons pumpkin pie spice
- 1 cup chopped pecans
- Maple Frosting

Preheat oven to 375°. Cream margarine, gradually add brown sugar and beat well at medium speed of an electric mixer. Add eggs, one at a time, beating after each addition. Stir in sweet potato and flavorings. In a separate bowl, combine flour, baking powder, salt and pumpkin pie spice. Gradually add creamed mixture, mixing well. Stir in pecans. Drop dough by teaspoonful 2 inches apart onto greased cookie sheets. Bake for 12 minutes. Cool on wire racks. Frost with Maple Frosting. Yields 7½ dozen cookies.

Maple Frosting

- ¼ cup margarine, softened
- 1½ cups sifted powdered sugar
- 2 tablespoons milk
- ¾ teaspoon maple extract

Cream margarine; gradually add 1 cup powdered sugar, beating well at medium speed of electric mixer. Add remaining sugar alternately with milk, beating until smooth enough to spread. Add maple extract and beat well. Makes about 1 cup.

Georgia Sweet Potato Commission

Easy Sweet Potato Spears

- 2 medium sweet potatoes
- ½ cup crushed corn flakes
- ½ cup grated Parmesan cheese
- ¼ teaspoon garlic powder
- 2 tablespoons prepared ranch salad dressing

Pierce potatoes with fork and place in microwave-safe dish. Cook on high for 5 minutes, or until slightly firm. Cool slightly. In a small bowl, combine corn flakes, cheese and garlic powder. Peel potatoes and cut in eighths. Brush spears with dressing and roll in cornflake mixture. Broil until golden, 2 to 3 minutes. Serve hot. Yields 4 servings.

Jessica Tibbitts
Dallas, Georgia

Sweet Potato Pie

Looks like pumpkin, but sweeter

2	cups cooked, mashed sweet potatoes
1	cup sugar
2	eggs
¼	cup melted butter or margarine
¼	teaspoon salt
1	teaspoon vanilla extract
¾	cup milk
1	teaspoon ground cinnamon
1	teaspoon pumpkin pie spice or allspice
1	9-inch pie shell, unbaked

Preheat oven to 350°. Mix all ingredients well and pour into pie shell. Bake for 60 minutes or until toothpick inserted in center comes out clean. Yields 6 slices.

Agriculture Test Kitchen

Fried Tomatoes and Creamy Gravy

Serve on an English muffin topped with bacon

	Bacon, fried crisp; reserve drippings
½	cup cornmeal
3	tablespoons all-purpose flour
2	teaspoons sugar
2	teaspoons salt
¼	teaspoon pepper
4	large, firm tomatoes, sliced ½-inch thick
1	cup milk
½	teaspoon salt
	English muffins, toasted

Combine cornmeal, flour, sugar, salt and pepper. Coat tomato slices with mixture. Fry until golden brown in bacon drippings, turning once. Remove slices from pan and place on platter to keep warm. Over medium to low heat, heat milk and salt, adding 1 to 2 tablespoons of cornmeal mixture as needed, stirring until thick. Place bacon, tomato slices and gravy over English muffins. Yields 6 servings.

Shirley Berny
Dalton, Georgia

A Basket of Tomatoes Later

The tomato plant wasn't always such a garden favorite. In the early 1800s people of southern Europe and France were enjoying the "apple of love" as it was known, but England and the young United States considered it an ornamental plant. Physicians warned against eating it. "All that oxalic acid! One dose and you're dead."

Finally, to put the rumors to rest, Colonel Robert Gibbon Johnson, an eccentric gentleman from Salem, New Jersey, announced he was going to eat a whole basket of the "wolf peaches." On September 26, 1820, Colonel Johnson lifted a tomato before a crowd of two thousand gathered in front of the Salem courthouse steps and declared: "The time will come when this luscious, golden apple, rich in nutritive value, a delight to the eye, a joy to the palate, whether fried, baked, or eaten raw, will form the foundation of a great garden industry, and will be recognized, eaten, and enjoyed as an edible food.... And to help speed that enlightened day, to help dispel the tall tales, the fantastic fables that you have been hearing about the thing, to show you that it is not poisonous, that it will not strike you dead, I am going to eat one right now!"

A basket of tomatoes later, the band struck up the victory march and the crowd began to cheer. It was one small bite for Colonel Johnson, one large juicy bite for mankind.

Slightly used goose feathers, 50 cents lb.
Mrs. J. F. McCartley, Mesena.

Miscellaneous For Sale, Market Bulletin,
August 10, 1933

TOMATOES

Native to the Andes Mountains in South America, tomatoes were introduced to Central and North America by prehistoric Indian trade and migrations. European explorers returned to the Old World with tomatoes. A yellow variety was known in the sixteenth century as apples of gold. In England tomatoes weren't eaten but given as tokens of affection; legend has it that Sir Walter Raleigh presented one to Queen Elizabeth. Few early American settlers ventured to eat the tomato, which many thought poisonous. By the 1830s, however, tomatoes were widely recognized as edible.

One of the most popular foods today, the tomato nonetheless still suffers from one perception problem. Is it a fruit or a vegetable? Technically, it is a fruit, more specifically, one of only four true berries. (The others are bananas, cranberries and grapes.) In any case, tomatoes are low in fat and calories and a good source of vitamins C and A. Tomatoes are available from mid-May through mid-November in Georgia. Commercial production takes place mostly in southwest Georgia.

VEGETABLE CURRY

Serve this easy curry filled with fresh vegetables over rice

- 2 cups water
- 5 new potatoes, peeled
- 1 chicken bouillon cube
- 1/4 cup butter
- 1/4 cup vegetable oil
- 2 medium onions, chopped
- 2 tablespoons curry powder
- Pinch of paprika
- 1 medium red bell pepper, diced
- 1 medium green bell pepper, diced
- 4 medium zucchini, sliced
- 4 medium tomatoes, quartered
- 1 clove garlic, crushed
- 2 tablespoons flour
- 1 tablespoon tomato paste
- Salt and pepper to taste
- 4 cups cooked rice

In medium saucepan, bring water and potatoes to boil and reduce heat; simmer for 20 minutes. Strain the potatoes, reserving the liquid. Add the bouillon cube to the liquid, set aside.

Heat the butter and oil together over medium heat in large skillet; add the onion and cook for 5 minutes or until brown. Add the curry powder and paprika; cook for 2 minutes. Add the peppers, zucchini, tomatoes, garlic, flour and tomato paste. Simmer for 10 minutes.

Slice the potatoes; add to vegetable mixture. Pour in reserved liquid; simmer 20 minutes. Season as desired; serve over rice. Yields 8 servings.

Cynthia Gresham
Lawrenceville, Georgia

Hint: To reduce the fat in this recipe, reduce the butter and oil to 2 tablespoons each. Result: One serving with rice contains 268 calories and 7.3g fat (24% of calories).

Tomato Zucchini Bake

Easy to prepare and delicious

3	medium zucchini, thinly sliced
4	medium ripe tomatoes, peeled and thinly sliced
¾	cup grated Parmesan cheese, divided
2	cloves garlic, minced
1	teaspoon dried thyme
¼	teaspoon salt
¼	teaspoon pepper
2	tablespoons olive oil

Preheat oven to 400°. In 8-inch square baking dish, arrange half of zucchini slices. Top with half of tomato slices. Sprinkle with ¼ cup cheese. Top with remaining zucchini and tomato. Sprinkle garlic, thyme, salt and pepper over tomato; drizzle with olive oil. Sprinkle remaining ½ cup cheese over top. Bake for 20 to 25 minutes. Yields 6 servings.

Georgia Department of Agriculture Test Kitchen

Hint: To cut the fat and calories in this recipe, reduce Parmesan cheese to ½ cup and olive oil to 1 tablespoon. Result: Each serving contains 91 calories and 5.2g fat.

Buyer's Guide to Tomatoes

Look for well-formed tomatoes that are smooth, ripe and free of blemishes.

Fully ripe tomatoes will have a consistent, rich red color and be slightly soft.

For tomatoes not quite ripe, look for firm texture and color, ranging from pink to light red.

Tomatoes with stems attached retain moisture and stay fresh longer.

Avoid overripe and bruised tomatoes, which are soft and watery.

Tomatoes should not have green or yellow areas or cracks near the stem scar.

Don't store tomatoes in the refrigerator unless fully ripe. The cold temperatures might keep them from ripening.

Tangy Olive Salsa

Fresh, unforgettable flavors of summer!

1	cup peeled, seeded and diced ripe tomatoes
⅓	cup fresh parsley, chopped
¼	cup yellow bell pepper, chopped
2	tablespoons Greek olives, pitted
2	tablespoons fresh lime juice
1½	tablespoons drained capers
1½	tablespoons olive oil
1½	tablespoons chopped fresh basil
1	teaspoon balsamic vinegar
	Dash cayenne pepper
	Dash black pepper

In medium bowl, combine all ingredients. Cover and refrigerate for at least 1 hour to allow flavors to blend. Yields 8 servings.

National Turkey Federation

FRIED GREEN TOMATOES

Shortly after the Blue Willow Inn in Social Circle opened in 1992, columnist Lewis Grizzard came for dinner. On the buffet that evening were fried green tomatoes. At that time, owners Louis and Billie Van Dyke served the dish only once every week to ten days. Grizzard went on to write a column about the restaurant, its food and particularly the fried green tomatoes he had enjoyed. The Van Dykes claim that that newspaper column, which appeared in about 280 newspapers nationwide, turned their new, struggling establishment into a successful restaurant in just one weekend. The column is reprinted in full at the beginning of their *Blue Willow Inn Cookbook*, and the Van Dyke's now serve fried green tomatoes at every meal.

To prepare 8 servings of their famous fried green tomatoes, the Van Dyke's wash and slice 3 green tomatoes into slices approximately ¼ inch thick. Then, in a mixing bowl, they mix 1½ cups of buttermilk with 2 eggs, adding ½ teaspoon of salt and ½ teaspoon of pepper. Next they measure out 1½ cups of self-rising flour, add 1 tablespoon of the flour to the buttermilk/egg mixture and set the remaining flour aside. After mixing well, the Van Dyke's place the tomato slices in the buttermilk/egg mixture to soak.

While preheating 2 cups of vegetable oil to 350° in a heavy skillet or electric fryer, the Van Dykes take a second mixing bowl and mix together another ½ teaspoon of salt, ½ teaspoon of pepper and the remaining flour. Next they toss the tomato slices in the seasoned flour and then fry them in the oil until the tomatoes are golden brown, turning them 2 or 3 times until they are crisp.

PASTA WITH FRESH TOMATOES

A good use of tomatoes in a summertime pasta

- 1½ pounds (about 4 cups) fresh, ripe tomatoes
- ½ cup (4 ounces) sliced, pitted black olives
- 1 clove garlic, minced
- ¼ teaspoon salt
- ¼ teaspoon crushed red pepper
- ⅛ teaspoon black pepper
- ½ cup olive oil
- 3 tablespoons sliced, fresh basil leaves
- 3 tablespoons minced parsley or 1 tablespoon dried parsley
- 1 8-ounce package medium-sized pasta, cooked

Cut tomatoes into wedges. In medium bowl, toss tomatoes, olives, garlic, salt, red pepper and black pepper. Pour olive oil over mixture and toss gently. Let stand at room temperature in a covered container for 30 minutes. Just before serving, add basil and parsley, mixing well. Serve immediately over cold or warm pasta. Yields 4 servings.

Lauren McMann
Blairsville, Georgia

Hint: Recipe can be prepared using ¼ cup olive oil.

TOMATO PIE

Tomatoes, bacon and cheese make up this yummy pie

- 1 9-inch deep dish frozen pie shell
- 3 medium, ripe tomatoes, sliced
- 6 strips bacon, fried and crumbled
- 1 cup grated sharp Cheddar cheese
- 1 cup mayonnaise

Bake frozen pie shell following package directions. Preheat oven to 350°. Place tomatoes in bottom of pie shell; top with crumbled bacon. Combine cheese and mayonnaise; pour over tomatoes. Bake 35 to 40 minutes. Serves 4.

Ethel Strickland
Albany, Georgia

ZUCCHINI BARS

Zucchini combines with coconut and pecans to make this treat

BARS

- ¾ cup butter
- ½ cup packed brown sugar
- ½ cup sugar
- 2 eggs
- 1 teaspoon vanilla extract
- 2 cups all-purpose flour
- ½ teaspoon salt
- 1½ teaspoons baking powder
- 1 cup shredded coconut
- ¾ cup chopped pecans
- 3 cups shredded zucchini
- Vegetable cooking spray

Preheat oven to 325°. In large bowl, cream together first 5 ingredients. In separate bowl, combine flour, salt and baking powder. Add dry mixture to cream mixture, blending well. Fold in coconut, pecans and zucchini. Spread mixture on jellyroll pan coated with cooking spray. Bake approximately 25 minutes.

FROSTING

- 1 cup powdered sugar
- 1 tablespoon butter, melted
- 1½ tablespoons milk
- ½ teaspoon ground cinnamon

Combine all ingredients and mix thoroughly. Spread on bars while they are warm. Yields 24 bars.

Lucille Sieren
Atlanta, Georgia

Hint: To reduce calories and fat in bars, substitute ½ cup reduced-calorie margarine, 1 whole egg and 2 egg whites; reduce coconut to ½ cup and pecans to ½ cup. Result: One bar contains 137 calories and 4.8g fat (31% of calories).

After draining the tomatoes on paper towels, the Van Dyke's serve them immediately to their patrons.

The Van Dykes like to serve tomato chutney as an accompaniment to their fried green tomatoes. To make this, they mix together in a sauce pan or small stock pot: one 14-ounce can of undrained whole tomatoes which they have chopped, 1 cup of light brown sugar, ½ cup of granulated sugar, 2 finely chopped green bell peppers, 1 finely chopped medium onion, 2 tablespoons of tomato ketchup, 6 drops of Tabasco sauce and 1 teaspoon of black pepper. The Van Dykes bring this to a boil and simmer it for 2 hours or until it is cooked to a thick sauce.

High grade farm near Atlanta suitable for dairying and trucking. 130 acres of very fertile and productive land; 80 acres under cultivation; 10 acres in good bottoms; 30 acres in fine timber. 3 dwellings; barn and outbuildings. Plenty of fruit, grapes, strawberries, etc. Dwellings equipped with electric lights. Main 8 room dwelling equipped for water works. Sell or exchange for other property $55 per acre. Farm located at Riverdale 20 minutes drive from Atlanta. Address J. R. Allen, Owner, Gainesvile, Ga.

Farm Land For Sale, Market Bulletin, *February 26, 1931*

ZUCCHINI

One of the most prolific vegetables, zucchini is a member of the squash family, which are native to the Americas and were first cultivated by Indians. The vegetable is a flavorful, nutritious one that can be enjoyed raw, steamed, boiled, fried or baked. Zucchini seeds house most of the vegetable's flavor; the smaller the seed, the better the flavor.

Blending well with most vegetables and meats, zucchini is a regular part of the diet of millions of Americans. Zucchini, especially raw, is a good source of vitamin C and contains some vitamin A. It is low in sodium and has only about twelve calories per serving.

A variety of summer squash, its cousins include straightneck, cocozelle and yellow crookneck. Like other summer squashes, zucchini is harvested when immature, thus requiring a shorter growing season than winter squashes. The vegetable is grown commercially in southwest Georgia and harvested from May through November.

ZUCCHINI BURRITO

Zucchini replaces the meat and beans in this Mexican favorite

1	tablespoon olive oil
3	medium (about 4 cups) sliced zucchini
1	tablespoon Mexican seasoning
1	8-count package of 10-inch flour tortillas
1	cup chopped tomatoes
1	cup shredded Monterey Jack cheese
½	cup guacamole
½	cup sour cream
4	cups shredded lettuce
3	small, chopped green onions, including chives
1	cup salsa

Heat oil in frying pan on medium heat. Add zucchini and Mexican seasoning and sauté until tender (about 10 minutes). Meanwhile, heat tortillas according to package directions. Once tortillas are heated, top each with ½ cup zucchini and divide remaining ingredients between the 8 tortillas. Wrap up and eat. Yields 8 burritos.

Mariah Thompson
Smyrna, Georgia

Hint: To make this burrito lower in fat, choose reduced-fat or fat-free cheese and sour cream. To enhance nutritional value, use whole wheat tortillas and red leaf or romaine lettuce.

Chocolate Zucchini Bread

Delicious! With a taste similar to brownies

- 3 cups self-rising flour
- 2 cups sugar
- 1 teaspoon ground cinnamon
- ¼ cup cocoa
- 3 eggs, beaten
- 2 cups grated zucchini
- 1 cup vegetable oil
- 1 cup chopped pecans
- 1 teaspoon vanilla extract
- Vegetable cooking spray

Preheat oven to 325°. In a medium bowl, mix together flour, sugar, cinnamon and cocoa. In a large bowl, combine eggs, zucchini, oil, pecans and vanilla. Pour flour into batter and mix thoroughly. Spray 2 9x5-inch loaf pans with vegetable spray. Divide batter equally between the 2 pans.

Bake for 1 hour or until firm. Cool in pan 10 minutes; remove from pan. Allow to cool completely before slicing. Yields 2 loaves or 12 servings each.

Rosie Higgins
Lawrenceville, Georgia

Hint: To reduce the calories and fat in this recipe, use 2 whole eggs and 2 egg whites, reduce oil to ½ cup, add ½ cup applesauce and reduce pecans to ½ cup. Result: One slice of bread contains 190 calories and 6.5g fat (31% of calories).

Honey Baked Vidalia® Onions

Honey makes the onions even sweeter

- 6 medium-sized Vidalia® onions
- 1½ cups tomato juice
- 1½ cups water
- 3 tablespoons butter, melted
- 6 teaspoons honey

Preheat oven to 325°. Peel and trim onions, cut in half and place in a buttered 13x9-inch baking dish. Combine remaining ingredients and pour over onions. Bake for 1 hour or until tender. Yields 12 servings.

Sharon Davis
Fayetteville, Georgia

Buyer's Guide to Zucchini

Zucchini should be firm-fleshed and crisp, with a glossy color.

Look for zucchini with small stems and no wrinkles near the ends. Avoid zucchini with cuts or bruises in the flesh.

Zucchini is usually a deep-green color with faint stripes or specks of gray or gold.

The best-tasting zucchini is relatively small, up to seven inches long.

Zucchini will keep in the refrigerator for one to two weeks.

Want full information as to culture and prices on sufficient Kudzu plants to set 3-5 acres. W. C. Fleming, Blackshear

Kudzu Plants Wanted, Market Bulletin, *August 23, 1934*

Vidalia Onions

A member of the lily family, the onion's relatives include daffodils, tulips, lily-of-the-valley, wild hyacinth, leeks, garlic and chives. Wild onions may have grown all over Europe and West Asia, but they probably originated in Central Asia.

Onions have been an integral part of many cultures. Sacred to ancient Egyptians, they were as valuable as gold and used for rent payments and wedding gifts. When they took an oath, Egyptians placed their right hand on an onion, believing it a symbol of eternity. Builders of the great pyramids ate onions to give them strength. King Tut's tomb was adorned with onions as a farewell offering. The Greeks believed them to be an aphrodisiac and strength builder. The Romans valued them as medicine, recommending onions for snake bites and anyone who had been struck dumb. Romans spread the onion throughout Europe. It came with early immigrants to America. During the Civil War, General Grant declared, "I will not move my troops without onions," believing they prevented dysentery.

Vidalia onions, which have become one of the most recognized sweet onions in the world, were first grown in Toombs County in the 1930s by Mose Coleman. The farmer was surprised to find the onions he planted turned out mild and sweet instead of hot and pungent. Yet when his onions garnered a high price, other farmers began planting them. Tourists who bought them at the Vidalia Farmers' Market coined the name "Vidalia onion."

By the mid-1970s there were more than six hundred total acres of Vidalia onions. In 1986 the state gave the Vidalia onion legal

Marinated Onion and Cucumber Salad

Kidney beans are an addition to this old favorite

- 2 medium Vidalia® onions, sliced thin
- 3 large cucumbers, sliced thin, with peel left on
- 1 16-ounce can red kidney beans, rinsed and drained

Dressing

- ½ teaspoon salt (optional)
- 1 teaspoon sugar
- 1 tablespoon Italian seasoning
- 1 teaspoon fresh parsley, chopped fine
- 2 tablespoons olive oil
- ¼ cup vinegar
- ¼ cup water

In large bowl, combine onions, cucumbers and kidney beans. Toss together, separating onion rings. Set aside. In small jar with tight-fitting lid, combine dressing ingredients. Shake well; refrigerate for 30 minutes. Pour dressing over vegetable mixture. Refrigerate 2 hours and serve. Yields 10 servings.

Carol Nalley
Atlanta, Georgia

Vidalia® Onion and Pear Salsa

Great with grilled seafood, chicken or hamburgers!

- 2 cups chopped Vidalia® onions
- 1 cup diced, unpeeled pear
- ½ cup chopped roasted red pepper (from a 7-ounce jar)
- 2 tablespoons chopped fresh jalapeño pepper
- 2 tablespoons chopped fresh cilantro
- 2 tablespoons lime juice
- ¾ teaspoon salt

In a medium bowl, combine onions, pear, red pepper, jalapeño pepper, cilantro, lime juice and salt. Serve immediately or cover and refrigerate up to 2 days. Yields 3 cups.

Vidalia® Onion Committee

Vidalia® Onion Dip

A secret recipe

- 3 cups finely chopped Vidalia® onions
- 2 cups mayonnaise
- 2 cups grated Swiss cheese
- ¼ teaspoon Tabasco sauce
- 1 cup grated Parmesan cheese
- Paprika

Preheat oven to 350°. In medium bowl, mix onions, mayonnaise, Swiss cheese and Tabasco. Spread mixture into 13x9-inch glass baking dish. Sprinkle Parmesan cheese evenly over mixture and sprinkle with paprika to taste. Bake 30 minutes or until bubbly. Serve warm as a dip with your favorite chips or crackers. Yields 16 servings.

R. R. Whipkey
Acworth, Georgia

Hint: This is a very rich dip and works wonderfully as an appetizer. For a lower fat version, substitute low-calorie mayonnaise and low-fat Swiss cheese and reduce Parmesan cheese to ½ cup. Result: One serving contains 124 calories and 7.6g fat (55% of calories).

status and established a twenty-county region, the only place the onion may grow. Similar hybrids grow in other parts of the country, but the combination of sandy soil and mild climate provide the Vidalia onion with its distinct flavor. The official state vegetable, Vidalia onions have a higher water and sugar content than other onions. But they also have twice the vitamin C of apples and high levels of fiber, vitamin B6, potassium and other vitamins and minerals.

Available fresh from late April to mid-July, Vidalia onions continue to grow primarily in the twenty counties around the Vidalia area. They are cultivated today on more than ten thousand acres.

Onion Cheese Supper Bread

An easily prepared complement to any meal

- ½ cup chopped onion
- 2 tablespoons vegetable oil
- 1 egg, beaten
- ½ cup milk
- 1½ cups biscuit mix
- 1 cup grated sharp Cheddar cheese, divided
- 2 tablespoons parsley flakes
- 2 tablespoons butter, melted

Preheat oven to 400°. Sauté onion in oil until tender but not brown. Combine egg and milk; add to biscuit mix and stir just until moistened. Add onion, half of cheese and parsley. Spread dough in a greased 8-inch round cake pan. Sprinkle with remaining cheese and parsley. Drizzle butter over top. Bake for 20 minutes. Yields 8 servings.

Carolyn Crane
Stockbridge, Georgia

VIDALIA ONIONS BUYER'S GUIDE

Onions should have a light, golden brown bulb with a white interior, be rounded on the bottom and slightly flat on the top.

Vidalia onions bruise easily, so handle carefully.

To enjoy them longer than the ten to twelve weeks they're available each year, buy in large quantities and store them properly.

Keep them cool, dry and separate to ensure they stay fresh. One way is to store them in the legs of old pantyhose. Tie a knot between each onion and cut above the knot when you need an onion. Hang in a cool, dry, well ventilated place.

Onions can also be stored on racks or screens as long as they don't touch and are kept in a cool, dry place.

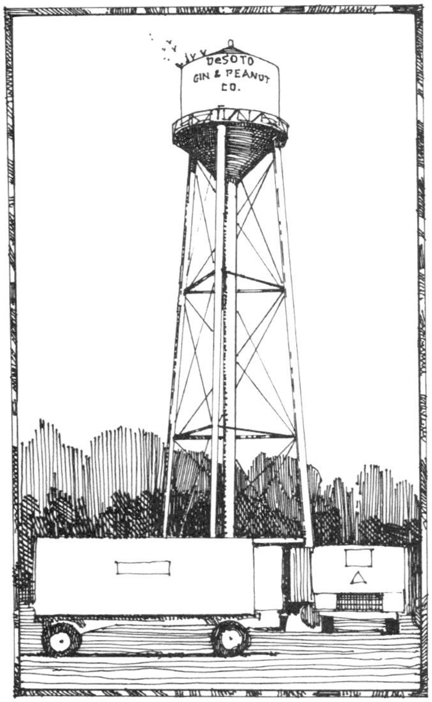

VIDALIA® ONION PIE SUPREME

1978 Vidalia® Onion Festival winner

- 3 cups thinly sliced Vidalia® onions
- 3 tablespoons melted butter
- 1 deep dish pie shell, baked
- ½ cup milk
- 1½ cups sour cream
- 1 teaspoon salt
- 2 eggs, beaten
- 3 tablespoons flour
- 4 bacon strips, fried crisp

Preheat oven to 325°. Cook onion in butter until lightly browned. Spoon into pie shell. In medium bowl, combine milk, sour cream, salt, eggs and flour. Mix well and pour over onion mixture. Top with bacon. Bake for 30 minutes or until firm in the center. Yields 6 to 8 servings.

Mrs. Franklin Conner
Vidalia, Georgia

GEORGIA-GROWN STIR FRY

Carrots add great color and crunch!

- 2 pounds chicken breasts
- 1 pound carrots
- 2 zucchini squash
- 1 pound yellow squash
- 2 large Vidalia® onions
- 2 to 3 ribs of celery
- ¾ pound mushrooms
- ½ pound snow peas (may use frozen)
- 4 tablespoons cooking oil
- 2 packages stir fry seasoning
- Lemon pepper seasoning

Dice chicken and vegetables. Heat oil in large, deep skillet or wok. Sauté chicken and carrots until chicken is done. Add remaining vegetables. Prepare stir fry seasoning packages according to package directions. Add to vegetables, along with lemon pepper seasoning. Stir until vegetables are tender. Yields 6 servings.

Sherry Cooler
Albany, Georgia

Marinated Vegetables

This is a colorful, vegetable-filled pasta side dish

- 1½ cups broccoli florets
- 1½ cups cauliflower florets
- 2 large Vidalia® onions, cut in half and sliced
- 1 cup sliced yellow squash
- ¾ cup sliced carrots
- 2 cups boiling water
- 1 cup sugar
- ½ cup cider vinegar
- ½ cup mayonnaise
- 2 teaspoons celery seed
- 1 14-ounce can artichoke hearts, drained and quartered
- 2 cups cooked small shell pasta

Combine first 5 vegetables in a large glass bowl; set aside. In small saucepan, heat water, sugar and vinegar, stirring to dissolve sugar. Pour hot mixture over vegetables. Cover and refrigerate for several hours. Drain liquid from vegetables, reserving ½ cup liquid; return vegetables to bowl.

Mix vinegar mixture, mayonnaise and celery seed; pour over vegetables. Add artichoke hearts and pasta. Toss gently to coat. Cover and chill until ready to serve. Yields 6 to 8 servings.

Ann Stallings
Nashville, Georgia

Harvey's South Georgia Vichyssoise

Sweet onions and potatoes combine in a delicious soup

- 3 large Vidalia® onions, sliced,
- 1 tablespoon butter
- 2½ cups peeled, diced potatoes
- 2 cups chicken broth
- ¼ teaspoon paprika
- Salt and pepper to taste
- 1½ cups milk
- 1 cup heavy cream
- Fresh chopped chives or dill

In a large skillet, sauté onions in butter until soft, but not brown. Add potatoes, chicken broth and seasonings; simmer covered for 45 minutes. In a food processor or blender, blend thoroughly. Chill well. When ready to serve, add milk, cream and stir. Garnish each bowl of soup with chopped fresh herbs. Yields 8 servings.

H. C. Mills
Atlanta, Georgia

The Vegetable Garden

From *Run with the Horsemen*, by Ferrol Sams …

"Comp adopted as his personal contribution to the family welfare the responsibility of the vegetable garden. The rows were laid out with geometric precision and plowed free of crab grass before it could become more than a green fuzz on the surface of the earth. The yearly yield was a deluge of agrarian wealth, and the family rarely bought food at the grocery store. There were beans, butter-beans, peas, tomatoes, okra, corn, squash, onions, potatoes, turnip greens, mustard, peppers, beets, radishes, carrots and eggplant. They grew prolifically and they poured into the large back porch and kitchen in an overwhelming volume in season. They were eaten and they were canned and they were dried for the winter. The boy's mother had a tendency toward excessive generosity with the produce and would lade city kin with enough vegetables for a week when they came visiting. This infuriated Comp, who thought two tomatoes comprised a handsome enough gift for a thank-you note."

Good looking blind mule, wt. about 1100 lbs. and another one, about the same size. $80 for the 2, or will exch. for a yoke of oxen in good shape, 6 or 8 yrs. old. C. M. Jackson, Lawrenceville.

Horses and Mules For Sale, Market Bulletin, *August 30, 1934*

A Short History of Georgia Farmers

When the first European explorers—probably Hernando DeSoto and his band of Spaniards in 1540—ventured into the land that would become Georgia, they expected to find the forest primeval. Instead, they discovered a land bearing marks of centuries of use by the Indians. Open woodland vistas stood where Indians had burned forests in order to encourage the growth of new vegetation; a network of trails, blazed first by animals and second by man, criss-crossed the region, connecting villages, rivers and streams and ecological signs pointed to centuries of planting. Farming had occurred in this new land ever since man had realized that a seed dropped on the ground would grow.

The Creeks and Cherokees who occupied the land at that time—the Cherokees basically north of the Fall Line and the Creeks to the south—grew many of the crops cultivated by the Mississippian cultures before them (see page 70). They tilled large fields in the river bottoms and tended garden patches in and around their towns. The Indian farmers grew different varieties of beans and peas, pumpkins, squash, onions, wild greens and tobacco. They hunted turkeys, possums, deer, rabbits, squirrels, ducks, geese and pigeons in the forest and harvested turtles, oysters, crabs, shrimp, clams, catfish, trout, herring mullet and shad from the rivers, streams and ocean. Corn was plentiful.

But the days of Georgia's first farmers were numbered.

Colonial Farmers

The first Europeans to settle in Georgia came under the auspices of a charter granted by England to the "Trustees for Establishing the Colony of Georgia in America." The Trustees were to administer the colony for twenty-one years and then it would revert to the Crown. They named the colony Georgia, in honor of the reigning King George. The English had a three-fold purpose for settling the region: the colony would be a place of new beginnings for England's deserving poor; it would serve as a buffer between the coastal plantations of the Carolina's and the Spanish territories of Florida, and it would be an agricultural experiment for producing a valuable range of tropical crops and silk.

From the beginning, these first settlers to Georgia were expected to farm. The Trust made a large grant to each in the form of free passage, equipment and food for the first year, seeds, agricultural implements and a plot of land to cultivate.

Once the settlers founded Savannah on the Savannah River in February 1733, their leader, James Edward Oglethorpe, surveyed and laid out the town in an arrangement of straight streets and open squares. Since it was planned that Georgia's settlers should be yeoman farmers rather than absentee plantation operators, Oglethorpe allotted each only fifty acres of land, broken into three separate parcels: a small town lot located on one of the squares; a five-acre garden plot near the town limits, and a forty-five-acre farm lot still farther out from town.

Within a month, Oglethorpe also plotted out the Trustees' experimental garden (see page 37). In this garden, the colonial farmers planted oranges, olives, apples, pears, figs vines, pomegranates, cotton, coffee, tea, bamboo and some medicinal plants.

An initial condition of land tenure required each colonial family to plant mulberry trees to feed the silkworms they were to raise for producing silk for England.

The Trustees placed a bounty on food crops, including wheat, peas, potatoes and especially, corn—the most important food crop grown. Most early colonial farmers farmed with the simplest of tools—an axe to clear the land, a hoe for cultivating, a spade and a rake. Plows and horses were scarce.

From the first, the Trustees prohibited slavery in the colonies. Morally, they believed it wrong, but also, it was antagonistic to their plan for a Georgia populated by a hard-working yeomanry of small landholders. It did not take long, however, for discontent to grow among the colonists. Other southern colonies had developed lucrative systems of production based on slave labor. Only the largest colonial families could effectively tend to their dispersed land holdings. And toiling in the mosquito infested fields was brutal in the heat and humidity. Eventually, the Trustees relented to the pressures for slavery, but by then it was too late. The relationship between the colonists and the Trust had deteriorated beyond repair, and the Trustees were forced to return the colony's charter back to the Crown before the end of the twenty-one-year term.

With that, the colonial farmer's life began to change. Parliament liberalized land grants. Tracts essential for plantation-scale agriculture were more easily acquired. Now, slavery was not only tolerated but clearly encouraged, since a grantee could obtain additional acreage proportional to the number of slaves he brought with his family.

By the late colonial period, the

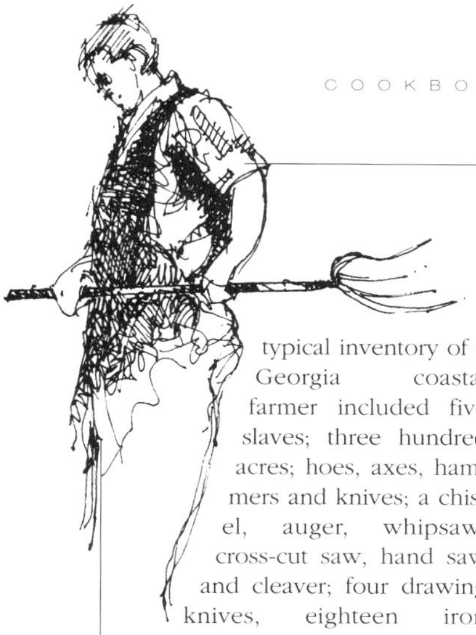

typical inventory of a Georgia coastal farmer included five slaves; three hundred acres; hoes, axes, hammers and knives; a chisel, auger, whipsaw, cross-cut saw, hand saw and cleaver; four drawing knives, eighteen iron wedges and a grinding stone. The farmer had on hand over two hundred pounds of indigo, thirty bushels of corn, five horses and thirty head of range cattle, a horse cart and a saddle, a still, twenty-five thousand shingles and three rawhides.

Large rice and indigo plantations rapidly developed along the coast. Rice production demanded tedious labor, skillful management and a heavy outlay of capital. To begin the enterprise, a planter needed an estimated forty slaves, two hundred acres of suitable swamp land, tools, equipment for cleaning and processing and food for the workers' upkeep for one year. Unlike rice, indigo lent itself to a diversified, family-scale enterprise. A visitor to Jekyll Island in August 1746, described the highly diversified farm of Major Horton, which was perhaps typical of the small plantation of the period. "A very Large Barn full of Barley not inferior to ye Barley in England, about 20 Ton of Hay in one Stack, as spacious House & Fine Garden, a plow was going with. Eight Horses, And above all I saw Eight Acres of Indigo of which he has made a good Quantity..."

The colonial farmers did their work well for the Crown. A 1763 list of Georgia exports consisted of 7,500 barrels of rice, 9,633 pounds of indigo and 1,250 bushels of corn; deer and beaver skins; cowhides, naval stores, timber and "other provisions" amounting to a total value of 27,021 English pounds. Ten years later, the total value of exports had increased almost fivefold and the list had expanded to include sago powder (a starch made from sweet potatoes), beeswax, tallow, hemp, tobacco, salt beef and pork.

By the end of the colonial period, Georgia farmers fell into three groups: small planters, subsistence farmers and plantation owners. The bulk of the colonists were small planters, who usually operated farms of some fifty acres with their families and a handful of slaves, and subsistence farmers, who had even smaller farms and no slaves.

Slaves were concentrated largely on the rice and indigo plantations. The typical plantation owner employed forty to fifty slaves on a landholding of four hundred fifty to five hundred acres. Aside from slavery, the most prominent social development to grow out of plantation agriculture was the rise of a landed aristocracy. This group, which came to make up about 5 percent of the population by the time of the Revolution, owned more than 20 percent of the best productive land and over 50 percent of the slaves. This statistic was one typical of Georgia farming up to the Civil War.

Tenants and Sharecroppers

The end of the Civil War and the emancipation of the slaves was a watershed moment for Georgia agriculture. Fighting and troop movement had destroyed much of the countryside, and Union troops had wrecked the railroads. Confederate money was worthless and three-quarters of the state's capital—the slaves—no longer existed. To rebuild this economy, which had been based on agriculture and slavery, would take many decades and would dominate the life lived by white and black alike. This would be the era of tenant farmers, sharecroppers and the crop-lien system; and it would last until after the Great Depression.

The southern tenancy system of farming was the result of thousands of former slaves and landless whites who had no work nor homes and moniless landowners who were unable to pay their workers. This system allowed workers to be paid with a portion of the crop. Owners, no longer able to operate their plantations without slave labor, divided them into twenty-to-forty-acre units that could be worked by a farm family. These families, contracted as either tenant farmers or sharecroppers, worked the owner's land for a specified portion of the crop.

The crop-lien system of credit was where a merchant extended credit to a tenant farmer or sharecropper for seed and fertilizer and even clothing and food in return for a lien or first claim on their portion of the crop. Oftentimes, the merchant was in the form of the landholder who ran a store from what was once the slave commissary.

The farmer's dependency upon the crop-lien system basically determined his level of tenancy. Very often tenant farmers owned mules or equipment, could supply some portion of seed or fertilizer, could provide their own living necessities and might need little supervision from their landlord. Their portion of the crop might be up to two-thirds of three-fourths. By contrast, the sharecroppers usually owned no workstock or tools and contributed only labor. They were highly supervised by the landowner and were dependent on lien credit for all their necessities. Sharecropping farmers usually received no more than half the crop they worked. Unfortunately, landowners who were hard pressed by taxes, mortgages, production costs and low crop prices could not profit except by cutting into the profits of their tenants.

The tenancy system was at its peak during the first three decades of the twentieth century with these farmers living in a poverty that epitomized the rural South for years. Once in the tenant system, there was little chance of escape. Often after paying the lien, there was little or no profit. Tenants and croppers rarely cleared more than a couple of hundred dollars a year, leaving no choice but to turn to credit again. Many lived in glassless, screenless pine-board cabins in the fields they worked with no electricity, plumbing, wells and privies. They had few household furnishings or clothes. The poorest croppers lived on salt pork, flour and meal. Few croppers owned cows or poultry nor could they plant a garden: not only were they too tired after a day in the fields but the landowner planted cotton right up to their doorsteps.

Farmers were growing corn, tobacco and peanuts, but cotton was by far the dominant crop. Not only was cotton cultivation labor intensive, it was rapidly depleting the topsoil of its nutrients. Farmers ignored agrarian leaders across the South who warned of cotton's effect on the soil and of the farmer's dependency on cash crops. Experiment stations were set up to introduce new farming methods, farm journals promoted plant and animal diversification and cooperative extension services proposed new ways to solve the problems. But despite the efforts of these reformers, markets, transportation, health, educational services and credit were all too inadequate to promote any change.

GEORGIA FARMER, c. 1920

Georgia's farm economy set on the brink of disaster throughout this entire period. Draught, flood or even a personal illness or accident could plunge tenants and landowners into economic disaster. A price fluctuation in the world cotton market was enough to produce economic depression in the entire state. The boll weevil attack in the early 1920s devastated families already on the edge of financial collapse, causing them to abandon their farms and leave the region. Tenant and sharecropper families loaded down with their few personal belongings and migrating toward cities with hopes of possible jobs was a common sight. Between 1920 and 1925, 3.5 million acres of cotton land were abandoned, and the number of farms in Georgia fell from 310,132 to 249,095.

When the Great Depression hit the country in 1929, many of Georgia's farmers had already been there for a decade or two.

THE PROGRESSIVE FARMER

In the end, the Depression helped to rid Georgia of the tenancy and crop-lien systems that the boll weevil and farm abandonment had begun. Programs created by the New Deal attacked the plight of Georgia farmers just as they helped all Americans. Credit was easier to obtain, allowing tenant farmers and sharecroppers to depend less on the crop-lien. The federal government began paying landowning farmers to restrict their production of certain crops which were glutting the market. With the crop reduction monies they received, farmers had the capital needed to buy tractors, milk machines, corn pickers and grain combines. Both of these factors decreased the number of workers needed to farm the land, which forced more and more laborers away from the farms and into the cities where they could find New Deal-created jobs. In the end, this was better for the laborers and further twindled the surplus of workers which had created the tenancy system in the first place.

This would be the beginning of massive changes to agriculture in Georgia as well as the rest of the south. Mechanization was the most revolutionary. In 1920 only about 1 percent of the farmers in the eleven cotton states had a tractor. From the 1930s onward, the number of tractors owned by farmers steadily increased.

Mechanization of the cotton

harvest had been one of the most perplexing technological problems in southern agriculture. In 1941, International Harvester Company built the first practical spindle picker. Mechanical pickers also harvested citrus fruits, and eight-row planters seeded the cotton crop.

World War II drew so many men and women to the armed services or industrial war-time jobs that it forced landowners to mechanize even more. At the end of the war, these men and women who had left the farm never returned. They now had the skills to seek employment elsewhere. The tenant farmer and sharecropper period of Southern agriculture had finally ended.

Tractor power now completely replaced human and animal muscle. Farmers could buy and farm larger tracts of land, using a lot less labor. As they had done for years, state and federal agencies continued to encourage agricultural diversification. Farmers started to listen and began to specialize.

Georgia farmers looked to peaches and peanuts—two crops that would become important to the state's agricultural system. Tobacco became more important and livestock rearing, dairying and chicken and egg production got underway. Cotton production moved into western states, and new crops, such as soybeans and peanuts, replaced King Cotton in many Georgia fields.

Scientific farming became accepted and necessary to survive in the new environment. Chemical weed control and crop and livestock diversification made farming less labor-intensive. Better roads and transportation systems opened up more markets.

After World War II, the Rural Electrification Administration concentrated on delivering electricity to rural areas. Electricity not only brought running water, lights, indoor toilets and radio to Georgia farmers, it also brought refrigeration—enabling dairy farming and poultry production to expand. As farm incomes rose, decent housing, schools and health facilities became a reality for Georgia farmers.

From 1949 to 1969, the number of farm families in Georgia dropped from 220,000 to 47,000. The remaining farmers tended to specialize. In 1970, soybeans and peanuts combined with traditional row crops like corn, cotton and tobacco to make up one-third of Georgia's farm income. Poultry accounted for one-third and livestock, dairying, fruit and other specialty products combined for the other one third.

By the late 1970s, tractors, combines, corn pickers or picker-shellers, pickup baler and field forage harvesters were common on Georgia farms. Mechanization had resulted in fewer and fewer farm workers producing more and more.

Agribusiness

In 1955 the term agribusiness was coined to describe the vertical integration of agriculture through a company's control of the production, processing and marketing of farm products. The term also includes industries that supply goods or services for agricultural production.

In the 1970s agribusiness became one of the major foundations for the economic prosperity of the Sunbelt. Mechanization, the emergence of large farm units, the loss of farm labor, crop diversification and changes in government farm policy have all contributed to the rise of agribusiness in the Georgia as well as the rest of the South.

Contract farming is a characteristic of agribusiness. An agricultural business contracts with individual farmers to produce and deliver produce for a set price. Then the company processes the farm commodity and distributes it for sale.

Agribusiness has transformed much of South Georgia into agricultural operations thousands of acres in size, devoted to major row crops like cotton, peanuts and soybeans. Some farms remain in the hands of multi-generational farm families. Others have become the property of non-resident corporations, large conglomerates such as Dole, Heinz or other agribusiness relating to the animal feed or food process industries that hire corporate farmers to run the operations.

More and more farmers now specialize, producing what the market demands—culinary herbs, wild rice, ostrich, catfish and alligator (see page 296). Poultry farmers produce thousands of chickens daily and rely on the agribusiness system to deliver their commodities to consumers concentrated in far-off large cities (see page 19). In the 1970s Gold Kist, an Atlanta corporation, became one of the leading corporate producers, processors and distributors of poultry in the South (see page 121).

Agriculture today is not just about farming; it's about feeding the nation. The concept of agribusiness reflects a trend that is steadily rising: farm operations involving larger numbers of people with only a small percentage of them actually raising livestock or farming the land.

Tractors through the Years

Beginning in the early 1900s, tractors revolutionized farming methods that had been practiced since prehistoric times. Technical innovations followed one after the other: steam, the internal combustion engine, adjustable wheel width, the three point hitch, each a revolution within the revolution, resulting in the computer intelligent farm machine of the twenty-first century.

(See Resources for tractor clubs and fairs and festivals information.)

1. This English Fordson turned soil in the late 1940s—long after Henry Ford stopped manufacturing it in the United States.
2. Steam traction engines were the first source of portable power to reach American farms.
3. Today's tractors are often cab-enclosed, air-conditioned and stereo-equipped. Where early mechanical planters planted only a row or two, modern planters take wide swaths, planting eight rows or more at a time.
4. Henry Ford's Fordson tractor, built between 1917 and 1928, was the first piece of machinery to replace mules on many Georgia farms. Known as Everyman's Tractor and priced around $500, it put tractor power within the average farmer's reach.
5. Motor cultivators were another early replacement for mules and horses.
6. By 1940, International Harvester's Farmall tractor had stylish hoods and grills. New features included rubber tires and hydraulic power to raise and lower implements.
7. Steam traction engines pulling wheat harvesters helped farmers move from subsistence farming to feeding dozens of families.
8. By 1935, the Oliver 70 had a sleek look, with a stylish grill and louvered panels covering the engine. The smooth running six-cylinder engine made the Oliver line popular with farmers. Oliver, like many other tractor companies, is no longer in business.

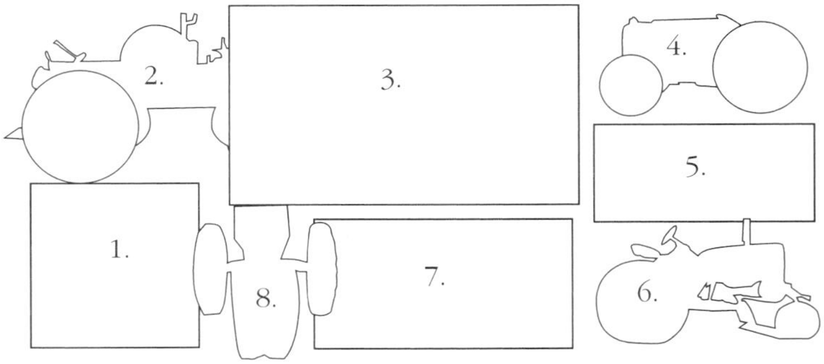

D.W. Brooks

Born September 11, 1901, in Royston, Georgia, D.W. Brooks founded the Cotton Producers Association in 1933. That early farmers cooperative eventually became Gold Kist, one of Georgia's largest corporations and one of the biggest farm co-ops in the world.

I was a professor of agriculture and economics at the University of Georgia. I enjoyed my teaching. It was wonderful. But I wasn't getting anything done, and I wasn't changing the world. I figured, if I could get out, I could change the world.

The per capita income of Georgia farmers was seventy-two dollars for a year's work. They were all starving to death. I decided with my training in economics that I could put a stop to that. I was young and impetuous and so I thought I could do it. So I resigned from the University and went to Carrollton. Carroll County was the largest county in the state of Georgia. Had the most farmers. And the most poverty. You can't realize what agriculture was like at that time. The farmers were doing everything backwards. They weren't doing anything right.

The first meeting I held, I had eight thousand farmers at Carrollton. In the courthouse, all outside. They didn't fully understand what I was doing. I put up all the money to start the co-op. The farmers didn't have any money. At seventy two dollars a year, they didn't have a dime to invest. I had saved my money teaching, so I had enough money to start Gold Kist.

One thing I felt was that I had to say to farmers, "You are crazy the way you are farming, and you ought to starve to death. You've got one denim shirt and it's patched, one pair of overalls and they're patched, no shoes, barefoot. And your wives and children are in worse shape than you are. I can prove what I'm telling you to do."

So I told them, "We are going to change everything. First, we are going to take all the sand out of the fertilizer."

Sand was cheaper than fertilizer so the folks who were selling them fertilizer loaded every ton with twelve to fourteen hundred pounds of sand. I held meetings with farmers and I said, "We are going to put a stop to this foolishness of buying sand."

That was the number one problem. Then I said, "In addition to that, I am going to get better seed. The seed you are using won't germinate. You are just getting a half stand out there. When you plant, only half of them come up. You can't make a big crop with half a stand." So I said, "We are going to do that."

Then, third, I said, "I am going to give you high yielding-seed."

The average yield of corn in the state of Georgia was ten and one-half bushels of corn per

Mr. Brooks is from Royston, Georgia, the hometown of baseball legend Ty Cobb, who was fifteen years Brooks's senior.

Ty Cobb thought I ought to be another Ty Cobb and when he came home from the big leagues he would come up to my house and train me. I was right-handed, but he made me bat left-handed 'cause he said I was two steps nearer to first base and I would make a hit instead of being thrown out. So he made me bat left-handed. I was captain of the baseball team in high school, and I was pretty good but not really that good. When I went to the university, I went out one or two afternoons.

The coach was a big league player and he said, "You look pretty good, can you come out every afternoon?"

I said, "No, I am studying agriculture. I've got laboratory every afternoon."

He said, "You can't do both. What are you going to do?"

I said. "I came over to go to college, I didn't come over here to play baseball."

So I just walked out and did not play any baseball.

acre. It had been that way for fifty years, no change. All you can produce on ten and one-half bushels of corn is poverty. And corn was the largest row crop in Georgia, over 5 million acres of corn. So I decided that I would begin to breed the corn to get high-yielding corn and then in time I got to hybrid corn. I started working on that and I brought it from ten and one-half bushels up to eighty-six bushels per acre. That's the way you do things. You increase productivity and the farmer begins to produce something and he had something to grow. It took about five years to really get it done.

I realized that the problem with the farmer was the average yield was a very small amount. In the case of cotton two to three hundred pounds per acre. That was in 1933. What I did then was increase its yield. I was able to demonstrate to farmers that if they would do it my way, they would double their yield, double their income. I put it up to over two bales per acre. That's over one thousand pounds. Consequently, I converted them—took time to do it—but I converted them from sorry fertilizer to good fertilizer, from sorry seed to good seed. The miracle of increasing production here was fantastic.

I soon realized that if you are going to increase production, you had to sell it. You couldn't just sit. I began to open markets not only in this country but throughout the world. I got on the plane and I went around the world and I stopped at every country. I got me an agent to represent me in that market and I'd sell cotton, for example, in Hong Kong. I would sell it in Japan. I opened all these markets all around the world. That way there was no end to how much you could produce because you keep selling it. You could open markets all around the world.

So Gold Kist became one of the largest exporters out of this country, and Gold Kist began to pour money into the communities. Everybody wanted a setup and so I spread out in a hurry all over the South. I had the knowledge to open these markets and to increase production and then market it and you put the two together and it made Gold Kist into a tremendous large institution.

Norman Borlaug—he was given the Nobel Prize for the Green Revolution—was down in Mexico working for the Rockefeller Foundation. I found out he was doing some research, and I went down there to see how it was doing and so I started working with him and we worked together finally all over the world. For example in India, for fifty years every time you picked up a newspaper in this country you would see pictures of people starving to death in India. Now I decided I could stop that. So I went over there, got some partners and built the largest fertilizer complex in the world. It took me seven years to build it, but it was perfect when I got it built and in one year I stopped hunger in India. They had been hungry for fifty years and I

In his years as head of Gold Kist, Mr. Brooks served as an agricultural and economic consultant to every president from Truman to Carter ...

Well, as a whole, the average president was not trained in economics, and they didn't know what was right and what was wrong. I was economic advisor to seven presidents. For forty years I was in the White House for four Democrats and three Republicans. I never went to celebrate anything at the White House. I went up there to settle troubles. If I got a telephone call that said, "The White House is calling," I said, "Oh, no, more trouble." So I'd have to get on a plane and go up there and explain to the President how to straighten this thing out that was going haywire.

Truman in many ways was the most dynamic President of all of them. Now Lyndon Johnson was a wheeler-dealer, but he knew more about agriculture than any of them because he had a ranch out in California and Texas. He had some experience out on the farm. But most of them had no farming experience. But Truman was a wonderful person and a great president. He once said, "I don't trust a man unless he really understands a pig."

stopped it in one year. I produced so much food they not only could not consume it all, they couldn't even store it all. I had to export some stuff out of India. Now for twenty years you have not seen a picture of anybody starving to death in India. For years I went around the world every year. I would stop in these countries and check and see what is going right and what is going wrong.

I am ninety-six so I have had to slow down. But Norman Borlaug is still going and he is working in Africa. He's got six countries now. Production is up 300 percent.

You are going to have to use better methods of production, but we could keep increasing the yield. We have not reached the top yet. For example, corn; we got it up over two hundred bushels per acre. We can feed the world for a long time yet to come. We have not exhausted all the methods of increasing productivity. We still have some room. Agricultural scientists can do this job if we can get the politicians out of the way. They're always messing you up and getting in your way. But if you can get them out of the way, you can solve the production problem.

As cotton farming moved west in the 1940s and '50s, Brooks began promoting the poultry business to Southern farmers.

We got poultry scientists and we found out it took twelve to fourteen weeks and four to four and a half pounds of feed per pound of meat to produce a three-pound bird. Through research and breeding, we brought the time down to five weeks. We brought the feed conversion from four and a half pounds to produce a pound of meat down to two pounds. I put a big farm over here in northeast Georgia and I hired top poultry people and put them in there and began to produce yields a whole lot better. I was soon the largest producer of broilers in the world. I was twice as large as anybody else. Through research, I knew how to do it.

I did that with everything I've touched with Gold Kist. I did research on it. Don't accept anything. You think everything is wrong until you prove it through research. You got to prove it first and then you know you are right and then you go ahead and do it.

THE ANTEBELLUM PLANTATION AT STONE MOUNTAIN PARK

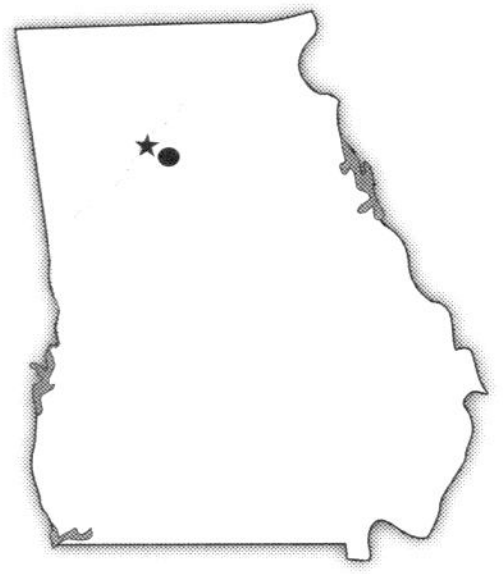

STONE MOUNTAIN PARK

The Antebellum Plantation sits within the boundaries of the 3,200-acre Stone Mountain Park, just east of Atlanta.

Facilities: Authentic non-working 100-year-old gristmill on a stream by the lake, tennis, golf, hotels, wildlife preserve and petting zoo, restaurants, paddleboat cruises, train rides, a laser show, a museum and both a trail and skylift to the top of the mountain.

Days/Hrs.: Park: daily 6am-midnight, Antebellum Plantation: summer, 10am-9pm, rest of year, 10am-5:30pm.

Fees: Vehicles, $6 daily parking permit or $25 yearly parking permit; plantation, adults $3.50, children $2.50. Prices may change as the park is in the midst of almost complete privatization.

Directions: From Atlanta, go east on US 78 for 16 miles. Follow signs to the park.

More Information: Antebellum Plantation, Stone Mountain Park, PO Box 778, Stone Mountain, GA 30086; 770/498-5664 or 5701, or 770/413-5085, plantation manager. Web site: www.stonemountain-park.org.

THE ANTEBELLUM PLANTATION AT STONE MOUNTAIN PARK IS ONE OF the best-preserved, most diverse collections of pre-Civil War plantation buildings in the state. Built between 1790 and 1845, the structures, chosen for their authenticity and historical value, were moved from their original sites around the state and then restored at the park. Providing a glimpse into how people of the early nineteenth century worked for their daily bread, the plantation has a corn crib, barn, period herb and vegetable garden, smokehouse, cookhouse and some rare wooden slave cabins. Moreover, the antebellum structures have exceptional furnishings. Almost every room, including those tucked away in the far reaches of attics and basements, are open to view and loaded with well-preserved artifacts.

This tour begins next to the country store, an 1830s structure moved from Orange in Cherokee County, and continues along a grass-covered rectangle in a counter-clockwise manner. Women in hoopskirts stroll the grounds and greet visitors in the homes, swinging unusual net purses they've knit according to 19th-century fashion. The first stop, directly to the right, is the overseer's house, or Kingston House (1), built in 1945 as the main house on the Allen Plantation near Kingston. After passing a log storage crib (2) and a well (3), typical of plantations that were not located near fresh-water streams, the tour reaches a log cabin (4), a circa 1826 dwelling belonging to Dr. Chapmon Powell, one of DeKalb County's first physicians. In the room are dozens of simple children's dolls, made from patterns and materials over one hundred years old. Next stop along the wide paved path is the Thornton House (5), one of the oldest restored dwellings in Georgia, built in Greene County around 1790. The boy's room upstairs contains original furnishings made entirely on the plantation: beds, chairs, desks, woven rugs and a hoop and stick—parts of an old children's game. Just past the Thornton House stand two circa 1830 wooden slave cabins (6) moved from the Graves plantation near Covington. Each is a simple, one-room wooden structure with single door, chimney and window. Next, a two hundred-year old barn (7) exhibits square strewn timbers and period farm equipment inside. To the left are a well-preserved moonshine still and several corn cribs (8). Next to a brick coach house (9) is the circa 1800 smokehouse (10), also from the Graves Plantation. Next is the outhouse (11) and then the kitchen gardens and cook house (12). Often isolated from towns, plantations grew and preserved most or all of their own food. The garden contains plants common to a nineteenth-century farm plot, including herbs, spices, melons, tomatoes, grape vines, fig trees, corn and sunflowers. Inside the cookhouse a cook in modest ankle-length dress, apron and bonnet watches over delicious-smelling cornbread made with corn, buttermilk and lard on a thick iron skillet over hot coals in the hearth. Scattered throughout the room are a wide variety of historic culinary appliances, including an ingenious apple peeler and cherry pitter. The neo-classical fourteen-room Dickey House (13) housed members of the same family for 120 years. Mint condition china, furniture, musical instruments and fine rugs fill the home. Formal gardens (14) and a plantation office (15) complete the tour.

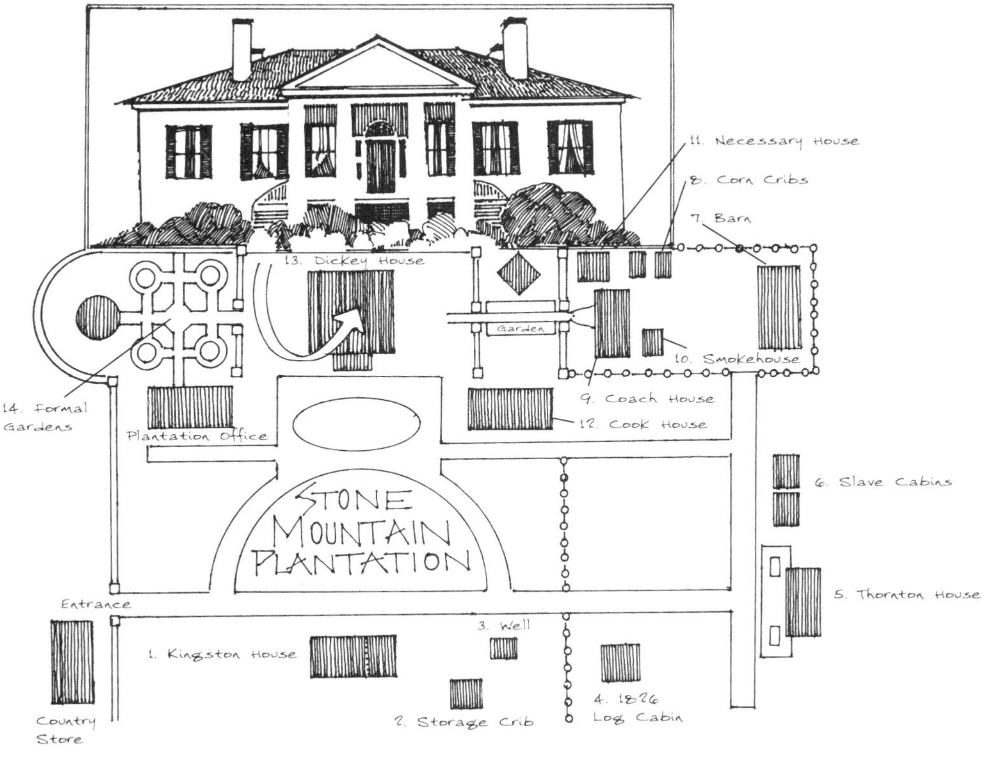

Corn: The Amazing Vegetable

Maize was a native American gift to colonial settlers. It became such an important food crop that it was given the English generic name for cereal plants: corn. During colonial and antebellum times, acreage in corn exceeded that of any other crop. Most of the corn produced wasn't sold but used by farm families and their animals. Southerners ate every possible variation of corn, then found hundreds of other uses for it, including a way to distill and drink it. Scots-Irish settlers in Appalachia adapted their Ulster distilling skills to create liquid corn — one of the mountain farmers few sources of cash income. Illegal moonshiners and licensed bourbon became legendary Southern products.

In Georgia, corn continues to be more widely grown than any other crop. Each county has some corn acreage. Yields were low until 1948, when hybrids better adapted to Southern growing conditions were developed. In 1994, 57.2 million bushels of corn were harvested from 540,000 acres. The average yield was 106 bushels per acre, with the value of crop production equaling $140 million.

Corn is still a major bread grain in the South, cooked in a skillet, pan or mold. Its continued popularity, once due to its affordability over wheat flour, is now more a matter of taste.

Cooking with Corn

Roasting ears, popcorn, hominy grits, cornbread, dodgers, hoecake, johnny cake, pone, mush, fritters, spoon bread, pudding, porridge, parched corn, fish-frying batter, Hoppin' John (with peas), succotash (with beans) and cornstarch

Traditional Corn Products

Pipes, torches, corn shellers, tool handles, jug stoppers, fishing corks, back scratchers, litter, hair curlers, salt and pepper shakers, knothole plugs, kindling, ornaments, Christmas tree strings and dolls

Industrial Corn Byproducts

Paint, insecticides, baby foods, chewing gum, soft drinks, hot dogs, cough drops, toothpaste, lipstick, shaving cream, shoe polish, detergents, tobacco, rayon, rubber tires, urethane foam, explosives, embalming fluid

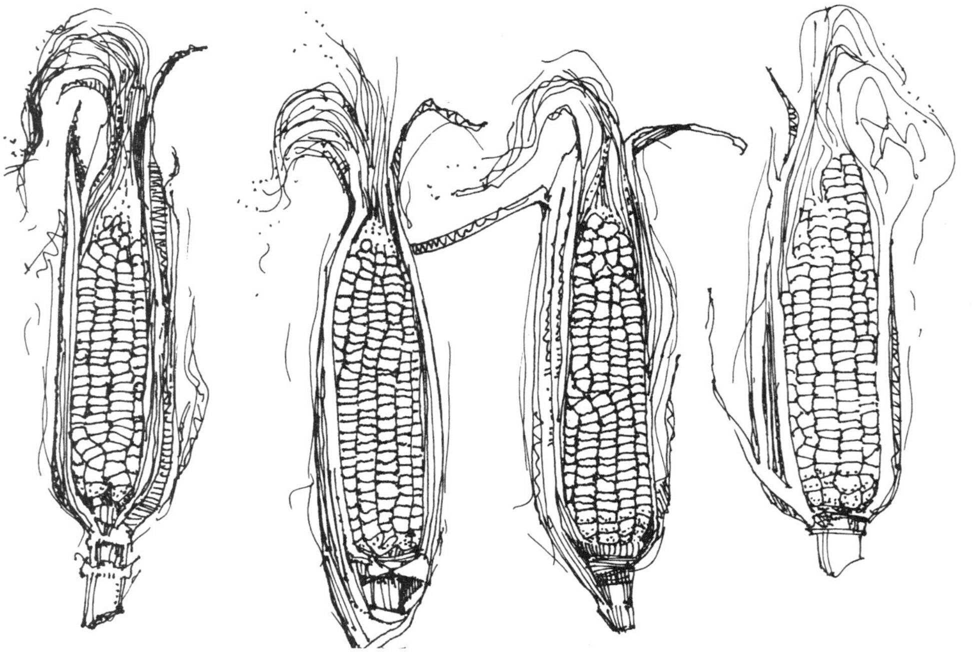

Corn

After Christopher Columbus landed in Cuba in 1492, two of his men returned from exploring the island to tell him about a "sort of grain called maiz." This was the white man's first experience with the North American plant we call corn. But corn was a staple in the diets of the ancient Inca, Mayan and Aztec civilizations. Fossilized pollen grains from corn plants have been found in Mexico that probably are more than sixty thousand years old. The earliest written record of corn dates back to eighth-century Guatemala. American Indians held elaborate ceremonies when planting and harvesting corn and used corn patterns to decorate pottery, sculpture and other art. An Indian named Squanto taught the Pilgrims how to grow corn. Most of the first mills along Georgia streams were for grinding corn into meal.

Corn is a member of a family of grasses which includes wheat, oats, barley, sorghum and rice. The word "corn" means grain of any kind, but in America the word is used for maize. It is the most valuable crop grown in the country and one of the most important crops in the world. Sweet corn, a warm-weather crop well-suited to Georgia's climate, is the state's most widely grown crop. It is low in fat and sodium, cholesterol free and a good source of vitamin C.

Grits Mystique

How has a hot breakfast cereal become so identifiable with the South? Could it be because grits have been the common ingredient of Southern society? After all, grits have crossed over every culture, from Indian to farmer, from white to black. Or maybe it's because grits simply can't be found anywhere else?

The American Indians, who depended on corn as a year-round staple, had different names for this softened corn dish. The Creek Indians called their version "sofki." The English colonists borrowed the name, "hommony corn," from the northern tribes. The colonists also borrowed the Indian cooking techniques, learning two ways of hulling the corn. They would either break the corn into pieces, then clear the hulls by winnowing; or clear the hulls by boiling the kernels in lye, which was made from sifted hardwood ashes dissolved in a pot of boiling water. Lye hominy was the popular choice among early settlers.

These days grits (Anglo-Saxon "grytt" for bran and "greot" for ground) are still produced by variations of each method. The corn in mass-produced grits, either instant or regular, is steamed to remove the hull, then dried and quickly milled. Stone-ground corn, on the other hand, is milled slowly and leaves behind more of the heart of the kernel, which has nutritional value.

How do you cook grits? Which foods should they accompany? Lewis Grizzard answered these questions for most southerners in his "Grits Billy Bob" recipe from *Gettin' It On, a Down-Home Treasury*:

"First, don't fool with no instant grits. The idiot who invented instant grits also thought of frozen fried chicken, and they

Spicy Grits in Red Pepper Cups

4	medium red bell peppers
	Olive oil
4	cups water
1	cup old-fashioned grits
4	tablespoons unsalted butter
1	medium jalapeño pepper, minced
1	cup heavy cream
	Salt and freshly ground black pepper
½	cup plain dry bread crumbs

Preheat broiler. Halve bell peppers crosswise. Remove and discard stems, seeds and ribs. Lightly rub the peppers with olive oil. Place them cut-side down on a lightly greased baking sheet and broil, turning once until lightly charred.

In large saucepan, bring 4 cups lightly-salted water to a boil over high heat. Gradually whisk in the grits. Reduce heat to low, cover and simmer, stirring occasionally until grits are tender, smooth and thick--about 20 minutes. Meanwhile, melt butter in small skillet over medium-high heat. Add jalapeño and cook until slightly softened, about 2 minutes. Stir in the butter and jalapeno into the grits along with the heavy cream. Season well with salt and black pepper.

Preheat oven to 375°. Sprinkle half of bread crumbs in the bottom of the 8 red bell pepper cups. Divide grits among the pepper cups, mounding them slightly. Sprinkle the remaining bread crumbs on top. Bake for 15 minutes or until hot. Serve immediately. Yields 8 servings.

Julie Green
Savannah, Georgia

Baked Cheese Grits

6	cups water
2½	teaspoons salt
1½	cups uncooked old-fashioned grits
½	cup butter or margarine
4	cups (1 pound) shredded Cheddar cheese, divided
3	eggs, beaten
1	teaspoon garlic

Combine water and salt; bring to a boil. Stir in grits; cook until done, following package directions. Remove from heat. Preheat oven to 350°. Add butter and 3¾ cups cheese; stir until completely melted. Add a small amount of hot grits to eggs, stirring well. Stir egg mixture into remaining grits. Pour grits into a lightly greased 2½ quart baking dish; sprinkle with remaining ¼ cup cheese. Bake for 1 hour and 15 minutes. Yields 8 servings.

Polly Boggs
Lawrenceville, Georgia

Columbus Grits

Sausage and cheese makes this a Sunday brunch dish

- 4 cups water
- 1 teaspoon salt
- 1 cup quick grits
- 4 eggs, well beaten
- 1 pound hot (or medium) lite sausage, browned and drained
- 1½ cups reduced calorie shredded Cheddar cheese, divided
- ⅛ teaspoon coarsely ground black pepper
- ⅛ teaspoon garlic powder
- 1 cup milk
- ⅔ cup reduced-calorie margarine
- Vegetable cooking spray

Preheat oven to 350°. Bring water and salt to a boil and slowly stir in grits. Cook 5 to 6 minutes, stirring occasionally. Remove from heat. In small bowl, combine eggs and ½ cup of cooked grits. In medium bowl, combine egg/grits mixture, remaining grits, sausage, 1 cup cheese, pepper, garlic powder, milk and margarine. Blend well. Coat 3-quart baking dish with vegetable cooking spray and add grits mixture. Top with remaining cheese and bake for 45 to 50 minutes. Let stand for 12 to 15 minutes before serving. Yields 10 servings.

Lynne Weeks
Columbus, Georgia

Grits Cornbread

Add a little grits to traditional cornbread for texture

- ½ cup cooked grits
- 1½ cups self-rising cornmeal mix
- 1 egg, beaten
- 1 cup buttermilk
- ½ cup butter, melted

Preheat oven to 425°. Preheat 8-inch baking pan or iron skillet in the oven and grease while hot. Combine above ingredients and pour into preheated pan. Bake for 30 to 35 minutes. Yields 8 servings.

Georgia Department of Agriculture Test Kitchen

ought to lock him up before he tries to freeze-dry collards.

"Get yourself some Aunt Jeminas or some Jim Dandys. Cook 'em slow and stir every chance you get. Otherwise, you'll have lumps, and you don't want lumps.

"Salt and pepper and stir in enough butter to choke a goat. Fry some bacon and sausage on the side and crumble that in, and then come right on top of that with all the cheese the law will allow.

"Grits Billy Bob ought not to run out of the pot. They ought to crawl. Serve hot. Cold Grits Billy Bob are harder than a steel-belted radial."

1 corn mill complete. Rocks are 42 in. top runner, all good cond. In operation now. $75.00 at my place. Oscar Smith, Martin, Rt. 2.

Second-Hand Machinery For Sale, Market Bulletin, *June 1, 1937*

Buyer's Guide to Corn

Select corn with bright green, snug husks.

Kernels should be fresh, tender, plump and just firm enough to offer slight resistance to pressure.

To store, cut away the base of the ear to the bottom kernels.

Ears of corn will keep for several days in the refrigerator if wrapped tightly in plastic wrap or stored in airtight containers.

Squash Dressing

Cornbread is a key to this great side dish!

- 2 cups sliced yellow squash, cooked and drained
- 2 cups crumbled cornbread
- 1 10.75 ounce can cream of chicken soup
- 1 small onion, chopped
- ½ cup melted margarine
- 3 eggs, beaten
- Sage to taste (approximately ½ teaspoon)

Preheat oven to 350°. Combine all ingredients and pour into a greased 8-inch pan. Bake for 40 minutes. Yields 6 servings.

Mrs. M. F. Eller
Atlanta, Georgia

Cornbread Salad

Sweet Vidalias® make this dish a winner!

- 1 6-ounce box cornbread mix
- 1 12-ounce package bacon
- ½ cup sweet pickle relish
- ½ cup sweet pickle juice
- 3 large tomatoes, chopped
- 1 large bell pepper, chopped
- 1 large Vidalia® onion, chopped
- 1 cup mayonnaise or to taste

Prepare cornbread according to package directions. Cool; crumble into very small pieces. Cook bacon; drain and crumble or chop.

In large glass bowl, layer half of cornbread. Top with half each of pickle relish, juice, tomatoes, pepper, onion and bacon and ½ cup mayonnaise. Repeat layers, reserving small amount of tomatoes and bacon for garnish. Refrigerate; serve chilled. Yields 12 servings.

Lynn Lamb
Statesboro, Georgia
First Place Side Dish,
1994 Savannah Great Tastes of Georgia Recipe Contest

Hint: All ingredients can be mixed together rather than layered if desired.

Crock Pot Dressing

Slow cooking creates a moist and tasty dressing

½	cup margarine
1	cup chopped onion
1	cup chopped celery
¼	cup chopped parsley
1	8-ounce can mushrooms, drained
8	cups dry bread crumbs (16 ounces)
½	teaspoon poultry seasoning
½	teaspoon salt
¾	teaspoon rubbed sage
½	teaspoon rubbed thyme
¼	teaspoon pepper
¼	teaspoon marjoram leaves
2 to 3	cups chicken broth
1	egg, beaten

Melt margarine in skillet and sauté onion, celery, parsley and mushrooms until onions are transparent. Place bread crumbs in a very large bowl; add vegetable mixture and seasonings and toss together well. Pour in enough broth to moisten mixture; add beaten egg and mix together. Pack lightly in crock pot. Cover and set to high for 45 minutes then reduce to low and cook for 4 to 8 hours. Yields 16 servings.

Variations: You may want to create your own dressing by adding some of the following ingredients: ground sausage, chopped apples, water chestnuts, almonds or pecans and turkey giblets.

Georgia Department of Agriculture Test Kitchen

Hint: If using seasoned bread crumbs, omit herbs and salt. Cornbread crumbs may be substituted.

Calamus root, slipperyelm, bearfoot, yellowroot, Birdock, yellow dock, rattle root, Kueen of the Meadow, Witchhazel, horsemint, pennyroyal, sassafras, 30 cents per lb. or ex. for sacks, 100 lb capacity. Mrs. R. C. Stower, Ralston.

Miscellaneous For Sale, Market Bulletin, *August 1, 1939*

Corn-on-the-Cob Etiquette
From *Story of Corn* by Betty Fussell …

1890: From *Good Form: Dinners Ceremonious and Unceremonious*—Corn may be eaten from the cob. Etiquette permits this method, but does not allow one to butter the entire length of an ear of corn and then gnaw it from end to end. To hold an ear of corn, if it be a short one, by the end, with the right hand, and bite from the ear is good form. A little doily, or very small napkin, is sometimes served with corn to fold about the end of a cob that is to be grasped by the hand, but this arrangement is as inconvenient as it is unnecessary.

1982: From *Miss Manners' Guide to Excruciatingly Correct Behavior*—Dear Miss Manners: The advent of the corn-on-the-cob season raises the disturbing question of nibbling etiquette. I have been dismayed at the lack of uniformity in nibbling styles. The two most commonly observed have been variously described, but I shall term them the "piano" and the "rotary" techniques. The former involves nibbling horizontally across the cob, reminiscent of one attempting to play all the octaves of the keyboard in a single stroke with one's teeth. The latter involves holding the teeth stationary, while rotating the cob in a fashion similar to honing a knife on a spinning stone. I would appreciate definite guidelines on the relative social acceptability of these, or other preferred techniques.

Gentle Reader: Miss Manners is partial to the typewriter method, which involves a strict progress in orderly rows. It is a social error to say "Bing!" at the end of each line. However, she is willing to allow for such creativity as you describe, provided one does not leave odd kernels on the cob when one is finished. Odd kernels drive Miss Manners berserk.

Cheesy Vidalia® Onion Cornbake

Onions and cream-style corn produce a winner

- 4 tablespoons butter
- 1 large Vidalia® onion, chopped (1 to 1½ cups)
- 1 egg, lightly beaten
- ⅓ cup milk
- 1 cup cream-style corn
- 1½ cups of corn muffin mix (1 small package is usually perfect)
- 1 8-ounce container sour cream
- ½ teaspoon salt
- 1¼ cups finely shredded mild Cheddar cheese, divided

Preheat oven to 425°. Melt the butter in skillet and sauté onions over medium heat until tender and slightly transparent. Remove from stove and allow to cool. In large bowl, mix egg, milk and cream-style corn with spoon. Fold in onion and cornbread; mix until blended. Spread evenly in 9-inch square baking pan. In separate bowl, thoroughly mix sour cream, salt and 1 cup of cheese. Drop gently by large tablespoons over top of batter in 9-inch square pan. Use a knife or spatula to gently "frost" the batter with the sour cream and cheese mixture. Sprinkle the remaining ¼ cup of shredded cheese on top of this "frosting" layer. Bake for 30 minutes. Serve warm. Yields 9 servings.

Kathie Montgomery
Marietta, Georgia
Second Place Side Dish,
1995 Atlanta Great Tastes of Georgia Recipe Contest

Hint: May be made ahead; reheats beautifully! (If using a glass baking dish, lower oven temperature 25°.)

Cornmeal Soufflé

Kitchen staples create a unique side dish

- ⅓ cup cornmeal
- 1½ cups milk
- ½ teaspoon salt
- ½ cup grated cheese
- 2 eggs, separated

Preheat oven to 325°. Combine cornmeal, milk and salt; cook in top of double boiler for 25 minutes, stirring occasionally. Remove from heat and add cheese; stir until melted. Separate eggs and beat whites until stiff; beat yolks using same beaters. Add yolks to cornmeal mixture and fold in egg whites. Place in a 1-quart casserole. Bake for 40 minutes. Yields 4 servings.

Bonnie Seaton
Stone Mountain, Georgia

Vegetable Kebobs

Fresh vegetables make up these colorful kebobs

- ⅓ cup butter, melted
- 1 tablespoon lemon juice
- ¼ teaspoon crushed red pepper
- ½ teaspoon garlic powder
- ⅛ teaspoon paprika
- ⅛ teaspoon black pepper
- Salt to taste
- 2 small ears of corn, cut into 1-inch pieces
- 1 small red bell pepper, cut into 1-inch squares
- 1 small green bell pepper, cut into 1-inch squares

Combine butter and next 6 ingredients. Alternate vegetables on skewers. Grill over medium coals for 10 to 15 minutes, basting with butter mixture. Serve with remaining butter mixture. Yields 2 servings.

Georgia Department of Agriculture Test Kitchen

Stewed Corn

From *Raney* by Clyde Edgerton ...

I was shaving the corn kernels off the cob because Charles said he was having stewed corn.

"What in the world are you doing that for?" he asks.

"You said you wanted stewed corn, didn't you?"

"Why are you cutting it off the ear?"

"Because that's the way you fix stewed corn."

"No, it's not."

This really took the cake. I'd been watching my mother fix stewed corn for over twenty years and suddenly here's Charles – a librarian, and a man – telling me how to fix stewed corn. "Well, how do you fix stewed corn, Mr. Chef Boy Are Dee?"

"You boil it on the cob and then you cut it off."

That was like somebody telling me you cook string beans in a peach pie. Charles was getting too big for his pants.

"No, you don't, Charles. You cut it off first. Call Mama if you don't believe me. Then you put it in a pot with a little water, salt, a pinch of sugar—"

"Raney. Just let me do this."

286A farm, good country home, one 4 room tenant, creek and branch, 50A pasture, plenty wood, some timber, school bus, mail. 2 miles from main paved highway on state kept road. Suitable for farming and stock raising. Must sell. Half cash. $7.00 per acre. 12 miles from Gainesvile. Mrs. Helen Ledford, E. Spring St., Gainesville

Land For Sale, Market Bulletin, *October 15, 1938*

SEARCHING FOR TARA *by Sherri M. L. Smith*

When I was twelve, my Aunt Madeleine gave me a copy of *Gone with the Wind* for Christmas. I had seen the movie the previous summer, and when she told me that there was a book—that I could actually curl up in my own room and read to my heart's content about Scarlett, Rhett, the Civil War and Tara—I was beside myself with amazement and anticipation. And then I got it and saw that there were hundreds of pages that I could pour over—passages describing the red clay countryside, the march from Resaca to Atlanta, Rhett and Scarlett fleeing Atlanta's flames and the billowy, green-flowered muslin dress Scarlett wore to the barbeque.

During all my teenage summers, my family headed out of Indiana for Daytona Beach, Florida, each time passing through Atlanta, where I would peer from the car window at the skyline, dominated by the blue Hyatt dome, as we maneuvered our way through the construction and detours of the new interstate highway. Was there a trace of the railroad depot or Aunt Pittypat's house? Would I catch a glimpse of a sign with an arrow pointing to Tara?

By the time I was twenty-one, I had read the book ten times. Then I put it down—life got in the way. But my perception of the South, and particularly Georgia, was fixed: it was a long-gone place of cotton fields, huge houses with white columns and pretty, flirtatious Southern belles with eighteen-inch waists and swaying hooped skirts.

Over the years I learned that I was not alone in my fascination with Tara and *Gone with the Wind*. In the preface of the book's sixtieth anniversary edition, author Pat Conroy writes about his mother's passion for the novel and how she raised him up to be a "Southern" novelist because *Gone with the Wind* "set her imagination ablaze." Albert Castel, Civil War historian and author of the widely acclaimed *Decision in the West: The Atlanta Campaign of 1864*, tells of being mesmerized by the movie and the book at the age of thirteen. From that time on the Civil War became a passion of his "inseparable from what had inspired it—*Gone with the Wind*." Back in the '70s I taught a high school student in North Carolina who told me how she and her father, with a copy of the book and county road maps, had driven the back roads of Clayton County one vacation looking for signs of Tara. And, of course, there's the Georgia Department of Tourism claiming that thousands of tourists, both foreign and out-of-state, visiting each year will invariably ask for directions to Tara. Somehow this all comforted me.

In my late twenties I moved to

THE MOVIE VERSION OF TARA, BUILT ON A HOLLYWOOD BACK LOT

Atlanta—to Fayette County, that is. This Hoosier girl had gone from Indiana to California to Texas to North Carolina only to end up within twenty miles of where Gerald O'Hara's plantation sat along the swamp bottoms of the Flint River. In fact, Scarlett had received her meager education from the Fayetteville Female Academy—just nine miles down the road in Fayetteville.

I could NOT believe this twist of fate. But—WHERE WAS TARA—exactly?

The receptionist at the Clayton County Visitor's Center looked at me strangely.

"Well, yes, I know that Gone with the Wind is a novel—but it's so real." After all, I expected to find something. "What? There isn't any Tara?"

The Tarleton twins never sat on Tara's porch with Scarlett? Scarlett and Cathleen Calvert never spied Rhett looking up at them from the bottom of the Twelve Oaks winding staircase? Rhett never gave Scarlett a farewell kiss on the road near Rough and Ready? Scarlett never led her half-dead horse up the driveway to find Tara, desolate but standing, spared by the Yankee invaders? And movie producer David O. Selznick put white columns on Tara—Margaret Mitchell never mentioned white columns in her book? Not only is there no Tara—but my vision of it is just a celluloid Hollywood version of the South?

Margaret Mitchell couldn't have made all of this up. I decided to combat my disillusionment with action. Forget Scarlett—what was Margaret thinking of?

Born in 1903, Margaret Mitchell was spoon-fed stories about the War of Northern Aggression. Her grandmother, Annie Fitzgerald Stephens, had been an Atlanta wartime bride. Stories were told and battles were fought over and over again in living rooms and on porches as Margaret sat on her relatives' knees. According to Mitchell biographer Darden Asbury Pyron in his book *Southern Daughter*, Mitchell wrote the first draft of her book from memory. So, if Mitchell had written from memory—what memory had sparked Tara? How did she envision Gerald O'Hara's plantation? What had been her inspiration?

My search for Tara began again.

With county maps in hand, I have wandered Fayette and Clayton County roads along the Flint River searching for the hills of Tara—or more accurately, the plantation land where Margaret Mitchell had spent her childhood summers, the land belonging to Mitchell's Irish great-grandfather, Philip Fitzgerald.

Like Tara, Fitzgerald's plantation lay along the Flint River swamp bottoms. Flint River land in the Georgia Piedmont was some of the finest cotton land in the state. It had been Creek Indian territory up until 1821 when the Creeks ceded this portion of their land to the federal government. Georgia held a lottery to divide up this vast territory, an area that eventually would become Fayette, Clayton, Henry, Houston, Dooly and Monroe Counties. Land lottery winners cleared trees and carved cotton fields out of a frontier. With family members and possibly a few slaves, they planted a manageable amount of crops.

For the most part, plantations here were extremely rural and backwoods in the years leading up to the Civil War. These were not the great cotton plantations of the South; although in terms of numbers, Georgia had more "plantations" than any other Southern state. This was not the landed aristocracy who grew thousands of acres of cotton or rice and owned hundreds of slaves. That class comprised less than 2 percent of the 62,003 farms listed in Georgia's 1861 census.

The "typical" planter of the northern Piedmont, as well as Georgia and the South as a whole, was the small planter who owned two to three hundred acres of land and five to twenty slaves. Later on, historians would not even designate these properties as plantations since their acreage did not total five hundred acres. But these planters did not hesitate to refer to their holdings as "plantations" and considered their interests as important as that small percentage of elite planters who controlled vast amounts of land, possessed great wealth and yielded huge social and political power.

Like the fictional Gerald O'Hara, Philip Fitzgerald was born in Ireland—in Tipperary County, however, rather than County Meath. After migrating to America, Fitzgerald settled in Fayetteville, Georgia, in 1831, began operating a store with his brother James and started buying property.

Founded in 1823, Fayetteville was a thriving center for the surrounding farm community by the time Fitzgerald arrived. There was no Atlanta and no railroad connecting the region to cotton markets. Farmers carried cotton and other marketable farm products caravan style to Savannah, returning with the goods they could not produce themselves on their self-contained properties.

Fitzgerald, like the fictional Gerald O'Hara, bought at least part of his property from another local land owner. A deed dated August 9, 1853, and recorded in Fayette County Deed Book G, shows Fitzgerald purchasing

THE FITZGERALD PLANTATION – MARGARET MITCHELL'S INSPIRATION FOR TARA IN GONE WITH THE WIND

twelve hundred acres from Henry McElroy for forty-eight hundred dollars. One family story says this property, which had a home and slave cabins, lay between two other parcels Fitzgerald had previously purchased.

The 1861 Tax Digest for Clayton County shows Fitzgerald owning 2,527 acres and thirty five slaves. The 1860 census valued his total estate at sixty-one thousand dollars, making him the richest man, though not the largest slaveholder, in Clayton County at that time. By 1860 standards this put him far above the "typical" planter—but his was still a middle-sized plantation, nowhere close to the status of the great planters.

The Fitzgerald plantation home, originally built by McElroy, was primitive—a typical Piedmont farm house. As Fitzgerald and his wife Eleanor's family and wealth grew, the house, which they called Rural Home, evolved—a second story, porches, separate guests houses encircling it—but it always remained plain.

Rural Home was, in fact, much closer to Margaret Mitchell's mental image of Tara than David Selznick's white-columned movie lot facade. Pine board, instead of the book's "whitewashed brick," —but no columns. Darden Pyron recounts a letter Mitchell wrote to a friend: "...this section of North Georgia was new and crude compared with other sections of the South, and white columns were the exception rather than the rule...."

Also, like Tara, the house was spared during Sherman's March to the Sea, while the farmlands and cotton fields were destroyed. In her book *Road to Tara: The Life of Margaret Mitchell*, Anne Edwards wrote that the family story young Margaret heard over and over was that "when the battle was over, the Fitzgerald farm stood raped and silent, its fields stripped, its slaves and animals gone, the house emptied of most valuables. But Eleanor Fitzgerald's dark velvet drapes still hung defiantly at the windows, and her few small personal treasures, including her sacred gold cross, were buried under the pig house in an old tea caddy." Philip Fitzgerald, then sixty-six, said Edwards "began all over again with no slaves, no food and only three of his daughters and an ailing wife at home to help with the work."

My obsession with the mythical Tara came to an official end. Now I had to find what I believed to be the true inspiration of Margaret Mitchell's novel—Rural Home.

My search suddenly became easier.

I called Betty Talmadge. I knew that Ms. Talmadge had purchased the crumbling Tara movie facade from the MGM backlot years ago.

I had often wondered about it—what it would be like to see it restored to its 1939 glory. I also knew that in 1981 Ms. Talmadge had moved Rural Home, in great disrepair, to her own property for safekeeping—but only now did I care about that.

"I want to see the old Fitzgerald homestead," I said.

"Oh, Honey, you don't want to see that. It's a mess."

"No, Ms. Talmadge, I really want to see it."

From my home in Fayette County, the road to Tara heads east on Georgia 54 through Fayetteville, onto McDonough Road and straight to Lovejoy Plantation.

I inspected the movie facade first. Pieces of roof, window frames, peeling dark green shutters, doors and the infernal square, white, faux brick columns were piled in stacks—dirty and desolate looking but tagged and labeled with letters and numbers. The Atlanta History Center had taken the double palladium-style front door, and it was now enclosed behind glass in a *Gone with the Wind* exhibit. But these other pieces—which once made up a movie facade so classy it was featured in the November 1939 issue of House & Garden magazine—lie sadly waiting for the time when they, too, might be reconstructed again.

"Are you ready for Rural Home?" Ms. Talmadge broke the silence. I nodded and we turned away.

Betty Talmadge saved Rural Home from destruction back in 1981. "I bought it over the telephone in thirty minutes," she told me. "One thousand dollars, and I had to move it and clean up the mess left behind."

She said she went out to see what she had purchased and as she stood looking at it, wondering how she was going to move it, all she could think of was "what have I done" and "why have I done it?"

The oldest portions of Rural Home stood in sections raised on cement blocks in the back of her pasture: a two-story structure with broken window frames and panes; a smaller one-story section stood a few feet away. One entire end of this section was open where it was once attached to the main house and a gaping hole took the place of what was once a chimney. Weather-and-age-worn clapboard—very plain—definitely, no columns.

In the *History of Clayton County*, Stephens Mitchell, Margaret's brother, wrote that the "old house was ugly, but comfortable and surrounded by huge oaks of great age."

The original portions dated from the 1820s Ms. Talmadge told me. Just four rooms. "I took down the Victorian trim," she said.

It was hard to imagine Scarlett chattering away to the lounging Tarletons here after seeing Selznick's white-columned splendor; but it was easy to imagine a young Margaret Mitchell spending her summers here and returning to this house and the story of her great grandparents when she wrote her great Civil War novel.

I looked at Betty Talmadge, wondering what inner voice of hers had led her to the ownership of these symbols of the antebellum south.

"Just think, I whispered. "You have the 'real' Tara and the 'mythical' Tara."

"I know," she replied softly.

As I left Betty Talmadge, I knew I had just one more thing to do and then nearly forty years of "searching" would be over.

In 1938 Mitchell provided a description of Tara and its environs for an artist drawing up a plot plan of the plantation to aid in the movie production. She placed the plantation on the north side of a road that headed west to the Flint River, Twelve Oaks and Fayetteville and east to Lovejoy and Jonesboro. I pulled out my copy of the plot plan and my county road maps. Now, it was time to match the house to the land where it belonged.

I headed west toward Fayetteville on McDonough Road. On Folsom Road, called Fitzgerald on an old topo map, I took a left. As I drove my car up the road's incline, I thought of how Gerald O'Hara's Tara was "a clumsy sprawling building that crowned the rise of ground overlooking the green incline of pasture land running down to the river." At the end of Folsom, where it dead ends into Tara Road, I came to the top of the hill. Straight ahead, I looked out onto the rooftops of what is now a huge recently built subdivision with roads winding down the north side of the hill. To the west was the incline down to what I knew was the bottom land of the Flint River. I turned my head directly to the right and there, along the side of the road, were the crumbling remains of a brick chimney. And to my left, among the briars and weeds, were traces of an old foundation...Tara.

I've been asked if maybe its time to take down the posters of Clark Gable and *Gone with the Wind* that hang on the walls in my office. Funny, I had thought of that myself. Kind of an end of an era for me. I've spent nearly forty years and traveled hundreds of miles to realize a myth. The "real" ended up sitting practically in my own back yard. And that "real," in some unexplainable way that I still haven't sorted through yet, has been the much more satisfying experience.

Jarrell Plantation State Historic Site

Jarrell Plantation is the story of a farm family's fortitude and resourcefulness over a period of more than 140 years. The estate of John Fitz Jarrell and his descendants has become one of the best preserved nineteenth-century farms in the state's Piedmont region. Virtually everything on this historic site belonged to the family, which managed to keep the farm together through wars, economic depressions, soil erosion, boll weevils and epidemics.

A self-guided tour of the property begins at the visitor center (1) where detailed tour information is available. Even though a tour of the twenty historic buildings, dating between 1847 and 1945, is interesting, what is even more fascinating is how the Jarrells diversified in order to survive through hard times. The Jarrells, among the county's most prosperous citizens before and after the Civil War, did not live extravagantly. Three homes built over eighty years are modest and simple.

In 1847, John Fitz Jarrell, with his first wife, Elizabeth, built the first dwelling (5). By 1860, the house was the center of a cotton plantation where fields, worked by forty-five slaves, stretched three quarters of a mile west to the Ocmulgee River. Slave cabins, barns, a blacksmith shop, a mule-driven cotton gin and a syrup mill made up the plantation. The Civil War brought hardship: Elizabeth died of typhoid fever; and a Sherman raiding party burned the cotton gin, poured out a year's supply of cane syrup and confiscated food, livestock and wagons. But until his death in 1884, John Fitz Jarrell retained his acreage with tenants doing the farming.

By 1900 Dick, John's son by his second wife, Nancy, had bought several acres from his mother and built a second house, the 1895 Dick Jarrell home (3). Dick and his wife Mamie planted corn, squash, peas, beans, tomatoes, okra, collards, potatoes, sunflowers and gourds in the family garden (2). Dick, who had attended Mercer University, also built a steam-powered mill complex (6). Using scrap wood as fuel, Jarrell heated water from a nearby spring in a forty-horsepower

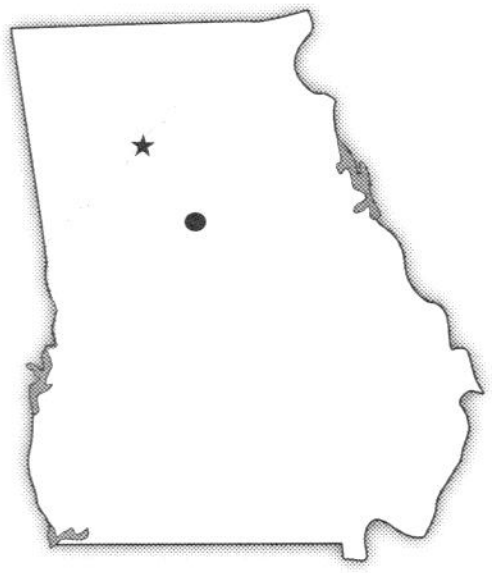

Jarrell Plantation

Jarrell Plantation State Historic Site is an original middle Georgia plantation consisting of twenty historic buildings dating between 1847 and 1945.

Facilities: Living history plantation farm; visitor center with interpretive exhibits, slide show and books.

Days/Hrs.: Open year-round, Tues.-Sat., 9am-5pm; Sun., 2pm-5:30pm. Closed Christmas, Thanksgiving, and Mondays, except some legal holidays, in which case it often closes the following day (Tues.).

Fees: Adults $3, children 6-18 $1.50, 5 and under free.

The Jarrell 1920 House Bed and Breakfast: Tours, adults $5, accompanying children free, on Sundays from April-Oct. and days when the park puts on living history programs. Accommodations, $95 a night, includes breakfast, a tour of the home and tickets to the state historic site.

Directions: From Macon, go north on I-75 to Macon Exit 55. Continue north on US 23, go east on GA 18 and follow the signs. Total one-way trip is about 20 miles.

More Information: Jarrell Plantation State Historic Site, Route 2, Box 220, Juliette, GA 31046; 912/986-5172. Jarrell 1920 House, Route 2 Box 225, Jarrell Plantation Road, Juliette, GA 31046; 912/986-3972.

boiler and ran it to one of two steam engines. By switching a few belts, either machine might power a gristmill, cane mill, cotton gin, timber saw or wooden shingle maker, all housed in adjacent wooden buildings. Like most millers, Dick took a small portion of the finished product as payment, not cash. In 1917 Dick Jarrell constructed a sugar evaporator (7), which made sugar cane syrup much more efficiently than his father's mule-driven kettle and chimney operation. During this same time period, Dick's sister Mattie ran the Cardsville post office and a country store out of a bedroom in the 1847 home, selling such items as matches, flour, kerosene, starch, soda, soap and candy.

In the 1920s Jarrell built another home (4), elegant and spacious enough for him and Mamie's twelve children. Little or no cash went into the plantation-style house. They made or bartered for all the construction materials.

Despite their fortitude, economic forces eventually drove the last of John's grandchildren off the land. They donated the property to the state in 1974, preserving it for future generations. The 1920 house remained in the family, and Dick's grandson Phillip Jarrell Haynes and his wife, Amelia, presently run it as a weekend bed and breakfast.

Scarlett on Hunger
From *Gone with the Wind*, by Margaret Mitchell ...

Hunger gnawed at her empty stomach again and she said aloud: "As God is my witness, as God is my witness, the Yankees aren't going to lick me. I'm going to live through this, and when it's over, I'm never going to be hungry again. No, nor any of my folks. If I have to steal or kill—as God is my witness, I'm never going to be hungry again."

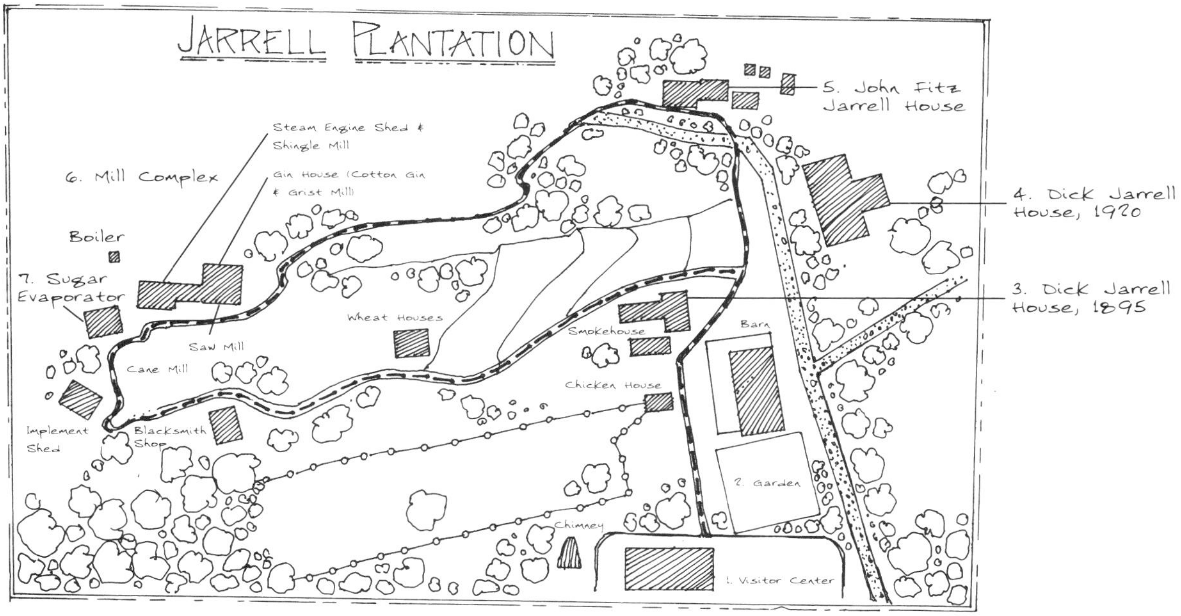

Nothing Worked Like a Mule

A domestic animal and beast of burden, a mule is the offspring of a mare (a female horse) and a jackass (a male donkey). The offspring of a male horse (stallion) and a female ass (jenny) is called a hinny.

A mule looks somewhat like its parents. It has long ears, a short mane, small feet and a tail with a tuft of long hairs at the end like a jackass. From the mare, it gets a large, well-shaped body and strong muscles. The mare also gives the mule its horse's ease in getting used to being harnessed. From the jackass, it gets a braying voice, sure-footedness, and endurance.

Mules can remain strong under hard conditions and rough use, but they work better if they are treated with kindness. When properly taken care of, mules will do as much work as horses and under harder conditions. In the United States, most mules worked on farms and plantations in the South.

Mule Folk Tale

From *Storytellers: Folktales and Legends from the South*, edited by John A. Burrison …

An' then there was a mule that was supposed to be so well trained. Man had him down at the trade day tryin' to trade him off, an' he said, "Why, this mule's the best-trained mule;" said, "you don't have ta say anything to him, just one little inclination of what you want him to do and he just does it." Said, "You never have ta speak harshly to him or anything."

But it so happened he didn't sell the mule, an' he had to take him on back home. An' a neighbor happened by one day just in time to see him just beatin' the tar out of the ol' mule. And he hollered up there to him, said, "Neighbor," said, "I thought that mule was well trained."

An' he said, "He is, he is; but," said, "you have ta git his attention first!"

A Good Mule

From *A Childhood: The Biography of a Place* by Harry Crews …

In all the years in Bacon County, I never saw any rows straighter than the ones Willalee's daddy put down. He would take some point of reference at the other end of the field, say, a tree or a post, and then keep his eye on it as the mule dragged the row marker over the freshly broken ground, laying down those first critical rows. If the first four rows were straight, the rest of the field would be laid off straight, because the outside marker would always run in the last row laid down.

It didn't hurt to have a good mule. As was true of so many other things done on the farm, it was much easier if the abiding genius of a good mule was brought to bear on the job.

There were mules in Bacon County that a blind man could have laid off straight rows behind. Such mules knew only one way to work: the right way. To whatever work they were asked to do, they brought a lovely exactitude, whether it was walking off rows, snaking logs, sledding tobacco without a driver, or any of the other unaccountable jobs that came their way during a crop year.

Eggs

The chicken is believed to have first been domesticated about 3000 BC in India. In the United States, most chickens were raised in small flocks on individual farms—at least until the 1940s. Then came the modern age, when egg laying was transformed into a high-tech industry with the latest mechanical facilities.

Georgia averages 4.6 billion eggs a year from 18.6 million layers. In 1996, each commercially owned chicken produced an average of 246 eggs. Georgia ranked third in value of eggs produced in 1996, behind California and Ohio. That year the total farm value of egg production, which takes place primarily in the northern part of the state, was $348 million.

Eggs are one of the most versatile, nutritious, inexpensive and easiest-to-use foods available. They can be prepared in a variety of ways or used as essential ingredients in many dishes. One of nature's most nutritionally complete foods, eggs contain all the essential nutrients, minerals and vitamins except C. They are also an excellent source of high-quality protein. Although rich in dietary cholesterol, eggs in moderation are an important part of a nutritious diet.

Buyer's Guide to Eggs

Look for eggs with shells that are clean and whole. Breakage can occur during handling. Don't use a cracked, broken or unclean egg.

Refrigeration is essential to maintain egg quality. Buy eggs only from refrigerated cases and refrigerate immediately.

Store in the original carton and keep them on the inside shelf in the refrigerator. If kept in the door, eggs are more likely to experience temperature changes and breakage.

If refrigerated properly, eggs will keep two to three weeks beyond the expiration date.

Eggs will age more in one day at room temperature than one week in the refrigerator.

Egg shell and color may vary, but color has nothing to do with quality. The hen breed determines egg color.

There are five basic cooking methods for eggs: baked, cooked in the shell, fried, poached and scrambled.

Never Fail Popovers

A cold oven is the key to these low-fat and fun popovers

	Vegetable cooking spray
1	cup all-purpose flour
¼	teaspoon salt
2	eggs, slightly beaten
1	cup milk
1	teaspoon butter, melted

Coat 6 custard cups with vegetable spray. Place custard cups in freezer for 10 minutes or chill in refrigerator for 1 to 2 hours. In medium bowl, sift flour with salt. In separate bowl, mix eggs, milk and butter. Pour liquid into flour mixture; stir until smooth. Fill chilled custard cups half full with batter. Place custard cups on a cookie sheet and put in cold oven. Bake at 400° for 45 to 60 minutes. Yields 6 popovers.

Margaret Hiller
Atlanta, Georgia

Hint: The secret to the success of this popover recipe is using chilled custard cups and a cold oven to begin the baking process.

Pickled Eggs

Just like Grandma used to make!

1¼	cup white vinegar
1	tablespoon sugar
½	teaspoon salt
1	teaspoon mixed pickling spices
1	small onion, sliced
1	clove garlic, minced
1	bay leaf
6 to 8	eggs, hard-cooked

Simmer all ingredients, except eggs, uncovered, for 10 minutes. Peel hard-cooked eggs and put them in a 1-quart jar, loosely, so that the pickling solution can circulate freely. Pour hot mixture over eggs, seal and refrigerate. The pickling process takes several days.

Variation: For red pickled eggs, add ½ cup beet juice to the pickling mixture.

Georgia Egg Commission

HEALTHY LASAGNA

Spinach and cottage cheese fill this low-fat lasagna

8	ounces lasagna noodles
20	ounces frozen, chopped spinach, thawed
24	ounces 1% fat cottage cheese
4	egg whites, beaten
½	cup grated Parmesan cheese
½	teaspoon pepper
2	tablespoons parsley flakes
	Vegetable cooking spray
8	ounces shredded low-fat mozzarella cheese
1	30-ounce jar spaghetti sauce (low-sodium variety)

Preheat oven to 375°. Cook lasagna noodles as directed on package, omitting oil. While noodles are cooking, cook spinach in microwave about 10 minutes; drain well. Combine cottage cheese, egg whites, Parmesan cheese, pepper and parsley flakes in separate bowl. Coat a 9x13-inch pan with vegetable cooking spray. Place half of cooked noodles in bottom of dish. Spread half of cottage cheese mixture over noodles; top with half of cooked spinach, followed by half of mozzarella cheese. Top this with half of the spaghetti sauce. Repeat layers. Bake for 30 minutes. Let stand 10 minutes. Yields 8 servings.

Lucy Lepley, R.D.
East Point, Georgia

Hint: This is a delicious low-fat entreé (28% of calories from fat); however, it is very high in sodium. To reduce the sodium content, you may choose low-sodium cheeses and prepare your own low-sodium spaghetti sauce.

NATHALIE ON EGGS

Renown Southern cook Nathalie Dupree has written numerous articles about Georgia crops over the years. Some of her thoughts on eggs appeared in her "Good Cooking" column for *Brown's Guide to Georgia* in September 1978:

Eggs are the most magical of our foods. One minute they are light and fluffy, helping a soufflé rise, the next they are cold and firm—hard cooked....

Eggs leaven, thicken, tenderize, bind, enrich, glaze; they form custards, delicate yet nourishing, ready to heal an invalid; they are used as liaisons, to thicken mixtures, and are the major ingredient in soufflés, quiches, and cakes. In addition to their taste, delights, eggs are eminently practical. Not only inexpensive, they are such a high source of protein that they are the gauge against which other proteins are measured. Eggs contain all the vitamins except vitamin C, as well as many minerals and all the essential amino acids....

The magic of the egg whites comes from beating, developing their rising and leavening powers. Because the egg white is elastic, air can be beaten into it. Grandmother took a large platter, some egg whites, and a fork, then used the fork to whisk the egg whites in the platter, patiently and firmly, until the egg whites became solid-looking, glossy, white castles of air....

1 real good Jersey cow, soon to freshen; 1 reg. Black Poland China sow, ready bred; or will swap for good meat hogs. Eight nice black Poland China shoats. Brooks Green, Gray.

Cattle For Sale, Market Bulletin, *December 16, 1940*

MRS. DULL'S SOUTHERN COOKING

The 1928 edition of Mrs. S. R. Dull's *Southern Cooking* defined life in kitchens across Georgia for decades. Many of the traditional recipes of the South in use today evolved from the classic work of Mrs. Dull, the food editor for many years at the *Atlanta Constitution*. Before her book, few recipes, or receipts as they were then called, had been written down. Most stayed locked away in the memories of their creators until verbally passed on to a friend or daughter. Her work was the first to include a comprehensive written account of how to make fried chicken, cornbread, fluffy biscuits and other southern staples.

"I think Mrs. Dull contributed a lot to Georgia and southern cooking. For a long time her cookbook was the only one available that showed people cooking in their day," says Nathalie Dupree, one of Georgia's premier chefs in print and television.

"She's been a big influence on us, probably the guiding influence for a long time," echoes John Dillard, owner of the Dillard House in Rabun County. "She had such a wide grasp of everything that was being done at the time. Most of her methods are still pretty good. We just have to substitute the heavier type things."

In 1968 Grosset and Dunlap reprinted the classic book, which included this recipe for fried chicken with cream gravy:

Select a young chicken weighing from 1½ to 2 pounds. Dress and disjoint, chill. When ready, have a deep fry pan with grease at least 2 inches deep. Sift enough flour in which to roll the chicken pieces (1½ to 2 cups). Add salt and pepper to the flour, roll each piece in flour and place in the hot grease. Put the largest pieces in first and on the hottest part of the

"EGGS"CELLENT CASSEROLE

Grits combine with eggs for the perfect breakfast.

6	eggs, lightly beaten
1	15-ounce can cream-style corn
1	4-ounce can chopped green chilies, drained
1	cup shredded, extra sharp Cheddar cheese
1	cup shredded Monterey Jack cheese
1½	teaspoons instant grits
¾	teaspoon Worcestershire sauce
⅛	teaspoon pepper

Preheat oven to 325°. In large bowl, combine all ingredients; stir until well-mixed. Pour into ungreased 9x9-inch baking dish. Casserole can be refrigerated up to 24 hours before baking. Remove from refrigerator 1 hour before baking. Bake 1 hour or until firm to the touch and lightly browned. Yields 6 servings.

Gail Hooks
Swainsboro, Georgia

Broccoli Cornbread

Eggs add great texture to this tasty cornbread

1 8.5-ounce box cornbread mix

1 10-ounce package frozen, chopped broccoli, thawed and drained

1 small onion, chopped

1 green onion, chopped

1 cup grated sharp Cheddar cheese or cottage cheese

4 eggs, slightly beaten

1 stick (½ cup) butter, softened

Preheat oven to 350°. Combine all ingredients and pour into a greased iron skillet. Bake for 45 minutes or until golden brown. Yields 8 to 10 servings.

Mrs. Bill Tate
LaFayette, Georgia

pan. When all is in, cover for 5 minutes. Remove top and turn when the underside is well browned. Replace top for another 5 minutes, remove and cook in open pan until the bottom side is browned. About 30 minutes in all will be required for cooking chicken if it is not too large. Do not turn chicken but once; too much turning and too long cooking will destroy the fine flavor which is there when well cooked. The fat should be deep enough to cover the pieces when it boils up. To make cream gravy: Pour off all the grease, leaving 2 to 3 tablespoons in the pan with the browned crumbs. Add 2 tablespoons butter, 4 tablespoons flour, blend and cook until golden brown; add 1 cup milk and 1 cup hot water. Stir until smooth and the right thickness and add salt and black pepper. Pour into a gravy boat and serve with hot biscuit or dry rice. Never pour gravy over chicken if you wish Georgia fried chicken.

I definitely believe the turning point has been reached in Georgia farming and that from now on during the succeeding years, better crops will be grown and the income of the farmer will gradually increase. This will be brought about by the changed methods of farming being followed in Georgia and the South. I confidently believe that if the soil saving methods, adopted by the Roosevelt administration are followed for the next ten years as they have for the last four or five years, that the Georgia and southern farming area will be completely re-made, which will mean a new day for the farmer.

Editorial by Columbus Roberts, Georgia Commissioner of Agriculture, Market Bulletin, *January 1, 1940*

Habersham Winery

Habersham Winery produced its first two thousand cases of wine in 1983. Since then, it has become the largest winery in the state, winning over one hundred awards in national and international competition; and its annual production figure has risen to over twelve thousand cases. Habersham wines come from the classic grape types of the old world, native southern grapes, such as the popular muscadine, and other North American varieties. Most of Habersham's grapes are grown three miles northwest of Clarkesville at the thirty-two-acre Stonepile Vineyard where fifteen varieties of grapes, including classic European viniferas such as Merlot and Cabernet Sauvignon as well as French-American hybrids such as Seyval and Chambourcin, yield one hundred fifty tons annually. Habersham also manages the ten-acre Mossy Creek Vineyard in Hall County which adds another forty tons of Chardonnay, Merlot and Cabernet Sauvignon to Habersham's annual harvest. Habersham has recently moved its entire winery operation from Baldwin to Helen and the Nacoochee Valley area. Habersham, with eight tasting rooms around the state (see page 297), only sells its wines in Georgia.

Miracle Pie

This pie is a longtime favorite among Southern cooks!

- 1 cup Jeremiah 6:20 (sugar)
- ¼ cup Genesis 18:8 (butter)
- 4 Deuteronomy 22:6 (eggs)
- ½ cup 2 Kings 7:18 (all-purpose flour)
- 2 cups Hebrew 5:13 (milk)
- 1 cup Genesis 43:11 (coconut)
- ¼ teaspoon Matthew 5:13 (salt)
- ½ teaspoon 2 Kings 23:15 (baking powder)
- 1 teaspoon vanilla extract

Preheat oven to 350°. Put all ingredients into a blender. Blend thoroughly. Pour into a 10-inch pie plate that has been greased and floured. Bake for 60 minutes. A crust will form on the bottom, pie filling in the center and a coconut topping above. Yeilds 8 servings.

Make it a family project to look up the ingredients. All are found in the King James version of the Bible.

Azilee Edwards
Atlanta, Georgia

Make Its Own Crust Coconut Pie

The cook as well as the kids will enjoy watching this pie bake

- 4 eggs
- 1¾ cups sugar
- ½ cup self-rising flour
- 2 cups 2% milk
- 1 teaspoon vanilla extract
- ½ stick (¼ cup) margarine, melted
- 1½ cups flaked coconut
- Vegetable cooking spray

Preheat oven to 350°. In medium mixing bowl, combine eggs and sugar. Add flour and milk, alternating each. Stir in vanilla, margarine and coconut until well-blended. Pour mixture into 10-inch pie plate, coated with cooking spray. Bake for 45 to 50 minutes or until crust is golden brown. Yields 8 servings.

Irene Parrish
Monroe, Georgia

Mississippi Lemon Chess Pie

All across the South, this pie is a tradition!

- 2 cups sugar
- 1 tablespoon all-purpose flour
- 1 tablespoon cornmeal
- ¼ teaspoon salt
- ¼ cup butter or margarine, melted
- ¼ cup lemon juice
- Grated rind of 2 lemons
- ¼ cup milk
- 4 eggs
- Unbaked 9-inch pastry shell

Preheat oven to 350°. Combine sugar, flour, cornmeal and salt. Add butter, lemon juice, lemon rind and milk. Mix well. Add eggs one at a time, beating well after each addition. Pour into pastry shell. Bake for 50 minutes. Yields 8 servings.

Lois Knight
Jeffersonville, Georgia

Mexican Brunch Pie

Green chilies and Monterey Jack add the "Mexican" to this pie

- 5 eggs, beaten
- 2 tablespoons butter or margarine, melted
- ¼ cup all-purpose flour
- ½ teaspoon baking powder
- 1 8-ounce carton cream-style cottage cheese
- 2 cups (8 ounces) shredded Monterey Jack cheese
- 1 4-ounce can chopped green chilies, drained

Preheat oven to 400°. Combine first 4 ingredients in a mixing bowl; beat well. Stir in remaining ingredients and pour into a well-greased 9-inch pie plate. Bake for 10 minutes; reduce heat to 350° and bake about 20 minutes or until set. Cut into wedges to serve. Yields 6 servings.

Gail McNeely
Smyrna, Georgia

Breakfast

From *The Taste of Country Cooking* by Edna Lewis ...

Breakfast was about the best part of the day. There was an almost mysterious feeling about passing through the night and awakening to a new day. Everyone greeted each other in the morning with gladness and a real sense of gratefulness to see the new day. If it was a particularly beautiful morning, it was expressed in the grace. Spring would bring our first and just about only fish-shad. It would always be served for breakfast, soaked in salt water for an hour or so, rolled in seasoned cornmeal, and fried carefully in home-rendered lard with a slice of smoked shoulder for added flavor. There were crispy fried white potatoes, fried onions, batter bread, any food left over from supper, blackberry jelly, delicious hot coffee, and cocoa for the children. And perhaps if a neighbor dropped in, dandelion wine was added. With the morning feeding of the animals out of the way, breakfast was enjoyable and leisurely.

A nation's strength in war is no greater than its food supply. It is just as imperative to build up reserves of food and all agricultural crops as it is to build up reserves of soldiers, guns and ammunition. The American farmer will provide the food for America and feed the hungry nations of Europe if given an opportunity to do so.

Editorial by Tom Linder, Georgia Commissioner of Agriculture, Market Bulletin, *December 10, 1941*

FOOD IN THE FAMILY

Here's a Georgia trivia question. What do Mary Mac's Tea Room in Atlanta, Spano's Restaurant in Columbus and Atlanta's Peasant Restaurants have in common? Family ties. Margaret Lupo founded legendary Southern restaurant Mary Mac's on Ponce de Leon Avenue, while her sister, Sara Spano, operated the continental-style cuisine Spano's Restaurant in Columbus and was a food editor for the *Columbus Ledger-Enquirer*. Steve Nygren, co-founder of the Peasant Restaurants in Atlanta, married Mrs. Lupo's daughter, Marie. After years of establishing and running such restaurants as the Pleasant Peasant, the Country Place and Mick's, the Nygrens have settled in the Palmetto countryside where they now operate the Serenbe Bed and Breakfast.

By the way, a cousin of Margaret and Sara went into the writing business. Her name is Margaret Mitchell, author of *Gone with the Wind*.

OLD FASHIONED EGG CUSTARD PIE

An old-time favorite that never goes out of style

1	cup sugar
2½	tablespoons flour
⅛	teaspoon ground nutmeg
4	egg yolks
2	egg whites
1	cup milk
2	tablespoons melted butter or margarine
1	9-inch unbaked pie crust
2	egg whites
2	tablespoons sugar

Preheat oven to 400°. Combine sugar, flour and nutmeg. Beat 4 egg yolks and 2 egg whites; add to dry ingredients. Beat well. Add milk and stir in melted butter. Pour into crust and bake for 10 minutes. Reduce heat to 325° and bake 30 minutes longer. Beat 2 egg whites and 2 tablespoons sugar to make meringue. Spread on custard and brown. Yields 8 servings.

Mrs. Guy Duckett
Royston, Georgia

Orange Salad Supreme

Congealed salads are a Southern family tradition

1	6-ounce package orange gelatin
1	20-ounce can crushed pineapple, drained
1	cup chopped pecans
1	8-ounce container whipped topping
1	8-ounce package cream cheese, softened
1	cup pineapple juice
2	tablespoons lemon juice
¾	cup sugar
2	tablespoons all-purpose flour
2	eggs, beaten

In small bowl, mix gelatin as directed on package but use ½ cup less water. Pour gelatin into 9x13-inch dish. Chill until gelatin begins to thicken; add pineapple and pecans. Allow to congeal thoroughly. In medium bowl, cream the cheese and whipped topping. Spread on congealed mixture. In small saucepan, combine remaining ingredients. Cook over low heat until thick. Cool somewhat and spread over cream cheese layer. Refrigerate for at least 2 hours. Yields 12 squares.

Sara T. Dukes
Bartow, Georgia

Hint: When the recipe says "cook over low heat," don't try to "hurry" it by cranking up the fire! Why? Well, the first hurry-up batch of cooked topping resembled egg drop soup with strands of cooked egg whites throughout! The second try cooked quite nicely — but only with a little patience added.

Gardening for Two

In her book, *The Story of Corn*, Betty Fussell relates a story about Indian couples working in the garden together that was told by Indian Wolf Dan in 1910 to Gilbert L. Wilson for his 1917 book, *Buffalo Bird Woman's Garden:*

In my tribe in old times, some men helped their wives in their gardens. Others did not. Those who did not help their wives talked against those who did, saying, "That man's wife makes him her servant!"

And the others retorted, "Look, that man puts all the hard work on his wife!"

Men were not all alike; some did not like to work in the garden at all, and cared for nothing but to go around visiting or to be off on a hunt.

My father, Small Ankle, liked to garden and often helped his wives.... My father said that that man lived best and had plenty to eat who helped his wife. One who did not help his wife was likely to have scanty stores of food.

Want camomile, Lavender, Hop, Rue, Caraway, Savory, Thyme, Balm, sweet fennell and other herbs. Exc. Elecampane, Mints, rosemary, comfrey, catnip, sage, hoarhound, feverfew or pay cash. Mrs. Ralph Williams, Cumming.

Miscellaneous Wanted, Market Bulletin, *April 15, 1942*

Tea Cakes

Elizabeth Harris, wife of former Georgia Governor Joe Frank Harris, fondly recalls this treasured family recipe often made by the governor's mother, Nanny Harris. "All the family loves what we called Nanny's Tea Cakes. We have so many cherished memories of Nanny and her grandson, Joe Frank Jr., in the kitchen making them. Joe Frank, wearing an apron almost as big as he was, would stand on a stool to reach the counter to roll and cut out the tea cakes, scattering flour everywhere, especially on himself. When the tea cakes popped out of the oven, it was his delight to sprinkle them with sugar."

To make her tea cakes, Nanny Harris would cream 1 cup of sugar, 1 cup of solid shortening, 2 eggs, 1 teaspoon of vanilla extract and ½ teaspoon of lemon extract in a large mixing bowl. Gradually, she would add 4 cups of self-rising flour, kneading the mixture until it was stiff enough to roll. Then she would roll the dough ¼ inch thick and cut it into the desired shapes. She would place the dough shapes on a greased cookie sheet and bake them in a 350° preheated oven for 10 to 12 minutes. Nanny's recipe made about 72 tea cakes, which the family loved to spread with peanut butter.

Old Fashioned Tea Cakes

These cakes are a perfect end to any special occasion

- 1 cup butter
- 2 cups sugar
- 5 eggs
- 5½ cups all-purpose flour
- 3 teaspoons baking powder
- ¼ cup milk
- 1 teaspoon vanilla flavoring

Preheat oven to 350°. In a large mixing bowl, cream butter and sugar. Add eggs one at a time. In a separate bowl, combine flour and baking powder. Add to butter mixture alternately with milk. Add vanilla and mix well. Place dough on a floured board and knead to cutting consistency (add up to ¼ cup flour if needed). Roll dough to ½-inch thick and cut as for biscuits. Place on an ungreased cookie sheet and bake for 12 to 15 minutes. Makes 36 tea cakes.

Joy Puckett
Newnan, Georgia

Ginger Snaps

Molasses and ginger combine in this old-time favorite

- ¼ cup margarine, softened
- ¾ cup sugar
- ⅓ cup molasses
- 1½ tablespoons lemon rind
- 1 egg
- 2 cups all-purpose flour
- 1½ teaspoons baking soda
- 1 tablespoon ground ginger
- ½ teaspoon ground cinnamon
- Dash salt

Beat margarine with electric mixer until creamy; gradually add sugar, beating well. Add molasses, lemon rind and egg; beat well. In small bowl, combine flour and next 4 ingredients; stir well. Gradually add flour mixture to margarine mixture, stirring well. Cover dough and chill for 1 hour.

Preheat oven to 350°. Shape dough into 35 balls. Place 2 inches apart on greased cookie sheets. Bake for 12 minutes or until golden. Remove from cookie sheets and let cool completely on wire racks. Yields 35 cookies.

Georgia Egg Commission

Basic Eggnog

Vary this creamy homemade eggnog to suit your taste

- 6 eggs
- ¼ cup sugar
- ¼ teaspoon salt
- 1 quart milk
- 1 teaspoon vanilla extract
- 1 cup whipping cream, whipped
- Garnish or stir-ins, optional

In large saucepan, beat together eggs, sugar and salt. Stir in milk. Cook over low heat, stirring constantly, until mixture thickens and just coats a metal spoon. Stir in vanilla. Cool quickly by setting pan in bowl of ice or cold water and stirring for a few minutes. Cover and refrigerate until thoroughly chilled, several hours or overnight. Pour into bowl or pitcher. Fold in whipped cream, if desired. Garnish or add stir-ins if desired. Serve immediately.

Variation: For Fluffy Eggnog, separate eggs. Omit whipping cream and prepare custard as above using egg yolks, 2 tablespoons of the sugar, salt, milk and vanilla. Chill as above. Just before serving, in large mixing bowl, beat egg whites with ¾ teaspoon cream of tartar at high speed until foamy. Add remaining 2 tablespoons sugar, 1 tablespoon at a time, beating constantly until sugar is dissolved* and whites are glossy and stand in soft peaks. Gently, but thoroughly, fold chilled custard into whites. Pour into bowl or pitcher. Serve immediately. Yields 3 quarts or 24 servings.

* Rub just a bit of meringue between thumb and forefinger to feel if sugar has dissolved.

Georgia Egg Commission

Eggnog Elegant

Peach liqueur makes this a truly elegant holiday drink

- 4 eggs
- ½ cup sugar
- ¼ teaspoon salt
- 2 cups milk
- ⅓ cup peach liqueur
- 2 tablespoons frozen orange juice concentrate

In medium saucepan, beat together eggs, sugar and salt. Stir in milk. Cook over low heat, stirring constantly, until mixture thickens and just coats a metal spoon. Cool quickly by setting pan in a bowl of ice or cold water and stirring for a few minutes. Cover and refrigerate until thoroughly chilled, several hours or overnight. Stir in liqueur and orange concentrate. Pour into bowl or pitcher. Serve immediately. Yields six servings.

Georgia Egg Commission

250 acres in Fayette Co., 100 A. tillable, bal. pasture and young pasture. Good 7 and 4 R. houses, out-bldgs., 19 A. cotton. Good roads, church, school and mail facilities. Elec. available. 2 wells, 3 springs, creek. Clear title. Possession now. $4,000.00 easy terms. 4 percent interest. John W. Clements, Dalton, Box 254.

Farm Land For Sale, Market Bulletin, *March 24, 1943*

THE AGRIRAMA

THE EARLIEST PIONEERS ARRIVED TO THE PINE BARRENS OF SOUTH Georgia in the mid-1800s, bringing livestock herds to vast estates they bought for as little as twenty-five cents an acre. The railroads soon brought more settlers, mostly small farmers, millers, ginners, clergy and teachers.

Most of the South Georgia population practiced subsistence agriculture, raising only what they needed to survive with a mule or horse or two. They planted corn, peas, greens, sugar cane, sweet potatoes and enough cotton to make a few bales for cash. Farmers commonly could only work a small portion of land because clearing the thick stands of virgin yellow pine proved extremely labor intensive. Each year rangers would round up the cattle, hogs and sheep left to forage in the wiregrass and pines. With hostile Indians, lawless men and free range cattle roaming the wiregrass, this part of the state resembled the Wild West more than the Plantation South. Added to the mix was a class of transient sharecroppers and laborers, struggling to survive with no property of their own.

In the late 1800s, lumberjacks and mostly African American turpentiners from the Carolinas began to clear the forests of the timber and pine sap that would ride the newly laid railroads crisscrossing South Georgia, like the Brunswick & Albany and Macon & Albany. By the turn of the century, with much of the forests cleared, large-scale commercial agriculture began replacing the traditional farm practices of the original settlers two generations prior. Farmers planted mostly cotton, which promised quick returns, but also depleted the already nutrient-poor sandy soil and rendered them helpless in producing their own basic food. Progressive agricultural leaders began preaching the economic philosophy of "hogs and hominy," a movement calling for the return to self-sufficiency through diversification of crops and livestock, which would free farmers from dependence on King Cotton. But a commercial farmer could never be totally self-sufficient, and the rural towns of the late 1800s and early 1900s reflected the

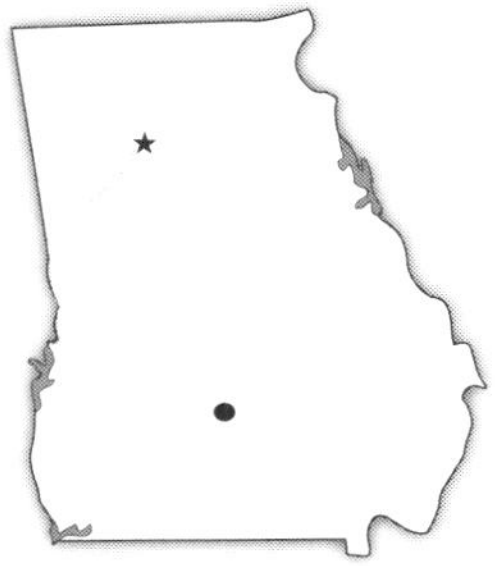

THE AGRIRAMA

The Georgia Agrirama reflects Georgia's agricultural heritage, particularly life lived in the South Georgia wiregrass. It is the state's flagship living history museum with thirty-five structures relocated to a ninety-five-acre site and faithfully restored or preserved as they appeared at the turn of the century. Costumed interpreters explain and demonstrate the lifestyle and activities of the period.

Facilities: Living history museum; educational workshops for schools, churches and other youth groups; seminars, family reunions, company picnics and birthday parties in certain historic buildings; on and off-site traditional country meal catering and overnight camping for scout groups

Days/Hrs.: Year-round, Tues.-Sat., 9am-5pm; Sun., 12:30pm-5pm. Closed on Mon., New Year's Day, Thanksgiving and 4 days for Christmas.

Fees: Adults $8, seniors over 55 $6, youths 4-18 $4, children 3 and under free, family pass $22

Directions: Located just west of I-75 at Exit 20 in Tifton.

More Information: Georgia Agrirama, P.O. Box Q, Tifton, GA 31793; 912/386-3344.

needs of the rural community: merchants who provided credit for equipment and low-priced common goods for cash; professionals such as doctors, dentists and lawyers; support industries like sawmills, turpentine stills, gins and gristmills.

The Agrirama, Georgia's flagship living history museum, presents a convincing recreation of life in rural South Georgia at the turn of the twentieth century. It consists of four distinct areas: a traditional farm community of the 1870s, a progressive farmstead of the 1890s, an industrial sites complex and a rural town. All of the buildings, furnishings and farm equipment date from 1870 to 1910 and are donated from around the state.

Every building is historic. The Visitor Center (1) is a circa 1850 log cabin from Tift County and the concession stand (3) once served as a farm commissary in the city of Hat. The Opry Shelter is a structure based on a traditional tabernacle located in Ashburn. The Country Store (5), which sells old-fashioned children's books, crafts and foods, is located in a reconstructed brick cotton warehouse. The massive nineteenth-century

continued on page 158

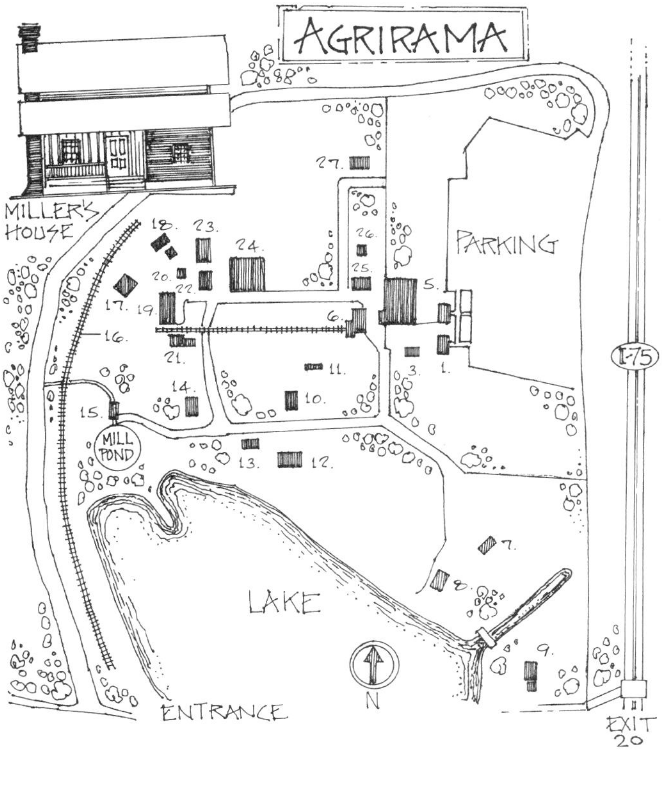

A Dairy Farm

On a typical dairy farm, the first of two milk production shifts can begin as early as 4 am. Before the milking, the cows are cleaned with watery soap sprayed on them by sprinklers. The animals drip dry and their udders are dipped in an iodine solution to prevent infections. The farmer then hooks the cows to computerized machines that begin the milking process. The milk is suctioned out through the clear plastic tubes and into large bottles where the exact amount of milk each cow gives is recorded. The milk then flows into a refrigerated tank until it is transported, generally once a day.

1. Katie Kinnett, the big cow, stands in front of Kinnett Dairies in Columbus.
2. The average cow consumes roughly eighteen pounds of grain, thirty pounds of silage, eight pounds of hay and twenty to twenty-five gallons of water each day. One common source of feed is grain from local breweries, which the dairy farmer mixes with hay silage, peanut hulls, peanut meal and other ingredients.
3. Cagle Dairies, which has operated in Cherokee County since 1951, is one of the last family-owned-and-operated dairies in the state.
4. The average dairy cow can produce more than six gallons of milk per day.
5. A dairy cow gives birth to one calf a year and produces milk for about the next ten months as long as she is milked regularly.
6. The modern milking process is highly mechanized and sanitized. The suction cups use the same gentle pulsing action that hand-milkers used for years.
7. Len Cagle carries an armload of yellow plastic milk jugs. Cagle Dairies was one of the first dairies in the nation to bottle milk in plastic jugs.
8. At one time cows were always milked by hand, using a gentle pulsing action that mimics the suckling of a calf.

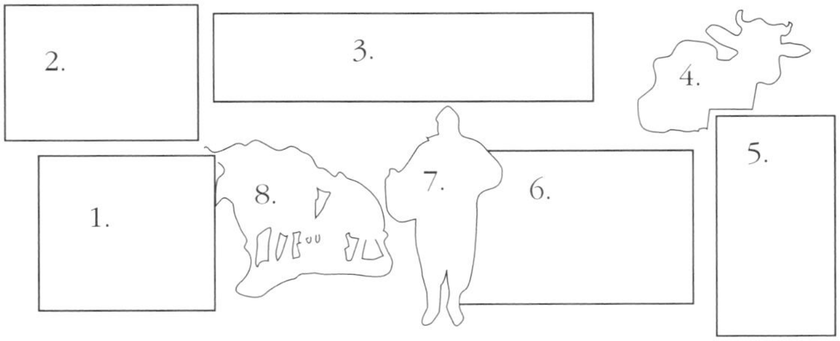

Nathalie Dupree

Along with the presidency of Jimmy Carter and the 1996 Olympics in Atlanta, Nathalie Dupree is one of the most important influences focusing national attention on the foods of the South. Her books and public television cooking shows have made "Nathalie" a household name throughout the South and across much of the United States. Her 1986 cookbook, New Southern Cooking, *published by Knopf, and the public television show of the same name, produced by Georgia Pubic Television and distributed nationally, caused Southerners and many other Americans to realize that Southern cooking was a true regional cuisine, rather than one long steamtable of collard greens, fatback, cornbread, grits and sweet tea. As part of her television series, Nathalie and her crew traveled to locations where farm products originated.*

We talked in the combination living room and kitchen of her home in Ansley Park, one of Atlanta's most fashionable intown neighborhood. Nathalie sat on a floral print sofa, her test kitchen in the background.

The idea was to break up the show. We decided nobody could take a half hour of Nathalie Dupree alone, that it needed to be broken up in some way and that we would put a two-minute information segment in each show where people would finish watching and say, "I didn't know that."

We wanted to connect people with how food is grown and show them the process, under the theory that a lot of children just see milk coming out of a bottle, or corn in a grocery store and they don't realize it is grown on a stalk. Or Brussels sprouts, how they grow. I wanted to show how it originated before it becomes an end product. Then part of it was to feature the South, to make it clear to people where the foods of the South come from. We did turnip greens, hot peppers; we did okra; we did zucchini and eggplant; we did cantaloupes, shrimp, oysters. It just kept going. You name something. Mushrooms in Georgia; we saw peanuts growing; Cordele for watermelons. Cordele was important to me.

Other people bring back diamonds and jewels and furs. What I do is load up the car or plane with cantaloupes and watermelons and zucchini and eggplants and corn and flour and cornmeal and all the things I saw produced and bring them back. The reality of the matter is that when you taste something that has been picked that day and bring it home, when you taste it, even when its several days older, it just tastes better.

One of the things that helped Southern cooking was the affluence prior to the Civil War and the poverty after. The affluence gave us a broad base and a memory of good food. After the war we didn't have the kind of distribution system that the North had, so consequently we had to eat what we grew. You didn't have the cash money to pay for turnip greens. If you didn't grow them yourself, you went without. Look at fried green tomatoes. I mean we learned that we had to do something with those green tomatoes. It takes poverty. When you're poor you learn to do the best with what you have.

The weather helped. We have a longer growing season. You can do two crops, sometimes three. You can't get a second crop in a lot of places.

I do think our hospitable nature added to it. I don't want to say Minnesota isn't hospitable. But at the same time I think our natural gregariousness and our never-meet-a-stranger—in a sense feeling the obligation for others' welfare. That was a part of it.

Southern food was always fresh. I never subscribed to that thing that it's fresher now.

Southern food was always fresh. Because you had your own garden. We always ate primarily vegetables in the south. We were practically a vegetarian society. So everybody's just going back now to the way Southerners have always cooked. They're even arguing that vegetables can be cooked a long time as long as you eat their water, their liquid, their "pot likker" so you haven't lost any nutrition. There was a time when we were told that the best thing to do about vegetables was to blanch them because cooking for a long time broke down the nutrients, but that's been proven not true. A whole bunch of stuff was done naturally in the South. Saving all the liquids that the greens were cooked in. That certainly makes sense.

Southern cooking is primarily home cooking, not chef's art. It certainly ain't "nouvelle" or precious. It's just good food, fit for savoring, not simply pretty to look at. The foods of the South for generations were meant to nourish hardworking families as they came together at mealtimes. Foods were always served family style in big bowls at the table. I've never had a plated meal in a Southern home, except in the kitchen when you could go back to the pot for refills. Perhaps that's a poor people's way to avoid looking stingy. We wanted to make a show of abundance and served a number of vegetables.

Nathalie on...

Collards: Collards are a very common Southern green. Unlike some turnip greens, collards have no root vegetable. They are related to cabbage and kale. A very old vegetable, probably with African origins, they are fleshy and have a little "bite" to them. The silver-green leaves grow large and are thicker than turnip greens. They should be well washed and the stems, ribs and thick center veins removed before cooking. When cooked in the traditional way, they have an affinity for hot pepper sauce. Since turnip greens and collards are considered antidotes for indigestion, it is no wonder Southerners always serve them on New Year's Day. You can often substitute collards for turnip greens in recipes.

Grits: Grits in their purest form are just corn ground into grist, or "grits." However, in some varieties of grits the bran and germ have been removed. In the past, grits had to be prewashed and soaked, but now, with the packaged variety, all you have to do is boil the grits in liquid for a shorter time. You must take care to stir frequently to avoid scorching. Southerners have grits as standard breakfast fare, served with bacon, ham sausage, eggs and biscuits. Grits are also a good accompaniment for fried fish and may be served as a side dish and a substitute for rice or potatoes at any meal. Leftover grits are often pressed into a tall glass, chilled, then cut into patties, dipped into cracker or corn meal, and fried in hot fat. Grits are never served as a cereal with sugar and cream. They are traditionally eaten with a pat of butter melting on top. Grits come in many different versions, each varies slightly as to the amount of liquid and cooking time needed. There are speckled grits, regular grits, quick grits and instant grits, for instance. I never seem to have the right kind of grits on hand for the recipe I'm doing, so I've adapted the recipes to the grits on hand by following the package directions for cooking them, substituting liquid amounts and time for cooking. I also cook my grits in liquids other than water—whipping cream, chicken stock, yogurt, or any liquid that complements the occasion.

Turnip Greens: Some turnip greens are attached to the round turnip that is eaten as a vegetable, while some greens are grown only for the leaf. Both varieties are cooked the same way. The leaves are a deep green color and curly. They should be well washed because they grow in sandy soil. Always stem and remove the ribs and large veins before cooking. The traditional method calls for cooking them with fatback for a long time and the odor is very strong. I cook my turnip greens a shorter time, blanching them first for some recipes.

Nathalie's Favorite Recipes for Grits and Greens

Greens and Pot Likker, Old Style

Both collard and turnip greens were traditionally cooked in this manner. They have always been an important stable and source of calcium in out diets. And, since they like poor soil, they're often found growing along side a road or in a hilly, rocky place where nothing else will grow.

4 pounds turnip or collard greens, stemmed
Salt
¼ pound fatback (salt pork) or streak-o-lean
Freshly ground black pepper

Rinse the greens thoroughly several times, then put them in a large pot of boiling water and boil for 2 minutes. Drain, discarding the water to remove the bitter taste. Fill the pot again with water and bring to the boil. Place the greens back in the pot. Cut into the fatback in several places without slicing it into pieces, and add to the pot. Bring to the boil, cover, turn down to a simmer, and cook 2-3 hours. Taste and add salt and pepper as desired. Serve greens in their juices or serve "potlikker" separately as a soup with cornbread.

Stir-Fried Collards, Chicken Breasts and Peanuts

You may decide to change the mood and flavor of this completely by adding a slice of ginger the size of a quarter, chopped and 2 tablespoons of soy sauce rather than the Hot Sauce. It's and easy and healthful supper!

1 pound collards or turnip greens, washed, stemmed and sliced
1 or 2 chicken or vegetable bouillon cubes
3 tablespoons peanut oil
⅓ cup chopped roasted peanuts
4 chicken breasts halves, boned
2 tablespoons Hot Sauce or Tabasco
1 tablespoon butter

Place the greens in a large pot of boiling water with the bouillon cubes. Boil for 5 minutes, then drain. Meanwhile, cut the chicken breasts into 1-inch pieces. Heat the peanut oil in a large frying pan and add the chicken breasts. Toss over medium heat for 3-5 minutes,until nearly done. Add the greens and Hot Sauce or Tabasco and toss until the greens are heated through and coated with the juices of the chicken and the Hot Sauce or Tabasco. In a separate pan, melt the butter and stir in the peanuts. Sprinkle over the chicken and greens before serving.

Grits with Cream and Cheese

Many people have had grits only for breakfast with butter, unless they live here where grits are eaten at all times and for all meals. This recipe is for dinner and is a very special dish you'll always remember.

½ cup quick grits
2-3 tablespoons butter
Freshly ground white pepper
2 cups heavy cream
Salt
½ cup freshly grated Parmesan, Swiss, or Monterey jack cheese

Place the grits and cream in a heavy saucepan, stirring. Cook the grits according to package directions, substituting cream for water. Stir occasionally, being careful they don't burn. If grits begin to separate and turn lumpy, add water to keep them creamy. Remove from the heat, taste, add the butter and salt and pepper to taste, then stir in the cheese. May be made ahead and reheated over low heat or in a microwave.

Fried Spicy Cheese Grits Pieces

This is a good use for leftover grits, and can be eaten like bread, as a snack, first course, or side dish. It's easy to make the base ahead and reheat later the same day.

2 cups grits, cooked
⅔ cup grated extra-sharp Cheddar or Monterey jack cheese
Salt to taste
4 tablespoons bacon drippings or peanut oil
1 cup bread crumbs
3 cloves garlic, chopped
Freshly ground black pepper to taste
1 hot pepper, finely chopped
1 tablespoon Hot Sauce or Tabasco
1 egg, lightly beaten

Butter an 8-inch square pan and refrigerate or freeze until cold. Reheat the grits and add garlic and cheese. Taste and add the pepper, hot pepper, salt, and Hot Sauce or Tabasco. Spread the grits in the buttered pan and place in the freezer for 30 minutes, or refrigerate overnight until solid. When ready to eat, heat the drippings or oil in a large, heavy frying pan. Cut the cold grits into squares. Dip the squares into the egg, then coat with bread crumbs, and fry until crisp on each side, 3-4 minutes.

PREACHERS AND SUNDAY DINNER

Dr. John Burrison, professor of English at Georgia State University, estimates there are dozens of stories involving preachers and chicken, but he selected the best of the bunch for his book *Storytellers: Folktales and Legends from the South*. This story was told by Don Buchanan of Decatur, who heard it from his father, a Baptist minister:

Once there was this preacher who loved fried chicken, as all preachers are supposed to love fried chicken. And he was invited to eat at the house of one of his parishioners one Sunday. After church he made his way through the country to this house, and it so happened, as he was crossing this particular creek, right in the middle of the bridge he stumbled and he lost his false teeth, and they fell in the creek.

Well, 'course he couldn't eat, but he couldn't turn down this invitation either, so he went on to the house. And, as they ate dinner, he ate what he could eat – mash potatoes an' things that weren't so hard to chew – but he didn't touch the fried chicken. Well, he had a great reputation for eating fried chicken, and so, of course, everybody at the table was amazed and couldn't understand why he wasn't eating any fried chicken. So finally they asked him. And he said, "Well, I just have to tell you the truth. I lost my teeth goin' across the creek down here, an' I just can't eat any."

Well, he no sooner got the words out of his mouth than a little boy 'bout twelve years old jumped up from the table, grabbed a chicken leg from off the platter, got him a piece of string, and went out the door.

cotton gin (6) represents a milestone in American agriculture (see page 65). The 110-horsepower, steam-powered 1898 Lummis gin, complete with duct, elevator, feeder, gin stand, condenser and cotton press in a two-story building, dramatically illustrates a typical gin house from the time. Still operational, the gin makes five hundred-pound bales most weekdays in October.

The 1882 Methodist church (7) represents what was an integral part of a rural settlement. It has its original pulpit, pews and railings and window panes of hand-poured glass. In the circa 1895 school house (8) from Ty Ty, an interpreter in long dress, old-fashioned hat and bonnet describes life for children in the late 1800s. All ages attended the one-room structure an average of six months of the year, arranged around the farm calendar year; classes began after harvest and ended before planting. Beyond a small creek is the circa 1870 traditional farmstead (9). With bricks scarce, the chimney consists of sticks chinked with mud. The wide overhang of the roof protects the chimney from rain. The blocks underneath the house protect it from rotting, a risk in the region because the water table remains so high. Inside the kitchen-dining room, separated by a walkway to keep the kitchen fire and heat out, a woman shells peas for a real dinner she plans to cook. Period furnishings fill the house, like a corn husk broom propped against the porch. Outside, corn and other staples grow on in a large garden, harvested in September by mule.

Offering cool breezes and shade in summer, a breezeway connects the rooms in the 1896 Gibbs farm house (10), part of the Agrirama's progressive farmstead area. The farm house incorporates other modern elements, like turned porch rails, fancy bracket work and a multicolor paint scheme. Yet, despite such luxuries, most rooms served as work areas in the day and sleeping quarters at night. Rows of cotton, cane and heirloom vegetables and greens grow on a small plot outside.

The cane mill (11) operates most weekdays in November. A mule powers the mill, which crushes stalks fed between two rollers, sending the cane juice into a waiting barrel. The staff boils most down into a thick sweet syrup or brown sugar, available along with the cane juice at the country store. The adjacent smokehouse stored pork cured by salt or smoke. Hogs were butchered in the cooler months, salted in a trough, then laid on pine boughs to cool and dry a month before winding up in the smokehouse. The 1889 reconstructed barn (12) houses equipment, animals and feed. The seed storage (13), relocated from Hat, used to house newly picked cotton seed before it headed to the gin.

The 1877 miller's house (14) and the 1879 gristmill (15) were important community centers in early Georgia settlements. Farmers trekked for miles to go to the mill to grind grain, saw timber, hull rice or gin cotton. They also caught up on the local news or fished in the mill pond while they waited their turn. Before the 1880s, most mills used running water from a nearby stream to power its gears and machinery. Inside the mill, two grinding flint stones crush corn into grits and meal. Like most, these stones probably came from Germany or France, brought by skilled European millers. At the Agrirama a miller works most days. He releases water from the small reservoir pond, which moves the gears and massive stones to grind the corn. Signs advertise meal or grits, two-pound bags for $2.00, five-pound for $3.50.

The narrow gauge logging tram (16) is an example of a very common steam engine utilized by medium or large lumbering operations throughout the region.

Steam replaced water for heavy jobs as the agriculture in South Georgia evolved from small farms to large timber and turpentining operations beginning in the early twentieth century. Whining, grinding metal and bellowing, whistling steam often announce the open sawmill shed (17), where sweating sawyers cut timber used at the Agrirama. The imposing 25-horsepower Deloach circular saw can cut up to ten thousand board feet a day. The operation is portable. Sawmills frequently had to pick up and move after exhausting the local timber supply. Starting in the Carolinas, they slowly migrated west or south over decades in search of virgin stands in Georgia, Alabama and Florida.

A turpentine still stands to the right of the sawmill (18). Like timber, the turpentine or naval store industry, so called because many of the rosin and sap products from pine trees were used

'Bout half an hour later he came back in, and he had the teeth in his hand. An' the preacher said, "How in the world did you get those teeth out of the creek?"

He said, "Well, I just took this chicken leg and tied the string on it and dipped it down in the water, and those teeth bit right on it!"

Captain Tift

Tifton boasts the state's leading crop and livestock research complex, some of the most productive fields and one of the richest farming heritages in Georgia. But the city may never have risen had not a seafarer from Mystic, Connecticut, eyed the land. Growing up the son of a merchant who often traded in southern cities, Henry Harding Tift drifted South. He became an engineer, running steam ships along the coast from Apalachicola to Key West and paddle-wheelers up the Chattahoochee and Flint from Apalachicola all the way to Albany, where his Uncle Nelson Tift had a general store and thousands of acres of pecans.

He joined his uncle in Albany in 1870 and two years later bought five thousand acres, forty miles to the east. His trained seaman's eye knew good mast material; and from the long leaf yellow pine, used for ship siding by the shipyards of New England, "the Captain" made a fortune. He named his sawmill village Lena, but most referred to the settlement as Tift's Town. It is said that a sawmill worker, who wanted to honor Captain Tift, climbed a pine tree and nailed a placard with the name, Tifton, a contraction of "Tift's Town." In 1905, the legislature followed suit, naming the county Tift, another honor for the Captain.

Tift County was such a rich land that agriculture soon superseded sawmilling as the main industry. In 1906 when South Georgia communities battled to secure the new coastal plain experiment station promised by the state, Tift took twenty-five thousand dollars out of pocket to ensure his city would get it. By his death in 1922, the Captain had amassed sixty-five thousand acres and a net worth of $7 million.

on ships, arrived in South Georgia in the 1870s. Once a year in April the Agrirama makes turpentine in the still, a ten-foot high vat that resembles a giant hot tub. Adjacent to the still, the cooper shed served as the working quarters for the cooper, or wooden barrel-maker.

Most of the remaining buildings, demonstrating life in the city, stand on a nearby town square. Inside the circa 1888 print shop (19), a man dressed as a nineteenth-century printing clerk hand presses the Whitlock Flatbed press to make museum guides and the Georgia Recorder, a nostalgic newspaper with articles and classified ads from the turn of the century. Farmers took their plowshares, wagon wheels and horseshoes for mending to the circa 1900 blacksmith shop (20). The train depot (21), built between 1895 and 1905 in Montezuma, is an example of an early prefabricated building. All the studs, eaves and shingles came assembled and were shipped along the line.

The 1889 commissary or company store (22) was where laborers from the turpentine or sawmill camps bought essentials. Any item which was purchased was entered in the store ledger as a debit and tallied against the laborer's wages. The variety works (23), which is under construction, was a woodworking shop that produced a variety of wood items for the community, such as doors, sashes, blinds, decorative trim and molding, as well as cabinet work and furniture. The drug store (24) serves old-fashioned sodas and homemade snacks from a long countertop. In the same storefront to the right, the general store houses many interesting agricultural artifacts. An old iron cream separator remains by the door. Hand-held reapers hang from the ceiling. Three mule yokes hang on a wall in a row. Nearby sits a stately oak-wood bin, tiny drawers separating about one hundred varieties of seed. Two women in the back sell piping hot corn bread made from grits ground on site.

A fraternal hall building, such as the 1909 Masonic Hall (25), was among the first structures built in a small town, and a doctor's office (26) was vital to the settlement and growth of a rural community. The Tift-Willingham House (27), built in 1887 by Captain Henry Tift (see sidebar this page), represents an upper-class dwelling in a developing rural town.

HERITAGE FARM
GENERAL COFFEE STATE PARK

THE AGRICULTURAL HISTORY OF SOUTH GEORGIA IS VERY DIFFERENT from other parts of the state. No rich planters with slave estates lived in these counties. The farmers who worked this soil lived off their vegetable crops and sold tobacco and cotton to get money to buy clothes and other necessities. Many farm families did well to have a roof over their heads.

The harsh realities of this South Georgia farm life is interpreted at the Heritage Farm, General Coffee State Park's living history museum. About a dozen structures make up the farm. Start a self-guided tour at the Relihan Cabin (1), built by a local sheriff in 1933. The front room, filled with century-old antiques, contains a quilting frame used by a local sewing group. Visitors are encouraged to try their hand.

The circa 1828 Meeks Cabin (2), a hand-hewn log home, is one of the oldest standing in South Georgia and has virtually all the original lumber. Up to eleven family members at a time lived until 1976 in the house with its two rooms and one loft. The building contains no chink or mortar between its walls. A broom made of thin gallberry branches rests against the door, used to sweep the dirt around the house. The yard of a well-kept home had no grass—a haven for biting bugs in the semi-tropical climate. The interior, which visitors can enter only during a regular tour or special event, retains its original, simple character. On a wooden table sits a worn dough bowl, the heart of the old Southern kitchen, used to make biscuits and bread; and gourds, which early Georgians learned from the Indians made excellent storage containers for dried foods. An iron swing arm, made on-site by a blacksmith, swivels over the fireplace. The only reading material rural Georgians kept in their homes, if they could afford it, was the Bible.

After the smokehouse (3) and outhouse comes the shed with old farm equipment (4), including a crop duster, crop sprayer, middle buster, fertilizer distributor, one row stalk cutter, one row turning plow and cane mill. The one row planter could plant two different seeds at different intervals, for

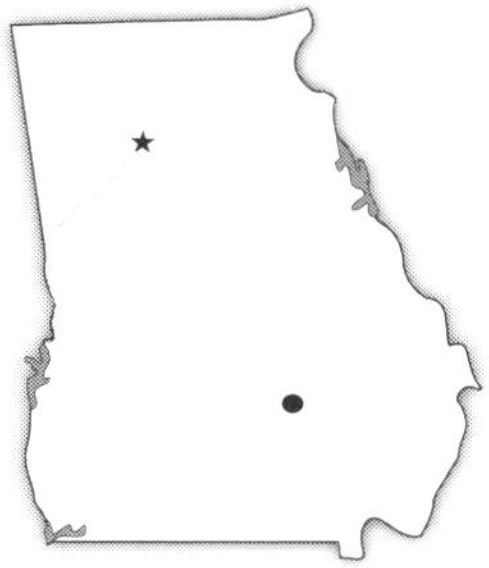

HERITAGE FARM

Heritage is an agricultural living history museum located within the boundaries of the 1,510-acre General Coffee State Park in Southeast Georgia.

Facilities at State Park: 51 tent, trailer and RV sites; 5 rental cottages; winterized group shelter, 6 picnic shelters; 4-acre lake, swimming pool and bath house; nature preserve; heritage farm, archery range; 15-mile nature trail.

Days/Hrs.: Park: daily, 7am-10pm. Office: daily, 8am-5pm.

Fees: Parking fee $2. All state parks are free.

Directions: From Douglas, go 6 miles east on GA 32. The entrance is on the left.

More Information: General Coffee State Park, 46 John Coffee Road, Nicholls, GA 31554; 912/384-7082.

THIRTY ACRES AND TWO MULES
From *A Childhood: The Biography of a Place* by Harry Crews ...

The farm had sixty acres in cultivation, and so Luther Carter furnished Uncle John and daddy each a mule. Thirty acres was as much as one man and one mule could tend, and even then they had to step smart from first sun to last to do it. They had no cows or hogs and no smokehouse, and that first year they lived—as we did for much of my childhood—on fatback, grits, tea without ice, and biscuits made from flour and water and lard.

1. Relihan Cabin, 1933
2. Meeks Log Cabin
3. Smokehouse
4. Old farm equipment display
5. Blacksmith Shop
6. Turpentine Industry display
7. Moonshine Still
8. Sugar cane syrup kettle and mill
9. 100-year old tobacco barn
10. Equipment storage barn

example, velvet beans every twelve feet and corn every one. In the old days, farmers grew corn, then hogged out the fields when they harvested, letting the pigs or cows loose to forage for beans. On the one-row riding cultivator, a farmer used foot levers to turn and guide mules as he drove them with the reigns in his hands. On the hay rake, one of the most common antique agricultural machines seen rusting in fields all over Georgia, farmers worked their feet to raise the line of curved rakes, dumping a bale of collected hay on the ground.

In the blacksmith shop (5), craftsmen perform their trade on open house days, making nails, horseshoes and repairing metal tools. The naval store display (6) offers thorough interpretations of old-fashioned turpentine and rosin making, a major industry in South Georgia a century ago. Besides the display models of small pails underneath cuts in tree trunks to catch sap, pines a few feet away outside show well-preserved, "cat-face" scars, which resemble cat whiskers, from where they were tapped years ago. Nearby a syrup shed (8) shows where cane juices were boiled down in a large cauldron to make sugar cane syrup. The Kirkland tobacco barn (9), over one hundred years old, housed tobacco, hung on sticks from the rafters. Two fireplaces heated and cured the gold leaf, which today remains an important cash crop in South Georgia. The center floor of the corn crib and pen, just past the tobacco barn, was elevated to keep out dampness. The sides contain a shelter for the animals, a tool storage bin and a long log trough used to water the horse and wash the laundry—and possibly the children.

Heritage Farm plants tobacco and other traditional crops like corn, cotton and sugar cane around the village. It also keeps goats, pigs, sheep, mules and birds, such as donimicker hens, roosters, peacocks and turkeys, which often venture from the chicken coop and hen house, pecking at loose corn and other morsels around the village. Guests can rent the historic Burnam Cottage, a nineteenth-century farm cabin built with gun portholes for aiming rifles at attacking Indians, active in South Georgia during the 1830s. The log dwelling, back on the main road heading toward the park entrance contains antebellum furnishings, three bedrooms and modern conveniences.

Dairy Products

No one knows when people first used animal milk for food. However, the people of ancient Babylon, Egypt and India raised dairy cattle as early as 4000 BC Norwegian Vikings may have brought the first cattle to the Americas in the early 1000s. Historians are certain that Columbus brought cattle on his second voyage to America in 1493. English colonists brought dairy cows to Jamestown in 1611, helping to end terrible starvation. In the late 1600s, the colonists began feeding grain and hay to cattle during the winter so that the cows could give milk all year, rather than just the warm months when they fed in open pastures. The family cow was common during those times, and as pioneers moved west, almost every family traveled with a covered wagon and a cow—their mobile food source. When local laws prohibited cows within city limits, rural farmers increased their herds and established dairy businesses.

The commercial dairy and creamery industry began in Georgia in the 1930s. The number of dairy farms have declined over the last several years, but the amount of milk produced per cow has increased greatly. Today, Georgia is home to 437 dairy farms and one hundred thousand dairy cows, producing more than 1.5 billion pounds of raw milk.

Buyer's Guide to Milk

When selecting milk, examine containers for leaks and other damage. Only purchase milk products that are in perfect condition.

Check sell-by dates on milk. If stored properly, milk will usually stay fresh for seven days past the sell-by date.

Pick up milk just before checking out of the supermarket so it stays as cold as possible.

Take milk home after purchase and refrigerate immediately in the coldest part of the refrigerator.

Don't let milk remain at room temperature any longer than necessary. Pour only what milk is needed and return the rest to the refrigerator.

Exposure to light destroys milk's flavor and riboflavin.

Freezing affects the quality of milk and isn't recommended.

Store canned milk in a cool, dry place. Once canned milk is opened, pour into a clean container; cover and refrigerate.

Holiday Cheese Ring

A memorable mix of onion, red pepper and strawberry flavors

- 4 cups shredded extra sharp Cheddar cheese
- 4 cups shredded medium Cheddar cheese
- 1 small onion, grated
- 1 cup mayonnaise
- 1 teaspoon red pepper
- 1 cup chopped pecans, divided
- Strawberry preserves

Combine first 5 ingredients, mixing well. Sprinkle ¼ cup pecans into a greased 7-cup ring mold* and press cheese mixture into mold; chill until firm. Unmold onto platter and pat remaining pecans into cheese ring. Spread strawberry preserves on top of ring. Serve with crackers. Yields 6 cups.

*If you do not have a ring mold, use a spring-form pan with a custard cup placed in the center to form a ring. Cheese ring unmolds very easily from this.

Marianna Pedrick
Savannah, Georgia

Hawaiian Loaf

Real butter adds to this unforgettable taste!

- 1 cup butter
- 2 cups sugar
- 4 eggs
- 1 cup mashed ripe banana
- 4 cups all-purpose flour
- 2 teaspoons baking powder
- 1 teaspoon baking soda
- ¾ teaspoon salt
- 1 20-ounce can undrained crushed pineapple
- 1 cup flaked coconut

Preheat oven to 350°. In medium bowl, beat butter with electric mixer until light and fluffy; gradually beat in sugar until creamy. Add eggs and beat well. Stir in mashed banana. In another medium bowl, combine the dry ingredients. Add to butter mixture, mixing just until smooth. Fold in pineapple and coconut. Spoon batter into 2 greased and floured 9x5-inch loaf pans. Bake until tooth pick inserted comes out clean. Bake 60 to 70 minutes. Each loaf yields 10 slices.

Estelle Neighbors
Hoganville, Georgia

Hint: This is a delicious quickbread! For a lower calorie version, use these suggestions: an egg substitute, ½ cup coconut, ½ cup butter and ½ cup applesauce.

Baking Powder Biscuits

Every cook needs a good biscuit recipe!

- 2 cups sifted all-purpose flour
- 2 teaspoons baking powder
- ½ teaspoon salt
- ⅓ cup shortening
- ¾ cup milk

Preheat oven to 450°. Sift dry ingredients into a bowl; cut in the shortening until mixture resembles coarse crumbs. Make a well; add milk all at once. Stir quickly with fork just until dough follows fork around the bowl. Turn onto lightly floured surface. (Dough should be soft.) Knead gently 10 to 12 strokes. Roll or pat dough ½-inch thick. Dip 2½-inch biscuit cutter in flour; cut dough straight down. Bake on ungreased baking sheet for 12 minutes. Yields 10 biscuits.

Agriculture Test Kitchen

Hot Tomato Pan Bread

This unusual bread is easy to prepare

- ⅔ cup self-rising flour
- ¾ cup milk
- ¼ cup olive oil
- 1 4-ounce container liquid egg product
- 1 10-ounce can of diced tomatoes with green chilies
- Vegetable cooking spray

Preheat oven to 350°. In large bowl, combine all ingredients; mix until well-blended. Pour batter into preheated 9-inch cake pan coated with vegetable spray. Bake for 30 minutes or until bread tests done with wooden pick. Remove from pan and cool on a wire rack. Serve warm. Yields 10 servings.

Lewis Holladay
Concord, Georgia

Hint: This is a tasty, quick bread containing a moderate amount of fat. To reduce calories and fat, substitute skim milk and reduce oil to 2 tablespoons. Result: One serving of bread contains 134 calories and 3.5g fat (23% of calories).

Boarding House Biscuits

On any fine day in Savannah, the line spills out onto Jones Street in front of Mrs. Wilkes's Boarding House, where people are waiting to sample the fine southern food from this well-known Savannah inn. From her own cookbook, *Famous Recipes from Mrs. Wilkes' Boarding House*, Sema Wilkes shares the recipe for her famous biscuits.

Mrs. Wilkes sifts 2 cups of self-rising flour and ½ teaspoon of baking powder into a bowl. Next, she cuts in 1 tablespoon of shortening and 2 tablespoons of unmelted margarine until the mixture resembles coarse corn meal. She fills a measuring cup with ⅓ cup buttermilk, ⅓ cup whole milk and enough water to make ¾ cup of liquid. She makes a well in the center of the dry flour and pours in the liquid. With her hands, she mixes the ingredients lightly and quickly to form dough that is moist enough to leave the sides of the bowl. She then turns the dough onto a lightly floured surface. To knead the dough, she picks it up by its sides, pulling the dough towards her, and presses down with the palms of her hands, pushing the dough away. She repeats this kneading action 6 or 7 times, working the dough into a large ball and dipping her fingers into dry flour frequently to keep them dry. After the dough is kneaded, she pinches off portions of it to make about 16 biscuits. She places these on a well-greased pan and presses them lightly to make the biscuits appear flat. Sema Wilkes then bakes the biscuits for 12 to 15 minutes in a 450° preheated oven and serves them to her guests.

VARIETIES OF MILK

Whole milk must contain at least 3.25 percent milkfat and at least 8.25 percent milk solids, not fat.

Reduced-fat milk has a milk fat content of 2 percent.

Low-fat milk has had enough fat removed to reduce milkfat content to 0.5, 1 or 1.5 percent. All contain at least 8.25 percent milk solids, not fat. Because vitamin A is removed with milkfat, it's added to low-fat and reduced fat milk.

Skim milk, also called non-fat or fat-free milk, has a fat content of less than 0.5 percent. It must contain at least 8.25 percent milk solids, not fat, and be fortified with vitamin A.

Chocolate milk is made by adding chocolate or cocoa and sweetener to whole or lowfat milk.

Evaporated milk is made by evaporating enough water from whole milk to reduce the volume by half. It contains at least 7.25 percent milkfat and 25.5 percent milk solids.

Evaporated skim milk is concentrated, vitamins A and D fortified skim milk, containing up to 0.5 percent milkfat and at least 20 percent milk solids.

Sweetened condensed milk is a canned milk concentrate (whole or skim) with a sweetener added.

Eggnog is a mixture of milk, eggs, sugar and cream. It may include flavorings like rum extract, vanilla and nutmeg.

Cultured buttermilk is made by adding a bacterial culture to milk, most often skim. Salt is added for flavor.

ROASTED GARLIC POTATO SOUP

This soup is a tasty way to get the health benefits of garlic

- 5 whole garlic heads (or bulbs)
- ½ pound bacon, diced
- 1 cup diced onion
- 1 cup diced carrot
- 2 garlic cloves, minced
- 6 cups diced baking potato (about 2 pounds)
- 4 cups chicken broth
- ½ teaspoon salt
- ¼ teaspoon pepper
- 1 bay leaf
- 1 cup 2% milk
- ¼ cup chopped fresh parsley

Preheat oven to 350°. Remove white papery skin from each garlic head (do not peel or separate cloves). Wrap each head separately in aluminum foil. Bake for 1 hour. Let cool for 10 minutes. Separate cloves and squeeze ¼ cup garlic pulp; discard the skins.

Cook bacon in a large saucepan over medium-high heat until crisp. Discard all but 1½ tablespoons of bacon grease. Add onion, carrot, minced garlic and sauté 5 minutes. Add potato, broth, salt, pepper and bay leaf; bring to a boil. Cover; reduce heat and simmer 20 minutes or until potatoes are tender; remove bay leaf.

In food processor or blender, combine garlic pulp and 2 cups potato mixture; process until smooth. Return purée to pan; stir in milk and cook over low heat until thoroughly heated. Remove from heat and stir in chopped parsley. Yields 10 servings.

Shannon Souvinette
Forest Park, Georgia

Hint: To reduce the fat and cholesterol in this recipe, reduce the amount of bacon to 3 slices. Result: Each serving contains 194 calories, 6g fat and 10mg cholesterol.

BANANA BREAKFAST BOOSTER

Start the day with this healthy drink

- 3 ripe bananas
- 3 cups cold milk
- 3 tablespoons honey
- 1 teaspoon vanilla extract

Peel and slice bananas. Put in blender container. Add milk, honey and vanilla. Blend and mix just until smooth and frothy. Serve immediately. Yields 4 servings.

Southeast United Dairy Industry Association, Inc.

Veggie Pizza

Everyone will love this healthy, vegetarian pizza

1	12-inch thin prepared pizza crust
½	cup prepared pizza sauce
1	cup thinly sliced mushrooms
1	small zucchini (about 4 ounces), thinly sliced
1	medium green or red bell pepper, cut into thin strips
2	cups (8 ounces) shredded part-skim mozzarella cheese
2	tablespoons grated Parmesan cheese
½	teaspoon basil leaves
½	teaspoon oregano leaves

Preheat oven to 400°. Place pizza crust on baking sheet or pizza pan. Spread pizza sauce on crust to within ½ inch of edge. Arrange vegetables over sauce. Combine mozzarella, Parmesan and seasonings. Sprinkle over vegetables. Bake 15 to 20 minutes or until cheese has melted and crust is crisp. To serve, cut pizza into 8 wedges. Yields 1 12-inch pizza, or 8 servings.

Southeast United Dairy Industry Association, Inc.

Pineapple Au Gratin

Sharp Cheddar can't be beat!

2	20-ounce cans crushed pineapple, drained
2	cups grated sharp Cheddar cheese
1	cup sugar
6	tablespoons all-purpose flour
1	cup buttery rich cracker crumbs
½	cup margarine, melted

Preheat oven to 350°. Combine pineapple and cheese. In a separate bowl, combine sugar and flour; stir into pineapple mixture. Pour into a 2-quart casserole; top with cracker crumbs. Pour melted margarine on top. Bake for 30 minutes. Yields 6 servings.

Mary Kempton
Atlanta, Georgia

Border Collies

One of the most important members of a dairy farm work force is the border collie. These dogs run, walk, circle, nip—anything to herd livestock. Border collies have perfected their collecting skills over hundreds of years on the border of England and Scotland, thus giving them their name. The instinct runs so deep that the dogs will attempt to herd most anything—cattle, sheep, chickens, children and even bees.

Two collies can do the equivalent of ten men when gathering up a pasture of cows or sheep to move to another field, truck or holding pen. Fifty years ago only a handful of Georgia farmers had purebred border collies; today, an estimated five hundred Georgia farmers have border collies, which range in price from five hundred dollars for a puppy to four thousand dollars for a fully trained dog.

Three major stock dog competitions in Georgia showcase the talents of border collies and other livestock breeds. Patterned after the original dog trials in England, the events draw hundreds of spectators each year. Directed by the call and whistle of their handlers, the dogs corral livestock, usually sheep, through a complex maze of fences, rings and posts, as if pushing balls through a field of croquet gates.

Mule, good looker and hard worker; eats well. $65. T. L. Osiecki, Atlanta, Box 224 (Fairburn Rd) (Adamsville Dist.)

Horses and Mules For Sale, Market Bulletin, *August 16, 1944*

COOPERATIVE EXTENSION SERVICE

"Putting Knowledge to Work" is the motto of the University of Georgia Cooperative Extension Service, and that is exactly what it does—whether the knowledge needed concerns soil and water quality, pesticide use, food safety, financial stability or parenting and building strong relationships. Through a unique partnership with the U.S. Department of Agriculture, the state of Georgia and virtually every county government in the state, the University of Georgia Cooperative Extension Service has offered a wealth of information to farmers and the general public alike since 1914.

An outgrowth of the federally supported agricultural experiment stations (see page 207), cooperative extension services were set up across the country to pass along unbiased, research-based information from experiment stations and public agricultural schools to farmers. In Georgia, extension agent offices are administered by the University of Georgia and are located in every county except Chattanooga County (which consists primarily of Fort Benning). Backed up by specialists and a network of resources, county agricultural extension agents (see sidebar next page) are the public officials from the extension offices who provide the one-on-one contact with farmers and the public.

ZUCCHINI CASSEROLE

Milk, cheese and butter add richness to this casserole!

- 3 cups sliced cooked zucchini or yellow squash (preferably a mixture of both for color)
- 2 eggs
- 2 cups seasoned cornbread crumbs
- 1 cup milk
- 1 cup grated Cheddar cheese
- 1 cup chopped onions
- 6 tablespoons (¾ stick) butter, softened
- 1 teaspoon salt
- ¼ teaspoon pepper
- ½ teaspoon celery salt

Preheat oven to 375°. In a large bowl, mix all ingredients thoroughly. Bake in 11x7-inch baking dish for 40 minutes. Yields 8 servings.

Glenda Reyes
Stone Mountain, Georgia

Hint: To reduce calories, fat and sodium, reduce butter to 4 tablespoons, substitute 2 egg whites for 1 egg, reduce cheese to ½ cup and eliminate 1 teaspoon salt. Result: One serving contains 174 calories, 9.2g fat, 50mg cholesterol and 551mg sodium.

CREAM OF BROCCOLI VEGGIE SOUP

Easy to prepare and a great source of calcium!

- 1 cup chopped celery
- 1 cup chopped onion
- 1 10-ounce package frozen chopped broccoli
- 1 10.75-ounce can condensed chicken broth
- 1 cup cottage cheese
- 2 cups milk
- 2 10-ounce packages frozen mixed vegetables, cooked and drained
- ¼ teaspoon seasoned salt
- ⅛ teaspoon pepper

Combine celery, onion, frozen broccoli and chicken broth in a medium-sized saucepan. Bring to boil and cover. Reduce heat and simmer 10 minutes or until vegetables are tender. Place half the soup mixture and half the cottage cheese in blender container; cover. Blend until smooth. Pour into a 3-quart saucepan. Repeat with remaining vegetable mixture and cottage cheese. Stir in milk, cooked vegetables, seasoned salt and pepper. Heat through but do not boil. Serve immediately. Yields 8 servings.

Georgia Milk Commission

Sugarless Pink Lemonade Pie

This sugar-free pie is a perfect summertime dessert

- ½ cup graham cracker crumbs
- 2 tablespoons honey
- Vegetable cooking spray
- 1 cup evaporated skim milk
- 1 envelope unflavored gelatin
- ½ cup water
- 1 .46-ounce packet sugar-free pink lemonade drink mix
- 1 teaspoon lemon extract
- ½ teaspoon lemon peel
- 1 teaspoon vanilla extract
- 6 packets sugar substitute
- 1 cup fat-free cream cheese

Combine crumbs and honey in a small bowl, stirring well. Press crumb mixture into bottom and 1 inch up sides of a 9-inch pie plate coated with cooking spray. Bake at 350° for 5 minutes. Let cool on a wire rack.

Pour evaporated milk into a bowl and freeze until ice forms around edges. In medium saucepan, soften gelatin in water for 2 minutes. Place over medium heat until gelatin is dissolved. Remove from heat and stir in drink mix, lemon extract, lemon peel, vanilla extract, sugar substitute and cream cheese. Mix well with spoon. Chill mixture in refrigerator until gelatin begins to set (about 30 minutes).

Remove bowl of chilled evaporated milk from freezer and immediately place bowl in larger bowl of ice. Whip chilled milk until stiff peaks form, 8 to 10 minutes. Fold whipped milk into chilled gelatin mixture. Pour mixture into graham cracker pie crust. Chill pie in refrigerator for 30 minutes prior to serving. Yields 8 servings.

Nutrition Information Per Serving: Calories 135 / Protein 12.5g / Carbohydrates 17.2g / Fat 1g / Cholesterol 11mg / Fiber 0g / Calcium 142mg / Iron .5mg / Sodium 425mg

Diabetic Exchanges: 1 bread, ½ milk

"KATIE KINNETT"...THE BIG COW—COLUMBUS, GA

County Agents

Most people know of the cooperative extension service through their local contact, the county agricultural extension agent, better known as the county agent. Nearly every county in the United States has at least one agent, and these public officials fulfill a variety of job responsibilities. First and foremost, county agents help farmers. They constantly learn about the latest advances in seed varieties, fertilizers, tilling methods and mechanized equipment from the agricultural experiment stations (see page 207), then share that information with farmers through radio shows, seminars, newspaper columns and house calls to the farm.

The specific duties of each agent vary as much as the crops in their counties. A county agent in Barrow County might show farmers how to compost dead chickens; in Carroll how to sell cattle over televised markets; in Sumter how to apply a peanut fungicide; in Newton how to grow organics; and in DeKalb how to grow ornamentals.

But the county agent also serves the general public as well. County agents and their offices have hundreds of pamphlets, books and classes dealing with everything from canning and preserving foods to pruning shrubs; from communicating with children to cleaning drapes. Most handouts are free, but some books and classes have a small fee. County agents also advise 4-H organizations (see page 248) and work with local civic leaders to improve community living.

Onion Chive Muffins

Shirley Miller, Governor Zell Miller's wife, uses Georgia-grown Vidalia onions in this muffin recipe—one of her favorites.

In a small skillet over medium heat, Mrs. Miller sautés ¾ cup of chopped Vidalia onions in 1 teaspoon of vegetable oil until they are crisp-tender and then sets them aside. She then lightly spoons all-purpose flour into a 1½ cup measuring cup and levels it off. In a large bowl, she combines the flour with ¼ cup of chopped, fresh chives, 2 tablespoons of granulated sugar, 2 teaspoons of baking powder, ½ teaspoon of salt and ¼ teaspoon of baking soda. In a small bowl, Mrs. Miller combines the cooked onions, ¼ cup of buttermilk, ¼ cup of vegetable oil and 1 lightly beaten egg, mixing them together well.

Next, she adds these to the dry ingredients, stirring just until the dry ingredients are moistened. She then fills 12 greased muffin cups ¾ of the way full and places them in an oven preheated to 375°. Mrs. Miller bakes the muffins for 10 to 12 minutes or until a pick inserted in the center of one of the muffins comes out clean. She says the muffins will be very light in color. She then removes the muffins from the pan and cools them on a rack, ready for dinner to be served.

Fresh Fruit Salad

Pasta combines with fruit and yogurt for a refreshing salad!

- 8 ounces medium shell pasta
- 1 8-ounce container plain nonfat yogurt
- ¼ cup frozen orange juice concentrate, thawed
- 1 15-ounce can pineapple chunks, drained
- 1 large orange, peeled and sectioned
- 1 cup seedless red grapes, halved
- 1 cup seedless green grapes, halved
- 1 large apple, chopped
- 1 medium banana, sliced

Prepare pasta according to package directions. Rinse with cold water and drain. In a small bowl blend yogurt and orange juice concentrate. In a large bowl, combine shell pasta with fruit and mix well. Stir in yogurt mixture; toss to coat. Cover and chill thoroughly. Yields 10 servings.

Banana Pudding

This is a must-have recipe for every Southern cook

- 3 cups milk
- 1 5.1-ounce package instant vanilla pudding mix
- 1 8-ounce container sour cream
- 1 8-ounce container whipped topping
- 1 12-ounce box vanilla wafers
- 4 large bananas, peeled and sliced

In large mixing bowl, combine the milk and pudding mix and mix on low speed until it thickens. Add the sour cream and mix well, about 2 minutes. Fold the whipped topping into this mixture. Place a layer of vanilla wafers on the bottom of a 2-quart deep dish, then a layer of sliced bananas. Cover this with half of the pudding mixture. Repeat with another layer. Sprinkle some vanilla wafer crumbs on top. Refrigerate until ready to serve. Yields 6 to 8 servings.

Mrs. Howard Patterson
Chestnut Mountain, Georgia

OLD MILL AT BERRY COLLEGE, ROME—

ANATOMY OF A GRISTMILL

All along the rivers and streams of Georgia are reminders of one of the state's first industries—the mill. Sometimes only place names, like Mundy's Mill, remain. At other sites, the abandoned structure still looms over the mill town, like the cotton and grist mills in Juliette (see page 172). And still there are mills like Barker's Creek Mill and Nora's Mill Granary that still grind out corn meal and grits.

At one time all of these mills served as important community centers. Farmers traveled for miles to the nearest mill to grind grain, saw timber, hull rice or gin cotton. They fished the pond, swapped news and stories, or picked up some supplies as they waited their turn to grind their corn. On weekends and rainy days when farmers couldn't work the fields, business picked up at the mill.

Until the early twentieth century, most mills used running water from a nearby stream to power its gears and machinery. The state's hilly Piedmont or the Fall Line section of a river, where the water rushes over rock outcroppings and shoals, were ideal locations for mills.

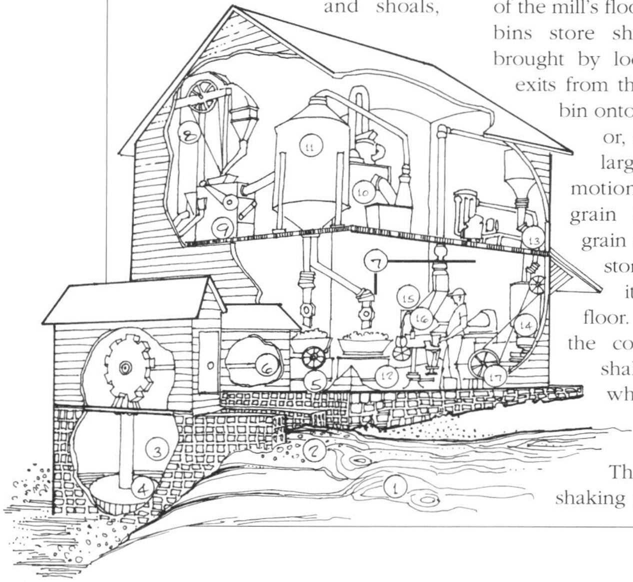

The diagram illustrates how a typical gristmill worked. To harness the river's power, a mill owner first dammed it to form a millpond (1), or reservoir, for storing water to power the mill. Water, flowing from the pond, runs over the millrace (2) and pours down into the turbine house (3), where it turns the fins on the turbine wheel (4), which activates the mill's machinery.

Next a mill worker turns a crank (5) that connects to a shaft leading to the turbine wheel that sits at the bottom of the millrace. The shaft activates machinery that opens the fins of the turbine wheel. The force of water rushing against the fins turns the wheel. The power goes via a long shaft to the turbine house to the cogwheel, whose cogs mesh with those attached to a long, horizontal shaft (6) that runs into the mill itself. The force of the falling water, thus transmitted through the initial wheels and shafts, brings the mill to life, powering a second maze of whining, creaking wheels, shafts and belts in the mill. Occupying almost one-third of the mill's floor space, two large bins store shucked corn (7), brought by local farmers. Corn exits from the bottom of each bin onto an augur conveyor, each resembling a large screw, whose motion transports the grain to a belt-driven grain elevator (8), three stories high, that lifts it to the mill's top floor. There it empties the corn into the first shaking machine (9), which shakes out large pieces of foreign matter. Then the second shaking machine (10) in a similar fashion removes smaller particles of trash.

The corn moves to a storage bin (11) on the top floor, located directly above the heart of the mill: the millstones (12), also called "rocks" by the millers, which actually grind the corn into meal. A mill might contain three pairs of stones. When in operation, one stone in each set remains stationary while the other slowly turns, grinding the corn between them. The corn, poured through an opening in the top stone of each set, is ground between the stones and channeled by grooves cut into the bottom stone into a collection bin. The distance between stones can be adjusted, which produces meal of greater or lesser fineness. The old fashioned, water powered method keeps the stones grinding at a consistent speed, preventing the corn from becoming too hot or too dry, which can spoil the flavor.

Fans blow the corn through a set of pipes to the top floor, where it goes through a sifting machine (13), which separates the chaff and bran from the good meal, which is blown back downstairs to the blender (14). Here the meal is blended into a homogeneous texture. Soda, phosphate and salt are added if the meal is to be sold as a self-rising product. From the blender, the meal goes via a conveyor belt to the scales (15) and the bagging machine (16). The bags, labeled with the mill's name, are then stacked on the floor ready for sale (17).

JULIETTE

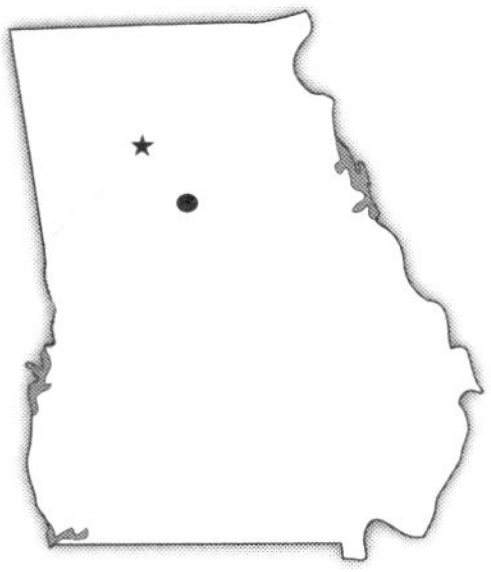

JULIETTE

This former mill town sits on the banks of the Ocmulgee River in Middle Georgia.

Facilities: Mill ruins, short street of cafes, gift shops and antique stores.

Days/Hrs.: Whistle Stop Cafe: Mon.-Sat., 8am-2pm; Sun., noon-5pm. Most businesses close by nightfall.

Directions: From Forsyth, take Exit 61 on I-75, go east 8 miles on Juliette Road, CR 271, for 8 miles. Right before the Ocmulgee River bridge turn right on McCrackin Street and park.

More Information: President Mark Goolsby, The River Club, McCrackin Street, Juliette, GA 31046; 912/994-3771. Forsyth-Monroe County Chamber of Commerce, 267 Tift College Drive, Forsyth, GA 31029; 912/994-9239. The Whistle Stop Cafe, 912/994-3670.

"I may be sitting here at the Rose Terrace Nursing Home, but in my mind I'm over at the Whistle Stop Cafe having a plate of fried green tomatoes."
Mrs. Cleo Treadgoode, June 1986

Fannie Flagg, Fried Green Tomatoes at the Whistle Stop Cafe

WHISTLE STOPS AND MILL TOWNS ALONG GEORGIA RIVERS WERE A vital part of the agricultural economy. Surrounded by farms and plantations, they were the place where the local farmers brought their cotton and grains for processing and shipping, bought their supplies and caught up on county events. All across the South, many of these towns slowly and painfully died as economics pushed people off of farms and into cities.

To visit Juliette is to visit a once-bustling place that found itself on the brink of disappearing. The best perspective from which to see how geography and man came together to produce this town is to stand on the site of the concrete ruins of the Juliette mills, looking toward the town. At your back is the Ocmulgee River, the source of power for this gigantic rock-grinding mill. The shoaled river site was perfect to harness this power. Joe Smith built the original mills and wooden dam, the first across the Ocmulgee River. Sherman's Union troops spared the site on their march through Georgia. When the Southern Railroad built a rail line by the river in 1882, a company official named McCrackin named the station after his wife, Juliette.

At the turn of the century, W. P. Glover purchased the mill and renamed it the Juliette Milling Company. Hearing of another mill in Europe with the same number of large grinding stones, he added one more set, making his the largest such mill in the world. Each stone was forty-eight inches in diameter. There were twenty pairs of them, lined in two rows. Each row had a separate water wheel that moved the gears, which in turn moved the stones that crushed the corn. Altogether the mill could grind cornmeal at the rate of three hundred bushels an hour. Glover replaced the original mill with a new building in 1904, but it burned to the ground in 1926. One year later, a new fireproof building went up, the concrete and steel ruins of today. It was a monumental, modern complex. In all, the storage bins and steel tank could hold 77,400 bushels of grain; in an hour it could process 5,000 bushels of corn, turning half into grits and half into meal. Each month forty-five to fifty railway cars of corn were brought to the mill; about seven cars of corn meal left each day. Glover also built a cotton mill directly across the river in Jones County. In September when cotton season opened, country wagons from all over came loaded with cotton. The farmers shopped in Juliette, further boosting the economy. By the 1930s, the company pretty much ran the town, whose main street stretched west of the tracks, providing cottages, electricity and water free to most of the three hundred citizens, the majority of whom worked at the mills.

Despite its technological advancements, the mill still relied on the river's natural flow to stone-grind meal the traditional way, a fact underscored during the area's 1954 drought. The wheels didn't turn for two months. A year later, Martha White Mills acquired the Juliette landmark; but eventually, the train left town and the mills closed. After that, virtually every other business faded and died.

Until the movie. The producers needed an old whistle stop to locate their movie based on Fannie Flagg's novel, *Fried Green Tomatoes at the Whistle Stop Cafe.* From a helicopter, they spotted Juliette. They transformed an antique store near the south end of McCrackin Street, one of the town's last businesses, into the Whistle Stop Cafe, where much of the movie's plot unfolds. Today, the cafe serves country food and fried green tomatoes to tourists, and about a dozen antique stores and gift shops operate from behind the movie facades and grey wooden storefronts on both sides of McCrackin Street. Juliette breathes life again.

JON AVNET ON JULIETTE

Jon Avnet is the producer/director of *Fried Green Tomatoes,* which was filmed in Juliette:

When I first saw Juliette, Georgia, I wondered whether Kudzu ever had it so good. The whole town was being engulfed by that leafy predator. It was hot—Georgia summer hot and humid. So much so that when I went into the antique store that would become the Whistle Stop Cafe in my film *Fried Green Tomatoes,* my glasses fogged up so badly I couldn't see a thing inside. When I went outside, I was perspiring so badly that my glasses kept sliding off my nose.

It was a town that time forgot. When I walked out on the dam and looked back over the lake towards the town, I knew I had found my Southern home. It was so tiny, so devoid of people and so clearly a town where memories were far richer than the today's comings and goings. I could smell the barbecue. I could hear the laughter of children running up the muddy street. I could see that old Model T pickup being dredged out of the lake. I knew I could put Evelyn Couch (Kathy Bates in the movie) by those train tracks and she would hear the ghost trains of yesteryear—and the spell would be set for my movie to begin.

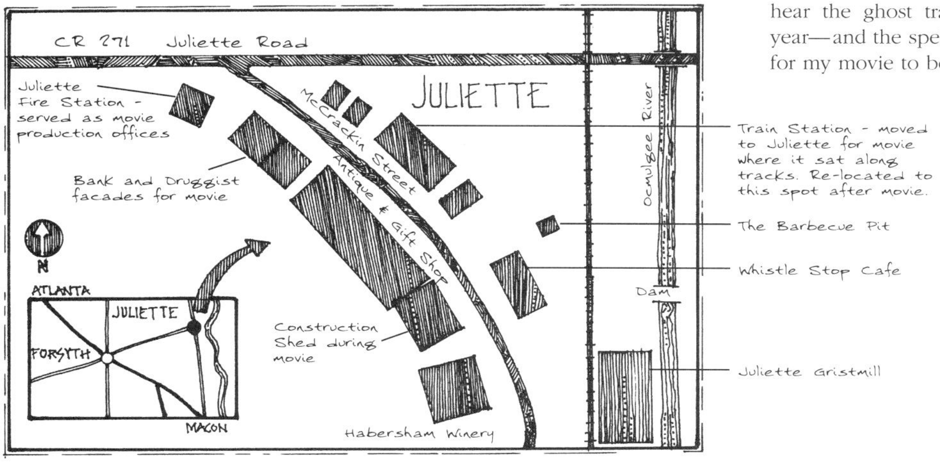

BAINBRIDGE

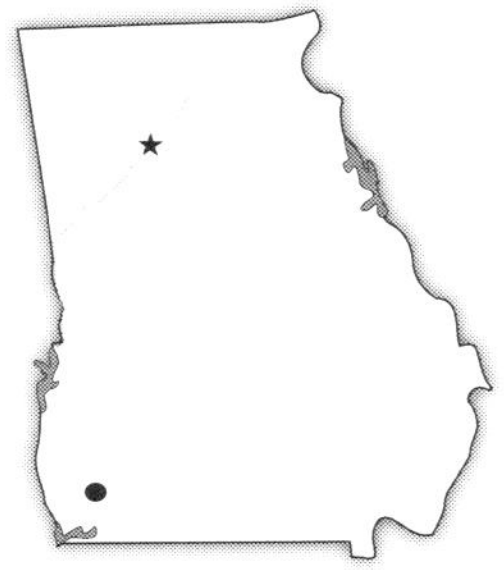

BAINBRIDGE

Bainbridge, with a population of twelve thousand, sits on the banks of the Flint River in Decatur County.

Directions: Located at the intersections of US 27 and US 84 in southwest Georgia.

More Information: Bainbridge-Decatur County Chamber of Commerce, P.O. Box 736, Bainbridge, GA 31717; 912/246-4774, fax 912/243-7633. Bainbridge Auction Market, 912/246-0680. Attapulgus Research Farm, 912/465-3843.

WITH ITS LOCATION AT THE HEAD OF NAVIGATION ON THE FLINT River, Bainbridge has always been a river town in a prime position for transporting the agricultural goods of South Georgia. For much of the 1800s and early 1900s, steamboats rode the Flint down to the Gulf of Mexico, carrying products from the region and returning with fresh seafood. First, timber was shipped. But after sawyers depleted the forests in the late 1880s, farmers planted cotton in the cleared fields. Steamboats now left Bainbridge piled high with bales of the cash crop. When an act of nature—in the form of the boll weevil—dethroned King Cotton in the early 1920s, tobacco replaced cotton as the leading crop shipped from the river town. Today, massive barges have replaced the steamboats that paddled the river a hundred years ago. Now the trip to Apalachicola Bay transports livestock feed while the return trip brings petroleum-based products to be used in the manufacture of fertilizers.

Feed mills and peanut processing plants sprang up along the river and US 27 during the early and mid 1900s and continue to dominate the economy. Monumental-sized signs of agriculture appear on the northern outskirts of town. Near the Flint River on US 27 stands the Elberta Crate Company (1), one of the nation's largest makers of produce crates. About four hundred employees make around one hundred thousand food crates, cartons or boxes a day. The crates will carry everything from cucumbers to peaches to tomatoes to fish. A little further south is the Flint River Mills (2). This sprawling series of connected blue warehouses is topped with tall towers with spreading chutes that collect and disperse mixes of chemicals, grains and other substances to make animal feeds. The Bainbridge Auction Market (3) has held livestock sales since before the 1940s when mules were still sold on the lot.

The Bainbridge Hardware Company (4), right off the town square, occupies an old tobacco warehouse. Owner Lofton Willis has assembled an astounding variety of products reflecting rural southwest Georgia–catfish and cotton baskets hang from the ceiling; iron skillets and tack for farm animals are stacked on shelves. But the majority of his business is big business–equipping area farms, peanut processing plants and feed mills. Across the street, pecan brokers once occupied the Callahan Builder's Mart building (5) back in the 1920s and '30s when pecan orchards were an important crop of the region. Willis Park (6), the original Bainbridge town square, reflects the best of southern town squares. Stop to look at the bell from the steamboat John W. Callahan Jr., one of the many steamboats that carried cash crops and seafood between Bainbridge and Apalachicola. Cheney Griffin Park (7) offers a scenic view of the Flint through Spanish moss-draped live oaks. A dirt road following the river leads from the park to Earl May Boat Basin (8), where a turn-of-the-century steam saw mill is displayed.

Just south of town is the Golden Arrow Dairy (9), reflecting the evolution of agriculture in South Georgia. Dairies, as well as poultry and cattle farms, have started up over the past several decades in much of the region to handle the rising demand for their products. Ten miles south of Bainbridge is the Attapulgus Research Farm (10), one of several small experiment stations run by the Georgia Agricultural Extension Service. The public farm conducts tests on the latest research involving seeds, fertilizers, pesticides and irrigation, all specific to the region's unique conditions and common crops.

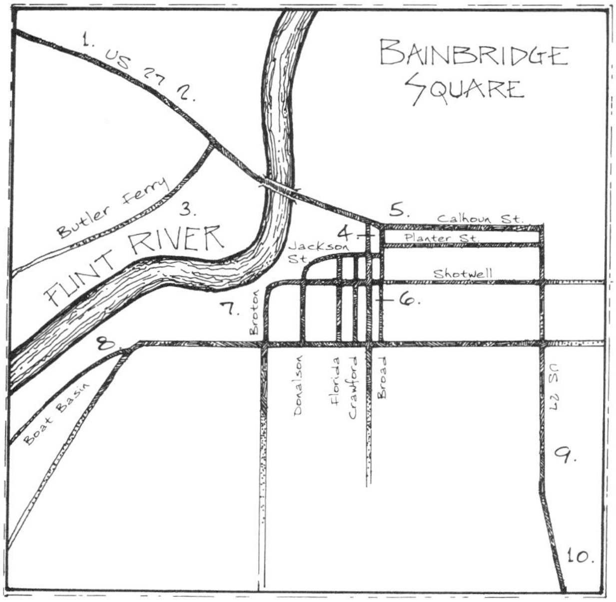

DIAMOND JOE

First recorded by the Georgia Crackers in 1927, Diamond Joe is an old-time mountain tune that is known as a "knockdown tune," a rough-and-tumble banjo song that is usually played at a break-neck tempo. The identity of the character, Diamond Joe, is unknown.

I'm gonna buy me a sack of flour
Cook a hoecake every hour.
Diamond Joe, you better come
get me, Diamond Joe.

CHORUS:
Diamond Joe come and get me.
My wife now done quit me.
Diamond Joe, you better come
get me, Diamond Joe.

I'm gonna buy me a piece of meat,
Cook me a slice once a week.
Diamond Joe, you better come
get me, Diamond Joe.

I'm gonna buy me a sack of meal.
Take a hoecake to the field.
Diamond Joe, you better come
get me, Diamond Joe.

I'm gonna buy me a jug of
whiskey,
I'm gonna make my baby frisky,
Diamond Joe, you better come
get me, Diamond Joe.

I'm gonna buy me a jug of rum,
I'm gonna give my Ida some.
Diamond Joe, you better come
get me, Diamond Joe.

FOXFIRE CENTER AND MUSEUM

FOXFIRE IS NOT A PLACE, MEMBERS EMPHASIZE, BUT A PROCESS, A WAY of teaching that gives students a firsthand experience in learning about their culture and beyond. Started in the 1970s by a local teacher and some high school students, Foxfire began interviewing elderly citizens in Rabun County to document and preserve traditional knowledge and lore. The organization struck a chord across the world. Its books have sold millions internationally. Network television made a movie based on the life of a local farm woman. Three decades later, the students continue to do the work of interviewing, reconstructing buildings and writing magazine articles, a process that allows them to personally learn about their heritage.

Foxfire conducts seminars throughout the country and hosts workshops at the Foxfire Center, a reconstructed Appalachian village on Black Rock Mountain. Visitors are welcome to tour this collection of historic and reconstructed log cabins and wooden buildings, many directly related to early Georgia agriculture, the trade of virtually all settlers.

The Foxfire students have recorded in great detail the personal histories of many who lived in the village's cabins. Foxfire interprets the structures not only by when they were built, moved or modified; but why: children were born, parents died, husbands returned from war. The Savannah House (1) is the first of many interesting Foxfire cabins. Built in the early nineteenth century, it is complete with rope beds, feather mattresses, spinning wheels, chairs with cornshuck and white oak split bottoms and beegums, or hollow sections of the black gum tree, which stored staples like sugar and flour. In the Savannah house, one of Manson Wilson's descendants recalled being able to see the sun and stars through the roof. Rain did not fall through the slits between the shingles, but once a layer of snow blew into his bed. Another spoke of having to pick a shoe full of cotton seed before going to bed. Adjacent to the house, an iron pot sitting in the middle of a large, rectangular stone oven is a hog scalder (2). When not used to soften a pig's

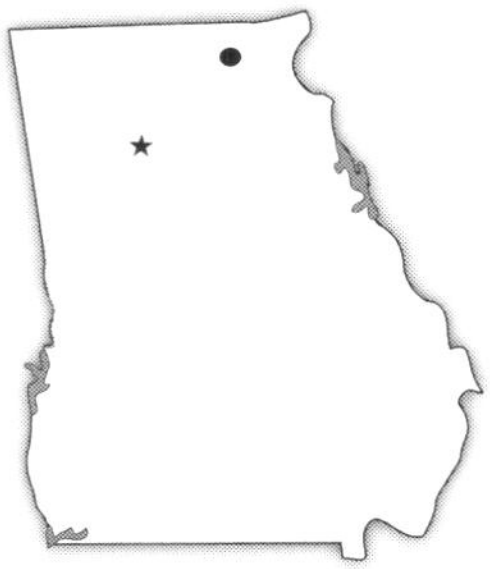

FOXFIRE CENTER AND MUSEUM

Foxfire Center is located on Foxfire's 110-acre property on the side of Black Rock Mountain in Northeast Georgia. The Foxfire Museum is housed in a replica of a log cabin built by Foxfire students.

Facilities: Foxfire Museum has an adjoining gift shop, bookstore and restrooms. The Foxfire Center has no facilities or staff on-site unless part of a group tour. A conference center is available for education seminars.

Days/Hrs.: Mon.-Sat., 9am-4:30pm

Fees: Museum, free. Self-guided tour books for the Center cost $1.50. Guided tours of the village for educational or similar groups are by appointment only, run about two hours and cost $7.50 a person.

Directions: Foxfire Museum borders the west side of US 441 in Mountain City. To reach the Foxfire Center, go south from the museum on US 441 for less than two blocks, turn right on Cross Street, then left on Foxfire Road. Proceed up a steep, gravel road which dead ends into the center.

More Information: Foxfire Museum, P.O. Box 541, Mountain City, GA 30562; 706/746-5828. Web site: http://www.foxfire.com

skin to remove the hair, it might have been used to wash clothes, make lye soap or cook large amounts of soup.

The Phillips Cabin (3) is where Hardy Ledford charged a bucket of corn to grind cornmeal. Further behind it is the Warwoman Cabin (4), where Nellie Turpin couldn't sleep because the neighbor's pigs huddled and grunted under her cabin at night. The holes in the walls of the circa 1900 Ingram mule barn (5) formerly held pegs to form a hay catch, keeping the grass off the ground to prevent trampling and spoiling.

To the right of the mill is the root cellar (6), a common mountain structure, for storing root crops like potatoes, turnips and other vegetables and fruit. This one is above ground, but many were dug into the earth. Sod and dirt often covered the roof. Underground cellars maintained a temperature of 50 degrees in the summer and 38 degrees in the winter.

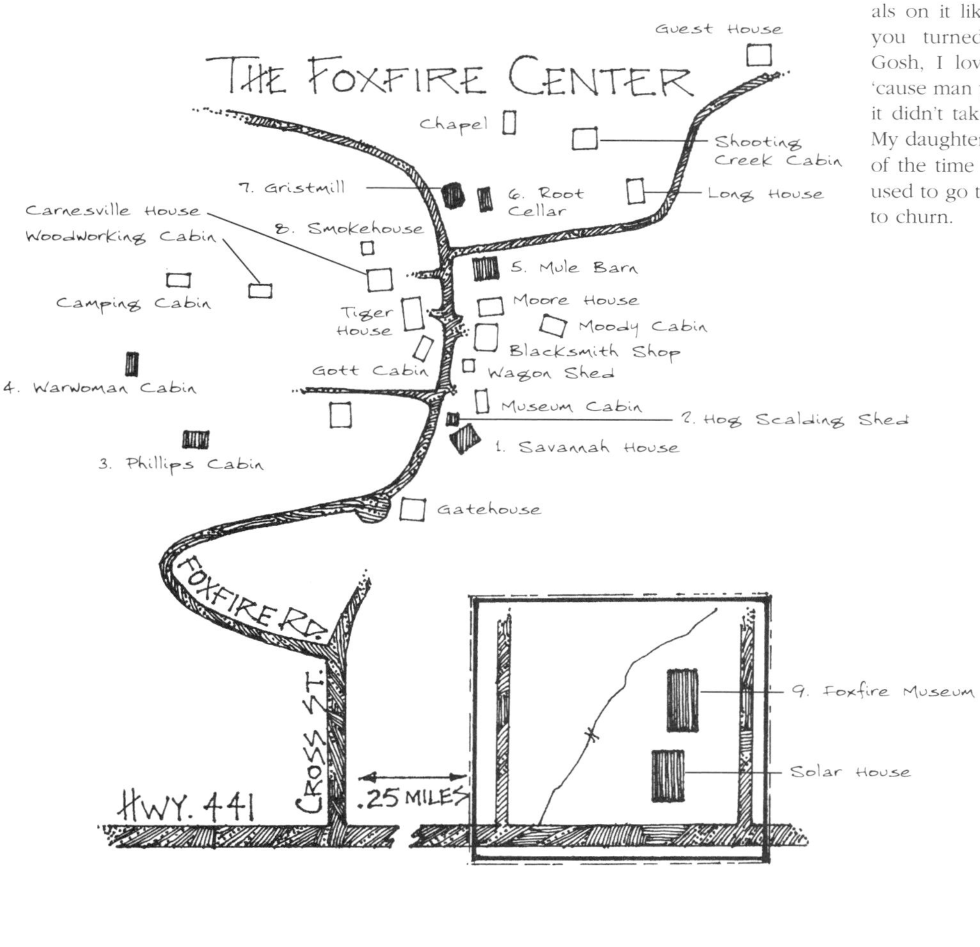

CHURNING

Interview with Ruth Ledford in *The Foxfire Book of Appalachian Cookery* edited by Linda Garland Page and Eliot Wigginton …

My mother taught me how to churn. It really wasn't hard when I was learning, but churning is never *easy*. Some milk is harder to churn than others. It is according to the kind of cow it is, I reckon. My mother churned a lot—about every other day. I churn about three times a week.

My grandmother had a churn and it was square. It had two big dashers of the thing that went in the middle of it and it had a wheel like thing and you turned it around and around. It had pedals on it like bicycle pedals that you turned with your hands. Gosh, I loved to churn for her 'cause man you could just fly and it didn't take you long to churn. My daughter Liz used to churn all of the time and I was like her. I used to go to Granny's just to get to churn.

HOMINY

From the *Foxfire Book of Appalachian Cookery* edited by Linda Garland Page and Eliot Wigginton ...

Hominy is served as a starchy vegetable, like rice, and is made from the kernels of dried corn. The outer husks of the kernels are removed by boiling the shelled corn in lye water. It is usually prepared outdoors in a large cast-iron pot over an open fire.

"Granny" Gibson briefly explained this time-consuming process:

"People used to tie ashes and corn in a sack and boil them a pretty long time in an old iron pot. The water going through the ashes makes lye. That's what makes the outer part of the corn kind of scale off, and what you have left is hominy. You just wash it and wash it to get the lye out, and then you put it back in the pot with just pure water and cook it until it gets tender. Keep adding water to it because it just keeps swelling. Then you take it out, put some grease in it and fry it. It takes all day to make, but it was good."

The reconstructed gristmill (7) has a complete overshot water wheel, which means the water went over the top of the wheel, turning it in the same direction as its flow. Using gravity, this is the most efficient type of wheel.

The smokehouse (8) preserved and stored meat, commonly the ham, shoulder and middling of pig. Soon after slaughter, a farmer took the meat to the smokehouse, thoroughly salted it and set it up on waist-high shelves or down in barrels to "take the salt." The process often took place in winter when the weather provided refrigeration. Hung from wooden poles in the smokehouse, the meat cured slowly for two to six days from the billowing smoke of a green chip, hickory or oak fire on the dirt floor. The meat took on a brown crust, desired for its flavor and ability to keep out insects.

The Foxfire Museum (9) displays a treasure of implements used by Southern Appalachian pioneers. The centerpiece is the inner workings of a gristmill, complete with interlocking gears spiked with wooden peg teeth and a massive grinding stone. An astounding variety of well-displayed and well-marked artifacts cover the walls of the museum, many made from household scraps: toy horses from corn cobs and shucks, lye soap from bacon grease, dishrags from gourd skeletons resembling natural sponges. Other domestic conveniences: a sausage grinder, coffee grinder and tree bark bucket, used to gather berries and nuts. An apple butter stir stick, oak egg basket, and fireless cooker, which used hot iron wafers to slow cook a meal, allowing a family to leave the house without worrying about it burning down. A farming collection: ox yokes, cow bells and bull leads, which are nose rings used to control the beasts of burden. A goat yoke, cornshucker and grain cradle, which is a harvesting tool with a long blade to cut the stems with wooden fingers to catch them. A rabbit box, meal bin and calf weaner, which is a spiked device placed in a little one's nose. When the hungry calf nudged and stuck its mother she would kick him away, eventually weaning the calf.

The list is of unusual and fascinating contraptions is endless. And amazing is Foxfire's ability to find, identify and explain these folk technologies.

Fruit

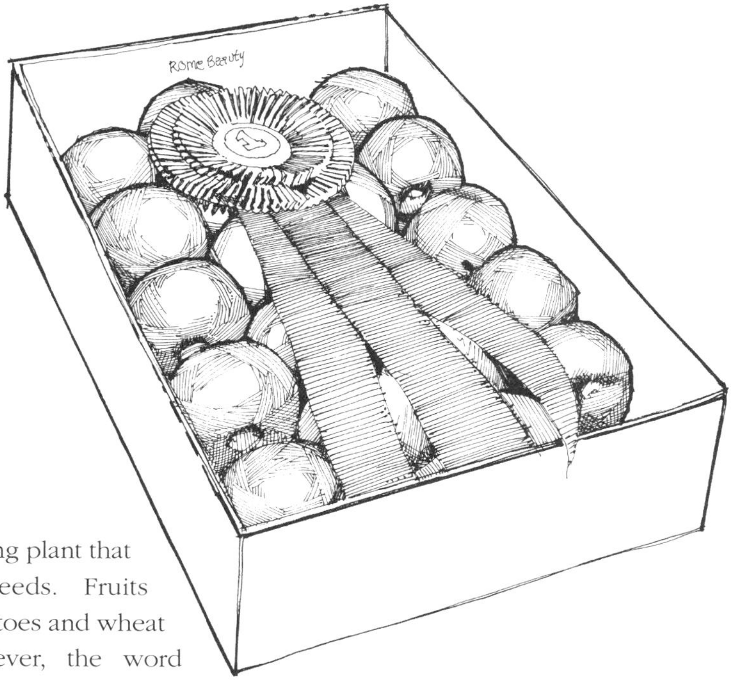

Fruit is the part of a flowering plant that contains the plant's seeds. Fruits include acorns, cucumbers, tomatoes and wheat grains. Most commonly, however, the word "fruit," from the Latin word *frui*, meaning enjoy, refers to the juicy, sweet or tart kinds that people eat as desserts or snacks.

Wild fruits, nuts and seeds were some of the earliest plant food found by prehistoric people. Indians in the southeastern United States were eating fruits like muscadines and blueberries when explorers and early settlers arrived. Much of the fruit grown in Georgia today, however, came from other regions.

Almost all species of fruit grow on plants that have a woody stem, like trees, bushes or wood vines. Fruit crops, unlike most other crops, are not grown from seeds, but rather from grafting or from cuttings and are perennials, so they do not have to be replanted annually.

The world's fruit growers raise millions of tons of fruit annually. In Georgia the total value of fruit production is over $75 million in a normal year. Apples, blueberries, grapes and peaches are the main fruits harvested.

Apples

Jarvas Van Buren, one of the state's first apple enthusiasts, collected apple seedlings from old Cherokee Indian orchards and cultivated them in a Habersham County orchard near Clarkesville in the 1840s. Apple production surged during the Civil War as the fruit was grown to keep Confederate soldiers from developing scurvy. Commercial production was delayed until the railroads opened in North Georgia, but H. R. Straight of Cornelia is believed to have established the state's first commercial orchard in 1895. Today the state's apple industry continues to concentrate in North Georgia, in particular Gilmer County, where the fruit thrives in the cool nights and warm days of the mountains (see page 216).

The old saying, "an apple a day keeps the doctor away," has some nutritional validity. Apples are a good source of dietary fiber, pectic and potassium, are low in calories and have virtually no fat or sodium. Best of all, apples taste great. Variety determines the size, shape and color of an apple. Georgia varieties offer distinctive tastes from sweet to tart. From July to December, North Georgia orchards offer Arkansas Blacks, Empires, Fujis, Golden Delicious, Granny Smiths, Jonagolds, Jonathons, Mutzus, Ozark Golds, Paulareds, Red Delicious, Rome Beauties, Stayman Winesaps and Yates.

Georgia Apple Cake

Chopped apples and pecans abound in this delicious cake

- 3 cups all-purpose flour
- 1½ teaspoons baking soda
- ½ teaspoon salt
- 1 teaspoon ground cinnamon
- 2 eggs
- 2 cups sugar
- 1¼ cups vegetable oil
- 2 teaspoons vanilla extract
- 5 cups chopped apples
- 1 cup chopped pecans

Preheat oven to 350°. Sift together twice, the flour, baking soda, salt and cinnamon. In a separate bowl, beat eggs and sugar until creamy; add oil and vanilla, beating until smooth. Add dry ingredients and mix until a stiff dough forms. Stir in apples and pecans. Pour into a greased and floured 10-inch tube pan. Bake 60 to 70 minutes or until brown. Yields 16 slices.

Nutrition Information Per Serving: Calories 430 / Protein 3.9g / Carbohydrates 54g / Fat 23g / Cholesterol 26mg / Fiber 2.7g / Calcium 15mg / Iron 1.4mg / Sodium 154mg

Georgia Apple Commission

Light Georgia Apple Cake

Less calories and fat, but all the flavor you expect

Recipe Makeover

We lightened traditionally rich Georgia Apple Cake without sacrificing the wonderful flavor and moistness that makes this popular dessert so hard to resist. The lighter version of our apple cake is full of fresh apples and pecans and is elegant enough to serve to family and friends during the holidays!

- 3 cups all-purpose flour
- 1½ teaspoons baking soda
- ½ teaspoon salt
- 2 teaspoons ground cinnamon
- 2 eggs
- 1½ cups sugar
- ⅓ cup vegetable oil
- 1 cup unsweetened applesauce
- 2 teaspoons vanilla extract
- 5 cups peeled and chopped apples
- ½ cup finely chopped pecans, toasted
- Vegetable cooking spray

Preheat oven to 350°. Sift together twice the flour, baking soda, salt and cinnamon. In a separate bowl, beat eggs and sugar until creamy with a wire whip. Add oil, applesauce and vanilla; beat until smooth. Add dry ingredients and mix until a stiff dough forms. Stir in apples and pecans. Pour into a 10-inch tube pan coated with vegetable cooking spray and lightly dusted with flour. Bake for 1 hour and 10 minutes or until brown. Yields 20 slices.

Nutrition Information Per Serving: Calories 215 / Protein 2.8g / Carbohydrates 37.2g / Fat 6.5g / Cholesterol 21mg / Fiber 1.7g / Calcium 11mg / Iron 1.1mg / Sodium 122mg

HOW WE DID IT: To lower fat and calories, we reduced the amount of vegetable oil from 1¼ cups to ⅓ cup. We then added 1 cup unsweetened applesauce to add back moisture and tenderness. We cut additional calories by reducing the sugar from 2 cups to 1½ cups. Extra cinnamon was added to enhance the flavor. Finally, we used half the original amount of chopped pecans to reduce fat and calories. The pecans were toasted to increase their flavor.

Georgia Apple Commission

Buyer's Guide to Apples

Look for apples that are firm and free of bruises.

Sort apples often. One bad apple can spoil the rest.

Buy apples in bulk to cut down on costs. Most will stay fresh for several months if stored at cool temperatures.

To keep the flavor longer, store apples in vented plastic bags.

If necessary, apples can be allowed to ripen for up to two weeks at room temperature.

To enjoy apples year-round, try canning, freezing or drying.

Adding lemon juice to cut apples prevents discoloration.

72 A farm, 6 r. house, barn, chicken house, Elec. pump, lake site. Bottom land. 50,000 ft. saw timber, good pasture and orchard, on Hopewell Rd. 7 mi. No. Alpharetta, 2 mi Church. (Am too old to continue farming.) Bargain. Write J. M. Day, Alpharetta, Rt. 1.

Farm Land For Sale, Market Bulletin, *October 10, 1945*

BLUEBERRIES

Native to the Northern Hemisphere, blueberries were an important food for many North American Indians, particularly in the winter when they relied on dried berries in their diet. American settlers gave many names to the fruit; besides blueberries there was hurtleberries, buckleberries, bilberries and blaeberries. Although small, blueberries pack a lot of taste and vitamins. The blue-black fruit, which vary in size from one-eighth an inch to more than an inch in diameter, mature several months after flowering, and are a good source of vitamin C, iron, fiber and potassium.

Although native rabbiteye blueberries have grown wild for years along Georgia's streams and rivers, the fruit was not cultivated until the twentieth century. Mixing dozens of varieties of native fruit from the 1920s through the 1960s, scientists at the Coastal Plain Experiment Station in Tifton (see page 206) came up with an incredible assortment of large-sized, sweet blueberries, such as Ruby, Black Giant, Tifblue and Woodward, that are grown around the world. Blueberries are harvested in Georgia from late-May to July, mostly around Alma, the state's blueberry capital. In the 1970s, the Bacon County city, beginning its ambitious and ultimately successful blueberry cultivation program, bought almost every available plant in Georgia and Florida for stock.

Of the twenty blueberry varieties in the eastern United States, the rabbiteye strains remain the most important in Georgia. The annual blueberry harvest in Georgia can bring in over 10 million pounds. The blueberry industry is expanding, some of it due to pick-your-own farms (see page 95) all over the state.

YE OLD APPLE PECAN PIE

Using an iron skillet is part of the fun in making this winner

5 to 6	crisp apples
3	tablespoons margarine
2	tablespoons sugar
3	cups all-purpose flour
1	teaspoon salt
3	tablespoons sugar
1	cup shortening
1	egg
	Cold milk
1	cup sugar
	Water
	Pecans
	Ground cinnamon

Preheat oven to 375°. Peel, core and slice apples. In "ye old" iron skillet, melt margarine, add apples and sprinkle with 2 tablespoons sugar. Cook over medium heat until lightly browned and crisp-tender. Transfer apples to plate to cool.

Sift flour, salt and 3 tablespoons sugar together. Cut shortening into flour mixture. Beat egg with enough cold milk to yield ½ cup liquid. Add egg mixture to flour mixture; stir well to form a ball. Roll out and place in pie dish. Add apples to pastry-lined pie dish.

In heavy pan, combine 1 cup sugar with enough water to cover. Bring to boil over high heat, stirring to dissolve sugar. Stop stirring and boil until light brown. Immediately remove from heat and pour over apples. Sprinkle with pecans and a little cinnamon. Pull pastry from sides of pie pan and fold over apples. Bake for 30 to 40 minutes. Serve warm. Yields 6 to 8 slices.

Merle Bates
Buckhead, Georgia
First Place, Apple Pie Recipe Contest,
1992 Ellijay Apple Festival

HOT APPLE TEA

A festive fireside drink

1	quart water
2 to 3	tablespoons instant tea, flavored with lemon
2	cups apple cider or juice
	Cinnamon sticks

Combine all ingredients except cinnamon sticks and bring to a boil. Place cinnamon sticks in mug and pour hot apple mixture over them. Yields 6 servings.

Nancy McCullough
Kennesaw, Georgia

Double Apple Pie

This no-sugar pie is healthy and delicious

6	cups peeled, sliced baking apples (about 2 pounds prior to peeling)
2½	tablespoons all-purpose flour
⅔	cup unsweetened apple juice concentrate
2	teaspoons cornstarch
1	teaspoon ground cinnamon
¼	teaspoon ground nutmeg
1	9-inch pastry shell top and bottom crust

Preheat oven to 425°. Place sliced apples in large bowl. Sprinkle flour over apples and stir gently until slices are evenly coated. In small saucepan, combine apple juice concentrate, cornstarch, cinnamon and nutmeg. Stir until smooth. Place over medium heat and stir constantly until thickened. Pour apple juice mixture over apples, mixing gently until apples are coated. Line 9-inch pie pan with bottom half of ready-made crust. Spoon apple mixture into pie crust. Place top half of ready-made pie crust over pie and seal crust edges together. With a knife, cut several slits in the top crust to allow steam to escape while cooking. Place pie in oven and bake for 10 minutes. Reduce heat to 375° and bake 35 to 40 minutes. Yields 8 slices.

Louise Davis Haynes
Bainbridge, Georgia

Nutrition Information Per Serving: Calories 341 / Protein 2.6g / Carbohydrates 4.8g / Fat 16g / Cholesterol 0 mg / Fiber 2.7g / Calcium 21.5mg / Iron 1.6mg / Sodium 312mg

Diabetic Exchanges: 1 bread, 2½ fruit and 3 fat

Hint: To reduce the fat and calories in this recipe, omit the top pie crust. Result: One serving contains 220 calories and 8g fat (33% of calories).

Diabetic Exchanges: ½ bread, 2 fruit and 1½ fat

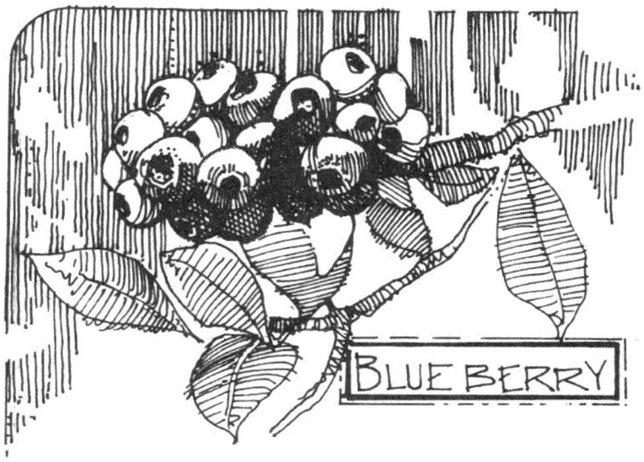

Buyer's Guide to Blueberries

Look for plump, firm, fresh blueberries that are a light powdery blue-gray color. Over-ripe blueberries are dull and lifeless in appearance.

If covered properly and refrigerated, fresh blueberries will keep up to three weeks.

Wash blueberries just before using.

Frozen blueberries can last up to two years, if stored properly.

To reduce color streaking when baking with blueberries, use hard frozen blueberries.

When preparing fresh fruit salads, add blueberries last to avoid coloring other fruit.

Want small acreage and small house for standing rent by ex-GI of World War 2. Near Atlanta, preferably to Northwest. Milton K. Kelly, Kingston, Rt. 1.

Positions Wanted, Market Bulletin, *July 24, 1946*

Blueberry Pie

In the *Dillard House Cookbook and Mountain Guide,* Henry Dillard of the Dillard House in Rabun County reminisced about his mother, Carrie, and the wonderful blueberry pies she used to make:

Back in the W.P.A. days Mother started the county's first school lunch program. Before she finished, she established six lunchrooms. She prepared the best meals for the lowest cost anywhere. Kids would bring what they could from home, like jelly, jams, cornmeal, and so on, then W.P.A. set up some money to help pay for other food.

One day they had blueberry pie. Mother asked one little boy named Jack Darnell to say grace, which they did before every meal.

Mother said, "Jack would you say the prayer?"

Old Jack said, "Oh, Lord, look on us this blueberry pie. Open our mouths and eat blueberry pie. One more time we thank you, Lord, for this blueberry pie."

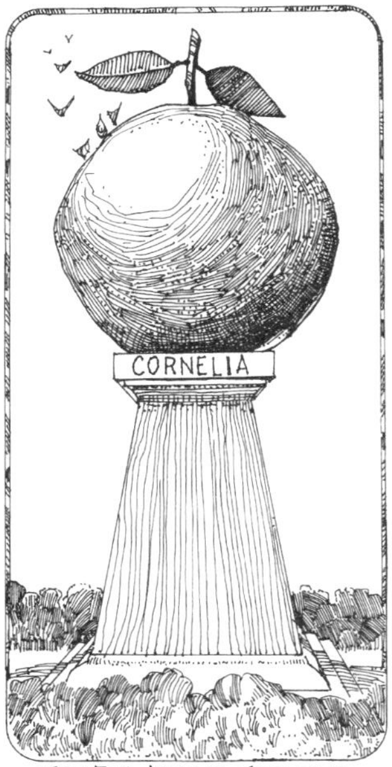

THE BIG APPLE, CORNELIA

French Apple Dessert

A streusel topping adds crunch to this dessert

- 6 cups thinly sliced peeled apples (tart or sweet)
- 1 cup sugar
- ¾ cup baking mix
- ¾ cup milk
- 2 tablespoons butter or margarine, softened
- 1¼ teaspoons ground cinnamon
- ¼ teaspoon ground nutmeg
- 2 eggs
- Streusel Topping

Preheat oven to 350°. Grease 9-inch baking dish. Prepare Streusel Topping and reserve. Spread apples in baking dish. Beat remaining ingredients in blender on high speed about 15 seconds or with wire whisk or hand beater about 1 minute, until smooth. Pour over apples. Sprinkle with streusel topping. Bake about 55 minutes or until knife inserted in center comes out clean. Cool. May add a drizzle icing if desired. Serve at room temperature. Yields 6 servings.

Streusel Topping

- 1 cup baking mix
- ½ cup chopped nuts
- ⅓ cup packed brown sugar
- 3 tablespoons butter or margarine

Mix baking mix, nuts and brown sugar. Cut in butter or margarine with a fork or pastry blender until mixture is crumbly.

Kay Moore, Hawkinsville, Georgia
First Place, Georgia Apple Recipe Contest, 1993 Georgia National Fair

---

Apple Fritters

- 1 cup all-purpose flour
- 1 teaspoon baking powder
- 1 teaspoon powdered sugar
- ¼ teaspoon salt
- ¼ cup milk
- 1 egg, beaten
- 2 fresh apples, peeled and chopped
- Vegetable oil
- Powdered sugar

Combine dry ingredients in a medium mixing bowl. Combine milk and egg; stir into dry ingredients. Stir in apples. Drop batter by teaspoonful into deep hot oil; fry until brown, turning once. Drain on absorbent paper; sprinkle with powdered sugar. Yields 1 dozen.

Georgia Apple Commission

Apple Cheese Crisp

A tasty cheese crust tops this dessert

4	cooking apples
1/4	cup water
1	teaspoon lemon juice
3/4	cup sugar
1/2	teaspoon ground cinnamon
1/2	cup all-purpose flour
3/4	cup shredded cheese
1/2	teaspoon salt
1/4	cup shortening

Preheat oven to 350°. Core, peel and slice apples into eighths and place in a shallow buttered baking dish. Pour water and lemon juice over apples. Combine sugar, cinnamon, flour, cheese and salt; cut in shortening and sprinkle over top of apples. Bake for 30 to 40 minutes or until apples are tender. Yields 5 servings.

Dot Comer
Norcross, Georgia

Ellijay Apple Bread

	Vegetable cooking spray
2	cups sugar
1	cup oil
3	eggs
3	cups all-purpose flour
1	teaspoon salt
1	teaspoon baking soda
1	teaspoon ground cinnamon
2	teaspoons vanilla extract
2	cups chopped, peeled baking apples
1	cup chopped pecans

Preheat oven to 325°. Spray two 9x5-inch loaf pans with vegetable cooking spray. In a large bowl using an electric mixer, beat together sugar, oil and eggs. In a separate bowl, stir together dry ingredients. Add dry mixture to batter and mix just until blended. Stir vanilla, apples and pecans into batter. Pour batter into prepared loaf pans. Bake for 1 hour or until inserted knife comes out clean. Yields 2 loaves, 16 servings each.

Diane Hutchens
Leslie, Georgia

Hints: To reduce fat and calories in this recipe, use 2/3 cup vegetable oil and 1/2 cup pecans. Result: Each serving contains 156 calories and 6.4g fat (36% of calories).

Canning and Preserving

Is it better to use a dial gauge pressure canner or a weight gauge pressure canner to preserve a favorite mixture of vegetables? Should food be re-canned if the lid doesn't seal? Are canned foods that have been frozen during storage safe to eat? Is it really necessary to leave head space in the jar?

So Easy to Preserve, published by the Cooperative Extension Service, is a veritable encyclopedia of food preservation, giving the answer to these and other canning questions. Continuing to sell briskly since its first publication in 1984, the book covers an exhaustive list of subjects: canning fruits, vegetables, seafood, meats, soups and pie fillings; pickling cucumbers, produce, chutneys and relishes; making jams, jellies, marmalades, fruit butters, honeys and preserves; freezing foods; and drying seeds. It discusses canning green peanuts in the shell, drying homemade fruit rolls and making pectin syrups, and offers hundreds of recipes for preservable foods, everything from spaghetti sauce to Brussels sprouts. There are diagrams on how to place lids and pare apples, graphs that show the pH values of foods and illustrations on how to butcher wrap animal products before freezing them.

To order this valuable resource, contact the local extension agent or the main office of the University of Georgia Cooperative Extension Service (see page 285).

STRAWBERRIES

Strawberries have grown in the wild on coasts, in forests and on mountains in the Northern and Southern Hemispheres for thousands of years. Cato, a senator in ancient Rome, mentioned strawberries in his writings. Literature from the first millennium described the medicinal value of the strawberry plant, not the food value of its fruit. Twelfth-century Saint Hildegard von Binger pronounced strawberries unsuitable to eat; they grew too close to the ground where snakes and toads could contaminate the fruit by touching them, she said. A few centuries later famed botanist Charles Linnaeus helped debunk the myth by prescribing a diet of only the fruit for himself.

Explorers to the Americas found strawberry plants that surpassed all European varieties in appearance and taste. In the eighteenth century, agricultural experimenters on both sides of the Atlantic crossed various American varieties and improved the strawberry further.

Strawberries are not really fruit or berry, but rather the enlarged receptacles of flowers. This member of the rose family is grown in every state in the United States.

Besides the pleasantly sweet flavor, strawberries offer plenty of nutrition. They are low-calorie, fat free and a good source of vitamin C, potassium and antioxidants. The Georgia strawberry harvest takes place from around March to July. The crop is scattered all over the state, much of it on pick-your-own farms. It yields about fifteen thousand to twenty thousand pounds per acre.

SUGAR CREEK CHICKEN

Apple juice adds a wonderful flavor to this tender chicken

- 2 tablespoons oil
- 2 small chicken breasts
- ½ cup all-purpose flour
- Salt and pepper to taste
- 1 small onion, chopped
- ½ cup apple juice
- ½ cup water
- ½ teaspoon ground cumin seed

Heat oil in frying pan. Coat chicken breasts with seasoned flour. Brown on all sides; add chopped onion and brown lightly. Reduce heat to simmer and add apple juice, water and cumin. Cover and simmer for about 30 minutes or until chicken is done. Yields 2 main dish servings.

Doug Dowdy
Atlanta, Georgia

FARMHOUSE APPLE SALAD

Chicken and sweet onions combine with apples in this dish

- 3 cups (about 1 pound) diced, unpeeled sweet red apples
- 2 cups diced cooked chicken breast
- 1 cup coarsely chopped Vidalia® onion
- 1 cup sliced celery
- ¼ cup dark raisins
- ¼ cup chopped toasted* pecans
- Creamy Apple Dressing

In a large serving bowl, place apples, chicken, Vidalia® onion, celery, raisins and pecans. Top with Creamy Apple Dressing; toss to coat. Serve immediately or cover and refrigerate until ready to serve. Yields 8 cups or 4 servings.

CREAMY APPLE DRESSING

- ½ cup plain yogurt
- ¼ cup reduced-calorie mayonnaise
- ¼ cup frozen apple juice concentrate, thawed
- 1 tablespoon lemon juice
- 1¼ teaspoons salt
- ⅛ teaspoon ground black pepper

In a small bowl, combine yogurt, mayonnaise, apple juice concentrate, lemon juice, salt and black pepper. Yields about 1 cup.

* To toast pecans: Place in a single layer on a baking sheet. Bake at 300°, until light brown and crisp, about 10 minutes.

Georgia Department of Agriculture Test Kitchen

Apple and Plum Pork Tenderloin

Deliciously different with apples and vegetables

- 1/4 cup soy sauce
- 1/2 teaspoon ground ginger
- 1/4 teaspoon pepper
- 1 pound pork tenderloin, cut into 1/4-inch slices
- 2 tablespoons brown sugar
- 1 tablespoon cornstarch
- 1 tablespoon water
- 1 teaspoon oil
- 1/4 cup chopped celery
- 1/2 cup julienne-sliced red bell pepper
- 1/2 cup chopped green onions
- 1/2 cup apple cider
- 1 cup cored, sliced cooking apples, unpeeled
- 1 cup pitted, sliced plums, unpeeled

In medium bowl, combine soy sauce, ginger, pepper and pork. Refrigerate mixture for 2 hours. Meanwhile, in a small bowl, combine brown sugar, cornstarch and water. Heat oil in large skillet over medium-high heat. Add pork and discard marinade. Cook pork 5 to 7 minutes or until browned. Add celery, red pepper, green onions and apple cider. Cover and simmer for 3 minutes. Add apples, plums and cornstarch mixture. Cook 5 minutes on very low heat, stirring constantly, until mixture is thickened and fruit is crisp-tender. Yields 4 servings.

Georgia Department of Agriculture Test Kitchen

Peach Preserves

A simple recipe every Southern cook needs

- 2 quarts sliced and peeled ripe peaches (about 10 large)
- 6 cups sugar

Combine fruit and sugar; let stand 12 to 18 hours in refrigerator. Sterilize canning jars. Bring fruit and sugar mixture slowly to boiling; stirring frequently. Boil gently until fruit becomes clear and syrup thick, about 40 minutes. As mixture thickens, stir frequently to prevent sticking. Skim, if necessary. Pour hot preserves into hot jars, leaving 1/4-inch head space. Wipe jar rims and adjust lids. Process 5 minutes in a boiling water bath. Carefully remove jars from water and do not tighten lids. Allow jars to cool untouched for 12 to 24 hours. Yields approximately 7 half pints.

The University of Georgia Cooperative Extension Service

Buyer's Guide to Strawberries

Select firm, but not hard, fruit, with a pleasant fragrance, deep red color and green caps attached. Avoid or remove badly bruised or moldy strawberries.

Place strawberries in a single layer in a clean container covered with wax paper in the refrigerator.

Remove caps and wash thoroughly with water just before using. Wash strawberries by placing them in a colander and spraying them with water.

Atlanta Farmer's Market

The Atlanta Farmer's Market is the largest produce destination and distribution center in the region. Produce from all over the world comes into the farmer's market and goes out all over the Southeast (see page 280). Before dawn each day, eighteen-wheeler tractor trailers pull up to the docks of the permanent wholesale buildings to unload California grapes or load up Vidalia onions. Georgia farmers work six of the open-air stalls during the season, selling an infinite variety of produce, including peanuts, pecans, corn and peaches. Restaurant owners, grocery stores and consumers alike reap the benefits—a chance to buy fresh fruits and vegetables straight from the farm.

1. Georgia-grown vegetables, like sweet Vidalia green salad onions, can be found at the farmer's market.
2. Richard Branan is just one of the many farmers selling fresh produce at the market.

3 and 7. Farmers and retailers rent market stalls and sheds to sell produce to consumers.

4. At 146 acres, the Atlanta Farmer's Market is the largest in the state.
5. Virginia Debard, a market personality for more than twenty-seven years, sells customers her fresh boiled peanuts.
6. A farmer's truck transports tomatoes between market stalls.

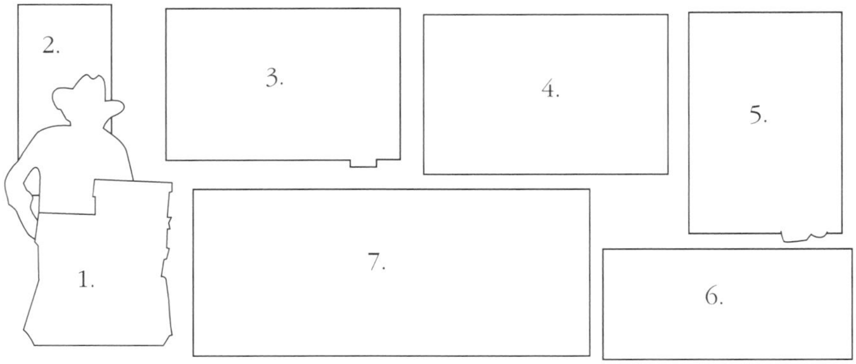

TIM MERCIER

My dad, Bill Mercier, originally came from a place outside of Athens called Ila, Georgia. He attended the University of Georgia, majored in agronomy. He came to Fannin County in the early 1940s as a county agent and purchased the orchard in 1943. We've been developing and planting apple trees ever since.

I was born in 1945. I attended the University of Georgia, got my B.S. in horticulture from the university and went on to get my master's in pathology from Clemson University. I spent a couple of years with Uncle Sam in the Army in the early seventies. When I came home from the service, which was 1972, I came back into the business. My wife, Sandra, teaches school. We have two children. One of my daughters, Melissa, and her husband entered the business this summer. We have one grandson, which will be the fourth generation, we hope to train into this business—unless he is smarter. My youngest daughter, Amanda, is a senior at the university.

We farm about two hundred acres. I guess we are pretty close to the largest, if not right at the largest, in the state as apple orchards go. Most orchards in the past have been in the fifty to seventy five acre range. We started out as a small operation. When my dad purchased it, there were maybe twenty-five acres of apples here that were originally planted in the early twenties. Since that time, we have expanded it to our present acreage and many of our acres have been replanted three to four times.

We consider the life of an orchard to be about eighteen years. So we are constantly reworking. At any one time there is only—out of 200 acres—about 125 that is in actual full-bearing capacity. The rest of it is in some state of being reclaimed.

We are running about thirty different varieties. Of course the old standbys, the Red and Golden Delicious, Rome and Winesaps, and then the Gala, Ginger Gold, Jonagold, Fugi, Brayburn, Yate, Arkansas Black and quite a few others.

We have abut eighty thousand trees. In the older days we would plant seventy-five to one hundred trees on an acre of ground. Today we have seven hundred to eight hundred trees on an acre of ground. That is considered the low scale of high density. There are a lot of plantings in this country that are over one thousand trees per acre. In Europe they are growing as high as two thousand trees per acre of ground, so we've got a long way to go to catch up with the intensity the Europeans have. They developed root stocks to allow them to produce as many apples on one acre of ground as we would produce in this country on ten acres of ground. The land over there for many many centuries has been more precious. They had little land to farm on so they had to learn to use the land they had. Where as in this country, we have had broad expanses of land. We could be a little more wasteful with the way we use the land. In the old days you might let that tree get twenty-five-feet tall and have to use a very long ladder to climb it and do all the work. Today, a lot of our work is done standing on the ground. Our trees at a maximum may be eight or nine feet tall. They have to have a post to hold them up. We are getting everything the big tree gets, except it comes in a smaller package. The apple itself would be exactly the same.

All those trees are pruned by hand. All the trees, every year. Sometimes twice. We try to do summer and winter pruning. We stopped picking apples this year about the first part of November. Our crews started pruning the second of November and they prune all the time until we start picking again.

We run about twelve to fourteen employees all year long. In our peak harvest season from July to Christmas that gets up to fifty employees. All our work is hand labor. Our full-time crew, we couldn't operate without them. Our people are most important to us. All our work is hand labor. Even though we have a lot of machinery, when you are in the fruit business, it is not as mechanized as other types of agriculture. It takes a lot of manpower, a lot of hand type work to do the job. There are no machines to pick with. There are no machines basically that would prune as we would prune. Our work is outside all year long. It's either too hot or too cold or too wet. When a guy is offered a chance to go into a plant and work making the same or more money, it doesn't take very long before he will do that. So labor is one of our biggest concerns.

Because Georgia is a relatively small apple producing state, much of the marketing is directed to consumers at roadside stands. While Mercier Farms continues to ship apples all over the Southern region, more and more customers are showing up at Tim Mercier's orchard, buying his apples and at the same time increasing the value of his land.

Most of the farms are no longer shipping apples. They have a farm market. They grow and sell their apples direct to the customers that drive up in the fall of the year. We are about the only shipper left in the state because of our size and acreage and also because my dad had a lot of foresight. He planted these new varieties, and by doing that, we were able to stay competitive to a certain extent and continue to wholesale.

We also have a very good roadside market. In the last few years we've had this influx of people moving into the mountains. You have the urban sprawl around Atlanta with a couple of new roads. One is I-575. That road opened up this area to development. We have a lot of second homes and people moving into the area now. To that extent we are gaining a lot of customer base and that's helping us in our direct marketing.

With this though you also get problems as any agriculture venture does. It is obvious that poultry and second-home development don't always go hand in hand and are not always compatible as neighbors. For the most part, we in the fruit industry have not experienced too much of this, but, as we get more people, then maybe the noises of our spray machine running, our equipment running will not be welcome by our neighbors. So as these things occur and more development comes, this could become a bigger problem for us.

Most of us would probably be better off if we just sold out. We could sell our land out now for much more than we could realize from farming. That's probably the one little niche that sits in the back of your mind that says, "Well, I can continue to do this to a certain point and then we are going to have to quit." We've been very fortunate in Georgia because of the ability to sign up our land under the covenants in which you can agree to maintain your land as a farm, not to sell it without facing certain penalties, and they have to value your land as farm land for your tax base. Here in our own county there are acres of ground that border our orchards that they were selling for phenomenal prices because of the fact that we are on a very high side. You can see three states from our orchard. People are paying big prices to put a cabin on that type of terrain. Up here the land is probably six to seven thousand dollars an acre and that would be a very cheap piece of property now. And we have tracts of land, if it is on the high tops, individual tracts may sell for twenty-five to thirty thousand dollars a lot. If it's on a lake area, like around Blue Ridge Lake, half-acre lots are selling for around a hundred thousand dollars. Beyond what we consider it to be worth, but obviously someone thinks it's worth that. Most of our land was bought for fifty dollars an acre. We couldn't farm it if we didn't have those protections.

Like other farmers who have occupied the same piece of land for generations, Mercier sees his role as a caretaker of the earth.

People say you wear out the ground, you wear out the soil. You are just constantly farming and you are using all this high-tech stuff and you are wearing out Mother Earth. Well, the piece of ground that was originally planted in 1925, that my father bought in 1943, we just replanted two years ago. That's probably the fifth time its been replanted in that period of time. It is more productive today than it's ever been before, even back in the twenties when it was originally cleared and planted. That is one of the most productive pieces of land we have on our place. To me that's great. We have taken a resource in the earth and we have protected the environment. We have protected our soil and we are constantly producing products. We are not destroying the earth. We are working hand in hand with the earth, and I think that's true of all agriculture when it's done proper.

Peaches

Georgia's most recognizable fruit traveled all over the world before reaching the Peach State. First cultivated in ancient China, peaches went to Greece with Alexander the Great's soldiers around 322 BC. A peach in Rome around 100 AD cost the equivalent of more than four dollars; in Victorian England about five. Spanish explorers traveling through Mexico and Florida brought the first peaches to North America, where they spread through missionary and Indian populations. The original settlers to the colony planted peaches in the Trustees Garden in Savannah in the 1700s. Highly perishable, the fruit was grown mostly for home use; its often hard and bitter fruit was fed to hogs or made into brandy.

In the 1850s growers like Robert Nelson and R. J. Moses, experimenting in Middle Georgia nurseries, developed better tasting peaches that they shipped on a limited basis on the railroads. In 1872, Samuel Rumph of Marshallville cultivated the Elberta, a peach unrivaled in taste, color and size, that when shipped by rail in newly invented refrigerated boxes sold extremely well in Northern markets. The region, notably Peach County, continues to produce most of the state's peaches (see page 234).

Georgia peaches, which number about 2.5 million trees on about twenty thousand acres, can produce 160 million pounds of fruit in a good year.

A refreshing taste for summer, peaches have a perfect blend of flavor and nutrition. They can be enjoyed as appetizers, desserts and everything in between. And they contain important nutrients like fiber, riboflavin and beta carotene, which has been linked

Fort Valley Peach Cobbler

Served with vanilla ice cream, this cobbler is always a hit!

- 8 cups sliced peaches
- 2 cups sugar
- 3 tablespoons all-purpose flour
- ½ teaspoon ground nutmeg
- 1 teaspoon vanilla extract
- ⅓ cup butter or margarine
- Pastry for double-crust pie
- Vanilla ice cream

Combine peaches, sugar, flour and nutmeg in a Dutch oven; set aside to allow syrup to form (about 15 minutes). Bring peach mixture to a boil; reduce heat to low and simmer 10 minutes or until peaches are tender. Remove from heat and stir in vanilla and butter.

Preheat oven to 475°. Roll half of pastry to ⅛-inch thickness; cut into a circle to fit a 2-quart baking dish. Spoon half of peach mixture into lightly buttered baking dish; top with pastry. Bake for 12 minutes or until lightly browned. Spoon remaining peach mixture over baked pastry. Roll remaining pastry to ⅛-inch thickness and cut into 1-inch strips; arrange in lattice design over peaches. Bake an additional 15 to 20 minutes until browned. Allow to cool slightly before serving. Serve with vanilla ice cream. Yields 8 servings.

Georgia Peach Commission

Grilled Peaches and Berries

Grilled or baked, this is a beautiful combination of color

- Large ripe peaches
- Fresh or frozen blueberries
- Brown sugar
- Lemon juice

Select peaches; wash, peel and halve. Remove pit. Place each half on a double thickness of heavy-duty aluminum foil. Fill peach halves generously with fresh or frozen blueberries. Sprinkle 2 teaspoons brown sugar and 1 teaspoon lemon juice on each. Wrap securely with the foil. Cook on grill 18 to 20 minutes, turning once. Serve right out of the foil.

These peaches also could be baked in the oven and served in stemmed glasses to dress up a meal. Bake in foil or glass dish for about 15 minutes at 350° or until peaches are done. Allow ½ peach for each serving.

Georgia Peach Commission

Peach Harvest Salad

A peach vinegar and basil dressing highlights this pasta salad

1	9-ounce package refrigerated cheese-filled tortellini
3	cups sliced peaches
1	medium red bell pepper, cut into match sticks
¼	cup basil peach vinaigrette (more to taste)
4	cups mixed fresh salad greens

Cook tortellini according to package directions. Rinse until cool; drain well. In medium bowl, combine tortellini, peaches and red pepper. Chill until ready to serve. Drizzle dressing over mixture; toss gently. Place salad greens on large serving platter or 4 individual salad plates. Arrange peach tortellini mixture over greens. Yields 4 servings.

Basil Peach Vinaigrette

½	cup peach preserves
¼	cup peach vinegar
1	tablespoon seeded, finely chopped jalapeno pepper
1	tablespoon finely chopped fresh basil
½	cup olive oil

Combine all ingredients in bowl of food processor; process until smooth. Refrigerate until ready to use. Yields 1¼ cups.

Georgia Peach Commission

Peach Salsa

This versatile salsa is good with chips, chicken, pork or fish

2	cups peeled and chopped peaches
¾	cup chopped red or green sweet pepper
¼	cup chopped, seeded cucumber
¼	cup sliced green onion
1 to 2	jalapeño peppers, seeded and finely chopped
2	tablespoons honey
2	tablespoons lime juice
1	tablespoon chopped fresh cilantro

In medium mixing bowl, combine all ingredients. Cover; chill for up to 4 hours, stirring once or twice. Yields about 2½ cups or 10 servings.

Georgia Peach Commission

to a reduced cancer risk. Peaches are one of the lowest calorie fruits.

Georgia produces more than forty commercial varieties of peaches, available fresh from mid-May to early August. They are divided into two main categories. Clingstone, the earlier variety, have fruit that cling to the stone, or pit. The fruit of the latter one, freestone, readily breaks from the pit.

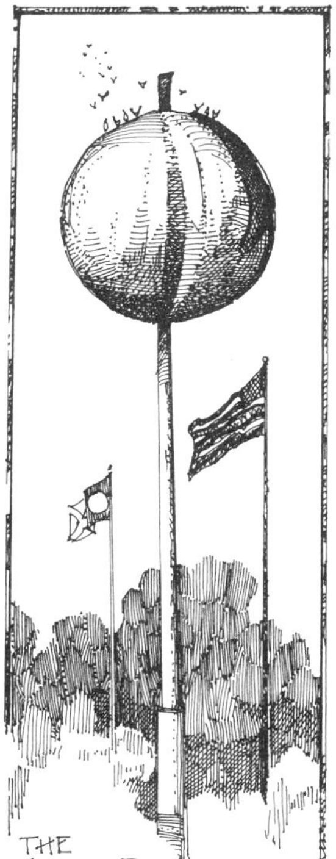

THE GIANT PEACH SEEN ALONG I-75 IN PEACH COUNTY, IS 100 FEET HIGH AND 25 FEET IN DIAMETER.

Want for own use and not re-sale, side of country cured boiling meat. Advise full particulars. Josie Gibert, Atlanta, 761 Piedmont Ave., NE

Miscellaneous Wanted, Market Bulletin, *July 2, 1947*

Buyer's Guide to Peaches

When selecting peaches, smell the fruit. A member of the rose family, peaches should have a pleasant, sweet fragrance.

Look for a creamy gold or yellow under-color. The red or "blush" of a peach indicates variety, not ripeness.

Peaches should be soft to the touch, but not mushy.

Look for a well-defined crease that runs from the stem to the point.

Don't squeeze peaches. They bruise easily.

Place firm peaches on the counter for a day or two to ripen.

Promptly refrigerate ripe peaches and eat them within a week of purchase.

To peel a peach, dip it into boiling water for thirty seconds, then cold water. The peel should slide off easily.

To keep sliced peaches from darkening, add lemon juice or ascorbic acid.

Georgia Peach Pound Cake

A traditional Southern pound cake with peaches added

1	cup plus 2 tablespoons butter
2¼	cups sugar, divided
4	eggs
1	teaspoon vanilla extract
3	cups all-purpose flour, divided
1	teaspoon baking powder
½	teaspoon salt
2	cups chopped, fresh peaches

Preheat oven to 350°. Grease a 10-inch tube pan with 2 tablespoons of butter. Sprinkle pan with ¼ cup sugar. Cream remaining butter; gradually add remaining sugar, beating well. Add eggs, one at a time, beating well after each addition. Add vanilla and mix well. Combine 2¾ cups flour, baking powder and salt; gradually add to creamed mixture, beating until well-blended. Dredge peaches with remaining ¼ cup flour. Fold peaches into batter. Pour batter into prepared pan. Bake for 1 hour 10 minutes. Remove from pan and cool completely. Yields 16 slices.

Nutrition Information Per Serving: Calories 336 / Protein 4.4g / Carbohydrates 48.5g / Fat 14.5g / Cholesterol 86mg / Fiber 1g / Calcium 19mg / Iron 1.3mg / Sodium 214mg

Georgia Peach Commission

Low-Fat Peach Pound Cake

A low-fat version of the same delicious pound cake

- Vegetable cooking spray
- ⅓ cup vegetable oil
- ½ cup plain low-fat yogurt
- 1½ cups sugar, divided
- 3 eggs
- 2 egg whites
- 1 teaspoon vanilla extract
- 3 cups all-purpose flour, divided
- 1½ teaspoons baking powder
- ½ teaspoon salt
- 2 cups chopped, fresh peaches

Preheat oven to 350°. Spray a 10-inch tube pan with cooking spray. Sprinkle with 1 teaspoon sugar. Combine oil, yogurt and gradually add remaining sugar, beating well. Add whole eggs and whites, one at a time, beating well after each addition. Add vanilla and mix well. Combine 2¾ cups flour, baking powder and salt. Gradually add to yogurt mixture; beat until well-blended. Dredge peaches with remaining ¼ cup flour. Fold peaches into batter. Pour batter into prepared pan. Bake for 1 hour. Remove from pan and cool completely. Yields 16 slices.

Nutrition Information Per Serving: Calories 228 / Protein 4.6g / Carbohydrates 39g / Fat 5.8g / Cholesterol 39mg / Calcium 29mg / Iron 1.2mg / Sodium 122mg

Georgia Peach Commission

Peach Bowl

Enjoy all of your favorite fruits in this summer delight!

- 2 cups sliced peaches
- 1 cup blueberries
- 2 cups cubed watermelon
- 1 banana, sliced
- 1 medium-sized cantaloupe, cubed
- 1 pint strawberries, hulled
- 1 kiwi fruit, peeled and sliced
- 1 6-ounce can frozen orange juice, thawed

In a decorative glass bowl, layer fruit. Pour orange juice over mixture; cover and let marinate in refrigerator for two hours. Yields 10 servings.

Georgia Peach Commission

Pickled Peaches

From *Run with the Horsemen* by Ferrol Sams ...

He had dried peas, dried butterbeans, cole slaw, and a scoop of mashed potatoes with gravy. Sitting in the middle was a pickled peach, its beautiful amber surface interrupted by the star of a fragrant clove. He loved pickled peaches and for a moment forgot his anxiety about table manners in appreciative anticipation.

The pickled peaches his mother made were cooked until they were soft and practically fell off the seed while being served. This peach on his plate was firm to the point of hardness. Relaxed and unsuspecting, he confidently speared it with his fork and gave a downward snap of his wrist to cut off a bite. To his horror the enticing fruit shot forth like a chinaberry from an elderberry gun.

It skidded across his plate, scattering peas and butterbeans on the tablecloth, and shot all the way across the table between Marietta and the curly-haired boy to land with an audible thud on the linoleum floor. Marietta and the boys were so absorbed in each other that they did not even notice the intrusion. The waitress, on her way between tables, gave the boy a swift look and then kicked the peach with one deft motion into the corner.

Want farm family to help on large irrigated vegetable farm near Atlanta. Nice 4 R house with elec., wood, garden, pasture, $3 daily to man able to cut turnip salad and drive truck. R. F. Sams, Clarkston, Phone C I 2211

Farm Help Wanted, Market Bulletin, *May 19, 1948*

MUSCADINES

The muscadine, a dark reddish, musky-flavored grape, grows naturally in much of the Southeastern United States. In his *Travels,* plant explorer William Bartram noted that Indians in Georgia and the Carolinas gathered great quantities of the tough-skinned fruit, some of which they dried for winter use. Since muscadines primarily grew around Indian villages, some researchers believe the Indians brought the fruit into Georgia.

Bearing clusters of grapes from one half to one inch in diameter, the muscadine ripens in late summer and early autumn. The naturally sweet muscadine is often used for jellies, syrups, sauces and wines.

One popular variety of domesticated muscadine is the scuppernong, distinguished by its silvery green color and sweeter flavor. The two thick-skinned vine fruit have much in common, and some folks refer to large specimens of both as bullets.

Muscadine is a popular crop across the South because of its natural adaptability, resistance to diseases and insects and long vine life, which may survive for decades. Muscadine is often planted by home gardeners on fence rows or homemade trellises. Muscadine and similar varieties are sometimes called slipskin because the flesh and the skin separate easily; the skin is usually not eaten.

Unlike grapes that ripen in and remain in clusters when harvested, muscadines produce fruit in clusters but are removed berry by berry when ripe. The fruit is often shaken from the vines onto a cloth. Muscadines are harvested from late August to October. Commercial production concentrates in the southern part of the state, as the fruit cannot be grown in areas where the temperature drops below 10°.

PEACH CUSTARD ICE CREAM

An easy and refreshing summertime dessert

1	quart whole milk
1	cup heavy cream
3	eggs
1¼	cups sugar, divided
1	tablespoon all-purpose flour
⅛	teaspoon salt
6	cups mashed peaches
1	tablespoon vanilla extract

In large, heavy saucepan, heat milk and cream just below boil. In medium bowl, beat eggs and combine with ½ cup sugar. In small bowl, mix flour and salt with remaining ¾ cup sugar. Add egg mixture and flour mixture to hot milk. Cook until mixture thickens and lightly coats the back of a metal spoon. Remove from heat, add peaches and vanilla. Chill in refrigerator before freezing in ice cream maker. Yields 1 gallon or 20 servings.

Georgia Peach Commission

GEORGIA PEACH CHUTNEY

Peaches and raisins are key ingredients in this versatile chutney

1	medium onion, finely chopped
1	clove garlic, minced
1	cup seedless raisins, chopped
8	pounds peaches, peeled and chopped
2	tablespoons mustard seed
2	tablespoons chili powder
1	cup crystallized ginger, chopped
1	teaspoon salt
1	quart vinegar
2¼	cups dark brown sugar

Combine all ingredients in a Dutch oven; bring to a boil and simmer uncovered for 1 hour and 15 minutes or until mixture is thickened and deep brown. Pour hot chutney into hot canning jars, leaving ½-inch head space. Remove air bubbles. Wipe jar rims. Adjust lids. Process for 10 minutes in a boiling water bath. Remove jars from bath and let cool untouched for 12 to 24 hours. Yields 6 pint jars.

The University of Georgia Cooperative Extension Service

Hint: Serve peach chutney with pork or chicken dishes. Also, place several tablespoons of peach chutney over cream cheese and serve with crackers for a unique appetizer.

Peach Bread

Serve one loaf of this delicious bread tonight—freeze the other

1½	cups sugar
½	cup shortening
2	eggs
2¼	cups puréed, fresh peaches (6 to 8 medium size)
2	cups all-purpose flour
1	teaspoon ground cinnamon
1	teaspoon baking soda
1	teaspoon baking powder
¼	teaspoon salt
1	teaspoon vanilla extract
1	cup finely chopped pecans

Preheat oven to 325°. In large bowl, cream sugar and shortening. Add eggs and mix thoroughly. Add peach purée and dry ingredients. Mix thoroughly. Add vanilla and chopped pecans and stir until blended. Pour into 2 loaf pans that have been well-greased and floured. Bake for 55 to 60 minutes. Let bread cool a few minutes before removing from pan. Yields 2 loaves, 8 servings per loaf.

Georgia Peach Commission

Grandma's Peach Shortcake

A timeless Southern dessert

½	cup butter
2	cups self-rising flour
¾	cup buttermilk
4	tablespoons sugar, divided
	Vegetable cooking spray
3	cups sliced peaches
1½	cups fresh whipped cream

In medium bowl, cut butter into flour with pastry blender until mixture resembles coarse meal. Add buttermilk and 1 tablespoon sugar until all dry ingredients are moistened. Turn dough out onto lightly floured surface and knead 3 to 4 times.

Preheat oven to 425°. Roll dough to ¾-inch thickness; cut with a 2-inch biscuit cutter. Place pieces close together on a lightly greased baking sheet. Bake for 13 to 15 minutes. While shortcake is baking, place sliced peaches in medium bowl and stir in remaining 3 tablespoons sugar. To serve, split shortcake in half and place peaches on the bottom half. Place the other half on top and spoon on 2 tablespoons whipping cream. Yields 12 servings.

Georgia Peach Commission

Buyer's Guide to Muscadines

Select fruit that has ripened fully on the vine to produce the best flavor from grapes used in desserts, juices and wines.

Choose grapes that are a little underripe for making jelly. They have a higher pectin content then and produce a clearer jelly.

Fresh grapes stored dry in the refrigerator will remain good for one or two months.

Fully ripe grapes will be firm and sweet. Wash before using.

Print sacks, washed and ironed, 100 lb cap., 30 cents ea; Unwashed 25 cents each; Odds 20 cents each. Add postage. No holes nor mildew. Mrs. Sam Ridings, Ball Ground, Rt. 1.

Miscellaneous For Sale, Market Bulletin, *July 1949*

FIGS

People have eaten figs since the earliest of times. Native to the Mediterranean region, the fig plant may grow as a low spreading bush or as a tree, depending on how it is pruned. Sometimes called a fruit without a flower, the inside of the fig has several hundred tiny flowers. An opening at the top of the fruit permits a small wasp to enter and pollinate the flowers.

People eat figs fresh, canned, preserved or pickled. But most figs are eaten dried. Dried figs contain large amounts of sugar, calcium and iron.

Once upon a time in ancient Greece, figs were stolen from trees sacred to the gods. Later, certain people were accused and were found to have the figs in their homes. According to Samuel Taylor Coleridge, the word "sycophant" (from *sykos* (fig) and *phanein* (to show) refers to "a wretch who flatters the prevailing party by informing against his neighbours the pretense that they are exporters of prohibited figs or fancies."

FIG COBBLER

This unique cobbler will soon become a favorite

5 to 6	cups peeled fresh figs
¾	cup sugar
3	tablespoons flour
2 to 3	teaspoons butter or margarine
1	pie crust for 8-inch pie

Preheat oven to 375°. In medium bowl combine figs, sugar and flour; mix well. Spoon into an 8-inch square baking pan; dot with butter. Roll pastry into ¼-inch thickness on lightly floured surface; cut into 9 ½-inch strips. Arrange strips in lattice pattern over fig mixture. Trim edges as needed. Bake for 45 minutes or until golden brown. Yields 6 servings.

Cobb County Cooperative Extension Service

MUSCADINE OR SCUPPERNONG JELLY

This jelly is a staple in all farm kitchens

4	cups muscadine or scuppernong juice
3	cups sugar

TO PREPARE JUICE

Select about 1 gallon of grapes that are in the just-ripe stage. Wash and crush grapes. Without adding water, boil and simmer for about 10 minutes, stirring constantly. Press juice from the heated grapes. Pour the cool juice into glass containers and set in refrigerator. The next day strain the juice through a flannel bag. Do not squeeze the bag.

TO MAKE JELLY

Sterilize canning jars. Heat 4 cups juice to boiling in a sauce pot. Add 3 cups sugar and stir until the sugar dissolves. Then boil rapidly over high heat to 8° above the boiling point of water or until jelly mixture sheets from a spoon. Remove from heat; quickly skim off foam. Pour jelly immediately into hot canning jars, leaving ¼-inch head space. Wipe jar rims and adjust lids. Process 5 minutes in a boiling water bath. Yields 3 to 4 pint jars.

The University of Georgia Cooperative Extension Service

Blueberry Buckle

- ¼ cup butter or margarine
- 1 cup sugar, divided
- 1 teaspoon vanilla extract
- 1 egg, lightly beaten
- 1⅓ cups sifted all-purpose flour, divided
- 1 teaspoon baking powder
- ¼ teaspoon salt
- ⅓ cup milk
- 2 cups blueberries
- ½ teaspoon ground cinnamon
- ¼ cup margarine

Preheat oven to 375°. Cream butter, ½ cup sugar and vanilla and add beaten egg. Sift together 1 cup flour, baking powder and salt. Add dry ingredients alternately with milk to the creamed mixture. Pour into a 10x5x2-inch greased baking dish. Cover with berries. Combine remaining sugar, flour, cinnamon and margarine. Blend together to form a crumb topping and sprinkle over berries. Bake for 40 to 50 minutes. Yields 6 servings.

Major C. Collins, Tifton, Georgia

Very Blueberry Muffins

These low-fat muffins are full of berries!

- 2⅔ cups all-purpose flour
- 2 cups quick oats
- 1 cup dark brown sugar
- 1 tablespoon baking powder
- 2 teaspoons baking soda
- 1 teaspoon salt
- 2 teaspoons ground cinnamon
- 2 cups skim milk
- 2 eggs, lightly beaten
- 3 tablespoons vegetable oil
- 4 cups blueberries

Preheat oven to 425°. Line large muffin tins with paper muffin cups. In large bowl, combine all dry ingredients. Add milk, eggs and oil. Stir until dry ingredients are moistened. Fold in blueberries. Fill muffin cups ¾ full. Bake 25 minutes or until light golden brown. Yields 36 large muffins.

Susette Wilson, Chula, Georgia

Hint: After baking, cool the muffins then freeze. Remove the paper muffin cups while still frozen and before microwaving to re-heat. This way the low-fat batter won't stick to the paper.

In recent days, cold weather has done tremendous damage to crops, especially peaches, early vegetables and early planted field crops. The weather man tells us that April 15, 1950, showed the lowest temperature of any April 15, on record.

From a news story, Market Bulletin, *April 19, 1950*

PEARS

The first colonists in Georgia planted pear trees along with dozens of other experimental crops in the Trustees' Garden in Savannah. Some miles to the south, the LeContes, one of the most prominent planting families in Georgia (see page 36), developed what became the state's first successful commercial pear variety.

Major LeConte, a relative living up North, hoped that a combination of the hardy but unsavory Chinese Sand Pear and weak the but tasty French Dessert Pear would exhibit the best qualities of both. He sent a hybrid seedling to his niece, Jane LeConte Hardin, who lived on Woodmanston Plantation near Midway. After the Civil War, Leander L. Varnedoe, a former superintendent of the Hardin lands, returned to discover that the specimen had grown into "a handsome tree ... loaded with the most delicious fruit." Planting some of the cuttings near Thomasville, the ex-Confederate colonel began the pear industry in the South.

Eventually, the number of LeConte pear trees in Thomas County exceeded one hundred thousand. Blight, neglect and poor marketing brought an end to the commercial pear industry in Georgia by World War I. Yet, limited pear production continues in many parts of the state. The pear harvest takes place from about August 1 to November 1.

PLUM BREAD

Make this in five mini-loaves for a delicious gift

- 2 cups sugar
- 3 eggs
- 2 cups self-rising flour
- ¾ cup oil
- ½ teaspoon ground cinnamon
- ¼ teaspoon ground cloves
- Dash of salt
- 2 4-ounce jars of strained baby food plums
- 1¼ cups chopped pecans
- Vegetable cooking spray
- Glaze

Preheat oven to 325°. Combine first 8 ingredients in large mixing bowl. Beat 4 minutes on medium speed. Add pecans and mix for 1 minute. Pour batter into a tube pan coated with vegetable cooking spray. Bake for 1 hour. Cool in pan 10 minutes.

GLAZE

- ½ cup sugar
- ¼ cup water
- 1 teaspoon margarine

In small saucepan, bring sugar and water to a boil; boil 1 minute. Remove from heat and stir in margarine. Remove bread from pan. Pour glaze over bread while warm. Yields 16 servings.

Hint: This is a delicious bread, and it is ideal to bake in mini-loaf pans and wrap up for gifts (yields 5 mini-loaves). To reduce the calories and fat in this recipe, reduce oil to ½ cup, use 2 whole eggs and 2 egg whites, reduce pecans to ½ cup and reduce sugar in glaze to ¼ cup. Result: One serving contains 270 calories and 10g of fat (33% of calories).

Cindy Anderson
Mableton, Georgia

PEAR AMBROSIA

The addition of pears makes this Southern classic unique

- 5 pears
- 4 oranges
- 1 cup flaked coconut
- 1 16-ounce can crushed pineapple, drained
- 1 small jar maraschino cherries, halved

Cube pears, cut up oranges and combine with remaining ingredients. Chill until serving time. Yields 10 servings.

Virginia Hogan
Ocilla, Georgia

BAKED PEARS

Chunks of pineapple bring added taste to this pear recipe

- 1 20-ounce can chunk pineapples, drained, reserving 1 cup juice
- 1½ tablespoons cornstarch
- ½ cup sugar
- 6 to 8 medium-sized pears, peeled and sliced
- 6 tablespoons butter, melted
- 6 tablespoons dark brown sugar
- ¾ cup coarse bread crumbs

Preheat oven to 375°. Combine one cup pineapple juice and cornstarch. Add sugar and cook over medium heat until thickened. Place pears in the bottom of a greased or buttered 8-inch baking dish. Pour pineapple chunks over pears. Combine butter and brown sugar, add bread crumbs and stir lightly until well-coated. Pour juice mixture over pears and pineapple; sprinkle with bread crumbs. Bake for 30 minutes or until bubbly. Yields 6 servings.

Liza Jameson
Stone Mountain, Georgia

SUGAR-FREE STRAWBERRY PIE

Everyone will love this sugar-free pie

- 1 9-inch frozen pie crust
- 1 package (4-serving size) sugar-free vanilla cook n' serve pudding mix
- 1 package (4-serving size) sugar-free strawberry gelatin
- 2 cups cold water
- 4 cups sliced strawberries

Bake pie crust according to package directions. Set aside.

In medium saucepan, combine pudding mix, gelatin mix and water. Stir to dissolve; continue stirring over medium heat until mixture comes to full boil. Remove from heat. Cool glaze in refrigerator until slightly thickened. Arrange strawberries in pie shell. Pour cooled glaze over strawberries. Chill until set. Yields 8 slices.

Nutrition Information Per Serving: Calories 119 / Protein 2.2g / Carbohydrates 17.8g / Fat 5.3g / Cholesterol 5mg / Fiber 2.2g / Calcium 13mg / Iron .3mg / Sodium 160mg

Diabetic Exchanges: ½ bread, ½ fruit, 1 fat

Hint: For variation, try this recipe with a graham cracker crust. For one pie shell, combine 1 cup graham cracker crumbs with 2 tablespoons reduced-calorie melted margarine. Press mixture into pie tin and bake at 350° for 7 to 9 minutes. One serving of strawberry pie with graham cracker crust contains 120 calories and 3g fat.

Diabetic exchanges: 1 bread, ½ fruit, ½ fat.

Georgia Department of Agriculture Test Kitchen

BUYER'S GUIDE TO PEARS

Always ripen pears in a bowl at room temperature. Once they have reached desired ripeness, place them in the refrigerator to slow further ripening.

Green and firm pears will take four to six days to ripen at room temperature.

Pears turning from green to yellow and losing their firmness are ready to eat in two to three days. When pears are golden yellow, they are at their ripest, juiciest, most flavorful stage.

Depending on their ripeness, pears can be stored in the refrigerator for almost a week.

To prevent sliced pears from darkening, dip them into a mixture of one tablespoon of lemon juice and one cup of water.

WATERMELONS

Famed explorer Dr. David Livingston found watermelons growing wild in the central part of Africa where this large, sweet, watery fruit originated in the 1850s. Today, cultivated in the warm regions of every part of the world, watermelon is served differently by various cultures. Russians make a beer from its juice. Iraqis use the flesh as an animal feed and water source. Asians roast its seeds and eat them from the hand.

As early as 1853 Georgia farmers shipped melons by boat to Northern states. Commercial production took root in the southern part of the state were settlers often planted watermelon—which thrives on newly cleared soil—as their first crop after they had cleared the land of timber. Because of the state's success in watermelon production, in 1914 the National Watermelon Association set up its headquarters in Morven, Georgia, where the organization continues to promote the interests of watermelon growers.

Georgia farmers began trucking watermelons to Northern markets as highways improved. Watermelons remain an important truck farming crop and the state, with over forty thousand acres in cultivation, is among the leaders in United States production. Crisp County, where the warm climate and good soils ensure consistent yields of sweet melons, claims the title of Watermelon Capital of the World.

Watermelons are low in calories, virtually fat free, and a good source of vitamins A and C.

There are about fifty different varieties of watermelons in the United States. Those grown in Georgia are available from June to August. Popular ones include Crimson Sweets and Jubilees.

STRAWBERRY PIZZA

This pizza can be eaten for dessert!

1 cup self-rising flour
¼ cup powdered sugar
½ cup melted butter or margarine
1 8-ounce package cream cheese, softened
1 14-ounce can sweetened condensed milk
⅓ cup lemon juice
1 teaspoon vanilla extract
½ cup sugar
2 tablespoons cornstarch
½ cup water
2 pints strawberries, hulled and halved
A few drops red food coloring (optional)

Preheat oven to 350°. Combine flour and powdered sugar; add butter, mixing well. Pat this dough out in a 14-inch pizza pan; bake for 10 minutes or until lightly browned. In a medium bowl, combine cream cheese, condensed milk, lemon juice and vanilla; mix well and spread on cooled crust. Chill thoroughly. In a large saucepan, combine sugar and cornstarch; add water, mixing until smooth. Cook over medium heat until thickened (about 5 minutes), stirring constantly. Add strawberries; if desired, stir in food coloring. Cool completely. Spread strawberry mixture over cream cheese layer and chill. Cut into wedges to serve. Yields 8 to 10 servings.

Gwen W. Bentley
Lyerly, Georgia

Hint: For a different recipe, use peach slices (3 cups) and substitute almond flavoring for the vanilla.

WATERMELON SALSA

Great with tortilla chips, fish or grilled chicken

2 cups seeded and finely chopped watermelon
2 tablespoons chopped onion
2 tablespoons chopped water chestnuts
3 tablespoons chopped green chilies
2 tablespoons balsamic vinegar
¼ teaspoon garlic salt

In medium bowl, combine all ingredients and stir until blended. Cover and place in refrigerator for 1 hour. Serve cold. Yields 2 cups, 8 servings.

National Watermelon Board

Watermelon Pie

1	10-ounce box mixed-fruit gelatin
¼	cup water
1	12-ounce non-dairy whipped topping
2	cups watermelon balls
	Graham cracker crust

Fold together gelatin, water and non-dairy whipped topping. Fold in watermelon balls. Place mixture into graham cracker crust. Chill for 2 hours. Yields 8 slices.

National Watermelon Board

Tri-Color Salad

Layers of lime, lemon and strawberry gelatin color this salad

Layer One

1	4-serving package lime-flavored gelatin
1¼	cups hot water
	Pineapple tidbits, cherries, etc. for design

Layer Two

1	4-serving package lemon-flavored gelatin
1	cup hot water
6	ounces cream cheese
⅓	cup mayonnaise
1	tablespoon lemon juice

Layer Three

1	4-serving package strawberry or cherry-flavored gelatin
1	cup hot water
¾	cup cold water
	Chopped pears

Dissolve lime gelatin in hot water. Place in clear bowl or mold. Chill till partially set. Arrange pineapple and cherries and allow to set completely.

In another bowl, dissolve lemon gelatin in hot water. Mix in cream cheese, mayonnaise and lemon juice until thoroughly blended. Pour on top of thoroughly set lime gelatin layer.

Dissolve strawberry or cherry gelatin layer in hot water. Add cold water. Pour on top of thoroughly set lemon layer and arrange pears or other desired fruits attractively. Refrigerate until set or overnight. Unmold onto a decorative serving plate. Yields 8 servings.

Virginia Long
Atlanta, Georgia

Buyer's Guide to Watermelons

When buying a whole watermelon, look for a firm, slightly dull rind and fully-rounded sides.

If buying cut watermelon, look for firm, juicy, red flesh with no white streaks.

Watermelon seeds vary in color from white to black, depending on variety, and should be fully mature and hard.

The lower side of watermelon should be yellow in color where the melon came in contact with the soil.

If a melon is hard, white or very pale green on the underside, it's probably immature.

Watermelon can be stored at room temperature until cut. Once cut, it should be refrigerated.

PROVIDENCE CANYON

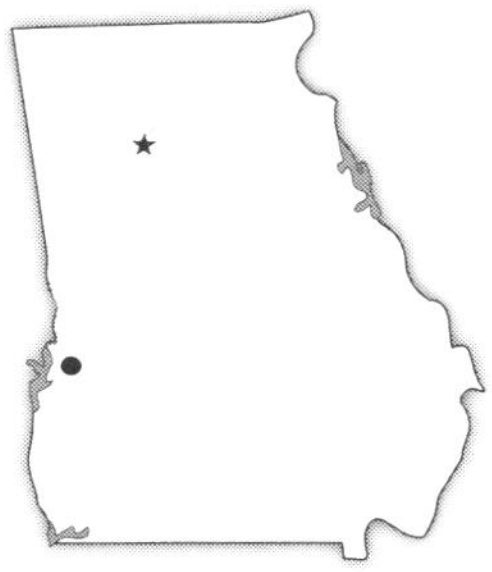

PROVIDENCE CANYON

Providence Canyon is a 1,108-acre state conservation park located in the Chattahoochee River Valley.

Facilities: Visitor center with interpretive displays about the canyon's formation, pioneer camping, 2 picnic shelters, 3 miles of hiking trails and a 7 mile-backcountry trail.

Days/Hrs.: Sept. 15-Apr. 14, 7am-6pm; Apr. 15-Sept. 14, 7am-9pm. Visitor Center, daily 8am-5pm.

Fees: Park, $2 per vehicle; primitive backpacking $3 a night; pioneer camping for groups $30 a night, winter, and $15 a night, summer.

Directions: From Lumpkin, go west on GA 39C for 7 miles and follow the signs.

More Information: Providence Canyon State Conservation Park, Route 1, P.O. Box 158, Lumpkin, GA 31815; 912/838-6202.

TWO HUNDRED YEARS AGO, PROVIDENCE CANYON DID NOT EXIST. The pink, red, orange and purple maze of sheer walls, buttes and cliffs that rise 150 feet above the main canyon floor of what is sometimes called "Georgia's Little Grand Canyon" was just ordinary farm land owned by three families, the Worthingtons, the Woodalls and the Humbers. Legend has it that the canyons began with water dripping from the roof of a barn. But historical accounts suggest that it was really the result of poor soil management practices. During the early 1800s—before the development of contour plowing and strip cropping, standard measures which protect the soil today—farmers growing cotton stripped the forests and worked the top soil to sheer exhaustion. With the natural vegetation removed, there was nothing to diminish the erosive action from the rainfall that flowed unimpeded across the barren landscape, cutting into the sandy soils of this Coastal Plain region and forming gullies. The gullies deepened rapidly in the soft soil and served to concentrate the runoff into small wet weather streams, increasing the rate of erosion even further. By 1850, the gullies reached down vertically three to five feet. Today, many are as deep as 150 feet.

Much of the canyon can be seen from Canyon Rim Drive, which runs along its rim; but the best way to see it is to hike the Canyon Loop Trail which encircles the main canyon maze. Numerous overlooks provide views of the canyon walls, which, like a Neapolitan ice cream sandwich, divide into three separate layers, each with unique coloring and qualities. These three layers make up two distinctive geologic formations (recognizable bodies of rock or sediment), the Providence formation and the Clayton formation.

Look closely at the canyon's bottom: a 3-9 foot, brownish to dark gray, silt and sand layer, geologically known as the Perote member of the Providence formation. It feels like a mixture of play-dough and beach sand, and contains pieces of the shiny, flaky, glittering mineral known as mica, used in the manufacture of table tops and other board surfaces.

The next layer, about 120 feet high, is the Providence formation member known as the Providence Sand. This sandy soil contains streaks of white, buff, tan, pink and lavender. Within these massive horizontal layers are smaller layers with a different angle, a sign that an ocean deposited the sand millions of years ago. This section contains a white clay, known as kaolin. When rubbed between the hands it feels gritty and leaves a slippery stain like baby powder, but it's mined for many industrial uses. Kaolin is found in a rich belt just south of the fall line, which runs east to west in the middle of the state from Augusta to Columbus, marking the ancient coastline.

Above the Providence Sand at the top of the canyon, a thin layer called the Clayton formation appears as a red-orange sand-and-clay mix. Near the bottom of the Clayton, a hard heavy layer resembling rusted metal indicates a layer of high-grade iron ore, which is mined in some areas for the manufacture of steel. Once the newly formed gullies cut through the red-orange sand and clay of the Clayton, they easily erode away the Providence Sand. The canyon continually widens as nature works away the walls, at a rate of about six feet per year.

Crop Rotation

Georgia's Cooperative Extension Service suggests that gardeners should rotate their crops to reduce losses to several soil-borne diseases, including bean root rot, clubroot of cabbage, bacterial diseases of tomatoes and various potato diseases. In rotating crops, try not to plant the same vegetable or a related vegetable in the same location year after year. Groups or related vegetables are:

Cole Crops - Cabbage, cauliflower, collards, Brussels sprouts and broccoli

Cucurbit Crops - Cucumbers, gourds, melons, pumpkins and squash

Legumes - Beans and peas

Root Crops - Radishes, turnips, beets, carrots and sweet potatoes

Salad Greens - Lettuce, endive, mustard and turnips (tops)

Solanaceous Crops - Tomato, pepper, eggplant and potato

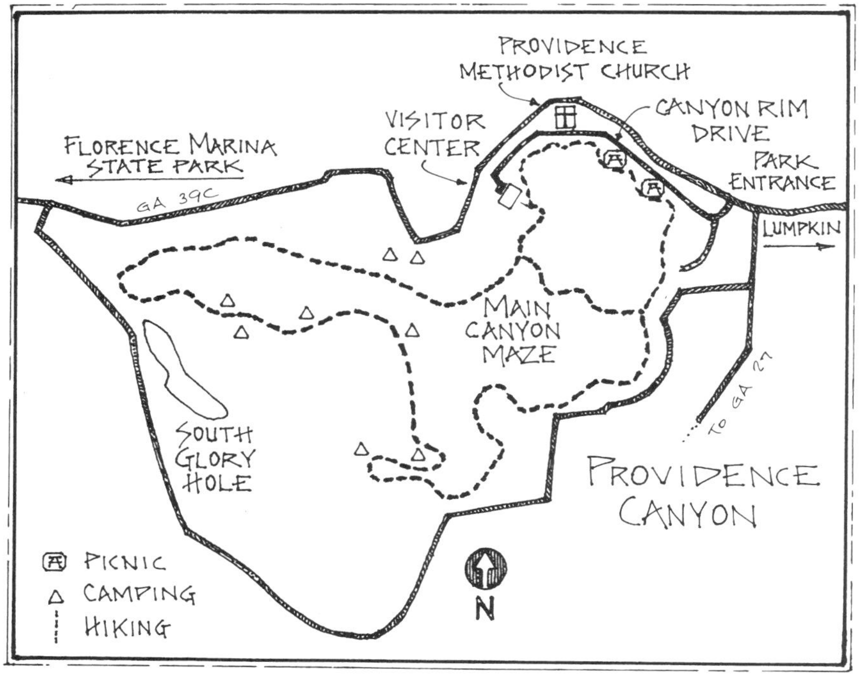

Coastal Plain Experiment Station

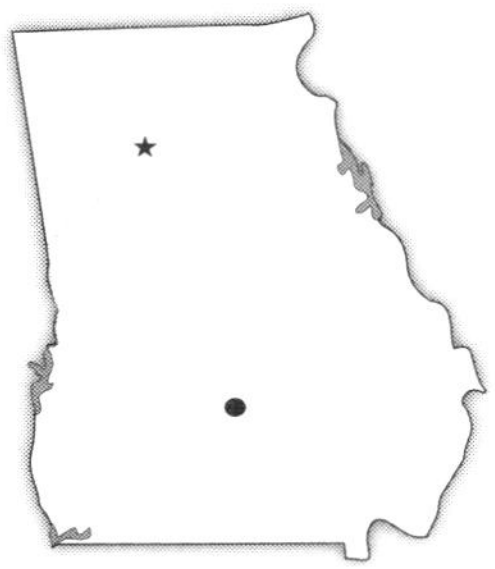

CPES

The Coastal Plain Experiment Station in Tifton is one of Georgia's largest agricultural research centers.

Facilities: Experimental labs, conference space, livestock barns and research plots with row crops, orchards and grasses.

Days/Hrs.: Offices, Mon.-Fri. ,8am-12pm and 1pm-5pm. Closed public holidays.

Directions: From I-75 in Tifton, take Exit 21 to US 41 north. Turn left on RDC Road then left on Moore Highway. CPES administration offices are on the right.

More Information: Coastal Plain Experiment Station, P.O. Box 748, Tifton GA 31793; 912/386-7080 or 3351.

Created in 1918 to help farmers in South Georgia, the Coastal Plain Experiment Station (CPES) has developed agricultural advances that have changed the world. Its discoveries, made at the molecular level in laboratories and in field demonstration plots hundreds of acres in size, have improved the way farmers harvest and people eat. Experimental row crops, orchards and shrubs, old farm buildings and several livestock centers cover the two thousand-acre research property.

To reach the station's entrance, take US 41 to RDC Road. To the left is the Rural Development Center (1), where the station has offices and conference rooms. Across the road, acres of cotton (2) form a random quilt of different shades, heights and textures of green. Divided into subplots, the cotton undergoes tests relating to irrigation schedules, fungicides, fertilizers, pesticides, natural biological controls and weather conditions. Take the dirt road between the plots to reach the peanuts (3). Technicians regularly examine the vines and place tiny blue, red, yellow, pink and white markers to record different levels of attack by blight, a common pest with many crops. North of the peanuts grows pearl millet (4), so named because of its pearly-white seeds in the stalks. In India, where the grain serves as one of the primary staples, millet production increased more than 30 percent in the 1930s, in large part from a variety developed here. Return to RDC Road, turning right on Moore Highway to the Abraham Baldwin Agricultural College (6) campus. Among residential junior colleges, ABAC boasts the most acres in Georgia, the only rodeo club east of the Mississippi and dormitories for students' horses.

Turn left on Moore Highway to reach the livestock centers (5). The swine center conducts tests in nutrition, breeding and antibiotics. In the beef cattle barn, Black Angus and Polled Herefords feed, standing on wooden slats, their waste collecting underneath. Sprayed as liquid irrigation, the manure promotes three corn plantings in one year. In the dairy barn,

Jerseys and Holsteins drink cow gatorade, a project to protect them from the heat of South Georgia.

Head back south on Moore Highway to the blueberry fields (7). CPES scientist Tom Brightwell crossed a tasty rabbiteye blueberry, so named for the size of its fruit, with a wild relative having large, deep blue berries. The resulting Tifblue has parented blueberries varieties that grow all over the world. Dozens of round metal outlines, each about two yards across and filled with different grasses, designate the experimental turf plots (8). Although seemingly unrelated to agriculture, turf research goes back to the early twentieth century when CPES crossed southern bermuda grasses with ones from as far as Indiana and Germany to develop pasture forage for cattle, which at the time in South Georgia ranged free. The Vidalia Onion Research Lab (9) tests the onions in cold storage rooms where in a controlled atmosphere of 5 percent oxygen, the delicate onions stay fresh for many months longer than usual. The National Environmentally Sound Production Agriculture Laboratory (NESPAL), a new fifty-thousand-square foot complex (10), has taken on the ambitious job of redesigning agriculture from the ground up, moderating its effects on the environment by breeding disease-resistant crops, studying natural predators of harmful insects, recycling farm wastes as fertilizer, devising steps to protect groundwater and using computers and satellites to reduce chemical applications.

Experiment Stations

In 1887, Congress passed the Hatch Act, legislation to create and support state agricultural experiment stations, research centers for conducting farm-improving scientific investigations. Today, each state has at least one main station, usually at a state college or university. Scientists at each experiment station study crops and livestock raised in their state. Some larger stations have branches that study special, localized problems. In Georgia, stations have sprung up in every geographical region of the state.

Farmers can directly benefit from these stations' work by merely contacting their area station with questions. A farmer might send a soil sample for analysis or ask for advice on irrigation or poultry raising. Experiment stations provide farmers with the desired information, either directly or through a county agricultural extension agent (see page 169). The stations also prepare free bulletins on many farm subjects.

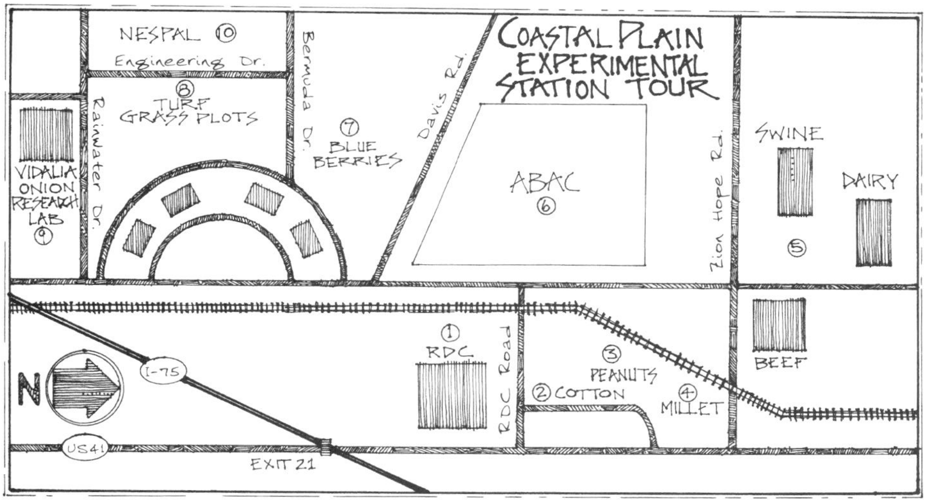

MR. CASON'S VEGETABLE GARDEN

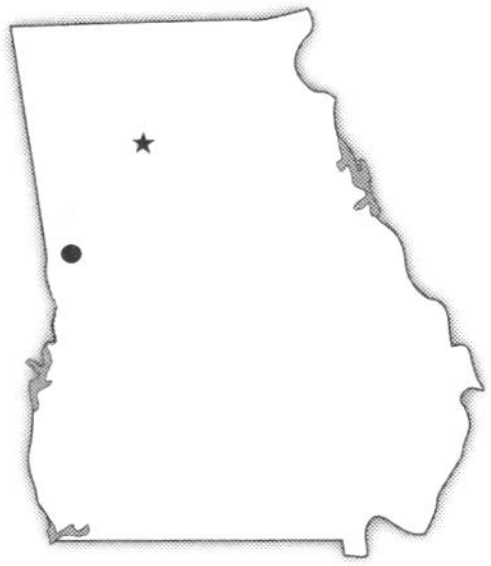

CALLAWAY GARDENS

Mr. Cason's Vegetable Garden is part of Callaway Garden's 14,000 acres situated in west Georgia just north of the Fall Line in the last rolling foothills of the Appalachian Mountains.

Facilities: Five-acre indoor-outdoor horticulture center with seasonal floral displays, largest glass-enclosed butterfly conservatory in North America, circa 1830s log cabin, Robin Lake beach for swimming, bicycle rentals, a 7.5-mile bike trail, walking trails, fishing, tennis, chapel, visitor center, hotel, cottages, villas, golf, shops and restaurants.

Days/Hrs.: Attractions: daily, Mar. 21-Aug. 30, 9am-7pm; Sept., 9am-6pm; Oct. 1-Mar. 20, 9am-5pm. Main entrance usually opens an hour earlier than attractions, weather permitting.

Fees: General admission, adults $10, children $5, children under 6 free.

Directions: From Pine Mountain, go south on US 27 for several miles. The main entrance is on the right. To reach Country Kitchen in the Callaway Country Store, return to main entrance, turn right and continue on US 27 for 0.25 mile. It is on the right.

More Information: Callaway Gardens, Pine Mountain, GA 31822; 1-800-CALLAWAY. Website: www.callawaygardens.com.

When Cason Callaway, leading businessman of Georgia, personal friend of President Franklin Roosevelt and international emissary for trade, stepped down as leader of the family empire, the LaGrange textile magnate decided to pursue a longtime dream to farm. His dream first took shape when his wife Virginia and he, while exploring Pine Mountain in the 1920s, spotted the deep, clear pool of Blue Springs underneath a granite cliff. Enchanted, they visited frequently and found on one trip the azalea prunifolium, a rare plumleaf flower that became the symbol of Callaway Gardens.

Buying twenty-five hundred acres surrounding the springs, they built a lake and a cottage and transformed the land into Blue Springs Farm. Using innovative methods, the former cotton textile king sought to repair the earth from the damage of cotton, a crop grown to extreme at the turn of the century, leaving in its wake eroded gullies, depleted soils and dispirited farmers. Using improved varieties of nitrogen fixers like clover, kudzu and alfalfa, the latest mechanized equipment and fertilizers and modern methods of soil conservation, Callaway astonished farmers from across the region, who came to see the amazing harvests of legumes, nuts, berries and native grapes, as well as his cattle and poultry.

After the success of the farm program, Callaway and Virginia focused on another project, Callaway Gardens. Near Blue Springs, in the scenic woodland valley of Mountain Creek, they built a golf course, hotel, restaurants and lakes, and planted an unprecedented number and variety of flowering plants like azaleas, camellias, dogwoods and magnolias. A fourteen thousand-acre resort, Callaway Gardens, opened in 1952, but Cason had more work to do. He began his last major project, a demonstration vegetable garden, shortly before his death in 1961.

Today Mr. Cason's Vegetable Garden produces four hundred varieties of colorful fruits, vegetables, nuts, herbs and flowers. The perimeter of the 7.5-acre site is marked by a low stone wall in the foreground with a tall line of neatly clipped shrubs in the background. Three large, semi-circular terraces define the interior of the garden. Entering on the light brown pebble path, which runs straight through the center from the entrance to the back, visitors see muscadine grapevines and blueberry shrubs on the upper terrace. A little forward and to the left of the main path, a picket fence surrounds a small barn, shed, patio and garden. Further on the main path is the middle terrace, where stalks of flowering okra stand next to rows of collards, cabbage, corn, tomatoes, squash, peppers and other seasonal crops. Old farm staples like cotton and sugar cane, unusually robust this far north, tower over black eye peas and turnips. Cool season vegetables like cauliflower, broccoli, lettuce and radishes are planted twice, once in early spring and again in early autumn. Slightly further the walkway reaches the lowest terrace. Rosemary, basil and sage attract butterflies and hummingbirds in a raised bed herb garden, displaying year-round a variety of culinary, medicinal and fragrant plants, annual and perennial. On either side of the herb garden there are usually narrow lines of apple and peach trees. Seasonal bounty from the garden is served in the Callaway restaurants.

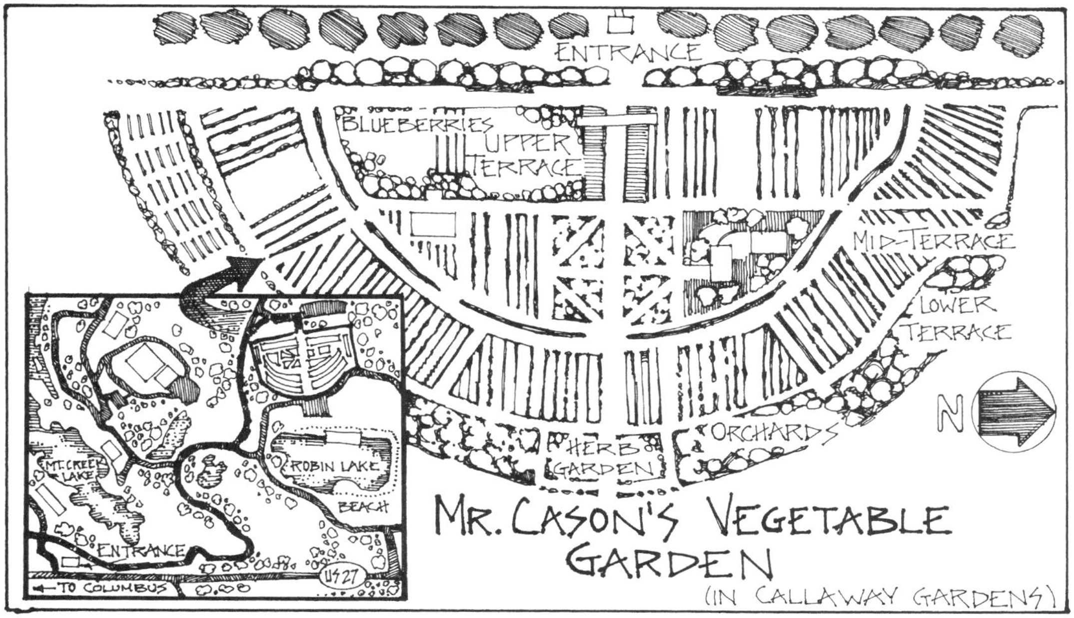

BEEKEEPING

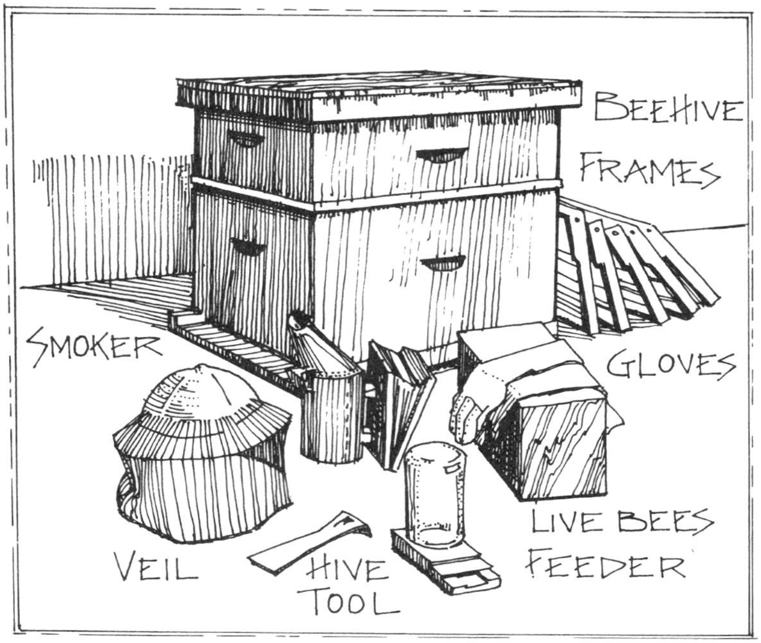

When people look to return to the land, they might consider another hobby besides growing gardens. A vocation that dates back to antiquity, beekeeping serves as an enjoyable, productive hobby as well as a nice income booster. A small colony of bees can supply a neighborhood with all the honey it can eat, plus more to sell on the side. In the world of agriculture, bees offer far more than honey. Their value as pollinators of fruit, trees and vegetables far exceeds that of their honey production.

The basic beekeeper needs a hive, smoker, veil, hive tool, a pair of gloves and some bees. The cost might not exceed $140 when ordered from a hardware store or mail order supply house. Used hives, with or without bees, from an experienced beekeeper often represent a good buy. Package or starter bees, which literally come in a package, can be obtained from a number of suppliers in the state.

The best time of year to start a hive is early spring when fruit trees bloom. After the beekeeper assembles a hive, complete with the foundation for the combs, and paints the exterior with a coat of paint, he places the package bees inside. After "hiving a swarm" of bees, as it is called, he feeds the bees for a short time with damp, granulated sugar dripped into the hive. As the colony expands, the bees then require new "supers," or sections on the hive. During the spring and summer, the bees collect flower nectar and pollen which they store in their hive as honey, sealing it in wax in honeycombs. A beekeeper then brushes the bees off the honeycomb, cuts the comb from the frame, chops it up and strains the pieces through a colander into jars. Preparations must be made to feed the bees over the winter. Usually, late fall flowers provide enough raw materials for them to make their own food.

For more information on beekeeping and supplies, contact Rossman Apiaries in Moultrie at 912/985-7200, York Bee Company in Jesup at 912/427-7311, the Speedy Bee monthly newsletter at 912/427-4281, or the Department of Agriculture Honey Commission at 404/656-3678.

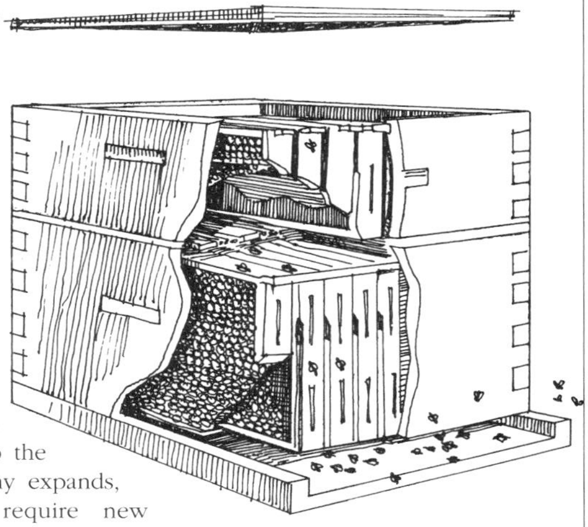

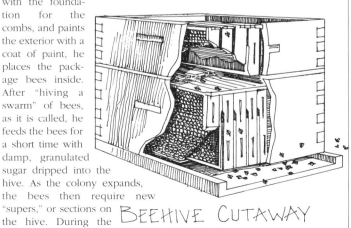

BEEHIVE CUTAWAY

Honey

Honey cultivation is as old as civilization. In 4000 BC Egyptians used honey as a sweetener. The Bible refers to Palestine as "the land of milk and honey" (Exodus 3:8). Spaniards, in the sixteenth century, found Central American Indians practicing beekeeping. About seventy years ago Georgia began raising bees to ship to beekeepers, and has since become one of the nation's top suppliers of bees. The industry has flourished particularly in the southeast, where the mild climate and extensive flora offer the conditions and food source necessary to produce bees year round. In 1996 about seventy-five thousand colonies of bees in Georgia produced 5.1 million pounds of honey valued at $4.5 million.

Honey is a natural, wholesome sweetener produced in a natural factory, the beehive. It is a good source of carbohydrates. There are more than three hundred kinds of honey in the country, each originating from a different flower. Some common ones in Georgia include gallberry, from coastal flowers; sourwood, from the southern Appalachians; and tulip poplar and wildflower, from many areas in the state.

Buyer's Guide to Honey

Select mild honeys to use with foods that have a delicate flavor. Use strong-flavored honeys in spreads or other recipes where a distinct honey flavor is desired.

You should store honey at room temperature.

If honey crystallizes, remove lid and place jar in warm water until crystals dissolve. Don't boil.

Honey can be used as a binding or coloring agent as well as a sweetener.

For easy removal, spray a measuring cup with vegetable cooking spray before adding honey.

Honey helps prevent baked goods from drying out and becoming stale because of its ability to absorb and retain moisture.

Honey has more sweetening power than sugar because of its high fructose content.

Honey Barbecue Sauce

1	10.5-ounce can condensed tomato soup
2	tablespoons Worcestershire sauce
2 to 3	tablespoons vegetable oil
1	tablespoon lemon juice
1	teaspoon ground mustard
	Dash cayenne or bottled hot pepper sauce (optional)
½	cup honey

In saucepan, combine all ingredients and bring to boil. Reduce heat and simmer, uncovered 5 minutes. Yields about 2 cups.

Georgia Beekeepers Association

Hint: This sauce can be served as a dipping sauce for chicken pieces. Preparation time is less than 15 minutes.

Fruit and Cheese Sandwich

Honey adds a touch of sweetness to this yummy sandwich!

1	cup cream cheese, softened
1	fresh peach, puréed
½	cup chopped pecans
1	tablespoon honey
8	slices raisin bread

Combine cream cheese, fresh peach purée, pecans and honey. Stir until fairly smooth. Chill for at least one hour. Serve on raisin bread for a healthy sandwich or snack. Yields 4 whole sandwiches.

Deborah Williams
Kennesaw, Georgia

Grilled Honey Chicken with Thyme

¼	cup honey
3	tablespoons Dijon mustard
1	tablespoon orange juice
1	tablespoon olive oil
½	teaspoon red pepper flakes
2	teaspoons dried thyme
2	chicken thighs
2	chicken legs

In small bowl, mix honey, mustard, orange juice, oil, red pepper and thyme. Brush over chicken. Prepare grill. Grill until done, turning once. Grilling time is from 20 to 25 minutes. Yields 2 servings.

Georgia Beekeepers Association

Honey Sponge Cake

Honey sweetens the coffee in this unusual cake

Vegetable cooking spray
6 eggs, separated
¾ cup sugar
½ cup coffee, freshly made, slightly hot
2 cups cake flour
2 tablespoons cornstarch
1 teaspoon baking powder
1 teaspoon baking soda
½ teaspoon salt
½ teaspoon cream of tartar
½ cup honey
Seven-Minute Frosting

Preheat oven to 350°. Spray 3 9-inch cake pans with vegetable spray and line each with wax paper. With an electric mixer, beat egg yolks until thick. Add sugar gradually while beating. Add coffee slowly and continue to beat. In separate bowl, sift flour, cornstarch, baking powder, baking soda and salt. Gradually add to moist mixture while beating with mixer. In another bowl, with electric mixer, beat egg whites until they form stiff peaks. Add cream of tartar and beat well. Pour honey into beaten egg whites slowly in a fine stream while beating. Carefully fold egg white mixture into moist batter. Pour batter into prepared pans and spread evenly. Bake for 20 minutes. Remove cakes from pans and cool on wire rack.

Seven-Minute Frosting

3 egg whites
1 cup sugar
½ cup water
¼ teaspoon cream of tartar

With electric mixer, beat egg whites until they form stiff peaks. In medium saucepan over medium heat, boil sugar and water for 7 minutes or until syrup dripped from a height spins a thread (240° on candy thermometer). Pour syrup in a thin stream into egg whites while beating. Add cream of tartar and beat well (approximately 5 minutes). Spread on cooled cake. Yields 20 servings.

Annamae Anderson
Savannah, Georgia

Hint: Instead of the frosting, serve this cake with fruit or toasted pecans.

The Florida Aquifer

Perhaps the most important contributor to farming in the Southeast is the Florida Aquifer, underlying about one hundred thousand square miles in southeastern Georgia, southern Alabama, southern South Carolina and all of Florida. An aquifer is a water bearing-geologic formation that yields usable amounts of water, and this is one of the largest and most productive underground water systems in the world.

The Florida Aquifer supplies about 50 percent of the ground water used in the state. It constantly replenishes the water table underneath farms in the Southeast, giving farmers a steady, reliable water supply with which to irrigate their crops. Together farmers and city dwellers take out 3 billion gallons from it each year, a startling amount that nature nevertheless soon replaces. A vital cog in the hydraulic cycle, the Florida Aquifer alternately draws water from and feeds water to rivers, creeks and springs.

Geologically, the aquifer consists mostly of saturated, permeable limestone sandwiched between surface soil and nearly impermeable anhydrite rock below. From its northern limits just south of the Fall Line, the aquifer generally increases in thickness from several hundred feet to thirty-four hundred feet in south Florida.

5 Bee Hives with bees and honey $15.00. No letters answered, nor delivery made. Come after. Milton P. Minchew Jr., Macon, Rt. 3

Honey Bees and Bee Supplies for Sale, Market Bulletin, *March 12, 1952*

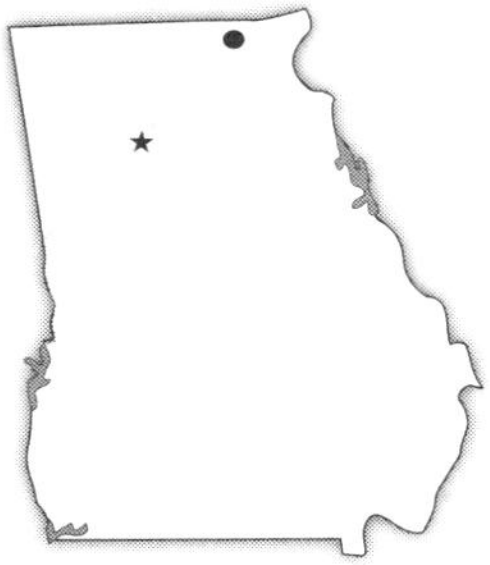

Rabun County Cabbage

Rabun County

Located in the lower Blue Ridge Mountains of the Southern Appalachians, Rabun County is in the most northeast corner of Georgia.

Facilities: Cabbage patches and pick-your-own farms are scattered throughout this area. The Dillard House in Clayton is a year-round resort with modern rooms, suites, cottages, swimming, tennis, petting zoo, horseback riding, gift shop and restaurant. The town of Dillard has dozens of mountain shops, cafes, antique stores and art galleries.

Days/Hrs.: Best time to tour is from late spring into October. Babyland General Hospital: Mon.-Sat., 9am-5pm; Sun. 10am-5pm.

Directions: Take US 441 into Rabun County. The tour begins in Clayton. Cleveland is located on US 129, 70 miles north of Atlanta and 9 miles south of Helen.

More Information: Rabun County Convention and Visitors Bureau, PO Box 750, Clayton, GA 30525; 706/782-4812. Web site: www.gamountains.com/rabun. Gillespie Farm, 706/746-2380. The Dillard House, Dillard, GA 30537; 800/544-0671 or 706/746-5348. Babyland General Hospital, 19 Underwood Street, Cleveland, GA 30528; 706/865-5862.

From late spring until October, both sides of US 441 through Rabun County, from Clayton north to Dillard, become a giant cabbage patch. Row after row of the green heads color the slopes of this large expanse of flatland, known as the Valley. This is the heart of cabbage country in Northeast Georgia. In fact, cabbage is the county's leading crop. It's grown in patches as small as two acres and as large as four hundred. The rich mountain soil, watered by one of the highest concentrations of annual rainfall in the country, offers cabbages a haven.

In the early 1900s, most farmers in the county raised cabbage. The most prominent cabbage growers were the Gillespies. Begin this tour by driving north from Clayton on US 441, through Mountain City to Rabun Gap, where a sign to the right marks the entrance to the Gillespie farm. Earl Gillespie began peddling cabbage from a horse-drawn wagon in his youth in the early 1900s. His father sent him up to Scaly Mountain, northeast of Dillard, to buy cabbage to sell in the cities. The cabbage growers would cut the cabbages, put them in tubs and transport them down the mountain on a mule-drawn sled. Sellers then loaded the cabbage on wagons, sorted them along with other vegetables and hauled the produce by horse on narrow dirt roads to small towns in Northeast Georgia, like Athens and Watkinsville. Along the way, they camped alongside the road under their wagon. People would show up at their campfires and buy off the wagon. The round trip took up to two weeks. In the 1920s and 1930s when trucks arrived, sellers took the cabbage to Atlanta, whose wholesale markets kept Rabun County farmers going. The cabbage sold at a market on Piedmont Avenue, anywhere from fifty cents to two dollars per hundred head.

Later Earl Gillespie, having opened a produce store in Clayton in 1932, sold cabbage to supermarkets such as Kroger and Winn-Dixie, who remain customers of the family today. Currently, Earl's son Jim runs this four hundred-acre farm, the county's largest cabbage operation. The Gillespies offer freshly

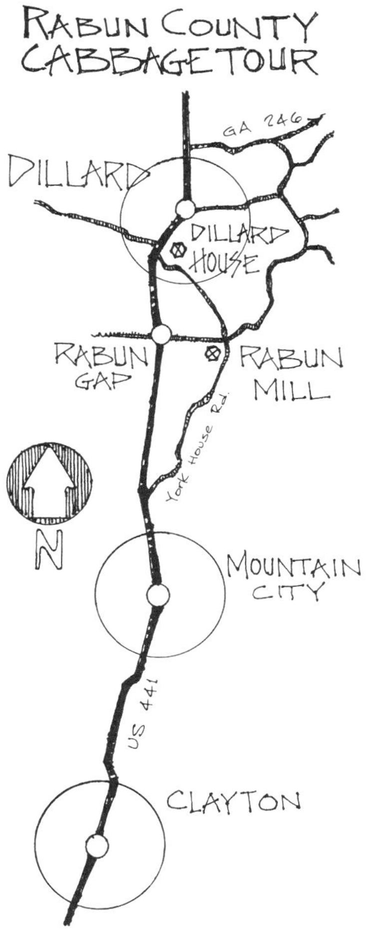

cut cabbage from early July to late October to individual buyers, but they don't let anyone into their cabbage fields. The family grows other vegetables, like tomatoes, that visitors can self-harvest on their pick-your-own farm, open seasonally from spring to autumn.

Leave the Gillespie farm and continue north to Dillard. Turn right at the Dillard House sign. Here is where Dillard House cook Lazell Vinson prepares her award-winning cabbage casserole (see page 78).

To view cabbage on some less-traveled mountain roads, turn east off of US 441 onto GA 246 just north of the Dillard city limits. Bear right at the fork about 0.25 mile later. Pass the Kelly Cemetery and bear right again. Continue about 1 mile to the intersection with Rabun Mills and turn left onto the gravel road. The road continues about 2 more miles, passes the York House restaurant, then reaches US 441 a little north of Mountain City. All along this stretch of roads, cabbage grows on the outer reaches of the Valley, in the floodplain of the Little Tennessee River and its tributary creeks.

If children are along and the time is available, a fun ending to the cabbage tour is a stop at the Babyland General Hospital in Cleveland to see how Cabbage Patch Kids are "born."

"There's a cabbage in labor! All staff, to delivery room" is a common announcement at the hospital as little Selma Jeans, Naomi Callas, Nell Nessies and Nigel Sheas are born in the cabbage patch and "adopted" each day by children nationwide. Weather that effects the region's annual cabbage crop can also effect Cabbage Patch "deliveries." One year a drought reportedly caused the dolls to have wavy hair. An early frost during another year brought about a lot of premature births.

Creator Xavier Roberts began making the soft-sculpture dolls in 1976. The art student combined his interest in sculpture with the quilting skills passed down for generations in the Appalachian Mountains to make his first life-size cloth "babies" that were "so homely they were adorable." In 1978 he opened his "hospital." Since then, more than 650,000 of these hand-stitched original babies have found homes around the world.

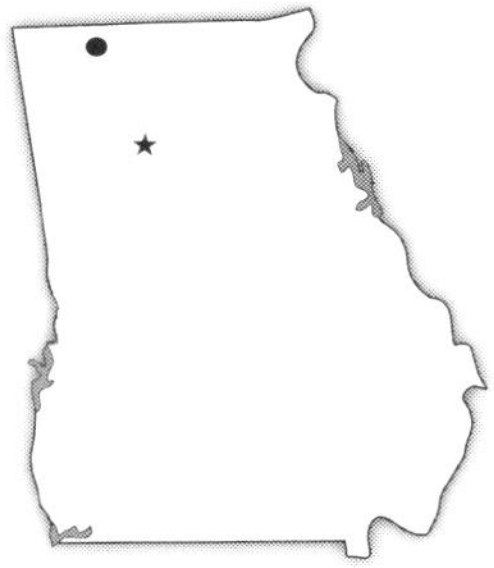

APPLE ALLEY

The Apple Alley region of Georgia winds through Gilmer County in the foothills of the Chattahoochee National Forest in the Appalachian Mountain Range.

Facilities: Roadside outlets and orchards in the Ellijay area.

Days/Hrs.: Apple harvest generally takes place from mid-Aug. to late-Nov. Call the Chamber of Commerce or the individual apple orchards for specifics. Most orchards in the area grow other items like blueberries, vegetables and peaches, which usually are picked in early July.

Directions: From Atlanta, take 400 North or I-75 North.

More Information: Gilmer County Chamber of Commerce, 5 Westside Square, Ellijay, GA 30540; 706/635-7400. Hillcrest Orchards, 706/273-3838. Apple Barrel, 706/273-3767. R & A Orchards, 706/273-3821. Mercier Orchards, 706/632-2364. Life's Little Pleasures, 706/635-7818. Panorama Orchards, 706/276-3813. Red Apple Barn, 706/635-5898.

APPLE ALLEY

APPLES, A TEMPERATE ZONE CROP, THRIVE IN THE UNIQUE geography of the mountains. Their color and flavor relates to temperature. They prefer cool nights, warm days, adequate rainfall and south-facing ridges, where maximum sunlight prevents frosts. From late August to December, the roadside stands of North Georgia overflow with fresh local apples. Some twenty orchards in the mountains offer harvests of Granny Smiths, Solid Golds, Rome Beauties, Arkansas Blacks and more than a dozen other varieties.

Gilmer County is the heart of apple production in Georgia. The county produces four hundred thousand bushels a year, about 70 percent of the state's annual harvest. Numerous apple houses and outlets are located along a ten-mile stretch of a scenic mountain highway east of Ellijay known as Apple Alley. Begin a tour of this region by stopping at Hillcrest Orchards (1), a seventy-five-acre orchard with an impressive number of first place ribbons for apple varieties from the Georgia National Fair. Heward Reece started the orchard back in 1946 with fifteen acres, selling apples from his garage. In the retail outlet section, bushels of apples crowd the floor, along with apple bread, old-fashioned cider, jams and jellies. In the warehouse, a ten-minute video about apple growing discusses how Hillcrest rents bees to cross-pollinate the orchard flowers in the spring and how the orchard has replaced much of its standard-sized trees with dwarf ones, which are easier to handle and harvest. In the back of the warehouse outlet is a large apple sorter and washer. In March and April, visitors might see a mechanical tree planter setting down a few new trees in the orchard. To allow for optimal growing, limbs must be constantly trained, clipped and directed, giving the bearing limbs the maximum room and light. From July to December, Hillcrest Orchards gives hayride tours of the orchards. The tour winds through several acres of apples and a children's park before ending up at a petting zoo with chickens, rabbits and goats.

The Apple Barrel (2), with its new barn and other farm buildings, draws family tourists looking for petting zoos and farm tours for the children. R & A Orchards (3) has sixty acres and a roadside outlet. The family has grown apples since 1947. The orchard organizes apple picking days for preferred customers in September.

Just north of Blue Ridge, Mercier Orchards (4) is the largest and one of the oldest apple producers in the state (see page 189). Three generations of Merciers have worked the orchards since 1943. It's the only apple operation in Georgia that packs and ships apples out of state. A good Mercier harvest can bring in one hundred thousand bushels. For months the packing house in the rear of the outlet warehouse churns out apples earmarked for out-of-state delivery. Then in mid-autumn the Merciers, like all the other growers in north Georgia, cater their roadside stand to the tourists streaming into the mountains for fresh apples and fall foliage. Besides two dozen varieties of apples, Mercier sells apple products such as breads, slushees, doughnuts, heavy cider and regional jams, jellies and relishes.

At Ellijay (5), a small mountain town of red brick storefronts on winding, curving streets, the Chamber of Commerce hands out apples and information on local apple orchards, including maps, brochures and a driving tour tape of Apple Alley. Life's Little Pleasures (6), a popular apple bakery, makes apple bread, full of apple chunks, laced in cinnamon and drenched in glaze. From their store and roadside outlets, the bakery sells up to 4,000 loaves a day and 125,000 a year.

At Panorama Orchards (7) visitors can watch apple pies, fried apple pies, apple sauce bread and apple brandy cake bake through a viewing window into the kitchen. The outlet also has an apple packing line, cold storage for ten thousand bushels, old antiques and retail sales. The orchard is actually ten miles away from the packing facility and retail store, but Panorama welcomes guests there. It's one of the few orchards to offer pick-your-own apples on a regular basis, from Labor Day until early October. The Red Apple Barn (8) has apples, cider, dried apples, fried apple pies, honey, candied apples, pickled peaches and other products. Call to schedule a guided tour of the orchard, which includes free samples of apples and cider.

Hot Apple Pie

In his book *Crackers*, Roy Blount Jr., relates this story by country comedian Jerry Clower:

Uncle Versy was outside in the yard one day when his wife Aunt Pet Ledbetter asked him would he like to come inside and have a piece of apple pie with the church ladies. Uncle Versy said he believed he would.

Now, one of the church ladies had told Aunt Pet about a new way of serving apple pie, where you served it hot.

And Uncle Versy never had had apple pie hot. He'd always had it cooled. So he came in there to the parlor and took a big old bite of that pie right into his mouth, and WAAAWWWW, it like to have burnt the whole roof of his mouth off, and AWWWWWW, Uncle Versy gathered that big old mouthful of pie up in his mouth and went WOWR...phoo. And spit.

And there was a great big quivering gob of steaming hot apple pie right out on Aunt Pet's best tablecloth in front of the church ladies.

And Uncle Versy said, "You know there's a many a damn fool woulda swallered that."

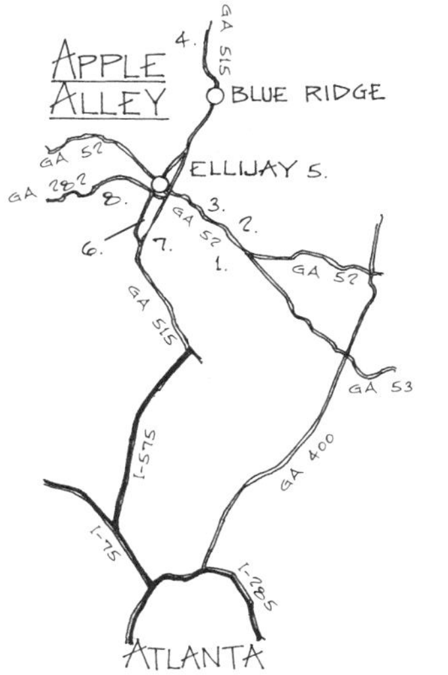

VIDALIA ONION COUNTRY

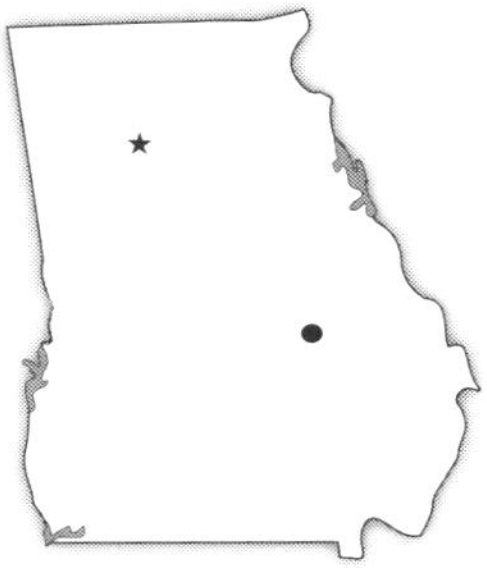

VIDALIA ONION COUNTRY

Toombs County, the heart of Vidalia onion country, is in Georgia's coastal plain region.

Days/Hrs.: During onion season, The Vidalia Onion Factory offers guided tours throughout the day and evening as time and space permits. Call in advance to find the best time to visit. During the off-season, the factory store and cafe are open from 8:30am-5pm.

Directions: From Vidalia, go about 4.5 miles east of downtown on US 280 to reach the Vidalia Onion Factory.

More Information: Vidalia Onion Factory, P.O. Box 310, Vidalia, GA 30474; 912/526-3466 or 800/227-ONION. Vidalia Onion Committee, P.O. Box 1609, Vidalia, GA 30474; 912/537-1918. Bland Farms, 800/VIDALIA.

MOST PEOPLE DO NOT KNOW THE NAME OF MOSE COLEMAN, BUT a historical marker (1) bearing his name sits on the late farmer's property in Toombs County. Here is where Mose planted onions in 1931. But oddly, they turned out sweet, not hot like he had predicted. Nevertheless, the Toombs County farmer got a decent price for his novelty onions at the market. He managed to sell each fifty-pound bag for $3.50. Over the years other farmers in the region tried their luck with the onions, which sold well in the Toombs County seat of Vidalia. Motorists traveling on nearby US 280 and Route 1 who tried the onions liked their sweet, mild taste. They bought them by the bagload and referred to them by the name of the town. Soon Vidalia onions appeared in Piggly Wiggly and A&P grocery stores all over the East. Today, the Vidalia onion industry is worth an estimated $30 million. Each autumn and winter more than two hundred farmers plant the sweet onions on about fourteen thousand acres. When harvested in the spring and early summer, each acre produces up to seventy thousand plants.

Within site of the late Mose Coleman property is the five thousand-acre Stanley Farms (2) and Vidalia Onion Factory (3). Like most Vidalia onion farms, the Stanleys run a family-owned, multi-generation business. Their onion acreage, however, is much larger than most, about one thousand acres. Visitors can walk through their fields on either side of the factory. In early September the Stanleys start seed beds for the onions and from November to February they plant the seedlings by hand. Then come the hazards of the growing season. Too much rain can rot the stems. Too much cold can harden the centers. Too much heat can bring stifling weeds. In the spring, a straight blade behind a tractor digs up the onions. Then between one and two hundred migrant workers cut off the tops, which reach up to three feet in height, and put the onions in bags, which remain in the field for a day or two to dry in the sun. Then they are taken into the Vidalia Onion Factory for processing.

Visitors can also tour the processing plant, which serves as the family's headquarters. Onions fresh from the field go into large, green metal driers, heated by gas, for a day or so of curing. Then they are moved to a conveyor belt where they roll up and down a long line of chutes, canals and tunnels as workers inspect them for soft spots or bruises. Next, the onions are sorted into peewee, medium and jumbo sizes and bagged, ready for delivery to roadside stands, grocery stores and mail boxes all over the world. Others go into controlled atmospheric storage units. Inside each of the tightly sealed rooms, where the temperature remains 34 degrees and the humidity 70 percent, is a mix of 92 percent nitrogen, 5 percent carbon dioxide and 3 percent oxygen. The combination puts onions into a deep sleep that keeps them fresh longer, dramatically lengthening the selling season. The Stanleys sell Vidalia onion products like jams, relishes and salad dressings in their gift shop and offer onion specialities in season in the shop's cafe.

Over the years the nearby city of Glennville in Tattnall County has feuded with Vidalia over the origin of the Georgia sweet onion. And in 1979 when Vidalia conducted a test that determined its onions were sweeter than those in the Glennville area, the latter city responded with an experiment of its own that concluded their onions to be less pungent. Farmers who grow sweet onions in Tattnall County produce more than twice as many as those in Toombs. One of the largest Tattnall County Vidalia onion farms is Bland Farms (4), which the Bland family has owned since the 1940s. During April the farm employs one thousand people to harvest onions on its twenty-four thousand acres. Visitors can tour the onion fields and packing facility.

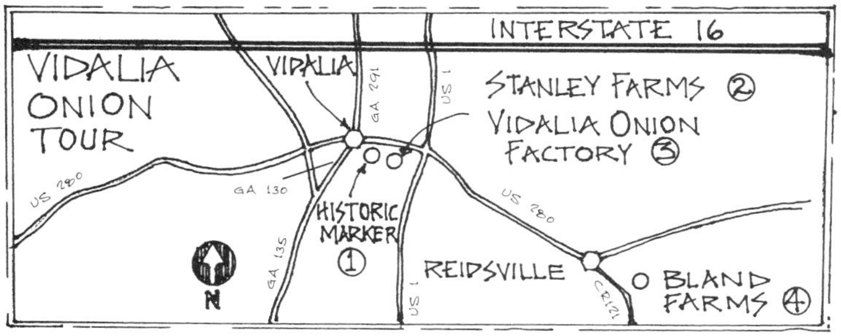

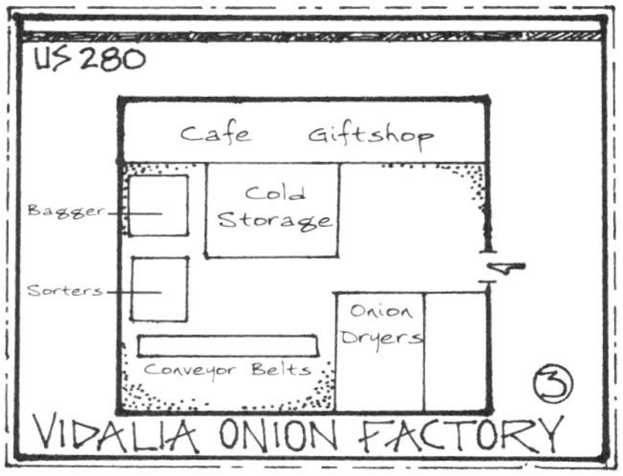

The Vidalia Onion Trademark

Over the years onion farmers have raged a persistent battle as to whose onions can wear the Vidalia trademark. In the early 1980s one man was taken to court for selling out-of-state onions as Vidalias. His defense was that genetics, not location, made the onion sweet; because they were of the yellow granex hybrid variety, the onions would grow sweet anywhere.

While some agricultural researchers quietly concede that variety has something to do with it, Vidalia farmers, nonetheless, have always maintained that the soil and climate of the region are primarily responsible to make their product unique. The specific blend of sandy loam soil with low sulphur content and mild winters gives character to the onions, which have higher sugar and water contents than ordinary ones. One 1979 experiment determined that a Vidalia onion has more sugar than orange juice, apple juice and Coca-Cola.

To put an end to the feuding, the state determined in 1986 that only onions grown in thirteen counties and portions of seven others can wear the Vidalia label. Sweet onion growers across the nation have challenged the commercial supremacy of the original Georgia sweets, but none have come close to the marketing success of those with the label Vidalia.

FARM IRRIGATION

Even though Georgia has a humid climate, agricultural drought commonly affects most of the state. In the 1970s when commodity prices reached historic peaks, farmers in Georgia, mostly in the Coastal Plain, installed expensive irrigation systems to reduce the damage of drought. Agricultural irrigation withdrawals in 1980 ran an estimated 400 million gallons of water a day, roughly half the groundwater withdrawals for the state. Ninety percent of it was in the southern half of the state. As agricultural prices leveled off in the 1980s, the development of irrigation did as well, leaving about 1 million acres in Georgia under irrigation. In the 1990s prices have increased again slightly and so has the amount of irrigated fields to about 1.2 million acres in Georgia.

In Georgia, nearly all irrigation systems are sprinkler types, usually center pivots like the one in the illustration below. The long, segmented pipe irrigation sprinklers, which can extend in length more than one thousand feet, slowly work their way on thick squat wheels, well under one mile per hour, across row crop fields in a full circle, or more commonly a half circle. The overhead pipe stands about fifteen feet off the ground, spraying water about twelve hundred gallons a minute per thousand feet of pipe.

The water usually comes from deep well or large springs, sometimes stored in a small impoundment pond, where a pump draws the water and runs it through underground pipes to water hydrants installed throughout the farm. The irrigation system resembles that of a golf course, only on a much larger scale. The systems are expensive, over one thousand dollars an acre to install. Yet most farmers recoup their investment within a couple of years due to yield increases.

Another common irrigation system are tow-cable sprinklers. They look essentially like a lawn sprinkler pivot, only the water jets stream over fifty feet into the air. They have wheels at their bases and are reeled in by a thick metal ground cable, which gets its power by diverting some of the water stream. They move slowly, about one hundred feet over ten hours, along a line between the crop rows.

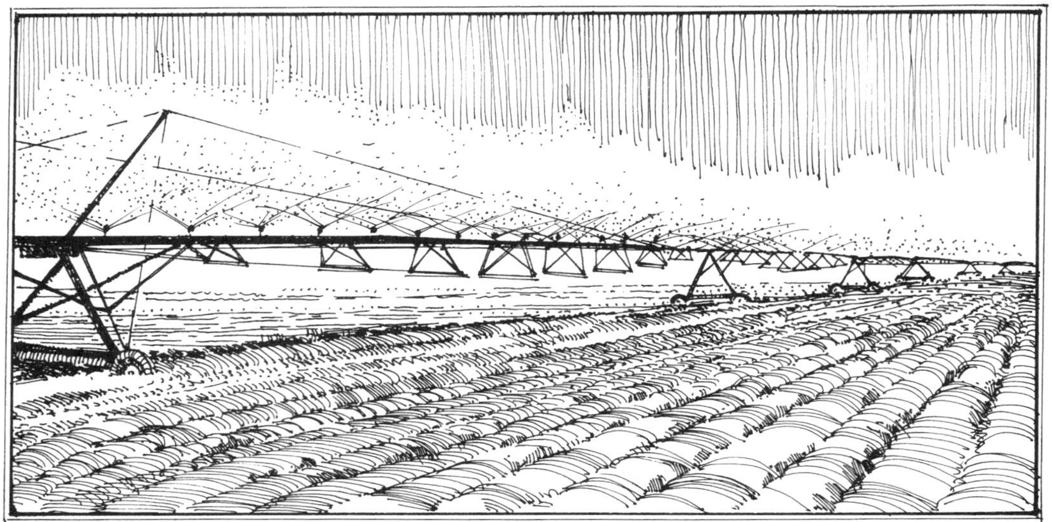

IRRIGATING CROPS

Pecans

Pecans, members of the hickory family, grew along the Flint and other major rivers in the South for centuries, brought by Native Americans from the Mississippi Delta. Thought to derive from the indigenous word "pacan," meaning a hard nut to crack, the pecan was used to season hominy, thicken venison broth and ferment into an intoxicating drink. Over much of the continent early settlers planted and traded pecans, sometimes known as Mississippi nuts.

In 1890 Nelson Tift planted twenty-five thousand pecan trees near Albany. In 1920, with more than 1 million trees planted in the vicinity, Albany brought in a harvest of 2.5 million pounds of the nut. By the 1950s the state led the nation in pecan harvests and continues to do so. There are more than five hundred varieties of pecans harvested from the middle of October to late December, including Desirable, Elliott, Stuart and Schley.

A popular all-season nut, pecans can be used in summer ice creams, fall baked goods, winter confections or spring vegetables. Pecans are a good source of protein and are loaded with essential vitamins and nutrients, including iron, calcium, potassium, phosphorus, the B vitamins and fiber.

The Heritage of Farm Crafts

At one time, crafts made by hand on the farm served a specific purpose—weaving and spinning produced clothes; quilts were stitched for warmth; baskets were woven to hold cotton and produce; pottery enabled farmers to store cane syrup, whiskey, water, lard, butter, milk, fruit, vegetables and meat; furniture and musical instruments were sometimes unobtainable otherwise. In this modern day, there is less necessity for making these crafts; but the craftsmen who continue to demonstrate, create, display and sell these works of art at craft shows and fairs are preserving a vital part of the Southern heritage. For information on craftsmen, see Resources.

1. Tobe Wells from Elberton splits strips of wood and weaves them into cotton baskets of all sizes.
2. The Georgia Piedmont's good clay soil has always provided potters with an abundance of raw material.
3. Many eighteenth-century quilts were insulated with cotton seeds, pounded flat so they weren't felt.
4. Quilting guilds continue the art form throughout Georgia.
5. Glazed stoneware pottery—like this four-handle vase, jug and pitcher—are beautiful in form and function.
6. Today, a glazed stoneware churn and casserole are considered works of art.

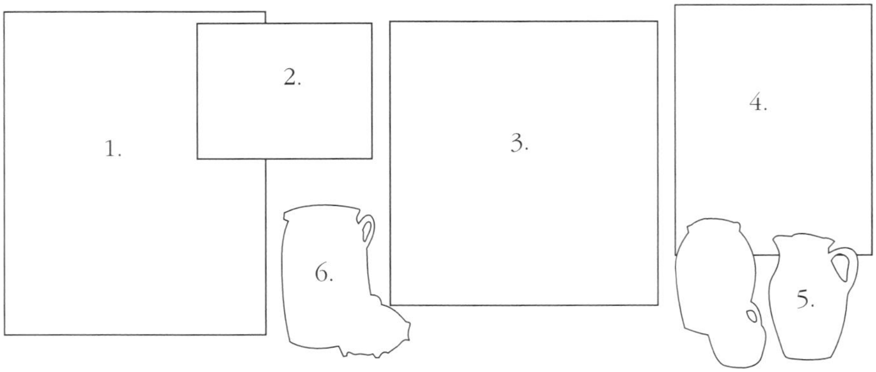

JAMES LEE ADAMS

Our family came into the area in the 1840s and 1850s, and we have about six or seven generations buried in Mitchell County today. They were primarily farmers, and in fact, we are farming some of the same land that my great-grandfather farmed. It passed through other hands before my father obtained it and I have obtained it along with some other land. So our roots are fairly deep in Mitchell County.

We have several thousand acres of crop at present—I guess right at five thousand if you take all the different entities that we farm together. We have close to two thousand acres of pecans we are running. We grow cotton. We grow peanuts. All these are irrigated crops. We grow wheat. We grow cattle. We have fifteen hundred to two thousand head of stockers. We bring in young steers and young heifers, one year old that have just been weaned, bring them in at four hundred pounds and run them up to around six or seven hundred pounds in the wintertime. We run them in pecan groves and use those fields when they don't really have any other use.

We have twenty poultry houses on this farm, which is a large number. We have three to four thousand alligators on this farm that are raised for hides and meat. What we are doing there is taking the two or three thousand pounds of chickens that die naturally every day and feeding them to the alligators so we have a source of feed there that is not really restrictive. There is no cost associated with it.

Our property is relatively big, but it includes timberland. But there are quite a few operations that are quite larger. We are probably in the top 5 or 10 percent of the farms in the United States.

I never will forget a young lady came down, Pam Martin from Atlanta's WAGA-TV 5. She came down one year and she was talking about our farm in her introduction. I never will forget, she was walking across the field and she said, "Now we've come to a farm that is making a lot of money. In fact, last year they made over a million dollars." I said, "Pam, stop right there." I said, "There is a profound difference between gross and net." Sales may be over a million dollars, but we surely did not even come close to netting that figure. I think sometimes we have a misconception of what really constitutes large.

At the time of the Civil War, people were planting cotton and after a few years they would deplete the soil or literally mine it of the nutrients and they would have to move on to other areas. It left the soil washed out and eroded. The modern-day farmer knows that his major asset is his soil and he has to protect it—making sure it does not wash away and also making sure that the nutrient level stays high so that he can have a good productive crop.

We are also very much aware that we need to rotate our crops. They used to have a monoculture where it was cotton crop after cotton crop ad infinitum. And the soil, because of the monoculture was depleted even faster because one particular crop will pull down certain nutrients that it specializes in using. Now we rotate in peanuts to restore the nitrogen in the soil, that love residual fertilizer. Then you go to cotton. Then you go to corn and so your pest pressure is lowered and also you have a balanced use of nutrients.

Now we go out and test the soil—pull samples of soil, run them through the laboratory and so we are able to check for pests that you can't see which feed on the roots of plants. We are also able to test for nutrients in the soil, the phosphorus, potash and the magnesium and the sulfur and every other ingredient that allows crops to grow well. And we are able to replenish it to a large degree with naturally occurring organic fertilizer such as chicken litter and what have you and also occasionally with the chemical fertilizers that are mined and spread on our farms, too. But this is something that you have to constantly monitor. I think we are going to be moving away from chemical fertilizers in the future. It makes no sense for us to put out chemicals and fertilizers that can't be sustained 100, 150 and 200 years from today. We don't need to put out things on our land which are going to harm it on a cumulative basis. My family, my wife, my kids, my grandkids drink the water that comes off this land. They eat the crops that are grown on this land.

We are in a global economy whether we like it or not. We cannot compete in agriculture by being a low labor cost producer anymore. We've got to be the most efficient producer, and the way you achieve efficiency today is through technological breakthroughs. You've got to be at the cutting edge of changes and be able to adapt to new technologies. Right now on our farm the combine goes though the field. Each foot it moves, it is evaluating a crop on that particular foot of land. It is detecting its position by reading off at least two satellites. So what you get is a map, drawn in real time, showing the production of that field as the combine moves across it. So now what we are able to do is take this global position satellite technology and identify our strong spots in the field and the weak spots in the field. We go back with a chicken litter spreader that puts fertilizer or nutrients on the field. We take these computer derived maps and this information and put it into a device that relocates where it is in that field, reading again off these satellites that are going over in the air. And when it comes to the spots that are weak, then it opens the gates and applies more fertilizer in those spots as predetermined at the proper rate. We had in that particular field I'm talking about, variations on corn yields from an excess of three hundred bushels an acre down to eighty bushels an acre. The field itself averaged 225 bushels an acre. But now we are able to identify to the foot where our good areas are and where our bad areas are and now for the first time we can go back and start correcting those weak areas, hopefully to bring them up to some semblance of percentage of 85 or 90 percent of production of our strongest areas.

Farming is high-tech. It has dramatically changed since I've been farming. I've got two son-in-laws who have advanced degrees from Georgia Tech. One is handling alligators and poultry; the other son-in-law is handling cattle and pecans and working with me in row crops. But these are the types of folks that are going to be able to take advantage of the technology that is coming down the pike and that's how we are going to compete in this country. My father's world ended at the gate post of his farm to a large degree. Today the limits of our world in agriculture are out of space, literally.

The biggest revolution in the history of the world's going to be a genetic revolution where we will be able to manipulate genes on a scientific basis.

Several years ago, scientists were able to take a tobacco plant and cross it with a lightening bug. So literally, you go out into the tobacco field at night and see the tobacco plant that had been genetically manipulated beep its light.

With genetic manipulation we are able to put naturally occurring genes into our crops that make these crops unattractive to pests and, in some cases, literally make the insect sick. So now we are able to eliminate or diminish insect pressure and other pest pressure by these advances that are going on at the University of Georgia and other universities in the South and all over the world.

We have a soybean breeding program. Probably one of the preeminent breeders in the world is Dr. Roger Boemer at the University of Georgia. In the past we've had plants that were defoliated. Now these insects will not eat the leaves because of genetic material that Dr. Bonner's put in them.

He is finding other genes that allow soybeans to withstand drought.

Now we are able to go in and change the very structure of the plant. For example, soybeans are able to take nitrogen out of the air, and they use fixation of that nitrogen to produce their own nitrogen. So you don't have to have nitrogen fertilizer on soybeans. Peanuts are the same way. Corn, however, and wheat does not have the nitrogen fixation to take the nitrogen out of the air; and therefore, we have to go out and put our chemical fertilizers on them. Sometime in the next few years, we are going to see a scientist take nodules or roots of soybean plants and use genetic guns or manipulation and put those roots on corn or wheat. And then, instead of applying nitrogen by chemical means, you will have that plant itself go out and fixate nitrogen and allow it to come down those roots.

The limits we are going to have tomorrow are going to be those moral limits that we put upon ourselves which are proper as to what we can do with this new ability. It is a frightening possibility. It's a Promethean possibility. But if we have the wisdom to do it correctly...

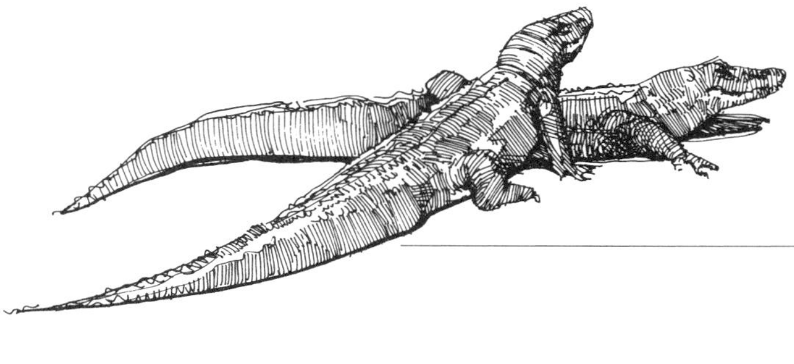

BUYER'S GUIDE TO PECANS

The best time to buy pecans is during the fall harvest season.

Look for plump pecans, uniform in color and size. The shell should be smooth and light brown in color.

Pecans are perishable and must be properly stored to maintain optimum quality.

Keep shelled or unshelled pecans in airtight containers in the refrigerator or freezer. Pecans can be kept in the refrigerator for about nine months or the freezer for up to two years.

GEORGIA PECAN PIE

A year-round favorite

- 3 eggs
- 1 cup sugar
- 1 cup light or dark corn syrup
- 1 teaspoon vanilla extract
- 3 tablespoons butter, melted and cooled
- 1½ cups coarsely chopped pecans (or halves)
- 1 9-inch unbaked pie crust

Preheat oven to 350°. Place eggs in a medium mixing bowl and whisk lightly. Add sugar, corn syrup, vanilla and melted butter. Stir with a wooden spoon to combine well. Stir in pecans. Pour filling into prepared unbaked pie crust. Bake 45 to 55 minutes or until toothpick inserted in center comes out clean. Cool on wire rack. Yields 8 servings.

Georgia Pecan Commission

Hint: If using a frozen pie crust, be forewarned that they brown easily. You may want to shield the crust with strips of aluminum foil cut about 3 inches wide and about 12 to 15 inches long. Wrap these around the edge of the pie pan to cover the edge of the crust.

SUGAR SPICED PECANS

Good for parties or just as a snack

- 1 pound pecan halves
- 1 cup sugar
- ¾ teaspoon salt
- 1 teaspoon ground cinnamon
- 1 cup water
- 1 teaspoon vanilla extract

Toast pecans 10 minutes at 300°. In a small saucepan, combine all ingredients except pecans and vanilla. Cook until syrup spins a small thread, about 5 minutes. Remove from heat; add pecans and vanilla. Stir quickly until syrup crystallizes. Pour onto buttered platter. Rapidly, but gently, separate pecans. Yields about 4 cups or 16 appetizer servings.

Georgia Pecan Commission

Chewy Bread

This bread tastes like a dessert!

½	cup butter, melted
1	16-ounce box light brown sugar
3	eggs
2	cups self-rising flour
1	teaspoon vanilla extract
2	cups chopped pecans

Preheat oven to 325°. Combine butter and sugar; add eggs one at a time, beating well after each addition. Blend in flour and vanilla. Add pecans and mix well. Pour into a greased and floured 9x13-inch pan. Bake for 45 minutes or until brown. Yields 36 servings.

Frances Worley
Commerce, Georgia

Sawdust Pie

This is a popular recipe among Market Bulletin *readers*

7	egg whites, unbeaten
1½	cups sugar
1½	cups graham cracker crumbs
1½	cups finely chopped pecans
1½	cups flaked coconut
1	9-inch deep dish unbaked pie shell

Preheat oven to 325°. In large deep-dish bowl, mix first 5 ingredients together and stir by hand. Pour into pie shell and bake for 25 to 30 minutes until glossy and set. Do not overbake! Serve warm with sliced bananas and whipped cream. Yields 8 slices.

Etta Gore
Walthourville, Georgia

Trilba Cordell
Wildwood, Georgia

Hint: The baked pie is firm near the edges but moist and chewy in the center.

Pecan Meringue Pie

Senator Sam Nunn, who served in the United States Senate for four consecutive terms, grew up in Perry, a small middle Georgia town that is right in the heart of pecan country. His wife Colleen likes to make pecan meringue pie, not only because it reflects the senator's heritage but because it is a true family favorite.

To make the pie, Mrs. Nunn beats until frothy the egg whites from 3 large room temperature eggs and then adds 1 teaspoon of baking powder. Next, she adds 1 cup of sugar, gradually beating the mixture until it is stiff. Then she takes 1 cup of pecans and chops them and 20 Ritz crackers and crushes them. She then folds the pecans, crackers and 1 teaspoon of vanilla extract into the mixture. Mrs. Nunn pours all of this into a greased 8 or 9-inch pie pan and bakes it for 40 minutes in a 300° preheated oven. After the pie cools, she covers it with whipped cream and refrigerates it overnight.

Want unencumbered, refined woman, health card, sober, for light farm work on farm; for room, board, bath, salary. No snuff users. 2 in family. Letters answered. No cards. Mrs. V. A. Locke, Toccoa, 520 E. Doyle St.

Farm Help Wanted, Market Bulletin, *June 3, 1953*

Pecan Chicken Kiev

Adding pecans to a traditional Kiev makes this a winner

½	cup butter or margarine
1	teaspoon lemon juice
1	tablespoon chopped parsley
1	tablespoon chopped chives
1	clove garlic, crushed
1	teaspoon salt
⅛	teaspoon pepper
3	whole chicken breasts
⅓	cup cornflake crumbs
1	cup finely chopped pecans
½	cup all-purpose flour
1	egg, lightly beaten

Beat butter until soft. Stir in lemon juice, parsley, chives, garlic, salt and pepper until well combined. Spread mixture onto wax paper to a 4x3-inch rectangle, about ½-inch thick. Place in freezer to chill, about 20 minutes.

Split chicken breasts and remove skin. Carefully cut meat from bones, keeping meat in whole pieces (6 in all). Place each piece, smooth side down, between 2 sheets of wax paper. Flatten with wooden mallet or heavy object to about ½-inch thickness, being careful not to break meat. (This pounding stage is essential for recipe success.) Remove papers.

Remove herb-butter from freezer; cut lengthwise into six ½-inch-wide sticks, then half across to make 12 "fingers." Place a "finger" of herb butter in center of each flattened chicken breast. Bring long sides of chicken over butter; then fold ends over, making sure butter is completely covered. Fasten with wooden picks. Combine cornflake crumbs and pecans in shallow bowl. Roll chicken in flour, dip in beaten egg, then roll in crumb mixture to coat completely and evenly with crumbs. Wrap individually or a few together in foil; freeze.

Preheat oven to 425°. Unwrap chicken rolls; place in single layer in jellyroll pan. Bake for 5 minutes. Lower heat to 400°. Bake 20 minutes longer. Yields 6 servings.

Delores Little
Albany, Georgia
Grand Prize Winner,
National Pecan Festival Cooking Sweepstakes

Recipe Fame and Fortune

Do you have a great-tasting recipe? Do your friends and family rave, saying it's the best they've ever tasted? Do you think it's got that special something that will undoubtedly win a recipe contest? Well, you might be right, but before you go off seeking fame and fortune, there are a few simple tips you should follow when entering.

Obey the rules. Don't take anything for granted. Read the rules very carefully and follow them exactly. For example, if the contest requires entries to be submitted on one side of an 8.5 x 11-inch sheet of paper, don't turn it in on an index card. Contest judges will think that if you can't follow the rules, you don't deserve to win!

Keep it simple. Make sure that your recipe is easy to follow. List the ingredients in order of use and have the preparation steps flow in a logical order. Have several friends "test" your recipe to make sure that they can follow the instructions. If they have questions or troubles, you can be sure that the judges will, too.

Be specific. Judges are not mind readers. If your recipe says to add "3 cups of cooked squash," does this mean zucchini squash, yellow squash, yellow crookneck or butternut, and should it be sliced, cubed or julienned? Don't leave things to someone else's interpretation. In general, providing too many details is much better than too few!

Practice makes perfect. Everyone thinks that they have that special recipe and competition is tough! Get an edge by practicing your recipe. Prepare your recipe over and over. Do the flavors blend? Does it need a little more or less spice? Don't rely solely on your own taste buds. Serve your

Tomato Soup Cake

This cake is similar to spice cake and has a great texture

1 cup sugar
½ cup shortening or margarine
2 cups sifted all-purpose flour
2 teaspoons baking powder
½ teaspoon salt
1 teaspoon ground cinnamon
½ teaspoon ground nutmeg
1 10.75-ounce can tomato soup
1 teaspoon baking soda
½ cup chopped pecans
½ cup raisins
1 teaspoon vanilla extract

Preheat oven to 350°. In large bowl, cream sugar and shortening. In separate bowl, combine flour, baking powder, salt, cinnamon and nutmeg. In small bowl, mix tomato soup and baking soda. Add flour mixture to sugar and shortening alternating with tomato soup. Mix well. Fold in pecans, raisins and vanilla. Pour batter into greased and floured 8x8x2-inch pan. Bake for 45 minutes or until cake tests done. Cool in pan 10 minutes. Remove from pan and cool completely. Yields 9 squares.

Margaret Huller
Atlanta, Georgia

Hint: Notice that this cake doesn't include eggs. Watch the tomato soup and baking soda foam! (That step is great for kids!) Sprinkle the cake with powdered sugar for a nice finishing touch.

recipe to a variety of people and ask for their opinions.

Enhance what you've got. Winning a recipe contest requires skill and is not simply a matter of whose recipe tastes the best. There are several subtle, but extremely important, ways to make your recipe even more alluring to the judges, including: using a catchy title, following food trends and making the meal eye appealing.

Susan Lewis, Home Economist, Georgia Department of Agriculture

80 A Fayette Co., 6 mi Fairburn, 4 mi Tyrone, 8 mi Fayetteville road being paved. 2 good houses, both wired, 2 barns, fine lakesite, 2 large branches never fail; 30 A imp. pasture, page wire and locust post; 20 A swamp, pasture, barbwire A under cultivation. 3/4 mi. road frontage. All on mail and school bus rt. Atlanta phone available. $8,500.00 M. E. West, Fayetteville, Rt. 2.

Farm Land For Sale, Market Bulletin, *October 20, 1954*

Harvesting Pecans

Pecan harvesting offers a fascinating spectacle to the motorist who spots the unusual mechanized gadgets that are part of this operation: shakers, sweepers and harvesters.

Resembling a post-nuclear war age hot rod, the shaker has a looming hydraulic arm, twenty feet in length, that reaches up with a massive set of claws, literally shaking the fully grown pecan trees and sending down torrents of pecans. They plunk down softly on the ground or land on shag carpet stuck all over the machine, then roll down to the ground, swept harmlessly aside by one of six round brushes attached underneath the shaker like those on a street sweeper.

A bona fide full-time sweeper follows. Its brush-like rubber teeth strain and push the nuts into large piles between the rows, which are later scooped up by a harvester, which shoots them into a collector bin on its back.

The pecans are ready to leave the orchard.

Fruitcake Squares

A colorful holiday treat!

6	tablespoons butter, melted
1½	cups graham cracker crumbs
1	cup flaked coconut
1	cup chopped dates
⅛	cup all-purpose flour
1½	cups diced, mixed candied fruit
½	cup golden raisins
1½	cups chopped pecans
1	14-ounce can sweetened condensed milk

Preheat oven to 350°. Pour melted butter into a 15x10x1-inch (jelly-roll) pan. Distribute butter evenly. Sprinkle graham cracker crumbs in pan and shake to distribute evenly. Press to form a firm crust. Begin layering ingredients by sprinkling on coconut. In small bowl, toss dates in flour so they do not stick together. Discard extra flour. Pour dates over coconut. Add candied fruit and raisins for next layer. Sprinkle pecans and press lightly with hands to level mixture in the pan. Pour condensed milk evenly over top. Bake about 30 minutes. Cool completely; cut and remove from pan. Yields approximately 35 squares.

Georgia Pecan Commission

Pecan French Toast

Making the night before means a quick and delicious breakfast

4	eggs
⅔	cup orange juice
⅓	cup milk
¼	cup sugar
¼	teaspoon ground nutmeg
½	teaspoon vanilla extract
1	8-ounce loaf French bread, cut in 1-inch slices
⅓	cup butter or margarine, melted
½	cup chopped pecans

Combine eggs, orange juice, milk, sugar, nutmeg and vanilla; mix with a wire whisk. Place bread in a single layer in a tight-fitting casserole; pour milk mixture over bread. Cover and refrigerate overnight, turning once.

Preheat oven to 400°. Arrange soaked bread slices in single layer in an oblong casserole. Pour butter over top and sprinkle with pecans. Bake for 20 to 25 minutes or until brown. Serve with maple syrup and butter. Yields 4 servings.

Kay Meyer
Fort Valley, Georgia

Pecan Apple Cake

Cream cheese icing tops this cake filled with pecans and apples

1	18.25-ounce yellow cake mix
1	3.5-ounce package instant vanilla pudding
1	cup vegetable oil
½	cup cold water
4	eggs
3	medium apples, peeled, cored and diced
1	cup chopped pecans
	Vegetable cooking spray

Preheat oven to 350°. Blend cake mix, pudding, oil, water and eggs. Beat at medium speed for 2 minutes. Add apples and pecans and combine. Spray 4 8-inch round cake pans with vegetable spray and pour in batter. Bake for 25 to 35 minutes, until done. Cool for 10 minutes in pans. Turn cakes out of pans and cool completely.

Frosting

12	ounces cream cheese, softened
1½	boxes powdered sugar (24-ounces total weight)
¾	cup chopped pecans
2	tablespoons milk (as needed)

Cream cheese and powdered sugar. Beat at medium speed for 2 minutes, adding milk as needed to give a creamy consistency. Add pecans to cream cheese mixture and frost each layer, sides and top of cake. Yields 10 slices.

Alice Blackwell
Warwick, Georgia
First Place Dessert,
1994 Macon Great Tastes of Georgia Recipe Contest

Hint: Cake may be frosted with cream cheese icing and nuts sprinkled on top.

The Business of Farming

The concept of agribusiness—the production, sale and distribution of farm products—reflects the national trend toward larger numbers of people being involved in farm operations. According to a recent University of Georgia study, one in every six Georgians works in an agriculturally related sector of the economy. Together, agriculture and agribusiness contribute over $46 billion to the state's annual economic output, making it Georgia's largest industry.

The farm input and machinery sector contributes $0.8 billion and employs more than 14,000 people. Farm inputs include seeds, feeds, fertilizers and machinery, plus the specialized firms that provide services to farmers and foresters.

The food and fiber processing sector provides almost 170,000 jobs and contributes $31 billion to the economic output. Food wholesale and retail outlets, including the large grocery store chains and their suppliers, contribute $2.3 billion and more than 98,000 jobs to Georgia's economy. The food service industry, including restaurants and institutions, is responsible for more than 212,000 jobs and $6.1 billion of output.

The farm and forestry production sector represents over 85,000 jobs and contributes $5.1 billion in output.

As an aid to farmers hard hit by the recent freeze, the plantings of soybeans is recommended by the Georgia Cottonseed Crushers Association. Farmers planting soybeans can expect a return of $30 to $50 per acre.

News Item, Market Bulletin, *April 13, 1955*

Orange Pecan Salad with Toasted Pecan Dressing

Toasted Pecan Dressing is a great finish to this refreshing salad

2	small heads (about 8 cups) Bibb lettuce, torn into bite-size pieces
½	pound (about 8 cups) spinach, torn into bite-size pieces
2	oranges, peeled, seeded and sectioned
½	medium red onion, thinly sliced and separated into rings
	Toasted Pecan Dressing
½	cup chopped pecans, toasted

Place lettuce, spinach, orange sections and onion in large bowl and toss to distribute evenly. Drizzle pecan dressing over salad and toss again until all ingredients are lightly coated. Serve salad on individual serving plates and top each with 1 tablespoon toasted pecans. Yields 8 servings.

Toasted Pecan Dressing

¼	cup chopped pecans, toasted
2	garlic cloves
1	teaspoon dry mustard
2	tablespoons white wine vinegar
¼	teaspoon hot sauce
1	teaspoon soy sauce
1	teaspoon sugar
⅓	cup olive oil
¼	teaspoon salt
¼	teaspoon pepper

Place all ingredients in food processor or blender; process for 1 minute at high speed. Serve with Orange Pecan Salad. Yields ½ cup dressing.

Organic Farming

Over the last few years, the label "organically grown" has become one that more and more consumers look for at the grocery store. Organics is the art of farming without the use of manufactured materials, such as fertilizers and pesticides. Organic farming demands healthy plants, pain-staking soil preparation and vast knowledge. "You have to know plants, the life cycles of the insects. You don't just see the land when you plant, spray and harvest," says Cynthia Hizer, a veteran organic farmer who writes for the *Atlanta Journal-Constitution* food section.

Many growers have flocked to Newton County, home to over a half dozen organic farms. Hizer explains the appeal of the Covington area: good soil, much lighter than most Georgia clay types; reasonably priced land; and beautiful scenery. "We're calling it the new Napa Valley," she says.

Organic growing requires a passion for the earth, but the rewards are great. Most organic gardeners and farmers believe the satisfaction of producing food without the use of synthetic chemicals more than compensates for any drawbacks.

The strongest characteristic of an organic garden is good soil, one of the single most important pest control methods. But good soil does not come easily. The job is labor intensive. Crops have to be rotated frequently; composting and mulching must be done religiously; and weeds have to be controlled and old plants destroyed immediately, because both harbor bugs and disease.

A handful of maverick Georgia farmers have raised produce without pesticides and herbicides for decades. About fifteen years ago Larry Conklin, a part-time

Lemon Pecan Pie

Lemon custard texture inside with a crunchy outside

3 eggs
1½ cups sugar
⅓ cup melted butter
Juice of ½ lemon (approximately 2 tablespoons)
1 teaspoon lemon extract
1 9-inch unbaked pie shell
¾ cup chopped pecans

Preheat oven to 350°. In medium bowl, beat eggs, add sugar then melted butter, lemon juice and extract. Mix well. Pour into pie shell. Top with chopped pecans. Bake for 45 to 50 minutes. Yields 8 slices.

Marjorie Deitsch

No Cook Fudge

A unique use of processed cheese in an old favorite!

4 16-ounce boxes powdered sugar, sifted
1 cup cocoa, sifted
1 pound margarine, melted
1 pound processed American cheese, melted
1 tablespoon vanilla extract
3 cups chopped pecans

In very large bowl, sift powdered sugar and cocoa. (Use bread beaters on mixer if desired.) Set aside. In large bowl, combine melted margarine and melted cheese until smooth. Stir in vanilla. Combine sugar mixture and cheese mixture, stirring by hand or using heavy-duty mixer until smooth. Fold in pecans. Pour into a 9x13-inch dish and refrigerate 3 to 4 hours before serving. Yields 100 servings.

Wyndee Council
Winston, Georgia

Hint: This recipe can easily be halved. Be patient when combining the sugar with the cheese. The mixture is very thick and difficult to mix. The resulting fudge is creamy and great tasting and worth the extra work!

farmer in Coweta County, began organizing what became the Georgia Organic Growers Association, or GOGA, a federation of about three hundred gardeners and forty certified organic farmers. They include apple growers in Habersham County and a pecan orchard tender and Vidalia onion producer in South Georgia. State certification requires that farmers pass stringent tests before their produce can wear the organic label, prized by upscale consumers for both taste and health. Soon Georgia may join with other states in implementing national organic standards.

GOGA members sell produce at the Morningside Organic Farmers Market Saturday mornings from April to November and meet the first Sunday of every month at the Atlanta Botanical Gardens. All are welcome to attend meetings of GOGA, whose member-farmers are mostly of the garden variety. GOGA coordinates seasonal organic farm tours, an apprentice program for organic novices and an educational and outreach organization, the Georgia Land Stewardship Association. (see page 285). The University of Georgia Cooperative Extension Service publishes several booklets on organic gardening (see page 288).

Pretty Sue Walker, Georgia's 1958 Corn Meal Queen, reminds you that October 5, through October 11, is Corn Bread Week in Georgia. The annual observance is sponsored throughout the state by the Georgia Corn Miller's Association.

Front page photo caption, Market Bulletin, *October 8, 1958*

PEACH BLOSSOM TRAIL

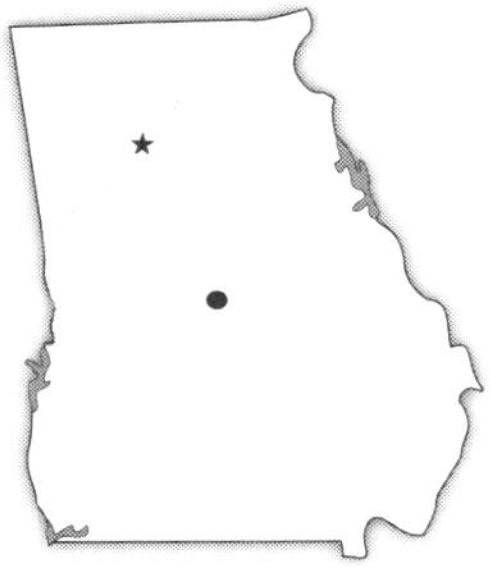

PEACH BLOSSOM TRAIL

In its entirety Georgia's Peach Blossom Trail winds from Clayton County down to Perry through the farmland and orchards of Middle Georgia.

Directions: From Atlanta, take I-75 south to Exit 66 (GA 36). Turn west and go to Barnesville. Just past Barnesville, turn south on US 341.

More Information: Peach Blossom Trail Association, P.O. Box 1619, Perry, GA 31069; 912/988-8000. Roberta-Crawford County Chamber of Commerce, P.O. Box 417, Roberta, GA 31078; 912/836-3825. Peach County Chamber of Commerce, P.O. Box 1238, Fort Valley, GA 31030; 912/825-3733. Perry Area Convention and Visitors Bureau, P.O. Box 1619, Perry, GA 31069; 912/988-8000. Lane Packing Company, GA 96 East and Lane Road, Fort Valley, GA 31030; 912/825-3592.

FOR MOST OF THE NINETEENTH CENTURY, COTTON WAS KING IN Middle Georgia. Highly perishable peaches were essentially a secondary crop, used to feed hogs and make brandy. But the building of railroads, improvements in shipping methods and experimentation in peach varieties led to peach orchards replacing cotton fields by 1900. Today, acres of orchards, roadside stands and towns built on peaches, like Musella, Fort Valley and Roberta, line a fifty-mile portion of the Peach Blossom Trail between Barnesville and Perry. Here pink blossoms carpet roadsides in early March when the trees bloom, turning into deep orange and red fruit in late spring until the peaches are finally harvested from May to August.

Crawford and Peach counties make up the heart of Georgia peach country, past and present. Heading south into Crawford County on US 341, twenty miles south of Barnesville, turn left at the sign for Musella. Musella is a living monument to Georgia's peach past. Just a block from the main highway on Old Highway 341 is the town, a handful of aging homes, farm sheds and warehouses where an old A & F Railroad line once ran. On the east side of Old 341 stands the roadside outlet and packing plant of Dickey Farms, the oldest peach packing operation in the state, established in 1890. The 1936 packing plant, a long white shed shaded by a large awning, had the first hydro-cooling system and brushing machine to remove peach fuzz in Georgia. Open from mid-May to August, the outlet offers many kinds of peaches, including Springgold, Express, Sunbrite, June Gold, Gold Prince, Candor, Dixie Red, Sure Crop, Coronet, Harvester, Red Haven, Topaz, Ted Globe and Blake. To the left of the stands is the Musella Gin and Cotton Company. Established in 1913, and burned and re-built in 1930, it still gins more than two thousand bales of cotton each year. Beyond the gin is the two hundred-acre peach orchard belonging to the Dickey family. On the west side of the road is the C. F. Hayes Jr., building, a small general merchandise store, and the 1884 Musella Baptist Church, a picturesque, white New England-style structure with a steeple in the front and a steeply slanted roof.

Return to US 341 and continue south to Roberta. The area between Musella and Roberta is one of the most remarkable physiographical areas of the state. It is where the Fall Line (see page 11), which runs mostly east and west across the state, intersects with US 341, which sits on the Eastern Continental Divide that runs north and south, or parallel, between the Ocmulgee and the Flint River watersheds. Water falling east of the ridge flows into the Ocmulgee and eventually into the Atlantic. Water falling west of the ridge flows into the Flint and then to the Gulf. Thus, a farmer in this area could have part of his farm in the Piedmont and part on the Coastal Plain. He could also have land that drained in both directions.

On the left just past GA 80 stands the site of Roberta's first railroad depot, where peaches from nearby orchards started their trip to urban markets. It was part of the A & F Railroad, built in 1889, connecting Atlanta to Fort Valley. Because the fruit was so perishable, agriculture experts urged farmers to grow peaches near the railroad lines that were springing up in South Georgia, allowing swift transportation to the major cities of the East. The present depot replaced the original one, destroyed by fire. Directly behind it stands a monument to Benjamin Hawkins, who in his role as chief Federal Indian Agent for the southeast region is said to be the first white man to have settled in Crawford County. As national migration and treaties forced the Creeks to give up their lands, Hawkins attempted without success to transform the Indians into farmers. He established a model farm on the east bank of the Flint River where he raised crops and animals to show the Creeks how to make a better living.

Continue south on US 341, which from this point parallels the rail line, about 15 miles to Fort Valley, the county seat of Peach County. Turn left onto GA 96 and continue about 3 miles to the Lane peach orchards and packing plant where rows of seven-foot high trees line both sides of the road for several miles. For almost one hundred years the Lane family has grown peaches here. Founded in the early 1900s by John David Duke, the Diamond D Fruit Farm grew some of the first peaches that

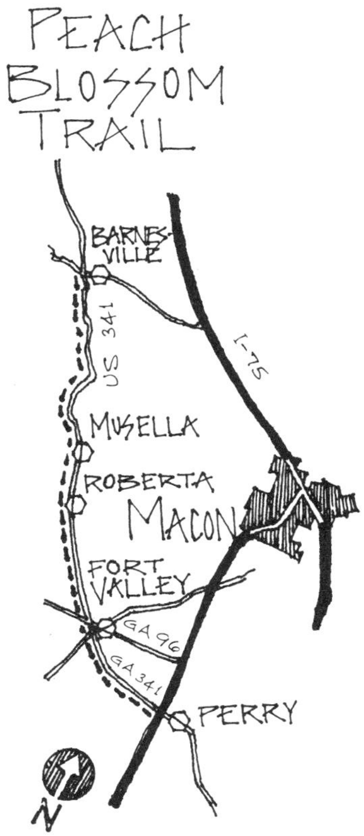

Crop Capitals of Georgia

It's safe to assume that Vidalia is the Vidalia® onion capital of the world and it might even be figured that Peach County would take the honors for peaches, but what about some of the other title holders in the state? Whether official or not, here are some of the Georgia cities or counties that have claimed to be the capital for a particular Georgia-grown food or food product.

Apples - Ellijay
Blueberries - Alma
Broilers - Habersham County
Cattle and calves - Morgan County
Chicken pie - Smithville
Hens and pullets - Hall County
Hogs - Colquitt County
Honey bees - Hahira
Milk cows - Putnam County
Peaches - Peach County
Peanuts - Worth County
Pecans - Dougherty County
Organic farms - Newton County
Vidalia® onions - Vidalia
Watermelons - Cordele
Wine - Habersham County

went to northern markets on the railroads. By the mid 1920s, two hundred seasonal pickers were working the farm, which had its own peach-packing plant, general store, dairy, syrup mill, hotel, church and commissary. Several generations later, the Diamond D Fruit Farm has become the Lane Packing Company, still family-owned-and-operated. The Lanes cultivate more than thirty varieties of peaches on about four hundred thousand trees, but in recent years have devoted some of their four thousand acres to other crops. Pecans grow on over six hundred acres, and they plant melons, cantaloupe and sweet corn and onions for their retail outlet.

The packing plant is one of the most sophisticated and modern in the Eastern United States. Using computer-controlled, soft-handling equipment to reduce damage to the fruit, it can weigh, count, separate and pack into thirty-eight-or-twenty-five-pound boxes more than three hundred thousand fruits an hour. Visitors are welcome to view the entire packing process from an elevated platform in the plant.

Return to US 341 and continue south, following the rail lines and passing peach orchards all the way, to Perry, a historically important town at the crossroads of highways 127, 341 and 41. In the late 1800s and early 1900s, Perry was a central market and distribution point for all crops from Middle Georgia. Peaches, cotton, pecans, grain, cattle, hogs and timber all rode the rail from Perry to large city markets. To reach the old cotton warehouses by the tracks, stay on US 341 until it intersects with GA 41 in downtown Perry and turn right onto GA 41. Continue about 0.25 mile and turn left on Jernigan Street, which soon runs along the tracks. The Tolleson Lumber Company, one of biggest in the state, occupies one of the warehouses.

Perry's most significant agricultural center is the Georgia National Fairgrounds and Agricenter (see page 18), a state-owned, multipurpose facility designed to host agricultural events, livestock shows, concerts, trade shows and meetings. Go back to GA 41 and turn left, or south, for about 1 mile. The fairgrounds are on the left.

ANDERSONVILLE TRAIL

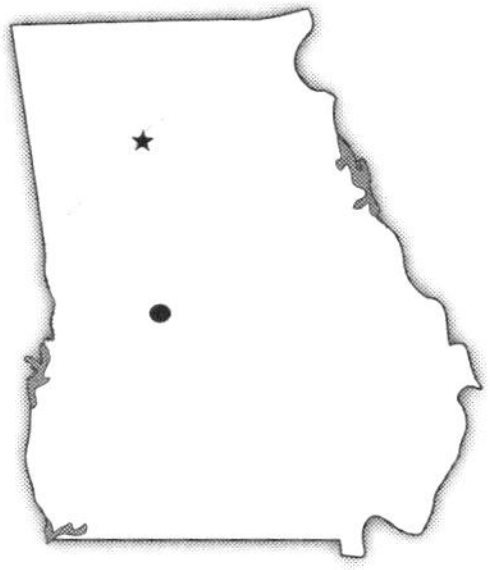

COUNTRY ROADS, EARTHY FARM SMELLS, ABANDONED PEANUT MILLS and rusting old-fashioned hay balers are all part of this leisurely drive which offers a scenic history of Georgia agriculture. Roadside signs mark the entire Andersonville Trail, which runs seventy-five miles from Byron to Cordele, primarily on GA 49.

Byron, in Peach County, was originally a whistle stop known as Number One and One Half Station. To reach the old railroad depot, turn right off of GA 49 onto GA 42 and go 0.25 mile to the railroad tracks. Built in 1870, the Byron Depot is located in the exact center of town. According to local reports, more peaches were shipped from here each day in the 1920s and '30s than from anywhere else in the world.

From Byron, GA 49 begins winding through countless pecan and peach orchards as it makes its way south. Roadside stands selling in-season fruits and vegetables reflect the county's agricultural base—617,000 peach trees, 73,000 pecan trees and annual harvests of over 1 million pounds of peanuts. The Andersonville Trail intersects with the Peach Blossom Trail in Fort Valley (see page 234). On the left, heading south out of Fort Valley is the state's agricultural school, Fort Valley State University. More than one hundred years old, the school has more acres than all but one other institution in the University System of Georgia. Between Fort Valley and Marshallville is the Massee Lane Gardens, home of the American Camellia Society. Of the total 160 acres, 10 are devoted to a landscaped camellia garden. Additional acres include a Japanese garden, a rose garden, a greenhouse, a peach orchard and a pecan grove.

Three miles further south in Monroe County is Marshallville, a town little changed in the last century. Like much of Middle Georgia, cotton covered the land around Marshallville in the mid-1800s; but by the end of the century, peach orchards had replaced most of the cotton, primarily due to the contributions of resident Samuel Rumph. Heeding the advice of contemporary agricultural journals, Rumph

ANDERSONVILLE TRAIL

The Andersonville Trail travels through the farmland, orchards and historic sites of Middle Georgia and the Flint River watershed.

Days/Hrs.: The Andersonville National Cemetery: daily, 8am-5pm. Park visitor center: daily, 8:30am-5pm except Christmas and New Years Day. Andersonville Visitor Center and Museum: daily, 9am-5pm except Christmas. The Nut House: Mon.-Fri., 8am-5pm

Fees: Andersonville National Historic Site, taped driving tour rental, $1.

Directions: To travel the entire trail from north to south, access it from I-75, Exit 46 (GA 49) at Byron.

More Information: The Andersonville Trail, P.O. Box 48, Andersonville, GA 31711; 912/928-2303. Massee Lane Gardens, One Massee Lane, Fort Valley, GA 31030; 912/967-2358. The Nut House, 912/874-1200.

SEED-SPITTING CHAMP

A talent show, fishing rodeo and photo contest take place every year at the annual watermelon festival in Cordele. But there's just one real competition, the one people talk about the rest of the year—the expectoration of the watermelon ovules, better known as the seed-spitting contest.

Skill, style, technique and luck all have their role in the main event, drawing competitors from as far away as China and press from as far away as England. Greg Leger, a local melon grower with national and Georgia spitting titles under his belt, offers some insight to those seeking to unseat the champion:

What are some of your best performances?

I spit forty-two feet one time in the state finals. The Georgia Watermelon Association sponsors that. The National Watermelon Association (in Morven, Georgia) hosts a national convention for watermelon growers and I won that two years ago. It was in Nashville, Tennessee, at the Opryland hotel. They put out a big sheet of paper in the lobby. That was a big deal. Bragging rights are fun.

How about your competitors?

One guy from Chicago spit sixty feet on top of a hotel in New Orleans. He spit between two buildings. He set it up in the wind and it caught it. No one ever spit that far, I think. The wind really got a hold of that one in what was left of a tropical storm.

Does the event draw a lot of press?

The BBC called one time. They were rather intrigued. I told them it's kind of similar to their Wimbleton. We have a foot fault occasionally.

diversified from cotton, tinkering with peaches at his Willow Lake Nursery three miles east of town. After ten years, he unveiled the bigger, tastier, more colorful Elberta, a major success with local customers. Rumph thought if he could figure out a way to prevent them from spoiling or bruising, he could market them across the nation. He came up with a way, inventing a shipping refrigerator and rigid packing crate specifically designed for peaches. Marshallville exploded into a national distribution center for Elbertas and Georgia Belles, the second invented by his Uncle Lewis. For decades the peaches rode the rails, beginning their trip from the Marshallville depot, one block east of GA 49 on Main Street (GA 127) where the current Central of Georgia depot now stands. Also on Main Street next to City Hall is the Vegetable Basket, owned by longtime resident Robert Barr. Inside the restaurant, the walls are plastered with business correspondences from Samuel Rumph's Willow Lake Nursery. Referring to subjects like the sale of apple cider or the purchase of fruit trees, the old documents give an interesting look into agricultural commerce one hundred years ago.

Twelve miles south of Montezuma (see page 240) is Andersonville. On the northern outskirts of town, on the left, is the Andersonville National Historic Site, where once stood the most notorious war prison in the Confederacy, Camp Sumter. Across GA 49 from the park is Andersonville, a small historic village town that sold supplies to the prison. Some of its nineteenth century structures were moved from other locations, like the restored railroad depot on Church Street that serves as a visitor center and museum. The town has a six-acre pioneer farm complete with mostly authentic structures such as a blacksmith shop, gristmill, liquor still, smokehouse and barn.

Nine miles south of Andersonville, GA 49 reaches Americus, a town with a number of impressive Victorian era commercial buildings and homes. From Americus, an optional side trip to President Jimmy Carter's home town of Plains can be taken (see page 252). From downtown Americus at its intersection with GA 49, take GA 280 east. Eleven miles east of Americus, a sign for DeRiso Farms, buyer of pecans, dominates the skyline of Leslie, an old whistle stop town changed only by time and the elements. Take a right onto GA 195 south to the main intersection to see a common site in the downtowns of old South Georgia settlements: the ruins of a large agricultural processing complex. In this case, on the edge of the Leslie business district stands a sprawling nut processing facility, littered with rusting warehouses, drooping chutes and countless red trailers like those still used in feed and nut mills across the South. Further east one mile on GA 280, is the DeSoto Confectionery and Nut Company, the source of much of the handmade peanut and pecan candy sold in outlets along I-75.

Heading east from DeSoto on GA 280 toward Cordele, where the Anderson Trail finishes at I-75, are some of the largest pecan orchards in the state. One visible from GA 280 to the west of the Flint River covers more than one thousand acres. Cordele, the official Watermelon Capital of the World, was the subject of a 1993 *Washington Post* feature story about the pleasures of eating out. The story described the glories of South Georgia dishes like peach cobbler, catfish, barbecue, cheese grits, fried chicken, ham, turnip greens, squash casserole, cornbread, sweet potatoes, rutabagas and butter peas.

Any tips for tenderlips in the event?

Some people try to bounce the seed if the wind is in their face. They try to aim low and let it roll. Bounces count for distance.

Do you have a personal spitting method?

I guess the technique I use is roll the tongue to blow seed through. You can't just put it between the teeth. From the back of tongue, direct air flow through the tube of the tongue. That works pretty good. Of course we're in the business. We're eating watermelon all year long and blowing seed.

Some rules of competition provided by the National Watermelon Association:

Official spitting seeds will be provided. No one will be permitted to use their own seed. Contestants who accidentally swallow seed while sucking in air prior to seed launch will be given one extra seed. Denture wearers whose teeth go farther than seed shall abide by the judge's decision. No running, jumping, skipping or lying down while spitting.

THE MENNONITES OF MONTEZUMA

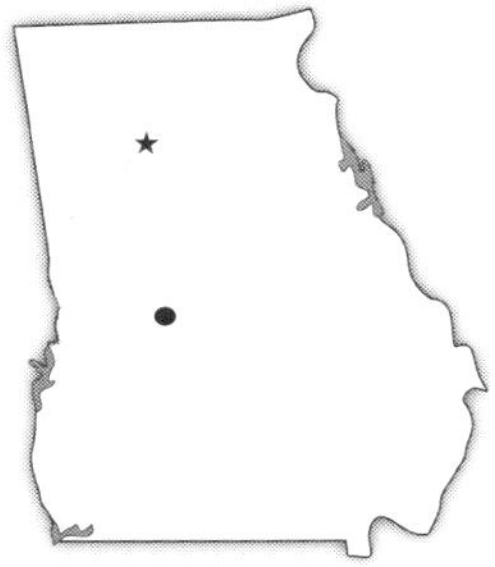

MONTEZUMA

Montezuma in Macon County is located on the banks of the Flint River.

Days/Hrs.: Yoder's Deitsch Haus restaurant and bakery: Tues., Thurs., Fri., 11:30am-2:30pm and 5pm-8:30pm; Wed., 11:30am-2pm, Sat., 11:30am-2:30pm and 4:30-8:30pm. Gift shop: Tues. and Thurs.-Sat., 10:30am-9pm, Wed., 10:30am-2:30pm. Both businesses are closed Sun. and Mon.

Directions: From Montezuma, take GA 26 east to begin a tour of the Mennonite area.

More Information: Yoder's Gift Shop or Yoder's Deitsch Haus Restaurant, Route 1, Montezuma, GA 31063; 912/472-7200 and 912/472-2024. Kauffman's Pick-Your-Own Strawberry Farm, 912/472-8833.

NOAH YODER LED THE FIRST MENNONITES TO GEORGIA FROM Norfolk, Virginia, in 1953. An ad in a dairy trade magazine for a farm near Vienna had caught his eye. The deal fell through; but while on the steps of the local courthouse, they happened to learn of a farmer selling near Montezuma. The pacifist, bearded and bonnet-wearing Mennonites made quite a stir in Montezuma at first, but today they are an integral part of the community, having grown to more than two hundred families, three churches and numerous schools and businesses, all within a five-square mile area of rolling pasture in Macon County.

Unwavering from a strict Christian code that prohibits many modern conveniences, the Mennonites have created one of the most successful and efficient dairy farming communities in Georgia. Despite their differences, their lives resemble those of their modern farmer counterparts in many ways. They drive modern combines and air-conditioned harvesters. Even the computer revolution has crept into some of their homes, as have fax machines, portable phones and walkie talkies used to call family members in the field.

Begin a tour of Mennonite country at the Myrtle Creek Dairies (1) run by Harley Yoder, one of the first Mennonites in South Georgia. His operation was once the largest dairy farm in the county and best in the state, according to a local extension agent. Inside Yoder's Deitsch Haus (2), patrons eat simple, Germanic cuisine that reflects the Mennonite heritage and buy fresh baked bread or sweets drenched in glaze. The adjacent Yoder's Gift Shop carries Amish and Mennonite cookbooks, calendars and handmade crafts like chairs and dolls. Bermuda Knolls Farm (3) is the dairy and corn operation owned by original settler Lloyd Swartzentruber, one of the area's most prominent Mennonite farmers. He and his wife Viola grow hundreds of acres of corn and cotton on either side of CR 27.

MENNONITE FARMER WORKING NEAR MONTEZUMA, GEORGIA

Montezuma Mennonite Church (4), also known as the Amish Mennonite Church, is the area's original Mennonite church. The church is simple and modest, made of basic brick and wood design. On the left, one mile past the intersection of CR 27 and CR 24 is the school (5) for the Clearview Mennonite Church, an offshoot of the Montezuma Mennonite Church. For a Mennonite hands-on farm experience, visit the pick-your-own strawberry farm (6) run by Marvin Kauffman. The five-acre field can be picked from April to June. Kauffman also sells vegetables grown on his farm for most of the summer.

The Clearview Mennonite Church (7) is a simply designed dark red brick building. There's little difference of opinion between the Mennonite churches. The Bible teaches them to be good stewards of the earth, and they attribute their higher-than-average yields to diligence and providence. But for the Mennonite, the ultimate goal of farming is not the growing of crops, but the cultivation and perfection of human beings. CR 269, a narrow dirt road, leads to the farm of Eli Kauffman (8), bishop of Montezuma Mennonite Church since 1980. Church members elected him by secret ballot, as they do pastors of all ranks. The Amish Mennonite School (9) takes students up to the eighth grade. Mennonites do not emphasize education, as too much schooling can tempt them to enter the outside world. They feel that higher education can wear a Mennonite down by keeping him from the land. Across from the school is an old church building (10) used by the Mennonites when they first arrived.

OLD SOUTH FARM MUSEUM

"Gathered over many years and with a great deal of love for farming and the South," Paul Bulloch, a retired county extension agent, brought together more than two thousand pieces of equipment from early-twentieth century farms to teach people about farming. Visitors to the Old South Farm Museum and Agricultural Learning Center can feel raw cotton, use a boll weevil catcher, see a milk bottling plant and even sign up for the popular hog killing classes.

This unique learning center, located in the small town of Woodland in central West Georgia, reflects southern agriculture from the 1900s to the 1960s. The museum, consisting of two warehouses with thirty-six thousand square feet of space, has everything from small hand tools and peach-packing equipment to hay balers and large harvesting machines, such as combines and tractors, lining the front yard.

For more information, call 706/674-2894.

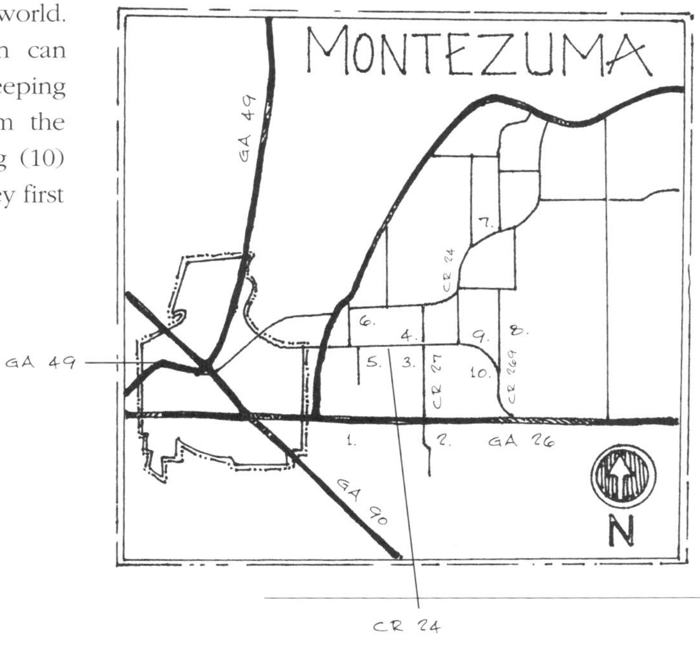

Cotton and the Boll Weevil

1892. Anthonomous grandis migrates from Mexico across the Rio Grande River. The boll weevil, as it is called, deposits its eggs in the cotton square, which then prevents the development of the cotton fiber.
1910. George Washington Carver in Tuskegee, Alabama, warns southern farmers, "The boll weevil is advancing this way at a rapid rate. Better get ready."
1914. The grayish, one-quarter-inch weevil officially arrives in Georgia.

Cotton is actually two crops, seed and fiber. Cotton seed are crushed in order to separate its three products: oil, meal and hulls. The oil is used for shortening, cooking oil and salad dressing. Some cotton seed is used as a high-protein concentrate for food products. The meal and hulls are used in products such as livestock, poultry and fish feed, while the stalks and leaves are plowed under to enrich the soil. The most important part of the cotton plant is the fiber or lint which is used to make textile products. The single-cell composition of each fiber, a characteristic science has yet to imitate, gives cotton its qualities of absorption and ability to breathe.

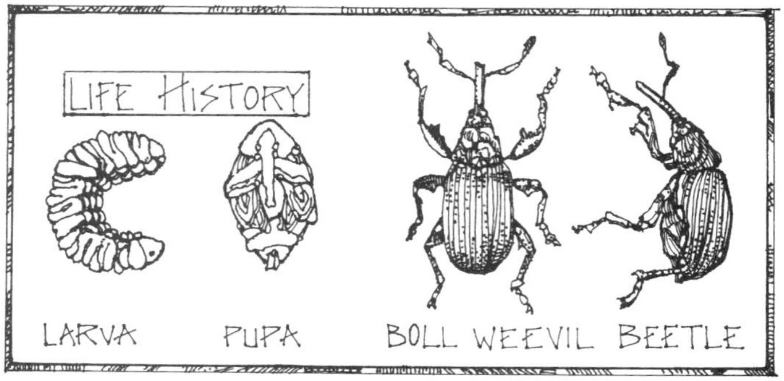

When the boll weevil arrived in Georgia, it compounded the existing problems of soil erosion and depletion in the Piedmont. Don Hastings, gardening author and nursery owner, says his grandfather had already warned farmers against depending solely on cotton. "H. G. Hastings used to lecture farmers against cotton on page one of his seed catalogue. He believed that Georgia agriculture was killing itself growing cotton (a bit of heresy in Georgia in the 1910s and '20s) when it should be planting corn, oats, wheat and legumes."

As a result of the boll weevil, the financially rewarding crop of cotton was wiped out. The ensuing years brought boll weevil panics and economic depression to rural communities; it also spurred farm workers to migrate and seek industrial work in northern cities (see page 118).

By the time help arrived, in the form of calcium arsenate in 1919, followed by synthetic insecticides after WWI, the weevil had destroyed farmers' confidence in relying on a single crop. It also helped southern farmers and businessmen become more receptive to new crops and opportunities.

To make sure that weevils run rampant only in memory, the agricultural authorities have asked that farmers plant the tiny, green boxes-on-a-stick seen all

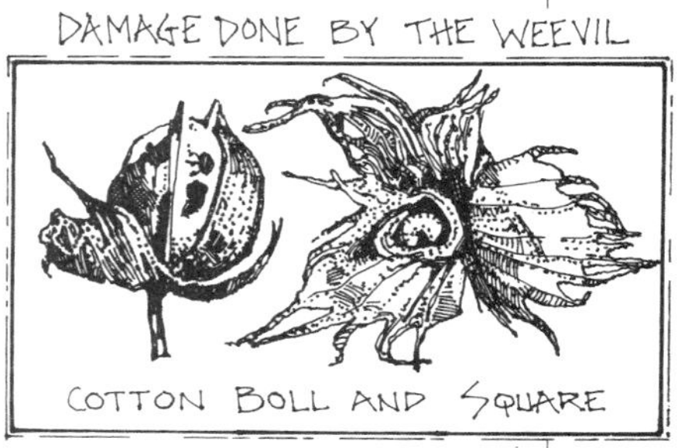

over South Georgia cotton fields. Should a maverick weevil turn up, they would fly to a box, attracted by the scent, and become trapped.

History of Cotton in Georgia

1734 - First cotton planted in Georgia
1793 - Development of Eli Whitney's gin
1811 - 1 million bales of cotton shipped from Georgia
1914 - Boll weevil appeared
1923 - Boll weevil destroyed half of the state's expected cotton yield
1994 - Boll weevil declared "insignificant;" Georgia crop at 1,537,000 bales, the largest since 1930

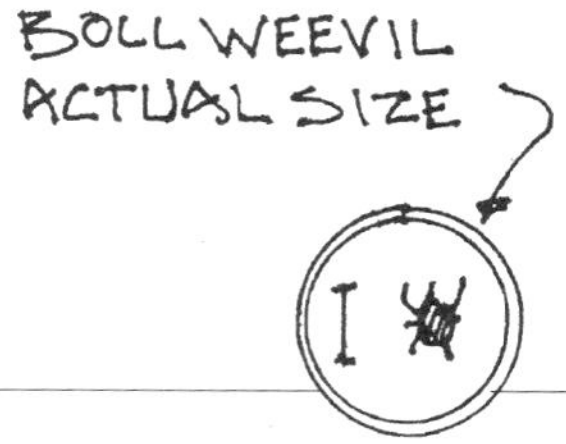

Peanuts

Believed to have originated in Peru or Brazil about 750 BC, peanuts filled jars placed in the graves of ancient Incas to provide food in the afterlife. Spanish explorers introduced the peanut to Europe, Asia and Africa. Slaves then brought the ground nut back to America where they planted them throughout the South. Although a staple for both Blue and Gray soldiers in the Civil War, peanuts were not grown much in the 1800s. But the groundbreaking work of George Washington Carver, an Alabama plant scientist who developed more than three hundred uses from peanuts, changed all that. Coupled with cotton's decline after the boll weevil epidemic, peanuts became an important cash crop for southern farmers in the early 1900s.

Also called ground nuts, ground peas, goobers and goober peas, peanuts, unlike other nuts, flower above ground, but the fruit develops below it. The nut, actually a legume like peas or beans, is an excellent source of protein, B vitamins, vitamin E, zinc, magnesium, potassium and phosphorus. Georgia, led by Early and Decatur counties, produces about 40 percent of the national output. Mostly of the runner variety used to make peanut butter, Georgia peanuts are harvested in autumn.

BUYER'S GUIDE TO PEANUTS

To maintain quality, store peanuts in a cool, dry place.

Peanuts stay fresh indefinitely when stored in a tightly closed container in the freezer.

When a recipe calls for raw peanuts, it should indicate the type required: in shell, shelled redskins or shelled blanched (redskins removed).

When roasted peanuts are called for, home-roasted (without redskins), cocktail or dry-roasted peanuts may be used interchangeably.

To chop peanuts, drop them in a blender or food processor a few at a time or use an inexpensive nut chopper.

GEORGIA 1ST
PEANUTS
SITTING HIGH
ATOP A PERCH, THIS
CONCRETE PEANUT
LOOMS 10 FEET TALL
OVER ASHBURN, GA

PEANUT CRUST BROWNIE SWIRL PIE

This pie is well worth the effort!

CRUST

- 1½ cups roasted, salted peanuts
- ½ cup firmly packed brown sugar
- 1½ tablespoons melted butter
- 1 egg white

Preheat oven to 350°. Place peanuts in ½ cup batches in food processor and pulse until peanuts are in crumbs. In small bowl, combine all ingredients and press mixture into bottom of lightly oiled 9½-inch spring-form pan. Place in freezer for 10 minutes. Bake for 10 minutes. Allow to cool to room temperature. Do not remove crust from pan.

PEANUT BUTTER MIXTURE

- ½ cup peanut butter
- 2 tablespoons softened butter
- 2 ounces cream cheese
- ¼ cup sugar
- 1 egg
- 1 tablespoon all-purpose flour
- ½ teaspoon vanilla extract

In medium bowl, combine peanut butter, butter and cream cheese. Microwave on high until all are soft and easily combined (about 20 to 30 seconds). Mix in sugar, egg, flour and vanilla; stir until smooth. Set aside.

BROWNIE MIXTURE

- ⅔ cup cake flour
- ½ teaspoon baking powder
- ¼ teaspoon salt
- 1 stick (½ cup) butter
- 2 squares unsweetened chocolate
- 1 cup sugar
- 2 large eggs
- 1 teaspoon vanilla extract

In medium bowl, combine flour, baking powder and salt. Set aside. In large bowl, place butter and chocolate. Microwave on high until butter is melted and chocolate is soft (about 60 to 90 seconds). Stir until chocolate is melted and combined with butter. Allow to cool slightly. After chocolate mixture has cooled, whisk in sugar, eggs and vanilla. Stir in flour mixture until combined. Set aside.

Garnish

- 2 tablespoons powdered sugar
- 1½ teaspoons cocoa
- 1 cup whipping cream
- Chocolate bar shavings
- A few roasted peanuts

In small bowl, combine powdered sugar and cocoa. Sift to remove lumps. With chilled medium bowl and beaters, whip cream until foamy. Slowly add sugar-cocoa mixture while continuing to beat cream until fluffy and combined. Refrigerate until pie is served.

To assemble pie: Preheat oven to 350°. Pour brownie mixture over crust in spring-form pan. Drop 1 large dollop of peanut butter mixture in middle of brownie mixture. Use remaining peanut butter mixture to make a ring about halfway between center and edge. To create swirled or decorative pattern, draw knife blade or toothpick from center to edge of pan, repeating about every inch as if you were cutting pie wedges. Be careful not to cut into crust. Bake for approximately 30 minutes or until outer edges are cooked and center is still moist. Before serving, garnish whipped cream with chocolate bar shavings and a few peanuts. Serve pie with whipped cream on the side. Yields 12 servings.

Tracy Gilbert
Columbus, Georgia
First Place Dessert,
1995 Great Tastes of Georgia Recipe Contest

Microwave Roasted Peanuts

Thirty-ninth United States President Jimmy Carter grew up on a farm near Plains (see pages 252 and 257) where he plowed and hoed his father's fields that grew watermelons, sweet potatoes, black-eyed peas, cotton, corn, tomatoes and, of course, peanuts. Today, one of President Carter's favorite ways of cooking peanuts from his farm is in the microwave.

"The key to success is the stirring of the peanuts. It is better for them to rotate, and they have to be stirred at regular intervals. At first, I cook them a maximum of 3 minutes, then remove them from the oven and stir them. Then cook them another 3 minutes. After this, 2-minute intervals are best. The total time depends on the quantity being cooked. For peanuts in the hull, it takes about 8 minutes for a small bowl the size of a softball, but up to 12 minutes for twice this many. When the husked kernels are *slightly* brown, they are done. They tend to cook a little more after being removed from the oven the last time."

Want cotton baskets, square bottoms and addresses of persons who make these.
Elwood Watkins, Cleveland, Ohio

Farm Products Wanted, Market Bulletin,
January 17, 1973

The Virtues of Kudzu

Kudzu. The word evokes frustration from those plagued by it, jokes from those who aren't and respect from those who understand its power. For, make no mistake about it, kudzu is powerful. Its leafy vines, called runners, can grow more than twelve inches in a single day, or between fifty and one hundred feet in a typical growing season. When the vines touch the ground, they form nodes, which become crowns once they send out roots. Roots radiate from the kudzu crown in all directions and drill as deep as twenty feet into the ground for water and nutrients. On these roots, potato-like tubers store carbohydrates. A single tuber may weigh as much as three hundred pounds. Try to imagine a three hundred-pound potato, growing beneath the ground and sending up new growth, to get some idea of kudzu's power. Scientists estimate there may be as many as ten thousand roots per acre of kudzu. As a member of the hard-working bean family, kudzu extracts nitrogen from the air and increases soil fertility by imparting the nitrogen to the soil. Few other plants have this ability; most plants feed on nitrogen in the soil.

First introduced in the United States at the 1876 Philadelphia Centennial Exposition, kudzu was initially cultivated as a shade plant on porches and arbors. Later, in the 1930s, the U.S. Department of Agriculture imported kudzu to control soil erosion. Problems with out-of-control kudzu growth began in the late 1940s. In its native land of Asia, kudzu had biological controls that kept it in check. In the southeastern United States, however, there were no controls on its growth, and it apparently grew much faster. So fast that it inspired Georgian bard James Dickey to write:

Potato Candy

Mashed potatoes and peanut butter make up this unique candy

- ½ cup cooked mashed Irish potatoes
- 1 teaspoon vanilla extract
- 2 boxes powdered sugar, sifted
- 1 16-ounce jar chunky peanut butter

Combine vanilla and potatoes; slowly add sugar into stiff dough. Take small portions and roll out thin on wax paper. Spread desired amount of peanut butter; roll in jellyroll fashion. Cool 1 hour; cut into small bite-size pieces. Yields approximately 7 dozen candies.

Cheryl Gibson
Dunwoody, Georgia

Corn Flake Candy

The kids will love this peanut butter and corn flake treat

- 1 cup sugar
- 1 cup corn syrup
- 1 cup peanut butter
- 6 cups corn flakes

Heat sugar and syrup until it boils and the sugar melts completely. Remove from heat and stir in peanut butter. Add corn flakes. Place on waxed paper with teaspoon. Roll into balls with hands if desired. Yields approximately 60 candies.

Mrs. Curtis Gibson
Fort Valley, Georgia

Chicken Curry Stir Fry

Peanuts add to this international flavor!

- 2 tablespoons olive oil
- ½ cup chopped Vidalia® onion
- 4 (about 1 pound) boneless, skinless chicken breasts, cut into small cubes
- 2 tablespoons water
- 2 tablespoons curry powder
- ¼ teaspoon salt
- ⅛ teaspoon pepper
- ⅓ cup chopped roasted peanuts
- 2 tablespoons currants or raisins
- 1 10-ounce package frozen mixed vegetables
- 2 cups cooked rice
- 1 green or red bell pepper, cut into strips

Heat oil in large skillet or stir fry pan over medium-high heat. Add onion, cook and stir until onion is clear. Add chicken, water, curry powder, salt and pepper; stir and cook 6 to 8 minutes or until chicken is no longer pink. Add peanuts, currants and frozen vegetables; cook and stir 7 to 8 minutes. Serve over hot rice; garnish with bell pepper strips. Yields 4 main dish servings.

Rachel G. Ramey
Cedartown, Georgia

Chocolate Peanut Clusters

A holiday classic!

- ½ cup cocoa
- 2 cups sugar
- ½ cup milk
- ½ cup margarine
- ¼ cup chopped, roasted peanuts
- 3 cups quick oats, uncooked
- ½ cup peanut butter
- 1 teaspoon vanilla extract

In a medium saucepan, combine cocoa, sugar, milk and margarine. Bring mixture to a boil. Add peanuts, oats, peanut butter and vanilla. Stir to blend. Form little clusters on waxed paper. Let stand to harden. Yields approximately 48 clusters.

Georgia Peanut Commission

"In Georgia, the legend says
That you must close your
windows
At night to keep it out of the
house.
The glass is tinged with green,
even so...."

Today, Americans are learning more about the edible and medicinal uses of kudzu. For two thousand years, Asians have used kudzu roots for cooking and for making medicinal teas to treat dysentery and fever. Starch made from the roots, called kuzu, can be used in place of other starches to create sauces, soups, puddings and pie fillings. Says Annemarie Colbin in her book *Food and Healing:*

"Kuzu is similar to arrowroot or cornstarch in that it must be dissolved in cold liquid and the mixture stirred while it heats, thickening as it reaches the boiling point. It has an alkalizing effect. One tablespoon kuzu starch will thicken 1 cup liquid to the consistency of Chinese vegetable sauce; 2½ tablespoons kuzu to 1 cup liquid makes pudding, which when cool is the consistency of soft tofu. As a remedy, kuzu can be used in two ways: shoyu-kuzu (salty, runny, like a thick broth) and apple juice-kuzu (thick and sweet like a pudding)." Colbin recommends kuzu mixes to relieve stress and for sore throats, earaches and other ailments.

In *The Kudzu Cookbook,* Carole Marsh has such recipes as Homemade Kudzu Noodles, Kudzu Gumbo and Kudzu Quiche. When deep frying kudzu leaves, Marsh says to "pick the tender, young leaves and avoid the older leaves and shoots which are very fibrous."

4-H Clubs

Pledging their "Head to clearer thinking, their Heart to greater loyalty, their Hands to larger service and their Health to better living," almost two hundred thousand students are part of Georgia's largest youth program, 4-H. Drawing from the success in the early 1900s of corn and tomato clubs, which encouraged farm boys and girls to improve crop yields on small plots, the University of Georgia Cooperative Extension Service established 4-H because they realized that young people would take to new farming methods better than their parents.

The Extension Service conducts the Georgia 4-H program through Extension Service agents in every county. Agents, program assistants and volunteer leaders teach youth nine through nineteen years old, using curriculum approved and endorsed by the Georgia State Board of Education. Over the years, local county agents have advised 4-H clubs by teaching farm classes, judging livestock shows and holding crop-growing contests. 4-H'ers can enroll in a wide variety of more than fifty projects. Classes are taught in many Georgia schools as an elective class. 4-H Clubs can be school classes, home schools, community clubs and special interest clubs.

The Georgia 4-H is a member of the Character Counts! Coalition, composed of fifty-six national and regional organizations and many individuals who have joined forces to promote character development through citizenship, caring, respect, fairness, trustworthiness and responsibility.

The 4-H Environmental Education Program, presently the

P. B. Swirls

Fun for kids!

- ½ cup shortening
- 1 cup sugar
- ½ cup crunchy peanut butter
- 1 egg
- 2 teaspoons milk
- 1¼ cup sifted all-purpose flour
- ½ teaspoon salt
- ½ teaspoon baking soda
- 1 6-ounce package semisweet chocolate chips

In medium bowl, cream shortening and sugar. Beat in peanut butter, egg and milk. In separate bowl, mix flour, salt and baking soda. Mix dry ingredients into peanut butter mixture. Place dough on lightly greased waxed paper. Using your hand, shape dough into a rectangle, approximately 9x13 inches. Melt chocolate chips and spread over dough. Roll dough like a jellyroll using long side of rectangle. Chill ½ hour.

Preheat oven to 350°. Slice into ¼-inch slices. Place on ungreased cookie sheet. Bake for 8 to 10 minutes. Yields 3 dozen cookies.

Peanut Advisory Board and the Georgia Peanut Commission

Peanut Butter Bread

Serve this bread plain or with fruit and whipped cream

- 1 egg
- ¾ cup peanut butter
- 1 cup firmly packed brown sugar
- 2 tablespoons vegetable shortening, melted
- 2 cups all-purpose flour
- ½ teaspoon baking powder
- ½ teaspoon baking soda
- 1 teaspoon salt
- 1 cup buttermilk

Preheat oven to 350°. Beat egg, then add peanut butter, sugar and shortening. Beat until creamy. Sift flour, baking powder, baking soda and salt. Alternately add sifted ingredients and buttermilk to peanut butter mixture, mixing well after each addition. Pour into a greased 8x4-inch loaf pan. Bake for 1 hour or until tester inserted in center comes out clean. Yields 10 servings.

Mame Doyle
Ludville, Georgia

Tasty Peanut Soup

Onion, celery and peanut butter produce a great soup!

- ¼ cup butter
- ¼ cup finely chopped onion
- ¼ cup finely chopped celery
- 1 cup creamy peanut butter
- 1 tablespoon flour
- 4 cups beef bouillon
- 2 teaspoons lemon juice
- Unsweetened whipped cream
- ½ cup chopped roasted peanuts

In a large saucepan, melt butter. Add onion and celery; sauté until tender. Stir in peanut butter and flour. Gradually stir in beef bouillon and lemon juice until smooth. Cook over medium heat, stirring occasionally, for 20 minutes. To serve, garnish with dollops of unsweetened whipped cream and sprinkle with chopped nuts. Yields 8 servings.

Bonnie Pirkle
Augusta, Georgia

largest residential environmental education program in the nation, was set up to develop an awareness, knowledge and appreciation for the natural environment. Four 4-H facilities—Rock Eagle, Jekyll Island, Tybee Island and Wahsega—have "living laboratories" of the mountain, coastal and piedmont habitats of Georgia. The facilities serves more than forty-one thousand students each school year and hosts teacher training workshops for hundreds of teachers annually.

Mrs. Justus L. Garrett, wife of a Monroe, Ga., minister and the mother of two girls, is the winner of the Georgia Chicken cook-off to determine the state's representative at the $10,000 stake National Chicken Cooking contest. Mrs. Garrett's winning recipe was Chicken Spaghetti Casserole, a tasty and attractive dish including chicken, spaghetti, noodles, green and pimiento peppers. The Winner received a set of luggage, an electric fry pan and various other gifts as well as the opportunity to compete in Little Rock, Arkansas, in September for the national chicken cook title.

News item, Market Bulletin, *July 11, 1973*

Boiled Peanuts

An old Southern favorite, boiled peanuts are found at roadside stands, church picnics, rural grocery stores and sporting events throughout Georgia. The salty snack even showed up once at a black-tie fundraiser at New York's Rockefeller Center. But nobody knew what to do with them, says Scott Peacock, a former chef at the Horseradish Grill. "We had 100 pounds of them in bags. You would've thought it was caviar, it was so exotic. Finally, people from the kitchen were showing the guests how to open the peanuts. They were clueless."

At the Atlanta Farmer's Market shed number seven, Tony Martin has the largest capacity operation at the market—yet he is barely able to keep up with the demand. A few years ago Martin began selling the briny goobers to people who resold them at Braves games.

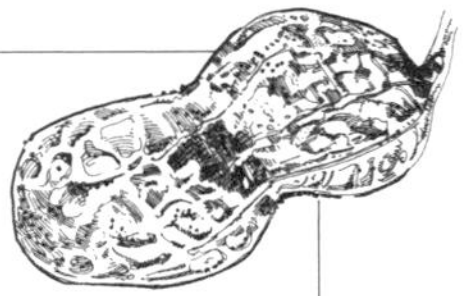

Since then he has set up half a dozen fifty-five gallon cookers that can boil up to three hundred pounds at a time. Mostly he uses dried peanuts, but when the season permits, usually from summer to early autumn, he cooks green peanuts, fresh ones taken directly from the field.

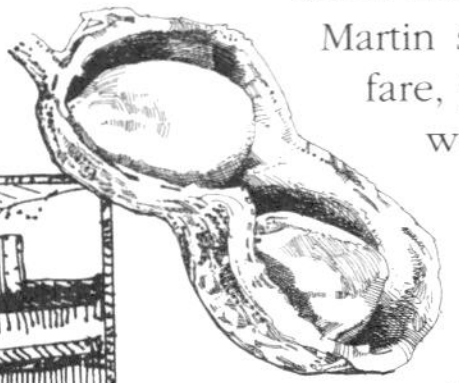

Martin serves up the basic fare, peanuts and salt, as well as cajun style, using twenty-two dollars worth of spices per twenty-five-pound bag. He keeps the details of the recipe a closely guarded secret. For more information on ordering Martin's peanuts, call 404/608-8048.

For those folks who prefer the information highway to a rural two-lane stretch of blacktop, boiled peanuts can be purchased over the Internet. Two days after submitting an electronic request, a delivery person will arrive with ten pounds of boiled peanuts that have been flash-cooled and packed in an insulated foam cooler to insure freshness.

Website: http://southernfood.com/boiledpea/boiledpea.htm or call 888/531-3663.

Georgia Boiled Peanuts

Boiling up a fresh batch of peanuts requires three basic ingredients: raw peanuts, water and a load of salt.

Wash peanuts thoroughly in cool water; then soak in clean cool water for about 30 minutes before cooking. Put peanuts in saucepan and cover completely with water. Add 1 tablespoon salt for each pint of peanuts.

Cooking time for boiled peanuts varies according to the variety and maturity of the peanuts used. Cooking time for "freshly pulled" green peanuts is shorter than for peanuts which have been stored for a time. The best way to prepare peanuts is to cook them as soon as they are picked.

There is no firm method for cooking boiled peanuts. The shells of some peanuts absorb more salt than others, so it is best to begin salt as prescribed above, then add more salt to taste later. When fully cooked, the texture of the peanut should be similar to that of a cooked dry pea or bean. Boil the peanuts for about 35 minutes, then taste. If they are not salted enough, add more salt. Taste again in 10 minutes, both for salt content and to see if the peanuts are fully cooked. If not ready, continue tasting every 5 minutes until they have a satisfactory texture. Drain peanuts after cooking, or they will continue to absorb salt and become oversalted.

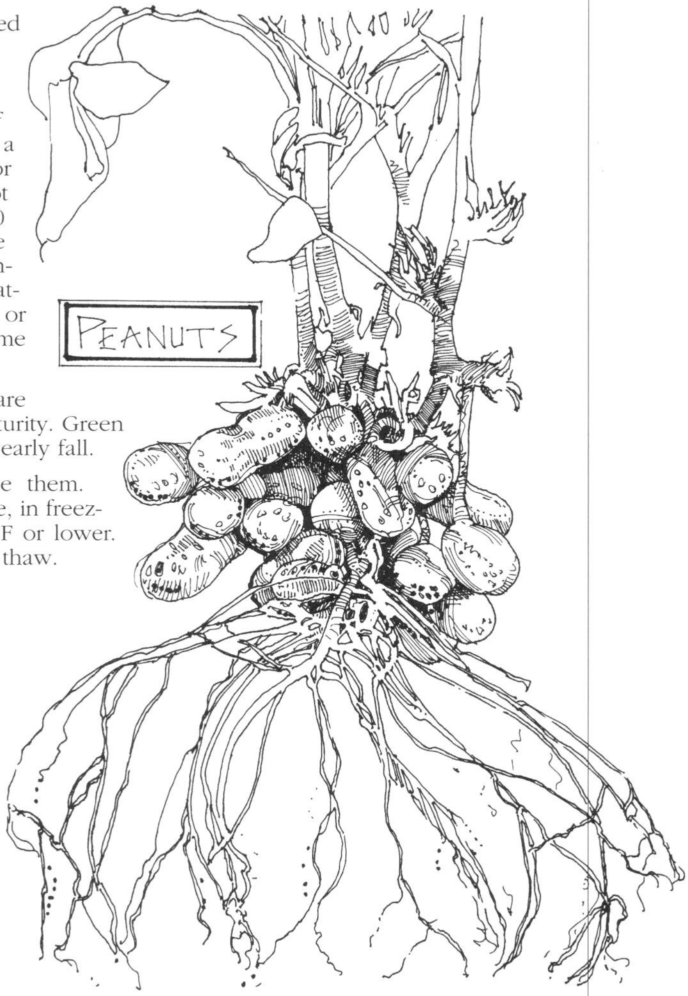

It is best to use only green peanuts, which are peanuts that are pulled before they reach maturity. Green peanuts are only available in late summer or early fall.

To have boiled peanuts year round, freeze them. Package the cooled peanuts, without the brine, in freezer-safe containers. Keep peanuts stored at 0°F or lower. When ready to eat, remove from freezer and thaw.

Georgia Peanut Commission

PLAINS

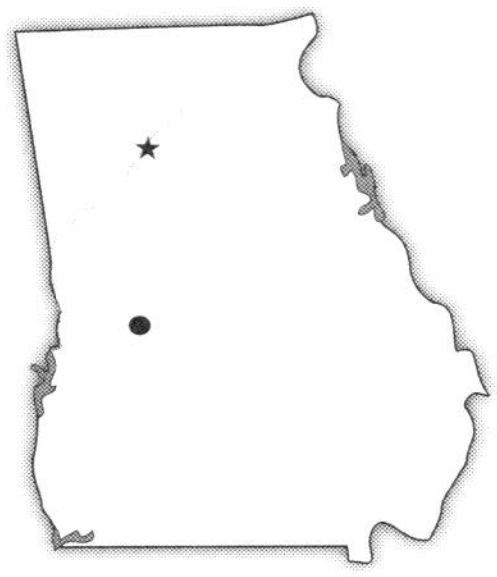

PLAINS

Located in the Coastal Plain farmland of Sumter County, Plains is home to President Jimmy Carter and site of the Jimmy Carter National Historic Site.

Facilities: The unstaffed railroad depot houses a self-guided museum that highlights Carter's 1976 presidential campaign. The Visitor Center has more exhibits on the life and career of the thirty-ninth U.S. President. Rangers guide tours of Plains to special groups that call and arrange in advance, and rent tours on tape to individual visitors for $1.

Days/Hrs.: Depot Museum and Jimmy Carter National Historic Site Visitor's Center in the former Plains High School: daily, 9am-5pm except New Years Day, Thanksgiving Day and Christmas.

Fees: None.

Directions: From Americus, take US 280 10 miles west to Plains. To reach the depot and business area, turn left onto South Hudson Street and cross the railroad tracks. The Carter boyhood home is southwest of Plains. Follow US 280 west for 0.5 miles and bear left on Old Plains Highway for 1.5 miles.

More Information: Jimmy Carter National Historic Site, P.O. Box 392, Plains, GA 31780; 912/824-3413.

American settlers founded the Plains of Dura in Sumter County in the mid-1830s on the Americus-Preston Road. The town's name was a biblical reference from Daniel 3:1, where Nebuchadnezzer set up a golden idol that the Israelites refused to worship, and according to biblical tradition, were cast into a burning furnace from which they emerged alive and unhurt as a sign of God's favor.

In 1884, the Americus, Lumpkin and Preston Railroad established a line south of the Plains of Dura. The town fathers moved the town to the track the next year, abandoning the original settlement site and shortening the name of the town to Plains by the late 1880s. With hopes of recovering from the Civil War's devastation, businessmen constructed a row of wood frame structures on the track's south side and a depot. Agriculture dominated the town. Cotton remained the cash crop, but a change in the agricultural profile of the region was beginning to take place. About 1910, an unknown "Yankee" planted a crop of peanuts in the Plains area as an experiment. Threshing machines not being available, his field hands picked the nuts by hand. At first, no one wanted to buy the product. But by 1916 candy manufacturers were regularly coming to Plains to purchase peanuts. Cotton gins took peanuts in as a side business, as the same equipment was used to crush both cottonseed and peanuts for oil. In 1916, the first peanut mill in Georgia was built in Coleman, to the west of Plains. By 1920, Americus, ten miles from Plains, had its own peanut sheller.

There are numerous sites to see in Plains; this tour points out those which demonstrate how one family, the Carters, have been both a witness to and a shaper of the agricultural history of this small South Georgia town.

In about 1850, Wiley Carter, great-great grandfather to President Jimmy Carter (see page 257), moved to a farm about eight miles north of present day Plains. In 1860, his farm produced about 147 bales of cotton. At his death in 1864, he left an estate of twenty-four hundred acres of farmland, thirty slaves and other substantial holdings to his eleven children and wife. In the 1920s, Earl Carter, great grandson of Wiley and father of Jimmy, invested in a variety of related business ventures, including cotton, timberland, peanuts, a grocery and a dry cleaning shop. In 1928, Earl Carter moved his wife Lillian, son Jimmy and daughter Gloria to a 360-acre farm (1) in Archery, southwest of Plains on the Old Plains Highway. They lived across the road from the long-gone whistle stop of Archery, growing peanuts, cotton and corn to sell and raising vegetables and livestock for their own use. On the farm, Earl operated a commissary (2) for his field hands, bringing surplus goods from the general store he opened in Plains to sell to the black sharecroppers. His inventory included cured ham and pork, overalls, comforters, snuff, tobacco, flour, sugar, meal, castor oil and homemade syrup, made on-site from sugar cane in his fields.

Two and one half miles from Earl Carter's farm is the circa 1888 Plains Depot (3). In 1919, sixty-six carloads of hogs and cows were shipped from here; and during the 1920s, up to ten thousand bales of cotton left this depot annually. It served as campaign headquarters for Governor Jimmy Carter as he campaigned for the White House, and in January 1977, the eighteen-car "Peanut Express" train departed from the depot filled with celebrants bound for the inauguration of the thirty-ninth president of the United States. The depot is now a museum for the Jimmy Carter National Historic Site.

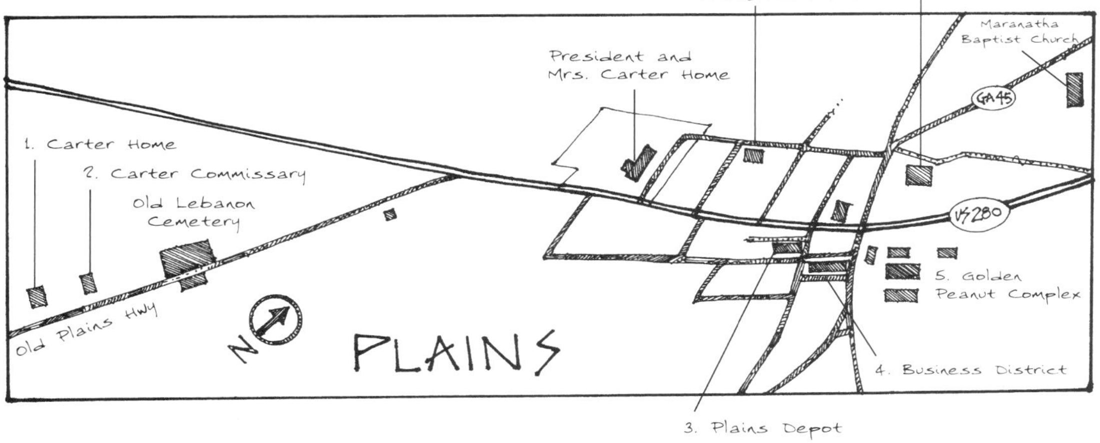

Farming in the Thirties

A hand-typed note from Jimmy Carter following his interview for *The Best From Georgia Farms:*

In the early or mid-thirties, farmers would plant an acre of peanuts. They would have to break their land with a mule. They would have to harrow the land. They would have to harrow twice before the peanuts came up to try to kill the weeds before the peanuts emerged. And then, they had to cultivate three or four times more—all with mules. They had to plow the peanuts up, shake them by hand, put them on stack poles that had to be cut and erected and let them dry for about eight to ten weeks. Take the stack poles to the peanut thresher and thresh them and then haul them to the marker.

And gross income off an acre was only seven dollars. Because peanuts at that time were only one cent a pound, and the average yield for the state was seven hundred pounds.

It was a back breaking and debilitating experience.

To understand the importance of agriculture and the Carters to Plains, park and walk around the one-block business district (4). These brick commercial buildings, constructed in the early 1900s, replaced the wood-frame structures built when Plains was relocated to the railroad tracks. Jimmy's uncle William Alton "Buddy" Carter, mayor of Plains in the 1920s, sold feed, fertilizer and cotton in the seventh building from the east for sixty years. His son Hugh now operates an antique store here. The circa 1901 bank building, fifth from the east, served as a post office in the 1920s. Hugh and Jimmy Carter sold burgers and boiled peanuts from the window in the 1930s. Later Hugh moved the Carter Worm Farm into the building. The sign remains, but the mail order fish bait company has closed. Earl Carter rented a portion of the third building from the east, formerly the Wise Sanitarium No. 1, when he began his peanut warehouse business in 1934. In this office Jimmy managed the family business after his father's death in 1953. A billboard for Carter covering the second-story windows went up during his gubernatorial campaign. The sign, which remains today, was repainted when he sought and won the presidency. From the circa 1902 storefront on the southwest corner of Hudson and Main, Earl Carter ran a general goods store and meat market. In the Depression, he closed it and moved most of his stock to his store on the farm in Archery. The building stored cotton in the 1950s and houses a barber shop in the back where Jimmy Carter has his hair cut. The Golden Peanut complex (5) of about eleven buildings, the most prominent feature in the Plains skyline, once housed the Carter Peanut Warehouse Company, started by Earl. The first year after the future president took over his late father's struggling wholesale peanut business, it cleared $187. Within two years, his fortunes improved and Carter built two of the large warehouses here.

Built in 1953, the Plains Public Housing Unit 9-A (6) was the home of the Carters when Jimmy resigned from the navy and returned home to run his late father's agricultural interests.

The General Store

According to the *Encyclopedia of Southern Culture* edited by Charles Reagan Wilson and William Ferris, "No rural southern institution gathered about itself a warmer aura of human nostalgia than the general or country store. Seated at crossroads all across the South, the stores were combination merchandising and farmers' markets; sources of credit, medicine, and simple bits of luxury; news centers; resorts for sage advice; and eternal places for gossiping and yarn spinning.... In large measure general stores in hundreds of isolated rural southern communities shaped the lives of their customers and served as a cardinal link between southern countrymen and the outside world of capital, industry, and contemporary technological and material advances."

The merchant was at the center of the country store. He was the link between the local townspeople and the northern and western manufacturers who supplied the needed goods. After the Civil War, merchants became powerful by extending credit to destitute whites and blacks with interest often as high as 40 percent and by way of crop liens where merchants supplied food and supplies based on the crop that was being planted. The merchant was basically the purchaser of the crop at the end of the growing season, taking the risks but sharing the profit. Much of the credit the merchant extended was in the form of coupon books which could only be used at his store.

The country store was the general gathering place for the community every day except Sunday. Men whittled, played checkers or pitched horseshoes out front in good weather and sat around the pot-bellied stove swapping stories in bad weather.

The store sold an amazing variety of items: overalls, blue jeans, hats, corsets, gloves, chewing tobacco, peppermint candy, crackers, cheese, axle grease, lard, kerosene, machinery, tools, coffins, fertilizer, seed and medicine.

Once the telephone was invented, the country store might possess the only one in the community.

Today, the country store is still found in rural areas, but with the addition of gas pumps outside and vending machines, soft drinks, candy bars and cash sales inside.

Grandpa's Store

From *Cold Sassy Tree* by Olive Ann Burns ...

Most folks thought, as Miss Effie Belle Tate put it, that Grandpa was "both rich and well-to-do." For sure he was one of Cold Sassy's leading merchants. Had him a big brick store with mahogany counters, beveled glass mirrors, and big colored signs for Coca-Cola, Mother's Friend (Take to Make Childbirth Easier), Fletcher's Castoria, Old Dutch Cleanser, McKesson and Robbins liniment, and all like that.

I liked to look at the advertisements in the mail-order catalogues he kept by the cash register....Grandpa had him a big sign out front over the entrance to the store, In fancy red letters outlined in gold it said: General Merchandise Mr. E. Rucker Blakeslee, Proprietor...

A third cousin of Papa's, Hopewell Stump, from out in Banks County, clerked and took care of the chickens that folks brought to trade out for nails, flour, sugar, coal oil, coffee, and chewing tobacco. There used to be smelly chicken coops out on the board sidewalk in front of every store in town....

Uncle Camp mostly swept the floor and put out stock, and in the wintertime broke up wooden shipping crates to burn in the stove....

Love Simpson was the first woman Grandpa ever hired...When I went inside, there was the new milliner, seated at a table littered with feathers, bird wings, satin bows, stiff tape, bolts of velvet, linen, silk, and so on, and several life-size dummy heads...

Peanut Processing

Peanuts, the world's most popular nut, and one of the top ten cash crops in the United States; and Georgia is the fourth largest producer of peanuts in the world. On the average, each American consumes about three and a half pounds of peanuts each year. Peanuts can be purchased raw in the shell, shelled with red skins intact or shelled and blanched with red skins removed. Most often, however, people buy processed peanuts—peanuts that are either roasted in the shell, roasted and salted in the shell, boiled in brine, oil roasted, oil roasted and salted or dry roasted.

Half of all edible peanuts in the United States are roasted and ground to make peanut butter. The average American eats six pounds of peanut butter a year.

1. Peanuts are sometimes stored in silos until they are ready to be shelled.
2. In Columbus during the early 1920s, Tom Huston perfected a method of processing toasted peanuts so they could be sold in small quantities for immediate consumption.
3. Tom Huston invented a novel bag that was narrow and elongated enabling the consumer to conveniently grasp it in one hand and pour the nuts directly into the mouth.

4 and 5. The O. A. Williams and Sons peanut processing plant is located in Plains.

6. Freshly harvested green peanuts boiled in brine at outdoor stands are a Georgia tradition (see page 250).
7. Most Georgia peanuts are used for making roasted and salted peanuts or peanut butter.
8. Botanist George Washington Carver (1859–1943) developed more than three hundred uses for peanuts. Dr. Carver once served a nine-course meal in which every dish, from salad to soup to coffee, was made with peanuts.
9. Consumers can purchase different-sized mesh bags of raw peanuts at roadside stands and farmer's markets.
10. Peanuts are not a nut; they are a legume, like beans and peas. The peanut plant is unusual because it flowers above the ground, but fruits below the ground.
11. Georgia's most famous peanut farmer, Jimmy Carter, worked on his peanut farm in pre-presidential days.

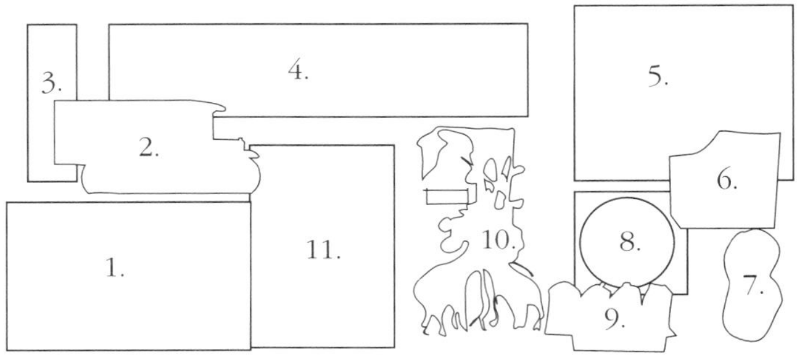

Jimmy Carter

Jimmy Carter was born in Plains, Georgia, October 1, 1924, to Earl and Lillian Carter. He was the oldest son in a family that would eventually include two sisters—Gloria, born in 1926, and Ruth, born in 1929—and a brother—Billy, born in 1937. In 1928 Earl Carter moved his family to Archery, two and one-half miles west of Plains on the old Preston-Americus Road. In 1941 Jimmy Carter would leave Archery and Plains for a career as a naval officer, farmer, state legislator, governor and eventually United States President. But for the first seventeen years of his life, the Carter farm, the settlement of Archery and the farming community of Plains composed the boundaries of his physical world.

Well, the farm itself, the whole thing, was about 360 acres. We grew cotton then shifted strongly to peanuts. We grew wheat, oats, rye as well as other things. In addition to cattle and sheep, we produced some of our own mules. Daddy always had about six mares, and he kept a very highly qualified and high-quality jackass to breed with the mares. We had about fifty geese that ran wild. We would harvest them twice a year; pick the breast feathers off. Daddy would often have down comforters made, which he sold for a pretty good price in our store, and he would peddle them around in other stores. We grew sugar cane and made syrup out of it, which Daddy sold under his brand name, which was "Plains."

We had it ingrained in us that hard work was an important part of life. Not a blemish on life but an asset to life. It was almost ingrained in us like our own religion was. It was the priority of and the honor of doing hard and successful work on the farm. Our bell rang every morning at four o'clock—before daybreak. We would get up, dress, go to the barn, catch the mules, put our plowstocks on the back of the wagon and drive the mules and wagons to the fields. And we would be standing at the end of the rows when daybreak came so that we could see where the cotton and peanuts were so we wouldn't plow them up. We would begin plowing, and we did that until sundown. Came back home and watered the livestock, ate supper and went to bed. So that was our day's work.

You would break the land first with mules and a turning plow and that would leave the earth broken down, I'd say an average of five inches. A tractor, now, can break it down to about eight inches. But after you broke the land down, you had a very uneven surface. So you would drag the harrow over it to smooth the top of the surface down to make it more effective when you laid off your rows and put out fertilizer and then planted your cotton, peanuts or corn on a smoother surface. We had a spring-tooth harrow that would go through the ground. And spikes were on a kind of spring. They were curved over and were about a foot off the ground, and they would kind of chop up the ground. The other one was a drag harrow and it had a spike like a railroad spike, and it would stick in the ground and just kind of smooth out the top of the ground.

The best job I had on the farm was pruning watermelons. A friend and I would go through Daddy's fields and my friend's father's fields with a pocketknife. We would select the deformed or small watermelons and cut them off the vine so they wouldn't sap the nutrients from the vine. We would leave the good watermelons on the vine. We would probably do that two or three times during the growing season. That was the most pleasant small chore I had.

The worse by far was mopping cotton. Boll weevils were becoming more and more of a problem then as they spread throughout the South, and the worse place they could be was in the bud of a growing cotton plant. When cotton plants were maybe a foot high, less than about knee high, we would have to go through the fields and mop the cotton. We mixed arsenic and molasses and water, and we carried a small bucket in our hands. Daddy would haul a barrel of this mixture to the end of the rows. Long rows. And we would go down the row and, with

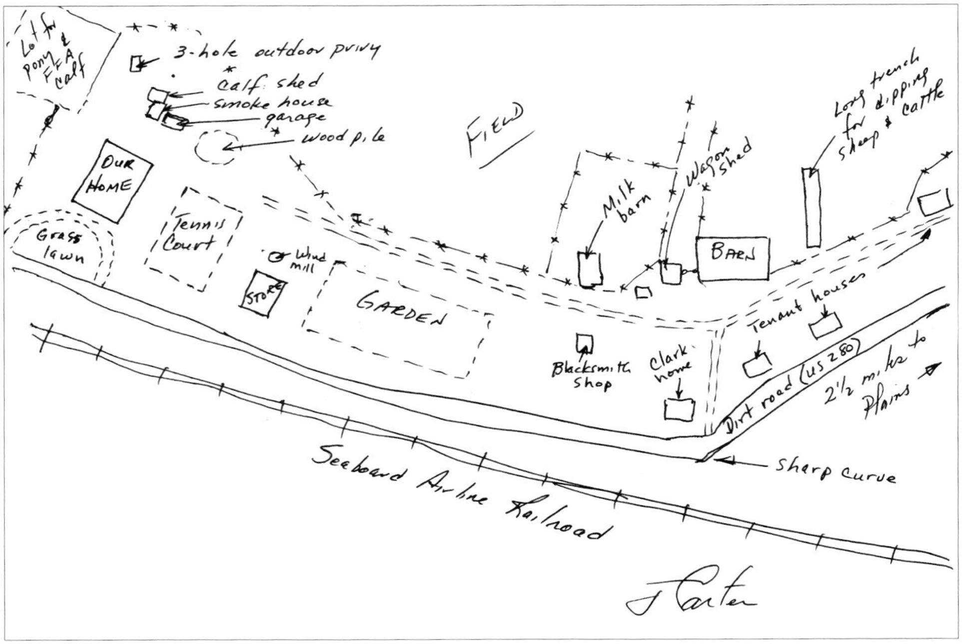

A hand-drawn map by Jimmy Carter of his home place in Archery, two and one-half miles west of Plains.

a stick with a little rag mop on the end, dip the rag mop in the bucket of this poison and put a dab of it in the bud of each growing cotton stalk. As we walked through the fields, we would be almost covered with flies—as they were attracted to the molasses. When we would get home at night and take off our pants—we wore long pants in the field and went barefooted—you could just stand them up in the corner. Once you messed up a pair of pants, you had to go with it. By the next morning they were sticky but stiff, and they would even crackle sometimes when we started walking early in the morning. Then, of course, with the warmer weather and the fresh application of spattered molasses, water and arsenic on them, they would loosen up some. I started doing this when I was about eight years old. When I wasn't at school, I would be mopping cotton.

We didn't have anything on the farm that was mechanized except a small gasoline motor that drove a pump near the barn to pump water. We would crank that little motor up—it had a fly wheel on it—and it would pump water. When you couldn't crank it, you had to pump it by hand.

We had a windmill to provide water for the house. That was installed several years after we moved out to the farm. At first we didn't have any running water in the house; but the windmill provided water and then, of course, when I was fourteen years old, in 1938, we got electricity. We had an outdoor toilet.

All of the cultivation, all of the breaking of land, all of the harvesting was done with hand labor and mules. We didn't get our first truck until the year I went off to college which was in the winter of 1941.

It was very difficult at that time to make a living. During the Depression years, there was no money to amount to anything. We were mutually interdependent, not only with each other in the family, but also with our neighbors.

The seasons came and went. We took pride always in the care of our land and with the principle that we were caretakers for God and protecting the world that he had given us. At least once a year, we would have a Sunday in all three major churches in Plains for honoring the natural beauty of our countryside and our farm. So the stewardship of nature, of preserving the quality of our land, the beauty of our woodlands, protection of wildlife was immediately and dramatically tied in with our belief in God.

Farm touring with Jimmy and Rosalynn Carter:

We go back and forth to the Carter Center in Atlanta from Plains. We generally go one route and come back another. One route we take is I-85 from the airport going toward Alabama. We go through Columbus down through Richland and back over eastward to Plains. Another route is on GA 85 and US 41, going through Manchester and down through Buena Vista. Another way that we go is right up GA 19 through Thomaston and Griffin. Another one is GA 36 over and run into I-75 at Barnesville. When we go to the coast like Savannah or Brunswick, sometimes we go all the way across the state on GA 32. Sometimes we go a little bit further south down I-75 and turn off through Tifton towards Brunswick.

So we try to take a different route so I can look at the farmland, see what different people are doing, see how they are harvesting their trees, planting their trees. I can make a pretty good judgement of how many more farmers or less farmers are raising cattle, chickens. I am still fascinated with farming.

THE "BULLETIN"

December 26, 1929: Want to exchange 2 teacupsful of heavy bearing English pea seed for 3 teacupsful of white Bunch butter-bean seed.

September 3, 1997: Want dwarf cannas, all colors, in exchange for thinning out.

Think of it as a running dialogue. Nearly every week since 1917, the Department of Agriculture has published a running dialogue for Georgia's farmers and consumers. It's called the *Farmers and Consumers Market Bulletin*, a twelve-page tabloid that is the largest circulating weekly in the state, with more than 250,000 readers in Georgia alone.

For more than eighty years, farm machinery, livestock, seed plants, flowers and miscellaneous goods and services have been bought, sold or swapped in the Market Bulletin. In addition, the Department of Agriculture publishes timely articles ("Muscadine Crop Running Late this Year") and recipes (Pork Roast with Georgia Peach Sauce) and answers questions from an agricultural hot line (Can apricot trees grow in Georgia?).

The original intention of the bulletin—to help farmers market their products and locate useful items—continues today, but with a twist. These days many of the readers are consumers, with 26 percent of the readers in the ten-county metro Atlanta area. Over thirteen hundred classified ads appear in the bulletin each week, free of charge to all Georgians. The bulletin accepts no commercial advertising.

This free, weekly dialogue has survived two World Wars and the Great Depression, but in 1972 was threatened by state budget cuts. Reacting swiftly, Commissioner of Agriculture Tommy Irvin, with the help of columnist Celestine Sibley, encouraged the public to contact their legislators and share their feelings about the *Market Bulletin*. Perhaps Sibley expressed the majority opinion best when she wrote, years later: "I'd rather the dear old Capitol, which I love, would go. They can get rid of the expressways for all I care, and I wouldn't give a bean for the dispute over the flag. But please, please don't take the *Market Bulletin* away!" As a result of the outpouring of calls and letters, legislators spared the bulletin from its budget trimming axe.

And so with the help of a nine-person staff, the weekly dialogue continues. Do you need bush hogging, disc plowing or your beaver pond siphoned? See the listings under Farm Services. Are you looking for non-smoking couples to take care of fifty horses? See Farm Employment. Need heart pine tongue and groove flooring or stainless steel hog feeders? Farm Supplies. Jersey cows, Simmental bulls, African pygmy goats or Hampshire hogs? Livestock. Pink poppies, Black-eyed Susans or Sweet Williams? Flowers for sale. Old-fashioned multiplying white onions, red pear tomatoes or tall fescue seeds? Seeds and Plants. Lye soap, Alpaca Llama wool or gourds? See Oddities.

Regular features in the bulletin include "Georgia Cookin,'" recipes from Georgia cooks tested in department kitchens; "Grandpa," an advice columnist for aspiring gardeners; and seasonal planting charts. Also, there are special editions that cover topics like horses, folk crafts, real estate, pick-your-own farms and recipes.

Cakes

Whether it's a Sunday dinner pound cake, a passed along, secret recipe, brandied friendship cake or a holiday fruit cake, cakes play a central and memorable role in many Southern celebrations. A prized cake can elevate its baker in the eyes of family and community and perhaps that's why cake recipes have long been a favorite of *Market Bulletin* readers.

Through the years these recipes have reflected the way readers eat and entertain. In the early years, cakes were fancy, often featuring multiple layers filled with frosting and elaborate decoration. Later, simplicity was in vogue with more cakes baked in single-layer pans, self-frosted or not frosted at all. Rather surprising is a recent revival of show-off desserts which are baked from scratch.

The pound cake, gracing Southern sideboards for more than two centuries, was an English invention of the mid-1700s and is one of the most basic of Southern sweets. It is appropriately named because it originally included one pound each of butter, sugar, eggs and flour. Modern Southern bakers sometimes enrich the cake with sour cream, whipping cream, chocolate, nuts or fruit flavors.

POUND CAKE
By Susan S. Lewis, Home Economist, Georgia Department of Agriculture:

I stared intently, frozen. Across the dining table he paused in serious contemplation. She had asked the ultimate question of the year, the year so far anyway, it being only January, and now he got to answer. He had the best of choices. I knew he would say "pound cake"—and I wasn't happy. Why not the devil's food with "white" icing as we called it. No, he was a pound cake man, my brother; and she, my mother, would have baked any cake for his birthday.

The choices were only limited by the cakes she had perfected for thirty-three years. We had our favorites: Pound Cake (plain, no frosting) for him and Devil's Food with Seven-Minute Frosting for me. He had lingered only to taunt me, or so I thought. Why had I not been there for my birthday the previous August? he asked. I had missed my cake—my choice.

Suddenly, the years came rolling back, and I saw her standing at the mixer and then over the double boiler in the house where we grew up. She was always happy to bake our favorites, and my brother and I and the rest of the family were always happy to eat them.

Daddy had to participate in this ritual and brought me back when he grinned and quipped, "Will the mixer go one more year?"

It was on its last leg, a Hamilton Beech, received as a wedding present thirty-five years ago. Though, it had been on its last leg since I was sixteen or so. She knowingly smiled, and we new the mixer would make it.

I consoled myself with the memories of her pound cake, pic-

CARAMEL PECAN POUND CAKE

Enjoy Georgia pecans in this elegant dessert

1	cup butter
1	pound box light brown sugar
1	cup sugar
5	eggs
½	teaspoon baking powder
½	teaspoon salt
3	cups all-purpose flour
1	cup milk
1	tablespoon vanilla extract
1	cup finely chopped pecans
	Powdered sugar

Preheat oven to 325°. In large bowl, cream butter and brown sugar thoroughly at medium speed of an electric mixer. Gradually add sugar and continue creaming. Add eggs one at a time, beating thoroughly after each addition. In medium bowl, combine baking powder, salt and flour. Alternately add flour mixture and milk to creamed mixture, beginning and ending with flour. Mix just until well blended after each addition. Stir in vanilla and pecans. Pour batter into a greased and floured 10-inch tube pan. Bake for 1 hour and 30 minutes. Cool cake for 15 minutes before removing from pan. If desired, dust lightly with powdered sugar. Yields 20 slices.

Georgia Pecan Commission

Great Depression Cake

This cake has the flavor of an old fashioned spice cake

2 cups sugar
½ cup vegetable shortening
2 cups strong coffee
2 cups raisins
2 cups all-purpose flour
1 teaspoon baking soda
1 teaspoon baking powder
1 teaspoon ground cinnamon
1 teaspoon ground allspice
1 teaspoon ground cloves
1 teaspoon ground nutmeg
1 cup chopped pecans
Vegetable cooking spray
Powdered sugar (optional)

In large saucepan, cream together sugar and shortening. Add coffee and raisins; bring mixture to boil. Reduce heat and simmer 10 minutes, stirring occasionally. Cool for 10 minutes.

Preheat oven to 350°. Meanwhile, combine flour, baking soda, baking powder and spices in separate bowl. Add flour mixture to liquid mixture, blending thoroughly. Stir in pecans. Pour batters into a 9x13-inch pan coated with vegetable spray and dusted with flour. Bake for 30 to 35 minutes or until cake tests done. Cool and dust with powdered sugar if desired. Yields 20 squares.

Alice Mayfield
Cusseta, Georgia

Hint: This is an old recipe which was popular during the Depression when milk, eggs and butter were hard to come by. To lower the fat content in this recipe, substitute ⅓ cup vegetable oil for the shortening (this also reduces the saturated fat content) and reduce pecans to ½ cup. Result: Each serving contains 220 calories and 5.9g fat (23% of calories).

turing it in the domed glass, footed cake stand. It had a perfect texture, was always baked in a bundt pan and had a crusty, cracked surface.

But it wouldn't hurt to try to sway my brother, and I blurted, "but what about the devil's food?" with a pleading sing-songy voice. No, he could not be moved.

"Don't you want pecans (PEA-cans) in it?" It was my last shot. Nah, he shook his head. He was sure. So for this birthday dinner, there will be pound cake.

I can't wait for August.

Freshman student wants part time job near Abraham Baldwin Agricultural College on farm, experienced. Kevin Johnson, Rt. 1, Monkton, Maryland

Farm Positions Wanted, Market Bulletin, *April 23, 1975*

RED VELVET CAKE

Lynda Talmadge, wife of former Georgia Governor and U.S. Senator Herman Talmadge, has been making a red velvet cake with a cream cheese frosting for her son's birthday ever since he was a year old. She even made it for his groom's cake at his April 1996 wedding. "It took ten recipes to make three four-inch tiers. I used a milk chocolate frosting and dark chocolate trim for this occasion," Lynda said.

To make her traditional cake, Lynda creams 1 cup of butter and 2 cups of sugar in a large bowl. She then adds 2 eggs and beats the mixture until it is light and fluffy. Next, she makes a paste from 1 tablespoon of cocoa and 1 tablespoon of vinegar and adds it to the mixture. Lynda then sifts together 2½ cups of cake flour, 1½ teaspoons of baking soda and ½ teaspoon of salt and alternately adds this and 1 cup of buttermilk to the butter/sugar mixture. Last, she adds ½ teaspoon of vanilla and three 1-ounce bottles of red food coloring. Lynda then pours the batter into 3 9-inch pans and bakes it for 25 minutes in her oven, which she has preheated to 325°.

While the cake is baking, Lynda makes her frosting. She mixes 1 8-ounce package of cream cheese with ½ cup of sugar in a large bowl until the ingredients are smooth. Next, she adds 1 cup of 4-X confectioners sugar and blends it well. After that, she folds in one 12-ounce container of whipped topping. After the cake has cooled, Lynda spreads the frosting on top of the 2 bottom layers, sprinkling about 1 cup of chopped pecans on them. She then puts the top layer in place and spreads frosting on the entire cake. Her red velvet cake is ready for any special occasion.

INTERSTATE 45 CAKE

This cake is baked with the cream cheese topping on it!

CAKE

	Vegetable cooking spray
1	yellow cake mix, pudding in the mix
2	eggs, beaten
½	cup margarine, melted

TOPPING

1	egg
8	ounces cream cheese
1	teaspoon vanilla extract
1	cup brown sugar
1	cup plus 2 tablespoons powdered sugar, divided

Preheat oven to 325°. Spray 9x13-inch pan with vegetable cooking spray. In medium bowl, mix together cake mix, beaten eggs and margarine. Spread mixture evenly into prepared pan. In separate bowl, beat egg, cream cheese, vanilla, brown sugar and 1 cup powdered sugar with electric mixer. Pour evenly over cake batter in pan. Bake for 45 minutes. Sprinkle with 2 tablespoons powdered sugar and serve. Yields 16 slices.

Shirley Berry
Dalton, Georgia

Hints: To reduce fat and calories, use ⅓ cup margarine in the cake and use low-fat cream cheese in the topping. Result: One serving contains 283 calories and 10.4g fat (33% of calories).

WHIPPING CREAM POUND CAKE

Out of this World!

- 2½ cups sugar
- 1 cup shortening
- 6 eggs
- 1 teaspoon lemon flavoring
- 1 teaspoon vanilla extract
- 3 cups sifted all-purpose flour
- 1 teaspoon baking powder
- ½ pint whipping cream

Preheat oven to 275°. Cream sugar and shortening. Add eggs one at a time; beat well after each addition. Add lemon and vanilla flavorings. Sift dry ingredients. Alternately add flour and whipping cream to sugar and shortening. Mix slowly. Place in a greased and floured tube pan or a 16.5x5x4-inch pan. Bake 40 minutes, then adjust temperature to 325° for 30 minutes without opening oven door or moving pan. Test for doneness by inserting wooden pick. Cake may need to cook for 5 to 10 additional minutes. Do not overcook. Cake should be very moist. Yields 16 slices.

Theo Corvette
Atlanta, Georgia

EARTHQUAKE CAKE

Pecans and coconut cover bottom of this easy-to-make cake

- 1½ cups chopped pecans
- 1½ cups shredded coconut
- 1 box German chocolate cake mix (prepared according to package directions)
- ½ cup margarine
- 1 8-ounce package cream cheese
- 4 cups powdered sugar

Preheat oven to 350°. Grease and flour a 9x13-inch pan. Combine pecans and coconut; sprinkle in bottom of pan. Pour prepared cake mix over pecan and coconut mixture. Melt margarine and cream cheese together in saucepan. Add powdered sugar; mix well. Pour mixture over cake batter. Bake for 45 minutes or until cake tests done. Remove from oven. Cool and cut into squares. Yields 16 squares.

Dorothy Conner
Jefferson, Georgia

Research has shown that top soybean yields are usually achieved with plantings made during May-Early June. The type of weather expected at and after planting is a major factor in determining the optimum time to plant. Many Georgia soybean growers get land prepared for planting by May 5, and begin planting as soon thereafter as soil moisture and temperature become favorable. Planting should be delayed until the surface soil temperature reaches 68 degrees for an extended 5-day period. Planting early in April causes very short plants and reduces yield in some years.

Soybean planting tip, Market Bulletin, *April 30, 1975*

Okra and Cotton

Okra, a member of the hibiscus family, has a well-known southern relative—cotton. Both cotton and okra share a delicate, light blue blossom. Beyond that, however, the resemblance is hard to see at times. Okra is long, green and slender; cotton is round, white and fluffy. Okra is a good source of vitamin A and vitamin C; cotton is a good source for shirts and jeans. As a natural thickening agent, okra (in Angolan it's called "ngombo") is found in southern gumbo and stews. Cotton, on the other hand, is rarely found in southern dishes—unless someone has accidentally dipped his shirt-sleeve into a serving dish.

Chocolate Syrup Cake

Butter and cream create a chocolate syrup-like icing

- 1 cup sugar
- ½ cup butter
- 4 eggs
- 1 16-ounce can chocolate syrup
- 1 teaspoon vanilla extract
- 1 cup self-rising flour
- Chocolate Icing

Preheat oven to 325°. Combine sugar and butter in a large bowl. Add eggs, beating well after each addition. Add remaining ingredients and mix well. Pour into a greased and floured 9x13-inch cake pan. Bake for 35 to 45 minutes or until done.

Chocolate Icing

- 1½ cups sugar
- 6 tablespoons butter
- ½ cup cream
- 8 ounces chocolate chips
- 1 teaspoon vanilla extract
- 1 tablespoon marshmallow cream

Place sugar, butter and cream in a medium-sized saucepan. Bring to a boil; add remaining ingredients. Stir to prevent sticking. Pour over cooled cake. Yields 8 slices.

Irene Parrish
Monroe, Georgia

Fresh Apple Cake

A rich brown-sugar glaze covers this delicious apple cake

- 3 cups all-purpose flour
- 1 teaspoon baking soda
- 1 teaspoon salt
- 1½ cups vegetable oil
- 3 eggs
- 2 cups sugar
- 2 teaspoons vanilla extract
- 1¼ cups chopped pecans
- 2 cups fresh apples, finely chopped
- 1 teaspoon apple pie spice or ground cinnamon (optional)
- Topping

Preheat oven to 325°. Sift flour, soda and salt. Add oil, eggs (one at a time), and sugar and beat until mixed. Dough will be stiff. Add vanilla, pecans, apples and apple spice if desired. Grease and flour tube or bundt pan; pour batter into pan. Bake 1 hour and 20 minutes. Cool.

Topping

- ½ cup margarine
- ½ cup dark brown sugar
- 2 teaspoons milk

Mix topping ingredients in a saucepan. Bring to a boil and cook for 2 minutes. Pour over cake. Yields 16 slices.

Olen Rosebrayh
Baxley, Georgia

Red Wigglers, many prices, worm casting miracle dirt. Mrs. John B. Aterbolt, Sr. Powder Springs

Miscellaneous For Sale, Market Bulletin, *July 16, 1986*

CARROT CAKE WITH SAUCE

Bernice Irvin, wife of Georgia Department of Agriculture Commissioner Tommy Irvin, says the most important thing to her about cooking is pleasing her family. "If I make them happy, my recipe is a 'prize winner.'"

One "prize winner" that Mrs. Irvin makes often for her family is her carrot cake with buttermilk-vanilla sauce.

To prepare it, Mrs. Irvin creams 2 cups of sugar and 1¼ cups of vegetable oil at medium speed with an electric mixer. She then adds 4 eggs, 1 at a time, mixing them well. Next, she adds 2 cups of finely grated carrots and 1 cup of chopped black walnuts. In a separate bowl, Mrs. Irvin combines 3 cups of self-rising flour with 2 teaspoons of ground cinnamon. She adds this to the creamed mixture. She then pours the batter into a greased and floured bundt or tube pan and bakes it for 1 hour, or until a wooden pick inserted in the center comes out clean, in a preheated 325° oven. When the cake is done, she cools it in the pan for 10 to 15 minutes before removing it to a platter.

To make her buttermilk sauce, Mrs. Irvin melts ½ cup of butter in a saucepan over low heat. Next, she stirs in ⅓ cup of sugar and 3 tablespoons of cornstarch. She adds 1½ cups of water and, stirring occasionally, brings the liquid to a rapid boil. She lets this boil for 1 minute and then stirs in 1 tablespoon of vanilla. The sauce is ready to serve over her carrot cake.

TASTY PINEAPPLE CAKE

All the flavor of your traditional upside-down cake!

- ½ cup reduced-calorie margarine
- Sugar substitute equivalent to 1 cup sugar
- 2 eggs
- 1½ cups all-purpose flour
- 1 teaspoon baking powder
- ½ teaspoon baking soda
- ¼ teaspoon salt
- ½ cup skim milk
- 4 slices unsweetened pineapple, drained
- Vegetable cooking spray
- ½ cup unsweetened pineapple juice
- Sugar substitute to taste

Preheat oven to 350°. In large bowl, cream margarine and sugar substitute until light and fluffy. Add eggs one at a time, beating well at medium speed of an electric mixer. In small bowl, combine flour, baking powder, baking soda and salt. Add flour mixture to creamed mixture alternating with milk, beginning and ending with flour mixture. Beat at low speed after each addition. Cut pineapple into ½-inch pieces; gently fold into batter. Spoon batter into a 6-cup bundt pan coated with vegetable cooking spray. (Either an 8-inch square pan or an 8-inch round cake pan can be used also.) Bake for 45 to 50 minutes or until cake tests done. Combine pineapple juice and sugar substitute equivalent to ¼ to ½ cup sugar; stir until dissolved. Pour juice mixture over cake when it is removed from the oven. Let stand 5 minutes. Remove cake from pan. Yields 10 slices.

Cheryl Presnal
Carrollton, Georgia

Nutrition Information Per Serving: Calories 151 / Protein 6.6g / Carbohydrates 18.6g / Fat 6g / Cholesterol 43mg / Fiber .6g / Calcium 31mg / Iron 1.1mg / Sodium 227mg

Dietary Exchanges: 1 bread, 1 fat

Hint: An aspartame-based artificial sweetener is recommended in this recipe.

Deluxe Carrot Cake

What! No sugar? Juice concentrates provide the sweetness!

4	eggs
½	cup vegetable oil
1	cup unsweetened pineapple juice concentrate
¼	cup unsweetened orange juice concentrate
2¼	teaspoons ground cinnamon
1½	cups packed, grated carrot
2½	cups all-purpose flour
2½	teaspoons baking soda
	Cream Cheese Frosting

Preheat oven to 325°. Grease and flour a 13x9x2-inch baking pan. In large bowl, combine eggs, oil and concentrates. Beat mixture until foamy on medium speed of electric mixer. Add cinnamon, carrots and flour; stir by hand until mixed thoroughly. Add baking soda; stir quickly to mix. Immediately pour batter into prepared pan. Bake 30 to 35 minutes. Cool on wire rack. Spread with cream cheese frosting. Yields 24 slices.

Cream Cheese Frosting

1	3-ounce package cream cheese, softened
¼	cup reduced-calorie margarine, softened
*32	packets artificial sweetener
1	teaspoon vanilla extract

In small bowl, cream together cheese and margarine until smooth. Slowly add sweetener; mix until smooth. Stir in vanilla and mix thoroughly. Spread over cooled cake.

(*32 packets is equivalent to 3 tablespoons plus ¾ teaspoon granulated sugar substitute.)

Cheryl Presnal
Carrollton, Georgia

Nutrition Information Per Serving: Calories 159 / Protein 4.3g / Carbohydrates 17.5g / Fat 6.2g / Cholesterol 39mg / Fiber .7g / Calcium 19mg / Iron 1mg / Sodium 121mg

Dietary Exchanges: 1 bread, ½ fruit, 1 fat

Hint: This is a delicious treat, especially if you're cutting back on sugar and calories. Icing may be prepared with reduced-fat or fat-free cream cheese.

When squash plants grow big and begin to fall over, pile more soil over bent stems. In a week or so the plants will put out new sprouts and you can enjoy a late squash crop.

Gardening tip, Market Bulletin, *July 16, 1986*

ORANGE POUND CAKE

You'll love the flavor and texture of this low-fat treat!

	Vegetable cooking spray
1	teaspoon all-purpose flour
1¾	cups all-purpose flour
2	teaspoons baking powder
¼	teaspoon salt
½	cup granulated fructose
2	teaspoons grated orange rind
⅔	cup orange juice
¼	cup vegetable oil
4	egg whites

Preheat oven to 325°. Coat bottom of 9x5-inch loaf pan with vegetable cooking spray; dust pan with 1 teaspoon flour. Set aside. Combine 1¾ cups flour and next 3 ingredients in a large bowl. Combine orange rind, juice and oil; add to flour mixture. Beat at medium speed of an electric mixer just until smooth. (Batter will be thick.)

Beat egg whites at high speed of an electric mixer until stiff peaks form. Fold ⅓ of beaten egg whites into batter; gently fold in remaining beaten egg whites. Pour batter into prepared pan. Bake for 60 minutes or until a wooden pick inserted in center comes out clean. Cool in pan 10 minutes; remove from pan and let cool on a wire rack. Yields 16 slices.

Georgia Department of Agriculture Test Kitchen

Nutrition Information Per Serving: Calories 114 / Protein 2.4g / Fat 3.6g / Carbohydrates 18g / Cholesterol 0 / Sodium 88mg / Calcium 11mg / Fiber .4g / Iron .7mg

Diabetic Exchanges: 1 bread, 1 fat

Out of this World Chocolate Cake

Dates and nuts make this a family dessert favorite!

1	cup vegetable oil
1½	cups sugar
3	eggs
1	cup buttermilk
2	cups all-purpose flour
1	teaspoon baking soda
1	teaspoon vanilla extract
1	cup chopped dates
1	cup chopped nuts
	Buttermilk Glaze
	Chocolate Frosting

Preheat oven to 350°. In a large bowl, combine oil and sugar. Add eggs one at a time, mixing well after each. Add buttermilk, flour, baking soda and vanilla. Fold in dates and nuts. Pour batter into a greased and floured 9x13-inch baking pan. Bake for 35 to 40 minutes. Remove from oven and top with buttermilk glaze. Return cake to oven for additional 10 minutes. Cool and frost with chocolate icing. Yields 12 slices.

Buttermilk Glaze

¼	cup butter
1	cup sugar
½	cup buttermilk
½	teaspoon baking soda
½	teaspoon vanilla extract
1	tablespoon light corn syrup

In a small saucepan, combine all ingredients and bring to a boil.

Chocolate Frosting

1	stick butter
4	tablespoons milk
3	tablespoons cocoa
1	tablespoon vanilla extract
1	16-ounce box powdered sugar

In a medium saucepan, combine butter, milk, cocoa and vanilla. Bring to a boil; remove from heat. Add powdered sugar to mixture, stirring well to remove lumps.

Kathleen Reed
Oakwood, Georgia

We have twenty geese and wish to pluck them for their down and feathers. However, this is a totally new experience and we are asking for help. We would appreciate any of the Market Bulletin readers writing us or calling us collect as to the most suitable time of year for plucking and the best method. E. C. Macfie, Route 1, Box 62 Crawfordsville

Reader inquiry, Market Bulletin, *February 13, 1980*

Sunday Dinner
From *Leaving Cold Sassy* by Olive Ann Burns …

Everybody in Cold Sassy used the good tablecloths and the good china, silver, and goblets on Sunday, and usually invited kinfolks or the preacher's family or neighbors. Mama was always saying she "owed" somebody a meal, and if Mama's watermelon pickle or sweet tomato sauce or fried eggplant was their favorite, you could count on that being on the table along with eight or ten more dishes, hot yeast rolls, and everything good you ever thought of eating. But it was just called Sunday dinner, not dinner party. If you had a party at night, it was a barbecue or fish fry.

Jam Cake

A Market Bulletin *tradition!*

- ½ cup butter, softened
- 1 cup sugar
- 4 eggs, reserve 2 egg whites for icing
- 1½ cups all-purpose flour
- 1 teaspoon baking soda
- 2 tablespoons ground cinnamon
- 1 teaspoon ground allspice
- 1 teaspoon ground nutmeg
- ½ cup buttermilk
- ½ teaspoon vanilla extract
- ¾ cup blackberry or strawberry jam
- Creole Icing

Preheat oven to 350°. In a large mixing bowl, cream butter and sugar. Add 2 eggs plus 2 egg yolks, beating well. Sift together flour, soda and spices; add alternately with buttermilk to butter mixture. Stir in vanilla and jam. Pour batter into 2 greased and floured 9-inch round cake pans; bake for 35 minutes or until cake tests done. Cool 10 minutes and remove from pans; cool completely and frost with Creole Icing. Yields 16 slices.

Creole Icing

- ½ cup water
- 1⅔ cups brown sugar
- ½ teaspoon cream of tartar
- 2 egg whites, beaten
- ½ cup chopped pecans

In a small saucepan, combine water, sugar and cream of tartar, stirring until smooth. Slowly boil without stirring until syrup reaches 260° or the hard ball stage. Pour syrup slowly over beaten egg whites; beat until mixture pulls away from sides of bowl. Stir in pecans and spread on cake.

Mrs. O. J. Capps
Augusta, Georgia

SCRIPTURE CAKE

A classic!

1) 1 cup Judges 5:25 (butter)
2) 2 cups Jeremiah 6:20 (sugar)
3) 6 Jeremiah 17:11 (eggs)
4) 2 tablespoons Samuel 14:25 (honey)
5) 4½ cups I Kings 4:22 (all-purpose flour)
6) 2 teaspoons Amos 4:5 (baking powder)
7) 1 pinch Leviticus 2:15 (salt)
8) 1 cup Judges 4:19 (milk)
9) 2 cups I Samuel 30:12 (raisins)
10) 2 cups Nahum 3:12, chopped (figs)
11) 2 cups Numbers 17:8, slivered (almonds)

Make it a family project to look up the ingredients. All are found in the King James version of the Bible.

Preheat oven to 350°. Cream first 2 ingredients. Add 3rd ingredient one at a time; add 4th ingredient and beat well. Mix ingredients 5, 6 and 7 and add alternately with ingredient number 8. Stir in ingredients 9, 10 and 11. Bake in 2 greased loaf pans for 1 hour or until done. Yields 20 slices.

A Market Bulletin *Favorite*

CANDY BAR POUND CAKE

Chocolate and pecans are the highlight of this pound cake

- 1 cup butter or margarine, softened
- 2 cups sugar
- 4 eggs
- 2½ cups all-purpose flour
- ¼ teaspoon baking soda
- 1 cup buttermilk
- 1 8-ounce milk chocolate candy bar, melted
- 2 teaspoons vanilla extract
- 1 cup chopped pecans

Preheat oven to 325°. Cream butter until light and fluffy; gradually add sugar. Add eggs one at a time, beating well after each addition. Add sifted dry ingredients alternately with buttermilk. Add remaining ingredients and pour into prepared bundt pan. Bake for 1 hour and 15 minutes or until cake tests done. Yields 12 slices.

Jeanette Beard
Montezuma, Georgia

GEORGIA WEDDING CEREMONY

The 1948 book, the *Southern Country Editor*, a collection of newspaper articles from across the south, relates the text of a *Choctaw Plain-dealer* newspaper story about a justice of the peace in Sandersonville who delivers this wedding ceremony:

By the authority vested in me as an officer of the State of Georgia, which is sometimes called the Empire State of the South; by the fields of cotton that spread out in snowy whiteness around us; by the howl of coon dogs, and the gourd vine, whose clinging tendrils will shade the entrance to your humble dwelling place; by the red and luscious heart of the watermelon, whose sweetness fills the heart with joy; by the heavens and earth, in the presence of these witnesses, I pronounce you man and wife.

My husband and I are collecting tips about the simple living lifestyle. We would appreciate hearing from any of your readers who would like to share "old time" simpler ways of doing things. We publish a newsletter for people who want to de-stress, down-scale, control spending, and gain more autonomy in their employment, finances and their lives in general.

Reader inquiry, Market Bulletin,
March 22, 1995

Cola Cake

This cake is a cola and marshmallow treat

- 2 cups all-purpose flour
- 2 cups sugar
- 1 cup butter
- 3 tablespoons cocoa
- 1 cup cola
- ½ cup buttermilk
- 2 eggs, beaten
- 1 teaspoon baking soda
- 1 teaspoon vanilla extract
- 1½ cups miniature marshmallows
- Icing

Preheat oven to 350°. Combine flour and sugar in a large mixing bowl. In a small saucepan, heat butter, cocoa and cola to boiling. Pour over flour mixture. Mix thoroughly and add buttermilk, eggs, soda, vanilla and marshmallows. Mix well. Place in a greased and floured 9x13-inch pan. Bake 35 minutes.

Icing

- ½ cup butter
- 3 tablespoons cocoa
- 6 tablespoons cola
- 1 16-ounce box powdered sugar
- 1 cup broken pecans

Combine butter, cocoa and cola in a medium saucepan and heat to boiling point. Place powdered sugar in mixing bowl and pour cola mixture over sugar. Beat well and stir in pecans. Pour over cake. Yields 12 slices.

Jan Ragland
Lyerly, Georgia

Do Nothing Cake

2 cups all-purpose flour
2 eggs, slightly beaten
½ teaspoon salt
1 20-ounce can crushed pineapple, undrained
2 cups sugar
1 teaspoon vanilla extract
1 teaspoon baking soda
Topping

Preheat oven for 350°. Combine all ingredients and mix by hand. Do not use an electric mixer. Pour into a greased 9x13-inch pan and bake for 30 to 35 minutes. Spread topping over cake while warm. Yields 12 squares.

Topping

1 5-ounce can evaporated whole milk
½ cup butter or margarine
1 cup sugar
1½ cups coconut
1 cup chopped pecans

In medium saucepan, mix milk, butter and sugar; boil 5 minutes. Stir in coconut and pecans.

Bertha Smith
Demorest, Georgia

Plum Nut Cake

3 eggs
2 cups sugar
1 cup vegetable oil
2 cups self-rising flour
1 teaspoon ground cinnamon
1 teaspoon ground cloves
2 4-ounce jars plum baby food
1 cup chopped nuts

Preheat oven to 350°. In large mixing bowl, combine eggs, sugar and oil. In medium bowl, sift together flour and spices; add to egg mixture. Stir until thoroughly blended. Add remaining ingredients and beat well. Pour batter into greased and floured tube pan. Bake for 45 to 55 minutes or until cake tests done. Yields 20 slices.

Georgia Department of Agriculture Test Kitchen

Hint: To reduce calories and fat in this cake, reduce sugar to 1½ cups and oil to ½ cup. Use 2 whole eggs plus 2 eggs whites and use ½ cup chopped and toasted nuts. Result: One slice of cake contains 187 calories and 8.1g fat.

Although I was born and raised in the South, I have always had an inordinate fascination with kudzu. My granddaddy was paid to plant it on his land back during the Depression when it was dubbed as the "savior" for eroding pastureland and hillsides throughout Georgia. And I've also read stories about young ladies being crowned as "Kudzu Queens," during the vine's heyday. (I wonder if any of these people are still around?) It seems that today, all folks want to do is "cuss" this aggressive green vine. But I am convinced that there are resourceful people who have come up with some unique ways to utilize kudzu and channel its energy. I would love to hear from anyone who has some clever uses for kudzu or who has a tale to tell about their experience with this infamous Southern Vine. Judy Jones, Chamblee

Reader inquiry, Market Bulletin, *April 10, 1996*

Crazy Cake

Grace Hartley served as food editor of the *Atlanta Journal* for more than forty years, a period where she received numerous local and national awards for her contributions to the regional cooking of the Southeast. Her book, *Grace Hartley's Southern Cooking*, is a collection of recipes from her readers, as well as her own research and remembered favorites passed down to her by her mother and grandmother.

"I grew up on a farm in middle Georgia where my family was a self-sustained unit, growing all the food we needed.... Many of the practical things I know about cooking I learned while sitting on the kitchen stove wood box and keeping my eyes on Mama."

To make Crazy Cake, one of her favorite cake recipes, Grace stirs together 2 cups of all-purpose flour, ½ teaspoon of salt and 2 cups of sugar in a large bowl. She places 1 stick of margarine, ½ cup of shortening, 4 tablespoons of cocoa and 1 cup of water in a saucepan, brings it to a rapid boil and then pours it over the flour mixture. She stirs this well and adds ½ cup of buttermilk, 2 lightly beaten eggs, 1 teaspoon of baking soda, 1 teaspoon of ground cinnamon and 1 teaspoon of vanilla extract. Next, she pours the batter, which is thin, into a greased 16 x 11-inch pan. Grace says she likes to use a broiler pan. She bakes the cake for 20 minutes in a preheated 400° oven.

While the cake is baking, Grace makes her icing. She combines 1 1-pound box of confectioners sugar with 1 teaspoon of vanilla extract and 1 cup of chopped nuts in a large bowl. She brings 1 stick of margarine, 4 tablespoons of cocoa and 6 tablespoons of milk to a rapid boil in a saucepan, stirring the mixture

Hummingbird Cake

Bananas, pineapple and nuts fill this very Southern cake

3	cups all-purpose flour
1½	teaspoons vanilla extract
2	cups mashed bananas
1	teaspoon salt
1	teaspoon ground cinnamon
1	8-ounce can crushed pineapple, undrained
2	cups sugar
1½	cups oil
3	eggs
1	teaspoon soda
½	cup chopped nuts
	Cream Cheese Icing

Preheat oven to 325°. Mix all ingredients together in a large mixing bowl. Pour batter into a greased and floured bundt or tube pan. Bake for 1½ hours. Cool in pan 1 hour before removing. Allow to cool completely and ice, if desired, with cream cheese icing. Yields 20 slices.

Cream Cheese Icing

1	8-ounce package cream cheese, softened
½	cup margarine, softened
1	16-ounce box powdered sugar
1	teaspoon vanilla extract

Cream cheese and margarine. Add sugar and vanilla. Beat until creamy and smooth.

Martha Sims
Auburn, Georgia

Hint: This cake could also be baked in 3 9-inch layer pans if desired. Bake only 30 minutes. This cake can be frozen.

often. Grace pours the cocoa mixture into the sugar mixture and beats them together well.

While the icing is still warm, she spreads it over the baked cake. She lets the cake cool thoroughly before cutting it into 48 squares. For a variation, Grace sometimes uses coconut instead of nuts in the icing.

FRUIT CAKE

This fruit cake recipe will become a holiday tradition

- ½ pound (2 sticks) butter
- 1 cup sugar
- 5 eggs, well-beaten
- 1½ teaspoons baking powder
- 2 cups sifted all-purpose flour
- 5 cups chopped pecans
- 1 pound candied pineapple (all colors)
- 1 pound candied cherries
- 1 pound white raisins
- 1 teaspoon lemon flavoring
- 1 teaspoon vanilla extract
- ⅛ cup orange juice

Cream butter and sugar. Add well-beaten eggs. Add baking powder to flour. Then sift twice. Add 1 cup of flour to nuts and fruit. Add other cup of flour to creamed mixture; mix thoroughly and add lemon and vanilla. Mix flour, nuts and fruit together by hand. Add to creamed mixture, mixing well. Put into ungreased tube pan and place in cold oven. Put pan of water on bottom shelf. Bake at 325° for 2 hours.

After baking, prick top of cake with a fork. Using a teaspoon, pour orange juice on top of cake so that the juice seeps into the holes.

Herman Watts
Baxley, Georgia

Hint: If possible, wrap cake in wax paper, cover tightly with foil and let set in covered cake plate about 10 days before serving.

From 1950 to 1966, Georgia's farm output rose faster than that of the U.S. by 40%. Nationally the average increase was 52%, Georgia's was 92%. In addition, the farmer's efficiency has helped hold down the cost of food and fiber to the consumer. In 1959 one farmer supplied the food and fiber needs for 23 people. Today he supplies the same needs for more than 43 people. Editorial by Georgia Commissioner of

Agriculture Tommy Irvin, Market Bulletin, *July 8, 1970*

Miss Love's Pound Cake
From *Cold Sassy Tree* by Olive Ann Burns ...

Miss Love brought in the hot pound cake on Granny's best china plate, holding it high over her head, and set it down in front of Grandpa with a grand flourish. She was smiling big. "I hope it's just the very best you ever ate, Mr. B.," she said, as if she'd forgot me and wanted him to have the whole dang cake. "It's an old receipt, sir, but I added a little of this and that. I do hope you like it. The man who owns Cold Sassy's first Pierce deserves to eat Cold Sassy's best cake. Don't you think so, Will?"

Friendship Cake

Share this with a friend–it's a tried and true favorite!

- 1 cup butter or margarine, melted
- 1¾ cups sugar
- 3 cups all-purpose flour
- 1 teaspoon baking soda
- 1 teaspoon ground cinnamon
- ½ teaspoon salt
- ¼ teaspoon ground cloves
- ¼ teaspoon ground nutmeg
- 2 eggs
- 2 cups drained Brandied Fruit Starter
- 1 cup chopped pecans
- ¼ cup brandied fruit juice
- Powdered sugar (optional)

Preheat oven to 350°. In large bowl, combine butter and sugar; beat well. In medium bowl, combine next 6 ingredients; add to butter mixture, beating well. Add eggs; beat well. Coarsely chop Brandied Fruit Starter; stir into batter. Add pecans and juice; mix. Pour batter into greased and floured 10-inch bundt pan. Bake for 1 hour or until cake tests done. Cool in pan 10 minutes; remove from pan and cool completely. Sprinkle with powdered sugar if desired. Yields 20 slices.

Brandied Fruit Starter

- 1 15.25-ounce can pineapple chunks, drained
- 1 16-ounce can sliced peaches, drained
- 1 17-ounce can apricot halves, drained
- 1 10-ounce jar maraschino cherries, drained
- 1 ¼ cups sugar
- 1 ¼ cups brandy

In a clean non-metal bowl, combine all ingredients; stir gently. Cover and let stand at room temperature 3 weeks, stirring fruit twice a week. To replenish starter, add 1 cup sugar and one of the first 4 ingredients every 1 to 3 weeks, alternating fruit each time; stir gently. Cover and let stand at room temperature 3 days before using. Yields 6 cups.

Serve fruit over ice cream or pound cake, reserving at least 1 cup starter at all times.

Agriculture Test Kitchen

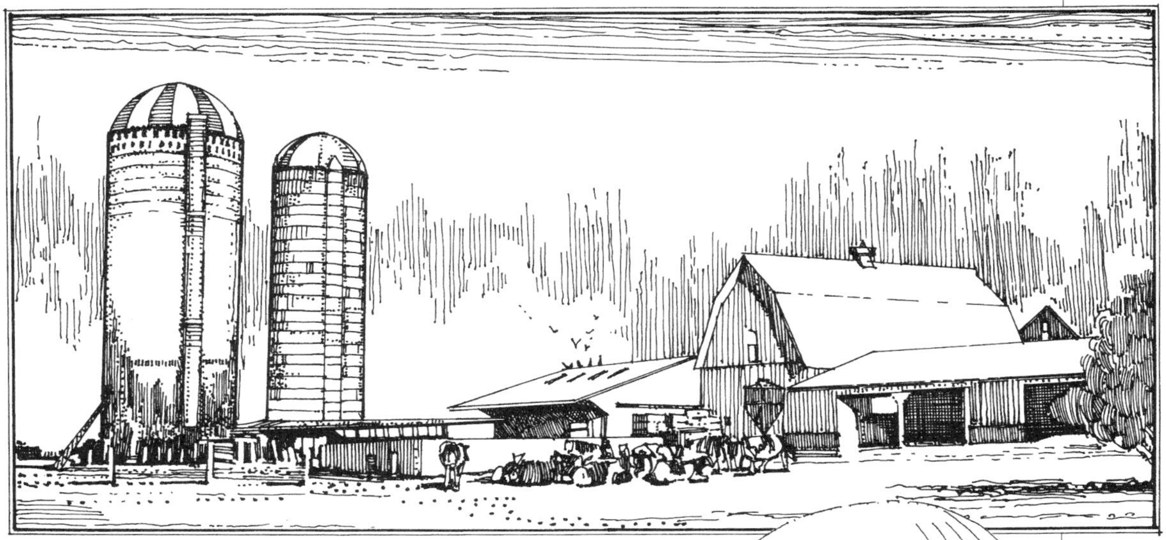

Silos

Tall cylinders that rise high above the farm, silos are as much a part of the rural landscape as the red barn. Silos store silage, the chopped up wheat, oats or hay that farmers feed their livestock over the winter months. Before silos were invented, cows gave less milk during the winter because they had no green grass to eat. Silos enable farmers to store a winter's supply of feed without it becoming spoiled.

Silos convert the grain or fodder through anaerobic acid fermentation into succulent feed, similar to sauerkraut, a soft and sweet dish which begins as hard cabbage. Usually made of concrete, ringed with steel reinforcements and capped with a metal dome, silos often are kept sealed airtight to allow microbial bacteria that don't use oxygen to begin the process of fermenting.

At the bottom of the silo, a compressed air blower sends the grain or fodder through a chute or pipe attached to the exterior up to the top, where it goes into the silo through a sealable door. Inside the silo, a machine that usually rests on top of the silage evenly scatters the silage and unloads it when needed. A winch on the outside pulls a cable that raises or lowers the unloader/distributor as needed inside the silo.

Natural combustion is a hazard when processing silage. Static electricity can ignite the gas from excessive fermentation. Sometimes silos catch on fire and occasionally they blow up.

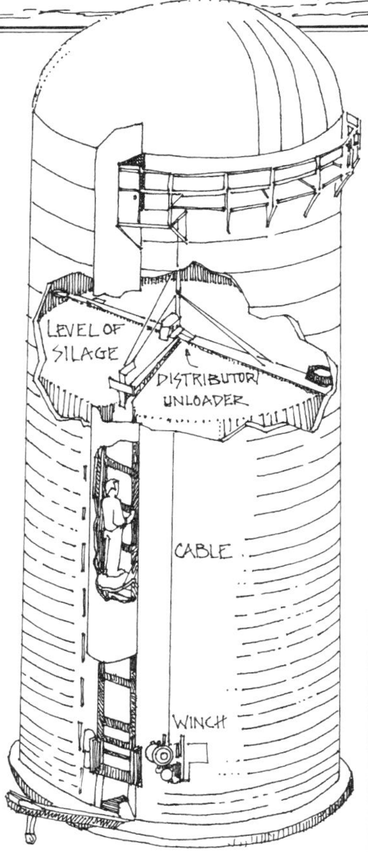

ATLANTA FARMER'S MARKET

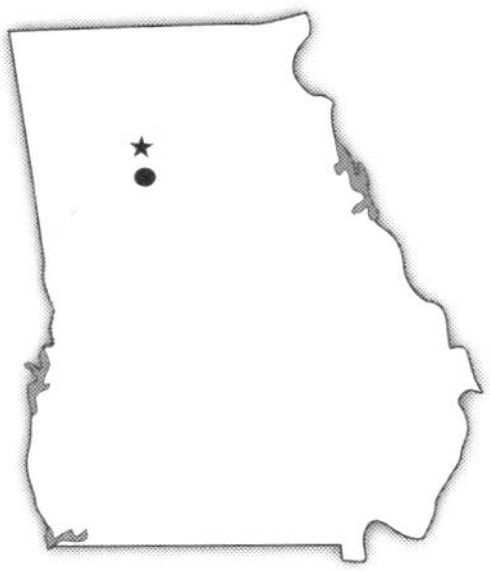

ATLANTA FARMER'S MARKET

Georgia produce comes to market from May through December at the Atlanta Farmer's Market, the largest farmer's market in the state.

Days/Hrs.: Daily, 24 hours a day. Market Grocery: Mon.-Sat., 8am-5pm. Hamper House: daily, 6am-5pm. Thomas' Restaurant: daily, 6am-9pm.

Fees: None for shopping. Exhibition Hall shows usually charge admission.

Directions: About 5 miles south of Atlanta on I-75, just past the airport. Take Forest Park Exit 78. Follow the signs. The Farmer's Market is right off the highway to the east.

More Information: Atlanta Farmer's Market, 16 Forest Parkway, Forest Park, GA 30297; 404/366-6910. Thomas' Restaurant, 404/361-1367.

AT 146 ACRES, THE ATLANTA FARMER'S MARKET IS THE WORLD'S largest produce market and one of the busiest. If grown in Georgia or much of the Southeast, vegetables usually go through this market, the largest produce destination and distribution center in the region. Market customers range from grocery chains to local housewives who come because of the low produce prices and for freshness and taste that is hard to beat.

Before dawn, supermarket transfer trucks from all over the nation dock at the long enclosed wholesale buildings to the right of the main market entrance. Railroad tracks snake around the area but are virtually unused now; trucks can bring a load of California produce in three days, five fewer than by rail. The long concrete sheds house companies like Seven Stars Produce, Lucas Tomatoes and Brito Produce. Inside building K is the Market Grocery, a privately owned wholesale store than sells almost anything a regular market does, minus alcohol and fresh produce.

By early morning sellers in the open-air sheds to the left of the main market entrance open up for business in the retail section of the market. Restaurant managers and roadside stand vendors look over fresh tomatoes and greens as produce merchants sing out "fresh snap peas" and "pecans cracked here." Many vendors shell beans, peas and nuts to order. Some of their produce comes from the wholesalers, which could mean peaches from South Carolina or grapes from Mexico. Yet a large portion comes from Georgia farms. The market reserves six of the twenty-eight open air sheds for in-state farmers.

From early morning until late evening, individual customers stream into the market. Using station wagons as shopping carts in what seems a giant drive-in supermarket, the regulars, many of them housewives, cruise up and down the aisle between the outdoor sheds. They drive slowly, car windows open, looking for the best produce and bargains. Some come at the end of the day to make deals as farmers close up shop for the night. Samples of the latest peaches or apples are handed out cheerfully. One seller talks to customers about folk terms for grapes, and asks them to taste the difference between muscadines and scuppernongs.

With all of its facilities, the market resembles a small city. The Hamper House, a gift shop, is filled with seasonal souvenirs, wicker oddities and picnic baskets. It has been selling crates, bags and baskets of all kinds to farmers and customers since the market opened here in 1958. A cannery still stands at the market, but it has been closed for several years. The increased use of freezing and commercially canned goods has caused most of the public canneries around the state to close their doors over the past two decades. The Georgia Department of Agriculture's Weights and Measures office is located here. The division checks weights used by supermarkets, restaurants and doctor's offices. There is also a thirty-five thousand-square-foot exhibition hall that hosts shows on birds, boats, guns and knives; a garden nursery; and Thomas' Restaurant, where farmers, businessmen, truckers and families eat traditional southern main courses and vegetables, straight from market wholesalers.

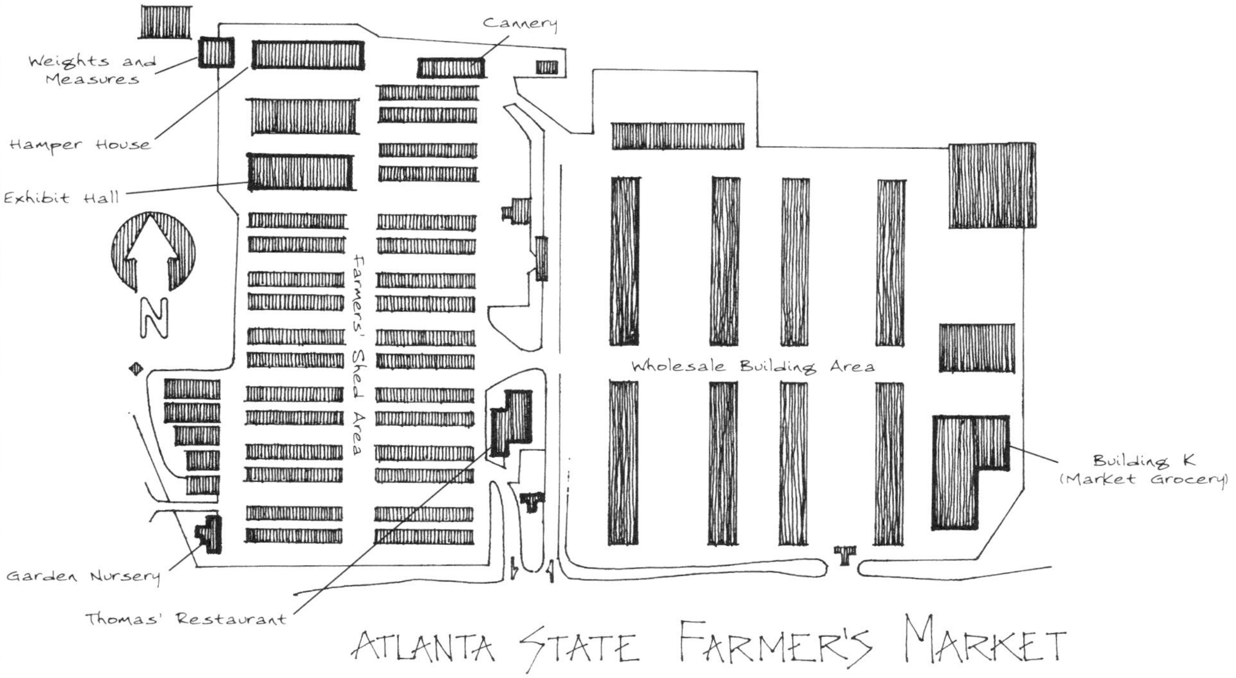

Buford Highway

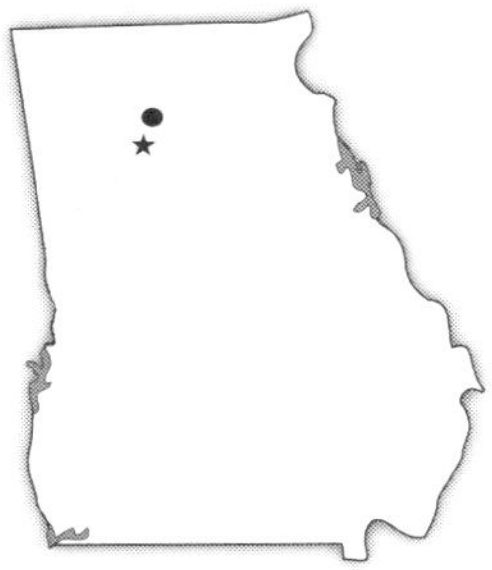

Buford Highway

From Lenox Road to the Gwinnett County line, Buford Highway in Atlanta is a seven-mile long highway that reflects the changing culture of Georgia.

Days/Hrs.: The best time to tour Buford Highway is the middle of the day during the week and the weekends. Avoid rush hour traffic in the morning and evening hours.

Directions: From I-85 north in Atlanta, take Clairmont Road, Exit 32, north to Buford Highway and continue north for 5 miles.

More Information: Asian-American Chamber of Commerce, 5455 Buford Highway, Suite B127, Atlanta, GA 30340; 770/452-0366.

A drive along Buford Highway north of Atlanta is testimony to an ethnicity that is new to Georgia culture. Thousands of immigrants have come to this area within the past two decades: Taiwanese, Koreans, Mainland Chinese, Vietnamese, Japanese, Malaysians, Filipinos, Indians and Hispanics. The Koreans alone have grown from a community of about three hundred in 1970 to around twenty thousand today. A five-mile stretch of Buford Highway around Doraville and Chamblee has become, essentially, a Chinatown or Koreatown, suburban style. These new Georgians have steadfastly kept many of their ethnic traditions, in particular their cuisine. A growing number of restaurants, food shops and large grocery stores have opened along Buford Highway, offering authentic foods from their home countries. Likewise, these same countries are a growing market for Georgia agricultural exports.

Inside the Oriental Mall, an Asian shopping complex, the largest business is the Hong Kong Market (1). In many ways it seems like a typical American grocery store with aisles full of boxed snacks, a meat department and a produce section. But here can be found roasted Malaysian green peas coated with fried flour and durains, a large fruit from Thailand with thick spikes like a giant kiwi crossed with a porcupine. In full view behind the meat counter, one dozen pigs hang from meat hooks as several Hispanics cut into them. A whole hog hangs in a small take-out food stand, completely glazed with a thick layer of salt. Adjacent to the pigs are six dark, bubbling pots, filled with pork tongues and intestines. Cooked whole ducks hang in a row. Seasoned bird feet lie in clear plastic bags in an open freezer. The fish counter displays octopus and squid.

Sitting among the Oriental law offices, jewelers, furniture and book stores at the Oriental Center shopping center is Harmony Vegetarian (2), which serves traditional Chinese beef, chicken and pork-flavored dishes, all made with soy tofu.

The International Farmer's Market (3) has products from every region of the world. Basmati rice, packed in ten-pound burlap bags, grew in the foothills of the Himalayas. Dates dried in the sun in Israel. Wheat-free breads baked in ovens in Ontario. Some of the products, like tupelo honey and quail eggs, come from Georgia farms. Hispanic foods include dried chili peppers with names like chile negro and chili ancho entero, cactus leaves, tomatillios and chayote. One item should look familiar to the Southerner: the chicharrones, or barbecue pork rinds. Bread takes the shape of circles, rolls and pretzels. And then there is Mexican sweet bread conchas, small, heavily textured loaves colored brown, white, pink and yellow.

The Ranch Market (4) in the Asian Square shopping complex serves primarily Chinese and Korean customers. Their inventory includes five-feet high bamboo sticks in a box and eel fish in an aquarium. A few doors to the left of the Ranch Market is a small herb shop that sells several hundred types of boxed herbs, mushrooms and roots. A traditional Chinese pharmacist takes herbs from any of two dozen drawers in a large wooden wall cabinet, mixes them in a mortar and pestle on a wooden counter and hands them out as medicines to customers. The Buford Highway Farmer's Market (5) is a big Asian market which leans heavily toward Korean products.

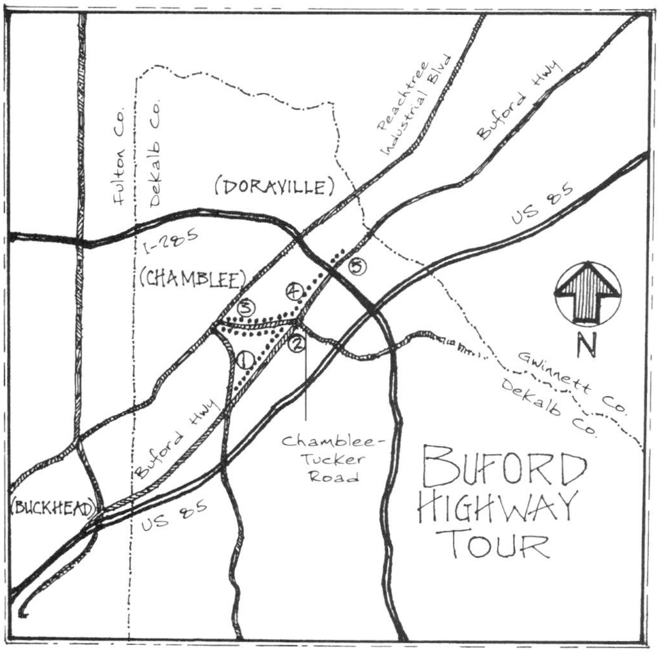

THE CHANGING FARM LANDSCAPE
From the lead front page story in the February 13, 1998, edition of the *Americus Times-Recorder* ...

A Leslie grower and landowner in late January completed what may be the single largest land deal in the history of Sumter County. According to deed records filed January 26 in the Sumter Superior Court Clerk's office, Neon Earl Bass Jr. sold seven tracts totaling 6,603.76 acres of land in the southeastern portion of the county north of Cobb to a Boston-based agriculture corporation for a figure estimated at just over $9 million. Complete financial terms of the deal between Bass and Goose Pond Ag. Inc. were not disclosed, but public records show a transfer tax of $9,050 was paid. The formula for the tax is $1 for every $1,000 exchanged in the sale of land. All property involved in the sale is agricultural, including some wooded areas.

Sumter County, the county where the sale took place, is Jimmy Carter's home county. Earl Bass, seller of the 6,630 acres, at one time cultivated thirty-five thousand acres of peanuts, making him the largest grower of peanuts in the country.

Baskets of the Hamper House

Before cardboard and styrofoam became popular, farmers shipped all their produce in wooden hampers, baskets and crates. Pegged with nails, bound with wire or simply glued, the containers are round or rectangular in shape and sized to hold a measured or weighed amount of produce.

Matthews Hamper House in the Atlanta Farmer's Market has been selling hampers, baskets, crates and bags to farmers and wholesale dealers for transporting produce since 1958. But the product is getting harder and harder to find. Only two places in the United States are still making the hampers that the Hamper House sells. Most are going out of business as farmers turn from wooden hampers to cardboard; cardboard costs half what wood costs.

Sellers used to bring their wooden crates to the Farmer's Market for re-use the next season. At one time two sheds would be filled with the recycled crates during the winter. Now, for sanitary reasons, the USDA encourages throwing away the crates instead of recycling. Once, grapes were shipped in small crates made in Mexico. Now grapes come in styrofoam cartons.

It's all another sign of the changing times in farming.

Today, more and more city folks buy Hamper House baskets to use for laundry baskets, yard work, flower arrangements, purses, book cases, storage and even lamp shapes. Everybody needs a few baskets around the house.

Hampers:
Bushel hamper $2
Bushel basket $3
Half-bushel basket $2.75
Peck basket $2.20
Bushel flat $3
Half-bushel flat $2.75

Round baskets with handles:
Half-bushel $2.75
Peck $2.20
Gallon $2.10

Market baskets made in Georgia:
Half-bushel market basket $2 each or $16.50 a dozen
4-quart market basket $1.50 each or $12 a dozen
2-quart market basket $1.25
1-quart market basket $1.25
Peck sized market basket $1.35

Tills (also called cups):
2-quart size $ .60
1-quart size $ .50

Napa crates (wooden crates made with nails):
1 1/2 bushel crate $9
Bushel crate $8.90
Half bushel crate $7.50

Wire-bound produce crates:
Bushel crate $ .80
Half-bushel crate $ .65

Mesh bags:
Green 50-lb cabbage bag $ .55
Purple 24-lb onion bag $.15 used
Red 15-lb onion bag $ .15 used
Red 10-lb onion bag $ .35

Burlap Sacks (jute, croker, gunny sack):
100-lb potato bag $ .50 each or $35 for 100

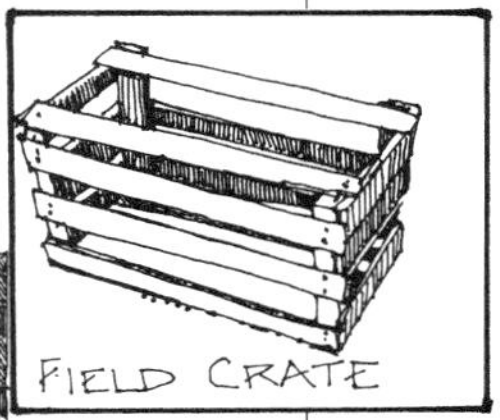

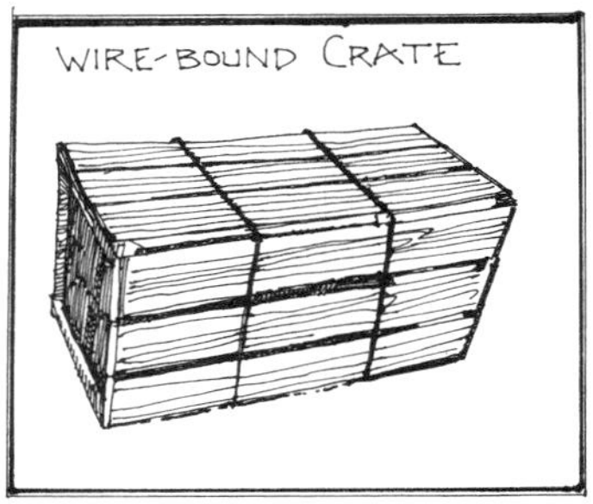

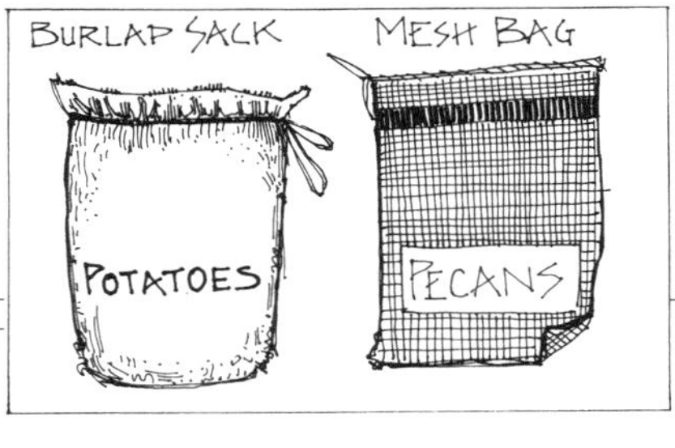

RESOURCES

GOVERNMENT AGENCIES AND ORGANIZATIONS

GEORGIA DEPARTMENT OF AGRICULTURE, Capitol Square, Atlanta, GA 30334; 404/656-3608.

GEORGIA AGRICULTURE COMMODITY COMMISSIONS (Apples, Canola, Corn, Cotton, Eggs, Milk, Peaches, Peanuts, Pecans, Soybeans, Sweet Potatoes and Tobacco Commissions), 328 Agriculture Building, Atlanta, GA 30334; 404/656-3678.

COTTON COMMISSION, P.O. Box 1464, 1019 Ball Street, Perry, GA 31069; 912/988-4235.

EGG COMMISSION, Atlanta's Farmer's Market, 16 Forest Parkway, Forest Park, GA 30050; 404/363-7661.

GEORGIA MILK PRODUCERS, Agriculture Building, Room 128, Capitol Square, Atlanta, GA 30334; 404/656-5647.

GEORGIA PEANUT COMMISSION, P.O. Box 967, Tifton, GA 31793; 912/386-3470 or 800/346-4993.

FARMERS AND CONSUMERS MARKET BULLETIN, Georgia Department of Agriculture, 19 Martin Luther King Jr. Drive, Atlanta, GA 30334-4250; 404/656-3722. Subscriptions are free for Georgia residents; out-of-state residents are charged $10 annually. The *Market Bulletin* is now available on the World Wide Web through the Georgia Department of Agriculture's Home Page at the following site: http://www.agr.state.ga.us. Just click on "What's New," look under Agency Directory and select Current Issue under the *Market Bulletin* heading.

COOPERATIVE EXTENSION SERVICE, University of Georgia, College of Agriculture, Athens, GA 30602; 706/542-3824.

COUNTY EXTENSION OFFICES. For the location and phone number of individual county extension offices, contact the Cooperative Extension Service (above).

4-H, Cooperative Extension Service, Hoke Smith Annex, Athens, GA 30602; 706/542-8804.

FUTURE FARMERS OF AMERICA, Georgia Department of Education, Twin Towers East, Room 1776, Atlanta, GA 30334; 404/656-4077.

GEORGIA FARM BUREAU FEDERATION, P.O. Box 7068, Macon, GA 31298; 912/474-8411 or 800/342-1196.

GEORGIA ORGANIC GROWERS ASSOCIATION, 770/253-0347 or 770/787-7300.

VIDALIA ONION COMMITTEE, P.O. Box 1609, Vidalia, GA 30474; 912/537-1918.

TRACTOR CLUBS

GEORGIA ANTIQUE ENGINE CLUB, C/O Zane Bristol, Bristol Boiler and Welding, 3267 Bachelor Street, Atlanta, GA 30344.

WEST GEORGIA TWO-CYLINDER CLUB, P.O. Box 982, Carrollton, GA 30117.

NORTH GEORGIA TWO-CYLINDER CLUB, c/o Mickey Miller, John Deere Co., 2001 Deere Drive, Conyers, GA 30013.

BIBLIOGRAPHY

The following books were used in the research for this book. We recommend them for anyone wanting more information.

COOKBOOKS

A Fresh Look at Figs: Traditions, Myths and Mouth-Watering Recipes by Pamela Allardice. Hill of Content Publishing Co., Melbourne, Australia. 1993.

Betty Talmadge's Lovejoy Plantation Cookbook by Betty Talmadge. Peachtree Publishers, Ltd., Atlanta, GA. 1983.
In her second cookbook, Betty Talmadge, a former first lady of Georgia and one of its most beloved personalities, has written an entertaining collection of recipes and personal stories about life on her plantation home.

Bread from Heaven or A Collection of African Americans' Home Cookin' and "Somepin' t' Eat" Recipes from down in Georgia by Sharon Hunt. 1992.

Everyday Meals from a Well-Stocked Pantry by Nathalie Dupree. Clarkson N. Potter, Inc., New York, NY. 1995.
Nathalie tells cooks how to stock their pantries in order to serve good meals every night of the week without continually going to the grocery store or resorting to packaged or convenience foods. Nathalie is featured on page 155.

Famous Recipes from Mrs. Wilkes' Boarding House in Historic Savannah by Mrs. L. H. Wilkes. Starr Toof, Memphis, TN. 1976.
Mrs. Wilkes has put together this collection of Southern recipes served at her historic inn in Savannah, one of which is featured on page 165.

Georgia Entertains: A Rich Heritage of Fine Food and Gracious Hospitality by Margaret Wayt DeBolt, Emma Rylander Law and Carter Olive. Rutledge Hill Press, Nashville, TN. 1983.
This cookbook, containing hundreds of traditional and modern Georgia recipes, is written by Margaret DeBolt, an award-winning cookbook reviewer and staff writer for the *Savannah News Press*.

Grace Hartley's Southern Cooking by Grace Hartley. Galahad Books, New York, NY. 1980 edition. Published by permission of Doubleday & Company, Inc., publishers of the first edition in 1976.
Grace Hartley, *Atlanta Journal* food editor for more than forty years, has put together a cookbook of recipes collected during those years. Many were sent from readers and friends, others were handed down from her mother and grandmother. One of Ms. Hartley's recipes is featured on page 276.

Guess Who's Coming to Dinner: Entertaining at the Governor's Mansion: Menus, Recipes and Anecdotes by Mary Beth Busbee and Jan Busbee Curtis. Peachtree Publishers, Ltd., Atlanta, GA. 1986.
These personal recipes and stories come from Mrs. Busbee's years as Georgia's first lady. One of her recipes is featured on page 62.

How to Cook a Pig and Other Back-To-The-Farm Recipes: An Autobiographical Cookbook by Betty Talmadge. Peachtree Publishers, Ltd., Atlanta, GA. 1978.
Good information written in her own humorous style, this is Ms. Talmadge's first cookbook about traditional Southern cooking and living.

Marion Brown's Southern Cookbook by Marion Brown. University of North Carolina Press, Chapel Hill, NC. 1968.
Originally published in 1951, this is a comprehensive histo-

ry of Southern cooking as well as a fine collection of traditional Southern recipes.

Nathalie Dupree Cooks for Family and Friends by Nathalie Dupree. William Morrow and Company, Inc., New York, NY. 1991.
Nathalie believes that "everyday meals are important meals" but it should not be "an onerous chore to prepare them." This cookbook, a companion to her PBS television series, features three hundred recipes that back her belief.

Nathalie Dupree's Matters of Taste by Nathalie Dupree. Alfred A. Knopf, Inc., Division of Random House, New York, NY. 1990.
The twenty-seven menus in this cookbook, from Nathalie's PBS television series *A Matter of Taste*, are accompanied with stories from her *Atlanta Journal-Constitution* newspaper column.

New Southern Cooking by Nathalie Dupree. Alfred A. Knopf, Inc., Division of Random House, New York, NY. 1986.
This cookbook contains over 350 recipes from Nathalie's twenty-six show public television series, *New Southern Cooking with Nathalie Dupree.*

Sara's Recipes: Through the Years by Sara Spano. Columbus Ledger-Enquirer, Columbus, GA. 1985.
This cookbook contains recipes published by Ms. Spano during her tenure as food editor of the *Columbus Ledger-Enquirer.*

Savannah Seasons: Food and Stories from Elizabeth on 37th by Elizabeth Terry with Alexis Terry. Doubleday, a division of Bantam Doubleday Dell Publishing Group, Inc., New York, NY. 1996.
Not only is this a collection of outstanding recipes and cooking tips by an award-winning chef, but it is also a wonderful collection of stories about food, life in Savannah and the experience of being a "family restaurant." Elizabeth and her recipes are featured on page 53.

Savannah Style, A Cookbook by the Junior League of Savannah. Kingsport Press. Junior League of Savannah, Inc., Savannah, GA. 1980.
This cookbook, loaded with traditional and updated Southern recipes with a Savannah flair, has a good seafood section reflecting the city's coastal location. A recipe from *Savannah Style* can be found on page 50.

Seasoned Skillets and Silver Spoons: A Culinary History of Columbus, Georgia by Mary Hart Brumby. The Columbus Museum Guild, Columbus, GA. 1993.
Mary Hart Brumby set out to record the family recipes and stories given to her by her grandmother, but the project soon grew to include other Columbus family friends as well. The result is a culinary history of the city. One of Mrs. Brumby's recipes is featured on page 26.

So Easy to Preserve by Susan Reynolds and Paulette Williams, revised by Judy Harrison. The University of Georgia Cooperative Extension Service, Athens, GA. Third Edition 1993.
This thoroughly researched guide to preserving covers canning, pickling, making jellied fruit products, freezing and drying. For more about this book, see sidebar on page 185.

Soul Food: Classic Cuisine from the Deep South by Sheila Ferguson. Grove Press, New York, NY. 1989.

Soul on Rice: African Influences on American Cooking by Patricia B. Mitchell. Historic Sims-Mitchell House, Chatham, VA. 1993.
This booklet of essays and recipes, written and collected by food historian Patricia Mitchell, spotlights "largely unrecognized legacies of Africa in American cooking." A recipe can be found on page 91.

Southern Cooking by Mrs. S. R. Dull. First edition 1928. Latest edition published by Grosset and Dunlap, 1968.
First printed in 1928, this classic Southern cookbook with more than thirteen hundred recipes has influenced many of Georgia's finest chiefs. Henrietta Stanley Dull, who was food editor of the *Atlanta Journal* magazine section for twenty years, gained a reputation all over the South for her skills in culinary art. One of her classic recipes is featured on page 144.

Southern Cooking from Mary Mac's Tea Room by Margaret Lupo. Cherokee Publishers. 1994.
Mary Lupo, one of the most experienced and well-known traditional Southern cooks in Georgia, wrote this cookbook about her midtown Atlanta tea room, known as Mary Mac's, a culinary cousin of the boarding house restaurants often started by war widows in the early twentieth century.

Southern Food: At Home, on the Road, in History by John Egerton. Alfred A. Knopf, Inc., Division of Random House, New York, NY. 1987.
More than a cookbook, this is the story of Southern food told through Egerton as well as other Southern writers, cooks and historical figures. Egerton visited more than two hundred restaurants across the south for his "Eating Out" section and selected the recipes for more than one hundred fifty time-honored foods for "Eating In."

The Blue Willow Inn Cookbook by Louis and Billie Van Dyke. St. Simons Press, Inc., Atlanta, GA. 1996.
The Van Dykes have put together this collection of recipes from their Blue Willow Inn in Social Circle, Georgia. A recipe from the restaurant, voted the best small town restaurant by readers of *Southern Living*, is featured on page 108.

The Callaway Cookbook by the Callaways, their Descendants and Friends. Calico Kitchen Press, Hartwell, GA. 1991.
Published to mark the two hundredth anniversary of the Callaway family's arrival in Wilkes County, this is a collection of heirloom recipes from Callaway family members and friends. A tour of the Callaway Plantation is on page 64.

The Dillard House Cookbook and Mountain Guide compiled and edited by Fred Brown. Longstreet Press, Inc., Marietta, GA. 1996.
This collection of family stories and recipes from the kitchen of the Dillard House, an all-you-can-eat Southern tradition in the North Georgia mountains for over eighty years, is interspersed with scenic drives, hikes and explorations of this beautiful mountain region. A recipe of Dillard House cook Lazell Vinson can be found on page 78.

The Foxfire Book of Appalachian Cookery edited by Linda Garland Page and Eliot Wigginton. The University of North Carolina Press, Chapel Hill, NC. 1992.
Prepared by Foxfire students, this is a book of more than five hundred Appalachian Mountain recipes and personal recollections of the people who have prepared and eaten these foods for generations. A tour of the Foxfire Center

can be found on page 176.
The Great American Tomato Book by Robert Hendrickson. Stein and Day Publishers, Briarcliff Manor, NY. Originally published by Doubleday & Co., Inc. 1977.
The Kudzu Cookbook by Carole Marsh. Gallopade Publishing Group's Podunk Publishing, Atlanta, GA. 1997.
Recipes and humorous anecdotes about the "miracle vine."
The Story of Corn by Betty Fussell. Alfred A. Knopf, Inc., Division of Random House, New York, NY. 1992.
The Taste of Country Cooking by Edna Lewis. Alfred A. Knopf, Inc., Division of Random House, New York, NY. 1976.
Ms. Lewis's love of food and cooking comes through clearly in this book of recipes and recollections. Raised in a community of black farm families, Ms. Lewis shares a lifetime's worth of information about food, the way it is prepared and eaten and the land where it grows.
Tullie's Receipts: Nineteenth-Century Plantation Plain Style Southern Cooking and Living compiled and edited by the Kitchen of the Tullie Smith House Restoration. Atlanta Historical Society, Inc., Atlanta, GA. Second Edition 1996.
Thoroughly researched and historically accurate, this book was created to preserve nineteenth-century recipes (known as receipts at that time) and cooking methods on the open-hearth and open-fire. Text, from individual family recipes, newspapers, scrapbooks, diaries and nineteenth-century cookbooks no longer in print, was transcribed exactly as it was written. A tour of the Tullie Smith Farm at the Atlanta History Center can be found on page 66.

FICTION

Cold Sassy Tree by Olive Ann Burns. Dell Publishing Co., Inc., New York, NY. 1984.
Crackers by Roy Blount Jr. Ballantine Books, Division of Random House, Inc., New York, NY. 1980.
Fried Green Tomatoes at the Whistle Stop Cafe by Fannie Flagg. Random House, New York, NY. 1988.
Gettin' It On, a Down-Home Treasury by Lewis Grizzard. Peachtree Publishers, Ltd, Atlanta, GA. 1989.
Gone with the Wind by Margaret Mitchell. Scribner, Unit of Simon & Schuster, New York, NY. 1936.
Leaving Cold Sassy by Olive Ann Burns. Ticknor & Fields, Houghton Mifflin Company, New York, NY. 1992.
Raney by Clyde Edgerton. Ballantine Books, Division of Random House, Inc., New York, NY. 1986.
Run with the Horsemen by Ferrol Sams. Peachtree Publishers Limited, Atlanta, GA. 1982.
The Color Purple by Alice Walker. Harcourt Brace Jovanovich, Orlando, FL. 1982.

HISTORICAL

A History of Georgia Agriculture 1732-1860 by James C. Bonner. University of Georgia Press, Athens, GA. 1964.
History of the state's agriculture from Oglethorpe up to the Civil War. This was particularly useful in researching the colonial period—how land was granted, what crops were grown and what tools and methods were used by the colonists.
David O. Selznick's Gone with the Wind by Ronald Haver. Bonanza Books. 1986.
Good text, drawings and photographs depicting how *Gone with the Wind* was translated from Margaret Mitchell's book to the big screen.
Decision in the West: The Atlanta Campaign of 1864 by Albert Castel. University Press of Kansas, Lawrence, KS. 1992.
The definitive historical account of this Civil War campaign.
Early Days on the Georgia Tidewater: The Story of McIntosh County and Sapelo by Buddy Sullivan. McIntosh County Board of Commissioners. 1990.
A detailed history of this area that we refer to again and again.
Principles and Privilege: Two Women's Lives on a Georgia Plantation by Frances A. Kemble and Frances A. Butler Leigh. Ann Arbor Paperbacks, The University of Michigan Press. 1995.
This edition contains Fanny Kemble's *Journal of a Residence on a Georgian Plantation*, depicting the horrific conditions of slaves on Butler Island, her husband's rice plantation, and the memoirs of her estranged daughter, Frances, who returned to Butler Plantation during Reconstruction.
Pickin' on Peachtree, A History of Country Music in Atlanta, Georgia by Wayne W. Daniel. University of Illinois Press. 1990.
The History of Fayette County 1821–1971 edited by Carolyn Cary. The Fayette County Historical Society, Inc. 1977.

BIOGRAPHICAL

A Harry Crews Reader by Harry Crews. Poseidon Press, Simon & Schuster Building, Rockefeller Center, New York, NY. 1993.
A Good Man...A Great Dream: D. W. Brooks of Gold Kist by Harold H. Martin. Gold Kist Inc., Atlanta, GA. 1982.
Armchair Tour of Jimmy Carter Country by Peggy Sheppard. Sheppard Publications, Andersonville, GA. 1977.
D. W. Brooks: Gold Kist and Seven U.S. Presidents, An Autobiography by D. W. Brooks. D. W. Brooks Family, Atlanta, GA. 1993.
Every Man a King by Huey P. Long, 1933.
In My Father's Garden by Lee May. Longstreet Press, Marietta, GA. 1995.
Jimmy Carter: American Moralist by Kenneth E. Morris. University of Georgia Press, Athens, GA. 1996.
Road to Tara: The Life of Margaret Mitchell by Anne Edwards. Ticknor and Fields, New Haven, CT. 1983.
Southern Daughter by Darden Asbury Pyron. Oxford University Press, Inc., New York, NY. 1991.
The Irish Roots of Margaret Mitchell's Gone with the Wind by David O'Connell. Claves and Petry, Ltd., Decatur, GA. 1996.
The Travels of William Bartram: Naturalist's Edition by William Bartram. The Beehive Press, Savannah GA. 1973.

GENERAL REFERENCE

A Field Guide to American Houses by Virginia and Lee McAlester. Alfred A. Knopf, Inc., Division of Random House, New York, NY. 1991.
A Treasury of Southern Folklore edited by B. A. Botkin. Bonanza Books, distributed by Crown Publishers, Inc., Division of Random House, New York, NY. 1980.
Architecture of Middle Georgia, The Oconee Area by John Linley. University of Georgia Press, Athens, GA. 1972.
Architecture of the Old South: Georgia by Mills Lane. A Beehive Press Book, Abbeville Press, New York, NY. 1986.

Contemporary Georgia edited by Lawrence R. Hepburn. Carl Vinson Institute of Government, The University of Georgia, Athens, GA. 1987.

Encyclopedia of Southern Culture edited by Charles Reagan Wilson and William Ferris. The University of North Carolina Press, Chapel Hill, NC. 1989.

Food and Healing by Annemarie Colbin. Ballantine Books, a division of Random House, Inc., NY. 1996.

Gardening in the South with Don Hastings, Volumes 1, 2 and 3 by Don Hastings. Taylor Publishing Company, Dallas, TX. 1988.

Georgia Agricultural Facts: 1997 Edition prepared by the Georgia Agricultural Statistics Service. Georgia Department of Agriculture, Atlanta, GA.

Georgia Folklife: A Pictorial Essay edited by Dr. Annie Archbold and Janice Morrill. The Georgia Folklife Program, State of Georgia. 1989.

Georgia Gardener's Guide by Erica Glasener and Walter Reeves. Cool Springs Press, Franklin, TN. 1996.

Growing Vegetables Organically prepared by Paul Colditz, Darbie Granberry and Charles Vavrina. The University of Georgia Cooperative Extension Service, Athens, GA. 1989.

Guide to Georgia Agriculture 1996 compiled by the Educational Support Services of The University of Georgia Cooperative Extension Service, Athens, GA.

Landmark Homes of Georgia 1733-1983 by Van Jones Martin and William Robert Mitchell, Jr. Golden Coast Publishing Company, Savannah, GA. 1982.

Miss Manners' Guide to Excruciatingly Correct Behavior by Judith Martin. Warner Books by arrangement with Atheneum Publishers. Warner Books, Inc., New York, NY. Atheneum Publishers, New York, NY. 1982.

Month-By-Month Gardening in the South by Don Hastings and Chris Hastings. Longstreet Press, Inc., Marietta, GA. 1996.

Organic Gardening and Pest Control by David B. Adams and Johnny Dan Gay. The University of Georgia Cooperative Extension Service, Athens, GA. 1993.

Storytellers: Folktales and Legends from the South, edited by John A. Burrison. The University of Georgia Press, Athens, GA. 1991.

The Atlas of Georgia by Thomas W. Hodler and Howard A. Schretter. The Institute of Community and Area Development, The University of Georgia, Athens, GA. 1986.

The Foxfire Book edited by Eliot Wigginton and His Students. An Anchor Book published by Doubleday, a division of Bantam Doubleday Dell Publishing Group, Inc., New York, NY. 1972.

The Georgia Catalog, Historic American Buildings Survey by John Linley. The University of Georgia Press, Athens, GA. 1982.

The Hog Book by William Hedgepeth. Dolphin Books, Doubleday and Company, Inc., New York, NY. 1978.

The New Georgia Guide produced by the Georgia Humanities Council. The University of Georgia Press, Athens, GA. 1996.

White Columns in Georgia by Medora Field Perkerson. American Legacy Press, distributed by Crown Publishers, Inc., by arrangement with Holt, Rinehart and Winston, Inc. (original publisher). Crown Publishing Group, Division of Random House, New York, NY. 1982.

SONG LYRICS

"Boll Weevil Blues" by Huddie Ledbetter. Folkways Music Publishers, Inc., New York. 1936. Excerpted from *The Blues Songbook* compiled by Paul Oliver. Wise Publications. 1982.

"Diamond Joe" recorded by the Georgia Crackers. 1927. Excerpted from Backpocket Old Time Song Book: Words and Music to 40 Timeless Mountain Tunes by Wayne Erbsen. Wayne Erbsen Music Company, Asheville, NC. 1992.

MAPS

TOPOGRAPHICAL MAPS FOR ALL STATES

POWERS ELEVATION CO., INC., P.O. Box 440889, Aurora, CO 80044-0889; 303/321-2217 or 800/824-2550; fax 303/321-2218. All USGA topos: $6, plus postage and handling charge from $2 to $10 per order. American Express, MasterCard and VISA accepted. Allow 5 to 10 days.

THE U.S. GEOLOGICAL SURVEY, Map Sales, Box 25286, Denver, CO 80225; 303/236-7477. Call 800/USA-MAPS first for a free index with order form. $2.50 for 1:24,000; $4 for 1:100,000, plus 6 percent sales tax and postage. Allow 3 to 5 days.

TOPOGRAPHICAL MAPS FOR GEORGIA

ENPRO ENGINEERING REPROGRAPHICS, 1800 Peachtree Street, Suite 210, Atlanta, GA 30309; 404/355-8520. $3 for 1:24,000, $4.50 for 1:100,000, plus postage and $1.89 if maps are rolled rather than folded. Allow 5 to 8 days.

THE GEORGIA GEOLOGICAL SURVEY, Agriculture Building, Room 406A, 19 Martin Luther King Jr. Drive SW, Atlanta, GA 30334; 404/656-3214. $2.50 for 1:24,000; $4 for 1:100,000, plus 6 percent sales tax and postage. Allow 3 to 5 days.

COUNTY ROAD MAPS AND STATE HIGHWAY MAPS

GEORGIA DEPARTMENT OF TRANSPORTATION, MAP SALES DIVISION, 2 Capitol Square, Atlanta, GA 30334; 404/656-5336.

FAIRS AND FESTIVALS

Fairs and festivals are a popular part of Georgia's culture, and numerous events take place most weekends in every part of the state. The fairs and festivals selected for the resource section of this book, pertain particularly to the state's agricultural history. Listed by season, each is a celebration of planting or harvesting, rural southern farm culture and skills, or just reminiscent of an old-fashioned country fair.

WINTER

WINTER HOMECOMING, during February at the Agrirama, features historical food traditions from the turn-of-the-century, gospel singing in the country church and a special "Dinner on the Ground." Contributions of African American culture in the development of South Georgia are also highlighted. *Location:* The Agrirama. Just west of I-75 at exit 20 in Tifton. *More Information:* Georgia Agrirama, P.O. Box Q, Tifton, GA 31793; 912/386-3344.

SPRING

OLD SOUTH FARM DAYS, two days in mid-March, takes place at the Tea Grove Plantation Farm Museum. Demonstration of cotton ginning, turpentine distilling, sawmilling, syrup-making, blacksmithing and gristmilling, arts and crafts, antique cars, steam and gas engines, flea market and gospel and country music. *Location:* Walthourville, 40 miles south of Savannah off US 84. *More Information:* 912/368-7412.

DARIEN'S ANNUAL BLESSING OF THE FLEET, the fourth weekend in March, celebrates the area's shrimping industry with decorated shrimp boats floating down the Darien River for their blessing on Sunday. Street parade, music, fireworks, crafts and children's carnivals. *Location:* Darien. *More Information:* McIntosh County Chamber of Commerce Visitor Center, 105 Fort King Drive (at the foot of the US 17 bridge), Darien, GA 31305; 912/437-4192 or 912/437-6684.

THE HAWKINSVILLE HARNESS HORSE FESTIVAL AND SPRING PIG RIBBIN' COOKOFF, usually the last weekend in March or the first weekend in April, a twenty-five-year old festival. Harness horse races, BBQ cookoff, art and crafts, 5K road race, carnival, country concert and golf tournament. *Location:* Hawkinsville. *More Information:* Hawkinsville-Pulaski County Chamber of Commerce, 912/783-1717.

THE BAXLEY TREE FEST, usually the first weekend in April, is an annual celebration of trees and tree products. Logging and loader competitions, chain saw carving, a lumberjack show, forestry expo, arts and crafts, carnival, fireworks and street dance. *Location:* Baxley. *More Information:* Baxley-Appling County Board of Tourism, 912/367-7731.

SHEEP TO SHAWL DAY, usually the first or second Saturday in April, demonstrates sheep shearing, washing, carding, spinning and weaving the yarn all in one day. *Location:* Tullie Smith Farm at the Atlanta History Center. *More Information:* Atlanta History Center, 130 W. Paces Ferry Road, Atlanta, GA 30305; 404/814-4000.

THE GRITS FESTIVAL, the third weekend in April, is a new celebration honoring the Southern staple—grits. Arts and crafts, a grits dive, a grits recipe contest, a fishing rodeo for disabled persons and entertainment. *Location:* Warwick. *More Information:* www.gritsfest.com.

THE MOSSY CREEK BARNYARD FESTIVAL, one in mid-April and another in mid-October, is considered one of the top one hundred events in North America. Pioneer demonstrations, nationally acclaimed artists and craftsmen, mule and wagon rides, music and storytelling. *Location:* In the "deep piney woods near Perry and Warner Robins." *More Information:* 912/922-8265.

THE AGRIRAMA FOLK LIFE FESTIVAL, usually the third Saturday in April, demonstrates turn-of-the-century crafts and leisure pursuits, including sheep shearing, log rolling, textile arts and turpentine making in the still. Music at the Wiregrass Opry Stage. *Location:* The Agrirama. Just west of I-75 at exit 20 in Tifton. *More Information:* Georgia Agrirama, P.O. Box Q, Tifton, GA 31793; 912/386-3344.

THE CRAWFISH FESTIVAL, usually the last Saturday in April, is annually held despite the closing of the local crawfish farm. *Location:* Woodbine. *More Information:* 912/576-3211.

THE VIDALIA ONION FESTIVAL, usually held the fourth weekend of April or first weekend in May, celebrates the harvest of the area's famous sweet onion. Cooking school, street dance, rodeo, beauty pageant, arts and crafts, air show, road races and tour of homes. *Location:* Vidalia. *More Information:* Vidalia Tourism Council, 2805 E. 1st Street, US 280 E., Vidalia, GA 30474; 912/538-8687.

WESTVILLE'S MAY DAY FESTIVAL takes place every May 1st. Inspired by Sir Walter Scott's *Ivanhoe*, people in the 1820s South began reviving the European celebration which marks the end of the planting season. The highlight of the day is the May Pole Dance. Traditionally, young adults danced around the tower until they completely wove their ribbons in hand around the pole. The trick was to unweave the strands successfully. *Location:* Westville. From downtown Lumpkin, go southeast about 1 mile on MLK Drive. Entrance is on the left. *More Information:* Westville, MLK Drive, Lumpkin, GA 31815; 912/838-6310 or 888/733-1850.

SAVANNAH SEAFOOD FESTIVAL, usually the first weekend in May, is one of the many Savannah River Street Festivals—this one celebrating the bounty of the sea. *Location:* Savannah River Walk. *More Information:* Savannah Waterfront Association, 912/234-0293.

THE COTTON PICKIN' FAIR, usually the first weekend in May and the first weekend in October, takes place on a turn-of-the-century cotton plantation. About three hundred craftsmen, artists and antique specialists; demonstrations, country cooking and family entertainment. *Location:* About 50 miles south of Atlanta on GA 85/74. *More Information:* Cotton Pickin' Fairs, Inc., P.O. Box 1, Gay, GA 30218; 706/538-6814.

THE PRATER'S MILL COUNTRY FAIR, usually the second weekend in May and the second weekend in October, is an arts and crafts festival with the atmosphere of an old-fashioned country fair. Demonstrating craftsmen, working gristmill, Southern foods, mountain music, country store and canoeing. *Location:* On GA 2 near Dalton, 7 miles from I-75. *More Information:* Prater's Mill Foundation, P.O. Drawer H, Varnell, GA 30756; 706/275-6455.

THE BRUNSWICK HABORFEST, usually the second weekend in May, is a celebration of the area's arts, music, seafood and heritage. Arts and crafts, boat tours, marine displays, entertainment, the blessing of the fleet and boat parade. *Location:* Brunswick. *More Information:* 912/265-4032.

THE OCMULGEE WILD HOG FESTIVAL OF ABBEVILLE, usually the second Saturday in May, has a wide range of activities mostly having to do with pigs. Arts and crafts, Hog Dog Baying Contest, Pig Chase, live wild hogs, Civil War reenactments, food and live entertainment. *Location:* Abbeville. *More Information:* Dean Clements, 912/467-21316.

TASTE OF THE SOUTH AT STONE MOUNTAIN PARK, usually Memorial Day weekend, celebrates the taste of Southern food. From boiled crawfish to vinegar-based BBQ, each southern state showcases its finest in food, entertainment, folk crafts and travel destinations. *Location:* Stone Mountain Park. *More Information:* 770/498-5702.

SUMMER

THE GEORGIA PEACH FESTIVAL, annually in June, is the state's official peach celebration. Arts and crafts, dancing, food, 5K Road Race and Fun Run, fireworks, peach shed tours and the Peach Ball. *Location:* Byron and Fort Valley. *More Information:* Peach County Chamber of Commerce, P.O. Box 1238, Fort Valley, GA 31030; 912/825-3733.

THE TUNIS CAMPBELL FESTIVAL, usually the fourth weekend in June, celebrates African American culture with music and food. *Location:* Darien. *More Information:* McIntosh County Chamber of Commerce Visitor Center, 105 Fort King Drive (at the foot of the US 17 bridge), Darien, GA 31305; 912/437-4192 or 912/437-3900.

WATERMELON DAYS FESTIVAL, from the end of June to mid-July, is a 3-week celebration of this native Southern delicacy in Cordele, the Watermelon Capital of the World. Fireworks, parade, arts and crafts and lots of watermelons.

Location: Cordele. *More Information:* Cordele-Crisp Chamber of Commerce, 912/273-1668.

THE NEW BLUEBERRY FESTIVAL, the last weekend in June, celebrates the state's blueberry crop. Arts and crafts and car show. *Location:* Alma. *More Information:* 912/632-5859.

THE INDEPENDENCE DAY FOLKLIFE CELEBRATION, July 4 on Jarrell Plantation, includes wood stove cooking, spinning, weaving, blacksmithing and old time games. *Location:* Jarrell Plantation in Juliette. *More Information:* Jarrell Plantation State Historic Site, Route 2, P.O. Box 220, Juliette, GA 31046; 912/986-5172.

TOBACCO SUNDAY, usually the third Sunday in July, brings back to life the old ways of tobacco harvesting. The festival coincides with the local tobacco harvest, the largest in the state. *Location:* Heritage Farm at General Coffee State Park. From Douglas, go 6 miles east on GA 32. The entrance is on the left. *More Information:* General Coffee State Park, 46 John Coffee Road, Nicholls, GA 31554; 912/384-7082.

OAK GROVE COUNTRY FAIR, usually a weekend in mid-August, features craft demonstrations, kiddie attractions and old-fashioned BBQ. *Location:* 2 miles north of Pine Mountain on US 27. *More Information:* Oak Grove Country Fair, 706/663-4327.

THE GEORGIA MOUNTAIN FAIR, usually the second and third week of August, is an old-fashioned fair that includes mountain arts and products. Craft demonstrations, midway rides, antiques, classic car show, parade, agricultural displays, flower show and live country music performances. *Location:* Georgia Mountain Fairgrounds off US 76 in Hiawassee. *More Information:* 706/896-4191.

THE CHATEAU ELAN HARVEST AND MUSIC CELEBRATION, usually the last weekend in August, is a celebration of the Georgia grape harvest. Hot-air balloons, music and food, wine games, seminars and tastings. *Location:* Chateau Elan in Braselton. *More Information:* 770/932-0900 or 800/233-WINE.

ANNUAL AG SHOWCASE, usually the fourth week of August, has demonstrations of latest farm technologies, a petting zoo, new ornamental flowering plants and samples of beef, goat or other livestock raised with innovative methods. *Location:* Coastal Plain Experiment Station. I-75 exit 21 west at Tifton. *More Information:* CPES, P.O. Box 748, Tifton, GA 31793; 912/386-3203.

FALL

POWERS CROSSROADS COUNTRY FAIR AND ART FESTIVAL, on Labor Day weekend, is a nationally recognized annual event. Three hundred artists and craftsmen, entertainment, country cooking and demonstrations of plantation skills. *Location:* Power's Crossroads. 12 miles southwest of Newnan on GA 34. *More Information:* Coweta Festivals, Inc., P.O. Box 899, Newnan, GA 30264; 770/253-2011.

KINGSLAND'S ANNUAL LABOR DAY CATFISH FESTIVAL, the biggest event in Camden County, is a celebration centering around "King Catfish," where locals fry up fillets and listen to free musical acts like the Charlie Daniels Band. Arts and crafts, parade and food. *Location:* Kingsland. *More Information:* Kingsland Convention and Visitors Bureau, P.O. Box 1928, Kingsland, GA 31548; 800/433-0225.

THE LABOR DAY COUNTY FAIR OF 1896 celebrates the summer harvest with fresh fruits and vegetables. Exhibit of handmade quilts and contests, including wagon driving, mule plowing and greased pole climbing. *Location:* The Agrirama. Just west of I-75 at exit 20 in Tifton. *More Information:* Georgia Agrirama, P.O. Box Q, Tifton, GA 31793; 912/386-3344.

LABOR DAY FOLKLIFE CELEBRATION, held on Labor Day at Jarrell Plantation, has craftspeople demonstrating old-time chores in an authentic farm setting. Blacksmithing, wood stove cooking, clothes washing, outdoor cooking, animal care, spinning, weaving, and others. *Location:* Jarrell Plantation in Juliette. *More Information:* Jarrell Plantation State Historic Site, Route 2, P.O. Box 220, Juliette, GA 31046; 912/986-5172.

THE CHATTAHOOCHEE MOUNTAIN FAIR, usually the second week of September, has been going on in Northeast Georgia for over twenty years. Arts and crafts, farm equipment, livestock and horse shows, calf ropings, antiques and carnival rides. *Location:* Lee Smith Memorial Park, GA 17 N, Clarkesville. *More Information:* 706/778-2294.

THE APPLE PICKING JUBILEE, usually the second and third weekends in September, is a pick-your-own apple harvesting celebration. Food, entertainment, wagon rides through the orchards and maybe an encore rendition of a recent year's tug-of-war contest over a big pool of apple sauce. *Location:* Hillcrest Orchards. *More Information:* 706/273-3838.

BARNESVILLE BUGGY DAYS, usually the third weekend in September, has been celebrating the buggy for twenty-five years. Arts and crafts, buggy displays, fireworks and parade. *Location:* Barnesville. *More Information:* 770/358-2732.

SAPELO CULTURAL DAY, usually the third Saturday in September, celebrates the Gullah and Geechee culture. Dance, music, storytelling, food, crafts and folklore. Location: Hog Hammock, Sapelo Island. *More Information:* 912/485-2126 or 2197.

INMAN FARM HERITAGE DAYS, the third weekend in September, drew over five thousand people its first year. Arts and crafts, antique tractors, demonstrations on threshing, baling and gristmilling, parade, storytelling and music. *Location:* Inman, 5 miles south of Fayetteville, off GA 92 on Hill's Bridge Road. *More Information:* 770/719-1596.

THE FALL HARVEST FESTIVAL, usually the third weekend in September, features a Fall Harvest Queen Contest. Arts and crafts, children's activities, food and live entertainment. *Location:* McDonough. *More Information:* 770/914-2269.

THE PLAINS PEANUT FESTIVAL, the fourth Saturday of September, celebrates the area's biggest crop. Arts and crafts, music, road race, parade peanut trailer backing contest, peanut education, peanut farming equipment and peanut museum. President and Mrs. Carter attend and participate. *Location:* Plains. *More Information:* 912/824-5445.

THE POSSUM HOLLOW COUNTRY FAIR, usually the last weekend in September, is a an old-fashioned country fair with three hundred artists and craftsmen. Fireworks, antique car show, 5K run, homemakers blue ribbon affair, "Best Possum Stew" and country music show. *Location:* Dexter. *More Information:* 912/875-3200.

THE HAHIRA HONEY BEE FESTIVAL, the end of September, celebrates its famous tupelo honey. Arts and crafts, 5K Honey Run, talent show, parade, canine show and gospel sing. *Location:* Hahira. *More Information:* 912/794-3617.

THE ATLANTA HISTORY CENTER'S FOLKLIFE FESTIVAL takes place

twice a year, usually two weeks in late September and early October and one week at the end of April. Demonstrations of traditional crafts like basket weaving, embroidering and candle making. *Location:* The Atlanta History Center. *More Information:* Atlanta History Center, 130 West Paces Ferry Road, NW, Atlanta, GA 30305; 404/814-4000.

THE ROCK SHRIMP FEST, the first Saturday in October, is named for the unusual, lobster-like and delicious crustacean caught far out in the Atlantic. Food and entertainment. *Location:* St. Marys. *More Information:* 912/882-6200.

THE FOXFIRE FALL FESTIVAL, the first Saturday of October, has craft demonstrations, village tours, music and children's activities. *Location:* Foxfire Center off US 441 in Mountain City. *More Information:* Foxfire Museum, P.O. Box 541, Mountain City, GA 30562; 706/746-5828.

MULE DAY AT CALLAWAY PLANTATION, usually the first weekend in October, celebrates the antebellum workhorse—the mule. Tours of plantation houses, primitives demonstrated, mule events, arts and crafts and antique show, children's plowing contest and Confederate encampment. *Location:* Callaway Plantation. *More Information:* Washington-Wilkes Chamber of Commerce, P.O. Box 661, Washington, GA 30673; 706/678-2013.

THE ANDERSONVILLE HISTORIC FAIR, usually the first weekend in October, boasts craftsmen, potters, glass blowers, quilters, basket makers and Civil War reenactors putting on a battle. *Location:* The Village of Andersonville. *More Information:* Andersonville Guild, P.O. Box 6, Andersonville, GA 31711; 912/924-2558.

GEORGIA NATIONAL FAIR, usually the second week in October, is the annual state-sponsored traditional fair. Livestock and horse shows; youth, home and fine arts competitions; concerts, circus, carnival rides, food and fireworks. *Location:* Georgia National Fairgrounds and Agricenter. I-75 Exit 42 at Perry. *More Information:* 800-YUR-FAIR or 912/987-3247.

THE BIG PIG JIG, for three days during the first part of October, is a nationally known event that awards twelve thousand dollars in prizes to the USA's top barbecuers. Arts and crafts, parade, pageants, 5K Hog Jog, hog calling contest, livestock shows and carnival rides. *Location:* I-75 exit 36 in Vienna. *More Information:* 912/268-8275.

ANNUAL HERITAGE HOLIDAYS FESTIVAL, usually the second weekend in October, celebrates Georgia's heritage with steam boat rides, a wagon train and trail rides. Exhibits and concerts. *Location:* Rome. *More Information:* 800/444-1834, Ext. 2.

THE ANNUAL SORGHUM FESTIVAL, lasting for three weekends in October, centers around grinding and cooking at the Sorghum Mill. Crafts, country and gospel music, square dancing, contests for biscuit eating, rock and horseshoe throwing, log sawing and pole climbing, parade and car show. *Location:* Blairsville. *More Information:* Blairsville Jaycees, P.O. Box 701, Blairsville, GA 30514; 706/745-4745 or 706/745-5789.

THE ANNUAL GEORGIA APPLE FESTIVAL, the second and third full weekend every October, celebrates the harvest with plenty of apple cider, apple bread, apple fritters, apple butter, and bagloads of different kinds of apples for sale. Arts and crafts, handicrafts, music, country dance, a petting zoo, pony rides and food. *Location:* Ellijay. *More Information:* Gilmer County Chamber of Commerce, 5 Westside Square, Ellijay, GA 30540; 706/635-7400.

THE BROWN'S CROSSING CRAFTSMEN FAIR, usually the third weekend in October, is located on the site of a former cotton ginning town. 175 exhibitors, demonstrations of nearly extinct crafts and skills, blues and bluegrass music, folksongs and storytelling. *Location:* Between Milledgeville and Macon on GA 22. *More Information:* 400 Brown's Crossing, Milledgeville, GA 31061; 912/452-9327.

THE GREAT PUMPKIN FESTIVAL, the last weekend in October, is home of Georgia's largest pumpkin competition and jack-o'-lantern contest. Arts and crafts, country and bluegrass music, clogging and carnival rides. *Location:* Lake Lanier Islands. *More Information:* 770/932-7200 or 800/840-LAKE.

THE CHICKEN PIE FESTIVAL, usually the last Saturday in October, celebrates a legendary chicken pie made at the McAfee Hotel when Smithville was a railroad hub in the early 1900s. Railroad passengers would order the famous chicken pie ahead of time and when the train stopped at Smithville, they would either go to the hotel for dinner or the hotel would deliver the pies to the train. Arts and crafts, chicken pie recipe contest, children's activities and entertainment. *Location:* Smithville. *More Information:* 912/846-2631 or 912/924-4399 or 912/846-4114.

THE GEORGIA PEANUT FESTIVAL, the fourth Saturday in October, takes place in Worth County, the peanut capital of the world. Parade, carnival and family entertainment. *Location:* Possom Poke Park, Sylvester. *More Information:* Worth County-Sylvester Chamber of Commerce, P.O. Box 60, Sylvester, GA 31791; 912/776-6657 or 912/776-7718.

THE BIG RED APPLE FESTIVAL, usually the last weekend in October, is in its eleventh year. Arts and crafts, car show, 5K run, food and entertainment. *Location:* City Park, Cornelia. *More Information:* Habersham County Chamber of Commerce, 706/778-8585.

WESTVILLE'S FAIR OF 1850, from mid-October through mid-November, is a month of harvest-time activity demonstrations, including syrup making and cane grinding and antebellum cotton ginning, both powered by mules. *Location:* Westville. From downtown Lumpkin, go southeast about 1 mile on MLK Drive. Entrance is on the left. *More Information:* Westville, MLK Drive, Lumpkin, GA 31815; 912/838-6310 or 888/733-1850.

THE ANNUAL TOCCOA HARVEST FESTIVAL, usually the first full weekend in November, has celebrated harvest time for twenty-two years. Country crafts, antique show and sale, quilt and art show, old-time demonstrations, children's activities, entertainment and food. *Location:* Toccoa. *More Information:* P.O. Box 577, Toccoa, GA 30577; 706/886—2132.

CANE GRINDING PARTIES, celebrating the annual cane grinding, take place at the Agrirama throughout November. Weather and cane supply permitting, cane grindings are scheduled most November weekdays. Mules turn the sweeps in the morning, grinding cane stalks to produce juice to be boiled into syrup in the afternoons in the sixty-gallon kettle. This is highlighted by two evening cane grinding parties, held a week apart, that include syrup cooking, music, dancing, wagon rides, storytelling, candy pulling and bonfires. *Location:* The Agrirama. Just west of I-75 at exit 20 in Tifton. *More Information:* Georgia Agrirama, P.O. Box Q, Tifton, GA 31793; 912/386-3344.

BEAVER CREEK AT IVEY STATION, usually the second weekend in November, celebrates the first Ivey Grey Watermelon, grown in the area and shipped in the mid-1800s. The festival site is located beside the railroad tracks. *Location:* Gordon. *More Information:* Beaver Creek Art Association, 912/628-2912.

THE ANNUAL COTTON HARVEST FESTIVAL AND FLY IN, the third weekend in November, has been celebrating the cotton harvest for almost twenty years. Arts and crafts, children's activities, food and entertainment. *Location:* Hazlehurst. *More Information:* Hazlehurst-Jeff Davis Chamber of Commerce, 912/375-4543.

HERITAGE FARM'S PIONEER SKILLS DAY, the third Saturday of November, includes farming, syrup making, corn shelling, basket weaving, lye soap making, blacksmithing, quilting and spinning that demonstrate life from a century ago. No modern crafts here. All the participants make authentic products from the past. Also period food, music, wagon rides and a Civil War camp and battle reenactment. *Location:* Heritage Farm at General Coffee State Park. From Douglas, go 6 miles east on GA 32. The entrance is on the left. *More Information:* General Coffee State Park, 46 John Coffee Road, Nicholls, GA 31554; 912/384-7082.

FARM TOURS

A handful of Georgia farmers are developing one of the newest trends in tourism—agritourism. By encouraging visitors to their farms, the farmers are bringing in some extra income, and the general public benefits by personally experiencing a broad spectrum of farm industries: dairy, apples, vegetables, pumpkins, corn, even llamas, emus and Christmas trees. Check the crop seasons and harvests to determine the best time to visit. All tours require appointments. Most require a minimum of ten or more persons on a tour.

ADAMS FARMS. Surprisingly close to Atlanta, this small produce farm with drip irrigation offers interpretive tours of its tomato, cantaloupe, corn and bean fields. *Location:* 1486 GA 54, Fayetteville, GA 30236. *More Information:* Virginia Adams, 770/461-9395.

ANIMAL CRACKERS LLAMAS. About thirty llamas, including babies and studs, are raised here by one of the state's veteran breeders. Two barns, eight pastures and one waterfall on the Little Toccoa Creek. *Location:* Route 3, Box 338, Toccoa, GA 30577. *More Information:* Myra Freeman, 706/886-7076.

BURT'S PUMPKIN FARM. Located within view of the Amicalola Falls near Dahlonega, Burt's offers a two-mile hayride through mountain woods, corn fields and pumpkins from September through Thanksgiving. Guests can pick from thousands of pumpkins in the field and try popcorn popped from corn grown on the farm. Large popcorn silo, barn and country store with boiled peanuts, gourds, jams, jellies, popcorn, corn bread and confections. Tours run on weekends in September, daily in October and weekends in November. Tours available year-round by appointment. *Location:* Box 210, Star Route, Dawsonville, GA 30534; on Hwy 52, 0.5 mile east of the Amicalola Park State Park entrance. *More Information:* Burt Cameron, 706/265-3701.

CAGLE'S DAIRY. The only milk producer/distributor in the state and one of the first marketers of plastic milk jugs in the nation, this dairy offers a close-up look at cow feeding and milking and milk processing. The Cagle sons lead hayrides and demonstrate their award-winning border collies (see page 167) for mostly school-age group tours. *Location:* 362 Stringer Road, Canton, GA 30115. *More Information:* Bernice Cagle, 770/345-5591.

CALHOUN PRODUCE. This tour goes through a 1.5-acre pick-your-own strawberry farm in season from early April to early June or an eighty-one hundred-square-foot packing shed for bean shelling from late June to late October. Covered picnic area and small retail outlet. *Location:* 5075 Hawpond Road, Ashburn, GA 31714; 6 miles east of I-20 off exit 30. *More Information:* Joyce or Brad Calhoun or Sheila Rice, 912/273-1887.

CHUCK-BAR EMU RANCH. One of the largest emu ranch operations in the Southeast, Chuck-Bar is a working ranch with Australian Emus, a slightly smaller cousin of the African ostrich and one of the newest livestock types in the United States. Tours by appointment cost $3.50 per person. Business tours available for those interested in getting started in emu ranching. *Location:* 15535 GA 219, West Point, GA 31883; the ranch is located a few miles south of Whitesville on the west side of GA 219. *More Information:* Chuck and Barbara Powell, 706/633-9127.

CIRCLE A FARM. Noted for its conservation techniques, this farm takes guests through Christmas tree orchards, gives out seedlings and goes by a small on-site cattle operation. *Location:* 3900 Freeman Road, Barnesville, GA 30204. *More Information:* Tom Aiken, 770/358-4184.

HARP'S FARM MARKET. In the farm tour business for ten years, this fifty-year-old family farm, complete with roadside market, showcases a four-acre nursery with hundreds of native plants and perennials, twenty acres of Christmas trees and cotton production. *Location:* 1692 GA 92 South, Fayetteville, GA 30215. More Information: Mickey or Tammy Harp, 770/461-1821 or 460-9180.

HILLCREST ORCHARDS. An educational video, wagon ride through an orchard and warehouse tour reveal the ins and outs of apple growing, sorting and packing and cider and pie making. Deluxe petting zoo. Tours available most of the summer and autumn. *Location:* Route 2, Box 1616, GA 52 E., Ellijay, GA 30540. *More Information:* Janice Smith, 706/273-3838.

JONES FARM. This large four-generation farm takes guests on a hay-ride tour of long fields of cotton, soybeans, peanuts, peas and corn and returns them to the barns to see chickens, hogs, goats and mules. Mule ride with covered wagon, meal in a cabin in the woods, a film on Georgia commodity products and a chance to talk with the family. Morning or afternoon tours. *Location:* 2979 Mt. Gilead Road, Tennille, GA 31089. *More Information:* Melton or Betty Jones, 912/552-7289.

SOUTHERN GRACE FARMS. This tour showcases the big three of Georgia row crops: tobacco, cotton and peanuts. Tour varies depending on time of year, but begins with a presentation on the crops, continues with a demonstration of farm equipment and visits to the fields and tobacco curing barns. A trip to a farmer-stocked peanut buying station is optional. *Location:* Route 1, Box 51-C, Enigma, GA 31749. *More Information:* Tim McMillan, 912/533-7965 or 8655.

USSERY FARM. There are donkey rides, goat petting, horses,

chickens, fields of sugar cane, corn, tomatoes, turnips, collards and cucumber; but the highlight remains the cane syrup making in the old syrup kettle and cane mill in November and December. Fishing, hay rides and seasonal cane juice available. *Location:* 173 Farr Road, Kathleen, GA 31047. *More Information:* Frank Ussery, 912/987-3331 or 951-2249.

WALLER FARMS. An all-day tour includes cattle farming, farm equipment demonstrations in the field, a traditional Southern lunch, boiled peanut snacks, petting zoo and optional pony rides and fishing. *Location:* 1289 Brantley Road, Harrison, GA 31082. *More Information:* Glenn or Rabun Waller, 912/552-9430 or 912/552-3491.

WALTERS FARM. Guests experience a modern swine operation from farrow to finish. Guests see samples of pig nutrition feeds and have an opportunity to hold baby pigs. Barbecue lunch also available. *Location:* 176 Walters Road, Barnesville, 30204 GA. *More Information:* John Waters, 770/358-1670.

OTHER FARM TOUR INFORMATION

The county extension agent, local farm bureau, or chamber of commerce often organizes annual all-day farm tours that stop at half a dozen or more farms and related agricultural operations in the county. The largest in the state, the Laurens County farm tour, exceeds three hundred visitors a year but welcomes more. 912/272-2277.

TATTNALL COUNTY, which grows, sells and ships more Vidalia onions than any other county, offers onion farm tours. For details contact the Tattnall County Development Authority, Alexander Hotel, Brazell Street, Reidsville, GA 30453; 912/557-6400.

TOURISM/PROMOTIONS in Douglas coordinates travel through greenhouses, fruit orchards and the tobacco roads of Coffee County, the buckle of the state's tobacco belt. 912/384-5978.

THE STATESBORO CONVENTION AND VISITORS BUREAU organizes tours of an historic farm house turned botanical gardens, an early 1900s turpentine still and seasonal visits to tobacco, cotton, peanut, watermelon and pick-your-own berry farms. 912/489-1869.

THE TIFTON COUNTY TOURISM ASSOCIATION puts together tours of peanut fields and a peanut butter factory. 912/386-0216.

THE LOWNDES COUNTY CONVENTION AND VISITORS BUREAU in Valdosta arranges a number of tours with agricultural themes: The "Cotton Picking Tour" includes a pick-your-own harvest and other experiences which explain the transformation of cotton from the fields to the clothing store. The "Nut and Honey Tour" highlights three major crops in the county—peanuts, pecans and honey. Other seasonal tours cover vegetable planting in the spring and tobacco auctioning in the summer. 912/245-0513.

VACATION FARMS

With cows or goats in the barn, fish in the pond and sometimes crops in the fields, vacation farms offer fresh air, picturesque scenery and quiet solitude. Georgia farms offering lodging and meals range from bona fide agricultural operations with livestock and crops to old cow pastures owned by retirees from the city. A sample includes:

GOD'S COUNTRY FARM. This fifty-acre ex-cow farm owned by Bill and Arlene Gray has a small stocked pond, a barn with goats, a few apple trees, a vegetable patch, a guest room in the farmhouse and three fully furnished and equipped log cabins in the woods. Open May-Oct., but call well in advance to reserve a time. *Location:* Near Brasstown Bald Mountain and Unicoi State Park. *More Information:* Rt. 4, Box 4380, Blairsville, GA 30512; 706/745-1560.

HIDDEN HOLLOW FARM. For a different vacation, this secluded mountain spot off GA 136 has log cabins, a country inn and camping cabins with nearby hiking and fishing. *More Information:* 463 Hidden Hollow Lane, Chickamauga, GA 30707; 706/539-2372.

PADGETT'S FARM. Traci Padgett's 610-acre spread of woods and pastures is ideal for family reunions, church outings and youth groups. Four cabins with dorm-style bunk beds and bathroom facilities, a lake house with three bedrooms, kitchen, television, washer and dryer, and a clubhouse with large commercial kitchen all overlook a twenty-acre lake. The farm offers bumper pool, tennis, basketball, volleyball, but NO fishing. Must bring own food and linens. *Location:* 20 miles south of Augusta. *More Information:* Rt. 4, Box 462, Waynesboro, GA 30830; 706/554-0590.

PINEFIELD PLANTATION. Charlie and Carole Ann Cannon's working farm with cattle, peanut, cotton and vegetable crops offers lake fishing, horseback riding, skeet shooting and nature walks. Accommodations include four fully furnished and equipped bedrooms with twin beds and three baths, a fully furnished kitchen, cook available, screened porch overlooking lake, wet bar and game room. *Location:* 10 minutes west of I-75 on GA 37. *More Information:* Rt. 2, Box 215, Moultrie, GA 31768; 912/985-2086.

SPARKLEBERRY FARM. This working horse farm on 105 acres has a two-bedroom, two-bath mobile home, two ponds for fishing, a pool, carriage rides, riding lessons and escorted trail rides for experienced riders. *Location:* 9 miles north of Metter off GA 121 on CR 222. *More Information:* Rt. 1, Box 121E, Metter, GA 30439; 912/865-5616.

TWIN OAKS. A twenty-three-acre farm in West Georgia, Twin Oaks has an old apple orchard, fig, pear and peach trees, fourteen grape vines, koi and goldfish ponds, game fowl, swans and geese and walking trails. Earl and Carol Turner's place also has a private guest cottage with covered patio and swimming pool. *More Information:* 9565 E. Liberty Road, Villa Rica, GA 30180; 770/459-4374.

For a complete listing of farm's offering vaction opportunites, get a copy of the Georgia Farm Vacations and Farm Tour Directory. *More Information:* Community Development Office, Cooperative Extension Service, The University of Georgia, Athens, GA 30602; 706/542-8935.

TROUT POND DIRECTORY

Trout farms generally are located in the northern part of the state since the fish need clean, cold water to survive and reproduce. These ponds offer a fun and convenient way to fish. Most are easily accessible, unlike many stocked streams and rivers that can be reached only by four-wheel drive. Many are open all year long and not just during trout season (from the last Saturday in March to October 31).

Some publicly managed impoundments on small mountain streams where the public can fish include:

DOCKERY LAKE. This scenic three-acre lake is stocked every other week during the trout season. Stocking is sometimes suspended in August if water temperatures get unusually high. Fishing is allowed only during the trout season. The

Forest Service operates a campground adjacent to the lake. *Location:* Lumpkin County, GA 60 north of Dahlonega.

Lake Winfield Scott. Trout are stocked in this eighteen-acre lake about every other week during the trout season. There is a Forest Service campground here. Also has a limited bass and bream fishery. *Location:* Union County on GA 180, south of Blairsville.

Nancytown Lake. This three-acre lake has a good population of bass and breams. It is stocked with trout during the first part of the trout season. Fishing is allowed year-round. The Forest Service operates a campground at nearby Lake Russell, and there is good stream fishing close by in the Middle Fork of the Broad River. *Location:* Habersham County, FSR 61, off US 123 east of Cornelia.

Some private pay lakes offering trout fishing include:

Eagle Mountain Trout Pond. This 0.5-acre lake stocked with trout provides bait and tackle and picnic tables. Fee based on the per-pound catch and includes fish cleaning. Open all year during daylight hours. *Location:* Towns County on Bell Creek Road 3 miles off GA 75, north of Hiawassee. *More Information:* 706/896-2323.

Ken's Ponds. Two lakes, each about 0.75 acre in size, offer trout in the wintertime and bass, bream, catfish and crappie the entire year. Bank fishing only; restrooms, bait and tackle. Fees are based on per-pound catch. Open all year, Mon.-Sat., 8am-7pm. *Location:* Berrien County, 3 miles north of Alapaha on US 129; 912/532-6135.

Rainbow Ranch. This 0.5-acre pond stocked with rainbow trout furnishes bait and tackle and picnic tables. Fee based on per pound fish catch. Cleaning is 10 percent more. Open year round, 9am-5pm. *Location:* Forsyth County on GA 20 adjacent to the Chattahoochee River bridge, between Buford and Cumming; 770/887-4947.

Twin Bridge Lakes. A fourteen-acre lake offers bank fishing only of winter trout, bass, bream, catfish and crappie. Restrooms, snacks, camping and bait and tackle. Daily use fee. Open year round Mon.-Thurs., 7am to 12pm; Fri. 7am until Sun. 7pm. *Location:* Gwinnett County, 2 miles north of Lawrenceville on GA 124; 770/963-6769.

The Fisheries Section, Wildlife Resources Division, Department of Natural Resources, has more information on trout fishing and pay lakes in Georgia. 404/918-6418.

Canning Facilities

Once, canning was a necessary summer chore because families depended on the preserved food to get through the lean winter months. But the large cannery at the Atlanta Farmer's Market and other public canning facilities run by the Cooperative Extension Service throughout the state have all closed over the past two decades as freezing became a more popular, inexpensive method to preserve foods. Yet some small canneries remain open in rural communities, administered by the Vocational-Agricultural section of the Georgia Department of Education. Located in county high schools in the vo-ag departments, the food processing plants, usually in rooms the size of large classrooms, generally open for about thirty-eight days each summer. Here canners partake in the traditional task, but with modern facilities that make it fun and easy.

To find out more about the nearest cannery, call one of the county high school vo-ag representatives from the following list: Appling, 912/367-8619; Bacon, 912/632-4414; Berrien, 912/686-3464; Brooks, 912/263-8923; Calhoun, 912/835-2473; Candler, 912/685-249; Colquitt, 912/890-6152; Dawson, 912/265-3938; Dooly, 912/268-818; Early, 912/723-3006; Emanuel, 912/763-2673; Fannin, 796/632-2081; Franklin, 706/384-4813; Gilmer, 706/276-5080; Habersham, 706/778-7161; Hart, 706/394-5461; Houston, 912/988-6312; Irwin, 912/468-9421; Jeff Davis, 912/375-6764; Jenkins, 912/982-4791; Lanier, 912/482-3869; Lowndes, 912/245-2260; McDuffie, 706/595-1481; Mitchell, 912/336-2172; Murray, 706/695-1414; Peach, 912/865-3402; Pickens, 706/692-2463; Rabun, 706/782-4186; Seminole, 912/524-8165; Stephens, 706/886-6825; Tattnall, 912/557-4375; Tift, 912/386-6591; Treutlen, 912/529-3842; Turner, 912/867-4378; Union, 706/745-6461; White, 706/865-4936; and Worth, 912/776-8625.

State Farmer's Markets

State farmer's markets are a good way for consumers to buy fresh vegetables and fruits direct from farmers or wholesalers. The Atlanta Farmer's Market (see page 188 and page 280) is the largest in the state, but there are numerous others. Some are seasonal only. Others, like the Atlanta market, are open year-round.

Albany Farmer's Market (seasonal), 701 Gaines Avenue, Albany, GA 31706; 912/430-4245.

Athens Farmer's Market (seasonal), 2160 W. Broad Street, Athens, GA 30603; no phone.

Atlanta Farmer's Market, 16 Forest Parkway, Forest Park, GA 30297; 404/366-6910.

Augusta Farmer's Market, 1150 5th Street, Augusta, GA 30901; 706/721-3004.

Cairo Farmer's Market (seasonal), 1110 North Broad Street, Cairo, GA 31728; no phone.

Columbus Farmer's Market, 318 10th Avenue, Columbus, GA 31901; 706/649-7448.

Cordele Farmer's Market (seasonal), 1901 US 41 North, Cordele, Georgia 31010; 912/276-2335.

Donalsonville Farmer's Market (seasonal), US 84, Donalsonville, GA 31745; no phone.

Glennville Farmer's Market (seasonal), US 301, Glennville, GA 30427; no phone.

Jesup Farmer's Market (seasonal), US 301, Jesup, GA 31545; 912/427-5773.

Macon Farmer's Market, 2055 Eisenhower Parkway, Macon, GA 31206; 912/752-1097.

Moultrie Farmer's Market (seasonal), Quitman Highway, Moultrie, GA 31768; 912/891-7240.

Pelham Farmer's Market (seasonal), US 19 North, Pelham, GA 31799; no phone.

Savannah Farmer's Market, 701 US 80 West, Savannah, GA 31408; 912/966-7800.

Thomasville Farmer's Market, 502 Smith Avenue, Thomasville, GA 31792; 912/225-4072.

Tifton Farmer's Market (seasonal), US 41, Tifton, GA 31794; no phone.

Valdosta Farmer's Market (seasonal), 1500 S. Patterson Street, Valdosta, GA 31601; no phone.

Georgia Gift Foods

Dozens of family farms and outlets across the state offer locally grown or made Georgia gift foods. Sweet Vidalia onions, traditional jams and jellies, luscious apple cakes and rich nut confections are some of the hundreds of specialty foods from Georgia, many of which can be shipped across the world with only a phone call.

Some Georgia gift food companies include:

ATKINSON PECAN CANDIES. Toasted and salted pecans and pecan confections. Garfield, GA. 912/763-2149.

CLAXTON BAKERY, INC. World famous old-fashioned fruit cake. Claxton, GA. 912/739-3441.

DESOTO CONFECTIONERY AND NUT COMPANY. Popcrickle, pecan crickle, peanut crickle. pralines, chocolates, candied and spiced nuts. DeSoto, GA. 912/874-1200.

DILLON CANDY COMPANY. Pecan divinity, handmade pecan candies, peanut and pecan brittles. Boston, GA. 912/498-2051.

GEORGIA GIFT PRODUCTS. Sauces, relishes, syrups, chocolates, jams and jellies. Buford, GA. 770/932-0509.

HILLSIDE ORCHARD FARMS. Sauces, salsas, juices, apple cider, fruit juices, jams and jellies. Tiger, GA. 706/782-7848.

KENDRICK PECAN. Spiced and chocolate covered pecans and pralines. Columbus, GA. 706/687-0161.

LANE PACKING COMPANY. Peaches, pecans. Fort Valley, GA. 912/825-3592.

LINDSAY FARMS. Peach and strawberry preserves; red pepper and muscadine jams and jellies, cakes and confections. Atlanta, GA. 404/305-0620.

LOUJIM'S SOUTHERN CUISINE. Ms. Louise Thompson-Childs' jams and jellies. Jonesboro, GA. 770/478-9638.

PLANTATION CANDY COMPANY. Divinity, pecan log rolls, nut brittles, pralines, caramel pecan clusters and other confections. Eastman, GA. 912/374-9940.

STANLEY FARMS. Vidalia onions, sauces and relishes. Vidalia, GA. 912/526-3466.

THE MAYHAW TREE COMPANY. Cucumber, hot pepper, mayhaw and Vidalia onion jams and jellies; syrups, salad dressings, gift baskets and mayhaw wine. Peachtree City, GA. 770/487-5230.

Growers who ship Vidalia onions include:

BLAND FARMS. Reidsville, GA. 912/654-1426.

EASTERLING FARMS. Montezuma, GA. 912/654-2599.

MORRIS FARMS. Uvalda, GA. 912/594-6275.

MCDONALD FARMS. Tarrytown, GA. 912/529-3383.

ROBISON FARMS. Ailey, GA. 912/583-4532.

HISTORIC MILLS

A handful of the gristmills scattered across Georgia have survived to the present. Farmers once traveled for miles to come here and grind grain or hull rice. Today these mills are still using power from a river or stream to produce corn meal and grits for consumers.

OGEECHEE RIVER MILL. Mills have stood on this spot in Hancock County since 1790 when the millpond was first built. The current structure, still in use, has ground meal since 1872. Historically, farmers fished the pond as they waited their turn to grind their corn. In recent years local children have used the pond as a favorite swimming hole. Charles Tackett owns the mill and lives in a nearby house. He offers tours by appointment and operates the mill on Monday and Wednesdays, using the historic machinery to make stone-ground cornmeal that he sells to local stores. *Location:* Hancock County, about 1 mile from Mayfield on the Ogeechee River. *More Information:* 706/465-2195.

BARKER'S CREEK MILL. Built in 1936 and restored in 1975, this picturesque, simple wooden gristmill with an overshot twelve-foot diameter wooden wheel stands next to a large waterfall on Betty's Creek in Rabun County. Owned by the nearby Hambidge Center, an artists' colony, the mill makes cornmeal and grits. *Days/Hrs.:* Open to the public the first Friday and Saturday of each month. *Location:* About 5 miles west on Betty's Creek Road off GA 441 in Dillard. *More Information:* 706/746-5718.

BERRY COLLEGE MILL. A forty-two-foot water wheel moves the machinery in this early twentieth century gristmill in a wooded section of the Berry College campus. Gravity-fed water from Berry's own reservoir powers the wheel, which has an iron hub moved to its current location by automobile magnate Henry Ford. *Location:* 1 mile north of Rome on US 27. *More Information:* 706/232-5374.

HAMBURG MILL. In 1921 the Gilmore Brothers built this gristmill. The staff still works the well-preserved gristmill, powered by the Ogeechee River, and sells bags of cornmeal. Alligators once patrolled the mill pond, now used by fishermen in Hamburg State Park. *Location:* 6 miles northeast of Warthen via Hamburg Road off GA 102. *More Information:* 912/552-2393.

PRATER'S MILL. At its peak in the late 1800s, Benjamin Prater's mill, situated strategically by a wagon crossing over Coahulla Creek, included a gristmill, sawmill, cotton gin, wool corder, blacksmith shop, general store and hotel. The still functional mill comes alive during two weekend arts and crafts festivals in mid-May and mid-October (see page 289). *Location:* About 10 miles north of Dalton on GA 2. *More Information:* 706/275-MILL.

NORA MILL GRANARY. Established in 1876, this authentic working mill, powered by the Chattahoochee River, has an adjacent country store that sells stone ground, speckled grits, cornmeal, wheat, rye and buckwheat flour, baking mixes, jellies, preserves and other mountain products. *Location:* Just south of Helen on GA 17/75. *More Information:* 706/878-2375.

SYLVAN FALLS MILL. A working gristmill has stood on this spot for more than 150 years, powered by springs from Black Rock Mountain. In 1946 a twenty-seven-foot high, ten thousand-pound steel wheel replaced the original chestnut wood one. The Sylvan Falls Mill has become a weekend bed and breakfast. It also sells its own stone-ground cornmeal. *Location:* Rabun Gap, 2 miles east of US 441 off Wolffork Valley Road. *More Information:* 706/746-7138

WATSON MILL. This circa 1880 building combines a gristmill with a covered bridge under a single spacious roof. Anglers and canoeists enjoy the mill pond, dotted with moss-draped cypress trees. Hubert Watson bought the property in 1943 and ran a successful business for over thirty years. Now part of the George L. Smith State Park. *Location:* 4 miles southeast of Twin City off GA 23. *More Information:* 912/763-2759.

Georgia mills that sell stone-ground grits by mail:

FIELDER'S MILL. Fielder's Old-Fashioned Water-Ground Grits. 706/269-3630.

GEORGIA AGRIRAMA COUNTRY STORE GIFTS. 912/386-3876.

LOGAN TURNPIKE. Old-Fashioned Speckled Grits. 706/745-5735.

NORA MILL GRANARY. Nora Mill Speckled Grits. 800/927-2375.

More information is available on the "y'all@the south" web site at http://www.yall.com.

More Information: For a complete listing of mills in the Southeast, contact the Society for the Preservation of Old Mills (SPOOM), which publishes a bimonthly newsletter and has a state-by-state directory of mills. 330/832-5130.

Pick-Your-Own Farms

Strawberries, blueberries, peaches, apples, muscadines, Vidalia onions, cabbage, pumpkins, watermelons, pecans and Christmas trees are just some of the Georgia crops that consumers can pick for themselves during harvest season (see page 95). Decide what vegetable or fruit to pick and when it's in season and look for the nearest pick-your-own farm. The *Farmers and Consumers Market Bulletin,* a periodical from the Georgia Department of Agriculture, offers three or four listings of pick-your-own farms each year. For more information call 404/656-3722. The Georgia Farm Bureau publishes a smaller yearly directory of certified farm markets that includes some pick-your-own farms. The number is 912/474-8411.

Specialty Crops

Besides commonly recognized farm products like chickens, peanuts, pecans and peaches, Georgia grows an incredible variety of lesser known crops. Gourmet mushrooms, culinary herbs, wild rice, alligators, ostriches and emus are only some of the unusual crops or livestock cultivated or raised in Georgia.

Some farmers of these unusual crops include:

Alligator Meat

Once a threatened species, alligators have made a major comeback in South Georgia and Florida. Described as tasting like chicken, one alligator farmer says much of his business comes from restaurants in Southeastern cities when the local university plays the Florida Gators in football.

James Lee Adams. A soybean farmer (see page 223), who has more than two thousand alligators. Camilla, GA. 912/336-8298.

Georgia Alligators Trappers Association. Moultrie, GA. 912/985-1148.

Prehistoric Ponds. Gator meat. 912/487-5878.

Culinary Herbs

Locally grown plants such as marjoram, thyme, rosemary, oregano and basil have become popular sellers to restaurants and supermarkets.

Frolicking Farms. Atlanta, GA. 888/252-4603.

Edible Flowers

Fancy restaurants and upscale produce markets are beginning to stock an ancient food source, wildflowers. Besides looking good, wildflower petals taste great and are loaded with nutrients. Roses, violets, violas and pansies are some of the more popular selections.

Morningside Farmers Market. Andrew and Bernadette Goldstein of Wildflower Organics Farm and other farmers sell flowers at this seasonal urban organic market. 1395 North Highland Avenue, Atlanta, GA. 770/621-4642.

Atlanta Farmer's Market. Coosemans at the state farmer's market sells a variety of edible flowers. Forest Park, GA. 404/366-7132.

Emu Meat

Low in fat and cholesterol and high in protein and iron, the meat of this flightless bird from Australia, a cousin of the ostrich, offers a healthy alternative to red meat.

Golden Creek Farms. Newnan, GA. 770/583-9933.

Komochi Food Products. Dewy Rose. 706/283-6504.

Gourmet Mushrooms

Shiitakes from Japan and portabellas from Italy are but two of the varieties cultivated by local fungus farmers.

Athena Mushrooms. Atlanta, GA. 404/362-9390.

Mayhaw Fruit

A tree that grows naturally in South Georgia swamps, the Mayhaw produces an apple-like fruit that makes what enthusiasts call the best jelly in the world. The taste is not particularly sweet or tart. Yet there's supposedly something about the understated, pleasant taste that allows one to use Mayhaw jelly every day indefinitely without tiring of it like other fruit spreads.

Swamp Treasure Products. Maurice Palmer began his Mayhaw orchard and jelly business because he loved the product so much. Camilla, GA. 912/336-8989.

Wild Rice

In an old rice field near Woodbine on the coast where slave labor once cultivated the grain, young farmer Charles Commander is raising wild grain rice for sale to restaurants and through custom orders. 904/399-0422.

Georgia Wineries

Vitaculture is presently a small, specialized part of Georgia agriculture. Several commercial vineyards and wineries operate in the state producing *vitis vinifera* grapes for European-style wines.

Chateau Elan Winery. Chateau Elan vineyards are planted with six *vitas vinifera* varieties and two French-American hybrids. The state-of-the-art winery has won over 140 awards in five years of competition. Vineyards, sidewalk cafe, art gallery, wine tasting, shopping areas, villas, golf course, nature trails, equestrian trail and picnic area. *More Information:* Chateau Elan Winery, 7000 Old Winder Highway, Braselton, GA 30517; 800/233-WINE.

Chestnut Mountain Winery. This fifteen-acre winery strives for the traditional dryness of West Coast vintages, producing Georgia-grown Chardonnay, Cabernet Sauvignon, Riesling, Chenin Blanc and Merlot. Cabernet vineyard, free tastings, cellar tour, rooftop patio, nature trail and picnic area. *More Information:* Chestnut Mountain Winery, P.O. Box 72, Braselton, GA 30517; 770-867-6915.

Fox Winery. The winery produces estate bottled wines with grape varieties Chardonnay, Cabernet Sauvignon, Sauvignon Blanc, Chenin Blanc, Orange Muscat, Seyval Blanc, Vidal Blanc and DeChaunac. Tastings, personalized tours and sales of award-winning wines and souvenirs. *More Information:* Fox Winery, 225 GA 11 S., Social Circle, GA 30279; 770/787-5402.

Georgia Wines. Established in 1983, this family-owned vineyard, located on the slopes of Lookout Mountain, is known for its Muscadine wines, Georgia Peach Wine and Concord. The Georgia Winery Tasting Center, at I-75 exit 141 in Ringgold, has free wine tastings with twelve varieties, customizes gift baskets and sells wine accessories and wine-making supplies. *Location:* Georgia Winery Tasting Center, Battlefield Parkway, Ringgold. *More Information:* Georgia Wines, 447 High Point Drive, Chickamauga, GA 30707; 706/937-2177.

HABERSHAM VINEYARDS AND WINERY. The largest winery in the state (see page 146), Habersham makes wine from traditional European and native Georgia grapes. The reds and whites come from several vineyards in the North Georgia mountains, the muscadines from suppliers in South Georgia. Habersham has recently moved their headquarters and all winery operations to the Nacoochee Valley. Their new tasting room, in the Martin House on GA 75 across from Nora Mill, carries an extensive selection of wine accessories and gourmet Georgia food products.

Other Habersham tasting rooms throughout the state include: Underground Atlanta, 404/522-WINE; Baldwin (the former main winery), 706/778-WINE; Commerce Factory Stores, 706/335-9403; Hiawassee, 706-896-WINE; Savannah Festival Mall, 912/927-3959; On the Square, Dahlonega, 706/864-8275; and Juliette Underground, 912/994-0057. *More Information:* Habersham Winery at Nacoochee Valley, Helen, GA 30545; 706/878-WINE.

FARM ANTIQUES

Several large antique flea markets that meet monthly in the Atlanta area are a good place to find the primitive farm antiques from rural Georgia that have become so popular with collectors. The sheer number of nationwide dealers in one location greatly improves the chance of digging up that perfect bread bowl, pie safe or spinning jenny.

LAKEWOOD ANTIQUES MARKET. This Atlanta market has from fifteen hundred to two thousand dealers. *Days/Hrs.:* Second full weekend of each month, Fri.-Sun. *Admission:* Weekend $3; $5 includes Thurs. early buyers day. *Directions:* Take I-75 to exit 88 east. Follow signs to Lakewood Fairgrounds. 404/622-4488.

SCOTT ANTIQUE MARKET. This Forest Park market was formerly known as Elcos Market. *Days/Hrs.:* Second full weekend of each month. *Admission:* Pass good for Fri., Sat. and Sun., $3 per person. *Directions:* Atlanta Exposition Center. Take I-285 exit 40 onto Jonesboro Road and follow signs to Atlanta Exposition Center. 770/569-4112.

PRIDE OF DIXIE ANTIQUE MARKET. With over eight hundred booths, this Norcross market has had tremendous growth in recent years. *Days/Hrs.:* Fourth weekend each month. *Admission:* Weekend, good for Sat. and Sun., $4. *Directions:* In Atlanta, take I-85 north to exit 38. Go east on Indian Trail, right on Oakbrook Parkway and right on Jeurgens Court to the North Atlanta Trade Center. 770/279-9899.

ANTIQUE ROW. The largest collection of antique dealers in Georgia, this Chamblee area is a good place to shop for primitives the remainder of the month. 150 dealers with over 250,000 square feet cram a short stretch of Broad and adjacent streets. *Directions:* From Atlanta, take I-85 north; turn west on I-285, then almost immediately go south on Peachtree Industrial Boulevard for 1.5 miles then turn left on Broad Street. 770/485-1614.

Check out issues of *Cotton and Quail, Southern Antiques* or the *Country Register* at local antique stores for information on regional dealers in Georgia.

FARM CRAFTS

What was once handmade on the farm for a specific purpose is now a treasured reminder of days past. These farm crafts are getting harder to find and the skills necessary to make them have become artforms.

COTTON BASKETS

Large, slightly square-shaped with rounded edges, hamper baskets have carried cotton and other crops through the fields of the South since the 1800s. Today, these containers remain popular for their usefulness and their decorator appeal.

TOBE WELLS. Wells demonstrates his unique craft of making cotton baskets completely by hand at festivals throughout Georgia. The retiree also sells them from his Elberton home. *Location:* 1829 Tobe Wells Road, Elberton, GA 30835. *More Information:* 706/283-1347.

THE REEVES FAMILY. Somewhat of a dynasty, this family has been making cotton baskets for over a generation. More than half a dozen family members practice the craft today, splitting strips of wood from white oak and demonstrating their weaving skills at craft shows throughout the South. *More Information:* 706/672-1225.

BARNIE JAMES. This Austell man works with many traditional wooden crafts, including cotton baskets. He shows his work at various festivals and sells from his home. 770/948-4518.

DOUGH BOWLS

To make bread or biscuits, women once turned to their wooden dough bowls. As they were always filled with flour, a cook had only to throw in a little lard, pour in some milk and go to work. When finished, she didn't clean the bowl but left a coat of flour inside, covered the top with a clean cloth and stored it in the pie safe. The constant presence of lard protected the wood from cracking.

The dark, smooth, gently bending lines of dough bowls make them popular collector's items. Finding bowls in good shape is difficult; but fortunately, several craftsman in the state have revived the art of making dough bowls, completely by hand without electric lathes and other modern tools. Craftsmen recommend that people oil the bowls twice a year, preferably with peanut oil and a napkin. Bowls should also be kept away from water, sun or heat, including the top of the refrigerator where hot air from the motor can dry them out.

RALPH HILS. From a family of wood workers, this Ellijay man demonstrates his art form for school and community groups on request and displays his dough bowls and a variety of other kitchenware made of walnut, cherry and poplar at the Foxfire Museum in Rabun Gap (see page 176). *More Information:* 706/635-5814.

BARNIE JAMES. James uses specialized hand-carving tools made by Judd Nelson, one of the last blacksmiths of North Georgia, now retired. The maple, cherry and poplar dough bowls are just a fraction of the work done by this traditional craftsman who also makes cotton baskets (see above). *More Information:* 770/948-4518.

FISH BASKETS

Borrowing techniques from Native Americans, some settlers made long wooden baskets to catch catfish and other fish in streams and rivers. Made of split wood, they look like teepees if stood on end. Placed in bottlenecks in the river, fish swim into the weir trap through the large opening in one end. Looking for the bait at the other narrow tipped end, they become trapped in a funnel.

Places to buy old-styled fish baskets:

BAINBRIDGE HARDWARE STORE. Metal fish baskets, along with cotton baskets and farm animal tack hang from the ceiling of Lofton Willis' unique store. *Location:* Bainbridge, on Broad Street near the square. *More Information:* 912/246-0404.

THOMAS TRAPPING COMPANY. George Thomas has been making wire catfish baskets by hand for about thirty-five years. He uses hand pliers to cut wire strands, pieces them together with loxit and pig rings and shapes them from designs and patterns that mostly come from his head. About six foot around and five foot long, the traps sell in bait and tackle and hardware stores across Georgia. The traps catch catfish up to thirty pounds in weight, using bait such as cotton seed, meal cake, fish food pellets and canned catfood, placed in one end of the basket. *Location:* Alamo, 30 miles south of Dublin. *More information:* 912/523-5807.

POTTERS

Long before plastic, glass and metal, farmers depended on potters to create an amazing variety of containers. Two clay families that have clung to the craft for generations, the Hewells and the Meaders, continue to pot using traditional methods. They dig clay by hand from local fields, mix it with a mill turned by a mule, wedge it into soft clumps like bread dough, shape it into different shapes on a wheel, dip it in a mixture of wood ash and broken glass, and bake it in a hot brick kiln fueled with wood.

HEWELL POTTERY. The Hewells host an annual "Turning and Burning Festival" to showcase pottery and other folk crafts, generally the fourth weekend in September. Location: just east of Gillsville on GA 52 and well-marked by signs and pots. *More Information:* 770/869-3469.

LANIER POTTERY. Georgia's famed folk potter, Lanier Meaders of Mossy Creek, recently passed away, but extended family namesake C. J. and wife Billie continue the craft. *Location:* Warner Robins. *More Information:* 912/953-3830.

To learn more about traditional pottery and other Southern folk crafts, visit the Atlanta History Center, 130 West paces Ferry Road, Atlanta, GA, 404/814-4000; or read *Brothers in Clay: The Story of Georgia Folk Pottery* by John Burrison, Georgia State University folklorist, 1983.

QUILTS

Quilts run the gamut from expensively made with incredibly well-constructed patterns to the common crazy quilts stitched together from scrap cloth such as bleached flour sacks. Although a historic practice, quilting continues to evolve as an art form. Patterns, stitches, dyes and applique or patchwork styles remain points of debate for collectors and quilters alike.

Places to buy antique quilts include:

GRANNY TAUGHT US HOW. Hundreds of works from all over the country crowd one of the oldest establishments that buys and sells antique quilts in Georgia. *Location:* 1921 Peachtree Road, Atlanta, GA 30309. *More Information:* 404/351-2942.

THE CO-OP CRAFT STORE. This store carries dozens of quilts in popular modern patterns. *Location:* 1 mile north of Tallulah Gorge on US 441. *More Information:* 706/754-6810.

For supplies, books, patterns, classes and referrals to quilters who do commissions:

VILLAGE QUILT SHOP. 975 Main Street, Stone Mountain, GA. 770/469-9883.

DREAM QUILTERS. 2343-A Main Street, Tucker, GA. 770/939-8034.

PATRICK'S FEED AND SEED. Corner of Elm and Williams Street, Covington, GA. 770/786-3220.

COLONIAL QUILTS. 11710-A Largo Drive, Savannah, GA. 912/925-0055.

A legacy of the 1996 Olympics, The Georgia Quilt Project continues to organize quilt-related activities. The project started by bringing together quilters from all over the state who knitted about 400 quilts to give to representatives of all the countries participating in the Centennial Summer Games in Atlanta. *The Olympics Games Quilts,* published by Oxmoor House, documents the work of the Project, which also has put out several calendars, available in bookstores. *More Information:* 770/662-0444 or 404/982-0523.

The Georgia Quilt Council provides information on guilds around the state. *More Information:* President, 770/889-0710.

EQUIVALENT AMOUNTS

IF INGREDIENT CALLED FOR IS:	ITS EQUIVALENT IS:
APPLES	
1 pound	3 medium (3 cups sliced)
BERRIES	
1 pint	1¾ cups
BREAD	
1 slice	½ cup soft bread crumbs
2 slices	1 cup soft bread crumbs
1 pound loaf	12 to 16 slices
BUTTER AND SHORTENING	
Butter or margarine, 1 ounce	2 tablespoons
Butter or margarine, ½ stick	¼ cup
Butter or margarine, 1 stick	½ cup
Butter or margarine, 1 pound	2 cups
Vegetable shortening, 1 pound	2 ½ cups
CANDIED FRUIT	
½ pound, chopped	1 ½ cups
CHEESE	
American cheese, 2⅔ cups cubed	1 pound
American cheese, 4 cups shredded	1 pound
Cottage cheese, 8 ounces	1 cup
Cream cheese, 3-ounce package	⅓ cup or 6 tablespoons
Cream cheese, 8-ounce package	1 cup
COCOA	
4 cups, ground	1 pound
COCONUT	
3½-ounce can, shredded	1⅓ cups
1 pound	5 cups
COFFEE	
5 cups, ground (80 tablespoons)	1 pound
CORNMEAL	
3 cups	1 pound
CORNSTARCH	
3 cups	1 pound
CRACKER CRUMBS	
Soda crackers, 23	1 cup
Graham crackers, 15	1 cup

IF INGREDIENT CALLED FOR IS:	ITS EQUIVALENT IS:
CREAM	
Cream, ½ pint	1 cup
Heavy or whipping cream, 1 cup	2 cups whipped cream
Sour cream, 8 ounces	1 cup
DATES	
1 pound, whole	2¼ cups
1 pound, chopped	1¾ cups
EGGS	
8 to 10 whites (large eggs)	1 cup
12 to 14 yolks (large eggs)	1 cup
5 to 6 whole eggs	1 cup
1 whole egg	4 tablespoons liquid
FIGS	
1 pound, whole	2¾ cups
1 pound, chopped	2⅔ cups
FLOUR	
All-purpose flour, 1 pound	4 cups sifted all-purpose
Cake flour, 1 pound	4¾ to 5 cups sifted cake flour
Whole-wheat flour, 1 pound	3½ to 3¾ cups unsifted whole-wheat flour
Rye flour, 1 pound	4½ to 5 cups
GELATIN	
Unflavored envelope, ¼ ounce	1 tablespoon
Flavored package, 3¼ ounces	½ cup
LEMON	
1 medium lemon	3 tablespoons juice
1 medium lemon	1 tablespoon grated rind
5 to 8 medium lemons	1 cup juice
LIME	
1 medium lime	2 tablespoons juice
MARSHMALLOWS	
¼ pound	16 large marshmallows
MILK	
Evaporated milk, 1 cup	3 cups whipped
Evaporated milk, 5⅓ to 6-ounce can	⅔ cup
Evaporated milk, 13 to 14¼ ounce can	1¼ to 1⅓ cups
Milk, 1 quart	4 cups
Heavy Cream, 1 cup	2 cups whipped
NUTS	
Almonds, 1 pound unshelled	1¼ cups shelled
Almonds, 1 pound shelled	3 cups
Peanuts, 1 pound unshelled	2 cups shelled
Peanuts, 1 pound shelled	4 cups
Pecans, 1 pound unshelled	2¼ cups shelled
Pecans, 1 pound shelled	4 cups
Walnuts, 1 pound unshelled	2 cups shelled
Walnuts, 1 pound shelled	4 cups

If ingredient called for is:	Its equivalent is:
ONION	
1 medium, chopped	¾ to 1 cup
ORANGE	
1 medium	⅓ to ½ cup juice
1 medium	2 to 3 tablespoons grated peel
PASTA	
Macaroni, 1 cup uncooked	2 cups cooked macaroni
Macaroni, 1 pound uncooked	5 cups cooked macaroni
Spaghetti, 1 cup uncooked	2 cups cooked spaghetti
Spaghetti, 1 pound uncooked	5 cups cooked spaghetti
Noodles, 1 cup uncooked	⅔ cup cooked noodles
PEACHES	
1 pound	4 medium
PEARS	
1 pound	3 medium
PLUMS	
1 pound	9 medium
POTATOES	
White, 1 pound	3 medium
PRUNES	
1 pound, whole	2⅓ cups
1 pound, chopped and cooked	3 cups
RAISINS	
1 pound	3 cups loosely packed
RICE	
Rice, 1 pound uncooked	2⅓ cups cooked rice
Quick-cooking rice, 1 cup uncooked	2 cups cooked rice
Converted rice, 1 cup uncooked	3 to 4 cups cooked rice
Long-grain rice, 1 cup uncooked	4 cups cooked rice
Wild rice, 1 cup uncooked	3 to 4 cups cooked wild rice
SUGAR	
Granulated sugar, 1 pound	2¼ cup
SWEET POTATOES	
1 pound	3 medium
SYRUP	
Corn syrup, 16 ounces	2 cups
Maple syrup, 12 ounces	1½ cups
TEA	
2 ounces	⅞ cup
1 pound	6 cups
TOMATOES	
1 pound	3 medium

Healthy and Simple: Ingredient Substitutions

To Reduce Fat, Cholesterol and Calories in Your Favorite Recipes

INSTEAD OF...	**USE...**
Whole or 2% milk	Skim milk, 1% milk, or evaporated skimmed milk diluted equally with water
Chocolate milk	Mix skim milk with cocoa
Whipping cream	Chilled evaporated skimmed milk, whipped; or whipped nonfat dry milk powder with a small amount of water
Cream or half-and-half	Evaporated skimmed milk
Cheddar, American, Swiss, and Monterey Jack cheese	Cheeses with 5 grams of fat or less per ounce; or reduce amount by ½ and use sharp flavored cheeses
Mozzarella cheese	Part-skim mozzarella cheese
Cream cheese	Light cream cheese products, Neufchâtel cheese; or mix in blender and chill: 1 cup dry lowfat cottage cheese, ¼ cup polyunsaturated margarine, skim milk if needed
Creamed cottage cheese	Nonfat or 1% fat cottage cheese, or farmer's cheese
Ricotta cheese	Nonfat, lite, or part-skim ricotta cheese
Sour cream	Nonfat or low-fat sour cream, or nonfat or low-fat plain yogurt (For baked goods, add 1½ teaspoons flour to each ½ cup yogurt or sour cream alternative.); or blend together 1½ cups dry lowfat cottage cheese, ½ cup skim milk, 1 tablespoon lemon juice (10 calories per tablespoon)
Whole egg	2 egg whites or ¼ cup egg substitute
Baking chocolate, 1-ounce square	3 tablespoons cocoa plus 1 tablespoon monounsaturated or polyunsaturated vegetable oil or margarine; or 3 tablespoons cocoa plus 2 teaspoons sugar and 1 tablespoon water
Fudge sauce	Chocolate syrup
White flour, 1 cup	½ cup whole wheat flour plus ½ cup white flour, or ⅔ cup white flour plus ⅓ cup oat bran
Sugar	Reduce amount by ⅓ to ½, substitute brown sugar or honey when flavor will not be affected
Salt	Reduce by half or eliminate

INSTEAD OF...	**USE...**
Margarine	Reduce amount by ½; or use a margarine made from monounsaturated or polyunsaturated oil; or use reduced-calorie margarine (In baked goods try an equal amount of unsweetened applesauce.)
Vegetable oil	Reduce amount by ½ and use a monounsaturated or polyunsaturated oil
Solid shortening	Use margarine made from polyunsaturated oil or use monounsaturated or polyunsaturated oil reducing amount by ¼
Mayonnaise	Fat-free, reduced-calorie, or low-cholesterol mayonnaise; or mix equal amounts of reduced-calorie mayonnaise with plain nonfat yogurt
Gravy	Gravy made with bouillon granules or broth and thickened with flour or cornstarch: (To remove fat from regular gravy, refrigerate until fat hardens on top or cool slightly and drop in several ice cubes. Fat will harden around ice cubes)
Condensed cream of mushroom soup	99% fat-free condensed cream of mushroom soup
Canned regular chicken broth	Ready to serve, reduced-sodium, fat-free, canned chicken broth
Egg noodles	Noodles made without egg yolks
White rice	Brown or wild rice
Pecans, walnuts	Reduce by ⅓ to ½ and toast (This works with any type of nut.)
Beef, pork, veal, or lamb	Lean cuts of red meat trimmed of all visible fat, or substitute with chicken or turkey
Ground beef	Lean ground turkey or lean ground round
Bacon strips	Turkey bacon or Canadian bacon
Poultry	Skinned poultry
Self-basting turkey	Baste turkey with fat-free chicken broth
Tuna packed in oil	Tuna packed in spring water
Syrup packed fruits	100% fruit juice or water packed fruits

PAN SIZES & CAPACITIES

13 x 9 inch baking dish	12 to 15 cups
10 x 4 inch tube pan	12 cups
10 x 3½ inch bundt pan	12 cups
9 x 3 inch tube pan	9 cups
9 x 3 inch Bundt pan	9 cups
11 x 7 inch baking dish	8 cups
8 inch square baking dish	8 cups
9 x 5 inch loaf pan	8 cups
9 inch deep-dish pie plate	6 to 8 cups
9 x 1½ inch cake pan	6 cups
7½ x 3 inch Bundt pan	6 cups
9 x 1½ inch pie plate	5 cups
8 x 1½ inch cake pan	4 to 5 cups
8 x 4 inch loaf pan	4 cups

USEFUL EQUIVALENTS

AMOUNT	YIELD
Dash or pinch	2-3 drops or less than ⅛ tsp.
Jigger	1½ fluid ounces
1 tablespoon	3 teaspoons ½ fluid ounce
¼ cup	4 tablespoons 2 fluid ounces
⅓ cup	5 tablespoons plus 1 teaspoon
½ cup	8 tablespoons 4 fluid ounces
1 cup	16 tablespoons 8 fluid ounces
1 pint	2 cups 16 fluid ounces
1 quart	4 cups 2 pints 32 fluid ounces
4 quarts	1 gallon 128 ounces
8 quarts	1 peck
4 pecks	1 bushel
16 ounces	1 pound

Identifying Causes of Common Cake-Baking Problems

Sometimes in trying out a new, recipe or even when preparing a long-time family favorite, "flops" occur. Here's a chart that lists the causes of some common cake-baking problems:

Sticky, sugary crust	Too much sugar or leavening Improper mixing Underbaked
Falls	Batter too thin Undermixed Too much sugar, leavening, or fat Too much batter in pan Oven temperature too low Underbaked Moving cake during baking
Uneven shape	Uneven oven heat Oven not level Warped pan
Peaked top	Too little fat or leavening Too much flour Oven temperature too high
Cracks on top	Batter too stiff Pan too deep Oven too hot early in baking time
Unevenly browned	Too little leavening Undermixed Uneven oven heat
Coarse texture	Too much sugar or leavening Undermixed Wrong oven temperature
Soggy	Too much sugar, liquid, or leavening Undermixed
Heavy	Too little leavening Too much fat, sugar or liquid Overmixed Pan too heavily greased Too much batter in pan Wrong oven temperature Underbaked Incorrect cooling
Dry	Too little fat, sugar or liquid Too much flour or leavening Egg whites over beaten Overbaked
Tough	Too little fat, sugar or leavening Too much flour Overmixed

Basic Cooking Pans

Loaf Pan

Multipurpose loaf pans are for breads, pound and fruit cakes, meat loaves and pates. They come in various sizes; but whatever their proportion, all are rectangular. They are made of tinned or black steel, aluminum, ovenproof glass or ceramic.

Springform Pan

This round baking pan with high sides is used for making cheesecake and other dense cakes that need special handling to be unmolded. A clamp releases the sides from the base, ensuring that the cake can be removed intact from the pan. These come in several sizes but usually are made of tinned steel.

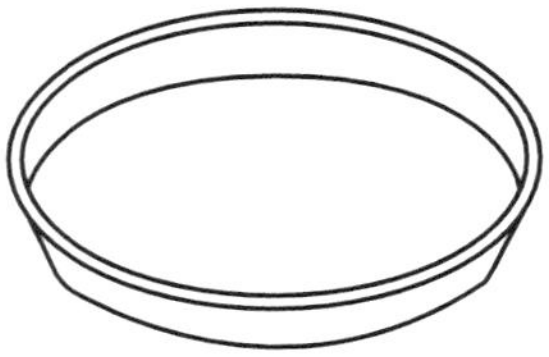

Round Cake Pan

Considered basic equipment, most kitchens have at least one of these. They are used for layer and other types of cakes and for breads. Most cake recipes call for round or square pans 8 or 9 inches by 1½ inches. The best quality are made of heavy-gauge aluminum.

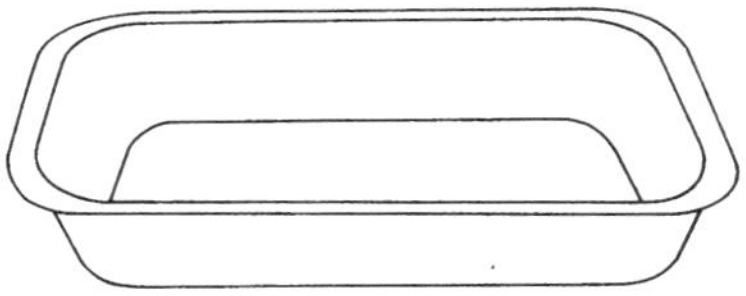

Baking Pan

These pans have straight sides, ¾ inch tall or higher, all the way around and are designed to contain runny batters. A kitchen essential, baking pans should be of the heaviest weight and best quality available; aluminum and heavy-gauge black steel are good choices.

Jellyroll Pan

A type of baking pan, a standard jellyroll pan measures approximately 11x15x¾ inches. These shallow pans are perfect for making Swiss rolls. Air-cushioned jellyroll pans sandwich a layer of air between two sheets of aluminum, preventing the dough from browning too quickly on the bottom.

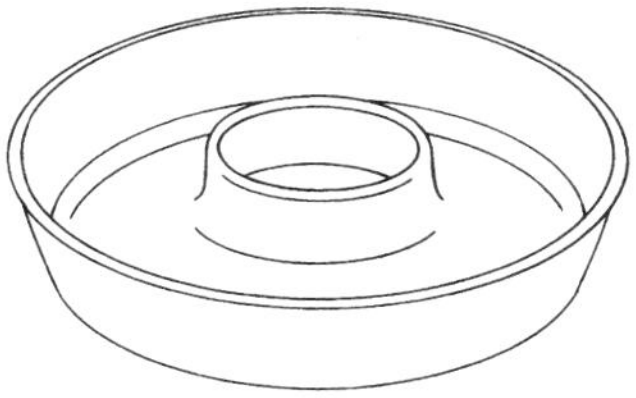

Ring Mold

The center hole of this pan is larger than that of a tube pan, making it suitable for breads, cakes, molded rice and gelatin desserts. Typically made of aluminum, it comes in a variety of sizes.

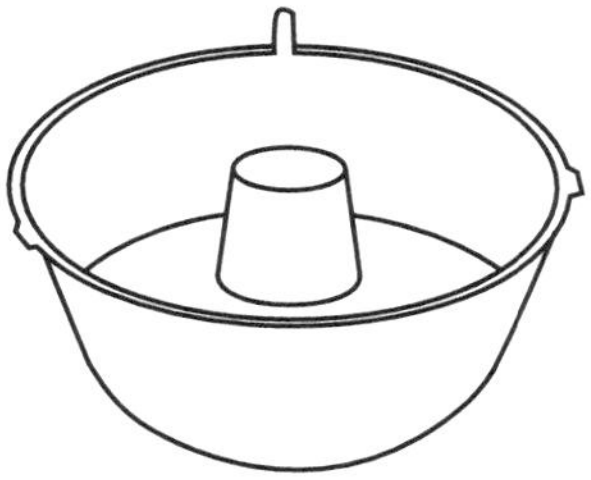

Angel Food Cake or Tube Pan

These pans have high sides and a center tube that promotes even distribution of heat and supports delicate batters as they rise in the oven. Most of these pans can hold a large amount of batter, anywhere from 9 to 12 cups. Made of aluminum, they often have a nonstick interior coating.

Bundt Pan

These deep tube pans are used to bake the popular, densely textured bundt cakes. The sides of the pan are curved and indented to produce a sculptured cake exterior. Usually bundt pans are made of colored cast aluminum and have nonstick interior coatings.

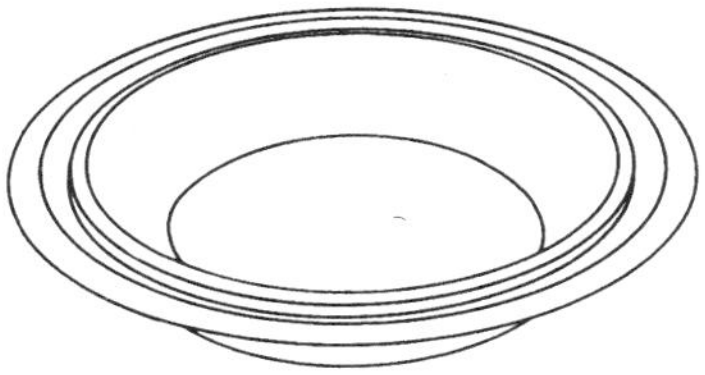

Pie Pan

Pie pans have sloping sides and wide, troughed rims that prevent juices from spilling out of the dish while baking. Heavyweight metal pie pans produce a more evenly browned product. Standard pie pans are 1 inch deep while deep-dish pie pans are 1½ to 2 inches deep.

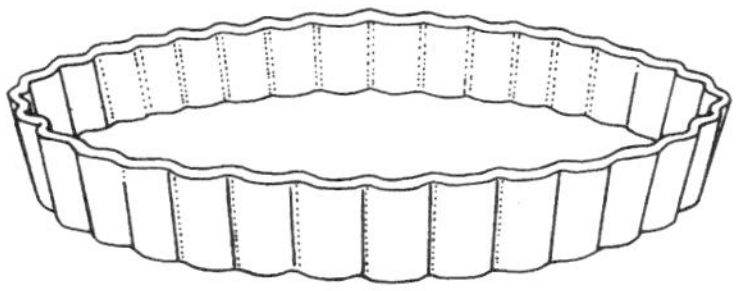

Tart Pan

Tarts are baked in shallow, fluted, straight-sided pans that usually have removable bottoms. These 1-to-2-inch deep pans are usually round, but can be found in square and rectangular shapes. Tinned or black steel are the most common materials.

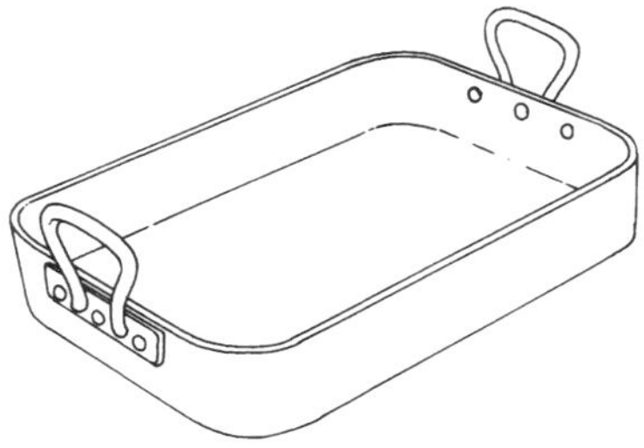

ROASTING PAN

Roasting pans come in a variety of shapes and styles but most have safe, strong handles for lifting heavy meats. Pans can be found in aluminum, stainless-steel and copper. Their open-rolled edges make for easier cleaning.

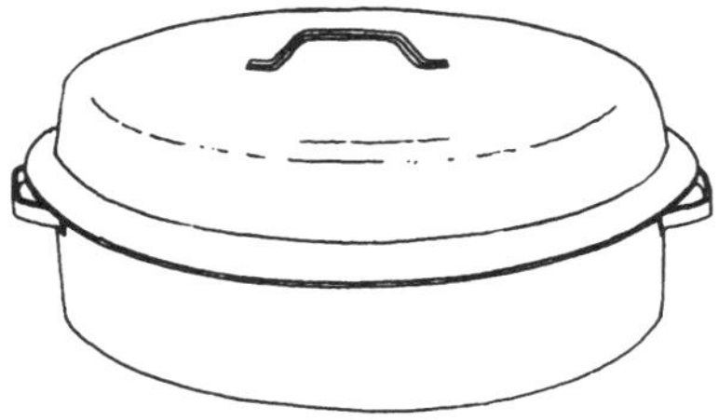

DUTCH OVEN ROASTER

These deep, covered pans magnify the heat, creating an oven within the oven.

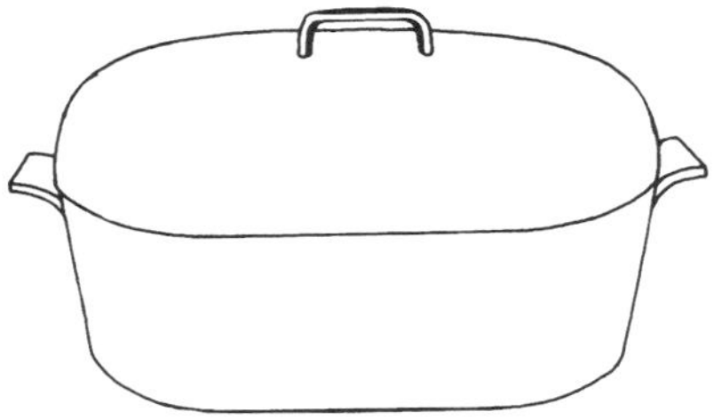

OVAL ROASTER

Oval roasters have domed lids and are sold in many sizes to encompass the smallest of chickens to the largest of turkeys.

Recipe Index

General Index

AFTERWORD

I was born in 1929 in northeast Georgia. As a farmer, businessman, and as Georgia's Commissioner of Agriculture for almost thirty years, I have seen the miracle of agriculture improve my life and the lives of millions in Georgia and throughout the world.

Our very existence is made possible because we have an abundant supply of wholesome food, pure water and clean air. Beginning there and with better farming methods, improved fertilizers, the introduction of the technology of cultivars and developments in plant and animal genetics, we are on the threshold of a new agricultural revolution. These changes will completely overshadow our accomplishments of the past.

As the pages of this book illustrate, Georgia Agriculture touches everyone and I want everyone who reads this book to have the opportunity to touch Georgia Agriculture.

The best of Georgia farms—the best of farms all over the world—starts with a seed. I hope you will plant these seeds and whether it's your first garden or your fiftieth, you will be a part of the miracle of agriculture.

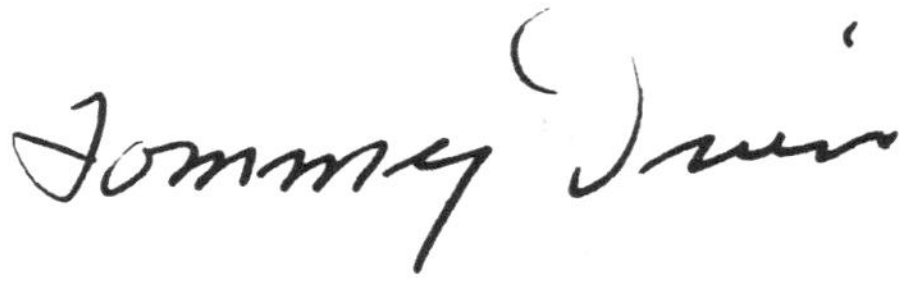